INSTRUCTOR'S SOLUTIONS MANUAL

Richard N. Aufmann
Palomar College

Vernon C. Barker
Palomar College

Joanne S. Lockwood
Plymouth State University

BASIC COLLEGE MATHEMATICS: AN APPLIED APPROACH

EIGHTH EDITION

Aufmann/Barker/Lockwood

HOUGHTON MIFFLIN COMPANY   BOSTON   NEW YORK

Senior Sponsoring Editor: Lynn Cox
Associate Editor: Melissa Parkin
Editorial Assistant: Noel Kamm
Senior Project Editor: Carol Merrigan
Editorial Assistant: Eric Moore
Assistant Manufacturing Coordinator: Karmen Chong
Senior Marketing Manager: Ben Rivera

Printed in the U.S.A.

ISBN: 0-618-50681-0

2 3 4 5 6 7 8 9-EB-09 08 07 06

Contents

Instructor's Solutions Manual

Chapter 1: Whole Numbers

Prep Test

1. 8
2. 1 2 3 4 5 6 7 8 9 10
3. a and D; b and E; c and A; d and B; e and F; f and C

Go Figure

On the first trip, the two children row over. The second trip, one child returns with the boat. The third trip, one adult rows to the other side. The fourth trip, one child returns with the boat. At this point, one adult has crossed the river. Repeat the first four trips an additional four times, one time for each adult. After completing the fifth time, there have been twenty trips taken, and the only people waiting to cross the river are the two children. On the twenty-first trip, the two children cross the river. There is a minimum of 21 trips.

Section 1.1

Objective A Exercises

1. 0 1 2 3 4 5 6 7 8 9 10 11 12
2. 0 1 2 3 4 5 6 7 8 9 10 11 12
3. 0 1 2 3 4 5 6 7 8 9 10 11 12
4. 0 1 2 3 4 5 6 7 8 9 10 11 12
5. $37 < 49$
6. $58 > 21$
7. $101 > 87$
8. $16 > 5$
9. $245 > 158$
10. $2701 > 2071$
11. $0 < 45$
12. $107 > 0$
13. $815 < 928$

Objective B Exercises

14. Thousands
15. Millions
16. Ten-thousands
17. Hundred-thousands
18. Two thousand six hundred seventy-five
19. Three thousand seven hundred ninety
20. Forty-two thousand nine hundred twenty-eight
21. Fifty-eight thousand four hundred seventy-three
22. Three hundred fifty-six thousand nine hundred forty-three
23. Four hundred ninety-eight thousand five hundred twelve
24. Three million six hundred ninety-seven thousand four hundred eighty-three
25. Six million eight hundred forty-two thousand seven hundred fifteen
26. 85
27. 357
28. 3456
29. 63,780
30. 609,948
31. 7,024,709

Objective C Exercises

32. $5000 + 200 + 80 + 7$
33. $6000 + 200 + 90 + 5$
34. $50,000 + 8000 + 900 + 40 + 3$
35. $400,000 + 50,000 + 3000 + 900 + 20 + 1$
36. $200,000 + 500 + 80 + 3$
37. $300,000 + 1000 + 800 + 9$
38. $400,000 + 3000 + 700 + 5$
39. $3,000,000 + 600 + 40 + 2$

Objective D Exercises

40. 930
41. 850
42. 1400
43. 4000
44. 44,000
45. 53,000
46. 390,000
47. 630,000
48. 650,000
49. 250,000

50. 37,000,000

51. 72,000,000

Applying the Concepts

52a. True

b. False. If the digit to the right of the rounded place value is greater than 5, then the rounded number will be greater than its exact value. For example, 8270 rounded to the nearest hundred is 8300.

53. 999; 10,000

54. The results are different.

3846 = 3850 to the tens = 3900 to the hundreds	3846 = 3800 to the hundreds (correct)

Section 1.2

Objective A Exercises

1. 28

2. 88

3. 125

4. 157

5. 102

6. 112

7. 154

8. 154

9. 1489

10. 1778

11. 828

12. 239

13. $\begin{array}{r} \scriptstyle 1 \\ 859 \\ +\ 725 \\ \hline 1584 \end{array}$

14. $\begin{array}{r} \scriptstyle 1 \\ 637 \\ +\ 829 \\ \hline 1466 \end{array}$

15. $\begin{array}{r} \scriptstyle 1 \\ 470 \\ +\ 749 \\ \hline 1219 \end{array}$

16. $\begin{array}{r} \scriptstyle 1 \\ 427 \\ +\ 690 \\ \hline 1117 \end{array}$

17. $\begin{array}{r} \scriptstyle 11\ 1 \\ 36{,}925 \\ +\ 65{,}392 \\ \hline 102{,}317 \end{array}$

18. $\begin{array}{r} \scriptstyle 1\ 11 \\ 56{,}772 \\ +\ 51{,}239 \\ \hline 108{,}011 \end{array}$

19. $\begin{array}{r} \scriptstyle 1\ 1 \\ 50{,}873 \\ +\ 28{,}453 \\ \hline 79{,}326 \end{array}$

20. $\begin{array}{r} \scriptstyle 1\ 11 \\ 34{,}872 \\ +\ 46{,}079 \\ \hline 80{,}951 \end{array}$

21. $\begin{array}{r} \scriptstyle 22 \\ 878 \\ 737 \\ +\ 189 \\ \hline 1804 \end{array}$

22. $\begin{array}{r} \scriptstyle 11 \\ 768 \\ 461 \\ +\ 669 \\ \hline 1898 \end{array}$

23. $\begin{array}{r} \scriptstyle 1 \\ 319 \\ 348 \\ +\ 912 \\ \hline 1579 \end{array}$

24. $\begin{array}{r} \scriptstyle 11 \\ 292 \\ 579 \\ +\ 315 \\ \hline 1186 \end{array}$

25. $\begin{array}{r} \scriptstyle 12 \\ 9409 \\ 3253 \\ +\ 7078 \\ \hline 19{,}740 \end{array}$

26. $\begin{array}{r} \scriptstyle 11 \\ 8188 \\ 8020 \\ +\ 7104 \\ \hline 23{,}312 \end{array}$

27. $\begin{array}{r} \scriptstyle 12 \\ 2038 \\ 2243 \\ +\ 3139 \\ \hline 7420 \end{array}$

28. $\begin{array}{r} \scriptstyle 11 \\ 4252 \\ 6882 \\ +\ 5235 \\ \hline 16{,}369 \end{array}$

29. $\begin{array}{r} \scriptstyle 11\ 11 \\ 67{,}428 \\ 32{,}171 \\ +\ 20{,}971 \\ \hline 120{,}570 \end{array}$

30. $\begin{array}{r} \scriptstyle 12\ 11 \\ 52{,}801 \\ 11{,}664 \\ +\ 89{,}638 \\ \hline 154{,}103 \end{array}$

31. $\begin{array}{r} \scriptstyle 11\ 1 \\ 76{,}290 \\ 43{,}761 \\ +\ 87{,}402 \\ \hline 207{,}453 \end{array}$

32. $\begin{array}{r} \scriptstyle 22 \\ 43{,}901 \\ 98{,}301 \\ +\ 67{,}943 \\ \hline 210{,}145 \end{array}$

33. $\begin{array}{r} \scriptstyle 1\ 11 \\ 20{,}958 \\ 3{,}218 \\ +\ 42 \\ \hline 24{,}218 \end{array}$

34. $\begin{array}{r} \scriptstyle 1\ 12 \\ 80{,}973 \\ 5{,}168 \\ +\ 29 \\ \hline 86{,}170 \end{array}$

35. $\begin{array}{r} \scriptstyle 111 \\ 392 \\ 37 \\ 10{,}924 \\ +\ 621 \\ \hline 11{,}974 \end{array}$

36. $\begin{array}{r} \scriptstyle 122 \\ 694 \\ 62 \\ 70{,}129 \\ +\ 217 \\ \hline 71{,}102 \end{array}$

37.

122
294
1029
7935
+ 65
9323

38.

121
692
2107
3196
+ 92
6087

39.

11 21
97
7,234
69,532
+ 276
77,139

40.

1 22
87
1,698
27,317
+ 727
29,829

41. 14,383

42. 13,666

43. 9473

44. 226,430

45. 33,247

46. 53,766

47. 5058

48. 47,787

49. 1992

50. 6926

51. 68,263

52. 34,217

53.

1234	≈	1200
9780	≈	9800
+ 6740	≈	+ 6700
Cal.: 17,754		Est.: 17,700

54.

919	≈	900
3642	≈	3600
+ 8796	≈	+ 8800
Cal.: 13,357		Est.: 13,300

55.

241	≈	200
569	≈	600
390	≈	400
+ 1672	≈	+ 1700
Cal.: 2872		Est.: 2900

56.

107	≈	100
984	≈	1000
1035	≈	1000
+ 2904	≈	+ 2900
Cal.: 5030		Est.: 5000

57.

32,461	≈	32,000
9,844	≈	10,000
+ 59,407	≈	+ 59,000
Cal.: 101,712		Est.: 101,000

58.

29,036	≈	29,000
22,904	≈	23,000
+ 7,903	≈	+ 8,000
Cal.: 59,843		Est.: 60,000

59.

25,432	≈	25,000
62,941	≈	63,000
+ 70,390	≈	+ 70,000
Cal.: 158,763		Est.: 158,000

60.

66,541	≈	67,000
29,365	≈	29,000
+ 98,742	≈	+ 99,000
Cal.: 194,648		Est.: 195,000

61.

67,421	≈	70,000
82,984	≈	80,000
66,361	≈	70,000
10,792	≈	10,000
+ 34,037	≈	+ 30,000
Cal.: 261,595		Est.: 260,000

62.

21,896	≈	20,000
4,235	≈	0
62,544	≈	60,000
21,892	≈	20,000
+ 1,334	≈	+ 0
Cal.: 111,901		Est.: 100,000

63.

281,421	≈	280,000
9,874	≈	10,000
34,394	≈	30,000
526,398	≈	530,000
+ 94,631	≈	+ 90,000
Cal.: 946,718		Est.: 940,000

64.

542,698	≈	540,000
97,327	≈	100,000
7,235	≈	10,000
73,667	≈	70,000
+ 173,201	≈	+ 170,000
Cal.: 894,128		Est.: 890,000

65.

28,627,052	≈	29,000,000
983,073	≈	1,000,000
+ 3,081,496	≈	+ 3,000,000
Cal.: 32,691,621		Est.: 33,000,000

66.

	1,792,085	≈	2,000,000
	29,919,301	≈	30,000,000
	+ 3,406,882	≈	+ 3,000,000
Cal.:	35,118,268	Est.:	35,000,000

67.

	12,377,491	≈	12,000,000
	3,409,723	≈	3,000,000
	7,928,026	≈	8,000,000
	+ 10,705,682	≈	+ 11,000,000
Cal.:	34,420,922	Est.:	34,000,000

68.

	46,751,070	≈	47,000,000
	6,095,832	≈	6,000,000
	280,011	≈	0
	+ 1,563,897	≈	+ 2,000,000
Cal.:	54,690,810	Est.:	55,000,000

Objective B Exercises

69. Strategy To find the total number of multiple births, add the four amounts (110,670, 6919, 627, and 79).

Solution

110,670
6,919
627
+ 79
118,295

The were 118,295 multiple births during the year.

70. Strategy To find the Census Bureau's estimate, add the amounts (296 and 281).

Solution

296
+ 281
577

The population estimate for 2100 is 577 million people.

71. Strategy To estimate the total income from the first four *Star Wars* movies, estimate each movie to the nearest hundred million and then add the estimates.

Solution

461,000,000	≈	500,000,000
290,200,000	≈	300,000,000
309,100,000	≈	300,000,000
431,100,000	≈	+ 400,000,000
		$1,500,000,000

The estimated income from the first four *Star Wars* movies was $1,500,000,000.

72. Strategy To find the total income from the first four *Star Wars* movies, add the four amounts ($461,000,000, $290,200,000, $309,100,000, and $431,100,000).

Solution

461,000,000
290,200,000
309,100,000
+ 431,100,000
$1,491,400,000

The total income was $1,491,400,000.

73a. Strategy To find the total income from the two movies with the lowest box-office incomes, add the incomes from Episode V ($290,200,000) and Episode VI ($309,100,000).

Solution

$290,200,000
+ 309,100,000
$599,300,000

The income from the two movies with the lowest box-office returns is $599,300,000.

b. The income from the 1977 *Star Wars* production is $461,000,000. The income from the two movies with the lowest box-office returns is $599,300,000 (from Exercise 73a). Yes, this income exceeds the income from the 1977 *Star Wars* production.

74. Strategy To find the perimeter, add the lengths of the three sides (12, 14, and 17 inches).

Solution

12
14
+ 17
43

The perimeter of the triangle is 43 inches.

75a. Strategy To find the total number of miles driven during the three days, add the three amounts (515, 492, and 278 miles).

Solution

515
492
+ 278
1285

1285 miles will be driven during the three days.

b. Strategy To find what the odometer reading will be by the end of the trip, add the total number of miles driven during the three days (1285) to the original odometer reading (68,692).

Solution

1,285
+ 68,692
69,977

At the end of the trip, the odometer will read 69,977 miles.

76. Strategy To find the total average amount invested for all Americans, add the amounts in checking accounts ($487), savings accounts ($3494), and U.S. Savings Bonds ($546).

Solution

$$\begin{array}{r} \$487 \\ 3494 \\ +\ 546 \\ \hline \$4527 \end{array}$$

All Americans have invested $4527 in these three investments.

77. Strategy To find the total average amount invested for Americans ages 16 to 34, add the amounts in checking accounts ($375), savings accounts ($1155), and U.S. Savings Bonds ($266).

Solution

$$\begin{array}{r} \$375 \\ 1155 \\ +\ 266 \\ \hline \$1796 \end{array}$$

Americans ages 16 to 34 have invested $1796 in these three investments.

78. Strategy To find the total average amount invested for Americans ages 16 to 34, add the amounts in checking accounts ($375), savings accounts ($1155), U.S. savings bonds ($266), money market ($4427), and stocks/mutual funds ($1615).

Solution

$$\begin{array}{r} \$375 \\ 1155 \\ 266 \\ 4427 \\ +1615 \\ \hline \$7838 \end{array}$$

The total of the five investments is $7838.

79. Strategy To find whether the sum of the average amount invested in home equity and retirement for all Americans is greater than or less than the sum of all categories for Americans between the ages of 16 and 34:

- Add the amount invested in home equity ($43,070) and retirement ($9016) for all Americans.
- Add all the values for all categories for Americans 16 to 34.
- Compare these sums.

Solution

$$\begin{array}{r} \$43,070 \\ +\ 9,016 \\ \hline \$52,086 \end{array} \qquad \begin{array}{r} \$375 \\ 1,155 \\ 266 \\ 4,427 \\ 1,615 \\ 17,184 \\ +\ 4,298 \\ \hline \$29,320 \end{array}$$

$52,086 > $29,320

The sum of the average amounts invested in home equity and retirement for all Americans is greater than the sum of all categories for Americans ages 16 to 34.

Applying the Concepts

80a. From 1 to 99, there are 99 numbers (one- and two-digit numbers).
From 1 to 9, there are 9 numbers (one-digit numbers).
Therefore, there are 99 – 9 = 90 two-digit numbers.

b. From 1 to 999, there are 999 numbers (one-, two-, and three-digit numbers).
From 1 to 99, there are 99 numbers (one- and two-digit numbers).
Therefore, there are 999 – 99 = 900 three-digit numbers.

81. There are 6 possible outcomes for each die (1, 2, 3, 4, 5, and 6).
The smallest sum on two dice is $1 + 1 = 2$. The largest sum on two dice is $6 + 6 = 12$. There are 11 different sums from 2 to 12 (2, 3, 4, 5, 6, 7, 8, 9, 10, 11, and 12).

82. No; $0 + 2 = 2$

83. No; $0 + 0 = 0$

84. Answers will vary. For example:
A part-time instructor is teaching two classes this term, with 34 students in one class and 28 students in the other. How many students is the part-time instructor teaching this term? 62 students.

85. Ten numbers that are less than 100 end in a 7. They are 7, 17, 27, 37, 47, 57, 67, 77, 87, and 97.

Section 1.3

Objective A Exercises

1. 4

2. 1

3. 4

4. 4

5. 10

6. 7

7. 4

8. 11

9. 9

10. 9

11. 22

12. 51

13. 60

14. 74

15. 66

16. 33

17. 31

18. 501

19. 901

20. 962

21. 791

22. 5002

23. 1125

24. 1513

25. 3131

26. 41

27. 47

28. 71

29. 925

30. 1244

31. 4561

32. 823

33. 3205

34. 4401

35. 1222

36. 2703

37. 3021

38. 9222

39. 3022

40. 3231

41. 3040

42. 3407

43. 212

44. 11,202

45. 60,245

Objective B Exercises

46.
611
71
−18
53

47.
813
93
−28
65

48.
317
47
−18
29

49.
314
44
−27
17

50.
217
37
−29
8

51.
410
50
−27
23

52.
610
70
−33
37

53.
813
993
−537
456

54.
14
1410
250
−192
58

55.
13
7310
840
−783
57

56.
616
768
−194
574

57.
61610
770
−395
375

58.
614
674
−337
337

59.
11
4116
3526
− 387
3139

60.
10
6012
1712
− 289
1423

61.
313410
4350
− 729
3621

62.
169
061012
1702
− 948
754

63.
159
051017
1607
− 869
738

64.
12
8213
5933
−3754
2179

65.
612813
7293
−3748
3545

66.
139
831017
9407
−2918
6489

67.
169
261016
3706
−2957
749

68.
159
751015
8605
−7716
889

69. 7 10 4 12
8052
−2709
5343

70. 9
7 10 2 10 15
80,305
− 9,176
71,129

71. 9
6 10 6 10 12
70,702
− 4,239
66,463

72. 9 9 9
0 10 10 10 14
10,004
− 9,306
698

73. 9 9
7 10 10 10
80,009
−63,419
16,590

74. 6 10
70,618
−41,213
29,405

75. 9
7 10 10 4 13
80,053
−27,649
52,404

76. 9
6 10 6 10 10
70,700
−21,076
49,624

77. 9
7 10 7 10 10
80,800
−42,023
38,777

78. 15 9
1 5 10 10
2600
−1972
628

79. 13 9
7 3 10 10
8400
−3762
4638

80. 9
8 10 10
9003
−2471
6532

81. 9
5 10 10
6004
−2392
3612

82. 11 9
7 1 10 12
8202
−3916
4286

83. 6 10 4 10
7050
−4137
2913

84. 9
6 10 11
7015
−2973
4042

85. 11
3 1 10
4207
−1624
2583

86. 9 9
6 10 10 15
7005
−1796
5209

87. 9 9
7 10 10 13
8003
−2735
5268

88. 9 9 9
1 10 10 10 15
20,005
− 9,627
10,378

89. 9 9 9
7 10 10 10 14
80,004
− 8,237
71,767

90. 4 11
10,051
− 9,027
1,024

91. 6 9 12 11
17,031
− 5,792
11,239

92. 9 9 13
1003
− 447
556

93. 7 17
29,874
−21,392
8,482

94. 5 17 9 9 15
68,005
−29,797
38,208

95. 6 9 9 9 14
70,004
−69,379
625

96. 1 14 13 12 12
25,432
− 7,994
17,438

97. 7 15 16 9 11
86,701
− 9,976
76,725

98. **Strategy** To find the amount that completes the statement, subtract the addend (39) from the sum (104).

Solution
104
− 39
65

Therefore 65 completes the statement, 65 + 39 = 104.

99. **Strategy** To find the amount that completes the statement, subtract the addend (67) from the sum (90).

Solution
90
−67
23

Therefore 23 completes the statement, 67 + 23 = 90.

100. Strategy To find the amount that completes the statement, subtract the addend (497) from the sum (862).

Solution
$$\begin{array}{r} 862 \\ -497 \\ \hline 365 \end{array}$$
Therefore 365 completes the statement, $365 + 497 = 862$.

101. Strategy To find the amount that completes the statement, subtract the addend (253) from the sum (4901).

Solution
$$\begin{array}{r} 4901 \\ -\ 253 \\ \hline 4648 \end{array}$$
Therefore 4648 completes the statement, $253 + 4648 = 4901$.

102.
$$\begin{array}{rcr} 80{,}032 & \approx & 80{,}000 \\ -19{,}605 & \approx & -20{,}000 \\ \hline \text{Cal.: } 60{,}427 & & \text{Est.: } 60{,}000 \end{array}$$

103.
$$\begin{array}{rcr} 90{,}765 & \approx & 90{,}000 \\ -60{,}928 & \approx & -60{,}000 \\ \hline \text{Cal.: } 29{,}837 & & \text{Est.: } 30{,}000 \end{array}$$

104.
$$\begin{array}{rcr} 32{,}574 & \approx & 30{,}000 \\ -10{,}961 & \approx & -10{,}000 \\ \hline \text{Cal.: } 21{,}613 & & \text{Est.: } 20{,}000 \end{array}$$

105.
$$\begin{array}{rcr} 96{,}430 & \approx & 100{,}000 \\ -59{,}762 & \approx & -\ 60{,}000 \\ \hline \text{Cal.: } 36{,}668 & & \text{Est.: } 40{,}000 \end{array}$$

106.
$$\begin{array}{rcr} 567{,}423 & \approx & 570{,}000 \\ -208{,}444 & \approx & -210{,}000 \\ \hline \text{Cal.: } 358{,}979 & & \text{Est.: } 360{,}000 \end{array}$$

107.
$$\begin{array}{rcr} 300{,}712 & \approx & 300{,}000 \\ -198{,}714 & \approx & -200{,}000 \\ \hline \text{Cal.: } 101{,}998 & & \text{Est.: } 100{,}000 \end{array}$$

Objective C Exercises

108. Strategy To find the amount left in the checking account, subtract the amount of the check ($139) from the original amount in the checking account ($304).

Solution
$$\begin{array}{r} \$304 \\ -\ 139 \\ \hline \$165 \end{array}$$
The amount left in the checking account is $165.

109. Strategy To find the increase in the number of identity theft complaints from 2001 to 2002, subtract the number of complaints for 2001 (86,198) from the number of complaints for 2002 (161,819).

Solution
$$\begin{array}{r} 161{,}819 \\ -\ 86{,}198 \\ \hline 75{,}621 \end{array}$$
The increase was 75,621 complaints.

110. Strategy To find the amount that remains to be paid, subtract the down payment ($180) from the cost ($1079).

Solution
$$\begin{array}{r} \$1079 \\ -\ 180 \\ \hline \$899 \end{array}$$
The amount that remains to be paid is $899.

111. Strategy To find the amount that remains to be paid, subtract the down payment ($950) from the cost ($11,225).

Solution
$$\begin{array}{r} \$11{,}225 \\ -\ \ \ 950 \\ \hline \$10{,}275 \end{array}$$
The amount that remains to be paid is $10,275.

112. Strategy To find the difference in maximum heights between the two geysers, subtract the height of the Valentine (75 feet) from the height of the Great Fountain (90 feet).

Solution
$$\begin{array}{r} 90 \\ -75 \\ \hline 15 \end{array}$$
The Great Fountain geyser erupts 15 feet higher than the Valentine geyser.

113. Strategy To find how much higher the Giant erupts than Old Faithful, subtract the height of Old Faithful (175) from the height of the Giant (200).

Solution
$$\begin{array}{r} 200 \\ -175 \\ \hline 25 \end{array}$$
The Giant erupts 25 feet higher than Old Faithful.

114. Strategy To find how many more women than men are expected to earn a bachelor's degree in 2012, subtract estimated number of men (587,000) who will earn a degree from the estimated number of women (850,000) who will earn a degree.

Solution
$$\begin{array}{r} 850{,}000 \\ -587{,}000 \\ \hline 263{,}000 \end{array}$$
263,000 more women than men will earn a bachelor's degree in 2012.

115. Strategy To find the expected increase over 10 years, subtract the population expected in 2010 (129,000) from the population expected in 2020 (235,000).

Solution
235,000
−129,000
106,000
The expected increase over 10 years is 106,000.

116a. Strategy To find which 2-year period has the smallest expected increase, find the difference for each of the 2-year periods and determine which is the smallest difference.

Solution For 2010 – 2012
146,000
−129,000
17,000
For 2012 – 2014
166,000
−146,000
20,000
For 2014 – 2016
187,000
−166,000
21,000
For 2016 – 2018
208,000
−187,000
21,000
For 2018 – 2020
235,000
−208,000
27,000
The smallest expected 2-year increase is 17,000 for 2010–2012.

b. Strategy To find which 2-year period has the greatest increase, find the difference for each of the 2-year periods and determine which is the greatest difference.

Solution Using the calculations from 116a, the greatest expected 2-year increase is 27,000 for 2018–2020.

117. Strategy To find the amount remaining in the sales executive's monthly expense account, subtract the sum of amounts already spent from the beginning account balance ($1500).

Solution
$479 transportation
268 food
317 lodging
$1064

$1500
−1064
$436
The amount remaining in the expense account is $436.

118. Strategy To find your new credit card balance, add the total amount of your purchases to the balance before the purchase ($409). Then subtract your payment ($350).

Solution Purchases : $168
36
97
$301
$409 + 301 = $710
$710 − 350 = $360
The new credit card balance is $360.

Applying the Concepts

119a. True
b. False
c. False

120. Answers will vary. For example:
Pat has earned 15 college credits, and Leslie has earned 8 college credits. How many more college credits has Pat earned? 7 college credits.

Section 1.4

Objective A Exercises

1. 6×2 or $6 \cdot 2$

2. 5×4 or $5 \cdot 4$

3. 4×7 or $4 \cdot 7$

4. 3×18 or $3 \cdot 18$

5. 12

6. 16

7. 35

8. 24

9. 25

10. 49

11. 0

12. 0

13. 72

14. 42

15. $\begin{array}{r} {}^{1} \\ 66 \\ \times\ 3 \\ \hline 198 \end{array}$

16. $\begin{array}{r} 70 \\ \times\ 4 \\ \hline 280 \end{array}$

17. $\begin{array}{r} {}^{3} \\ 67 \\ \times\ 5 \\ \hline 335 \end{array}$

18. $\begin{array}{r} {}^{26} \\ 127 \\ \times\ 9 \\ \hline 1143 \end{array}$

19. $\begin{array}{r} {}^{1} \\ 623 \\ \times\ 4 \\ \hline 2492 \end{array}$

20. $\begin{array}{r} {}^{1} \\ 802 \\ \times\ 5 \\ \hline 4010 \end{array}$

21. $\begin{array}{r} {}^{6} \\ 607 \\ \times\ 9 \\ \hline 5463 \end{array}$

22. $\begin{array}{r} 300 \\ \times\ 5 \\ \hline 1500 \end{array}$

23. $\begin{array}{r} 600 \\ \times\ 7 \\ \hline 4200 \end{array}$

24. $\begin{array}{r} {}^{4} \\ 906 \\ \times\ 8 \\ \hline 7248 \end{array}$

25. $\begin{array}{r} {}^{2} \\ 703 \\ \times\ 9 \\ \hline 6327 \end{array}$

26. $\begin{array}{r} {}^{13} \\ 127 \\ \times\ 5 \\ \hline 635 \end{array}$

27. $\begin{array}{r} 632 \\ \times\ 3 \\ \hline 1896 \end{array}$

28. $\begin{array}{r} {}^{23} \\ 559 \\ \times\ 4 \\ \hline 2236 \end{array}$

29. $\begin{array}{r} {}^{21} \\ 632 \\ \times\ 8 \\ \hline 5056 \end{array}$

30. $\begin{array}{r} {}^{1} \\ 524 \\ \times\ 4 \\ \hline 2096 \end{array}$

31. $\begin{array}{r} {}^{13} \\ 337 \\ \times\ 5 \\ \hline 1685 \end{array}$

32. $\begin{array}{r} {}^{2} \\ 841 \\ \times\ 6 \\ \hline 5046 \end{array}$

33. $\begin{array}{r} {}^{4\ 6} \\ 6709 \\ \times\ 7 \\ \hline 46{,}963 \end{array}$

34. $\begin{array}{r} {}^{3\ 4} \\ 3608 \\ \times\ 5 \\ \hline 18{,}040 \end{array}$

35. $\begin{array}{r} {}^{345} \\ 8568 \\ \times\ 7 \\ \hline 59{,}976 \end{array}$

36. $\begin{array}{r} {}^{132} \\ 5495 \\ \times\ 4 \\ \hline 21{,}980 \end{array}$

37. $\begin{array}{r} {}^{33} \\ 4780 \\ \times\ 4 \\ \hline 19{,}120 \end{array}$

38. $\begin{array}{r} {}^{34} \\ 3690 \\ \times\ 5 \\ \hline 18{,}450 \end{array}$

39. $\begin{array}{r} {}^{111} \\ 9895 \\ \times\ 2 \\ \hline 19{,}790 \end{array}$

40. $5 \times 7 \times 4 = 140$

41. $6 \times 2 \times 9 = 108$

42. $\begin{array}{r} 5304 \\ \times\ 9 \\ \hline 47{,}736 \end{array}$

43. $\begin{array}{r} 458 \\ \times\ 8 \\ \hline 3664 \end{array}$

44. $\begin{array}{r} 3208 \\ \times\ 7 \\ \hline 22{,}456 \end{array}$

45. $\begin{array}{r} 5009 \\ \times\ 4 \\ \hline 20{,}036 \end{array}$

46. $\begin{array}{r} 3105 \\ \times\ 6 \\ \hline 18{,}630 \end{array}$

47. $\begin{array}{r} 8957 \\ \times\ 8 \\ \hline 71{,}656 \end{array}$

Objective B Exercises

48. $\begin{array}{r} 16 \\ \times\ 16 \\ \hline 16 \\ 32\ \\ \hline 336 \end{array}$

49. $\begin{array}{r} 18 \\ \times\ 24 \\ \hline 72 \\ 36\ \\ \hline 432 \end{array}$

50. $\begin{array}{r} 35 \\ \times\ 26 \\ \hline 210 \\ 70\ \\ \hline 910 \end{array}$

51. $\begin{array}{r} 27 \\ \times\ 72 \\ \hline 54 \\ 189\ \\ \hline 1944 \end{array}$

52. $\begin{array}{r} 693 \\ \times\ 91 \\ \hline 693 \\ 6237\ \\ \hline 63{,}063 \end{array}$

53. $\begin{array}{r} 581 \\ \times\ 72 \\ \hline 1162 \\ 4067\ \\ \hline 41{,}832 \end{array}$

54. $\begin{array}{r} 419 \\ \times\ 80 \\ \hline 33{,}520 \end{array}$

55. $\begin{array}{r} 727 \\ \times\ 60 \\ \hline 43{,}620 \end{array}$

56. 8279
× 46
49674
33116
380,834

57. 9577
× 35
47885
28731
335,195

58. 6938
× 78
55504
48566
541,164

59. 8875
× 67
62125
53250
594,625

60. 7035
× 57
49245
35175
400,995

61. 6702
× 48
53616
26808
321,696

62. 3009
× 35
15045
9027
105,315

63. 6003
× 57
42021
30015
342,171

64. 809
× 530
24270
4045
428,770

65. 607
× 460
36420
2428
279,220

66. 800
× 325
4000
1600
2400
260,000

67. 700
× 274
2800
4900
1400
191,800

68. 987
× 349
8883
3948
2961
344,463

69. 688
× 674
2752
4816
4128
463,712

70. 312
× 134
1248
936
312
41,808

71. 423
× 427
2961
846
1692
180,621

72. 379
× 500
189,500

73. 684
× 700
478,800

74. 985
× 408
7880
39400
401,880

75. 758
× 209
6822
15160
158,422

76. 3407
× 309
30663
102210
1,052,763

77. 5207
× 902
10414
468630
4,696,714

78. 4258
× 986
25548
34064
38322
4,198,388

79. 6327
× 876
37962
44289
50616
5,542,452

80. 5763
× 45
28815
23052
259,335

81. 7349
× 27
51443
14698
198,423

82. $2 \times 19 = 38$
38
× 34
152
114
1292

83. $6 \times 73 = 438$
438
× 43
1314
1752
18,834

84. 376
×402
752
1504
151,152

85.
```
     842
   × 309
    7578
   2526
 260,178
```

86.
```
     233,489
   ×    3005
     1167445
    700467
 701,634,445
```

87.
```
       34,985
    ×    9007
       244895
    314865
  315,109,895
```

88.
```
        8745  ≈        9000
    ×     63  ≈    ×     60
  Cal.: 550,935    Est.: 540,000
```

89.
```
        4732  ≈        5000
    ×     93  ≈    ×     90
  Cal.: 440,076    Est.: 450,000
```

90.
```
        2937  ≈        3000
    ×    206  ≈    ×    200
  Cal.: 605,022    Est.: 600,000
```

91.
```
          8941  ≈          9000
    ×      726  ≈    ×      700
  Cal.: 6,491,166    Est.: 6,300,000
```

92.
```
          3097  ≈          3000
    ×     1025  ≈    ×     1000
  Cal.: 3,174,425    Est.: 3,000,000
```

93.
```
           6379  ≈           6000
    ×      2936  ≈    ×      3000
  Cal.: 18,728,744    Est.: 18,000,000
```

94.
```
         32,508  ≈         30,000
    ×       591  ≈    ×       600
  Cal.: 19,212,228    Est.: 18,000,000
```

95.
```
         62,504  ≈         60,000
    ×       923  ≈    ×       900
  Cal.: 57,691,192    Est.: 54,000,000
```

Objective C Exercises

96. **Strategy** To find the distance the car could travel on 12 gallons of gas, multiply the mileage per gallon (43) by the number of gallons (12).

Solution
```
   43
  ×12
   86
  43
  516
```
The car could travel 516 miles.

97. **Strategy** To find the number of gallons of fuel used on a 6-hour flight, multiply the number of gallons used in 1 hour (865) by 6.

Solution
```
   865
 ×   6
  5190
```
The plane used 5190 gallons of fuel in a 6-hour flight.

98. **Strategy** To find the perimeter, multiply the four by the length of the side (16 mi).

Solution
```
  16
 × 4
  64
```
The perimeter is 64 miles.

99. **Strategy** To find the area, multiply the length of one side (16 miles) by itself (16 miles).

Solution
```
   16
  ×16
   96
  16
  256
```
The area is 256 square miles.

100. **Strategy** To find the area, multiply the length (24 meters) by the width (15 meters).

Solution
```
   24
  ×15
  120
  24
  360
```
The area is 360 square meters.

101. **Strategy** To determine which company offers the lights for the lower total price:

- Find the total price each company would charge.
- Compare the two prices.

Solution

Company A	Company B
43 × 2 = 86	43 × 3 = 129
15 × 6 = 90	15 × 4 = 60
20 × 12 = 240	20 × 11 = 220
1 × 998 = 998	1 × 1089 = 1089
Total = 1414	Total = 1498

1414 < 1498

Company A offers the lower total price.

102. Strategy To determine how much the lighting consultant can save, find the difference between the total prices charged by the two companies. Use the prices from Exercise 101.

Solution
$$\begin{array}{r} 1498 \\ -1414 \\ \hline 84 \end{array}$$
The lighting consultant can save $84.

103. Strategy To estimate the cost for the electricians' labor, multiply the number of electricians (3) by the number of hours each works (50) by the wage per hour (34).

Solution Total cost = no. of electricians × no. of hours each works × wages per hour
= 3 × 50 × 34
= $5100
The estimated cost of the electricians' labor is $5100.

104. Strategy To find the total wages paid, multiply the number of plumbers (4) by the number of hours each works (23) by the wage per hour (30).

Solution Total wages = no. of plumbers × no. of hours each works × wages per hour
= 4 × 23 × 30
= $2760
The total wages paid to Carlos are $2760.

105. Strategy To find the total cost for the four components:
- Determine the costs for the electrician, the plumber, the clerical work, and the bookkeeper.
- Add to find the sum of the four costs.

Solution

Electrician =	1 × 30 × $34 =	$1020
Plumber =	1 × 33 × $30 =	$990
Clerk =	1 × 3 × $16 =	$48
Bookkeeper =	1 × 4 × $20 =	$80
	Total =	$2138

The total cost is $2138.

Applying the Concepts

106a. Always true
b. Always true
c. Sometimes true, c is a true statement except in the cases described in parts a and b.

107. There is one accidental death every 5 minutes.
There are 60 minutes in an hour.
5 × 12 = 60
There are 12 accidental deaths in an hour.
There are 24 hours per day.
12 × 24 = 288
There are 288 accidental deaths in a day.
There are 365 days in a year.
288 × 365 = 105,120
There are 105,120 accidental deaths in a year.

108. To find the increase per minute, subtract the number of people who die every minute from the number of people born every minute.
261 − 101 = 160
To find the increase every hour, multiply the increase per minute by 60 minutes per hour.
160 × 60 = 9600
The population increases by 9600 people every hour.
To find the increase every day, multiply the increase per hour by 24 hours per day.
9600 × 24 = 230,400
The population increases by 230,400 people every day.
To find the increase every week, multiply the increase per day by 7 days per week.
230,400 × 7 = 1,612,800
The population increases by 1,612,800 people every week.
To find the increase every year, multiply the increase per day by 365 days per year.
230,400 × 365 = 84,096,000
The population increases by 84,096,000 people every year.

109. 3 × 37,037 = 111,111
By the Multiplication Property of One, a number times 1 equals the number. Because the product of 3 and 37,037 is 111,111, the product of 111,111 and a number between 1 and 9 will be a six-digit number in which all digits equal the number between 1 and 9.

110. Answers will vary.

Section 1.5

Objective A Exercises

1. 2

2. 3

3. 6

4. 9

5. 7

6.
$$\begin{array}{r} 16 \\ 5\overline{)80} \\ \underline{-5} \\ 30 \\ \underline{-30} \\ 0 \end{array}$$

7.
$$\begin{array}{r} 16 \\ 6\overline{)96} \\ \underline{-6} \\ 36 \\ \underline{-36} \\ 0 \end{array}$$

8.
$$\begin{array}{r} 80 \\ 6\overline{)480} \\ \underline{-48} \\ 00 \\ \underline{-\ 0} \\ 0 \end{array}$$

9.
$$\begin{array}{r} 210 \\ 4\overline{)840} \\ \underline{-8} \\ 04 \\ \underline{-\ 4} \\ 00 \\ \underline{-\ 0} \\ 0 \end{array}$$

10.
$$\begin{array}{r} 230 \\ 3\overline{)690} \\ \underline{-6} \\ 09 \\ \underline{-\ 9} \\ 00 \\ \underline{-\ 0} \\ 0 \end{array}$$

11.
$$\begin{array}{r} 44 \\ 7\overline{)308} \\ \underline{-28} \\ 28 \\ \underline{-28} \\ 0 \end{array}$$

12.
$$\begin{array}{r} 29 \\ 7\overline{)203} \\ \underline{-14} \\ 63 \\ \underline{-63} \\ 0 \end{array}$$

13.
$$\begin{array}{r} 703 \\ 9\overline{)6327} \\ \underline{-63} \\ 02 \\ \underline{-\ 0} \\ 27 \\ \underline{-27} \\ 0 \end{array}$$

14.
$$\begin{array}{r} 530 \\ 4\overline{)2120} \\ \underline{-20} \\ 12 \\ \underline{-12} \\ 00 \\ \underline{-\ 0} \\ 0 \end{array}$$

15.
$$\begin{array}{r} 910 \\ 8\overline{)7280} \\ \underline{-72} \\ 08 \\ \underline{-\ 8} \\ 00 \\ \underline{-\ 0} \\ 0 \end{array}$$

16.
$$\begin{array}{r} 902 \\ 9\overline{)8118} \\ \underline{-81} \\ 01 \\ \underline{-\ 0} \\ 18 \\ \underline{-18} \\ 0 \end{array}$$

17.
$$\begin{array}{r} 21{,}560 \\ 3\overline{)64{,}680} \\ \underline{-6} \\ 04 \\ \underline{-\ 3} \\ 16 \\ \underline{-15} \\ 18 \\ \underline{-\ 18} \\ 00 \\ \underline{-\ 0} \\ 0 \end{array}$$

18.
$$\begin{array}{r} 12{,}690 \\ 4\overline{)50{,}760} \\ \underline{-4} \\ 10 \\ \underline{-\ 8} \\ 27 \\ \underline{-24} \\ 36 \\ \underline{-36} \\ 00 \\ \underline{-\ 0} \\ 0 \end{array}$$

19.
$$\begin{array}{r} 3{,}580 \\ 6\overline{)21{,}480} \\ \underline{-18} \\ 34 \\ \underline{-30} \\ 48 \\ \underline{-48} \\ 00 \\ \underline{-\ 0} \\ 0 \end{array}$$

20.
$$\begin{array}{r} 3{,}610 \\ 5\overline{)18{,}050} \\ \underline{-15} \\ 30 \\ \underline{-30} \\ 05 \\ \underline{-\ 5} \\ 00 \\ \underline{-\ 0} \\ 0 \end{array}$$

21.
$$\begin{array}{r} 482 \\ 3\overline{)1446} \\ \underline{-12} \\ 24 \\ \underline{-24} \\ 06 \\ \underline{-\ 6} \\ 0 \end{array}$$

22.
$$\begin{array}{r} 589 \\ 7\overline{)4123} \\ \underline{-35} \\ 62 \\ \underline{-56} \\ 63 \\ \underline{-63} \\ 0 \end{array}$$

23.
$$\begin{array}{r} 1075 \\ 7\overline{)7525} \\ \underline{-7} \\ 05 \\ \underline{-\ 0} \\ 52 \\ \underline{-49} \\ 35 \\ \underline{-35} \\ 0 \end{array}$$

24.
$$\begin{array}{r} 8{,}091 \\ 4\overline{)32{,}364} \\ \underline{-32} \\ 03 \\ \underline{-0} \\ 36 \\ \underline{-36} \\ 04 \\ \underline{-4} \\ 0 \end{array}$$

25.
$$\begin{array}{r} 52 \\ 7\overline{)364} \\ \underline{-35} \\ 14 \\ \underline{-14} \\ 0 \end{array}$$

26.
$$\begin{array}{r} 47 \\ 8\overline{)376} \\ \underline{-32} \\ 56 \\ \underline{-56} \\ 0 \end{array}$$

27.
$$\begin{array}{r} 34 \\ 5\overline{)170} \\ \underline{-15} \\ 20 \\ \underline{-20} \\ 0 \end{array}$$

28.
$$\begin{array}{r} 23 \\ 4\overline{)92} \\ \underline{-8} \\ 12 \\ \underline{-12} \\ 0 \end{array}$$

Objective B Exercises

29.
$$\begin{array}{r} 2 \text{ r1} \\ 4\overline{)9} \\ \underline{-8} \\ 1 \end{array}$$

30.
$$\begin{array}{r} 3 \text{ r1} \\ 2\overline{)7} \\ \underline{-6} \\ 1 \end{array}$$

31.
$$\begin{array}{r} 5 \text{ r2} \\ 5\overline{)27} \\ \underline{-25} \\ 2 \end{array}$$

32.
$$\begin{array}{r} 9 \text{ r7} \\ 9\overline{)88} \\ \underline{-81} \\ 7 \end{array}$$

33.
$$\begin{array}{r} 13 \text{ r1} \\ 3\overline{)40} \\ \underline{-3} \\ 10 \\ \underline{-9} \\ 1 \end{array}$$

34.
$$\begin{array}{r} 16 \text{ r1} \\ 6\overline{)97} \\ \underline{-6} \\ 37 \\ \underline{-36} \\ 1 \end{array}$$

35.
$$\begin{array}{r} 10 \text{ r3} \\ 8\overline{)83} \\ \underline{-8} \\ 03 \\ \underline{-0} \\ 3 \end{array}$$

36.
$$\begin{array}{r} 10 \text{ r4} \\ 5\overline{)54} \\ \underline{-5} \\ 04 \\ \underline{-0} \\ 4 \end{array}$$

37.
$$\begin{array}{r} 90 \text{ r2} \\ 7\overline{)632} \\ \underline{-63} \\ 02 \\ \underline{-0} \\ 2 \end{array}$$

38.
$$\begin{array}{r} 90 \text{ r3} \\ 4\overline{)363} \\ \underline{-36} \\ 03 \\ \underline{-0} \\ 3 \end{array}$$

39.
$$\begin{array}{r} 230 \text{ r1} \\ 4\overline{)921} \\ \underline{-8} \\ 12 \\ \underline{-12} \\ 01 \\ \underline{-0} \\ 1 \end{array}$$

40.
$$\begin{array}{r} 120 \text{ r5} \\ 7\overline{)845} \\ \underline{-7} \\ 14 \\ \underline{-14} \\ 05 \\ \underline{-0} \\ 5 \end{array}$$

41.
$$\begin{array}{r} 204 \text{ r3} \\ 8\overline{)1635} \\ \underline{-16} \\ 03 \\ \underline{-0} \\ 35 \\ \underline{-32} \\ 3 \end{array}$$

42.
$$\begin{array}{r} 309 \text{ r3} \\ 5\overline{)1548} \\ \underline{-15} \\ 04 \\ \underline{-0} \\ 48 \\ \underline{-45} \\ 3 \end{array}$$

43.
$$\begin{array}{r} 1347 \text{ r3} \\ 7\overline{)9432} \\ \underline{-7} \\ 24 \\ \underline{-21} \\ 33 \\ \underline{-28} \\ 52 \\ \underline{-49} \\ 3 \end{array}$$

44.
$$\begin{array}{r} 1160 \text{ r4} \\ 7\overline{)8124} \\ \underline{-7} \\ 11 \\ \underline{-7} \\ 42 \\ \underline{-42} \\ 04 \\ \underline{-0} \\ 4 \end{array}$$

45.
$$\begin{array}{r} 1720 \text{ r2} \\ 3\overline{)5162} \\ \underline{-3} \\ 21 \\ \underline{-21} \\ 06 \\ \underline{-6} \\ 02 \\ \underline{-0} \\ 2 \end{array}$$

46.
$$\begin{array}{r} 708 \text{ r2} \\ 5\overline{)3542} \\ \underline{-35} \\ 04 \\ \underline{-0} \\ 42 \\ \underline{-40} \\ 2 \end{array}$$

47. 409 r2
8)3274
−32
07
− 0
74
−72
2

48. 3,825 r1
4)15,301
−12
33
−32
10
− 8
21
−20
1

49. 6,214 r2
7)43,500
−42
15
−14
10
− 7
30
−28
2

50. 9,044 r2
8)72,354
−72
03
− 0
35
− 32
34
−32
2

51. 8,708 r2
5)43,542
−40
35
−35
04
− 0
42
−40
2

52. 388 r3
8)3107
−24
70
−64
67
−64
3

53. 1080 r2
8)8642
−8
06
− 0
64
−64
02
− 0
2

54. 11,434 r2
4)45,738
−4
05
− 4
17
−16
13
−12
18
−16
2
Round to 11,430.

55. 4,210 r6
9)37,896
−36
18
−18
09
− 9
06
− 0
6
Round to 4200.

56. 510 r2
7)3572
−35
07
− 7
02
− 0
2
Round to 510.

57. 19,586 r1
4)78,345
−4
38
−36
23
−20
34
−32
25
−24
1
Round to 19,600.

Objective C Exercises

58. 3 r15
27)96
−81
15

59. 1 r38
44)82
−44
38

60. 2 r3
42)87
−84
3

61. 1 r26
67)93
−67
26

62. 21 r36
41)897
−82
77
−41
36

63. 21 r21
32)693
−64
53
−32
21

64. 34 r2
23)784
−69
94
−92
2

65. 30 r22
25)772
−75
22
− 0
22

66. 8 r8
74)600
−592
8

67. 5 r40
92)500
−460
40

68. 4 r49
70)329
−280
49

69. 9 r17
50)467
−450
17

70. 200 r25
36)7225
−72
02
− 0
25
− 0
25

71. 200 r21
44)8821
−88
02
− 0
21
− 0
21

72. 203 r2
19)3859
−38
05
− 0
59
−57
2

73. 303 r1
32)9697
−96
09
− 0
97
−96
1

74. 35 r47
88)3127
−264
487
−440
47

75. 67 r13
92)6177
−552
657
−644
13

76. 271
33)8943
−66
234
−231
33
−33
0

77. 176 r13
27)4765
−27
206
−189
175
−162
13

78. 4,484 r6
22)98,654
−88
106
− 88
185
−176
94
−88
6

79. 1,086 r7
77)83,629
−77
66
− 0
662
−616
469
−462
7

80. 608
64)38,912
−384
51
− 0
512
−512
0

81. 403
78)31,434
−312
23
− 0
234
−234
0

82. 15 r7
206)3097
−206
1037
−1030
7

83. 12 r456
504)6504
−504
1464
−1008
456

84. 1 r563
654)1217
− 654
563

85. 4 r160
546)2344
−2184
160

86. 258 r14
21)5432
−42
123
−105
182
−168
14

87. 160 r27
53)8507
−53
320
−318
27

88. 517 r70
72)37,294
−360
129
− 72
574
−504
70

89. 1,669 r14
46)76,788
−46
307
−276
318
−276
428
−414
14

90.
```
     545  r22
43)23,457
  -215
    195
   -172
    237
   -215
     22
```
Round to 500.

91.
```
     7,948  r17
43)341,781
  -301
    407
   -387
     208
    -172
     361
    -344
      17
```
Round to 7950.

92. Cal.: 76)389,804 = 5,129 Est.: 80)400,000 = 5,000

93. Cal.: 53)117,925 = 2,225 Est.: 50)100,000 = 2,000

94. Cal.: 29)637,072 = 21,968 Est.: 30)600,000 = 20,000

95. Cal.: 67)738,072 = 11,016 Est.: 70)700,000 = 10,000

96. Cal.: 38)934,648 = 24,596 Est.: 40)900,000 = 22,500

97. Cal.: 34)906,304 = 26,656 Est.: 30)900,000 = 30,000

98. Cal.: 309)876,324 = 2,836 Est.: 300)900,000 = 3,000

99. Cal.: 642)323,568 = 504 Est.: 600)300,000 = 500

100. Cal.: 209)632,016 = 3,024 Est.: 200)600,000 = 3,000

101. Cal.: 614)332,174 = 541 Est.: 600)300,000 = 500

102. Cal.: 179)5,734,444 = 32,036 Est.: 200)6,000,000 = 30,000

103. Cal.: 374)7,712,254 = 20,621 Est.: 400)8,000,000 = 20,000

Objective D Exercises

104. Strategy To find the total amount spent annually, add all the expenses.

Solution
```
  $11,713
     5366
     1746
     1903
     3381
     4810
  +  6616
  $35,535
```
The total amount spent annually is $35,535.

105. Strategy To find the monthly expense for housing, divide annual housing expense ($11,713) by the number of months (12).

Solution
```
      976
12)11,713
  -108
     91
    -84
     73
    -72
      1
```
The average monthly expense for housing is $976.

106. Strategy To find the difference between the average monthly expense for food and health care, find the average monthly expense for food by dividing the annual expense for food ($4810) by the number of months in a year (12), find the average monthly expense for health care by dividing the annual expense for health care ($1903) by the number of months in a year (12), and then find the difference between the two by subtracting the average monthly expense for health care from the average monthly expense for food.

Solution
```
     400                 158
12)4810             12)1903
  -48                 -12
   01                  70
  - 0                 -60
    10                 103
   - 0                - 96
    10                   7
```
Round the quotient to 401. Round the quotient to 159.

The monthly expense for food is approximately $401, and the monthly expense for health care is approximately $159.
```
  $401
 -$159
  $242
```
The difference is $242.

107. Strategy To find the average monthly claim for theft, divide the annual claim for theft ($300,000) by the number of months (12).

Solution

```
      25,000
12)300,000
   −24
     60
    −60
      00
     − 0
       00
      − 0
        00
       − 0
         0
```

The average monthly claim for theft is $25,000.

108. Strategy To find the average claims per month for all the sources combined, add all the claims and divide the sum by the number of months (12).

Solution

```
   $560,000              95,000
    300,000       12)1,140,000
     80,000          −108
     50,000             60
     20,000            −60
     20,000              00
+   110,000             − 0
 $1,140,000               00
                         − 0
                           00
                          − 0
                             0
```

The average claims per month is $95,000.

109. Strategy To find the average hours worked by employees in Britain, divide the annual hours worked (1731) by the number of weeks (50).

Solution

```
      34
50)1731
  −150
     231
    −200
      31
```

Since 31 is greater than half of 50, the average number of hours worked by employees in Britain is 35 hours.

110. Strategy To find the difference in the average weekly work hours between an employee from France and the United States, find the average weekly work hours for a U.S. employee by dividing the annual work hours (1966) by the number of weeks in a year (50), find the average weekly work hours for a French employee by dividing the annual work hours (1656) by the number of weeks in a year (50), and then find the difference between the two by subtracting.

Solution

```
     39             33
50)1966       50)1656
  −150          −150
    466            156
   −450           −150
     16              6
```

The U.S. employee works approximately 39 hours, and the French employee works approximately 33 hours.

```
  39
 −33
   6
```

The difference is 6 hours.

111. Strategy To find the approximate number of pennies per person, divide the number of pennies in circulation (114,000,000,000) by the number of people (300,000,000).

Solution 380 pennies are in circulation for each person.

Applying the Concepts

112. Strategy To find the total of the three deductions, add the three deductions.

Solution

```
$225  Savings
  98  Taxes
  27  Insurance
$350
```

The total of the three deductions is $350.

113. Strategy To find the number of cases of eggs produced during the year, add all the values read from the graph.

Solution

```
111,100,000  Retail Stores
 61,600,000  Non-shell Products
 24,100,000  Food Service Use
  1,600,000  Exported
198,400,000
```

198,400,000 cases of eggs were produced during the year.

114. Strategy To find how many more cases of eggs were sold by retail stores than were used for non-shell products, subtract the number of non-shell products cases (61,600,000) from the number of cases sold in retail stores (111,100,000).

Solution

$$\begin{array}{r} 111{,}100{,}000 \\ -61{,}600{,}000 \\ \hline 49{,}500{,}000 \end{array}$$

Retail stores sold 49,500,000 more cases of eggs than were used for non-shell products.

115. Strategy To find the estimated amount the average U.S. household will spend on gasoline in 2020, divide the annual amount ($1562) by 12.

Solution

$$\begin{array}{r} 130 \\ 12\overline{)1562} \\ \underline{12} \\ 36 \\ \underline{36} \\ 2 \end{array}$$

Since 2 is less than half of 12, the average U.S. household will spend $130 (to the nearest dollar) on gasoline each month in 2020.

116. Strategy To find the difference between the starting salary for a computer science major and a biology major, subtract the starting salary for a biology major ($29,554) from the starting salary for a computer science major ($47,419).

Solution

$$\begin{array}{r} \$47{,}419 \\ -\$29{,}554 \\ \hline \$17{,}865 \end{array}$$

The difference in starting salary for a computer science major and a biology major is $17,865.

117. Strategy To find how much greater the average starting salary of an accounting major is than a psychology major, subtract the psychology major's starting salary ($27,454) from the accounting major's starting salary ($40,546).

Solution

$$\begin{array}{r} \$40{,}546 \\ -\$27{,}454 \\ \hline \$13{,}092 \end{array}$$

The average starting salary of an accounting major is $13,092 more than a psychology major.

118. Strategy To find a major's annual pay, multiply the monthly pay ($5528) by 12.

Solution

$$\begin{array}{r} \$5528 \\ \times\ \ 12 \\ \hline 11056 \\ 5528\ \\ \hline \$66336 \end{array}$$

A major's annual pay is $66,336.

119. Strategy To find the difference between a colonel's annual pay and a lieutenant colonel's annual pay:
- Subtract the lieutenant colonel's monthly pay ($6329) from the colonel's monthly pay ($7233) to find the monthly difference.
- Multiply the monthly difference by 12 to find the annual difference.

Solution

$$\begin{array}{r} \$7233 \\ -\$6329 \\ \hline \$904 \end{array} \qquad \begin{array}{r} \$904 \\ \times 12 \\ \hline 1808 \\ 904\ \\ \hline \$10848 \end{array}$$

The difference in annual pay for a colonel and a lieutenant colonel is $10,848.

120. Strategy To find the number of boxes needed to pack the avocados:
- Add the number of pounds from the two groves to find the total weight to be packed.
- Divide the total weight by the number of pounds in each box (24).

Solution

$$\begin{array}{r} \$48{,}290 \text{ pounds} \\ +\$23{,}710 \text{ pounds} \\ \hline \$72{,}000 \text{ pounds} \end{array} \qquad \begin{array}{r} 3000 \text{ boxes} \\ 24\overline{)72{,}000} \\ \underline{72} \\ 000 \end{array}$$

3000 boxes were needed to pack the avocados.

121. Strategy To find the total pay:
- Multiply the overtime rate ($13) by the number of extra hours worked (9).
- Add the extra wages to the amount for working a 40 hour week ($374).

Solution

$$\begin{array}{r} \$13 \\ \times\ 9 \\ \hline \$117 \end{array} \text{ additional pay} \qquad \begin{array}{r} \$374 \\ +\$117 \\ \hline \$491 \end{array}$$

The sales associate's total pay for the week was $491.

122. Strategy To find the total amount paid for the car:
- Multiply \$195 by 48 to find the amount paid in monthly payments.
- Add the total for the monthly payments to the down payment (\$2500).

Solution

$$\begin{array}{r} \$195 \\ \times 48 \\ \hline 1560 \\ 780 \\ \hline \$9360 \end{array} \qquad \begin{array}{r} \$2500 \\ +9360 \\ \hline \$11860 \end{array}$$

The total amount paid for the car was \$11,860.

123. The smallest three-digit palindrome number that is divisible by 4 is 212. Consider the list of the palindromic numbers 101, 111, 121, 131, ... 191, 202, 212, ...
The first ten numbers have an odd final digit and are thus not divisible by 4.

Section 1.6

Objective A Exercises

1. 2^3

2. 7^5

3. $6^3 \cdot 7^4$

4. $6^2 \cdot 9^4$

5. $2^3 \cdot 3^3$

6. $3^2 \cdot 10^2$

7. $5 \cdot 7^5$

8. $4^3 \cdot 5^3$

9. $3^3 \cdot 6^4$

10. $2^2 \cdot 5^3 \cdot 8$

11. $3^3 \cdot 5 \cdot 9^3$

12. $2^3 \cdot 4 \cdot 7^3$

13. $2 \cdot 2 \cdot 2 = 8$

14. $2 \cdot 2 \cdot 2 \cdot 2 \cdot 2 \cdot 2 = 64$

15. $2 \cdot 2 \cdot 2 \cdot 2 \cdot 5 \cdot 5 = 16 \cdot 25 = 400$

16. $2 \cdot 2 \cdot 2 \cdot 2 \cdot 2 \cdot 2 \cdot 3 \cdot 3 = 64 \cdot 9 = 576$

17. $3 \cdot 3 \cdot 10 \cdot 10 = 9 \cdot 100 = 900$

18. $2 \cdot 2 \cdot 2 \cdot 10 \cdot 10 \cdot 10 \cdot 10 = 8 \cdot 10{,}000 = 80{,}000$

19. $6 \cdot 6 \cdot 3 \cdot 3 \cdot 3 = 36 \cdot 27 = 972$

20. $4 \cdot 4 \cdot 4 \cdot 5 \cdot 5 = 64 \cdot 25 = 1600$

21. $5 \cdot 2 \cdot 2 \cdot 2 \cdot 3 = 5 \cdot 8 \cdot 3 = 120$

22. $6 \cdot 3 \cdot 3 \cdot 4 = 6 \cdot 9 \cdot 4 = 216$

23. $2 \cdot 2 \cdot 3 \cdot 3 \cdot 10 = 4 \cdot 9 \cdot 10 = 360$

24. $3 \cdot 3 \cdot 5 \cdot 5 \cdot 10 = 9 \cdot 25 \cdot 10 = 2250$

25. $0 \cdot 0 \cdot 4 \cdot 4 \cdot 4 = 0 \cdot 64 = 0$

26. $6 \cdot 6 \cdot 0 \cdot 0 \cdot 0 = 36 \cdot 0 = 0$

27. $3 \cdot 3 \cdot 10 \cdot 10 \cdot 10 \cdot 10 = 9 \cdot 10{,}000 = 90{,}000$

28. $5 \cdot 5 \cdot 5 \cdot 10 \cdot 10 \cdot 10 = 125 \cdot 1000 = 125{,}000$

29. $2 \cdot 2 \cdot 3 \cdot 3 \cdot 3 \cdot 5 = 4 \cdot 27 \cdot 5 = 540$

30. $5 \cdot 5 \cdot 7 \cdot 7 \cdot 7 \cdot 2 = 25 \cdot 343 \cdot 2 = 17{,}150$

31. $2 \cdot 3 \cdot 3 \cdot 3 \cdot 3 \cdot 5 \cdot 5 = 2 \cdot 81 \cdot 25 = 4050$

32. $6 \cdot 2 \cdot 2 \cdot 2 \cdot 2 \cdot 2 \cdot 2 \cdot 7 \cdot 7 = 6 \cdot 64 \cdot 49 = 18{,}816$

33. $5 \cdot 5 \cdot 3 \cdot 3 \cdot 7 \cdot 7 = 25 \cdot 9 \cdot 49 = 11{,}025$

34. $4 \cdot 4 \cdot 9 \cdot 9 \cdot 6 \cdot 6 = 16 \cdot 81 \cdot 36 = 46{,}656$

35. $3 \cdot 3 \cdot 3 \cdot 3 \cdot 2 \cdot 2 \cdot 2 \cdot 2 \cdot 2 \cdot 2 \cdot 5 = 81 \cdot 64 \cdot 5 = 25{,}920$

36. $4 \cdot 4 \cdot 4 \cdot 6 \cdot 6 \cdot 6 \cdot 7 = 64 \cdot 216 \cdot 7 = 96{,}768$

37. $4 \cdot 4 \cdot 3 \cdot 3 \cdot 3 \cdot 10 \cdot 10 \cdot 10 \cdot 10 = 16 \cdot 27 \cdot 10{,}000 = 4{,}320{,}000$

Objective B Exercises

38. $4 - 2 + 3 = 2 + 3 = 5$

39. $6 - 3 + 2 = 3 + 2 = 5$

40. $6 \div 3 + 2 = 2 + 2 = 4$

41. $8 \div 4 + 8 = 2 + 8 = 10$

42. $6 \cdot 3 + 5 = 18 + 5 = 23$

43. $5 \cdot 9 + 2 = 45 + 2 = 47$

44. $3^2 - 4 = 9 - 4 = 5$

45. $5^2 - 17 = 25 - 17 = 8$

46. $4 \cdot (5 - 3) + 2 = 4 \cdot 2 + 2 = 8 + 2 = 10$

47. $3 + (4 + 2) \div 3 = 3 + 6 \div 3 = 3 + 2 = 5$

48. $5 + (8 + 4) \div 6 = 5 + 12 \div 6 = 5 + 2 = 7$

49. $8 - 2^2 + 4 = 8 - 4 + 4 = 4 + 4 = 8$

50. $16 \cdot (3 + 2) \div 10 = 16 \cdot 5 \div 10 = 80 \div 10 = 8$

51. $12 \cdot (1 + 5) \div 12 = 12 \cdot 6 \div 12 = 72 \div 12 = 6$

52. $10 - 2^3 + 4 = 10 - 8 + 4$
$= 2 + 4 = 6$

53. $5 \cdot 3^2 + 8 = 5 \cdot 9 + 8$
$= 45 + 8 = 53$

54. $16 + 4 \cdot 3^2 = 16 + 4 \cdot 9$
$= 16 + 36 = 52$

55. $12 + 4 \cdot 2^3 = 12 + 4 \cdot 8$
$= 12 + 32 = 44$

56. $16 + (8 - 3) \cdot 2 = 16 + 5 \cdot 2$
$= 16 + 10 = 26$

57. $7 + (9 - 5) \cdot 3 = 7 + 4 \cdot 3$
$= 7 + 12 = 19$

58. $2^2 + 3 \cdot (6 - 2)^2 = 2^2 + 3 \cdot 4^2$
$= 4 + 3 \cdot 16$
$= 4 + 48 = 52$

59. $3^3 + 5 \cdot (8 - 6)^3 = 3^3 + 5 \cdot 2^3$
$= 27 + 5 \cdot 8$
$= 27 + 40 = 67$

60. $2^2 \cdot 3^2 + 2 \cdot 3 = 4 \cdot 9 + 2 \cdot 3$
$= 36 + 2 \cdot 3$
$= 36 + 6 = 42$

61. $4 \cdot 6 + 3^2 \cdot 4^2 = 4 \cdot 6 + 9 \cdot 16$
$= 24 + 9 \cdot 16$
$= 24 + 144 = 168$

62. $16 - 2 \cdot 4 = 16 - 8 = 8$

63. $12 + 3 \cdot 5 = 12 + 15 = 27$

64. $3 \cdot (6 - 2) + 4 = 3 \cdot 4 + 4 = 12 + 4 = 16$

65. $5 \cdot (8 - 4) - 6 = 5 \cdot 4 - 6 = 20 - 6 = 14$

66. $8 - (8 - 2) \div 3 = 8 - 6 \div 3 = 8 - 2 = 6$

67. $12 - (12 - 4) \div 4 = 12 - 8 \div 4 = 12 - 2 = 10$

68. $8 + 2 - 3 \cdot 2 \div 3 = 8 + 2 - 6 \div 3$
$= 8 + 2 - 2$
$= 10 - 2 = 8$

69. $10 + 1 - 5 \cdot 2 \div 5 = 10 + 1 - 10 \div 5$
$= 10 + 1 - 2$
$= 11 - 2 = 9$

70. $3 \cdot (4 + 2) \div 6 = 3 \cdot 6 \div 6 = 18 \div 6 = 3$

71. $(7 - 3)^2 \div 2 - 4 + 8 = 4^2 \div 2 - 4 + 8$
$= 16 \div 2 - 4 + 8$
$= 8 - 4 + 8$
$= 4 + 8 = 12$

72. $20 - 4 \div 2 \cdot (3 - 1)^3 = 20 - 4 \div 2 \cdot 2^3$
$= 20 - 4 \div 2 \cdot 8$
$= 20 - 2 \cdot 8$
$= 20 - 16 = 4$

73. $12 \div 3 \cdot 2^2 + (7 - 3)^2 = 12 \div 3 \cdot 2^2 + 4^2$
$= 12 \div 3 \cdot 4 + 16$
$= 4 \cdot 4 + 16$
$= 16 + 16 = 32$

74. $(4 - 2) \cdot 6 \div 3 + (5 - 2)^2 = 2 \cdot 6 \div 3 + 3^2$
$= 2 \cdot 6 \div 3 + 9$
$= 12 \div 3 + 9$
$= 4 + 9 = 13$

75. $18 - 2 \cdot 3 + (4 - 1)^3 = 18 - 2 \cdot 3 + 3^3$
$= 18 - 2 \cdot 3 + 27$
$= 18 - 6 + 27$
$= 12 + 27 = 39$

76. $100 \div (2 + 3)^2 - 8 \div 2 = 100 \div 5^2 - 8 \div 2$
$= 100 \div 25 - 8 \div 2$
$= 4 - 8 \div 2$
$= 4 - 4 = 0$

Applying the Concepts

77. $2^{10} = 1024$

78. In part a, the expression $\frac{14-2}{2}$ is first divided by 2 and then multiplied by 3. In part b, the same expression is divided by the product of 2 and 3. The difference between the two answers is $9 - 1 = 8$.

Section 1.7

Objective A Exercises

1. $4 \div 1 = 4$
$4 \div 2 = 2$
Factors are 1, 2, and 4.

2. $6 \div 1 = 6$
$6 \div 2 = 3$
$6 \div 3 = 2$
Factors are 1, 2, 3, and 6.

3. $10 \div 1 = 10$
$10 \div 2 = 5$
$10 \div 5 = 2$
Factors are 1, 2, 5, and 10.

4. $20 \div 1 = 20$
$20 \div 2 = 10$
$20 \div 4 = 5$
$20 \div 5 = 4$
Factors are 1, 2, 4, 5, 10, and 20.

5. $7 \div 1 = 7$
$7 \div 7 = 1$
Factors are 1 and 7.

6. $12 \div 1 = 12$
$12 \div 2 = 6$
$12 \div 3 = 4$
$12 \div 4 = 3$
Factors are 1, 2, 3, 4, 6, and 12.

7. $9 \div 1 = 9$
$9 \div 3 = 3$
Factors are 1, 3, and 9.

8. $8 \div 1 = 8$
$8 \div 2 = 4$
$8 \div 4 = 2$
Factors are 1, 2, 4, and 8.

9. $13 \div 1 = 13$
$13 \div 13 = 1$
Factors are 1 and 13.

10. $17 \div 1 = 17$
$17 \div 17 = 1$
Factors are 1 and 17.

11. $18 \div 1 = 18$
$18 \div 2 = 9$
$18 \div 3 = 6$
$18 \div 6 = 3$
Factors are 1, 2, 3, 6, 9, and 18.

12. $24 \div 1 = 24$
$24 \div 2 = 12$
$24 \div 3 = 8$
$24 \div 4 = 6$
$24 \div 6 = 4$
Factors are 1, 2, 3, 4, 6, 8, 12, and 24.

13. $56 \div 1 = 56$
$56 \div 2 = 28$
$56 \div 4 = 14$
$56 \div 7 = 8$
$56 \div 8 = 7$
Factors are 1, 2, 4, 7, 8, 14, 28, and 56.

14. $36 \div 1 = 36$
$36 \div 2 = 18$
$36 \div 3 = 12$
$36 \div 4 = 9$
$36 \div 6 = 6$
Factors are 1, 2, 3, 4, 6, 9, 12, 18, and 36.

15. $45 \div 1 = 45$
$45 \div 3 = 15$
$45 \div 5 = 9$
Factors are 1, 3, 5, 9, 15, and 45.

16. $28 \div 1 = 28$
$28 \div 2 = 14$
$28 \div 4 = 7$
$28 \div 7 = 4$
Factors are 1, 2, 4, 7, 14, and 28.

17. $29 \div 1 = 29$
$29 \div 29 = 1$
Factors are 1 and 29.

18. $33 \div 1 = 33$
$33 \div 3 = 11$
$33 \div 11 = 3$
Factors are 1, 3, 11, and 33.

19. $22 \div 1 = 22$
$22 \div 2 = 11$
$22 \div 11 = 2$
Factors are 1, 2, 11, and 22.

20. $26 \div 1 = 26$
$26 \div 2 = 13$
$26 \div 13 = 2$
Factors are 1, 2, 13, and 26.

21. $52 \div 1 = 52$
$52 \div 2 = 26$
$52 \div 4 = 13$
$52 \div 13 = 4$
Factors are 1, 2, 4, 13, 26, and 52.

22. $49 \div 1 = 49$
$49 \div 7 = 7$
Factors are 1, 7, and 49.

23. $82 \div 1 = 82$
$82 \div 2 = 41$
$82 \div 41 = 2$
Factors are 1, 2, 41, and 82.

24. $37 \div 1 = 37$
$37 \div 37 = 1$
Factors are 1 and 37.

25. $57 \div 1 = 57$
$57 \div 3 = 19$
$57 \div 19 = 3$
Factors are 1, 3, 19, and 57.

26. $69 \div 1 = 69$
$69 \div 3 = 23$
$69 \div 23 = 3$
Factors are 1, 3, 23, and 69.

27. $48 \div 1 = 48$
$48 \div 2 = 24$
$48 \div 3 = 16$
$48 \div 4 = 12$
$48 \div 6 = 8$
$48 \div 8 = 6$
Factors are 1, 2, 3, 4, 6, 8, 12, 16, 24, and 48.

28. $64 \div 1 = 64$
$64 \div 2 = 32$
$64 \div 4 = 16$
$64 \div 8 = 8$
Factors are 1, 2, 4, 8, 16, 32, and 64.

29. $95 \div 1 = 95$
$95 \div 5 = 19$
$95 \div 19 = 5$
Factors are 1, 5, 19, and 95.

30. $46 \div 1 = 46$
$46 \div 2 = 23$
$46 \div 23 = 2$
Factors are 1, 2, 23, and 46.

31. $54 \div 1 = 54$
$54 \div 2 = 27$
$54 \div 3 = 18$
$54 \div 6 = 9$
$54 \div 9 = 6$
Factors are 1, 2, 3, 6, 9, 18, 27, and 54.

32. $50 \div 1 = 50$
$50 \div 2 = 25$
$50 \div 5 = 10$
$50 \div 10 = 5$
Factors are 1, 2, 5, 10, 25, and 50.

33. $66 \div 1 = 66$
$66 \div 2 = 33$
$66 \div 3 = 22$
$66 \div 6 = 11$
$66 \div 11 = 6$
Factors are 1, 2, 3, 6, 11, 22, 33, and 66.

34. $77 \div 1 = 77$
$77 \div 7 = 11$
$77 \div 11 = 7$
Factors are 1, 7, 11, and 77.

35. $80 \div 1 = 80$
$80 \div 2 = 40$
$80 \div 4 = 20$
$80 \div 5 = 16$
$80 \div 8 = 10$
$80 \div 10 = 8$
Factors are 1, 2, 4, 5, 8, 10, 16, 20, 40, and 80.

36. $100 \div 1 = 100$
$100 \div 2 = 50$
$100 \div 4 = 25$
$100 \div 5 = 20$
$100 \div 10 = 10$
Factors are 1, 2, 4, 5, 10, 20, 25, 50, and 100.

37. $96 \div 1 = 96$
$96 \div 2 = 48$
$96 \div 3 = 32$
$96 \div 4 = 24$
$96 \div 6 = 16$
$96 \div 8 = 12$
$96 \div 12 = 8$
Factors are 1, 2, 3, 4, 6, 8, 12, 16, 24, 32, 48, and 96.

38. $85 \div 1 = 85$
$85 \div 5 = 17$
$85 \div 17 = 5$
Factors are 1, 5, 17, and 85.

39. $90 \div 1 = 90$
$90 \div 2 = 45$
$90 \div 3 = 30$
$90 \div 5 = 18$
$90 \div 6 = 15$
$90 \div 9 = 10$
$90 \div 10 = 9$
Factors are 1, 2, 3, 5, 6, 9, 10, 15, 18, 30, 45, and 90.

40. $101 \div 1 = 101$
$101 \div 101 = 1$
Factors are 1 and 101.

Objective B Exercises

41.

6	
2	3
3	1

$6 = 2 \cdot 3$

42.

14	
2	7
7	1

$14 = 2 \cdot 7$

43. 17 is prime.

44. 83 is prime.

45.

24	
2	12
2	6
2	3
3	1

$24 = 2 \cdot 2 \cdot 2 \cdot 3$

46.

12	
2	6
2	3
3	1

$12 = 2 \cdot 2 \cdot 3$

47.

27	
3	9
3	3
3	1

$27 = 3 \cdot 3 \cdot 3$

48.

9	
3	3
3	1

$9 = 3 \cdot 3$

49.

36	
2	18
2	9
3	3
3	1

$36 = 2 \cdot 2 \cdot 3 \cdot 3$

50.

40	
2	20
2	10
2	5
5	1

$40 = 2 \cdot 2 \cdot 2 \cdot 5$

51. 19 is prime.

52. 37 is prime.

53.

90	
2	45
3	15
3	5
5	1

$90 = 2 \cdot 3 \cdot 3 \cdot 5$

54.

65	
5	13
13	1

$65 = 5 \cdot 13$

55.

115	
5	23
23	1

$115 = 5 \cdot 23$

56.

80	
2	40
2	20
2	10
2	5
5	1

$80 = 2 \cdot 2 \cdot 2 \cdot 2 \cdot 5$

57.

18	
2	9
3	3
3	1

$18 = 2 \cdot 3 \cdot 3$

58.

26	
2	13
13	1

$26 = 2 \cdot 13$

59.

28	
2	14
2	7
7	1

$28 = 2 \cdot 2 \cdot 7$

60.

49	
7	7
7	1

$49 = 7 \cdot 7$

61. 31 is prime.

62.

42	
2	21
3	7
7	1

$42 = 2 \cdot 3 \cdot 7$

63.

62	
2	31
31	1

$62 = 2 \cdot 31$

64.

81	
3	27
3	9
3	3
3	1

$81 = 3 \cdot 3 \cdot 3 \cdot 3$

65.

22	
2	11
11	1

$22 = 2 \cdot 11$

66.

39	
3	13
13	1

$39 = 3 \cdot 13$

67. 101 is prime.

68. 89 is prime.

69.

66	
2	33
3	11
11	1

$66 = 2 \cdot 3 \cdot 11$

70.

86	
2	43
43	1

$86 = 2 \cdot 43$

71.

74	
2	37
37	1

$74 = 2 \cdot 37$

72.

95	
5	19
19	1

$95 = 5 \cdot 19$

73. 67 is prime.

74.

78	
2	39
3	13
13	1

$78 = 2 \cdot 3 \cdot 13$

75.

55	
5	11
11	1

$55 = 5 \cdot 11$

76.

46	
2	23
23	1

$46 = 2 \cdot 23$

77.

120	
2	60
2	30
2	15
3	5
5	1

$120 = 2 \cdot 2 \cdot 2 \cdot 3 \cdot 5$

78.

144	
2	72
2	36
2	18
2	9
3	3
3	1

$144 = 2 \cdot 2 \cdot 2 \cdot 2 \cdot 3 \cdot 3$

79.
$$\begin{array}{r|r} & 160 \\ \hline 2 & 80 \\ 2 & 40 \\ 2 & 20 \\ 2 & 10 \\ 2 & 5 \\ 5 & 1 \end{array}$$
$160 = 2 \cdot 2 \cdot 2 \cdot 2 \cdot 2 \cdot 5$

80.
$$\begin{array}{r|r} & 175 \\ \hline 5 & 35 \\ 5 & 7 \\ 7 & 1 \end{array}$$
$175 = 5 \cdot 5 \cdot 7$

81.
$$\begin{array}{r|r} & 216 \\ \hline 2 & 108 \\ 2 & 54 \\ 2 & 27 \\ 3 & 9 \\ 3 & 3 \\ 3 & 1 \end{array}$$
$216 = 2 \cdot 2 \cdot 2 \cdot 3 \cdot 3 \cdot 3$

82.
$$\begin{array}{r|r} & 400 \\ \hline 2 & 200 \\ 2 & 100 \\ 2 & 50 \\ 2 & 25 \\ 5 & 5 \\ 5 & 1 \end{array}$$
$400 = 2 \cdot 2 \cdot 2 \cdot 2 \cdot 5 \cdot 5$

83.
$$\begin{array}{r|r} & 625 \\ \hline 5 & 125 \\ 5 & 25 \\ 5 & 5 \\ 5 & 1 \end{array}$$
$625 = 5 \cdot 5 \cdot 5 \cdot 5$

84.
$$\begin{array}{r|r} & 225 \\ \hline 3 & 75 \\ 3 & 25 \\ 5 & 5 \\ 5 & 1 \end{array}$$
$225 = 3 \cdot 3 \cdot 5 \cdot 5$

Applying the Concepts

85. 3, 5; 5, 7; 11, 13; 41, 43; 71, 73; and 17, 19 are all the twin primes less than 100.

86. $8 = 3 + 5$

$24 = 11 + 13$

$72 = 31 + 41$ or $72 = 29 + 43$

87. 2 is the *only* even prime number because all other even numbers have 2 as a factor and thus cannot be prime.

88. Yes; 30 is a product of factors of 6 and 10 $(2 \cdot 3 \cdot 5)$.

Chapter 1 Review Exercises

1.
$$\begin{aligned} 3 \cdot 2^3 \cdot 5^2 &= 3 \cdot 8 \cdot 25 \\ &= 24 \cdot 25 = 600 \end{aligned}$$

2. $10{,}000 + 300 + 20 + 7$

3. $18 \div 1 = 18$

$18 \div 2 = 9$

$18 \div 3 = 6$

$18 \div 6 = 3$

Factors are 1, 2, 3, 6, 9, and 18.

4.
$$\begin{array}{r} {\scriptstyle 111} \\ 5894 \\ 6301 \\ +\ \ 298 \\ \hline 12{,}493 \end{array}$$

5.
$$\begin{array}{r} {\scriptstyle 11} \\ {\scriptstyle 8\,1\,16} \\ 4926 \\ -3177 \\ \hline 1749 \end{array}$$

6.
$$\begin{array}{r} 2{,}135 \\ 7\overline{)14{,}945} \\ -14 \\ \hline 09 \\ -\ 7 \\ \hline 24 \\ -21 \\ \hline 35 \\ -35 \\ \hline 0 \end{array}$$

7. $101 > 87$

8. $5 \cdot 5 \cdot 7 \cdot 7 \cdot 7 \cdot 7 \cdot 7 = 5^2 \cdot 7^5$

9.
$$\begin{array}{r} {\scriptstyle 6} \\ 2019 \\ \times\ \ 307 \\ \hline 14133 \\ 60570 \\ \hline 619{,}833 \end{array}$$

10.
$$\begin{array}{r} {\scriptstyle 9} \\ {\scriptstyle 0\,10\,11\,2\,14} \\ 10{,}134 \\ -\ \ 4{,}725 \\ \hline 5{,}409 \end{array}$$

11.
$$\begin{array}{r} {\scriptstyle 11} \\ 298 \\ 461 \\ +\ 322 \\ \hline 1081 \end{array}$$

12. $2^3 - 3 \cdot 2 = 8 - 3 \cdot 2 = 8 - 6 = 2$

13. 45,700

14. Two hundred seventy-six thousand fifty-seven

15.
```
     1306  r59
84)109,763
  - 84
    257
   -252
     56
    - 0
     563
    -504
      59
```

16. 2,011,044

17.
```
    488  r2
  8)3906
   -32
     70
    -64
     66
    -64
      2
```

18. $3^2 + 2^2 \cdot (5-3) = 3^2 + 2^2 \cdot (2) = 9 + 4 \cdot 2 = 9 + 8 = 17$

19. $8 \cdot (6-2)^2 \div 4 = 8 \cdot 4^2 \div 4 = 8 \cdot 16 \div 4 = 128 \div 4 = 32$

20. $72 = 2 \cdot 2 \cdot 2 \cdot 3 \cdot 3$

72	
2	36
2	18
2	9
3	3
3	1

21. 2133

22.
```
   32
   843
  × 27
  5901
 1686
22,761
```

23. Strategy To find the total pay for last week's work:
- Multiply the overtime rate ($24) by the number of hours worked (12).
- Add the total earned as overtime to the assistant's salary ($480).

Solution
```
 $24      $480
 ×12     + 288
  48      $768
 24
$288
```

The total pay for last week's work is $768.

24. Strategy To find the number of miles driven per gallon of gasoline, divide the total number of miles driven (351) by the number of gallons used (13).

Solution
```
    27
13)351
  -26
    91
   -91
     0
```

He drove 27 miles per gallon of gasoline.

25. Strategy To find the monthly car payment:
- Subtract the down payment ($3000) from the cost of the car ($17,880) to find the balance.
- Divide the balance by the number of equal payments (48).

Solution
```
$17,880          310
- 3,000     48)14,880
$14,880        -144
                  48
                 -48
                  00
                 - 0
                   0
```

Each monthly car payment is $310.

26. Strategy To find the total income from commissions, add the amounts received for each of the 4 weeks ($723, $544, $812, and $488).

Solution
```
$723
 544
 812
+488
$2567
```

The total income from commissions is $2567.

27. Strategy To find the total amount deposited, add the two deposits ($88 and $213). To find the new checking account balance, add the total amount deposited ($301) to the original balance ($516).

Solution
```
 $88
+213
$301
```

The total amount deposited is $301.

```
 $301
+ 516
 $817
```

The new checking balance is $817.

28. Strategy To find the total of the car payments over a 12-month period, multiply the amount of each payment ($246) by the number of payments (12).

Solution
$$\begin{array}{r} \$246 \\ \times\ 12 \\ \hline 492 \\ 246\ \ \\ \hline \$2952 \end{array}$$
The total of the car payments is $2952.

29. Strategy To find the year that there were more males involved in sports, read the values from the table and determine which number is larger.

Solution $208{,}866 > 170{,}384$
Since 208,866 is associated with the year 2001, there were more males involved in college sports in 2001 than in 1972.

30. Strategy To find the difference between the number of males involved in sports and the number of females involved in sports at U.S. colleges in 1972, subtract the values given in the table.

Solution
$$\begin{array}{rl} 170{,}384 & \text{males} \\ -\ 29{,}977 & \text{females} \\ \hline 140{,}407 & \end{array}$$
The difference between the numbers of male and female athletes in 1972 was 140,407 students.

31. Strategy To find the increase in the number of females involved in sports in U.S. colleges from 1972 to 2001, subtract the number in 1972 (29,977) from the number in 2001 (150,916).

Solution
$$\begin{array}{r} 150{,}916 \\ -\ 29{,}977 \\ \hline 120{,}939 \end{array}$$
The number of female athletes increased by 120,939 students from 1972 to 2001.

32. Strategy To find how many more U.S. college students were involved in athletics in 2001 than in 1972:
- Add the number of male and female athletes in 1972.
- Add the number of male and female athletes in 2001.
- Subtract these two sums to find the increase.

Solution
$$\begin{array}{rl} \underline{1972} & \\ 170{,}384 & \text{males} \\ 29{,}977 & \text{females} \\ \hline 200{,}361 & \end{array}$$
$$\begin{array}{rl} \underline{2001} & \\ 208{,}866 & \text{males} \\ 150{,}916 & \text{females} \\ \hline 359{,}782 & \end{array}$$
$$\begin{array}{rl} 359{,}782 & 2001 \\ -200{,}361 & 1972 \\ \hline 159{,}421 & \end{array}$$
159,421 more students were involved in athletics in 2001 than in 1972.

Chapter 1 Test

1. $3^3 \cdot 4^2 = 27 \cdot 16 = 432$

2. Two hundred seven thousand sixty-eight

3.
$$\begin{array}{r} {\scriptstyle 0\,17} \\ \not{1}\not{7}{,}495 \\ -8{,}162 \\ \hline 9{,}333 \end{array}$$

4. $20 \div 1 = 20$
$20 \div 2 = 10$
$20 \div 4 = 5$
$20 \div 5 = 4$
Factors are 1, 2, 4, 5, 10, and 20.

5.
$$\begin{array}{r} 9736 \\ \times\ \ 704 \\ \hline 38{,}944 \\ 681{,}520 \\ \hline 6{,}854{,}144 \end{array}$$

6.
$$\begin{aligned} 4^2 \cdot (4-2) \div 8 + 5 &= 4^2 \cdot (2) \div 8 + 5 \\ &= 16 \cdot (2) \div 8 + 5 \\ &= 32 \div 8 + 5 \\ &= 4 + 5 = 9 \end{aligned}$$

7. $900{,}000 + 6000 + 300 + 70 + 8$

8. 75,000

9.
$$\begin{array}{r} 1121\ \text{r27} \\ 97\overline{)108{,}764} \\ -\ 97 \\ \hline 117 \\ -\ 97 \\ \hline 206 \\ -194 \\ \hline 124 \\ -\ 97 \\ \hline 27 \end{array}$$

10. $3 \cdot 3 \cdot 3 \cdot 7 \cdot 7 = 3^3 \cdot 7^2$

11.

$$\begin{array}{r} \overset{2\ 21}{8{,}756} \\ 9{,}094 \\ +37{,}065 \\ \hline 54{,}915 \end{array}$$

12. $84 = 2 \cdot 2 \cdot 3 \cdot 7$

$$\begin{array}{r|l} & 84 \\ \hline 2 & 42 \\ 2 & 21 \\ 3 & 7 \\ 7 & 1 \end{array}$$

13.

$$\begin{aligned} 16 \div 4 \cdot 2 - (7-5)^2 &= 16 \div 4 \cdot 2 - 2^2 \\ &= 16 \div 4 \cdot 2 - 4 \\ &= 4 \cdot 2 - 4 \\ &= 8 - 4 = 4 \end{aligned}$$

14.

$$\begin{array}{r} \overset{6\ 52}{90{,}763} \\ \times \quad 8 \\ \hline 726{,}104 \end{array}$$

15. 1,204,006

16.

$$\begin{array}{r} 8710 \text{ r2} \\ 7\overline{)60972} \\ \underline{-56} \\ 49 \\ \underline{-49} \\ 07 \\ \underline{-\ 7} \\ 02 \\ \underline{-\ 0} \\ 2 \end{array}$$

17. $21 > 19$

18.

$$\begin{array}{r} 703 \\ 8\overline{)5624} \\ \underline{-56} \\ 02 \\ \underline{-\ 0} \\ 24 \\ \underline{-24} \\ 0 \end{array}$$

19.

$$\begin{array}{r} 25{,}492 \\ +71{,}306 \\ \hline 96{,}798 \end{array}$$

20.

$$\begin{array}{r} \overset{1\,1817}{\not{2}\not{9},\not{7}36} \\ -\ \ 9{,}814 \\ \hline 19{,}922 \end{array}$$

21. Strategy To find the difference between the total enrollment in 2012 and 2009:

- Add the numbers in the two columns for 2009 to find the total enrollment for 2009.
- Add the numbers in the two columns for 2012 to find the total enrollment for 2012.
- Subtract the two values to find the difference.

Solution

$$\begin{array}{rl} \underline{2009} & \\ 37{,}726{,}000 & \text{K–8} \\ +15{,}812{,}000 & \text{9–12} \\ \hline 53{,}538{,}000 & \end{array}$$

$$\begin{array}{rl} \underline{2012} & \\ 38{,}258{,}000 & \text{K–8} \\ +15{,}434{,}000 & \text{9–12} \\ \hline 53{,}692{,}000 & \end{array}$$

$$\begin{array}{rl} 53{,}692{,}000 & 2012 \\ -53{,}538{,}000 & 2009 \\ \hline 154{,}000 & \end{array}$$

The difference in projected total enrollment between 2012 and 2009 is 154,000 students.

22. Strategy To find the average enrollment in each of grades 9 through 12 in 2012, divide the total enrollment (15,434,000) in the four grades by 4.

Solution

$$\begin{array}{r} 3{,}858{,}500 \\ 4\overline{)15{,}434{,}000} \\ \underline{12}\phantom{{,}434{,}000} \\ 34\phantom{4{,}000} \\ \underline{32}\phantom{4{,}000} \\ 23\phantom{{,}000} \\ \underline{20}\phantom{{,}000} \\ 34 \\ \underline{32} \\ 20 \\ \underline{20} \\ 0 \end{array}$$

The average enrollment in each of grades 9 through 12 in 2012 is projected to be 3,858,500 students.

23. Strategy To find how many boxes were needed to pack the lemons:
- Find the total number of lemons harvested by adding the amounts harvested from the two groves (48,290 and 23,710 pounds).
- Divide the total number of pounds harvested by the number of pounds of lemons that can be packed in each box (24).

Solution

```
  48,290
 +23,710
  72,000

     3000
24)72,000
  -72
    00
   - 0
     00
    - 0
      00
     - 0
       0
```

3000 boxes were needed to pack the lemons.

24. Strategy To find the amount that the investor receives over the period, multiply the amount she receives each month ($237) by the number of months (12).

Solution

```
  $237
  × 12
   474
  237
 $2844
```

The investor receives $2844 over the 12-month period.

25a. Strategy To find the total number of miles driven during the 3 days, add the amounts driven each day (425, 187, and 243 miles).

Solution

```
  425
  187
 +243
  855
```

855 miles were driven during the 3 days.

b. Strategy To find the odometer reading at the end of the 3 days, add the number of miles driven during the 3 days (855) to the odometer reading at the start of the vacation (47,626).

Solution

```
  47,626
 +   855
  48,481
```

The odometer reading at the end of the 3 days is 48,481 miles.

Chapter 2: Fractions

Prep Test

1. 20
2. 120
3. 9
4. 10
5. 7
6.
$$\begin{array}{r} 2 \text{ r}3 \\ 30\overline{)63} \\ -60 \\ \hline 3 \end{array}$$
7. 1, 2, 3, 4, 6, 12
8. $8 \cdot 7 + 3 = 56 + 3 = 59$
9. 7
10. <

Go Figure

One lap is down to the end of the pool and back. If you swim one lap every 4 minutes and your friend swims one lap every 5 minutes, then a visual time reference might look like this

4	4	4	4	4

5	5	5	5

where each section represents one lap. As you can see, you meet up with your friend after you swim 5 laps and your friend swims 4 laps. Five 4-minute laps are 20 minutes ($5 \times 4 = 20$). From the visual reference, you can see that you pass each other 4 times for each lap during the 20 minutes. Since one lap is down and back, you pass each other twice per lap. So you pass each other 8 times ($4 \times 2 = 8$).

Section 2.1

Objective A Exercises

1.

	2	5
5 =		(5)
8 =	(2 · 2 · 2)	

$\text{LCM} = 2 \cdot 2 \cdot 2 \cdot 5 = 40$

2.

	2	3
3 =		3
6 =	(2)	(3)

$\text{LCM} = 2 \cdot 3 = 6$

3.

	2	3
3 =		(3)
8 =	(2 · 2 · 2)	

$\text{LCM} = 2 \cdot 2 \cdot 2 \cdot 3 = 24$

4.

	2	5
2 =	(2)	
5 =		(5)

$\text{LCM} = 2 \cdot 5 = 10$

5.

	2	3	5
5 =			(5)
6 =	(2)	(3)	

$\text{LCM} = 2 \cdot 3 \cdot 5 = 30$

6.

	5	7
5 =	(5)	
7 =		(7)

$\text{LCM} = 5 \cdot 7 = 35$

7.

	2	3
4 =	(2 · 2)	
6 =	2	(3)

$\text{LCM} = 2 \cdot 2 \cdot 3 = 12$

8.

	2	3
6 =	2	(3)
8 =	(2 · 2 · 2)	

$\text{LCM} = 2 \cdot 2 \cdot 2 \cdot 3 = 24$

9.

	2	3
8 =	(2 · 2 · 2)	
12 =	2 · 2	(3)

$\text{LCM} = 2 \cdot 2 \cdot 2 \cdot 3 = 24$

10.

	2	3
12 =	2 · 2	(3)
16 =	(2 · 2 · 2 · 2)	

$\text{LCM} = 2 \cdot 2 \cdot 2 \cdot 2 \cdot 3 = 48$

11.

	2	3	5
5 =			(5)
12 =	(2 · 2)	(3)	

$\text{LCM} = 2 \cdot 2 \cdot 3 \cdot 5 = 60$

12.

	2	3
3 =		(3)
16 =	(2 · 2 · 2 · 2)	

$\text{LCM} = 2 \cdot 2 \cdot 2 \cdot 2 \cdot 3 = 48$

13.

	2	7
8 =	(2 · 2 · 2)	
14 =	2	(7)

$\text{LCM} = 2 \cdot 2 \cdot 2 \cdot 7 = 56$

14.

	2	3
6 =	2	3
8 =	(2)	(3 · 3)

$\text{LCM} = 2 \cdot 3 \cdot 3 = 18$

15.

	3
3 =	3
9 =	(3 · 3)

$\text{LCM} = 3 \cdot 3 = 9$

16.

	2	5
4 =	2·2	
10 =	2	5

LCM = $2 \cdot 2 \cdot 5 = 20$

17.

	2
8 =	2·2·2
32 =	2·2·2·2·2

LCM = $2 \cdot 2 \cdot 2 \cdot 2 \cdot 2 = 32$

18.

	3	7
7 =		7
21 =	3	7

LCM = $3 \cdot 7 = 21$

19.

	2	3
9 =		3·3
36 =	2·2	3·3

LCM = $2 \cdot 2 \cdot 3 \cdot 3 = 36$

20.

	2	3	7
14 =	2		7
42 =	2	3	7

LCM = $2 \cdot 3 \cdot 7 = 42$

21.

	2	3	5	11
44 =	2·2			11
60 =	2·2	3	5	

LCM = $2 \cdot 3 \cdot 5 \cdot 11 = 660$

22.

	2	3	5
120 =	2·2	3	5
160 =	2·2·2·2·2		5

LCM = $2 \cdot 2 \cdot 2 \cdot 2 \cdot 2 \cdot 2 \cdot 3 \cdot 5 = 480$

23.

	2	3	17	23
102 =	2	3	17	
184 =	2·2·2			23

LCM = $2 \cdot 2 \cdot 2 \cdot 3 \cdot 17 \cdot 23 = 9384$

24.

	2	3	13	41
123 =		3		41
234 =	2	3·3	13	

LCM = $2 \cdot 3 \cdot 3 \cdot 13 \cdot 41 = 9594$

25.

	2	3
4 =	2·2	
8 =	2·2·2	
12 =	2·2	3

LCM = $2 \cdot 2 \cdot 2 \cdot 3 = 24$

26.

	2	3	5
5 =			5
10 =	2		5
15 =		3	5

LCM = $2 \cdot 3 \cdot 5 = 30$

27.

	2	3	5
3 =		3	
5 =			5
10 =	2		5

LCM = $2 \cdot 3 \cdot 5 = 30$

28.

	2	5
2 =	2	
5 =		5
8 =	2·2·2	

LCM = $2 \cdot 2 \cdot 2 \cdot 5 = 40$

29.

	2	3
3 =		3
8 =	2·2·2	
12 =	2·2	3

LCM = $2 \cdot 2 \cdot 2 \cdot 3 = 24$

30.

	2	3	5
5 =			5
12 =	2·2	3	
18 =	2	3·3	

LCM = $2 \cdot 2 \cdot 3 \cdot 3 \cdot 5 = 180$

31.

	2	3
9 =		3·3
36 =	2·2	3·3
64 =	2·2·2·2·2·2	

LCM = $2 \cdot 2 \cdot 2 \cdot 2 \cdot 2 \cdot 2 \cdot 3 \cdot 3 = 576$

32.

	2	3	7
18 =	2	3·3	
54 =	2	3·3·3	
63 =		3·3	7

LCM = $2 \cdot 3 \cdot 3 \cdot 3 \cdot 7 = 378$

33.

	2	3	5	7
16 =	2·2·2·2			
30 =	2	3	5	
84 =	2·2	3		7

LCM = $2 \cdot 2 \cdot 2 \cdot 2 \cdot 3 \cdot 5 \cdot 7 = 1680$

34.

	2	3	5
9 =		3·3	
12 =	2·2	3	
15 =		3	5

LCM = $2 \cdot 2 \cdot 3 \cdot 3 \cdot 5 = 180$

Objective B Exercises

35.

	3	5
3 =	3	
5 =		5

GCF = 1

36.

	5	7
5 =	5	
7 =		7

GCF = 1

37.

	2	3
6 =	2	3
9 =		3·3

GCF = 3

38.

	2	3
18 =	2	3·3
24 =	2·2·2	3

GCF = $2 \cdot 3 = 6$

39.

	3	5
15 =	3	5
25 =		$5 \cdot 5$

GCF = 5

40.

	2	7
14 =	2	7
49 =		$7 \cdot 7$

GCF = 7

41.

	2	5
25 =		$5 \cdot 5$
100 =	$2 \cdot 2$	$5 \cdot 5$

GCF = $5 \cdot 5 = 25$

42.

	2	5
16 =	$2 \cdot 2 \cdot 2 \cdot 2$	
80 =	$2 \cdot 2 \cdot 2 \cdot 2$	5

GCF = $2 \cdot 2 \cdot 2 \cdot 2 = 16$

43.

	2	3	17
32 =	$2 \cdot 2 \cdot 2 \cdot 2 \cdot 2$		
51 =		3	17

GCF = 1

44.

	2	3	7	11
21 =		3	7	
44 =	$2 \cdot 2$			11

GCF = 1

45.

	2	3	5
12 =	$2 \cdot 2$	3	
80 =	$2 \cdot 2 \cdot 2 \cdot 2$		5

GCF = $2 \cdot 2 = 4$

46.

	2	3
8 =	$2 \cdot 2 \cdot 2$	
36 =	$2 \cdot 2$	$3 \cdot 3$

GCF = $2 \cdot 2 = 4$

47.

	2	5	7
16 =	$2 \cdot 2 \cdot 2 \cdot 2$		
140 =	$2 \cdot 2$	5	7

GCF = $2 \cdot 2 = 4$

48.

	2	3	19
12 =	$2 \cdot 2$	3	
76 =	$2 \cdot 2$		19

GCF = $2 \cdot 2 = 4$

49.

	2	3	5
24 =	$2 \cdot 2 \cdot 2$	3	
30 =	2	3	5

GCF = $2 \cdot 3 = 6$

50.

	2	3
48 =	$2 \cdot 2 \cdot 2 \cdot 2$	3
144 =	$2 \cdot 2 \cdot 2 \cdot 2$	$3 \cdot 3$

GCF = $2 \cdot 2 \cdot 2 \cdot 2 \cdot 3 = 48$

51.

	2	3	11
44 =	$2 \cdot 2$		11
96 =	$2 \cdot 2 \cdot 2 \cdot 2 \cdot 2$	3	

GCF = $2 \cdot 2 = 4$

52.

	2	3
18 =	2	$3 \cdot 3$
32 =	$2 \cdot 2 \cdot 2 \cdot 2 \cdot 2$	

GCF = 2

53.

	3	5	11
3 =	3		
5 =		5	
11 =			11

GCF = 1

54.

	2	3	5
6 =	2	3	
8 =	$2 \cdot 2 \cdot 2$		
10 =	2		5

GCF = 2

55.

	2	7
7 =		7
14 =	2	7
49 =		$7 \cdot 7$

GCF = 7

56.

	2	3	5
6 =	2	3	
15 =		3	5
36 =	$2 \cdot 2$	$3 \cdot 3$	

GCF = 3

57.

	2	3	5
10 =	2		5
15 =		3	5
20 =	$2 \cdot 2$		5

GCF = 5

58.

	2	3	5
12 =	$2 \cdot 2$	3	
18 =	2	$3 \cdot 3$	
20 =	$2 \cdot 2$		5

GCF = 2

59.

	2	3	5
24 =	$2 \cdot 2 \cdot 2$	3	
40 =	$2 \cdot 2 \cdot 2$		5
72 =	$2 \cdot 2 \cdot 2$	$3 \cdot 3$	

GCF = $2 \cdot 2 \cdot 2 = 8$

60.

	3	17
3 =	3	
17 =		17
51 =	3	17

GCF = 1

61.

	3	17	31
17 =		17	
31 =			31
81 =	$3 \cdot 3 \cdot 3 \cdot 3$		

GCF = 1

62.

	2	3	7
14 =	2		7
42 =	2	3	7
84 =	2 · 2	3	7

GCF = 2 · 7 = 14

63.

	5
25 =	5 · 5
125 =	5 · 5 · 5
625 =	5 · 5 · 5 · 5

GCF = 25

64.

	2	3	17	23
12 =	2 · 2	3		
68 =	2 · 2		17	
92 =	2 · 2			23

GCF = 2 · 2 = 4

65.

	2	5	7
28 =	2 · 2		7
35 =		5	7
70 =	2	5	7

GCF = 7

66.

	3	7	17
1 =			
49 =		7 · 7	
153 =	3 · 3		17

GCF = 1

67.

	2	3	7
32 =	2 · 2 · 2 · 2 · 2		
56 =	2 · 2 · 2		7
72 =	2 · 2 · 2	3 · 3	

GCF = 2 · 2 · 2 = 8

68.

	2	3
24 =	2 · 2 · 2	3
36 =	2 · 2	3 · 3
48 =	2 · 2 · 2 · 2	3

GCF = 2 · 2 · 3 = 12

Applying the Concepts

69. Relatively prime numbers are numbers with no common factors except 1. Examples: 4 and 5, 8 and 9, and 16 and 21

70. After the life guard and his friend have a day off together, they will have another day off together in 12 days. The life guard has a 4-day cycle (3 workdays + 1 day off). His friend has a 6-day cycle (5 workdays + 1 day off). The least common multiple of 4 and 6 is 12.

71. The LCM of 2 and 3 is 6. The LCM of 5 and 7 is 35. The LCM of 11 and 19 is 209. The LCM of two prime numbers is the product of the two numbers. The LCM of three prime numbers is the product of the three numbers.

72. The GCF of 3 and 5 is 1. The GCF of 7 and 11 is 1. The GCF of 29 and 43 is 1. Because two prime numbers do not have a common factor other than 1, the GCF of two prime numbers is 1. Because three prime numbers do not have a common factor other than 1, the GCF of three prime numbers is 1.

73. Yes, the LCM of the two numbers is always divisible by the GCF of the two numbers. Two numbers are factors of their LCM. The GCF of the two numbers is a factor of the LCM of the same numbers. That is, the LCM of two numbers always is divisible by the GCF of the two numbers. For example, the GCF of 4 and 6 is 2, and the LCM of 4 and 6 is 12. 12 is divisible by 2.

74. 4, the GCF of 20, 36, and 60

Section 2.2

Objective A Exercises

1. Improper fraction

2. Mixed number

3. Proper fraction

4. Improper fraction

5. $\frac{3}{4}$

6. $\frac{4}{7}$

7. $\frac{7}{8}$

8. $\frac{3}{5}$

9. $1\frac{1}{2}$

10. $2\frac{2}{3}$

11. $2\frac{5}{8}$

12. $2\frac{3}{4}$

13. $3\frac{3}{5}$

14. $3\frac{5}{6}$

15. $\frac{5}{4}$

16. $\frac{7}{6}$

17. $\frac{8}{3}$

18. $\frac{9}{4}$

19. $\frac{28}{8}$

20. $\frac{18}{5}$

21.

22.

23.

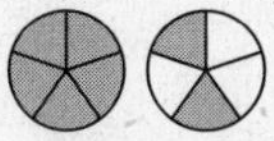

24.

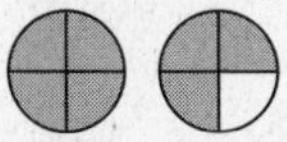

25.

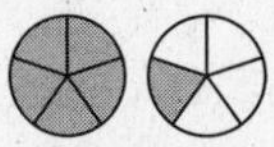

26.

27. $\begin{array}{r} 2 \\ 4\overline{)11} \\ \underline{-8} \\ 3 \end{array} \quad \frac{11}{4} = 2\frac{3}{4}$

28. $\begin{array}{r} 5 \\ 3\overline{)16} \\ \underline{-15} \\ 1 \end{array} \quad \frac{16}{3} = 5\frac{1}{3}$

29. $\begin{array}{r} 5 \\ 4\overline{)20} \\ \underline{-20} \\ 0 \end{array} \quad \frac{20}{4} = 5$

30. $\begin{array}{r} 2 \\ 9\overline{)18} \\ \underline{-18} \\ 0 \end{array} \quad \frac{18}{9} = 2$

31. $\begin{array}{r} 1 \\ 8\overline{)9} \\ \underline{-8} \\ 1 \end{array} \quad \frac{9}{8} = 1\frac{1}{8}$

32. $\begin{array}{r} 3 \\ 4\overline{)13} \\ \underline{-12} \\ 1 \end{array} \quad \frac{13}{4} = 3\frac{1}{4}$

33. $\begin{array}{r} 2 \\ 10\overline{)23} \\ \underline{-20} \\ 3 \end{array} \quad \frac{23}{10} = 2\frac{3}{10}$

34. $\begin{array}{r} 14 \\ 2\overline{)29} \\ \underline{-2} \\ 09 \\ \underline{-8} \\ 1 \end{array} \quad \frac{29}{2} = 14\frac{1}{2}$

35. $\begin{array}{r} 3 \\ 16\overline{)48} \\ \underline{-48} \\ 0 \end{array} \quad \frac{48}{16} = 3$

36. $\begin{array}{r} 17 \\ 3\overline{)51} \\ \underline{-3} \\ 21 \\ \underline{-21} \\ 0 \end{array} \quad \frac{51}{3} = 17$

37. $\begin{array}{r} 1 \\ 7\overline{)8} \\ \underline{-7} \\ 1 \end{array} \quad \frac{8}{7} = 1\frac{1}{7}$

38. $\begin{array}{r} 1 \\ 9\overline{)16} \\ \underline{-9} \\ 7 \end{array} \quad \frac{16}{9} = 1\frac{7}{9}$

39. $\begin{array}{r} 2 \\ 3\overline{)7} \\ \underline{-6} \\ 1 \end{array} \quad \frac{7}{3} = 2\frac{1}{3}$

40. $\begin{array}{r} 1 \\ 5\overline{)9} \\ \underline{-5} \\ 4 \end{array} \quad \frac{9}{5} = 1\frac{4}{5}$

41. $\begin{array}{r} 16 \\ 1\overline{)16} \\ \underline{-1} \\ 06 \\ \underline{-6} \\ 0 \end{array} \quad \frac{16}{1} = 16$

42. $\begin{array}{r} 23 \\ 1\overline{)23} \\ \underline{-2} \\ 03 \\ \underline{-3} \\ 0 \end{array} \quad \frac{23}{1} = 23$

43. $\begin{array}{r} 2 \\ 8\overline{)17} \\ \underline{-16} \\ 1 \end{array} \quad \frac{17}{8} = 2\frac{1}{8}$

44. $\begin{array}{r} 1 \\ 16\overline{)31} \\ \underline{-16} \\ 15 \end{array} \quad \frac{31}{16} = 1\frac{15}{16}$

45. $\begin{array}{r} 2 \\ 5\overline{)12} \\ \underline{-10} \\ 2 \end{array} \quad \frac{12}{5} = 2\frac{2}{5}$

46. $\begin{array}{r} 6 \\ 3\overline{)19} \\ \underline{-18} \\ 1 \end{array} \quad \frac{19}{3} = 6\frac{1}{3}$

47. $\begin{array}{r} 1 \\ 9\overline{)9} \\ \underline{-9} \\ 0 \end{array} \quad \frac{9}{9} = 1$

48. $\begin{array}{r} 5 \\ 8\overline{)40} \\ \underline{-40} \\ 0 \end{array} \quad \frac{40}{8} = 5$

49. $\begin{array}{r} 9 \\ 8\overline{)72} \\ \underline{-72} \\ 0 \end{array} \quad \frac{72}{8} = 9$

50. $\begin{array}{r} 1 \\ 3\overline{)3} \\ \underline{-3} \\ 0 \end{array} \quad \frac{3}{3} = 1$

51. $2\frac{1}{3} = \frac{6+1}{3} = \frac{7}{3}$

52. $4\frac{2}{3} = \frac{12+2}{3} = \frac{14}{3}$

53. $6\frac{1}{2} = \frac{12+1}{2} = \frac{13}{2}$

54. $8\frac{2}{3} = \frac{24+2}{3} = \frac{26}{3}$

55. $6\frac{5}{6} = \frac{36+5}{6} = \frac{41}{6}$

56. $7\frac{3}{8} = \frac{56+3}{8} = \frac{59}{8}$

57. $9\frac{1}{4} = \frac{36+1}{4} = \frac{37}{4}$

58. $6\frac{1}{4} = \frac{24+1}{4} = \frac{25}{4}$

59. $10\frac{1}{2} = \frac{20+1}{2} = \frac{21}{2}$

60. $15\frac{1}{8} = \frac{120+1}{8} = \frac{121}{8}$

61. $8\frac{1}{9} = \frac{72+1}{9} = \frac{73}{9}$

62. $3\frac{5}{12} = \frac{36+5}{12} = \frac{41}{12}$

63. $5\frac{3}{11} = \frac{55+3}{11} = \frac{58}{11}$

64. $3\frac{7}{9} = \frac{27+7}{9} = \frac{34}{9}$

65. $2\frac{5}{8} = \frac{16+5}{8} = \frac{21}{8}$

66. $12\frac{2}{3} = \frac{36+2}{3} = \frac{38}{3}$

67. $1\frac{5}{8} = \frac{8+5}{8} = \frac{13}{8}$

68. $5\frac{3}{7} = \frac{35+3}{7} = \frac{38}{7}$

69. $11\frac{1}{9} = \frac{99+1}{9} = \frac{100}{9}$

70. $12\frac{3}{5} = \frac{60+3}{5} = \frac{63}{5}$

71. $3\frac{3}{8} = \frac{24+3}{8} = \frac{27}{8}$

72. $4\frac{5}{9} = \frac{36+5}{9} = \frac{41}{9}$

73. $6\frac{7}{13} = \frac{78+7}{13} = \frac{85}{13}$

74. $8\frac{5}{14} = \frac{112+5}{14} = \frac{117}{14}$

Applying the Concepts

75. Students might mention any of the following: fractional parts of an hour, as in three-quarters of an hour; lengths of nails, as in $\frac{3}{4}$-inch nail; lengths of fabric, as in $1\frac{5}{8}$ yards of material; lengths of lumber, as in $2\frac{1}{2}$ feet of pine; ingredients in a recipe, as in $1\frac{1}{2}$ cups sugar; or innings pitched, as in four and two-thirds innings.

Section 2.3

Objective A Exercises

1. $\frac{1\cdot 5}{2\cdot 5} = \frac{5}{10}$

2. $\frac{1\cdot 4}{4\cdot 4} = \frac{4}{16}$

3. $\frac{3\cdot 3}{16\cdot 3} = \frac{9}{48}$

4. $\frac{5\cdot 9}{9\cdot 9} = \frac{45}{81}$

5. $\frac{3\cdot 4}{8\cdot 4} = \frac{12}{32}$

6. $\frac{7\cdot 3}{11\cdot 3} = \frac{21}{33}$

7. $\frac{3\cdot 3}{17\cdot 3} = \frac{9}{51}$

8. $\frac{7\cdot 9}{10\cdot 9} = \frac{63}{90}$

9. $\frac{3\cdot 4}{4\cdot 4} = \frac{12}{16}$

10. $\frac{5\cdot 4}{8\cdot 4} = \frac{20}{32}$

11. $\frac{3\cdot 9}{1\cdot 9} = \frac{27}{9}$

12. $\frac{5\cdot 25}{1\cdot 25} = \frac{125}{25}$

13. $\frac{1\cdot 20}{3\cdot 20} = \frac{20}{60}$

14. $\frac{1\cdot 3}{16\cdot 3} = \frac{3}{48}$

15. $\frac{11\cdot 4}{15\cdot 4} = \frac{44}{60}$

16. $\frac{3\cdot 6}{50\cdot 6} = \frac{18}{300}$

17. $\frac{2\cdot 6}{3\cdot 6} = \frac{12}{18}$

18. $\frac{5\cdot 4}{9\cdot 4} = \frac{20}{36}$

19. $\frac{5\cdot 7}{7\cdot 7} = \frac{35}{49}$

20. $\frac{7\cdot 4}{8\cdot 4} = \frac{28}{32}$

21. $\frac{5\cdot 2}{9\cdot 2} = \frac{10}{18}$

22. $\frac{11\cdot 3}{12\cdot 3} = \frac{33}{36}$

23. $\frac{7\cdot 3}{1\cdot 3} = \frac{21}{3}$

24. $\frac{9\cdot 4}{1\cdot 4} = \frac{36}{4}$

25. $\frac{7\cdot 5}{9\cdot 5} = \frac{35}{45}$

26. $\frac{5\cdot 7}{6\cdot 7} = \frac{35}{42}$

27. $\frac{15\cdot 4}{16\cdot 4} = \frac{60}{64}$

28. $\frac{11\cdot 3}{18\cdot 3} = \frac{33}{54}$

29. $\frac{3\cdot 7}{14\cdot 7} = \frac{21}{98}$

30. $\frac{5\cdot 24}{6\cdot 24} = \frac{120}{144}$

31. $\frac{5\cdot 6}{8\cdot 6} = \frac{30}{48}$

32. $\frac{7\cdot 8}{12\cdot 8} = \frac{56}{96}$

33. $\frac{5\cdot 3}{14\cdot 3} = \frac{15}{42}$

34. $\frac{2\cdot 14}{3\cdot 14} = \frac{28}{42}$

35. $\frac{17\cdot 6}{24\cdot 6} = \frac{102}{144}$

36. $\frac{5\cdot 13}{13\cdot 13} = \frac{65}{169}$

37. $\frac{3\cdot 51}{8\cdot 51} = \frac{153}{408}$

38. $\frac{9\cdot 17}{16\cdot 17} = \frac{153}{272}$

39. $\frac{17\cdot 20}{40\cdot 20} = \frac{340}{800}$

40. $\frac{9\cdot 40}{25\cdot 40} = \frac{360}{1000}$

Objective B Exercises

41. $\frac{4}{12} = \frac{\overset{1}{\cancel{2}}\cdot\overset{1}{\cancel{2}}}{\underset{1}{\cancel{2}}\cdot\underset{1}{\cancel{2}}\cdot 3} = \frac{1}{3}$

42. $\frac{8}{22} = \frac{\overset{1}{\cancel{2}}\cdot 2\cdot 2}{\underset{1}{\cancel{2}}\cdot 11} = \frac{4}{11}$

43. $\frac{22}{44} = \frac{\overset{1}{\cancel{2}}\cdot\overset{1}{\cancel{11}}}{\underset{1}{\cancel{2}}\cdot 2\cdot\underset{1}{\cancel{11}}} = \frac{1}{2}$

44. $\frac{2}{14}=\frac{\cancel{2}}{\cancel{2}\cdot 7}=\frac{1}{7}$

45. $\frac{2}{12}=\frac{\cancel{2}}{\cancel{2}\cdot 2\cdot 3}=\frac{1}{6}$

46. $\frac{50}{75}=\frac{2\cdot\cancel{5}\cdot\cancel{5}}{3\cdot\cancel{5}\cdot\cancel{5}}=\frac{2}{3}$

47. $\frac{40}{36}=\frac{\cancel{2}\cdot\cancel{2}\cdot 2\cdot 5}{\cancel{2}\cdot\cancel{2}\cdot 3\cdot 3}=\frac{10}{9}=1\frac{1}{9}$

48. $\frac{12}{8}=\frac{\cancel{2}\cdot\cancel{2}\cdot 3}{\cancel{2}\cdot\cancel{2}\cdot 2}=\frac{3}{2}=1\frac{1}{2}$

49. $\frac{0}{30}=0$

50. $\frac{10}{10}=\frac{\cancel{2}\cdot\cancel{5}}{\cancel{2}\cdot\cancel{5}}=\frac{1}{1}=1$

51. $\frac{9}{22}=\frac{3\cdot 3}{2\cdot 11}=\frac{9}{22}$

52. $\frac{14}{35}=\frac{2\cdot\cancel{7}}{5\cdot\cancel{7}}=\frac{2}{5}$

53. $\frac{75}{25}=\frac{3\cdot\cancel{5}\cdot\cancel{5}}{\cancel{5}\cdot\cancel{5}}=3$

54. $\frac{8}{60}=\frac{\cancel{2}\cdot\cancel{2}\cdot 2}{\cancel{2}\cdot\cancel{2}\cdot 3\cdot 5}=\frac{2}{15}$

55. $\frac{16}{84}=\frac{\cancel{2}\cdot\cancel{2}\cdot 2\cdot 2}{\cancel{2}\cdot\cancel{2}\cdot 3\cdot 7}=\frac{4}{21}$

56. $\frac{20}{44}=\frac{\cancel{2}\cdot\cancel{2}\cdot 5}{\cancel{2}\cdot\cancel{2}\cdot 11}=\frac{5}{11}$

57. $\frac{12}{35}=\frac{2\cdot 2\cdot 3}{5\cdot 7}=\frac{12}{35}$

58. $\frac{8}{36}=\frac{\cancel{2}\cdot\cancel{2}\cdot 2}{\cancel{2}\cdot\cancel{2}\cdot 3\cdot 3}=\frac{2}{9}$

59. $\frac{28}{44}=\frac{\cancel{2}\cdot\cancel{2}\cdot 7}{\cancel{2}\cdot\cancel{2}\cdot 11}=\frac{7}{11}$

60. $\frac{12}{16}=\frac{\cancel{2}\cdot\cancel{2}\cdot 3}{\cancel{2}\cdot\cancel{2}\cdot 2\cdot 2}=\frac{3}{4}$

61. $\frac{16}{12}=\frac{\cancel{2}\cdot\cancel{2}\cdot 2\cdot 2}{\cancel{2}\cdot\cancel{2}\cdot 3}=\frac{4}{3}=1\frac{1}{3}$

62. $\frac{24}{18}=\frac{\cancel{2}\cdot 2\cdot 2\cdot\cancel{3}}{\cancel{2}\cdot\cancel{3}\cdot 3}=\frac{4}{3}=1\frac{1}{3}$

63. $\frac{24}{40}=\frac{\cancel{2}\cdot\cancel{2}\cdot\cancel{2}\cdot 3}{\cancel{2}\cdot\cancel{2}\cdot\cancel{2}\cdot 5}=\frac{3}{5}$

64. $\frac{44}{60}=\frac{\cancel{2}\cdot\cancel{2}\cdot 11}{\cancel{2}\cdot\cancel{2}\cdot 3\cdot 5}=\frac{11}{15}$

65. $\frac{8}{88}=\frac{\cancel{2}\cdot\cancel{2}\cdot\cancel{2}}{\cancel{2}\cdot\cancel{2}\cdot\cancel{2}\cdot 11}=\frac{1}{11}$

66. $\frac{9}{90}=\frac{\cancel{3}\cdot\cancel{3}}{2\cdot\cancel{3}\cdot\cancel{3}\cdot 5}=\frac{1}{10}$

67. $\frac{144}{36}=\frac{\cancel{2}\cdot\cancel{2}\cdot 2\cdot 2\cdot\cancel{3}\cdot\cancel{3}}{\cancel{2}\cdot\cancel{2}\cdot\cancel{3}\cdot\cancel{3}}=4$

68. $\frac{140}{297}=\frac{2\cdot 2\cdot 5\cdot 7}{3\cdot 3\cdot 3\cdot 11}=\frac{140}{297}$

69. $\frac{48}{144}=\frac{\cancel{2}\cdot\cancel{2}\cdot\cancel{2}\cdot\cancel{2}\cdot\cancel{3}}{\cancel{2}\cdot\cancel{2}\cdot\cancel{2}\cdot\cancel{2}\cdot\cancel{3}\cdot 3}=\frac{1}{3}$

70. $\frac{32}{120}=\frac{\cancel{2}\cdot\cancel{2}\cdot\cancel{2}\cdot 2\cdot 2}{\cancel{2}\cdot\cancel{2}\cdot\cancel{2}\cdot 3\cdot 5}=\frac{4}{15}$

71. $\frac{60}{100}=\frac{\cancel{2}\cdot\cancel{2}\cdot 3\cdot\cancel{5}}{\cancel{2}\cdot\cancel{2}\cdot 5\cdot\cancel{5}}=\frac{3}{5}$

72. $\frac{33}{110}=\frac{3\cdot\cancel{11}}{2\cdot 5\cdot\cancel{11}}=\frac{3}{10}$

73. $\frac{36}{16}=\frac{\cancel{2}\cdot\cancel{2}\cdot 3\cdot 3}{\cancel{2}\cdot\cancel{2}\cdot 2\cdot 2}=\frac{9}{4}=2\frac{1}{4}$

74. $\frac{80}{45}=\frac{2\cdot 2\cdot 2\cdot 2\cdot\cancel{5}}{3\cdot 3\cdot\cancel{5}}=\frac{16}{9}=1\frac{7}{9}$

75. $\frac{32}{160}=\frac{\cancel{2}\cdot\cancel{2}\cdot\cancel{2}\cdot\cancel{2}\cdot\cancel{2}}{\cancel{2}\cdot\cancel{2}\cdot\cancel{2}\cdot\cancel{2}\cdot\cancel{2}\cdot 5}=\frac{1}{5}$

Applying the Concepts

76. $\frac{4}{6}, \frac{6}{9}, \frac{8}{12}, \frac{10}{15}$, and $\frac{12}{18}$ are fractions that are equal to $\frac{2}{3}$.

77. $\frac{3}{1}, \frac{6}{2}, \frac{9}{3}, \frac{12}{4}, \frac{15}{5}$ are fractions that are equal to 3.

78. $\frac{15}{24} = \frac{5}{8}$

$\frac{15}{24}$

1	2	3	4	5			
6	7	8	9	10			
11	12	13	14	15			

$\frac{5}{8}$

79a. $\frac{8}{50} = \frac{4}{25}$
Maine, Maryland, Massachusetts, Michigan, Minnesota, Mississippi, Missouri, Montana

b. $\frac{8}{50} = \frac{4}{25}$
Alabama, Alaska, Arizona, Idaho, Indiana, Iowa, Ohio, Oklahoma

Section 2.4

Objective A Exercises

1. $\frac{2}{7} + \frac{1}{7} = \frac{3}{7}$

2. $\frac{3}{11} + \frac{5}{11} = \frac{8}{11}$

3. $\frac{1}{2} + \frac{1}{2} = \frac{2}{2} = 1$

4. $\frac{1}{3} + \frac{2}{3} = \frac{3}{3} = 1$

5. $\frac{8}{11} + \frac{7}{11} = \frac{15}{11} = 1\frac{4}{11}$

6. $\frac{9}{13} + \frac{7}{13} = \frac{16}{13} = 1\frac{3}{13}$

7. $\frac{8}{5} + \frac{9}{5} = \frac{17}{5} = 3\frac{2}{5}$

8. $\frac{5}{3} + \frac{7}{3} = \frac{12}{3} = 4$

9. $\frac{3}{5} + \frac{8}{5} + \frac{3}{5} = \frac{14}{5} = 2\frac{4}{5}$

10. $\frac{3}{8} + \frac{5}{8} + \frac{7}{8} = \frac{15}{8} = 1\frac{7}{8}$

11. $\frac{3}{4} + \frac{1}{4} + \frac{5}{4} = \frac{9}{4} = 2\frac{1}{4}$

12. $\frac{2}{7} + \frac{4}{7} + \frac{5}{7} = \frac{11}{7} = 1\frac{4}{7}$

13. $\frac{3}{8} + \frac{7}{8} + \frac{1}{8} = \frac{11}{8} = 1\frac{3}{8}$

14. $\frac{5}{12} + \frac{7}{12} + \frac{1}{12} = \frac{13}{12} = 1\frac{1}{12}$

15. $\frac{4}{15} + \frac{7}{15} + \frac{11}{15} = \frac{22}{15} = 1\frac{7}{15}$

16. $\frac{3}{4} + \frac{3}{4} + \frac{1}{4} = \frac{7}{4} = 1\frac{3}{4}$

17. $\frac{3}{16} + \frac{5}{16} + \frac{7}{16} = \frac{15}{16}$

18. $$\begin{array}{r} \frac{5}{18}\\ \frac{11}{18}\\ +\frac{17}{18}\\ \hline \frac{33}{18}=1\frac{15}{18}=1\frac{5}{6} \end{array}$$

19. $$\begin{array}{r} \frac{3}{11}\\ \frac{5}{11}\\ +\frac{7}{11}\\ \hline \frac{15}{11}=1\frac{4}{11} \end{array}$$

20. $$\begin{array}{r} \frac{5}{7}\\ \frac{4}{7}\\ +\frac{5}{7}\\ \hline \frac{14}{7}=2 \end{array}$$

21. $\frac{4}{9}+\frac{5}{9}=\frac{9}{9}=1$

22. $\frac{5}{12}+\frac{1}{12}+\frac{11}{12}=\frac{17}{12}=1\frac{5}{12}$

23. $\frac{5}{8}+\frac{3}{8}+\frac{7}{8}=\frac{15}{8}=1\frac{7}{8}$

24. $\frac{4}{13}+\frac{7}{13}+\frac{11}{13}=\frac{22}{13}=1\frac{9}{13}$

Objective B Exercises

25. $$\begin{array}{r} \frac{1}{2}=\frac{3}{6}\\ +\frac{2}{3}=\frac{4}{6}\\ \hline \frac{7}{6}=1\frac{1}{6} \end{array}$$

26. $$\begin{array}{r} \frac{2}{3}=\frac{8}{12}\\ +\frac{1}{4}=\frac{3}{12}\\ \hline \frac{11}{12} \end{array}$$

27. $$\begin{array}{r} \frac{3}{14}=\frac{3}{14}\\ +\frac{5}{7}=\frac{10}{14}\\ \hline \frac{13}{14} \end{array}$$

28. $$\begin{array}{r} \frac{3}{5}=\frac{6}{10}\\ +\frac{7}{10}=\frac{7}{10}\\ \hline \frac{13}{10}=1\frac{3}{10} \end{array}$$

29. $$\begin{array}{r} \frac{8}{15}=\frac{32}{60}\\ +\frac{7}{20}=\frac{21}{60}\\ \hline \frac{53}{60} \end{array}$$

30. $$\begin{array}{r} \frac{1}{6}=\frac{3}{18}\\ +\frac{7}{9}=\frac{14}{18}\\ \hline \frac{17}{18} \end{array}$$

31. $$\begin{array}{r} \frac{3}{8}=\frac{21}{56}\\ +\frac{9}{14}=\frac{36}{56}\\ \hline \frac{57}{56}=1\frac{1}{56} \end{array}$$

32. $$\begin{array}{r} \frac{5}{12}=\frac{20}{48}\\ +\frac{5}{16}=\frac{15}{48}\\ \hline \frac{35}{48} \end{array}$$

33. $$\begin{array}{r} \frac{3}{20}=\frac{9}{60}\\ +\frac{7}{30}=\frac{14}{60}\\ \hline \frac{23}{60} \end{array}$$

34. $$\begin{array}{r} \frac{5}{12}=\frac{25}{60}\\ +\frac{7}{30}=\frac{14}{60}\\ \hline \frac{39}{60}=\frac{13}{20} \end{array}$$

35. $$\begin{array}{r} \frac{2}{3}=\frac{38}{57}\\ +\frac{6}{19}=\frac{18}{57}\\ \hline \frac{56}{57} \end{array}$$

36. $$\begin{array}{r} \frac{1}{2}=\frac{29}{58}\\ +\frac{3}{29}=\frac{6}{58}\\ \hline \frac{35}{58} \end{array}$$

37. $$\begin{array}{r} \frac{1}{3}=\frac{6}{18}\\ \frac{5}{6}=\frac{15}{18}\\ +\frac{7}{9}=\frac{14}{18}\\ \hline \frac{35}{18}=1\frac{17}{18} \end{array}$$

38. $$\begin{array}{r} \frac{2}{3}=\frac{8}{12}\\ \frac{5}{6}=\frac{10}{12}\\ +\frac{7}{12}=\frac{7}{12}\\ \hline \frac{25}{12}=2\frac{1}{12} \end{array}$$

39. $$\begin{array}{r} \frac{5}{6}=\frac{40}{48}\\ \frac{1}{12}=\frac{4}{48}\\ +\frac{5}{16}=\frac{15}{48}\\ \hline \frac{59}{48}=1\frac{11}{48} \end{array}$$

40. $$\begin{array}{r} \frac{2}{9}=\frac{70}{315}\\ \frac{7}{15}=\frac{147}{315}\\ +\frac{4}{21}=\frac{60}{315}\\ \hline \frac{277}{315} \end{array}$$

41. $$\begin{array}{r} \frac{2}{3}=\frac{40}{60}\\ \frac{1}{5}=\frac{12}{60}\\ +\frac{7}{12}=\frac{35}{60}\\ \hline \frac{87}{60}=1\frac{27}{60}=1\frac{9}{20} \end{array}$$

42. $$\begin{array}{r} \frac{3}{4}=\frac{45}{60}\\ \frac{4}{5}=\frac{48}{60}\\ +\frac{7}{12}=\frac{35}{60}\\ \hline \frac{128}{60}=2\frac{8}{60}=2\frac{2}{15} \end{array}$$

43. $\frac{1}{4}=\frac{45}{180}$, $\frac{4}{5}=\frac{144}{180}$, $+\frac{5}{9}=\frac{100}{180}$; $\frac{289}{180}=1\frac{109}{180}$

44. $\frac{2}{3}=\frac{80}{120}$, $\frac{3}{5}=\frac{72}{120}$, $+\frac{7}{8}=\frac{105}{120}$; $\frac{257}{120}=2\frac{17}{120}$

45. $\frac{5}{16}=\frac{45}{144}$, $\frac{11}{18}=\frac{88}{144}$, $+\frac{17}{24}=\frac{102}{144}$; $\frac{235}{144}=1\frac{91}{144}$

46. $\frac{3}{10}=\frac{45}{150}$, $\frac{14}{15}=\frac{140}{150}$, $+\frac{9}{25}=\frac{54}{150}$; $\frac{239}{150}=1\frac{89}{150}$

47. $\frac{2}{3}=\frac{48}{72}$, $\frac{5}{8}=\frac{45}{72}$, $+\frac{7}{9}=\frac{56}{72}$; $\frac{149}{72}=2\frac{5}{72}$

48. $\frac{1}{3}=\frac{24}{72}$, $\frac{2}{9}=\frac{16}{72}$, $+\frac{7}{8}=\frac{63}{72}$; $\frac{103}{72}=1\frac{31}{72}$

49. $\frac{3}{8}=\frac{15}{40}$, $+\frac{3}{5}=\frac{24}{40}$; $\frac{39}{40}$

50. $\frac{5}{9}=\frac{20}{36}$, $+\frac{7}{12}=\frac{21}{36}$; $\frac{41}{36}=1\frac{5}{36}$

51. $\frac{3}{8}=\frac{9}{24}$, $\frac{5}{6}=\frac{20}{24}$, $+\frac{7}{12}=\frac{14}{24}$; $\frac{43}{24}=1\frac{19}{24}$

52. $\frac{11}{12}=\frac{110}{120}$, $\frac{13}{24}=\frac{65}{120}$, $+\frac{4}{15}=\frac{32}{120}$; $\frac{207}{120}=1\frac{87}{120}=1\frac{29}{40}$

53. $\frac{1}{2}=\frac{36}{72}$, $\frac{5}{8}=\frac{45}{72}$, $+\frac{7}{9}=\frac{56}{72}$; $\frac{137}{72}=1\frac{65}{72}$

54. $\frac{5}{14}=\frac{15}{42}$, $\frac{3}{7}=\frac{18}{42}$, $+\frac{5}{21}=\frac{10}{42}$; $\frac{43}{42}=1\frac{1}{42}$

Objective C Exercises

55. $1\frac{1}{2}=1\frac{3}{6}$, $+2\frac{1}{6}=2\frac{1}{6}$; $3\frac{4}{6}=3\frac{2}{3}$

56. $2\frac{2}{5}=2\frac{4}{10}$, $+3\frac{3}{10}=3\frac{3}{10}$; $5\frac{7}{10}$

57. $4\frac{1}{2}=4\frac{6}{12}$, $+5\frac{7}{12}=5\frac{7}{12}$; $9\frac{13}{12}=10\frac{1}{12}$

58. $3\frac{3}{8}=3\frac{6}{16}$, $+2\frac{5}{16}=2\frac{5}{16}$; $5\frac{11}{16}$

59. 4, $+5\frac{2}{7}$; $9\frac{2}{7}$

60. $6\frac{8}{9}$, $+12$; $18\frac{8}{9}$

61. $3\frac{5}{8}=3\frac{25}{40}$, $+2\frac{11}{20}=2\frac{22}{40}$; $5\frac{47}{40}=6\frac{7}{40}$

62. $4\frac{5}{12}=4\frac{15}{36}$, $+6\frac{11}{18}=6\frac{22}{36}$; $10\frac{37}{36}=11\frac{1}{36}$

63. $7\frac{5}{12}=7\frac{20}{48}$, $+2\frac{9}{16}=2\frac{27}{48}$; $9\frac{47}{48}$

64. $9\frac{1}{2}=9\frac{11}{22}$, $+3\frac{3}{11}=3\frac{6}{22}$; $12\frac{17}{22}$

65. 6, $+2\frac{3}{13}$; $8\frac{3}{13}$

66. $\begin{array}{r} 8\frac{21}{40} \\ +\ 6 \\ \hline 14\frac{21}{40} \end{array}$

67. $\begin{array}{r} 8\frac{29}{30} = 8\frac{116}{120} \\ +7\frac{11}{40} = 7\frac{33}{120} \\ \hline 15\frac{149}{120} = 16\frac{29}{120} \end{array}$

68. $\begin{array}{r} 17\frac{5}{16} = 17\frac{15}{48} \\ +\ 3\frac{11}{24} = 3\frac{22}{48} \\ \hline 20\frac{37}{48} \end{array}$

69. $\begin{array}{r} 17\frac{3}{8} = 17\frac{15}{40} \\ +\ 7\frac{7}{20} = 7\frac{14}{40} \\ \hline 24\frac{29}{40} \end{array}$

70. $\begin{array}{r} 14\frac{7}{12} = 14\frac{49}{84} \\ +29\frac{13}{21} = 29\frac{52}{84} \\ \hline 43\frac{101}{84} = 44\frac{17}{84} \end{array}$

71. $\begin{array}{r} 5\frac{7}{8} = 5\frac{21}{24} \\ +27\frac{5}{12} = 27\frac{10}{24} \\ \hline 32\frac{31}{24} = 33\frac{7}{24} \end{array}$

72. $\begin{array}{r} 7\frac{5}{6} = 7\frac{15}{18} \\ +3\frac{5}{9} = 3\frac{10}{18} \\ \hline 10\frac{25}{18} = 11\frac{7}{18} \end{array}$

73. $\begin{array}{r} 7\frac{5}{9} = 7\frac{20}{36} \\ +2\frac{7}{12} = 2\frac{21}{36} \\ \hline 9\frac{41}{36} = 10\frac{5}{36} \end{array}$

74. $\begin{array}{r} 3\frac{1}{2} = 3\frac{6}{12} \\ 2\frac{3}{4} = 2\frac{9}{12} \\ +1\frac{5}{6} = 1\frac{10}{12} \\ \hline 6\frac{25}{12} = 8\frac{1}{12} \end{array}$

75. $\begin{array}{r} 2\frac{1}{2} = 2\frac{6}{12} \\ 3\frac{2}{3} = 3\frac{8}{12} \\ +4\frac{1}{4} = 4\frac{3}{12} \\ \hline 9\frac{17}{12} = 10\frac{5}{12} \end{array}$

76. $\begin{array}{r} 3\frac{1}{3} = 3\frac{35}{105} \\ 7\frac{1}{5} = 7\frac{21}{105} \\ +2\frac{1}{7} = 2\frac{15}{105} \\ \hline 12\frac{71}{105} \end{array}$

77. $\begin{array}{r} 3\frac{1}{2} = 3\frac{45}{90} \\ 3\frac{1}{5} = 3\frac{18}{90} \\ +8\frac{1}{9} = 8\frac{10}{90} \\ \hline 14\frac{73}{90} \end{array}$

78. $\begin{array}{r} 6\frac{5}{9} = 6\frac{20}{36} \\ 6\frac{5}{12} = 6\frac{15}{36} \\ +2\frac{5}{18} = 2\frac{10}{36} \\ \hline 14\frac{45}{36} = 15\frac{9}{36} = 15\frac{1}{4} \end{array}$

79. $\begin{array}{r} 2\frac{3}{8} = 2\frac{18}{48} \\ 4\frac{7}{12} = 4\frac{28}{48} \\ +3\frac{5}{16} = 3\frac{15}{48} \\ \hline 9\frac{61}{48} = 10\frac{13}{48} \end{array}$

80.
$$\begin{aligned} 2\tfrac{1}{8} &= 2\tfrac{9}{72} \\ 4\tfrac{2}{9} &= 4\tfrac{16}{72} \\ +5\tfrac{17}{18} &= 5\tfrac{68}{72} \\ \hline & 11\tfrac{93}{72} = 12\tfrac{21}{72} = 12\tfrac{7}{24} \end{aligned}$$

81.
$$\begin{aligned} 6\tfrac{5}{6} &= 6\tfrac{45}{54} \\ 17\tfrac{2}{9} &= 17\tfrac{12}{54} \\ +18\tfrac{5}{27} &= 18\tfrac{10}{54} \\ \hline & 41\tfrac{67}{54} = 42\tfrac{13}{54} \end{aligned}$$

82.
$$\begin{aligned} 4\tfrac{7}{20} &= 4\tfrac{84}{240} \\ \tfrac{17}{80} &= \tfrac{51}{240} \\ +25\tfrac{23}{60} &= 25\tfrac{92}{240} \\ \hline & 29\tfrac{227}{240} \end{aligned}$$

83.
$$\begin{aligned} 2\tfrac{4}{9} &= 2\tfrac{16}{36} \\ +5\tfrac{7}{12} &= 5\tfrac{21}{36} \\ \hline & 7\tfrac{37}{36} = 8\tfrac{1}{36} \end{aligned}$$

84.
$$\begin{aligned} 5\tfrac{5}{6} &= 5\tfrac{20}{24} \\ +3\tfrac{3}{8} &= 3\tfrac{9}{24} \\ \hline & 8\tfrac{29}{24} = 9\tfrac{5}{24} \end{aligned}$$

85.
$$\begin{aligned} 4\tfrac{3}{4} &= 4\tfrac{9}{12} \\ +9\tfrac{1}{3} &= 9\tfrac{4}{12} \\ \hline & 13\tfrac{13}{12} = 14\tfrac{1}{12} \end{aligned}$$

86.
$$\begin{aligned} 4\tfrac{8}{9} &= 4\tfrac{16}{18} \\ +9\tfrac{1}{6} &= 9\tfrac{3}{18} \\ \hline & 13\tfrac{19}{18} = 14\tfrac{1}{18} \end{aligned}$$

87.
$$\begin{aligned} 2 &= 2 \\ 4\tfrac{5}{8} &= 4\tfrac{45}{72} \\ +2\tfrac{2}{9} &= 2\tfrac{16}{72} \\ \hline & 8\tfrac{61}{72} \end{aligned}$$

88.
$$\begin{aligned} 1\tfrac{5}{8} &= 1\tfrac{15}{24} \\ 3 &= 3 \\ +7\tfrac{7}{24} &= 7\tfrac{7}{24} \\ \hline & 11\tfrac{22}{24} = 11\tfrac{11}{12} \end{aligned}$$

Objective D Exercises

89. **Strategy** To find the length of the shaft, add the three distances $\left(\frac{3}{8}, \frac{11}{16}, \text{ and } \frac{1}{4} \text{ inch}\right)$.

Solution
$$\begin{aligned} \tfrac{3}{8} &= \tfrac{6}{16} \\ \tfrac{11}{16} &= \tfrac{11}{16} \\ +\tfrac{1}{4} &= \tfrac{4}{16} \\ \hline & \tfrac{21}{16} = 1\tfrac{5}{16} \end{aligned}$$

The length of the shaft is $1\frac{5}{16}$ inches.

90. **Strategy** To find the length of the shaft, add the lengths of the three parts $\left(\frac{5}{16}, 6\frac{7}{8}, \text{ and } 1\frac{3}{8} \text{ inches}\right)$.

Solution
$$\begin{aligned} \tfrac{5}{16} &= \tfrac{5}{16} \\ 6\tfrac{7}{8} &= 6\tfrac{14}{16} \\ +1\tfrac{3}{8} &= 1\tfrac{6}{16} \\ \hline & 7\tfrac{25}{16} = 8\tfrac{9}{16} \end{aligned}$$

The length of the shaft is $8\frac{9}{16}$ inches.

91. **Strategy** To find the total thickness of the table after the veneer has been applied, add the table-top thickness $\left(1\frac{1}{8} \text{ inch}\right)$ to the veneer thickness $\left(\frac{3}{16} \text{ inch}\right)$.

Solution
$$\begin{aligned} 1\tfrac{1}{8} &= 1\tfrac{2}{16} \\ +\tfrac{3}{16} &= \tfrac{3}{16} \\ \hline & 1\tfrac{5}{16} \end{aligned}$$

The total thickness is $1\frac{5}{16}$ inches.

92a. Strategy To find the total number of hours of overtime worked, add the four amounts $\left(2\frac{2}{3}, 1\frac{1}{4}, 1\frac{1}{3}, \text{ and } 6\frac{3}{4} \text{ hours}\right)$.

Solution

$$\begin{aligned} 2\frac{2}{3} &= 2\frac{8}{12} \\ 1\frac{1}{4} &= 1\frac{3}{12} \\ 1\frac{1}{3} &= 1\frac{4}{12} \\ +6\frac{3}{4} &= 6\frac{9}{12} \\ \hline 10\frac{24}{12} &= 12 \end{aligned}$$

12 hours of overtime were worked during the week.

b. Strategy To find the overtime pay, multiply the hours of overtime worked (12) by the overtime salary ($22 per hour).

Solution

$$\begin{array}{r} \$22 \\ \times\ 12 \\ \hline 44 \\ 22 \\ \hline \$264 \end{array}$$

Fred receives $264 of overtime pay.

93a. Strategy To find the total number of hours worked, add the five amounts $\left(5, 3\frac{3}{4}, 2\frac{1}{3}, 1\frac{1}{4}, \text{ and } 7\frac{2}{3} \text{ hours}\right)$.

Solution

$$\begin{aligned} 5 &= 5 \\ 3\frac{3}{4} &= 3\frac{9}{12} \\ 2\frac{1}{3} &= 2\frac{4}{12} \\ 1\frac{1}{4} &= 1\frac{3}{12} \\ +7\frac{2}{3} &= 7\frac{8}{12} \\ \hline 18\frac{24}{12} &= 20 \end{aligned}$$

A total of 20 hours was worked.

b. Strategy To find the total salary for the week, multiply the number of hours worked (20) by the pay for 1 hour ($11).

Solution

$$\begin{array}{r} 11 \\ \times\ 20 \\ \hline \$220 \end{array}$$

Your total salary for the week is $220.

94. Strategy To find the total length of the course, add the three sides $\left(4\frac{3}{10}, 3\frac{7}{10}, \text{ and } 2\frac{1}{2} \text{ miles}\right)$.

Solution

$$\begin{aligned} 4\frac{3}{10} &= 4\frac{3}{10} \\ 3\frac{7}{10} &= 3\frac{7}{10} \\ +2\frac{1}{2} &= 2\frac{5}{10} \\ \hline 9\frac{15}{10} &= 10\frac{1}{2} \end{aligned}$$

The total length of the course is $10\frac{1}{2}$ miles.

95. Strategy To find the total length of the wood beams, add the three lengths $\left(25\frac{3}{4}, 12\frac{1}{2}, \text{ and } 17\frac{1}{2} \text{ feet}\right)$.

Solution

$$\begin{aligned} 25\frac{3}{4} &= 25\frac{3}{4} \\ 12\frac{1}{2} &= 12\frac{2}{4} \\ +17\frac{1}{2} &= 17\frac{2}{4} \\ \hline 54\frac{7}{4} &= 55\frac{3}{4} \end{aligned}$$

The total length of wood needed is $55\frac{3}{4}$ feet.

96. Strategy To find what fraction of the respondents named any of the three given types of doughnuts, add the three fractions $\left(\frac{2}{5}, \frac{8}{25}, \text{ and } \frac{3}{20}\right)$.

Solution

$$\begin{aligned} \frac{2}{5} &= \frac{40}{100} \\ \frac{8}{25} &= \frac{32}{100} \\ +\frac{3}{20} &= \frac{15}{100} \\ \hline & \ \frac{87}{100} \end{aligned}$$

$\frac{87}{100}$ of the respondents named glazed, filled, or frosted as their favorite type of doughnut.

97. Strategy To find what fractional part of those who changed homes moved outside the county, add the fractional part of those who moved to a different state $\left(\frac{1}{7}\right)$ to the fractional part of those who moved to a different county in the same state $\left(\frac{4}{21}\right)$.

Solution

$$\frac{1}{7}=\frac{3}{21}$$
$$+\frac{4}{21}=\frac{4}{21}$$
$$\frac{7}{21}=\frac{1}{3}$$

Those who changed homes outside the county were $\frac{1}{3}$ of the people who changed homes.

Applying the Concepts

98. A unit fraction is a fraction in which the numerator is 1 and the denominator is any natural number greater than 1.

$$\frac{1}{2}+\frac{1}{3}+\frac{1}{4}=\frac{6}{12}+\frac{4}{12}+\frac{3}{12}=\frac{13}{12}=1\frac{1}{12}$$

There is no smallest unit fraction. No matter how small the unit fraction is, we can always add 1 to the denominator to make it even smaller.

99. We can use 3 dimes and 1 quarter to model adding $\frac{3}{10}$ and $\frac{1}{4}$. Because the dime and the quarter are not the same unit, we change them to nickels and add.

3 dimes = 6 nickels
+1 quarter = 5 nickels
11 nickels

Now, consider the above problem in terms of dollars.

$$\frac{3}{10}=\frac{6}{20}$$
$$+\frac{1}{4}=\frac{5}{20}$$
$$\frac{11}{20}$$

Note that 1 dime = $\frac{1}{10}$ of a dollar,

1 quarter = $\frac{1}{4}$ of a dollar, and

1 nickel = $\frac{1}{20}$ of a dollar.

100. $\frac{1}{3}+\frac{1}{6}+\frac{1}{8}+\frac{1}{12}+\frac{2}{5}$

$=\frac{40}{120}+\frac{20}{120}+\frac{15}{120}+\frac{10}{120}+\frac{48}{120}=\frac{133}{120}=1\frac{13}{120}$

No, this is not possible. The total cannot be greater than 1, which represents all the people surveyed.

Section 2.5

Objective A Exercises

1. $\frac{9}{17}-\frac{7}{17}=\frac{2}{17}$

2. $\frac{11}{15}-\frac{3}{15}=\frac{8}{15}$

3. $\frac{11}{12}-\frac{7}{12}=\frac{4}{12}=\frac{1}{3}$

4. $\frac{13}{15}-\frac{4}{15}=\frac{9}{15}=\frac{3}{5}$

5. $\frac{9}{20}-\frac{7}{20}=\frac{2}{20}=\frac{1}{10}$

6. $\frac{48}{55}-\frac{13}{55}=\frac{35}{55}=\frac{7}{11}$

7. $\frac{42}{65}-\frac{17}{65}=\frac{25}{65}=\frac{5}{13}$

8. $\frac{11}{24} - \frac{5}{24} = \frac{6}{24} = \frac{1}{4}$

9. $\frac{23}{30} - \frac{13}{30} = \frac{10}{30} = \frac{1}{3}$

10. $\frac{17}{42} - \frac{5}{42} = \frac{12}{42} = \frac{2}{7}$

11. $\frac{13}{14} - \frac{5}{14} = \frac{8}{14} = \frac{4}{7}$

12. $\frac{17}{19} - \frac{7}{19} = \frac{10}{19}$

13. $\frac{7}{8} - \frac{5}{8} = \frac{2}{8} = \frac{1}{4}$

14. $\frac{7}{12} - \frac{5}{12} = \frac{2}{12} = \frac{1}{6}$

15. $\frac{18}{23} - \frac{9}{23} = \frac{9}{23}$

16. $\frac{7}{9} - \frac{3}{9} = \frac{4}{9}$

17. $\frac{17}{24} - \frac{11}{24} = \frac{6}{24} = \frac{1}{4}$

18. $\frac{19}{30} - \frac{11}{30} = \frac{8}{30} = \frac{4}{15}$

Objective B Exercises

19. $\frac{2}{3} = \frac{4}{6}$, $-\frac{1}{6} = \frac{1}{6}$; $\frac{3}{6} = \frac{1}{2}$

20. $\frac{7}{8} = \frac{14}{16}$, $-\frac{5}{16} = \frac{5}{16}$; $\frac{9}{16}$

21. $\frac{5}{8} = \frac{35}{56}$, $-\frac{2}{7} = \frac{16}{56}$; $\frac{19}{56}$

22. $\frac{5}{6} = \frac{35}{42}$, $-\frac{3}{7} = \frac{18}{42}$; $\frac{17}{42}$

23. $\frac{5}{7} = \frac{10}{14}$, $-\frac{3}{14} = \frac{3}{14}$; $\frac{7}{14} = \frac{1}{2}$

24. $\frac{5}{9} = \frac{25}{45}$, $-\frac{7}{15} = \frac{21}{45}$; $\frac{4}{45}$

25. $\frac{8}{15} = \frac{32}{60}$, $-\frac{7}{20} = \frac{21}{60}$; $\frac{11}{60}$

26. $\frac{7}{9} = \frac{14}{18}$, $-\frac{1}{6} = \frac{3}{18}$; $\frac{11}{18}$

27. $\frac{9}{14} = \frac{36}{56}$, $-\frac{3}{8} = \frac{21}{56}$; $\frac{15}{56}$

28. $\frac{5}{12} = \frac{20}{48}$, $-\frac{5}{16} = \frac{15}{48}$; $\frac{5}{48}$

29. $\frac{46}{51} = \frac{46}{51}$, $-\frac{3}{17} = \frac{9}{51}$; $\frac{37}{51}$

30. $\frac{9}{16} = \frac{18}{32}$, $-\frac{17}{32} = \frac{17}{32}$; $\frac{1}{32}$

31. $\frac{21}{35} = \frac{42}{70}$, $-\frac{5}{14} = \frac{25}{70}$; $\frac{17}{70}$

32. $\frac{19}{40} = \frac{38}{80}$, $-\frac{3}{16} = \frac{15}{80}$; $\frac{23}{80}$

33. $\frac{29}{60} = \frac{58}{120}$, $-\frac{3}{40} = \frac{9}{120}$; $\frac{49}{120}$

34. $\frac{11}{12} = \frac{55}{60}$
$-\frac{3}{5} = \frac{36}{60}$
$\frac{19}{60}$

35. $\frac{11}{15} = \frac{33}{45}$
$-\frac{5}{9} = \frac{25}{45}$
$\frac{8}{45}$

36. $\frac{11}{24} = \frac{33}{72}$
$-\frac{7}{18} = \frac{28}{72}$
$\frac{5}{72}$

37. $\frac{9}{14} = \frac{27}{42}$
$-\frac{5}{42} = \frac{5}{42}$
$\frac{22}{42} = \frac{11}{21}$

38. $\frac{11}{12} = \frac{55}{60}$
$-\frac{11}{15} = \frac{44}{60}$
$\frac{11}{60}$

39. $\frac{17}{20} = \frac{51}{60}$
$-\frac{7}{15} = \frac{28}{60}$
$\frac{23}{60}$

40. $\frac{13}{20} = \frac{39}{60}$
$-\frac{1}{6} = \frac{10}{60}$
$\frac{29}{60}$

41. $\frac{5}{6} = \frac{15}{18}$
$-\frac{7}{9} = \frac{14}{18}$
$\frac{1}{18}$

Objective C Exercises

42. $5\frac{7}{12}$
$-2\frac{5}{12}$
$3\frac{2}{12} = 3\frac{1}{6}$

43. $16\frac{11}{15}$
$-11\frac{8}{15}$
$5\frac{3}{15} = 5\frac{1}{5}$

44. $72\frac{21}{23}$
$-16\frac{17}{23}$
$56\frac{4}{23}$

45. $19\frac{16}{17}$
$-9\frac{7}{17}$
$10\frac{9}{17}$

46. $6\frac{1}{3}$
-2
$4\frac{1}{3}$

47. $5\frac{7}{8}$
-1
$4\frac{7}{8}$

48. $10 = 9\frac{3}{3}$
$-6\frac{1}{3} = 6\frac{1}{3}$
$3\frac{2}{3}$

49. $3 = 2\frac{21}{21}$
$-2\frac{5}{21} = 2\frac{5}{21}$
$\frac{16}{21}$

50. $6\frac{2}{5} = 5\frac{7}{5}$
$-4\frac{4}{5} = 4\frac{4}{5}$
$1\frac{3}{5}$

51. $16\frac{3}{8} = 15\frac{11}{8}$
$-10\frac{7}{8} = 10\frac{7}{8}$
$5\frac{4}{8} = 5\frac{1}{2}$

52. $25\frac{4}{9} = 24\frac{13}{9}$
$-16\frac{7}{9} = 16\frac{7}{9}$
$8\frac{6}{9} = 8\frac{2}{3}$

53. $8\frac{3}{7} = 7\frac{10}{7}$
$-2\frac{6}{7} = 2\frac{6}{7}$
$5\frac{4}{7}$

54. $16\frac{2}{5} = 16\frac{18}{45} = 15\frac{63}{45}$
$-8\frac{4}{9} = 8\frac{20}{45} = 8\frac{20}{45}$
$7\frac{43}{45}$

55. $23\frac{7}{8} = 23\frac{21}{24}$
$-16\frac{2}{3} = 16\frac{16}{24}$
$7\frac{5}{24}$

56. $6 = 5\frac{5}{5}$
$-4\frac{3}{5} = 4\frac{3}{5}$
$1\frac{2}{5}$

57. $65\frac{8}{35} = 65\frac{16}{70} = 64\frac{86}{70}$
$-16\frac{11}{14} = 16\frac{55}{70} = 16\frac{55}{70}$
$48\frac{31}{70}$

58. $82\frac{4}{33} = 82\frac{8}{66} = 81\frac{74}{66}$
$-16\frac{5}{22} = 16\frac{15}{66} = 16\frac{15}{66}$
$65\frac{59}{66}$

59. $101\frac{2}{9}$
-16
$85\frac{2}{9}$

60.
$$\begin{array}{r} 77\frac{5}{18} \\ -61 \\ \hline 16\frac{5}{18} \end{array}$$

61.
$$\begin{array}{rl} 17 & = 16\frac{13}{13} \\ -7\frac{8}{13} & = 7\frac{8}{13} \\ \hline & 9\frac{5}{13} \end{array}$$

62.
$$\begin{array}{rl} 8\frac{1}{9} = 8\frac{8}{72} & = 7\frac{80}{72} \\ -5\frac{3}{8} = 5\frac{27}{72} & = 5\frac{27}{72} \\ \hline & 2\frac{53}{72} \end{array}$$

63.
$$\begin{array}{rl} 23\frac{3}{20} = 23\frac{3}{20} & = 22\frac{23}{20} \\ -7\frac{3}{5} = 7\frac{12}{20} & = 7\frac{12}{20} \\ \hline & 15\frac{11}{20} \end{array}$$

64.
$$\begin{array}{rl} 9\frac{2}{7} & = 9\frac{8}{28} \\ -3\frac{1}{4} & = 3\frac{7}{28} \\ \hline & 6\frac{1}{28} \end{array}$$

65.
$$\begin{array}{rl} 12\frac{3}{8} = 12\frac{9}{24} & = 11\frac{33}{24} \\ -7\frac{5}{12} = 7\frac{10}{24} & = 7\frac{10}{24} \\ \hline & 4\frac{23}{24} \end{array}$$

66.
$$\begin{array}{rl} 10\frac{5}{9} = 10\frac{25}{45} & = 9\frac{70}{45} \\ -5\frac{11}{15} = 5\frac{33}{45} & = 5\frac{33}{45} \\ \hline & 4\frac{37}{45} \end{array}$$

67.
$$\begin{array}{rl} 6\frac{1}{3} = 6\frac{5}{15} & = 5\frac{20}{15} \\ -3\frac{3}{5} = 3\frac{9}{15} & = 3\frac{9}{15} \\ \hline & 2\frac{11}{15} \end{array}$$

Objective D Exercises

68.
$$\begin{array}{rl} 16\frac{2}{3} = 16\frac{16}{24} & = 15\frac{40}{24} \\ -7\frac{7}{8} = 7\frac{21}{24} & = 7\frac{21}{24} \\ \hline & 8\frac{19}{24} \end{array}$$

The missing dimension is $8\frac{19}{24}$ feet.

69.
$$\begin{array}{rl} 12\frac{3}{8} & = 11\frac{11}{8} \\ -2\frac{7}{8} & = 2\frac{7}{8} \\ \hline & 9\frac{4}{8} = 9\frac{1}{2} \end{array}$$

The missing dimension is $9\frac{1}{2}$ inches.

70. **Strategy** To find how much farther the horses run in the Kentucky Derby than in the Preakness Stakes, subtract the distance run in the Preakness Stakes $\left(1\frac{3}{16}\text{ miles}\right)$ from the distance run in the Kentucky Derby $\left(1\frac{1}{4}\text{ miles}\right)$.

Solution
$$\begin{array}{rl} 1\frac{1}{4} & = 1\frac{4}{16} \\ -1\frac{3}{16} & = 1\frac{3}{16} \\ \hline & \frac{1}{16} \end{array}$$

The horses run $\frac{1}{16}$ mile farther in the Kentucky Derby than in the Preakness Stakes.

Strategy To find how much farther the horses run in the Belmont Stakes than in the Preakness Stakes, subtract the distance run in the Preakness Stakes $\left(1\frac{3}{16}\text{ miles}\right)$ from the distance run in the Belmont Stakes $\left(1\frac{1}{2}\text{ miles}\right)$.

Solution
$$\begin{array}{rl} 1\frac{1}{2} & = 1\frac{8}{16} \\ -1\frac{3}{16} & = 1\frac{3}{16} \\ \hline & \frac{5}{16} \end{array}$$

The horses run $\frac{5}{16}$ mile farther in the Belmont Stakes than in the Preakness Stakes.

71. Strategy To find the difference between Meyfarth's distance and Coachman's distance, subtract Coachman's distance $\left(66\frac{1}{8}\text{ inches}\right)$ from Meyfarth's distance $\left(75\frac{1}{2}\text{ inches}\right)$.

Solution

$$\begin{array}{r} 75\frac{1}{2} = 75\frac{4}{8} \\ -66\frac{1}{8} = 66\frac{1}{8} \\ \hline 9\frac{3}{8} \end{array}$$

The difference between Meyfarth's distance and Coachman's distance was $9\frac{3}{8}$ inches.

Strategy To find the difference between Kostadinova's distance and Meyfarth's distance, subtract Meyfarth's distance $\left(75\frac{1}{2}\text{ inches}\right)$ from Kostadinova's distance $\left(80\frac{3}{4}\text{ inches}\right)$.

Solution

$$\begin{array}{r} 80\frac{3}{4} = 80\frac{3}{4} \\ -75\frac{1}{2} = 75\frac{2}{4} \\ \hline 5\frac{1}{4} \end{array}$$

The difference between Kostadinova's distance and Meyfarth's distance was $5\frac{1}{4}$ inches.

72a. Strategy To find the distance, add the distance to be traveled the first day $\left(7\frac{3}{8}\text{ miles}\right)$ to the distance to be traveled the second day $\left(10\frac{1}{3}\text{ miles}\right)$.

Solution

$$\begin{array}{r} 7\frac{3}{8} = 7\frac{9}{24} \\ +10\frac{1}{3} = 10\frac{8}{24} \\ \hline 17\frac{17}{24} \end{array}$$

The distance to be traveled during the first 2 days is $17\frac{17}{24}$ miles.

b. Strategy To find the distance, subtract the miles hiked $\left(17\frac{17}{24}\right)$ from the total miles $\left(27\frac{1}{2}\right)$.

Solution

$$\begin{array}{r} 27\frac{1}{2} = 27\frac{12}{24} = 26\frac{36}{24} \\ -17\frac{17}{24} = 17\frac{17}{24} = 17\frac{17}{24} \\ \hline 9\frac{19}{24} \end{array}$$

On the third day, $9\frac{19}{24}$ miles remain to be hiked.

73a. Strategy To find the distance, add the distance from the starting point to the first checkpoint $\left(3\frac{3}{8}\text{ miles}\right)$ to the distance from the first checkpoint to the second checkpoint $\left(4\frac{1}{3}\text{ miles}\right)$.

Solution

$$\begin{array}{r} 3\frac{3}{8} = 3\frac{9}{24} \\ +4\frac{1}{3} = 4\frac{8}{24} \\ \hline 7\frac{17}{24} \end{array}$$

The distance from the starting point to the second checkpoint is $7\frac{17}{24}$ miles.

b. Strategy To find the distance, subtract the distance from the starting point to the second checkpoint $\left(7\frac{17}{24}\text{ miles}\right)$ from the total distance (12 miles).

Solution

$$\begin{array}{r} 12 = 11\frac{24}{24} \\ -7\frac{17}{24} = 7\frac{17}{24} \\ \hline 4\frac{7}{24} \end{array}$$

The distance from the second checkpoint to the finish line is $4\frac{7}{24}$ miles.

74. Strategy To find how much weight must be lost during the third month:

- Add the weight lost during the first month $\left(8\frac{3}{4}\text{ pounds}\right)$ to the amount lost during the second month $\left(11\frac{5}{8}\text{ pounds}\right)$.
- Subtract the total lost during the first 2 months from the total goal (25 pounds).

Solution

$$\begin{array}{r} 8\frac{3}{4} = 8\frac{6}{8} \\ +11\frac{5}{8} = 11\frac{5}{8} \\ \hline 19\frac{11}{8} = 20\frac{3}{8} \end{array} \qquad \begin{array}{r} 25 = 24\frac{8}{8} \\ -20\frac{3}{8} = 20\frac{3}{8} \\ \hline 4\frac{5}{8} \end{array}$$

The patient has $4\frac{5}{8}$ pounds more to lose.

75a. The wrestler has lost $5\frac{1}{4}$ pounds the first week and $4\frac{1}{4}$ pounds the second week. Thus the wrestler has lost more than 9 pounds the first two weeks. Since less than 13 pounds needs to be lost, the wrestler can attain the weight class by losing less than 4 pounds. Yes, this is less than the $4\frac{1}{4}$ pounds lost in the second week.

b. Strategy To find how much weight must be lost to reach the desired weight:

- Add the amounts of weight lost during the first 2 weeks $\left(5\frac{1}{4}\text{ and }4\frac{1}{4}\text{ pounds}\right)$.
- Subtract the total weight lost so far from the amount that is required $\left(12\frac{3}{4}\text{ pounds}\right)$.

Solution

$$\begin{array}{r} 5\frac{1}{4} \\ +4\frac{1}{4} \\ \hline 9\frac{2}{4} = 9\frac{1}{2} \end{array} \qquad \begin{array}{r} 12\frac{3}{4} = 12\frac{3}{4} \\ -\ 9\frac{1}{2} = \ 9\frac{2}{4} \\ \hline 3\frac{1}{4} \end{array}$$

The wrestler needs to lose $3\frac{1}{4}$ pounds to reach the desired weight.

76a. Strategy To find the difference, subtract the fraction derived from corporate income tax from the fraction derived from personal income tax.

Solution

$$\begin{array}{rl} \frac{12}{25} = \frac{36}{75} & \text{Personal income taxes} \\ -\frac{8}{75} = \frac{8}{75} & \text{Corporate income taxes} \\ \hline \frac{28}{75} & \end{array}$$

The difference between the fraction derived from personal income taxes and that derived from corporate income taxes is $\frac{28}{75}$.

b. Strategy To find the difference, subtract the fraction derived from miscellaneous taxes from the fraction derived from the Social Security category.

Solution

$$\begin{array}{rl} \frac{1}{3} = \frac{25}{75} & \text{Social Security} \\ -\frac{2}{25} = \frac{6}{75} & \text{Miscellaneous} \\ \hline \frac{19}{75} & \end{array}$$

The difference between the fraction derived from in the Social Security category and that derived from miscellaneous taxes is $\frac{19}{75}$.

Applying the Concepts

77. To find the missing number, subtract $2\frac{1}{2}$ from $5\frac{1}{3}$.

$$\begin{array}{r} 5\frac{1}{3} = 5\frac{2}{6} = 4\frac{8}{6} \\ -2\frac{1}{2} = 2\frac{3}{6} = 2\frac{3}{6} \\ \hline 2\frac{5}{6} \end{array}$$

78. To find the missing number, add $1\frac{5}{8}$ and $4\frac{1}{2}$.

$$\begin{array}{r} 1\frac{5}{8} = 1\frac{5}{8} \\ +4\frac{1}{2} = 4\frac{4}{8} \\ \hline 5\frac{9}{8} = 6\frac{1}{8} \end{array}$$

79. Right diagonal: $\frac{3}{4}+\frac{5}{8}+\frac{1}{2}=\frac{6}{8}+\frac{5}{8}+\frac{4}{8}=\frac{15}{8}$

Left diagonal: $\frac{5}{8}+\frac{7}{8}=\frac{12}{8}$; $\frac{15}{8}-\frac{12}{8}=\frac{3}{8}$

Top across: $\frac{3}{8}+\frac{3}{4}=\frac{3}{8}+\frac{6}{8}=\frac{9}{8}$; $\frac{15}{8}-\frac{9}{8}=\frac{6}{8}=\frac{3}{4}$

Left down: $\frac{3}{8}+\frac{1}{2}=\frac{3}{8}+\frac{4}{8}=\frac{7}{8}$; $\frac{15}{8}-\frac{7}{8}=\frac{8}{8}=1$

Middle across: $1+\frac{5}{8}=\frac{8}{8}+\frac{5}{8}=\frac{13}{8}$;

$\frac{15}{8}-\frac{13}{8}=\frac{2}{8}=\frac{1}{4}$

Bottom across: $\frac{1}{2}+\frac{7}{8}=\frac{4}{8}+\frac{7}{8}=\frac{11}{8}$;

$\frac{15}{8}-\frac{11}{8}=\frac{4}{8}=\frac{1}{2}$

$\frac{3}{8}$	$\frac{3}{4}$	$\frac{3}{4}$
1	$\frac{5}{8}$	$\frac{1}{4}$
$\frac{1}{2}$	$\frac{1}{2}$	$\frac{7}{8}$

80. The electrician's income is 1, that is, 100%.

$$1=\frac{15}{15}$$
$$-\frac{4}{15}=\frac{4}{15}$$
$$\frac{11}{15}$$

$\frac{11}{15}$ of the electrician's income is not spent for housing.

Section 2.6

Objective A Exercises

1. $\frac{2\cdot 7}{3\cdot 8}=\frac{\overset{1}{\cancel{2}}\cdot 7}{3\cdot\underset{1}{\cancel{2}}\cdot 2\cdot 2}=\frac{7}{12}$

2. $\frac{1\cdot\overset{1}{\cancel{2}}}{\underset{1}{\cancel{2}}\cdot 3}=\frac{1}{3}$

3. $\frac{5\cdot 7}{16\cdot 15}=\frac{\overset{1}{\cancel{5}}\cdot 7}{2\cdot 2\cdot 2\cdot 2\cdot 3\cdot\underset{1}{\cancel{5}}}=\frac{7}{48}$

4. $\frac{3\cdot 6}{8\cdot 7}=\frac{3\cdot\overset{1}{\cancel{2}}\cdot 3}{\underset{1}{\cancel{2}}\cdot 2\cdot 2\cdot 7}=\frac{9}{28}$

5. $\frac{1\cdot 1}{6\cdot 8}=\frac{1\cdot 1}{2\cdot 3\cdot 2\cdot 2\cdot 2}=\frac{1}{48}$

6. $\frac{2\cdot 5}{5\cdot 6}=\frac{\overset{1}{\cancel{2}}\cdot\overset{1}{\cancel{5}}}{\underset{1}{\cancel{5}}\cdot\underset{1}{\cancel{2}}\cdot 3}=\frac{1}{3}$

7. $\frac{11\cdot 6}{12\cdot 7}=\frac{11\cdot\overset{1}{\cancel{2}}\cdot\overset{1}{\cancel{3}}}{\underset{1}{\cancel{2}}\cdot 2\cdot\underset{1}{\cancel{3}}\cdot 7}=\frac{11}{14}$

8. $\frac{11\cdot 3}{12\cdot 5}=\frac{11\cdot\overset{1}{\cancel{3}}}{2\cdot 2\cdot\underset{1}{\cancel{3}}\cdot 5}=\frac{11}{20}$

9. $\frac{1\cdot 6}{6\cdot 7}=\frac{1\cdot\overset{1}{\cancel{2}}\cdot\overset{1}{\cancel{3}}}{\underset{1}{\cancel{2}}\cdot\underset{1}{\cancel{3}}\cdot 7}=\frac{1}{7}$

10. $\frac{3\cdot 10}{5\cdot 11}=\frac{3\cdot 2\cdot\overset{1}{\cancel{5}}}{\underset{1}{\cancel{5}}\cdot 11}=\frac{6}{11}$

11. $\frac{1\cdot 5}{5\cdot 8}=\frac{1\cdot\overset{1}{\cancel{5}}}{\underset{1}{\cancel{5}}\cdot 2\cdot 2\cdot 2}=\frac{1}{8}$

12. $\frac{6\cdot 14}{7\cdot 15}=\frac{2\cdot\overset{1}{\cancel{3}}\cdot 2\cdot\overset{1}{\cancel{7}}}{\underset{1}{\cancel{7}}\cdot\underset{1}{\cancel{3}}\cdot 5}=\frac{4}{5}$

13. $\frac{8\cdot 27}{9\cdot 4}=\frac{\overset{1}{\cancel{2}}\cdot\overset{1}{\cancel{2}}\cdot 2\cdot\overset{1}{\cancel{3}}\cdot\overset{1}{\cancel{3}}\cdot 3}{\underset{1}{\cancel{3}}\cdot\underset{1}{\cancel{3}}\cdot\underset{1}{\cancel{2}}\cdot\underset{1}{\cancel{2}}}=6$

14. $\frac{3\cdot 3}{5\cdot 10}=\frac{3\cdot 3}{5\cdot 2\cdot 5}=\frac{9}{50}$

15. $\frac{5\cdot 1}{6\cdot 2}=\frac{5\cdot 1}{2\cdot 3\cdot 2}=\frac{5}{12}$

16. $\frac{3\cdot 5}{8\cdot 12}=\frac{\overset{1}{\cancel{3}}\cdot 5}{2\cdot 2\cdot 2\cdot 2\cdot 2\cdot\underset{1}{\cancel{3}}}=\frac{5}{32}$

17. $\frac{16\cdot 27}{9\cdot 8}=\frac{\overset{1}{\cancel{2}}\cdot\overset{1}{\cancel{2}}\cdot\overset{1}{\cancel{2}}\cdot 2\cdot\overset{1}{\cancel{3}}\cdot\overset{1}{\cancel{3}}\cdot 3}{\underset{1}{\cancel{3}}\cdot\underset{1}{\cancel{3}}\cdot\underset{1}{\cancel{2}}\cdot\underset{1}{\cancel{2}}\cdot\underset{1}{\cancel{2}}}=6$

18. $\frac{5\cdot 16}{8\cdot 15}=\frac{\overset{1}{\cancel{5}}\cdot\overset{1}{\cancel{2}}\cdot\overset{1}{\cancel{2}}\cdot\overset{1}{\cancel{2}}\cdot 2}{\underset{1}{\cancel{2}}\cdot\underset{1}{\cancel{2}}\cdot\underset{1}{\cancel{2}}\cdot 3\cdot\underset{1}{\cancel{5}}}=\frac{2}{3}$

19. $\frac{3\cdot 4}{2\cdot 9}=\frac{\overset{1}{\cancel{3}}\cdot\overset{1}{\cancel{2}}\cdot 2}{\underset{1}{\cancel{2}}\cdot\underset{1}{\cancel{3}}\cdot 3}=\frac{2}{3}$

20. $\frac{5\cdot\overset{1}{\cancel{3}}}{\underset{1}{\cancel{3}}\cdot 7}=\frac{5}{7}$

21. $\frac{7\cdot 3}{8\cdot 14}=\frac{\overset{1}{\cancel{7}}\cdot 3}{2\cdot 2\cdot 2\cdot 2\cdot\underset{1}{\cancel{7}}}=\frac{3}{16}$

22. $\frac{2\cdot 1}{9\cdot 5}=\frac{2\cdot 1}{3\cdot 3\cdot 5}=\frac{2}{45}$

23. $\frac{1\cdot 3}{10\cdot 8}=\frac{3}{2\cdot 5\cdot 2\cdot 2\cdot 2}=\frac{3}{80}$

24. $\frac{5\cdot 6}{12\cdot 7}=\frac{5\cdot\overset{1}{\cancel{2}}\cdot\overset{1}{\cancel{3}}}{\underset{1}{\cancel{2}}\cdot 2\cdot\underset{1}{\cancel{3}}\cdot 7}=\frac{5}{14}$

25. $\frac{15\cdot 16}{8\cdot 3}=\frac{\overset{1}{\cancel{3}}\cdot 5\cdot\overset{1}{\cancel{2}}\cdot\overset{1}{\cancel{2}}\cdot\overset{1}{\cancel{2}}\cdot 2}{\underset{1}{\cancel{2}}\cdot\underset{1}{\cancel{2}}\cdot\underset{1}{\cancel{2}}\cdot\underset{1}{\cancel{3}}}=10$

26. $\frac{5\cdot4}{6\cdot15}=\frac{\cancel{5}\cdot\cancel{2}\cdot2}{\cancel{2}\cdot3\cdot3\cdot\cancel{5}}=\frac{2}{9}$

27. $\frac{1\cdot2}{2\cdot15}=\frac{1\cdot\cancel{2}}{\cancel{2}\cdot3\cdot5}=\frac{1}{15}$

28. $\frac{3\cdot5}{8\cdot16}=\frac{3\cdot5}{2\cdot2\cdot2\cdot2\cdot2\cdot2\cdot2}=\frac{15}{128}$

29. $\frac{5\cdot14}{7\cdot15}=\frac{\cancel{5}\cdot2\cdot\cancel{7}}{\cancel{7}\cdot3\cdot\cancel{5}}=\frac{2}{3}$

30. $\frac{3\cdot15}{8\cdot41}=\frac{3\cdot3\cdot5}{2\cdot2\cdot2\cdot41}=\frac{45}{328}$

31. $\frac{5\cdot42}{12\cdot65}=\frac{\cancel{5}\cdot\cancel{2}\cdot\cancel{3}\cdot7}{\cancel{2}\cdot2\cdot\cancel{3}\cdot\cancel{5}\cdot13}=\frac{7}{26}$

32. $\frac{16\cdot55}{33\cdot72}=\frac{\cancel{2}\cdot\cancel{2}\cdot\cancel{2}\cdot2\cdot5\cdot\cancel{11}}{3\cdot\cancel{11}\cdot\cancel{2}\cdot\cancel{2}\cdot\cancel{2}\cdot3\cdot3}=\frac{10}{27}$

33. $\frac{12\cdot5}{5\cdot3}=\frac{2\cdot2\cdot\cancel{3}\cdot\cancel{5}}{\cancel{5}\cdot\cancel{3}}=4$

34. $\frac{17\cdot81}{9\cdot17}=\frac{\cancel{17}\cdot\cancel{3}\cdot\cancel{3}\cdot3\cdot3}{\cancel{3}\cdot\cancel{3}\cdot\cancel{17}}=9$

35. $\frac{16\cdot125}{85\cdot84}=\frac{\cancel{2}\cdot\cancel{2}\cdot2\cdot2\cdot\cancel{5}\cdot5\cdot5}{\cancel{5}\cdot17\cdot\cancel{2}\cdot\cancel{2}\cdot3\cdot7}=\frac{100}{357}$

36. $\frac{19\cdot48}{64\cdot95}=\frac{\cancel{19}\cdot\cancel{2}\cdot\cancel{2}\cdot\cancel{2}\cdot\cancel{2}\cdot3}{\cancel{2}\cdot\cancel{2}\cdot\cancel{2}\cdot\cancel{2}\cdot2\cdot2\cdot5\cdot\cancel{19}}=\frac{3}{20}$

37. $\frac{7\cdot15}{12\cdot42}=\frac{\cancel{7}\cdot\cancel{3}\cdot5}{2\cdot2\cdot3\cdot2\cdot\cancel{3}\cdot\cancel{7}}=\frac{5}{24}$

38. $\frac{32\cdot3}{9\cdot8}=\frac{\cancel{2}\cdot\cancel{2}\cdot\cancel{2}\cdot2\cdot2\cdot\cancel{3}}{\cancel{3}\cdot3\cdot\cancel{2}\cdot\cancel{2}\cdot\cancel{2}}=\frac{4}{3}=1\frac{1}{3}$

39. $\frac{5\cdot3}{9\cdot20}=\frac{\cancel{5}\cdot\cancel{3}}{\cancel{3}\cdot3\cdot2\cdot2\cdot\cancel{5}}=\frac{1}{12}$

40. $\frac{7\cdot15}{3\cdot14}=\frac{\cancel{7}\cdot\cancel{3}\cdot5}{\cancel{3}\cdot2\cdot\cancel{7}}=\frac{5}{2}=2\frac{1}{2}$

41. $\frac{1\cdot8}{2\cdot15}=\frac{1\cdot\cancel{2}\cdot2\cdot2}{\cancel{2}\cdot3\cdot5}=\frac{4}{15}$

42. $\frac{3\cdot12}{8\cdot17}=\frac{3\cdot\cancel{2}\cdot\cancel{2}\cdot3}{\cancel{2}\cdot\cancel{2}\cdot2\cdot17}=\frac{9}{34}$

Objective B Exercises

43. $\frac{4\cdot3}{1\cdot8}=\frac{\cancel{2}\cdot\cancel{2}\cdot3}{1\cdot\cancel{2}\cdot\cancel{2}\cdot2}=\frac{3}{2}=1\frac{1}{2}$

44. $\frac{14\cdot5}{1\cdot7}=\frac{2\cdot\cancel{7}\cdot5}{1\cdot\cancel{7}}=10$

45. $\frac{2\cdot6}{3\cdot1}=\frac{2\cdot2\cdot\cancel{3}}{\cancel{3}\cdot1}=4$

46. $\frac{5\cdot40}{12\cdot1}=\frac{5\cdot\cancel{2}\cdot\cancel{2}\cdot2\cdot5}{\cancel{2}\cdot\cancel{2}\cdot3\cdot1}=\frac{50}{3}=16\frac{2}{3}$

47. $\frac{1}{3}\times1\frac{1}{3}=\frac{1}{3}\times\frac{4}{3}=\frac{1\cdot2\cdot2}{3\cdot3}=\frac{4}{9}$

48. $\frac{2}{5}\times2\frac{1}{2}=\frac{2}{5}\times\frac{5}{2}=\frac{\cancel{2}\cdot\cancel{5}}{\cancel{5}\cdot\cancel{2}}=1$

49. $1\frac{7}{8}\times\frac{4}{15}=\frac{15}{8}\times\frac{4}{15}=\frac{\cancel{3}\cdot\cancel{5}\cdot\cancel{2}\cdot\cancel{2}}{\cancel{2}\cdot\cancel{2}\cdot2\cdot\cancel{3}\cdot\cancel{5}}=\frac{1}{2}$

50. $2\frac{1}{5}\times\frac{5}{22}=\frac{11}{5}\times\frac{5}{22}=\frac{\cancel{11}\cdot\cancel{5}}{\cancel{5}\cdot2\cdot\cancel{11}}=\frac{1}{2}$

51. $55\times\frac{3}{10}=\frac{55\cdot3}{1\cdot10}=\frac{\cancel{5}\cdot11\cdot3}{1\cdot2\cdot\cancel{5}}=\frac{33}{2}=16\frac{1}{2}$

52. $\frac{5}{14}\times\frac{49}{1}=\frac{5\cdot\cancel{7}\cdot7}{2\cdot\cancel{7}\cdot1}=\frac{35}{2}=17\frac{1}{2}$

53. $4\times2\frac{1}{2}=\frac{4}{1}\times\frac{5}{2}=\frac{2\cdot\cancel{2}\cdot5}{1\cdot\cancel{2}}=10$

54. $9\times3\frac{1}{3}=\frac{9}{1}\times\frac{10}{3}=\frac{\cancel{3}\cdot3\cdot2\cdot5}{1\cdot\cancel{3}}=30$

55. $2\frac{1}{7}\times3=\frac{15}{7}\times\frac{3}{1}=\frac{3\cdot5\cdot3}{7\cdot1}=\frac{45}{7}=6\frac{3}{7}$

56. $5\frac{1}{4}\times8=\frac{21}{4}\times\frac{8}{1}=\frac{3\cdot7\cdot\cancel{2}\cdot\cancel{2}\cdot2}{\cancel{2}\cdot\cancel{2}\cdot1}=42$

57. $3\frac{2}{3}\times5=\frac{11}{3}\times\frac{5}{1}=\frac{11\cdot5}{3\cdot1}=\frac{55}{3}=18\frac{1}{3}$

58. $4\frac{2}{9}\times3=\frac{38}{9}\times\frac{3}{1}=\frac{2\cdot19\cdot\cancel{3}}{\cancel{3}\cdot3\cdot1}=\frac{38}{3}=12\frac{2}{3}$

59. $\frac{1}{2}\times3\frac{3}{7}=\frac{1}{2}\times\frac{24}{7}=\frac{1\cdot\cancel{2}\cdot2\cdot2\cdot3}{\cancel{2}\cdot7}=\frac{12}{7}=1\frac{5}{7}$

60. $\frac{3}{8}\times4\frac{4}{5}=\frac{3}{8}\times\frac{24}{5}=\frac{3\cdot\cancel{2}\cdot\cancel{2}\cdot\cancel{2}\cdot3}{\cancel{2}\cdot\cancel{2}\cdot\cancel{2}\cdot5}=\frac{9}{5}=1\frac{4}{5}$

61. $6\frac{1}{8}\times\frac{4}{7}=\frac{49}{8}\times\frac{4}{7}=\frac{\cancel{7}\cdot7\cdot\cancel{2}\cdot\cancel{2}}{\cancel{2}\cdot\cancel{2}\cdot2\cdot\cancel{7}}=\frac{7}{2}=3\frac{1}{2}$

62. $5\frac{1}{3}\times\frac{5}{16}=\frac{16}{3}\times\frac{5}{16}=\frac{\cancel{2}\cdot\cancel{2}\cdot\cancel{2}\cdot\cancel{2}\cdot 5}{3\cdot\cancel{2}\cdot\cancel{2}\cdot\cancel{2}\cdot\cancel{2}}=\frac{5}{3}=1\frac{2}{3}$

63. $5\frac{1}{8}\times 5=\frac{41}{8}\times\frac{5}{1}=\frac{41\cdot 5}{2\cdot 2\cdot 2\cdot 1}=\frac{205}{8}=25\frac{5}{8}$

64. $6\frac{1}{9}\times 2=\frac{55}{9}\times\frac{2}{1}=\frac{5\cdot 11\cdot 2}{3\cdot 3\cdot 1}=\frac{110}{9}=12\frac{2}{9}$

65. $\frac{3}{8}\times 4\frac{1}{2}=\frac{3}{8}\times\frac{9}{2}=\frac{3\cdot 3\cdot 3}{2\cdot 2\cdot 2\cdot 2}=\frac{27}{16}=1\frac{11}{16}$

66. $\frac{5}{7}\times 2\frac{1}{3}=\frac{5}{7}\times\frac{7}{3}=\frac{5\cdot\cancel{7}}{\cancel{7}\cdot 3}=\frac{5}{3}=1\frac{2}{3}$

67. $6\times 2\frac{2}{3}=\frac{6}{1}\times\frac{8}{3}=\frac{2\cdot\cancel{3}\cdot 2\cdot 2\cdot 2}{1\cdot\cancel{3}}=16$

68. $6\frac{1}{8}\times 0=\frac{49}{8}\times 0=\frac{49\cdot 0}{8}=0$

69. $1\frac{1}{3}\times 2\frac{1}{4}=\frac{4}{3}\times\frac{9}{4}=\frac{\cancel{2}\cdot\cancel{2}\cdot\cancel{3}\cdot 3}{\cancel{3}\cdot\cancel{2}\cdot\cancel{2}}=3$

70. $2\frac{5}{8}\times\frac{3}{23}=\frac{21}{8}\times\frac{3}{23}=\frac{3\cdot 7\cdot 3}{2\cdot 2\cdot 2\cdot 23}=\frac{63}{184}$

71. $2\frac{5}{8}\times 3\frac{2}{5}=\frac{21}{8}\times\frac{17}{5}=\frac{3\cdot 7\cdot 17}{2\cdot 2\cdot 2\cdot 5}=\frac{357}{40}=8\frac{37}{40}$

72. $5\frac{3}{16}\times 5\frac{1}{3}=\frac{83}{16}\times\frac{16}{3}=\frac{83\cdot\cancel{2}\cdot\cancel{2}\cdot\cancel{2}\cdot\cancel{2}}{\cancel{2}\cdot\cancel{2}\cdot\cancel{2}\cdot\cancel{2}\cdot 3}=\frac{83}{3}=27\frac{2}{3}$

73. $3\frac{1}{7}\times 2\frac{1}{8}=\frac{22}{7}\times\frac{17}{8}=\frac{\cancel{2}\cdot 11\cdot 17}{7\cdot\cancel{2}\cdot 2\cdot 2}=\frac{187}{28}=6\frac{19}{28}$

74. $16\frac{5}{8}\times 1\frac{1}{16}=\frac{133}{8}\times\frac{17}{16}=\frac{133\cdot 17}{2\cdot 2\cdot 2\cdot 2\cdot 2\cdot 2\cdot 2}$

$=\frac{2261}{128}=17\frac{85}{128}$

75. $2\frac{2}{5}\times 3\frac{1}{12}=\frac{12}{5}\times\frac{37}{12}=\frac{\cancel{2}\cdot\cancel{2}\cdot\cancel{3}\cdot 37}{5\cdot\cancel{2}\cdot\cancel{2}\cdot\cancel{3}}=\frac{37}{5}=7\frac{2}{5}$

76. $2\frac{2}{3}\times\frac{3}{20}=\frac{8}{3}\times\frac{3}{20}=\frac{\cancel{2}\cdot\cancel{2}\cdot 2\cdot\cancel{3}}{\cancel{3}\cdot\cancel{2}\cdot\cancel{2}\cdot 5}=\frac{2}{5}$

77. $5\frac{1}{5}\times 3\frac{1}{13}=\frac{26}{5}\times\frac{40}{13}=\frac{2\cdot\cancel{13}\cdot 2\cdot 2\cdot 2\cdot\cancel{5}}{\cancel{5}\cdot\cancel{13}}=16$

78. $3\frac{3}{4}\times 2\frac{3}{20}=\frac{15}{4}\times\frac{43}{20}=\frac{3\cdot\cancel{5}\cdot 43}{2\cdot 2\cdot 2\cdot 2\cdot\cancel{5}}=\frac{129}{16}=8\frac{1}{16}$

79. $10\frac{1}{4}\times 3\frac{1}{5}=\frac{41}{4}\times\frac{16}{5}=\frac{41\cdot\cancel{2}\cdot\cancel{2}\cdot 2\cdot 2}{\cancel{2}\cdot\cancel{2}\cdot 5}=\frac{164}{5}=32\frac{4}{5}$

80. $12\frac{3}{5}\times 1\frac{3}{7}=\frac{63}{5}\times\frac{10}{7}=\frac{3\cdot 3\cdot\cancel{7}\cdot 2\cdot\cancel{5}}{\cancel{5}\cdot\cancel{7}}=18$

81. $5\frac{3}{7}\times 5\frac{1}{4}=\frac{38}{7}\times\frac{21}{4}=\frac{\cancel{2}\cdot 19\cdot 3\cdot\cancel{7}}{\cancel{7}\cdot\cancel{2}\cdot 2}=\frac{57}{2}=28\frac{1}{2}$

82. $6\frac{1}{2}\times 1\frac{3}{13}=\frac{13}{2}\times\frac{16}{13}=\frac{\cancel{13}\cdot\cancel{2}\cdot 2\cdot 2\cdot 2}{\cancel{2}\cdot\cancel{13}}=8$

83. $2\frac{1}{2}\times 3\frac{3}{5}=\frac{5}{2}\times\frac{18}{5}=\frac{\cancel{5}\cdot\cancel{2}\cdot 3\cdot 3}{\cancel{2}\cdot\cancel{5}}=9$

84. $4\frac{3}{8}\times 3\frac{3}{5}=\frac{35}{8}\times\frac{18}{5}=\frac{\cancel{5}\cdot 7\cdot\cancel{2}\cdot 3\cdot 3}{\cancel{2}\cdot 2\cdot 2\cdot\cancel{5}}=\frac{63}{4}=15\frac{3}{4}$

85. $2\frac{1}{8}\times\frac{5}{17}=\frac{17}{8}\times\frac{5}{17}=\frac{\cancel{17}\cdot 5}{2\cdot 2\cdot 2\cdot\cancel{17}}=\frac{5}{8}$

86. $12\frac{2}{5}\times 3\frac{7}{31}=\frac{62}{5}\times\frac{100}{31}=\frac{2\cdot\cancel{31}\cdot 2\cdot 2\cdot\cancel{5}\cdot 5}{\cancel{5}\cdot\cancel{31}}=40$

87. $1\frac{3}{8}\times 2\frac{1}{5}=\frac{11}{8}\times\frac{11}{5}=\frac{121}{40}=3\frac{1}{40}$

88. $3\frac{1}{8}\times 2\frac{4}{7}=\frac{25}{8}\times\frac{18}{7}=\frac{5\cdot 5\cdot\cancel{2}\cdot 3\cdot 3}{\cancel{2}\cdot 2\cdot 2\cdot 7}=\frac{225}{28}=8\frac{1}{28}$

Objective C Exercises

89. Strategy To find the cost of the salmon, multiply the amount of salmon $\left(2\frac{3}{4}\text{ pounds}\right)$ by the cost per pound ($4).

Solution $2\frac{3}{4}\times 4=\frac{11}{4}\times\frac{4}{1}=\frac{11\cdot 4}{4\cdot 1}=11$

The salmon costs $11.

90. Strategy To find how far a person can walk in $\frac{1}{3}$ hour, multiply the distance walked in 1 hour $\left(3\frac{1}{2}\text{ miles}\right)$ by $\frac{1}{3}$.

Solution $3\frac{1}{2}\times\frac{1}{3}=\frac{7}{2}\times\frac{1}{3}=\frac{7}{6}=1\frac{1}{6}$

A person can walk $1\frac{1}{6}$ miles in $\frac{1}{3}$ hour.

91a. No, $\frac{1}{3}$ of 9 feet is approximately 3 feet; therefore, $\frac{1}{3}$ of $9\frac{1}{4}$ feet is approximately 3 feet.

b. Strategy To find the length cut, multiply the length of the board $\left(9\frac{1}{4}\text{ feet}\right)$ by $\frac{1}{3}$.

Solution $\frac{1}{3} \times 9\frac{1}{4} = \frac{1}{3} \times \frac{37}{4} = \frac{1 \cdot 37}{3 \cdot 4} = \frac{37}{12} = 3\frac{1}{12}$

The length of the board cut off is $3\frac{1}{12}$ feet.

92. Strategy To find the perimeter of the square, multiply the length of one side $\left(16\frac{3}{4}\text{ inches}\right)$ by 4.

Solution

$16\frac{3}{4} \times 4 = \frac{67}{4} \times \frac{4}{1} = \frac{67 \cdot \overset{1}{\cancel{4}}}{\underset{1}{\cancel{4}}} = 67$

The perimeter of the square is 67 inches.

93. Strategy To find the area of the square, multiply the length of one side $\left(5\frac{1}{4}\text{ feet}\right)$ by itself $\left(5\frac{1}{4}\text{ feet}\right)$.

Solution $5\frac{1}{4} \times 5\frac{1}{4} = \frac{21}{4} \times \frac{21}{4} = \frac{21 \cdot 21}{4 \cdot 4}$

$= \frac{441}{16} = 27\frac{9}{16}$

The area of the square is $27\frac{9}{16}$ square feet.

94. Strategy To find the area of the rectangle, multiply the length $\left(4\frac{2}{5}\text{ miles}\right)$ by the width $\left(3\frac{3}{10}\text{ miles}\right)$.

Solution

$4\frac{2}{5} \times 3\frac{3}{10} = \frac{22}{5} \times \frac{33}{10} = \frac{\overset{1}{\cancel{2}} \cdot 11 \cdot 3 \cdot 11}{5 \cdot \underset{1}{\cancel{2}} \cdot 5}$

$= \frac{363}{25} = 14\frac{13}{25}$

The area of the rectangle is $14\frac{13}{25}$ square miles.

95a. Strategy To find the amount budgeted for housing and utilities, multiply the total monthly income ($4200) by $\frac{2}{5}$.

Solution $\frac{2}{5} \times \$4200 = \frac{2 \cdot 4200}{5} = \$1680$

The amount budgeted for housing and utilities is $1680.

b. Strategy To find the amount remaining for other than housing and utilities, subtract the amount for housing and utilities ($1680) from the total monthly income ($4200).

Solution

$$\begin{array}{r} \$4200 \\ -\ 1680 \\ \hline \$2520 \end{array}$$

The amount remaining for other than housing and utilities is $2520.

96a. Strategy To find the number of students passing the course, multiply the number of students (36) by the fraction of the students passing $\left(\frac{5}{6}\right)$.

Solution $36 \times \frac{5}{6} = \frac{36 \cdot 5}{6} = 30$

30 students passed the chemistry course.

b. Strategy To find the number of students receiving A grades, multiply the number passing by $\frac{1}{5}$.

Solution $30 \times \frac{1}{5} = \frac{30 \cdot 1}{5} = 6$

6 students received A grades.

97. Strategy To find the total cost of the capes, multiply the amount of material each cape requires $\left(1\frac{3}{8}\text{ yards}\right)$ by the cost of 1 yard ($12) and by the number of capes needed (22).

Solution $1\frac{3}{8} \times \$12 \times 22 = \frac{11}{8} \times 12 \times 22$

$= \frac{11 \times 12 \times 22}{8} = \$363$

The total cost is $363.

98. $6\frac{1}{2} \times \frac{3}{8} = \frac{13}{2} \times \frac{3}{8} = \frac{39}{16} = 2\frac{7}{16}$

The weight of the $6\frac{1}{2}$-foot steel rod is $2\frac{7}{16}$ pounds.

99. $12\frac{7}{12} \times 4\frac{1}{3} = \frac{151}{12} \times \frac{13}{3} = \frac{1963}{36} = 54\frac{19}{36}$

The weight of the $12\frac{7}{12}$-foot steel rod is $54\frac{19}{36}$ pounds.

100. $8\frac{5}{8}\times 1\frac{1}{4}=\frac{69}{8}\times\frac{5}{4}=\frac{345}{32}=10\frac{25}{32}$

$10\frac{3}{4}\times 2\frac{1}{2}=\frac{43}{4}\times\frac{5}{2}=\frac{215}{8}=26\frac{7}{8}$

$10\frac{25}{32}+26\frac{7}{8}=10\frac{25}{32}+26\frac{28}{32}=36\frac{53}{32}=37\frac{21}{32}$

The total weight of the $8\frac{5}{8}$- and $10\frac{3}{4}$-foot steel rods is $37\frac{21}{32}$ pounds.

101. $\frac{1}{2}\times\frac{3}{8}=\frac{3}{16}$

$\frac{3}{16}$ of the total portfolio is invested in corporate bonds.

Applying the Concepts

102. $\frac{1}{2}$. Any number multiplied by 1 is the number.

103. Student explanations should include the idea that every 4 years we must add 1 day to the usual 365-day year.

104. No, for example, $\frac{1}{4}\times\frac{1}{2}=\frac{1}{8}$ which is less than either $\frac{1}{4}$ or $\frac{1}{2}$. The product of any two positive rational numbers, each less than 1, is less than either of the two numbers.

105. *A*. See problem 104.

106.

$\frac{2}{3}$	$\frac{3}{4}$	$\frac{5}{9}$
$1\frac{1}{9}$	$\frac{1}{6}$	$1\frac{1}{2}$
$2\frac{1}{4}$	$\frac{5}{18}$	$\frac{4}{9}$

Other answers are possible.

Section 2.7

Objective A Exercises

1. $\frac{1}{3}\times\frac{5}{2}=\frac{1\cdot 5}{3\cdot 2}=\frac{5}{6}$

2. $\frac{3}{7}\times\frac{2}{3}=\frac{\cancel{3}\cdot 2}{7\cdot\cancel{3}}=\frac{2}{7}$

3. $\frac{3}{7}\times\frac{7}{3}=\frac{\cancel{3}\cdot\cancel{7}}{\cancel{7}\cdot\cancel{3}}=1$

4. $0\times\frac{2}{1}=0$

5. $0\times\frac{4}{3}=0$

6. $\frac{16}{33}\times\frac{11}{4}=\frac{\cancel{2}\cdot\cancel{2}\cdot 2\cdot 2\cdot\cancel{11}}{3\cdot\cancel{11}\cdot\cancel{2}\cdot\cancel{2}}=\frac{4}{3}=1\frac{1}{3}$

7. $\frac{5}{24}\times\frac{36}{15}=\frac{\cancel{5}\cdot\cancel{2}\cdot\cancel{2}\cdot\cancel{3}\cdot\cancel{3}}{\cancel{2}\cdot\cancel{2}\cdot 2\cdot\cancel{3}\cdot\cancel{3}\cdot\cancel{5}}=\frac{1}{2}$

8. $\frac{11}{15}\times\frac{12}{1}=\frac{11\cdot 2\cdot 2\cdot\cancel{3}}{\cancel{3}\cdot 5}=\frac{44}{5}=8\frac{4}{5}$

9. $\frac{15}{16}\times\frac{39}{16}=\frac{3\cdot 5\cdot 3\cdot 13}{2\cdot 2\cdot 2\cdot 2\cdot 2\cdot 2\cdot 2\cdot 2}=\frac{585}{256}=2\frac{73}{256}$

10. $\frac{2}{15}\times\frac{5}{3}=\frac{2\cdot\cancel{5}}{3\cdot\cancel{5}\cdot 3}=\frac{2}{9}$

11. $\frac{8}{9}\times\frac{5}{4}=\frac{\cancel{2}\cdot\cancel{2}\cdot 2\cdot 5}{3\cdot 3\cdot\cancel{2}\cdot\cancel{2}}=\frac{10}{9}=1\frac{1}{9}$

12. $\frac{11}{15}\times\frac{22}{5}=\frac{11\cdot 2\cdot 11}{3\cdot 5\cdot 5}=\frac{242}{75}=3\frac{17}{75}$

13. $\frac{1}{9}\times\frac{3}{2}=\frac{\cancel{3}}{\cancel{3}\cdot 3\cdot 2}=\frac{1}{6}$

14. $\frac{10}{21}\times\frac{7}{5}=\frac{2\cdot\cancel{5}\cdot\cancel{7}}{3\cdot\cancel{7}\cdot\cancel{5}}=\frac{2}{3}$

15. $\frac{2}{5}\times\frac{7}{4}=\frac{\cancel{2}\cdot 7}{5\cdot\cancel{2}\cdot 2}=\frac{7}{10}$

16. $\frac{3}{8}\times\frac{12}{5}=\frac{3\cdot\cancel{2}\cdot\cancel{2}\cdot 3}{\cancel{2}\cdot\cancel{2}\cdot 2\cdot 5}=\frac{9}{10}$

17. $\frac{1}{2}\times\frac{4}{1}=\frac{\cancel{2}\cdot 2}{\cancel{2}}=2$

18. $\frac{1}{3}\times\frac{9}{1}=\frac{\cancel{3}\cdot 3}{\cancel{3}}=3$

19. $\frac{1}{5}\times\frac{10}{1}=\frac{2\cdot\cancel{5}}{\cancel{5}}=2$

20. $\frac{4}{15}\times\frac{5}{2}=\frac{\cancel{2}\cdot 2\cdot\cancel{5}}{3\cdot\cancel{5}\cdot\cancel{2}}=\frac{2}{3}$

21. $\frac{7}{15}\times\frac{5}{14}=\frac{\cancel{7}\cdot\cancel{5}}{3\cdot\cancel{5}\cdot 2\cdot\cancel{7}}=\frac{1}{6}$

22. $\frac{5}{8}\times\frac{2}{15}=\frac{\cancel{5}\cdot\cancel{2}}{\cancel{2}\cdot 2\cdot 2\cdot 3\cdot\cancel{5}}=\frac{1}{12}$

23. $\frac{14}{3}\times\frac{9}{7}=\frac{2\cdot\cancel{7}\cdot\cancel{3}\cdot 3}{\cancel{3}\cdot\cancel{7}}=6$

24. $\frac{7}{4}\times\frac{2}{9}=\frac{7\cdot\cancel{2}}{\cancel{2}\cdot 2\cdot 3\cdot 3}=\frac{7}{18}$

25. $\frac{5}{9}\times\frac{3}{25}=\frac{\cancel{5}\cdot\cancel{3}}{\cancel{3}\cdot 3\cdot\cancel{5}\cdot 5}=\frac{1}{15}$

26. $\frac{5}{16}\times\frac{8}{3}=\frac{5\cdot\cancel{2}\cdot\cancel{2}\cdot\cancel{2}}{\cancel{2}\cdot\cancel{2}\cdot\cancel{2}\cdot 2\cdot 3}=\frac{5}{6}$

27. $\frac{2}{3}\times\frac{3}{1}=\frac{2\cdot\cancel{3}}{\cancel{3}}=2$

28. $\frac{4}{9}\times\frac{9}{1}=\frac{2\cdot 2\cdot\cancel{3}\cdot\cancel{3}}{\cancel{3}\cdot\cancel{3}}=4$

29. $\frac{5}{7}\times\frac{7}{2}=\frac{5\cdot\cancel{7}}{\cancel{7}\cdot 2}=\frac{5}{2}=2\frac{1}{2}$

30. $\frac{5}{6}\times\frac{9}{1}=\frac{5\cdot\cancel{3}\cdot 3}{2\cdot\cancel{3}}=\frac{15}{2}=7\frac{1}{2}$

31. $\frac{2}{3}\times\frac{9}{2}=\frac{\cancel{2}\cdot\cancel{3}\cdot 3}{\cancel{3}\cdot\cancel{2}}=3$

32. $\frac{5}{12}\times\frac{6}{5}=\frac{\cancel{5}\cdot\cancel{2}\cdot\cancel{3}}{\cancel{2}\cdot 2\cdot\cancel{3}\cdot\cancel{5}}=\frac{1}{2}$

33. $\frac{7}{8}\div\frac{3}{4}=\frac{7}{8}\times\frac{4}{3}=\frac{7\cdot\cancel{2}\cdot\cancel{2}}{\cancel{2}\cdot\cancel{2}\cdot 2\cdot 3}=\frac{7}{6}=1\frac{1}{6}$

34. $\frac{7}{12}\div\frac{3}{4}=\frac{7}{12}\times\frac{4}{3}=\frac{7\cdot\cancel{2}\cdot\cancel{2}}{\cancel{2}\cdot\cancel{2}\cdot 3\cdot 3}=\frac{7}{9}$

35. $\frac{5}{7}\div\frac{3}{14}=\frac{5}{7}\times\frac{14}{3}=\frac{5\cdot 2\cdot\cancel{7}}{\cancel{7}\cdot 3}=\frac{10}{3}=3\frac{1}{3}$

36. $\frac{6}{11}\div\frac{9}{32}=\frac{6}{11}\times\frac{32}{9}=\frac{2\cdot\cancel{3}\cdot 2\cdot 2\cdot 2\cdot 2\cdot 2}{11\cdot\cancel{3}\cdot 3}=\frac{64}{33}=1\frac{31}{33}$

Objective B Exercises

37. $\frac{4}{1}\times\frac{3}{2}=\frac{\cancel{2}\cdot 2\cdot 3}{\cancel{2}}=6$

38. $\frac{2}{3}\times\frac{1}{4}=\frac{\cancel{2}}{3\cdot\cancel{2}\cdot 2}=\frac{1}{6}$

39. $\frac{3}{2}\times\frac{1}{3}=\frac{\cancel{3}}{2\cdot\cancel{3}}=\frac{1}{2}$

40. $\frac{3}{1}\times\frac{2}{3}=\frac{\cancel{3}\cdot 2}{\cancel{3}}=2$

41. $\frac{5}{6}\times\frac{1}{25}=\frac{\cancel{5}}{2\cdot 3\cdot\cancel{5}\cdot 5}=\frac{1}{30}$

42. $\frac{22}{1}\times\frac{11}{3}=\frac{2\cdot 11\cdot 11}{3}=\frac{242}{3}=80\frac{2}{3}$

43. $\frac{6}{1}\div\frac{10}{3}=\frac{6}{1}\times\frac{3}{10}=\frac{\cancel{2}\cdot 3\cdot 3}{\cancel{2}\cdot 5}=\frac{9}{5}=1\frac{4}{5}$

44. $\frac{11}{2}\div\frac{11}{1}=\frac{11}{2}\times\frac{1}{11}=\frac{\cancel{11}}{2\cdot\cancel{11}}=\frac{1}{2}$

45. $\frac{13}{2}\div\frac{1}{2}=\frac{13}{2}\times\frac{2}{1}=\frac{13\cdot\cancel{2}}{\cancel{2}}=13$

46. $\frac{3}{8}\div\frac{9}{4}=\frac{3}{8}\times\frac{4}{9}=\frac{\cancel{3}\cdot\cancel{2}\cdot\cancel{2}}{\cancel{2}\cdot\cancel{2}\cdot 2\cdot\cancel{3}\cdot 3}=\frac{1}{6}$

47. $\frac{5}{12}\div\frac{24}{5}=\frac{5}{12}\times\frac{5}{24}=\frac{5\cdot 5}{2\cdot 2\cdot 3\cdot 2\cdot 2\cdot 2\cdot 3}=\frac{25}{288}$

48. $\frac{3}{2}\div\frac{11}{8}=\frac{3}{2}\times\frac{8}{11}=\frac{3\cdot\cancel{2}\cdot 2\cdot 2}{\cancel{2}\cdot 11}=\frac{12}{11}=1\frac{1}{11}$

49. $\frac{33}{4}\div\frac{11}{4}=\frac{33}{4}\times\frac{4}{11}=\frac{3\cdot\cancel{11}\cdot\cancel{2}\cdot\cancel{2}}{\cancel{2}\cdot\cancel{2}\cdot\cancel{11}}=3$

50. $\frac{32}{9}\div\frac{32}{1}=\frac{32}{9}\times\frac{1}{32}=\frac{\cancel{2}\cdot\cancel{2}\cdot\cancel{2}\cdot\cancel{2}\cdot\cancel{2}}{3\cdot 3\cdot\cancel{2}\cdot\cancel{2}\cdot\cancel{2}\cdot\cancel{2}\cdot\cancel{2}}=\frac{1}{9}$

51. $\frac{21}{5}\div\frac{21}{1}=\frac{21}{5}\times\frac{1}{21}=\frac{\cancel{3}\cdot\cancel{7}}{5\cdot\cancel{3}\cdot\cancel{7}}=\frac{1}{5}$

52. $\frac{62}{9}\div\frac{31}{36}=\frac{62}{9}\times\frac{36}{31}=\frac{2\cdot\cancel{31}\cdot 2\cdot 2\cdot\cancel{3}\cdot\cancel{3}}{\cancel{3}\cdot\cancel{3}\cdot\cancel{31}}=8$

53. $\frac{11}{12}\div\frac{7}{3}=\frac{11}{12}\times\frac{3}{7}=\frac{11\cdot\cancel{3}}{2\cdot 2\cdot\cancel{3}\cdot 7}=\frac{11}{28}$

54. $\frac{7}{8}\div\frac{13}{4}=\frac{7}{8}\times\frac{4}{13}=\frac{7\cdot\cancel{2}\cdot\cancel{2}}{\cancel{2}\cdot\cancel{2}\cdot 2\cdot 13}=\frac{7}{26}$

55. $\frac{5}{16}\div\frac{43}{8}=\frac{5}{16}\times\frac{8}{43}=\frac{5\cdot\cancel{2}\cdot\cancel{2}\cdot\cancel{2}}{\cancel{2}\cdot\cancel{2}\cdot\cancel{2}\cdot 2\cdot 43}=\frac{5}{86}$

56. $\frac{9}{14}\div\frac{22}{7}=\frac{9}{14}\times\frac{7}{22}=\frac{3\cdot 3\cdot\cancel{7}}{2\cdot\cancel{7}\cdot 2\cdot 11}=\frac{9}{44}$

57. $35\div\frac{7}{24}=\frac{35}{1}\times\frac{24}{7}=\frac{5\cdot\cancel{7}\cdot 2\cdot 2\cdot 2\cdot 3}{\cancel{7}}=120$

58. $\frac{3}{8}\div\frac{11}{4}=\frac{3}{8}\times\frac{4}{11}=\frac{3\cdot\cancel{2}\cdot\cancel{2}}{\cancel{2}\cdot\cancel{2}\cdot2\cdot11}=\frac{3}{22}$

59. $\frac{11}{18}\div\frac{20}{9}=\frac{11}{18}\times\frac{9}{20}=\frac{11\cdot\cancel{3}\cdot\cancel{3}}{2\cdot\cancel{3}\cdot\cancel{3}\cdot2\cdot2\cdot5}=\frac{11}{40}$

60. $\frac{21}{40}\div\frac{33}{10}=\frac{21}{40}\times\frac{10}{33}=\frac{\cancel{3}\cdot7\cdot\cancel{2}\cdot\cancel{5}}{\cancel{2}\cdot2\cdot2\cdot\cancel{5}\cdot\cancel{3}\cdot11}=\frac{7}{44}$

61. $\frac{33}{16}\div\frac{5}{2}=\frac{33}{16}\times\frac{2}{5}=\frac{3\cdot11\cdot\cancel{2}}{\cancel{2}\cdot2\cdot2\cdot2\cdot5}=\frac{33}{40}$

62. $\frac{38}{5}\div\frac{19}{12}=\frac{38}{5}\times\frac{12}{19}=\frac{2\cdot\cancel{19}\cdot2\cdot2\cdot3}{5\cdot\cancel{19}}=\frac{24}{5}=4\frac{4}{5}$

63. $\frac{5}{3}\div\frac{3}{8}=\frac{5}{3}\times\frac{8}{3}=\frac{5\cdot2\cdot2\cdot2}{3\cdot3}=\frac{40}{9}=4\frac{4}{9}$

64. $16\div\frac{2}{3}=\frac{16}{1}\times\frac{3}{2}=\frac{\cancel{2}\cdot2\cdot2\cdot2\cdot3}{\cancel{2}}=24$

65. $\frac{13}{8}\div\frac{4}{1}=\frac{13}{8}\times\frac{1}{4}=\frac{13}{2\cdot2\cdot2\cdot2\cdot2}=\frac{13}{32}$

66. $13\frac{3}{8}\div\frac{1}{4}=\frac{107}{8}\times\frac{4}{1}=\frac{107\cdot\cancel{2}\cdot\cancel{2}}{\cancel{2}\cdot\cancel{2}\cdot2}=\frac{107}{2}=53\frac{1}{2}$

67. $16\div\frac{3}{2}=\frac{16}{1}\times\frac{2}{3}=\frac{2\cdot2\cdot2\cdot2\cdot2}{3}=\frac{32}{3}=10\frac{2}{3}$

68. $\frac{9}{1}\div\frac{7}{8}=\frac{9}{1}\times\frac{8}{7}=\frac{3\cdot3\cdot2\cdot2\cdot2}{7}=\frac{72}{7}=10\frac{2}{7}$

69. $\frac{133}{8}\div\frac{5}{3}=\frac{133}{8}\times\frac{3}{5}=\frac{133\cdot3}{2\cdot2\cdot2\cdot5}=\frac{399}{40}=9\frac{39}{40}$

70. $\frac{124}{5}\div\frac{13}{5}=\frac{124}{5}\times\frac{5}{13}=\frac{2\cdot2\cdot31\cdot\cancel{5}}{\cancel{5}\cdot13}=\frac{124}{13}=9\frac{7}{13}$

71. $\frac{4}{3}\div\frac{53}{9}=\frac{4}{3}\times\frac{9}{53}=\frac{2\cdot2\cdot\cancel{3}\cdot3}{\cancel{3}\cdot53}=\frac{12}{53}$

72. $\frac{41}{3}\div0$

Division by zero is undefined.

73. $\frac{413}{5}\div\frac{191}{10}=\frac{413}{5}\times\frac{10}{191}-\frac{7\cdot59\cdot2\cdot\cancel{5}}{\cancel{5}\cdot191}$

$=\frac{826}{191}=4\frac{62}{191}$

74. $\frac{228}{5}\div\frac{15}{1}=\frac{228}{5}\times\frac{1}{15}=\frac{2\cdot2\cdot\cancel{3}\cdot19}{5\cdot\cancel{3}\cdot5}=\frac{76}{25}=3\frac{1}{25}$

75. $\frac{102}{1}\div\frac{3}{2}=\frac{102}{1}\times\frac{2}{3}=\frac{2\cdot\cancel{3}\cdot17\cdot2}{\cancel{3}}=68$

76. $0\div\frac{7}{2}=0$

77. $\frac{58}{7}\div1=\frac{58}{7}\times1=\frac{58}{7}=8\frac{2}{7}$

78. $\frac{105}{16}\div\frac{35}{32}=\frac{105}{16}\times\frac{32}{35}=\frac{3\cdot\cancel{5}\cdot\cancel{7}\cdot\cancel{2}\cdot\cancel{2}\cdot\cancel{2}\cdot\cancel{2}\cdot2}{\cancel{2}\cdot\cancel{2}\cdot\cancel{2}\cdot\cancel{2}\cdot\cancel{5}\cdot\cancel{7}}=6$

79. $\frac{80}{9}\div\frac{49}{18}=\frac{80}{9}\times\frac{18}{49}=\frac{2\cdot2\cdot2\cdot2\cdot5\cdot2\cdot\cancel{3}\cdot\cancel{3}}{\cancel{3}\cdot\cancel{3}\cdot7\cdot7}$

$=\frac{160}{49}=3\frac{13}{49}$

80. $\frac{51}{5}\div\frac{17}{10}=\frac{51}{5}\times\frac{10}{17}=\frac{3\cdot\cancel{17}\cdot2\cdot\cancel{5}}{\cancel{5}\cdot\cancel{17}}=6$

81. $\frac{59}{8}\div\frac{59}{32}=\frac{59}{8}\times\frac{32}{59}=\frac{\cancel{59}\cdot\cancel{2}\cdot\cancel{2}\cdot\cancel{2}\cdot2\cdot2}{\cancel{2}\cdot\cancel{2}\cdot\cancel{2}\cdot\cancel{59}}=4$

82. $7\frac{7}{9}\div5\frac{5}{6}=\frac{70}{9}\div\frac{35}{6}=\frac{70}{9}\times\frac{6}{35}=\frac{2\cdot\cancel{5}\cdot\cancel{7}\cdot2\cdot3}{\cancel{3}\cdot3\cdot\cancel{5}\cdot\cancel{7}}$

$=\frac{4}{3}=1\frac{1}{3}$

83. $2\frac{3}{4}\div1\frac{23}{32}=\frac{11}{4}\div\frac{55}{32}=\frac{11}{4}\times\frac{32}{55}=\frac{\cancel{11}\cdot\cancel{2}\cdot\cancel{2}\cdot2\cdot2}{\cancel{2}\cdot\cancel{2}\cdot5\cdot\cancel{11}}$

$=\frac{8}{5}=1\frac{3}{5}$

84. $8\frac{1}{4}\div1\frac{5}{11}=\frac{33}{4}\div\frac{16}{11}=\frac{33}{4}\times\frac{11}{16}=\frac{3\cdot11\cdot11}{2\cdot2\cdot2\cdot2\cdot2\cdot2}$

$=\frac{363}{64}=5\frac{43}{64}$

85. $\frac{14}{77}\div3\frac{1}{9}=\frac{14}{77}\div\frac{28}{9}=\frac{14}{17}\times\frac{9}{28}=\frac{\cancel{2}\cdot\cancel{7}\cdot3\cdot3}{17\cdot\cancel{2}\cdot2\cdot\cancel{7}}=\frac{9}{34}$

Objective C Exercises

86. **Strategy** To find how many boxes can be filled with 600 ounces of cereal, divide 600 by the amount in each box $\left(\frac{3}{4}\text{ ounce}\right)$.

Solution $600\div\frac{3}{4}=600\times\frac{4}{3}=\frac{600\cdot4}{3}=800$

800 boxes can be filled.

87. Strategy To find the number of servings in 16 ounces of cereal, divide 16 by the amount in each serving $\left(1\frac{1}{3}\text{ ounces}\right)$.

Solution
$$16 \div 1\frac{1}{3} = 16 \div \frac{4}{3} = 16 \times \frac{3}{4} = \frac{16 \cdot 3}{4} = 12$$

There are 12 servings in16 ounces of cereal.

88. Strategy To find the cost of a similar diamond weighing 1 karat, divide the cost of the purchased diamond (\$1200) by its weight $\left(\frac{5}{8}\text{ karat}\right)$.

Solution
$$\$1200 \div \frac{5}{8} = 1200 \times \frac{8}{5} = \frac{1200 \cdot 8}{5} = \$1920$$

The cost of a similar diamond weighing 1 karat is \$1920.

89. Strategy To find the cost of each acre, divide the total cost (\$200,000) by the number of acres $\left(8\frac{1}{3}\right)$.

Solution
$$\$200,000 \div 8\frac{1}{3} = 200,000 \div \frac{25}{3} = 200,000 \times \frac{3}{25} = \frac{200,000 \cdot 3}{25} = \$24,000$$

Each acre costs \$24,000.

90. Strategy To find how many miles the car can travel on 1 gallon of gasoline, divide the distance (275 miles) by the amount of gasoline used $\left(12\frac{1}{2}\text{ gallons}\right)$.

Solution
$$275 \div 12\frac{1}{2} = \frac{275}{1} \div \frac{25}{2} = \frac{275}{1} \times \frac{2}{25} = \frac{\overset{1}{\cancel{5}} \cdot \overset{1}{\cancel{5}} \cdot 11 \cdot 2}{\underset{1}{\cancel{5}} \cdot \underset{1}{\cancel{5}}} = 22$$

The car can travel 22 miles on 1 gallon of gasoline.

91. Strategy To find the number of turns, divide the distance for the nut to move $\left(1\frac{7}{8}\text{ inches}\right)$ by the distance the nut moves for each turn $\left(\frac{5}{32}\text{ inch}\right)$.

Solution
$$1\frac{7}{8} \div \frac{5}{32} = \frac{15}{8} \div \frac{5}{32} = \frac{15}{8} \times \frac{32}{5} = \frac{3 \cdot \overset{1}{\cancel{5}} \cdot \overset{1}{\cancel{2}} \cdot \overset{1}{\cancel{2}} \cdot \overset{1}{\cancel{2}} \cdot 2 \cdot 2}{\underset{1}{\cancel{2}} \cdot \underset{1}{\cancel{2}} \cdot \underset{1}{\cancel{2}} \cdot \underset{1}{\cancel{5}}} = 12$$

The nut will make 12 turns in moving $1\frac{7}{8}$ inches.

92a. Strategy To find the number of acres, subtract the number of acres set aside $\left(1\frac{1}{2}\right)$ from the total number of acres $\left(9\frac{3}{4}\right)$.

Solution
$$9\frac{3}{4} = 9\frac{3}{4}$$
$$-1\frac{1}{2} = 1\frac{2}{4}$$
$$8\frac{1}{4}$$

$8\frac{1}{4}$ acres are available for housing.

b. Strategy To find the number of parcels, divide the number of acres available $\left(8\frac{1}{4}\right)$ by the number of acres in one parcel $\left(\frac{1}{4}\right)$.

Solution
$$8\frac{1}{4} \div \frac{1}{4} = \frac{33}{4} \div \frac{1}{4} = \frac{33}{4} \times \frac{4}{1} = \frac{33 \cdot \overset{1}{\cancel{4}}}{\underset{1}{\cancel{4}} \cdot 1} = 33$$

33 parcels of land can be sold.

93a. Strategy To find the total weight of the fat and bone, subtract the weight after trimming $\left(9\frac{1}{3}\text{ pounds}\right)$ from the original weight $\left(10\frac{3}{4}\text{ pounds}\right)$.

Solution

$$\begin{array}{r} 10\frac{3}{4} = 10\frac{9}{12} \\ -9\frac{1}{3} = 9\frac{4}{12} \\ \hline 1\frac{5}{12} \end{array}$$

The total weight of the fat and bone was $1\frac{5}{12}$ pounds.

b. Strategy To find the number of servings, divide the weight after trimming $\left(9\frac{1}{3}\text{ pounds}\right)$ by the weight of one serving $\left(\frac{1}{3}\text{ pound}\right)$.

Solution

$$9\frac{1}{3} \div \frac{1}{3} = \frac{28}{3} \div \frac{1}{3} = \frac{28}{3} \times \frac{3}{1}$$
$$= \frac{28 \cdot \overset{1}{\cancel{3}}}{\underset{1}{\cancel{3}} \cdot 1} = 28$$

The chef can cut 28 servings from the roast.

94. Strategy To find the length of the remaining piece:

- Divide the total length (15 feet) by the length of each shelf $\left(3\frac{1}{2}\text{ feet}\right)$.
- Multiply the fraction left over by the length of one shelf.

Solution

$$15 \div 3\frac{1}{2} = 15 \div \frac{7}{2}$$
$$= \frac{15}{1} \times \frac{2}{7} = \frac{15 \cdot 2}{7} = \frac{30}{7}$$
$$= 4\frac{2}{7}$$
$$\frac{2}{7} \times 3\frac{1}{2} = \frac{2}{7} \times \frac{7}{2}$$
$$= \frac{2 \cdot 7}{7 \cdot 2} = 1$$

The length of the remaining piece is 1 foot.

95.

$$6\frac{1}{4} \div \frac{1}{2} = \frac{25}{4} \times \frac{2}{1} = \frac{5 \cdot 5 \cdot \overset{1}{\cancel{2}}}{\underset{1}{\cancel{2}} \cdot 2} = \frac{25}{2} = 12\frac{1}{2}$$

The actual length of wall a is $12\frac{1}{2}$ feet.

$$9 \div \frac{1}{2} = \frac{9}{1} \times \frac{2}{1} = 18$$

The actual length of wall b is 18 feet.

$$7\frac{7}{8} \div \frac{1}{2} = \frac{63}{8} \times \frac{2}{1} = \frac{3 \cdot 3 \cdot 7 \cdot \overset{1}{\cancel{2}}}{\underset{1}{\cancel{2}} \cdot 2 \cdot 2} = \frac{63}{4} = 15\frac{3}{4}$$

The actual length of wall c is $15\frac{3}{4}$ feet.

Applying the Concepts

96. Strategy To find the fractional part of money borrowed on home-equity loans that is spent in debt consolidation and home improvement, add the fraction spent on debt consolidation $\left(\frac{19}{50}\right)$ and the fraction spent on home improvement $\left(\frac{6}{25}\right)$.

Solution

$$\frac{19}{50} + \frac{6}{25} = \frac{19}{50} + \frac{12}{50} = \frac{31}{50}$$

$\frac{31}{50}$ of the money borrowed is spent on debt consolidation and home improvement.

97. Strategy To find the fractional part of money borrowed on home-equity loans that is spent on home improvement, cars, and tuition, add the fraction spent on home improvement $\left(\frac{6}{25}\right)$, the fraction spent on cars $\left(\frac{1}{20}\right)$, and the fraction spent on tuition $\left(\frac{1}{20}\right)$.

Solution

$$\frac{6}{25} + \frac{1}{20} + \frac{1}{20} = \frac{24}{100} + \frac{5}{100} + \frac{5}{100}$$
$$= \frac{34}{100} = \frac{17}{50}$$

$\frac{17}{50}$ of the money borrowed is spent on home improvement, cars, and tuition.

98. Strategy To find the bank-recommended maximum monthly house payment, multiply your monthly income (\$4500) by $\frac{1}{3}$.

Solution $4500 \times \frac{1}{3} = \frac{4500}{3} = \$1500$

The bank would recommend that your maximum monthly house payment be \$1500.

99. Strategy To find the capacity of the music center, divide the number of people attending (1200) by $\frac{2}{3}$.

Solution $1200 \div \frac{2}{3} = 1200 \cdot \frac{3}{2} = \frac{3600}{2} = 1800$

The capacity of the music center is 1800 people.

100. Strategy To find the difference between the average height of the grass in the 1980s and the 1950s, subtract the average height in the 1980s $\left(\frac{5}{32} \text{ inch}\right)$ from the average height in the 1950s $\left(\frac{1}{4} \text{ inch}\right)$.

Solution $\frac{1}{4} - \frac{5}{32} = \frac{8}{32} - \frac{5}{32} = \frac{3}{32}$

The difference between the average height of the grass in the 1980s and the 1950s is $\frac{3}{32}$ inch.

101. Strategy To find the fraction of the puzzle left to complete:

- Add the fraction completed yesterday $\left(\frac{1}{3}\right)$ to the fraction completed today $\left(\frac{1}{2}\right)$.
- Subtract that from 1.

Solution $\frac{1}{3} + \frac{1}{2} = \frac{2}{6} + \frac{3}{6} = \frac{5}{6} \qquad 1 - \frac{5}{6} = \frac{1}{6}$

$\frac{1}{6}$ of the puzzle is left to complete.

102. Strategy To find the dimensions of the game board when it is closed, multiply the length of one side (14 inches) by $\frac{1}{2}$ and multiply the thickness $\left(\frac{7}{8} \text{ inch}\right)$ by 2.

Solution $\frac{1}{2} \times 14 = 7$ inches on one side

The thickness is $2 \times \frac{7}{8} = \frac{7}{4} = 1\frac{3}{4}$ inches.

The other dimension (14 inches) remains the same.

The dimensions of the board when it is closed are 14 inches by 7 inches by $1\frac{3}{4}$ inches.

103. Strategy To find your total earnings for the week, add the four numbers representing the hours you worked and multiply the sum by your rate of pay (\$9 per hour).

Solution

$$\begin{aligned} 5 &= 5 \\ 3\frac{3}{4} &= 3\frac{9}{12} \\ 1\frac{1}{4} &= 1\frac{3}{12} \\ 2\frac{1}{3} &= 2\frac{4}{12} \\ \hline & 11\frac{16}{12} = 12\frac{4}{12} = 12\frac{1}{3} \text{ hours} \end{aligned}$$

$12\frac{1}{3} \times 9 = \frac{37}{3} \cdot 9 = 3.8 = \$1$

Your total earnings for last week's work are \$111.

104. Strategy To find the number of cans of soda per week the average teenage boy drinks, multiply the number of cans of soda per day $\left(3\frac{1}{3}\right)$ by 7.

Solution $3\frac{1}{3} \times 7 = \frac{10}{3} \times 7 = \frac{70}{3} = 23\frac{1}{3}$

The average teenage boy drinks $23\frac{1}{3}$ cans of soda per week.

105. Strategy To find the number of calories an average teenage boy consumes each week in soda:

- Multiply $3\frac{1}{3}$ by 7 to determine the number of cans of soda he drinks.
- Multiply that number by the number of calories per can (150).

Solution

$$3\frac{1}{3} \times 7 = \frac{10}{3} \times 7 = \frac{70}{3}$$

$$= 23\frac{1}{3} \text{ cans per week}$$

$$23\frac{1}{3} \times 150 = \frac{70}{3} \times 150 = 70 \times 50$$

$$= 3500 \text{ calories}$$

The average teenage boy consumes 3500 calories each week in soda.

106. Strategy To find how many more cans of soda per week the average teenage boy drinks than the average teenage girl, subtract the daily consumption for the teenage girls $\left(2\frac{1}{3}\text{ cans}\right)$ from the daily consumption for the teenage boys $\left(3\frac{1}{3}\text{ cans}\right)$. Then multiply that result by 7.

Solution $3\frac{1}{3} - 2\frac{1}{3} = 1$ more can per day
$1 \times 7 = 7 = 7$ more cans per week
The average teenage boy drinks 7 more cans of soda per week than the average teenage girl.

107. Strategy To find the number of miles:

- Find out how many units of $\frac{3}{8}$ inch there are in $4\frac{5}{8}$ inches.
- Multiply by 60.

Solution $4\frac{5}{8} \div \frac{3}{8} = \frac{37}{8} \times \frac{8}{3} = \frac{37}{3}$ units
Then, because each unit represents 60 miles, $\frac{37}{3} \times \frac{60}{1} = 740$
The distance is 740 miles.

108. No, for example, $4 \div \frac{1}{2} = 8$

109a. $\frac{1}{2} \div \frac{3}{4} = \frac{1}{2} \times \frac{4}{3} = \frac{2}{3}$
Factor 3 factor = product
In order to find a factor, divide the product by the known factor.

b. $1\frac{3}{4} \div \frac{2}{3} = \frac{7}{4} \times \frac{3}{2} = \frac{21}{8} = 2\frac{5}{8}$

110. First, find the spacing between the three columns.
$\frac{3}{8} \times 2 = \frac{3}{8} \times \frac{2}{1} = \frac{3}{4}$ inch
Second, find the remaining space for the columns.
$7\frac{1}{2} - \frac{3}{4} = 7\frac{2}{4} - \frac{3}{4} = 6\frac{6}{4} - \frac{3}{4} = 6\frac{3}{4}$ inches
Third, divide that space among the three columns.
$6\frac{3}{4} \div 3 = \frac{27}{4} \times \frac{1}{3} = \frac{9}{4} = 2\frac{1}{4}$ inches

111. The quotient. To divide by a proper fraction is to multiply by an improper fraction, which is greater than 1.
Examples:
$5 \times \frac{2}{3} = \frac{5}{1} \times \frac{2}{3} = \frac{10}{3} = 3\frac{1}{3}$
$5 \div \frac{2}{3} = \frac{5}{1} \times \frac{3}{2} = \frac{15}{2} = 7\frac{1}{2}$

Section 2.8

Objective A Exercises

1. $\frac{11}{40} < \frac{19}{40}$

2. $\frac{92}{103} > \frac{19}{103}$

3. $\frac{2}{3} = \frac{14}{21}, \frac{5}{7} = \frac{15}{21}, \frac{2}{3} < \frac{5}{7}$

4. $\frac{2}{5} = \frac{16}{40}, \frac{3}{8} = \frac{15}{40}, \frac{2}{5} > \frac{3}{8}$

5. $\frac{5}{8} = \frac{15}{24}, \frac{7}{12} = \frac{14}{24}, \frac{5}{8} > \frac{7}{12}$

6. $\frac{11}{16} = \frac{33}{48}, \frac{17}{24} = \frac{34}{48}, \frac{11}{16} < \frac{17}{24}$

7. $\frac{7}{9} = \frac{28}{36}, \frac{11}{12} = \frac{33}{36}, \frac{7}{9} < \frac{11}{12}$

8. $\frac{5}{12} = \frac{25}{60}, \frac{7}{15} = \frac{28}{60}, \frac{5}{12} < \frac{7}{15}$

9. $\frac{13}{14} = \frac{39}{42}, \frac{19}{21} = \frac{38}{42}, \frac{13}{14} > \frac{19}{21}$

10. $\frac{13}{18} = \frac{26}{36}, \frac{7}{12} = \frac{21}{36}, \frac{13}{18} > \frac{7}{12}$

11. $\frac{7}{24} = \frac{35}{120}, \frac{11}{30} = \frac{44}{120}, \frac{7}{24} < \frac{11}{30}$

12. $\frac{13}{36} = \frac{52}{144}, \frac{19}{48} = \frac{57}{144}, \frac{13}{36} < \frac{19}{48}$

Objective B Exercises

13. $\left(\frac{3}{8}\right)^2 = \frac{3}{8} \cdot \frac{3}{8} = \frac{9}{64}$

14. $\left(\frac{5}{12}\right)^2 = \frac{5}{12} \cdot \frac{5}{12} = \frac{25}{144}$

15. $\left(\frac{2}{9}\right)^3 = \frac{2}{9} \cdot \frac{2}{9} \cdot \frac{2}{9} = \frac{8}{729}$

16. $\left(\frac{1}{2}\right) \cdot \left(\frac{2}{3}\right)^2 = \left(\frac{1}{2}\right) \cdot \left(\frac{2}{3} \cdot \frac{2}{3}\right) = \frac{\overset{1}{\cancel{2}} \cdot 2}{\underset{1}{\cancel{2}} \cdot 3 \cdot 3} = \frac{2}{9}$

17. $\left(\frac{2}{3}\right) \cdot \left(\frac{1}{2}\right)^4 = \left(\frac{2}{3}\right) \cdot \left(\frac{1}{2} \cdot \frac{1}{2} \cdot \frac{1}{2} \cdot \frac{1}{2}\right)$
$= \frac{\overset{1}{\cancel{2}} \cdot 1 \cdot 1 \cdot 1 \cdot 1}{3 \cdot \underset{1}{\cancel{2}} \cdot 2 \cdot 2 \cdot 2} = \frac{1}{24}$

18. $$\left(\frac{1}{3}\right)^2\cdot\left(\frac{3}{5}\right)^3=\left(\frac{1}{3}\cdot\frac{1}{3}\right)\cdot\left(\frac{3}{5}\cdot\frac{3}{5}\cdot\frac{3}{5}\right)=\frac{1\cdot 1\cdot\cancel{3}\cdot\cancel{3}\cdot 3}{\cancel{3}\cdot\cancel{3}\cdot 5\cdot 5\cdot 5}=\frac{3}{125}$$

19. $$\left(\frac{2}{5}\right)^3\cdot\left(\frac{5}{7}\right)^2=\left(\frac{2}{5}\cdot\frac{2}{5}\cdot\frac{2}{5}\right)\cdot\left(\frac{5}{7}\cdot\frac{5}{7}\right)=\frac{2\cdot 2\cdot 2\cdot\cancel{5}\cdot\cancel{5}}{\cancel{5}\cdot\cancel{5}\cdot 5\cdot 7\cdot 7}=\frac{8}{245}$$

20. $$\left(\frac{5}{9}\right)^3\cdot\left(\frac{18}{25}\right)^2=\left(\frac{5}{9}\cdot\frac{5}{9}\cdot\frac{5}{9}\right)\cdot\left(\frac{18}{25}\cdot\frac{18}{25}\right)=\frac{\cancel{5}\cdot\cancel{5}\cdot\cancel{5}\cdot 2\cdot\cancel{3}\cdot\cancel{3}\cdot 2\cdot\cancel{3}\cdot\cancel{3}}{\cancel{3}\cdot\cancel{3}\cdot\cancel{3}\cdot\cancel{3}\cdot 3\cdot 3\cdot\cancel{5}\cdot\cancel{5}\cdot\cancel{5}\cdot 5}=\frac{4}{45}$$

21. $$\left(\frac{1}{3}\right)^4\cdot\left(\frac{9}{11}\right)^2=\left(\frac{1}{3}\cdot\frac{1}{3}\cdot\frac{1}{3}\cdot\frac{1}{3}\right)\cdot\left(\frac{9}{11}\cdot\frac{9}{11}\right)=\frac{1\cdot 1\cdot 1\cdot 1\cdot\cancel{3}\cdot\cancel{3}\cdot\cancel{3}\cdot\cancel{3}}{\cancel{3}\cdot\cancel{3}\cdot\cancel{3}\cdot\cancel{3}\cdot 11\cdot 11}=\frac{1}{121}$$

22. $$\left(\frac{1}{2}\right)^6\cdot\left(\frac{32}{35}\right)^2=\left(\frac{1}{2}\cdot\frac{1}{2}\cdot\frac{1}{2}\cdot\frac{1}{2}\cdot\frac{1}{2}\cdot\frac{1}{2}\right)\cdot\left(\frac{32}{35}\cdot\frac{32}{35}\right)=\frac{\cancel{2}\cdot\cancel{2}\cdot\cancel{2}\cdot\cancel{2}\cdot\cancel{2}\cdot\cancel{2}\cdot 2\cdot 2\cdot 2\cdot 2}{\cancel{2}\cdot\cancel{2}\cdot\cancel{2}\cdot\cancel{2}\cdot\cancel{2}\cdot\cancel{2}\cdot 5\cdot 7\cdot 5\cdot 7}=\frac{16}{1225}$$

23. $$\left(\frac{2}{3}\right)^4\cdot\left(\frac{81}{100}\right)^2=\left(\frac{2}{3}\cdot\frac{2}{3}\cdot\frac{2}{3}\cdot\frac{2}{3}\right)\cdot\left(\frac{81}{100}\cdot\frac{81}{100}\right)=\frac{\cancel{2}\cdot\cancel{2}\cdot\cancel{2}\cdot\cancel{2}\cdot\cancel{3}\cdot\cancel{3}\cdot\cancel{3}\cdot\cancel{3}\cdot 3\cdot 3\cdot 3\cdot 3}{\cancel{3}\cdot\cancel{3}\cdot\cancel{3}\cdot\cancel{3}\cdot\cancel{2}\cdot\cancel{2}\cdot 5\cdot 5\cdot\cancel{2}\cdot\cancel{2}\cdot 5\cdot 5}=\frac{81}{625}$$

24. $$\left(\frac{1}{6}\right)\cdot\left(\frac{6}{7}\right)^2\cdot\left(\frac{2}{3}\right)=\left(\frac{1}{6}\right)\cdot\left(\frac{6}{7}\cdot\frac{6}{7}\right)\cdot\left(\frac{2}{3}\right)=\frac{\cancel{2}\cdot\cancel{3}\cdot 2\cdot\cancel{3}\cdot 2}{\cancel{2}\cdot\cancel{3}\cdot 7\cdot 7\cdot\cancel{3}}=\frac{4}{49}$$

25. $$\left(\frac{2}{7}\right)\cdot\left(\frac{7}{8}\right)^2\cdot\left(\frac{8}{9}\right)=\left(\frac{2}{7}\right)\cdot\left(\frac{7}{8}\cdot\frac{7}{8}\right)\cdot\left(\frac{8}{9}\right)=\frac{\cancel{2}\cdot\cancel{7}\cdot 7\cdot\cancel{2}\cdot\cancel{2}\cdot\cancel{2}}{\cancel{7}\cdot\cancel{2}\cdot\cancel{2}\cdot\cancel{2}\cdot\cancel{2}\cdot 2\cdot 2\cdot 2\cdot 3\cdot 3}=\frac{7}{36}$$

26. $$3\cdot\left(\frac{3}{5}\right)^3\cdot\left(\frac{1}{3}\right)^2=\left(\frac{3}{1}\right)\cdot\left(\frac{3}{5}\cdot\frac{3}{5}\cdot\frac{3}{5}\right)\cdot\left(\frac{1}{3}\cdot\frac{1}{3}\right)=\frac{\cancel{3}\cdot\cancel{3}\cdot 3\cdot 3}{5\cdot 5\cdot 5\cdot\cancel{3}\cdot\cancel{3}}=\frac{9}{125}$$

27. $$4\cdot\left(\frac{3}{4}\right)^3\cdot\left(\frac{4}{7}\right)^2=\left(\frac{4}{1}\right)\cdot\left(\frac{3}{4}\cdot\frac{3}{4}\cdot\frac{3}{4}\right)\cdot\left(\frac{4}{7}\cdot\frac{4}{7}\right)=\frac{\cancel{2}\cdot\cancel{2}\cdot 3\cdot 3\cdot 3\cdot\cancel{2}\cdot\cancel{2}\cdot\cancel{2}\cdot\cancel{2}}{\cancel{2}\cdot\cancel{2}\cdot\cancel{2}\cdot\cancel{2}\cdot\cancel{2}\cdot\cancel{2}\cdot 7\cdot 7}=\frac{27}{49}$$

28. $$11\cdot\left(\frac{3}{8}\right)^3\cdot\left(\frac{8}{11}\right)^2=\left(\frac{11}{1}\right)\cdot\left(\frac{3}{8}\cdot\frac{3}{8}\cdot\frac{3}{8}\right)\cdot\left(\frac{8}{11}\cdot\frac{8}{11}\right)=\frac{\cancel{11}\cdot 3\cdot 3\cdot 3\cdot\cancel{2}\cdot\cancel{2}\cdot\cancel{2}\cdot\cancel{2}\cdot\cancel{2}\cdot\cancel{2}}{\cancel{2}\cdot\cancel{2}\cdot\cancel{2}\cdot\cancel{2}\cdot\cancel{2}\cdot\cancel{2}\cdot 2\cdot 2\cdot 2\cdot\cancel{11}\cdot 11}=\frac{27}{88}$$

Objective C Exercises

29. $$\begin{aligned}\frac{1}{2}-\frac{1}{3}+\frac{2}{3}&=\frac{3}{6}-\frac{2}{6}+\frac{2}{3}\\&=\frac{1}{6}+\frac{2}{3}\\&=\frac{1}{6}+\frac{4}{6}\\&=\frac{5}{6}\end{aligned}$$

30. $$\begin{aligned}\frac{2}{5}+\frac{3}{10}-\frac{2}{3}&=\frac{4}{10}+\frac{3}{10}-\frac{2}{3}\\&=\frac{7}{10}-\frac{2}{3}\\&=\frac{21}{30}-\frac{20}{30}\\&=\frac{1}{30}\end{aligned}$$

31. $$\begin{aligned}\frac{1}{3}\div\frac{1}{2}+\frac{3}{4}&=\frac{1}{3}\cdot\frac{2}{1}+\frac{3}{4}\\&=\frac{2}{3}+\frac{3}{4}\\&=\frac{8}{12}+\frac{9}{12}\\&=\frac{17}{12}=1\frac{5}{12}\end{aligned}$$

32. $$\begin{aligned}\frac{4}{5}+\frac{3}{7}\cdot\frac{14}{15}&=\frac{4}{5}+\frac{2}{5}\\&=\frac{6}{5}=1\frac{1}{5}\end{aligned}$$

33. $$\begin{aligned}\left(\frac{3}{4}\right)^2-\frac{5}{12}&=\frac{9}{16}-\frac{5}{12}\\&=\frac{27}{48}-\frac{20}{48}\\&=\frac{7}{48}\end{aligned}$$

34. $$\begin{aligned}\left(\frac{3}{5}\right)^3-\frac{3}{25}&=\frac{27}{125}-\frac{3}{25}\\&=\frac{27}{125}-\frac{15}{125}\\&=\frac{12}{125}\end{aligned}$$

35. $\frac{5}{6}\cdot\left(\frac{2}{3}-\frac{1}{6}\right)+\frac{7}{18}=\frac{5}{6}\cdot\left(\frac{4}{6}-\frac{1}{6}\right)+\frac{7}{18}$
$=\frac{5}{6}\cdot\frac{3}{6}+\frac{7}{18}$
$=\frac{5}{12}+\frac{7}{18}$
$=\frac{15}{36}+\frac{14}{36}$
$=\frac{29}{36}$

36. $\frac{3}{4}\cdot\left(\frac{11}{12}-\frac{7}{8}\right)+\frac{5}{16}=\frac{3}{4}\cdot\left(\frac{22}{24}-\frac{21}{24}\right)+\frac{5}{16}$
$=\frac{3}{4}\cdot\frac{1}{24}+\frac{5}{16}$
$=\frac{1}{32}+\frac{5}{16}$
$=\frac{1}{32}+\frac{10}{32}$
$=\frac{11}{32}$

37. $\frac{7}{12}-\left(\frac{2}{3}\right)^2+\frac{5}{8}=\frac{7}{12}-\frac{4}{9}+\frac{5}{8}$
$=\frac{21}{36}-\frac{16}{36}+\frac{5}{8}$
$=\frac{5}{36}+\frac{5}{8}$
$=\frac{10}{72}+\frac{45}{72}$
$=\frac{55}{72}$

38. $\frac{11}{16}-\left(\frac{3}{4}\right)^2+\frac{7}{12}=\frac{11}{16}-\frac{9}{16}+\frac{7}{12}$
$=\frac{2}{16}+\frac{7}{12}$
$=\frac{1}{8}+\frac{7}{12}$
$=\frac{3}{24}+\frac{14}{24}$
$=\frac{17}{24}$

39. $\frac{3}{4}\cdot\left(\frac{4}{9}\right)^2+\frac{1}{2}=\frac{3}{4}\cdot\frac{16}{81}+\frac{1}{2}$
$=\frac{4}{27}+\frac{1}{2}$
$=\frac{8}{54}+\frac{27}{54}$
$=\frac{35}{54}$

40. $\frac{9}{10}\cdot\left(\frac{2}{3}\right)^3+\frac{2}{3}=\frac{9}{10}\cdot\frac{8}{27}+\frac{2}{3}$
$=\frac{4}{15}+\frac{2}{3}$
$=\frac{4}{15}+\frac{10}{15}$
$=\frac{14}{15}$

41. $\left(\frac{1}{2}+\frac{3}{4}\right)\div\frac{5}{8}=\left(\frac{2}{4}+\frac{3}{4}\right)\div\frac{5}{8}$
$=\frac{5}{4}\cdot\frac{8}{5}$
$=2$

42. $\left(\frac{2}{3}+\frac{5}{6}\right)\div\frac{5}{9}=\left(\frac{4}{6}+\frac{5}{6}\right)\div\frac{5}{9}$
$=\frac{9}{6}\cdot\frac{9}{5}$
$=\frac{27}{10}$
$=2\frac{7}{10}$

43. $\frac{3}{8}\div\left(\frac{5}{12}+\frac{3}{8}\right)=\frac{3}{8}\div\left(\frac{10}{24}+\frac{9}{24}\right)$
$=\frac{3}{8}\div\frac{19}{24}$
$=\frac{3}{8}\cdot\frac{24}{19}$
$=\frac{9}{19}$

44. $\frac{7}{12}\div\left(\frac{2}{3}+\frac{5}{9}\right)=\frac{7}{12}\div\left(\frac{6}{9}+\frac{5}{9}\right)$
$=\frac{7}{12}\div\frac{11}{9}$
$=\frac{7}{12}\cdot\frac{9}{11}$
$=\frac{21}{44}$

45. $\left(\frac{3}{8}\right)^2\div\left(\frac{3}{7}+\frac{3}{14}\right)=\left(\frac{3}{8}\right)^2\div\left(\frac{6}{14}+\frac{3}{14}\right)$
$=\left(\frac{3}{8}\right)^2\div\frac{9}{14}$
$=\frac{9}{64}\cdot\frac{14}{9}$
$=\frac{7}{32}$

46. $\left(\frac{5}{6}\right)^2\div\left(\frac{5}{12}+\frac{2}{3}\right)=\left(\frac{5}{6}\right)^2\div\left(\frac{5}{12}+\frac{8}{12}\right)$
$=\left(\frac{5}{6}\right)^2\div\frac{13}{12}$
$=\frac{25}{36}\cdot\frac{12}{13}$
$=\frac{25}{39}$

47. $\frac{2}{5} \div \frac{3}{8} \cdot \frac{4}{5} = \frac{2}{5} \cdot \frac{8}{3} \cdot \frac{4}{5}$
$= \frac{16}{15} \cdot \frac{4}{5}$
$= \frac{64}{75}$

Applying the Concepts

48a. $\frac{13}{50} = \frac{26}{100}$ Location
$\frac{1}{4} = \frac{25}{100}$ Food Quality
More people choose location.

b. $\frac{1}{4} = \frac{25}{100}$ Food Quality
$\frac{13}{50} = \frac{26}{100}$ Location
$\frac{4}{25} = \frac{16}{100}$ Menu
$\frac{2}{25} = \frac{8}{100}$ Price
$\frac{3}{25} = \frac{12}{100}$ Speed
$\frac{3}{100} = \frac{3}{100}$ Other
The criterion that was cited by most people was location.

49. The "puzzle" works as it does because the sum of the fractions $\frac{1}{2}$, $\frac{1}{3}$, and $\frac{1}{9}$ is $\frac{17}{18}$, not 1. As a result,the first child actually received $\frac{9}{17}$ of the horses, not $\frac{1}{2}$; the second child received $\frac{6}{17}$ of the horses, not $\frac{1}{3}$; and the third child got $\frac{2}{17}$ of the horses, not $\frac{1}{9}$.

50. $\frac{2+3}{3+4} = \frac{5}{7}, \frac{5}{7} > \frac{2}{3}$, and $\frac{5}{7} < \frac{3}{4}$
Therefore, $\frac{2+3}{3+4}$ is between $\frac{2}{3}$ and $\frac{3}{4}$.

Chapter 2 Review Exercises

1. $\frac{30}{45} = \frac{2 \cdot \overset{1}{\cancel{3}} \cdot \overset{1}{\cancel{5}}}{3 \cdot \underset{1}{\cancel{3}} \cdot \underset{1}{\cancel{5}}} = \frac{2}{3}$

2. $\left(\frac{3}{4}\right)^3 \cdot \frac{20}{27} = \left(\frac{3}{4} \cdot \frac{3}{4} \cdot \frac{3}{4}\right)\left(\frac{20}{27}\right)$
$= \frac{\overset{1}{\cancel{3}} \cdot \overset{1}{\cancel{3}} \cdot \overset{1}{\cancel{3}} \cdot \overset{1}{\cancel{2}} \cdot \overset{1}{\cancel{2}} \cdot 5}{2 \cdot 2 \cdot 2 \cdot 2 \cdot \underset{1}{\cancel{2}} \cdot \underset{1}{\cancel{2}} \cdot \underset{1}{\cancel{3}} \cdot \underset{1}{\cancel{3}} \cdot \underset{1}{\cancel{3}}} = \frac{5}{16}$

3. $\frac{13}{4}$

4. $\frac{2}{3} = \frac{12}{18}$
$\frac{5}{6} = \frac{15}{18}$
$+\frac{2}{9} = \frac{4}{18}$
$\frac{31}{18} = 1\frac{13}{18}$

5. $\frac{11}{18} = \frac{44}{72}, \frac{17}{24} = \frac{51}{72}, \frac{11}{18} < \frac{17}{24}$

6. $18\frac{1}{6} = 18\frac{7}{42} = 17\frac{49}{42}$
$-3\frac{5}{7} = 3\frac{30}{42} = 3\frac{30}{42}$
$14\frac{19}{42}$

7. $\frac{2}{7}\left[\frac{5}{8} - \frac{1}{3}\right] \div \frac{3}{5} = \frac{2}{7}\left[\frac{15}{24} - \frac{8}{24}\right] \div \frac{3}{5}$
$= \frac{2}{7}\left[\frac{7}{24}\right] \div \frac{3}{5} = \frac{2 \cdot \overset{1}{\cancel{7}}}{\underset{1}{\cancel{7}} \cdot 24} \div \frac{3}{5}$
$= \frac{1}{12} \times \frac{5}{3} = \frac{5}{36}$

8. $2\frac{1}{3} \times 3\frac{7}{8} = \frac{7}{3} \times \frac{31}{8} = \frac{7 \cdot 31}{3 \cdot 8} = \frac{217}{24} = 9\frac{1}{24}$

9. $1\frac{1}{3} \div \frac{2}{3} = \frac{4}{3} \div \frac{2}{3} = \frac{4}{3} \times \frac{3}{2} = \frac{4 \cdot 3}{3 \cdot 2} = \frac{2 \cdot \overset{1}{\cancel{2}} \cdot \overset{1}{\cancel{3}}}{\underset{1}{\cancel{3}} \cdot \underset{1}{\cancel{2}}} = 2$

10. $\frac{17}{24} = \frac{34}{48}$
$-\frac{3}{16} = \frac{9}{48}$
$\frac{25}{48}$

11. $8\frac{2}{3} \div 2\frac{3}{5} = \frac{26}{3} \div \frac{13}{5} = \frac{26}{3} \times \frac{5}{13} = \frac{26 \cdot 5}{3 \cdot 13} = \frac{2 \cdot \overset{1}{\cancel{13}} \cdot 5}{3 \cdot \underset{1}{\cancel{13}}}$
$= \frac{10}{3} = 3\frac{1}{3}$

12.

	2	3	5
20 =	(2 · 2)		5
48 =	2 · 2 · 2 · 2	3	

GCF = 2 · 2 = 4

13. $\frac{2 \cdot 12}{3 \cdot 12} = \frac{24}{36}$

14. $\frac{15}{28} \div \frac{5}{7} = \frac{15}{28} \times \frac{7}{5} = \frac{15 \cdot 7}{28 \cdot 5} = \frac{3 \cdot \overset{1}{\cancel{5}} \cdot \overset{1}{\cancel{7}}}{2 \cdot 2 \cdot \underset{1}{\cancel{7}} \cdot \underset{1}{\cancel{5}}} = \frac{3}{4}$

15. $\frac{8 \cdot 4}{11 \cdot 4} = \frac{32}{44}$

16. $2\frac{1}{4}\times 7\frac{1}{3}=\frac{9}{4}\times\frac{22}{3}=\frac{9\cdot 22}{4\cdot 3}=\frac{3\cdot\overset{1}{\cancel{3}}\cdot\overset{1}{\cancel{2}}\cdot 11}{\underset{1}{\cancel{2}}\cdot 2\cdot\underset{1}{\cancel{3}}}$

$=\frac{33}{2}=16\frac{1}{2}$

17.

	2	3
18 =	2	3 · 3
12 =	(2 · 2)	(3 · 3)

LCM = 2 · 2 · 3 · 3 = 36

18. $\frac{16}{44}=\frac{\overset{1}{\cancel{2}}\cdot\overset{1}{\cancel{2}}\cdot 2\cdot 2}{\underset{1}{\cancel{2}}\cdot\underset{1}{\cancel{2}}\cdot 11}=\frac{4}{11}$

19.
$$\begin{array}{r}\frac{3}{8}\\ \frac{5}{8}\\ +\frac{1}{8}\\ \hline \frac{9}{8}=1\frac{1}{8}\end{array}$$

20.
$$\begin{array}{r}16=15\frac{8}{8}\\ -5\frac{7}{8}=5\frac{7}{8}\\ \hline 10\frac{1}{8}\end{array}$$

21.
$$\begin{array}{r}4\frac{4}{9}=4\frac{24}{54}\\ 2\frac{1}{6}=2\frac{9}{54}\\ +11\frac{17}{27}=11\frac{34}{54}\\ \hline 17\frac{67}{54}=18\frac{13}{54}\end{array}$$

22.

	3	5
15 =	3	(5)
25 =		5 · 5

GCF = 5

23.
$$\begin{array}{r}3\\ 5\overline{)17}\\ -15\\ \hline 2\end{array}\qquad \frac{17}{5}=3\frac{2}{5}$$

24. $\left[\frac{4}{5}-\frac{2}{3}\right]^2\div\frac{4}{15}=\left[\frac{12}{15}-\frac{10}{15}\right]^2\div\frac{4}{15}$

$=\left(\frac{2}{15}\right)^2\div\frac{4}{15}=\left(\frac{2}{15}\right)\left(\frac{2}{15}\right)\div\left(\frac{4}{15}\right)$

$=\frac{4}{225}\times\frac{15}{4}=\frac{4\cdot 15}{225\cdot 4}=\frac{1}{15}$

25.
$$\begin{array}{r}\frac{3}{8}=\frac{9}{24}\\ 1\frac{2}{3}=1\frac{16}{24}\\ +3\frac{5}{6}=3\frac{20}{24}\\ \hline 4\frac{45}{24}=5\frac{21}{24}=5\frac{7}{8}\end{array}$$

26.

	2	3
18 =	(2)	3 · 3
27 =		(3 · 3 · 3)

LCM = 2 · 3 · 3 · 3 = 54

27.
$$\begin{array}{r}\frac{11}{18}\\ -\frac{5}{18}\\ \hline \frac{6}{18}=\frac{1}{3}\end{array}$$

28. $2\frac{5}{7}=\frac{14+5}{7}=\frac{19}{7}$

29. $\frac{5}{6}\div\frac{5}{12}=\frac{5}{6}\cdot\frac{12}{5}=\frac{5\cdot 12}{6\cdot 5}=\frac{\overset{1}{\cancel{5}}\cdot\overset{1}{\cancel{2}}\cdot 2\cdot\overset{1}{\cancel{3}}}{\underset{1}{\cancel{2}}\cdot\underset{1}{\cancel{3}}\cdot\underset{1}{\cancel{5}}}=2$

30. $\frac{5}{12}\times\frac{4}{25}=\frac{5\cdot 4}{12\cdot 25}=\frac{\overset{1}{\cancel{5}}\cdot\overset{1}{\cancel{2}}\cdot\overset{1}{\cancel{2}}}{\underset{1}{\cancel{2}}\cdot\underset{1}{\cancel{2}}\cdot 3\cdot\underset{1}{\cancel{5}}\cdot 5}=\frac{1}{15}$

31. $\frac{11}{50}\times\frac{25}{44}=\frac{11\cdot 25}{50\cdot 44}=\frac{\overset{1}{\cancel{11}}\cdot\overset{1}{\cancel{5}}\cdot\overset{1}{\cancel{5}}}{2\cdot\underset{1}{\cancel{5}}\cdot\underset{1}{\cancel{5}}\cdot 2\cdot 2\cdot\underset{1}{\cancel{11}}}=\frac{1}{8}$

32. $1\frac{7}{8}$

33. **Strategy** To find the total rainfall for the 3 months, add the amounts of rain from each month $\left(5\frac{7}{8}, 6\frac{2}{3}, \text{ and } 8\frac{3}{4} \text{ inches}\right)$.

Solution
$$\begin{array}{r}5\frac{7}{8}=5\frac{21}{24}\\ 6\frac{2}{3}=6\frac{16}{24}\\ +8\frac{3}{4}=8\frac{18}{24}\\ \hline 19\frac{55}{24}=21\frac{7}{24}\end{array}$$

The total rainfall for the 3 months was $21\frac{7}{24}$ inches.

34. Strategy To find the cost of each acre, divide the total cost ($168,000) by the number of acres $\left(4\frac{2}{3}\right)$.

Solution

$$\begin{aligned}\$168,000 \div 4\frac{2}{3} &= 168,000 \div \frac{14}{3}\\ &= 168,000 \times \frac{3}{14}\\ &= \$36,000\end{aligned}$$

The cost per acre was $36,000.

35. Strategy To find how many miles the second checkpoint is from the finish line:

- Add the distance to the first checkpoint $\left(4\frac{1}{2} \text{ miles}\right)$ to the distance between the first checkpoint and the second checkpoint $\left(5\frac{3}{4} \text{ miles}\right)$.
- Subtract the total distance to the second checkpoint from the entire length of the race (15 miles).

Solution

$$\begin{array}{r} 4\frac{1}{2} = 4\frac{2}{4}\\ +5\frac{3}{4} = 5\frac{3}{4}\\ \hline 9\frac{5}{4} = 10\frac{1}{4}\end{array} \qquad \begin{array}{r} 15 = 14\frac{4}{4}\\ -10\frac{1}{4} = 10\frac{1}{4}\\ \hline 4\frac{3}{4}\end{array}$$

The second checkpoint is $4\frac{3}{4}$ miles from the finish line.

36. Strategy To find how many miles the car can travel, multiply the number of miles the car can travel on 1 gallon (36) by the number of gallons used $\left(6\frac{3}{4}\right)$.

Solution

$$36 \times 6\frac{3}{4} = 36 \times \frac{27}{4} = \frac{36 \cdot 27}{4} = 243$$

The car can travel 243 miles.

Chapter 2 Test

1. $\frac{9}{11} \times \frac{44}{81} = \frac{9 \cdot 44}{11 \cdot 81} = \frac{\cancel{3} \cdot \cancel{3} \cdot 2 \cdot 2 \cdot \cancel{11}}{\cancel{11} \cdot \cancel{3} \cdot \cancel{3} \cdot 3 \cdot 3} = \frac{4}{9}$

2.

	2	3	5
24 =	(2 · 2 · 2)	3	
80 =	2 · 2 · 2 · 2		5

GCF = 2 · 2 · 2 = 8

3. $\frac{5}{9} \div \frac{7}{18} = \frac{5}{9} \times \frac{18}{7} = \frac{5 \cdot 2 \cdot \cancel{3} \cdot \cancel{3}}{\cancel{3} \cdot \cancel{3} \cdot 7} = \frac{10}{7} = 1\frac{3}{7}$

4. $$\begin{aligned}\left(\frac{3}{4}\right)^2 \div \left(\frac{2}{3}+\frac{5}{6}\right) - \frac{1}{12} &= \left(\frac{3}{4}\cdot\frac{3}{4}\right) \div \left(\frac{4}{6}+\frac{5}{6}\right) - \frac{1}{12}\\ &= \frac{9}{16} \div \left(\frac{9}{6}\right) - \frac{1}{12}\\ &= \frac{9}{16} \div \frac{3}{2} - \frac{1}{12}\\ &= \frac{9}{16} \times \frac{2}{3} - \frac{1}{12}\end{aligned}$$
$$\frac{\cancel{3} \cdot 3 \cdot \cancel{2}}{2 \cdot 2 \cdot 2 \cdot \cancel{2} \cdot \cancel{3}} - \frac{1}{12} = \frac{3}{8} - \frac{1}{12} = \frac{9}{24} - \frac{2}{24} = \frac{7}{24}$$

5. $9\frac{4}{5} = \frac{45+4}{5} = \frac{49}{5}$

6. $5\frac{2}{3} \times 1\frac{7}{17} = \frac{17}{3} \times \frac{24}{17} = \frac{17 \cdot 24}{3 \cdot 17} = \frac{\cancel{17} \cdot 2 \cdot 2 \cdot 2 \cdot \cancel{3}}{\cancel{3} \cdot \cancel{17}} = 8$

7. $\frac{40}{64} = \frac{\cancel{2} \cdot \cancel{2} \cdot \cancel{2} \cdot 5}{\cancel{2} \cdot \cancel{2} \cdot \cancel{2} \cdot 2 \cdot 2 \cdot 2} = \frac{5}{8}$

8. $\frac{3}{8} = \frac{9}{24}, \frac{5}{12} = \frac{10}{24}, \frac{3}{8} < \frac{5}{12}$

9. $$\begin{aligned}\left(\frac{1}{4}\right)^3 \div \left(\frac{1}{8}\right)^2 - \frac{1}{6} &= \left(\frac{1}{4}\cdot\frac{1}{4}\cdot\frac{1}{4}\right) \div \left(\frac{1}{8}\cdot\frac{1}{8}\right) - \frac{1}{6}\\ &= \frac{1}{64} \div \frac{1}{64} - \frac{1}{6}\\ &= \frac{1}{64} \times \frac{64}{1} - \frac{1}{6}\\ &= 1 - \frac{1}{6}\\ &= \frac{6}{6} - \frac{1}{6} = \frac{5}{6}\end{aligned}$$

10.

	2	3	5
24 =	(2 · 2 · 2)	(3)	
40 =	2 · 2 · 2		(5)

LCM = 2 · 2 · 2 · 3 · 5 = 120

11. $$\begin{array}{r} \frac{17}{24}\\ -\frac{11}{24}\\ \hline \frac{6}{24} = \frac{1}{4}\end{array}$$

12. $$\begin{array}{r} 3\\ 5\overline{)18}\\ -15\\ \hline 3\end{array} \qquad \frac{18}{5} = 3\frac{3}{5}$$

13. $$\begin{aligned}6\frac{2}{3} \div 3\frac{1}{6} &= \frac{20}{3} \div \frac{19}{6} = \frac{20}{3} \times \frac{6}{19}\\ &= \frac{2 \cdot 2 \cdot 5 \cdot 2 \cdot \cancel{3}}{\cancel{3} \cdot 19} = \frac{40}{19} = 2\frac{2}{19}\end{aligned}$$

14. $\frac{5 \cdot 9}{8 \cdot 9} = \frac{45}{72}$

15.
$$\begin{array}{r} \frac{5}{6} = \frac{75}{90} \\ \frac{7}{9} = \frac{70}{90} \\ +\frac{1}{15} = \frac{6}{90} \\ \hline \frac{151}{90} = 1\frac{61}{90} \end{array}$$

16.
$$\begin{array}{r} 23\frac{1}{8} = 23\frac{11}{88} = 22\frac{99}{88} \\ -9\frac{9}{44} = 9\frac{18}{88} = 9\frac{18}{88} \\ \hline 13\frac{81}{88} \end{array}$$

17.
$$\begin{array}{r} \frac{9}{16} = \frac{27}{48} \\ -\frac{5}{12} = \frac{20}{48} \\ \hline \frac{7}{48} \end{array}$$

18.
$$\left(\frac{2}{3}\right)^4\left(\frac{27}{32}\right) = \left(\frac{2}{3}\cdot\frac{2}{3}\cdot\frac{2}{3}\cdot\frac{2}{3}\right)\left(\frac{27}{32}\right)$$
$$= \frac{\overset{1}{\cancel{2}}\cdot\overset{1}{\cancel{2}}\cdot\overset{1}{\cancel{2}}\cdot\overset{1}{\cancel{2}}\cdot\overset{1}{\cancel{3}}\cdot\overset{1}{\cancel{3}}\cdot\overset{1}{\cancel{3}}}{3\cdot\underset{1}{\cancel{3}}\cdot\underset{1}{\cancel{3}}\cdot\underset{1}{\cancel{3}}\cdot\underset{1}{\cancel{2}}\cdot\underset{1}{\cancel{2}}\cdot\underset{1}{\cancel{2}}\cdot\underset{1}{\cancel{2}}\cdot 2} = \frac{1}{6}$$

19.
$$\begin{array}{r} \frac{7}{12} \\ \frac{11}{12} \\ +\frac{5}{12} \\ \hline \frac{23}{12} = 1\frac{11}{12} \end{array}$$

20.
$$\begin{array}{r} 12\frac{5}{12} = 12\frac{25}{60} \\ +9\frac{17}{20} = 9\frac{51}{60} \\ \hline 21\frac{76}{60} = 22\frac{16}{60} = 22\frac{4}{15} \end{array}$$

21. $\frac{11}{4}$

22. Strategy To find the electrician's earnings, multiply daily earnings ($240) by the number of days worked $\left(3\frac{1}{2}\right)$.

Solution $\$240 \times 3\frac{1}{2} = 240 \times \frac{7}{2} = \frac{240 \cdot 7}{2} = \$840$

The electrician earns $840.

23. Strategy To find how many lots were available:

- Find how many acres were being developed by subtracting the amount set aside for the park $\left(1\frac{3}{4}\text{ acres}\right)$ from the total parcel $\left(7\frac{1}{4}\text{ acres}\right)$.
- Divide the amount being developed by the size of each lot $\left(\frac{1}{2}\text{ acre}\right)$.

Solution
$$\begin{array}{r} 7\frac{1}{4} = 6\frac{5}{4} \\ -1\frac{3}{4} = 1\frac{3}{4} \\ \hline 5\frac{2}{4} = 5\frac{1}{2} \end{array}$$

$5\frac{1}{2} \div \frac{1}{2} = \frac{11}{2} \times \frac{2}{1} = \frac{11 \cdot 2}{2} = 11$

11 lots were available for sale.

24. Strategy To find how many houses the developer plans to build:

- Subtract the amount of land set aside (3 acres) from the total purchased $\left(25\frac{1}{2}\text{ acres}\right)$ to determine the amount of land that can be used for houses.
- Divide the amount of land available for houses by $\frac{3}{4}$ to determine the number of $\frac{3}{4}$-acre plots that are available for houses.

Solution $25\frac{1}{2} - 3 = 22\frac{1}{2}$ acres

$22\frac{1}{2} \div \frac{3}{4} = \frac{45}{2} \cdot \frac{4}{3} = 15 \cdot 2 = 30$

The developer plans to build 30 houses on the property.

25. **Strategy** To find the total rainfall for the 3-month period, add the rainfall amounts for each of the months $\left(11\frac{1}{2}, 7\frac{5}{8}, \text{ and } 2\frac{1}{3} \text{ inches}\right)$.

Solution

$$\begin{array}{r} 11\frac{1}{2} = 11\frac{12}{24} \\ 7\frac{5}{8} = 7\frac{15}{24} \\ +2\frac{1}{3} = 2\frac{8}{24} \\ \hline 20\frac{35}{24} = 21\frac{11}{24} \end{array}$$

The total rainfall for the 3-month period was $21\frac{11}{24}$ inches.

Cumulative Review Exercises

1. 290,000

2. $$\begin{array}{r} 390{,}047 \\ -\ 98{,}769 \\ \hline 291{,}278 \end{array}$$

3. $$\begin{array}{r} 926 \\ \times\ 79 \\ \hline 8334 \\ 6482\ \\ \hline 73{,}154 \end{array}$$

4. $$\begin{array}{r} 540 \text{ r}12 \\ 57\overline{)30{,}792} \\ -285 \\ \hline 229 \\ -228 \\ \hline 12 \\ -0 \\ \hline 12 \end{array}$$

5. $4 \cdot (6-3) \div 6 - 1 = 4 \cdot 3 \div 6 - 1$
$= 12 \div 6 - 1$
$= 2 - 1$
$= 1$

6. $44 = 2 \cdot 2 \cdot 11$

44	
2	22
2	11
11	1

7.

	2	3	5	7
30 =	(2)	(3)	(5)	
42 =	2	3		(7)

LCM $= 2 \cdot 3 \cdot 5 \cdot 7 = 210$

8.

	2	3	5
60 =	(2 · 2)	3	(5)
80 =	2 · 2 · 2 · 2		5

GCF $= 2 \cdot 2 \cdot 5 = 20$

9. $7\frac{2}{3} = \frac{21+2}{3} = \frac{23}{3}$

10. $$\begin{array}{r} 6 \text{ r}1 \\ 4\overline{)25} \\ -24 \\ \hline 1 \end{array} \qquad \frac{25}{4} = 6\frac{1}{4}$$

11. $\frac{5 \cdot 3}{16 \cdot 3} = \frac{15}{48}$

12. $\frac{24}{60} = \frac{2 \cdot \cancel{2} \cdot \cancel{2} \cdot \cancel{3}}{\cancel{2} \cdot \cancel{2} \cdot \cancel{3} \cdot 5} = \frac{2}{5}$

13. $$\begin{array}{r} \frac{7}{12} = \frac{28}{48} \\ +\frac{9}{16} = \frac{27}{48} \\ \hline \frac{55}{48} = 1\frac{7}{48} \end{array}$$

14. $$\begin{array}{r} 3\frac{7}{8} = 3\frac{42}{48} \\ 7\frac{5}{12} = 7\frac{20}{48} \\ +2\frac{15}{16} = 2\frac{45}{48} \\ \hline 12\frac{107}{48} = 14\frac{11}{48} \end{array}$$

15. $$\begin{array}{r} \frac{11}{12} = \frac{22}{24} \\ -\frac{3}{8} = \frac{9}{24} \\ \hline \frac{13}{24} \end{array}$$

16. $$\begin{array}{r} 5\frac{1}{6} = 5\frac{3}{18} = 4\frac{21}{18} \\ -3\frac{7}{18} = 3\frac{7}{18} = 3\frac{7}{18} \\ \hline 1\frac{14}{18} = 1\frac{7}{9} \end{array}$$

17. $\frac{3}{8} \times \frac{14}{15} = \frac{3 \cdot 14}{8 \cdot 15} = \frac{\cancel{3} \cdot \cancel{2} \cdot 7}{2 \cdot 2 \cdot \cancel{2} \cdot \cancel{3} \cdot 5} = \frac{7}{20}$

18. $3\frac{1}{8} \times 2\frac{2}{5} = \frac{25}{8} \times \frac{12}{5} = \frac{25 \cdot 12}{8 \cdot 5}$
$= \frac{5 \cdot \cancel{5} \cdot \cancel{2} \cdot \cancel{2} \cdot 3}{\cancel{2} \cdot \cancel{2} \cdot 2 \cdot \cancel{5}} = \frac{15}{2} = 7\frac{1}{2}$

19. $\frac{7}{16} \div \frac{5}{12} = \frac{7}{16} \times \frac{12}{5} = \frac{7 \cdot 12}{16 \cdot 5}$
$= \frac{7 \cdot \cancel{2} \cdot \cancel{2} \cdot 3}{\cancel{2} \cdot \cancel{2} \cdot 2 \cdot 2 \cdot 5} = \frac{21}{20} = 1\frac{1}{20}$

20. $6\frac{1}{8} \div 2\frac{1}{3} = \frac{49}{8} \div \frac{7}{3} = \frac{49}{8} \times \frac{3}{7} = \frac{49 \cdot 3}{8 \cdot 7}$

$= \frac{7 \cdot \overset{1}{\cancel{7}} \cdot 3}{2 \cdot 2 \cdot 2 \cdot \underset{1}{\cancel{7}}} = \frac{21}{8} = 2\frac{5}{8}$

21. $\left(\frac{1}{2}\right)^3 \cdot \frac{8}{9} = \left(\frac{1}{2} \cdot \frac{1}{2} \cdot \frac{1}{2}\right) \cdot \frac{8}{9} = \frac{1}{8} \cdot \frac{8}{9} = \frac{1}{9}$

22. $\left(\frac{1}{2} + \frac{1}{3}\right) \div \left(\frac{2}{5}\right)^2 = \left(\frac{3}{6} + \frac{2}{6}\right) \div \left(\frac{2}{5} \cdot \frac{2}{5}\right)$

$= \frac{5}{6} \div \frac{4}{25} = \frac{5}{6} \times \frac{25}{4} = \frac{5 \cdot 25}{6 \cdot 4} = \frac{125}{24} = 5\frac{5}{24}$

23. Strategy To find the amount in the checking account:
- Find the total of the checks written by adding the check amounts ($128, $54, and $315).
- Subtract the total of the checks written from the original balance in the checking account ($1359).

Solution

$128	$1359
54	− 497
+ 315	$862
$497	

The amount in the checking account at the end of the week was $862.

24. Strategy To find the total income from the sale of the tickets:
- Find the income from the adult tickets by multiplying the ticket price ($10) by the number of tickets sold (87).
- Find the income from the student tickets by multiplying the ticket price ($4) by the number of tickets sold (135).
- Find the total income by adding the income from the adult tickets to the income from the student tickets.

Solution

87	135	$870
×$10	× $4	+540
$870	$540	$1410

The total income from the tickets was $1410.

25. Strategy To find the total weight, add the three weights $\left(1\frac{1}{2}, 7\frac{7}{8}, \text{ and } 2\frac{2}{3} \text{ pounds}\right)$.

Solution

$1\frac{1}{2} = 1\frac{12}{24}$

$7\frac{7}{8} = 7\frac{21}{24}$

$+2\frac{2}{3} = 2\frac{16}{24}$

$10\frac{49}{24} = 12\frac{1}{24}$

The total weight is $12\frac{1}{24}$ pounds.

26. Strategy To find the length of the remaining piece, subtract the length of the cut piece $\left(2\frac{5}{8} \text{ feet}\right)$ from the original length of the board $\left(7\frac{1}{3} \text{ feet}\right)$.

Solution

$7\frac{1}{3} = 7\frac{8}{24} = 6\frac{32}{24}$

$-2\frac{5}{8} = 2\frac{15}{24} = 2\frac{15}{24}$

$4\frac{17}{24}$

The length of the remaining piece is $4\frac{17}{24}$ feet.

27. Strategy To find how many miles the car can travel, multiply the number of gallons used $\left(8\frac{1}{3}\right)$ by the number of miles that the car travels on each gallon (27).

Solution $27 \times 8\frac{1}{3} = 27 \times \frac{25}{3} = 225$

The car travels 225 miles on $8\frac{1}{3}$ gallons of gas.

28. Strategy To find how many parcels can be sold:
- Find the amount of land that can be developed by subtracting the land donated for a park (2 acres) from the total amount of land purchased $\left(10\frac{1}{3} \text{ acres}\right)$.
- Divide the amount of land that can be developed by the size of each parcel $\left(\frac{1}{3} \text{ acre}\right)$.

Solution

$10\frac{1}{3}$

-2

$8\frac{1}{3}$

$8\frac{1}{3} \div \frac{1}{3} = \frac{25}{3} \div \frac{1}{3} = \frac{25}{3} \times \frac{3}{1} = 25$

25 parcels can be sold from the remaining land.

Chapter 3: Decimals

Prep Test

1. $\frac{3}{10}$
2. 36,900
3. Four thousand seven hundred ninety-one
4. 6842
5. 9394
6. 1638
7. $\begin{array}{r} 844 \\ \times\ 91 \\ \hline 844 \\ 7596 \\ \hline 76{,}804 \end{array}$
8. $\begin{array}{r} 278 \text{ r18} \\ 23\overline{)6412} \\ -46 \\ \hline 181 \\ -161 \\ \hline 202 \\ -184 \\ \hline 18 \end{array}$

Go Figure

There are 7 children in the family.
Maria has twice as many brothers as sisters. She has 4 brothers (including Pedro) and 2 sisters.
Pedro has as many brothers as sisters. He has 3 sisters (including Maria) and 3 brothers.

Section 3.1

Objective A Exercises

1. The digit 5 is in the thousandths place.
2. The digit 5 is in the tenths place.
3. The digit 5 is in the ten-thousandths place.
4. The digit 5 is in the hundred-thousandths place.
5. The digit 5 is in the hundredths place.
6. The digit 5 is in the millionths place.
7. $\frac{3}{10} = 0.3$ (three tenths)
8. $\frac{9}{10} = 0.9$ (nine tenths)
9. $\frac{21}{100} = 0.21$ (twenty-one hundredths)
10. $\frac{87}{100} = 0.87$ (eighty-seven hundredths)
11. $\frac{461}{1000} = 0.461$ (four hundred sixty-one thousandths)
12. $\frac{853}{1000} = 0.853$ (eight hundred fifty-three thousandths)
13. $\frac{93}{1000} = 0.093$ (ninety-three thousandths)
14. $\frac{61}{1000} = 0.061$ (sixty-one thousandths)
15. $0.1 = \frac{1}{10}$ (one-tenth)
16. $0.3 = \frac{3}{10}$ (three-tenths)
17. $0.47 = \frac{47}{100}$ (forty-seven-hundredths)
18. $0.59 = \frac{59}{100}$ (fifty-nine-hundredths)
19. $0.289 = \frac{289}{1000}$ (two hundred eighty-nine-thousandths)
20. $0.601 = \frac{601}{1000}$ (six hundred one-thousandths)
21. $0.09 = \frac{9}{100}$ (nine-hundredths)
22. $0.013 = \frac{13}{1000}$ (thirteen-thousandths)
23. Thirty-seven-hundredths
24. Twenty-five and six-tenths
25. Nine and four-tenths
26. One and four-thousandths
27. Fifty-three-ten-thousandths
28. Forty-one and one hundred eight-thousandths
29. Forty-five-thousandths
30. Three and one hundred fifty-seven-thousandths
31. Twenty-six and four-hundredths
32. 0.672
33. 3.0806
34. 9.0407
35. 407.03
36. 612.704

37. 246.024

38. 2067.9002

39. 73.02684

Objective B Exercises

40. *Given place value*
6.249
└ $4 < 5$
6.249 rounded to the nearest tenth is 6.2.

41. *Given place value*
5.398
└ $9 > 5$
5.398 rounded to the nearest tenth is 5.4.

42. *Given place value*
21.007
└ $0 < 5$
21.007 rounded to the nearest tenth is 21.0.

43. *Given place value*
30.0092
└ $0 < 5$
30.0092 rounded to the nearest tenth is 30.0.

44. *Given place value*
18.40937
└ $9 > 5$
18.40937 rounded to the nearest hundredth is 18.41.

45. *Given place value*
413.5972
└ $7 > 5$
413.5972 rounded to the nearest hundredth is 413.60.

46. *Given place value*
72.4983
└ $8 > 5$
72.4983 rounded to the nearest hundredth is 72.50.

47. *Given place value*
6.061745
└ $7 > 5$
6.061745 rounded to the nearest thousandth is 6.062.

48. *Given place value*
936.2905
└ $5 = 5$
936.2905 rounded to the nearest thousandth is 936.291.

49. *Given place value*
96.8027
└ $8 > 5$
96.8027 rounded to the nearest whole number is 97.

50. *Given place value*
47.3192
└ $3 < 5$
47.3192 rounded to the nearest whole number is 47.

51. *Given place value*
5439.83
└ $8 > 5$
5439.83 rounded to the nearest whole number is 5440.

52. *Given place value*
7014.96
└ $9 > 5$
7014.96 rounded to the nearest whole number is 7015.

53. *Given place value*
0.023591
└ $9 > 5$
0.023591 rounded to the nearest ten-thousandth is 0.0236.

54. *Given place value*
2.975268
└ $8 > 5$
2.975268 rounded to the nearest hundred-thousandth is 2.97527.

55. 0.1763668 rounded to the nearest hundredth is 0.18. The weight of a nickel to the nearest hundredth is 0.18 ounce.

56. 124.1093 rounded to the nearest cent is \$124.11. The amount paid for the parka is \$124.11.

57. 26.21875 rounded to the nearest tenth is 26.2. To the nearest tenth, the Boston Marathon is 26.2 miles.

Applying the Concepts

58a. The last zeros need not be entered on a calculator. 1.500

b. The first zero need not be entered on a calculator. 0.908

c. Both zeros must be entered on a calculator. 60.07

d. The first zero need not be entered on a calculator. 0.0032

59a. Answers will vary. For example, 0.11, 0.12, 0.13, 0.14, 0.15, 0.16, 0.17, 0.18, and 0.19 are numbers between 0.1 and 0.2. But any number of digits can be attached to 0.1, and the number will be between 0.1 and 0.2. For example, 0.123456789 is a number between 0.1 and 0.2.

b. Answers will vary. For example, 1.01, 1.02, 1.03, 1.04, 1.05, 1.06, 1.07, 1.08, and 1.09 are numbers between 1 and 1.1. But any number of digits can be attached to 1.0, and the number will be between 1 and 1.1. For example, 1.0123456789 is a number between 1 and 1.1.

c. Answers will vary. For example, 0.001, 0.002, 0.003 and 0.004 are numbers between 0 and 0.005. But any number of digits can be attached to 0.001, 0.002, 0.003, or 0.004, and the number will be between 0 and 0.005. For example, 0.00123456789 is a number between 0 and 0.005.

Section 3.2

Objective A Exercises

1. $\begin{array}{r} {}^{1}\ {}^{11} \\ 16.008 \\ 2.0385 \\ +\ 132.06 \\ \hline 150.1065 \end{array}$

2. $\begin{array}{r} {}^{1} \\ 17.32 \\ 1.0579 \\ +\ 16.5 \\ \hline 34.8779 \end{array}$

3. $\begin{array}{r} {}^{1}\ {}^{1} \\ 1.792 \\ 67 \\ +\ 27.0526 \\ \hline 95.8446 \end{array}$

4. $\begin{array}{r} {}^{11}\ {}^{1} \\ 8.772 \\ 1.09 \\ +\ 26.5027 \\ \hline 36.3647 \end{array}$

5. $\begin{array}{r} {}^{1} \\ 3.02 \\ 62.7 \\ +\ 3.924 \\ \hline 69.644 \end{array}$

6. $\begin{array}{r} {}^{211} \\ 9.06 \\ 4.976 \\ +\ 59.6 \\ \hline 73.636 \end{array}$

7. $\begin{array}{r} {}^{11}\ {}^{1} \\ 82.006 \\ 9.95 \\ +\ 0.927 \\ \hline 92.883 \end{array}$

8. $\begin{array}{r} {}^{11}\ {}^{1} \\ 0.826 \\ 8.76 \\ +\ 79.005 \\ \hline 88.591 \end{array}$

9. $\begin{array}{r} {}^{2111} \\ 4.307 \\ 99.82 \\ +\ 9.078 \\ \hline 113.205 \end{array}$

10. $\begin{array}{r} 0.3 \\ +\ 0.07 \\ \hline 0.37 \end{array}$

11. $\begin{array}{r} 0.29 \\ +\ 0.4 \\ \hline 0.69 \end{array}$

12. $\begin{array}{r} 1.007 \\ +\ 2.1 \\ \hline 3.107 \end{array}$

13. $\begin{array}{r} 7.3 \\ +\ 9.005 \\ \hline 16.305 \end{array}$

14. $\begin{array}{r} {}^{2}\ \ {}^{11} \\ 4.9257 \\ 27.05 \\ +\ 9.0063 \\ \hline 40.9820 \end{array}$

15. $\begin{array}{r} {}^{211} \\ 8.72 \\ 99.073 \\ +\ 2.9736 \\ \hline 110.7666 \end{array}$

16. $\begin{array}{r} {}^{111} \\ 62.4 \\ 9.827 \\ +\ 692.44 \\ \hline 764.667 \end{array}$

17. $\begin{array}{r} {}^{2} \\ 8. \\ 89.43 \\ +\ 7.0659 \\ \hline 104.4959 \end{array}$

18. $\begin{array}{rcr} 342.42 & \approx & 342 \\ 89.625 & \approx & 90 \\ +\ 176.2 & \approx & +\ 176 \\ \hline \text{Cal.: } 608.245 & & \text{Est.: } 608 \end{array}$

19.
219.9 ≈ 220
0.872 ≈ 1
+ 13.42 ≈ + 13
Cal.: 234.192 Est.: 234

20.
823.9 ≈ 824
82.65 ≈ 83
+ 46.923 ≈ + 47
Cal.: 953.473 Est.: 954

21.
678.92 ≈ 679
97.6 ≈ 98
+ 5.423 ≈ + 5
Cal.: 781.943 Est.: 782

Objective B Exercises

22a. Strategy To find the exact amount of the three bills, add the three amounts ($814.72, $216.60, and $87.32).

Solution
$ 814.72
216.40
+ 87.32
$1118.44

The total bill for the three services is $1118.44.

b. Strategy To estimate the total bill, round each number to the nearest 100, and then add the rounded numbers.

Solution
$ 814.72 ≈ $ 800
216.40 ≈ 200
+ 87.32 ≈ 100
$1100

The estimated amount of the three payments is $1100.

23. Strategy To find the length of the shaft, add the three measures on the shaft (1.87, 1.63, and 2.15 inches).

Solution
1.87
1.63
+ 2.15
5.65

The total length of the shaft is 5.65 inches.

24. Strategy To find the length of the shaft, add the three measures on the shaft (0.53 foot, 2.3 feet, and 1.52 feet).

Solution
0.53
2.3
+ 1.52
4.35

The total length of the shaft is 4.35 feet.

25. Strategy To find the amount in your checking account:

- Find the total amount of the four deposits ($210.98 + $45.32 + $1236.34 +$27.99).
- Add the total of the deposits to the previous balance ($2143.57).

Solution
$ 210.98
45.32
1236.34
+ 27.99
$1520.63

$1520.63
+ 2143.57
$3664.20

The amount in the checking account is $3664.20.

26. Strategy To find the perimeter of the triangle, add the three sides (4.9, 6.1, and 7.5 meters).

Solution
4.9
6.1
+ 7.5
18.5

The perimeter of the triangle is 18.5 meters.

27. Strategy To find total projected populations of Asia and Africa in 2050, add the expected population of Asia (5.3 billion) to the expected population of Africa (1.8 billion).

Solution
5.3
+ 1.8
7.1

The combined populations of Asia and Africa in 2050 are expected to be 7.1 billion people.

28. Strategy To find how many self-employed people earn less than $50,000, add the numbers of people from the chart who make less than $50,000 (5.1, 3.9, and 1.6 million).

Solution
5.1 Less than $5000
3.9 $5000 – $24,999
+ 1.6 $25,000 – $49,999
10.6

The number of self-employed people who earn less than $50,000 is 10.6 million.

29. Strategy To find how many self-employed people earn more than $5000, add the numbers of people from the chart who make more than $5000 (3.9, 1.6, and 1.0 million).

Solution

3.9	$5000–$24,999
1.6	$25,000–$49,999
+1.0	$50,000 or more
6.5	

The number of self-employed people who earn more than $5000 is 6.5 million.

30. Strategy To find the total number of people who are self-employed, add all the amounts from the chart (5.1, 3.9, 1.6, and 1.0 million).

Solution

5.1	Less than $5000
3.9	$5000–$24,999
1.6	$25,000–$49,999
+1.0	More than $50,000
11.6	

The total number of people who are self-employed is 11.6 million.

Applying the Concepts

31.

$3.29	Raisin bran
1.49	Bread
2.59	Milk
+ 2.79	Butter
$10.16	

No, $10 is not enough.

32. Three possible answers are bread, butter, and mayonnaise; raisin bran, butter, and bread; and potatoes, cola, and mayonnaise. Other answers are possible.

33. 1.4 × 4 = 5.6

No, a 4-foot rope cannot be wrapped around the box.

Section 3.3

Objective A Exercises

1.
13
1 3 10
24.037
−18.41
5.627

2.
15
1 5 10
26.029
−19.31
6.719

3.
12 9
1 2 10 6 10 10
123.0700
− 9.4273
113.6427

4.
13 9 9
0 3 10 10 10
214.000
− 7.143
206.857

5.
15 14 9 9
0 5 4 10 10 10
16.5000
− 9.7902
6.7098

6.
12 11 9 9
0 2 1 10 10 10
13.2000
− 8.6205
4.5795

7.
18
6 8 10
235.790
− 20.093
215.697

8.
16
1 6 10
463.270
− 40.095
423.175

9.
12 9 9 14
5 2 10 10 4 10
63.0050
− 9.1274
53.8776

10.
12 9 9 13
1 2 10 10 3 10
23.0040
− 7.2175
15.7865

11.
11 9 9 9
8 1 10 10 10 10
92.0000
−19.2909
72.7091

12.
10 11 13 9
3 0 1 3 10 15
41.2405
−25.2709
15.9696

13.
9
1 10 10
0.3200
−0.0058
0.3142

14.
9
7 10 10
0.7800
−0.0073
0.7727

15.
```
   9
 2 1010
 3.005
-1.982
 1.023
```

16.
```
   9
 5 1010
 6.007
-2.734
 3.273
```

17.
```
        1015
2151    0510
352.160
- 90.994
261.166
```

18.
```
        9 9
7171  101010
872.000
- 80.753
791.247
```

19.
```
   11
 6 114
 724.32
-  69.
 655.32
```

20.
```
 1114
 514  14510
 625.460
- 77.509
 547.951
```

21.
```
   11     13
  51  1383 10
 362.3940
- 19.4672
 342.9268
```

22.
```
  10      14
  10  137410
 421.3850
- 17.5293
 403.8557
```

23.
```
     9 9
   8 101010
 19.000
-10.372
  8.628
```

24.
```
    13 9
  2 31010
 23.400
- 0.921
 22.479
```

25.
```
  9 10
 6 10010
 7.010
-2.325
 4.685
```

26.
```
  9 16
 7 10610
 8.070
-5.392
 2.678
```

27.
```
   1214
 8  2410
 19.350
- 8.967
 10.383
```

28.
```
        93.079256   ≈      93
       -66.09249    ≈     -66
Cal.:  26.986766     Est.: 27
```

29.
```
        3.7529   ≈      4
       -1.00784  ≈     -1
Cal.:  2.74506     Est.: 3
```

30.
```
        76.53902  ≈      77
       -45.73005  ≈     -46
Cal.:  30.80897     Est.: 31
```

31.
```
        9.07325  ≈      9
       -1.924    ≈     -2
Cal.:  7.14925     Est.: 7
```

Objective B Exercises

32. **Strategy** To find the amount of sales between 1:00 P.M. and 2:00 P.M., subtract the reading on the tape at 1:00 P.M. ($967.54) from the reading on the tape at 2:00 P.M. ($1437.15).

Solution
```
  $1437.15
 -  967.54
  $ 469.61
```
The amount of sales between 1:00 P.M. and 2:00 P.M. was $469.61.

33. **Strategy** To find the missing dimension, subtract 6.79 from 14.34.

Solution
```
  14.34
 - 6.79
   7.55
```
The missing dimension is 7.55 inches.

34. **Strategy** To find the missing dimension, subtract 1.72 from 4.31.

Solution
```
  4.31
- 1.72
  2.59
```
The missing dimension is 2.59 feet.

35a. **Strategy** To find the total amount of the checks written, add the three amounts ($67.92, $43.10, and $496.34).

Solution
```
  $ 67.92
    43.10
 + 496.34
  $607.36
```
The total amount of the checks is $607.36.

35b. Strategy To find the new balance in your checking account, subtract the total amount of the checks written ($607.36) from the original balance ($1029.74).

Solution
$$\begin{array}{r} \$1029.74 \\ -\ \ 607.36 \\ \hline \$\ 422.38 \end{array}$$
Your new balance is $422.38.

36. Strategy To find the price of gasoline before the increases in price:
- Find the total increase by adding the two price increases ($.07 and $.12).
- Find the original price by subtracting the total increase from the price after the increase ($1.82).

Solution
$$\begin{array}{r} \$.07 \\ +\ .12 \\ \hline \$.19 \end{array} \qquad \begin{array}{r} \$1.82 \\ -\ \ .19 \\ \hline \$1.63 \end{array}$$
The price before the increases was $1.63.

37. Strategy To find the projected increase in the annual number of births from 2003 to 2012, subtract the number of projected births in 2003 (3.98 million) from the number of projected births in 2012 (4.37 million).

Solution
$$\begin{array}{rl} 4.37 & \text{million} \\ -3.98 & \text{million} \\ \hline 0.39 & \text{million} \end{array}$$
The increase is 0.39 million births.

38. Strategy To find the increase in shares, subtract the number of shares held in January (357.448) from the number of shares held in December (439.917).

Solution
$$\begin{array}{r} 439.917 \\ -357.448 \\ \hline 82.469 \end{array}$$
Grace Herrera owned 82.469 shares more at the end of the year.

39. Strategy To find the growth in online shopping, subtract the number of households shopping online in 2000 (17.7 million) from the number of households shopping online in 2003 (40.3 million).

Solution
$$\begin{array}{r} 40.3 \\ -17.7 \\ \hline 22.6 \end{array}$$
The growth in online shopping from 2000 to 2003 is 22.6 million households.

40. Strategy To find the growth in online shopping, subtract the number of households shopping online in 1998 (8.7 million) from the number of households shopping online in 2003 (40.3 million).

Solution
$$\begin{array}{r} 40.3 \\ -\ 8.7 \\ \hline 31.6 \end{array}$$
The growth in online shopping from 1998 to 2003 is 31.6 million households.

Applying the Concepts

41a. Rounding to tenths, the largest difference between a decimal and the decimal rounded to tenths is 0.05. Example: For numbers between 3.7 and 3.8,
(1) Any number between 3.7 and 3.75 (not including 3.75) is rounded to 3.7, so the largest difference is *less than* 0.05.
(2) Any number between 3.75 and 3.8 (including 3.75) is rounded to 3.8, so the largest difference is *equal to* 0.05.
Therefore, rounding to tenths, the largest amount by which the estimate of the sum of two decimals could differ from the exact sum is the sum of the largest differences for each decimal.
$0.05 + 0.05 = 0.1$.

b. For hundredths, $0.005 + 0.005 = 0.01$.

c. For thousandths, $0.0005 + 0.0005 = 0.001$.

Section 3.4

Objective A Exercises

1. $\begin{array}{r} 0.9 \\ \times\ 0.4 \\ \hline 0.36 \end{array}$

2. $\begin{array}{r} 0.7 \\ \times\ 0.9 \\ \hline 0.63 \end{array}$

3. $\begin{array}{r} 0.5 \\ \times\ 0.6 \\ \hline 0.30 \end{array}$

4. $\begin{array}{r} 0.3 \\ \times\ 0.7 \\ \hline 0.21 \end{array}$

5. $\begin{array}{r} 0.5 \\ \times\ 0.5 \\ \hline 0.25 \end{array}$

6. $\begin{array}{r} 0.7 \\ \times\ 0.7 \\ \hline 0.49 \end{array}$

7. $\begin{array}{r} 0.9 \\ \times\ 0.5 \\ \hline 0.45 \end{array}$

8. $\begin{array}{r} 0.2 \\ \times\ 0.6 \\ \hline 0.12 \end{array}$

9. $\begin{array}{r} 7.7 \\ \times\ 0.9 \\ \hline 6.93 \end{array}$

10. $\begin{array}{r} 3.4 \\ \times\ 0.4 \\ \hline 1.36 \end{array}$

11. $\begin{array}{r} 9.2 \\ \times\ 0.2 \\ \hline 1.84 \end{array}$

12. $\begin{array}{r} 2.6 \\ \times\ 0.7 \\ \hline 1.82 \end{array}$

13. $\begin{array}{r} 7.2 \\ \times\ 0.6 \\ \hline 4.32 \end{array}$

14. $\begin{array}{r} 6.8 \\ \times\ 0.4 \\ \hline 2.72 \end{array}$

15. $\begin{array}{r} 7.4 \\ \times\ 0.1 \\ \hline 0.74 \end{array}$

16. $\begin{array}{r} 3.8 \\ \times\ 0.1 \\ \hline 0.38 \end{array}$

17. $\begin{array}{r} 7.9 \\ \times\ 5 \\ \hline 39.5 \end{array}$

18. $\begin{array}{r} 9.3 \\ \times\ 7 \\ \hline 65.1 \end{array}$

19. $\begin{array}{r} 0.68 \\ \times\ 4 \\ \hline 2.72 \end{array}$

20. $\begin{array}{r} 0.83 \\ \times\ 9 \\ \hline 7.47 \end{array}$

21. $\begin{array}{r} 0.67 \\ \times\ 0.9 \\ \hline 0.603 \end{array}$

22. $\begin{array}{r} 0.84 \\ \times\ 0.3 \\ \hline 0.252 \end{array}$

23. $\begin{array}{r} 0.16 \\ \times\ 0.6 \\ \hline 0.096 \end{array}$

24. $\begin{array}{r} 0.47 \\ \times\ 0.8 \\ \hline 0.376 \end{array}$

25. $\begin{array}{r} 2.5 \\ \times\ 5.4 \\ \hline 13.50 \end{array}$

26. $\begin{array}{r} 3.9 \\ \times\ 1.9 \\ \hline 7.41 \end{array}$

27. $\begin{array}{r} 8.4 \\ \times\ 9.5 \\ \hline 79.80 \end{array}$

28. $\begin{array}{r} 7.6 \\ \times\ 5.8 \\ \hline 44.08 \end{array}$

29. $\begin{array}{r} 0.83 \\ \times\ 5.2 \\ \hline 166 \\ 415 \\ \hline 4.316 \end{array}$

30. $\begin{array}{r} 0.24 \\ \times\ 2.7 \\ \hline 168 \\ 48 \\ \hline 0.648 \end{array}$

31. $\begin{array}{r} 0.46 \\ \times\ 3.9 \\ \hline 414 \\ 138 \\ \hline 1.794 \end{array}$

32. $\begin{array}{r} 0.78 \\ \times\ 6.8 \\ \hline 624 \\ 468 \\ \hline 5.304 \end{array}$

33. $\begin{array}{r} 0.2 \\ \times\ 0.3 \\ \hline 0.06 \end{array}$

34. $\begin{array}{r} 0.3 \\ \times\ 0.3 \\ \hline 0.09 \end{array}$

35. $\begin{array}{r} 0.24 \\ \times\ 0.3 \\ \hline 0.072 \end{array}$

36. $\begin{array}{r} 0.17 \\ \times\ 0.5 \\ \hline 0.085 \end{array}$

37. $\begin{array}{r} 1.47 \\ \times\ 0.09 \\ \hline 0.1323 \end{array}$

38. $\begin{array}{r} 6.37 \\ \times\ 0.05 \\ \hline 0.3185 \end{array}$

39. $\begin{array}{r} 8.92 \\ \times\ 0.004 \\ \hline 0.03568 \end{array}$

40. $\begin{array}{r} 6.75 \\ \times\ 0.007 \\ \hline 0.04725 \end{array}$

41. $\begin{array}{r} 0.49 \\ \times\ 0.16 \\ \hline 294 \\ 49 \\ \hline 0.0784 \end{array}$

42. $\begin{array}{r} 0.38 \\ \times\ 0.21 \\ \hline 38 \\ 76 \\ \hline 0.0798 \end{array}$

43. $\begin{array}{r} 7.6 \\ \times\ 0.01 \\ \hline 0.076 \end{array}$

44. $\begin{array}{r} 5.1 \\ \times\ 0.01 \\ \hline 0.051 \end{array}$

45. $\begin{array}{r} 8.62 \\ \times\ 4 \\ \hline 34.48 \end{array}$

46. $\begin{array}{r} 5.83 \\ \times\ 7 \\ \hline 40.81 \end{array}$

47. $\begin{array}{r} 64.5 \\ \times\ 9 \\ \hline 580.5 \end{array}$

48. $\begin{array}{r} 37.8 \\ \times\ 8 \\ \hline 302.4 \end{array}$

49. $\begin{array}{r} 2.19 \\ \times\ 9.2 \\ \hline 438 \\ 1971 \\ \hline 20.148 \end{array}$

50. $\begin{array}{r} 1.25 \\ \times\ 5.6 \\ \hline 750 \\ 625 \\ \hline 7.000 \end{array}$

51. $$\begin{array}{r} 1.85 \\ \times\ 0.023 \\ \hline 555 \\ 370 \\ \hline 0.04255 \end{array}$$

52. $$\begin{array}{r} 37.8 \\ \times\ 0.052 \\ \hline 756 \\ 1890 \\ \hline 1.9656 \end{array}$$

53. $$\begin{array}{r} 0.478 \\ \times\ 0.37 \\ \hline 3346 \\ 1434 \\ \hline 0.17686 \end{array}$$

54. $$\begin{array}{r} 0.526 \\ \times\ 0.22 \\ \hline 1052 \\ 1052 \\ \hline 0.11572 \end{array}$$

55. $$\begin{array}{r} 48.3 \\ \times\ 0.0041 \\ \hline 483 \\ 1932 \\ \hline 0.19803 \end{array}$$

56. $$\begin{array}{r} 67.2 \\ \times\ 0.0086 \\ \hline 4032 \\ 5376 \\ \hline 0.57792 \end{array}$$

57. $$\begin{array}{r} 2.437 \\ \times\ 6.1 \\ \hline 2437 \\ 14622 \\ \hline 14.8657 \end{array}$$

58. $$\begin{array}{r} 4.237 \\ \times\ 0.54 \\ \hline 16948 \\ 21185 \\ \hline 2.28798 \end{array}$$

59. $$\begin{array}{r} 0.413 \\ \times\ 0.0016 \\ \hline 2478 \\ 413 \\ \hline 0.0006608 \end{array}$$

60. $$\begin{array}{r} 0.517 \\ \times\ 0.0029 \\ \hline 4653 \\ 1034 \\ \hline 0.0014993 \end{array}$$

61. $$\begin{array}{r} 94.73 \\ \times\ 0.57 \\ \hline 66311 \\ 47365 \\ \hline 53.9961 \end{array}$$

62. $$\begin{array}{r} 89.23 \\ \times\ 0.62 \\ \hline 17846 \\ 53538 \\ \hline 55.3226 \end{array}$$

63. $$\begin{array}{r} 8.005 \\ \times\ 0.067 \\ \hline 56035 \\ 48030 \\ \hline 0.536335 \end{array}$$

64. $$\begin{array}{r} 9.032 \\ \times\ 0.019 \\ \hline 81288 \\ 9032 \\ \hline 0.171608 \end{array}$$

65. $$\begin{array}{r} 4.29 \\ \times\ 0.1 \\ \hline 0.429 \end{array}$$

66. $$\begin{array}{r} 6.78 \\ \times\ 0.1 \\ \hline 0.678 \end{array}$$

67. $$\begin{array}{r} 5.29 \\ \times\ 0.4 \\ \hline 2.116 \end{array}$$

68. $$\begin{array}{r} 6.78 \\ \times\ 0.5 \\ \hline 3.390 \end{array}$$

69. $$\begin{array}{r} 0.68 \\ \times\ 0.7 \\ \hline 0.476 \end{array}$$

70. $$\begin{array}{r} 0.56 \\ \times\ 0.9 \\ \hline 0.504 \end{array}$$

71. $$\begin{array}{r} 1.4 \\ \times\ 0.73 \\ \hline 42 \\ 98 \\ \hline 1.022 \end{array}$$

72. $$\begin{array}{r} 6.3 \\ \times\ 0.37 \\ \hline 441 \\ 189 \\ \hline 2.331 \end{array}$$

73. $$\begin{array}{r} 5.2 \\ \times\ 7.3 \\ \hline 156 \\ 364 \\ \hline 37.96 \end{array}$$

74. $$\begin{array}{r} 7.4 \\ \times\ 2.9 \\ \hline 666 \\ 148 \\ \hline 21.46 \end{array}$$

75. $$\begin{array}{r} 3.8 \\ \times\ 0.61 \\ \hline 38 \\ 228 \\ \hline 2.318 \end{array}$$

76. $$\begin{array}{r} 7.2 \\ \times\ 0.72 \\ \hline 144 \\ 504 \\ \hline 5.184 \end{array}$$

77. $0.32 \times 10 = 3.2$

78. $6.93 \times 10 = 69.3$

79. $0.065 \times 100 = 6.5$

80. $0.039 \times 100 = 3.9$

81. $6.2856 \times 1000 = 6285.6$

82. $3.2954 \times 1000 = 3295.4$

83. $3.2 \times 1000 = 3200$

84. $0.006 \times 10{,}000 = 60$

85. $3.57 \times 10{,}000 = 35{,}700$

86. $8.52 \times 10^1 = 85.2$

87. $0.63 \times 10^1 = 6.3$

88. $82.9 \times 10^2 = 8290$

89. $0.039 \times 10^2 = 3.9$

90. $6.8 \times 10^3 = 6800$

91. $4.9 \times 10^4 = 49{,}000$

92. $6.83 \times 10^4 = 68{,}300$

93. $0.067 \times 10^2 = 6.7$

94. $0.052 \times 10^2 = 5.2$

95. $$\begin{array}{r} 3.45 \\ \times\ 0.0035 \\ \hline 1725 \\ 1035 \\ \hline 0.012075 \end{array}$$

96.
$$\begin{array}{r} 237 \\ \times\ 0.34 \\ \hline 948 \\ 711 \\ \hline 80.58 \end{array}$$

97.
$$\begin{array}{r} 0.00392 \\ \times\ 3.005 \\ \hline 1960 \\ 1176 \\ \hline 0.01177960 \\ \text{or } 0.0117796 \end{array}$$

98.
$$\begin{array}{r} 20.34 \\ \times\ 1.008 \\ \hline 16272 \\ 2034 \\ \hline 20.50272 \end{array}$$

99.
$$\begin{array}{r} 1.348 \\ \times\ 0.23 \\ \hline 4044 \\ 2696 \\ \hline 0.31004 \end{array}$$

100.
$$\begin{array}{r} 0.000358 \\ \times\ 3.56 \\ \hline 2148 \\ 1790 \\ 1074 \\ \hline 0.00127448 \end{array}$$

101.
$$\begin{array}{r} 23.67 \\ \times\ 0.0035 \\ \hline 11835 \\ 7101 \\ \hline 0.082845 \end{array}$$

102.
$$\begin{array}{r} 0.00346 \\ \times\ 23.1 \\ \hline 346 \\ 1038 \\ 692 \\ \hline 0.079926 \end{array}$$

103.
$$\begin{array}{r} 0.45 \\ \times 5 \\ \hline 2.25 \end{array} \qquad \begin{array}{r} 2.25 \\ \times 2.3 \\ \hline 675 \\ 450 \\ \hline 5.175 \end{array}$$

104.
$$\begin{array}{r} 23 \\ \times 0.03 \\ \hline 0.69 \end{array} \qquad \begin{array}{r} 9.45 \\ \times 0.69 \\ \hline 8505 \\ 5670 \\ \hline 6.5205 \end{array}$$

105.
$$\begin{array}{rcr} 28.5 & \approx & 30 \\ \times\ 3.2 & \approx & \times\ 3 \\ \hline \text{Cal.: } 91.2 & & \text{Est.: } 90 \end{array}$$

106.
$$\begin{array}{rcr} 86.3 & \approx & 90 \\ \times\ 4.4 & \approx & \times\ 4 \\ \hline \text{Cal.: } 379.72 & & \text{Est.: } 360 \end{array}$$

107.
$$\begin{array}{rcr} 2.38 & \approx & 2 \\ \times\ 0.44 & \approx & \times\ 0.4 \\ \hline \text{Cal.: } 1.0472 & & \text{Est.: } 0.8 \end{array}$$

108.
$$\begin{array}{rcr} 9.82 & \approx & 10 \\ \times\ 0.77 & \approx & \times\ 0.8 \\ \hline \text{Cal.: } 7.5614 & & \text{Est.: } 8 \end{array}$$

109.
$$\begin{array}{rcr} 0.866 & \approx & 0.9 \\ \times\ 4.5 & \approx & \times\ 5 \\ \hline \text{Cal.: } 3.897 & & \text{Est.: } 4.5 \end{array}$$

110.
$$\begin{array}{rcr} 0.239 & \approx & 0.2 \\ \times\ 8.2 & \approx & \times\ 8 \\ \hline \text{Cal.: } 1.9598 & & \text{Est.: } 1.6 \end{array}$$

111.
$$\begin{array}{rcr} 4.34 & \approx & 4 \\ \times\ 2.59 & \approx & \times\ 3 \\ \hline \text{Cal.: } 11.2406 & & \text{Est.: } 12 \end{array}$$

112.
$$\begin{array}{rcr} 6.87 & \approx & 7 \\ \times\ 9.98 & \approx & \times\ 10 \\ \hline \text{Cal.: } 68.5626 & & \text{Est.: } 70 \end{array}$$

113.
$$\begin{array}{rcr} 8.434 & \approx & 8 \\ \times\ 0.044 & \approx & \times\ 0.04 \\ \hline \text{Cal.: } 0.371096 & & \text{Est.: } 0.32 \end{array}$$

114.
$$\begin{array}{rcr} 7.037 & \approx & 7 \\ \times\ 0.094 & \approx & \times\ 0.09 \\ \hline \text{Cal.: } 0.661478 & & \text{Est.: } 0.63 \end{array}$$

115.
$$\begin{array}{rcr} 28.44 & \approx & 30 \\ \times\ 1.12 & \approx & \times\ 1 \\ \hline \text{Cal.: } 31.8528 & & \text{Est.: } 30 \end{array}$$

116.
$$\begin{array}{rcr} 86.57 & \approx & 90 \\ \times\ 7.33 & \approx & \times\ 7 \\ \hline \text{Cal.: } 634.5581 & & \text{Est.: } 630 \end{array}$$

117.
$$\begin{array}{rcr} 49.6854 & \approx & 50 \\ \times\ 39.0672 & \approx & \times\ 40 \\ \hline \text{Cal.: } 1941.069459 & & \text{Est.: } 2000 \end{array}$$

118.
$$\begin{array}{rcr} 2.00547 & \approx & 2 \\ \times\ 9.672 & \approx & \times\ 10 \\ \hline \text{Cal.: } 19.39690584 & & \text{Est.: } 20 \end{array}$$

119.
$$\begin{array}{rcr} 0.00456 & \approx & 0.005 \\ \times\ 0.009542 & \approx & \times\ 0.01 \\ \hline \text{Cal.: } 0.0000435152 & & \text{Est.: } 0.00005 \end{array}$$

120.
$$\begin{array}{rcr} 7.00637 & & 7 \\ \times\ 0.0128 & & \times\ 0.01 \\ \hline \text{Cal.: } 0.089681536 & & \text{Est.: } 0.07 \end{array}$$

Objective B Exercises

121. Strategy To find the cost of operating the electric motor, multiply the hourly cost ($.027) by the number of hours it is used (56).

Solution

$$\begin{array}{r} \$.027 \\ \times\ 56 \\ \hline 162 \\ 135 \\ \hline \$1.512 \end{array} \approx \$1.51$$

The motor costs $1.51 to operate.

122. Strategy To find the amount received for the cans, multiply the weight (18.75 pounds) by the cost per pound ($.75).

Solution

$$\begin{array}{r} 18.75 \\ \times\ \$.75 \\ \hline 9375 \\ 13125 \\ \hline \$14.0625 \end{array} \approx \$14.06$$

The amount received for the cans is $14.06.

123a. Strategy To estimate the amount received, round each number so that all the digits are zero except the first digit, and then multiply.

Solution

$$\begin{array}{rcr} 520 & \approx & 500 \\ \times\ \$.045 & \approx & \$.05 \\ \hline & & \$25.00 \end{array}$$

The estimated amount received is $25.00.

b. Strategy To find the payment for recycling the newspapers, multiply the number of pounds (520) by the payment per pound ($.045).

Solution

$$\begin{array}{r} 520 \\ \times\ \$.045 \\ \hline 2600 \\ 2080 \\ \hline \$23.400 \end{array}$$

The amount received was $23.40.

124. Strategy To find the perimeter of a square, multiply the length of a side (2.8 meters) by 4.

Solution

$$\begin{array}{r} 2.8 \\ \times\ 4 \\ \hline 11.2 \end{array}$$

The perimeter of the square is 11.2 meters.

125. Strategy To find the area of a square, multiply the length (6.75 feet) by the width (3.5 feet).

Solution

$$\begin{array}{r} 6.75 \\ \times\ 3.5 \\ \hline 3375 \\ 2025 \\ \hline 23.625 \end{array}$$

The area is 23.625 square feet.

126a. Strategy To find the amount of the payments, multiply the monthly payment ($399.50) by the number of payments (36).

Solution

$$\begin{array}{r} \$399.50 \\ \times\ \quad 36 \\ \hline 239700 \\ 119850 \\ \hline \$14,382.00 \end{array}$$

The amount of the payments is $14,382.

b. Strategy To find the total cost of the car, add the down payment ($5000) to the amount of the payments ($14,382).

Solution

$$\begin{array}{r} \$14,382 \\ +\ \ 5,000 \\ \hline \$19,382 \end{array}$$

The total cost of the car is $19,382.

127a. Strategy To find the amount of overtime pay, multiply the overtime rate ($43.35) by the number of hours worked (15).

Solution

$$\begin{array}{r} \$43.35 \\ \times\quad 15 \\ \hline 21675 \\ 4335 \\ \hline \$650.25 \end{array}$$

The amount of overtime pay is $650.25.

b. Strategy To find the nurse's total income for the week, add the overtime pay ($650.25) to the salary ($1156).

Solution

$$\begin{array}{r} \$\ 650.25 \\ +\ 1156.00 \\ \hline \$1806.25 \end{array}$$

The nurse's total income is $1806.25.

128. Strategy To find the total cost of renting the car:

- Find the cost of renting the car for 3 days by multiplying the daily rate ($15) by 3.
- Find the cost of the mileage by multiplying the cost per mile ($.15) by the number of miles (235).
- Find the total cost by adding the cost of the mileage to the cost of renting the car.

Solution

$$\begin{array}{r} \$15 \\ \times\ 3 \\ \hline \$45 \end{array} \qquad \begin{array}{r} \$.15 \\ \times\ 235 \\ \hline 75 \\ 45 \\ 30 \\ \hline \$35.25 \end{array} \qquad \begin{array}{r} \$45.00 \\ +\ 35.25 \\ \hline \$80.25 \end{array}$$

The total cost of renting the car is $80.25.

129. Strategy To find cost, multiply the rate for post office to addressee for up to $\frac{1}{2}$ pound ($13.65) by the number of packages (25).

Solution

$$\begin{array}{r} \$13.65 \\ \times\ 25 \\ \hline 6825 \\ 2730 \\ \hline \$341.25 \end{array}$$

The cost is $341.25.

130. Strategy To find the cost of hiring a taxi:

- Divide the distance traveled ($5\frac{1}{2}$ miles) by the increment of charge ($\frac{1}{8}$ mile).
- Find the charge for traveling the total distance by multiplying the cost ($.20) by the number of $\frac{1}{8}$-miles driven.
- Add the flat charge ($2.50) to the mileage charge.

Solution

$5\frac{1}{2} \div \frac{1}{8} = \frac{11}{2} \div \frac{1}{8} = \frac{11}{2} \times \frac{8}{1} = 44$

$44 \times (\$.20) = \$8.80$

$$\begin{array}{r} \$\ 8.80 \\ +\ 2.50 \\ \hline \$11.30 \end{array}$$

The total charge for hiring the taxi is $11.30.

131a.

$$\begin{array}{r} 2.2 \\ \times 8 \\ \hline 17.6 \\ \times 1.2 \\ \hline 352 \\ 176 \\ \hline 21.12 \end{array}$$

The total cost of grade 1 is $21.12.

b.

$$\begin{array}{r} 3.4 \\ \times\ 6.5 \\ \hline 170 \\ 204 \\ \hline 22.10 \\ \times\ 1.35 \\ \hline 11050 \\ 6630 \\ 2210 \\ \hline 29.8350 \end{array}$$

The total cost of grade 2 is $29.84.

c.

$$\begin{array}{r} 6.75 \\ \times\ 15.4 \\ \hline 2700 \\ 3375 \\ 675 \\ \hline 103.950 \\ \times\ 1.94 \\ \hline 415800 \\ 935550 \\ 103950 \\ \hline 201.66300 \end{array}$$

The total cost of grade 3 is $201.66.

d.

Grade 1	$ 21.12
Grade 2	29.84
Grade 3	+ 201.66
Total :	$252.62

The total cost is $252.62.

132a. Cost of product:

2 × 2.90	$ 5.80
1 × 5.25	5.25
3 × 6.25	18.75
4 × 3.70	+ 14.80
Total :	$44.60

Weight: $(2 \times 8) + 7 + (3 \times 8) + (4 \times 8) = 79$ oz

$\frac{79}{16} = 4\frac{15}{16} \approx 5$

5 lb to zone 4 is $8.30.

Total cost is $44.60 + $8.30 = $52.90.

b. Cost of product:

1×4.75	\$ 4.75
4×5.50	22.00
2×9.95	19.90
3×1.95	5.85
5×3.70	+ 18.50
Total :	\$71.00

Weight: 16 oz + 64 oz + 32 oz + 24 oz + 40 oz = 176oz

$\frac{176}{16} = 11$ lb

11 lb to zone 3 is \$8.60.

Total cost is \$71.00 + \$8.60 = \$79.60.

c. Cost of product:

3×5.50	\$16.50
1×9.95	9.95
2×4.80	9.60
4×1.95	7.80
1×3.70	3.70
3×1.90	+ 5.70
Total :	\$53.25

Weight: 48 oz + 16 oz + 16 oz + 32 oz + 8 oz + 24 oz = 144 oz

$\frac{144}{16} = 9$ lb

9 lb to zone 2 is \$7.80.

Total cost is \$53.25 + \$7.80 = \$61.05.

133. Car 1 $\frac{360}{367{,}921} < 0.001$

Car 2 $\frac{420}{401{,}346} > 0.001$

Car 3 $\frac{210}{298{,}773} < 0.001$

Car 4 $\frac{320}{330{,}045} < 0.001$

Car 5 $\frac{450}{432{,}989} > 0.001$

Cars 2 and 5 would fail the test.

Applying the Concepts

134a.

Quantity	Item number	Description	Unit price	Total
1	45837	Gasket set	\$174.90	\$174.90
1	29753	Ring set	\$169.99	\$169.99
8	54678	Valve	\$ 16.99	\$135.92
8	28632	Wrist pin	\$ 13.55	\$108.40
16	27345	Valve spring	\$ 9.25	\$148.00
8	34922	Rod bearing	\$ 4.69	\$ 37.52
5	41257	Main bearing	\$ 17.49	\$ 87.45
16	2871	Valve seal	\$ 1.69	\$ 27.04
1	23751	Timing chain	\$ 50.49	\$ 50.49

b. \$939.71

c. Total time spent = 7.0 + 7.5 + 6.5 + 8.5 + 9.0 = 38.5 hours

Cost of labor = 38.5 × \$46.75 = \$1799.88

d. Total cost for parts and labor = \$939.71 + \$1799.88 = \$2739.59

135. When a number is multiplied by 10, 100, 1000, 10,000, etc., the decimal point is moved as many places to the right as there are zeros in the multiple of 10. For example, the decimal point in a number multiplied by 1000 would be moved three places to the right.

136. Add the number of decimal places in each of the numbers being multiplied. The number of decimal places in the product is equal to this sum.

137. $1.3 = 1\frac{3}{10}$

$2.31 = 2\frac{31}{100}$

$$1\frac{3}{10} \times 2\frac{31}{100} = \frac{13}{10} \times \frac{231}{100} = \frac{3003}{1000} = 3\frac{3}{1000} = 3.003$$

Section 3.5

Objective A Exercises

1.
0.82
3)2.46
−24
06
− 06
0

2.
0.53
7)3.71
−35
21
− 21
0

3.
4.8
0.8.)3.8.4
−32
64
− 64
0

4.
7.7
0.9.)6.9.3
−63
63
− 63
0

5.
89.
0.7.)62.3.
−56
63
− 63
0

6.
132.
0.4.)52.8.
−4
12
−12
08
− 8
0

7.
60.
0.4.)24.0.
−24
00
− 0
0

8.
130.
0.5.)65.0.
−5
15
−15
00
− 0
0

9.
84.3
0.7.)59.0.1
−56
30
−28
21
− 21
0

10.
9.69
0.9.)8.7.21
−81
62
−54
81
− 81
0

11.
32.3
0.5.)16.1.5
−15
11
−10
15
−15
0

12.
97.
0.8.)77.6.
−72
56
−56
0

13.
5.06
0.7.)3.5.42
−35
04
− 0
42
−42
0

14.
4.06
0.6.)2.4.36
−24
03
− 0
36
−36
0

15.
1.3
6.3.)8.1.9
−63
189
−189
0

16.
2.2
3.2.)7.0.4
−64
64
−64
0

17.
0.11
3.6.)0.3.96
− 36
36
−36
0

18.
0.24
2.7.)0.6.48
− 54
108
−108
0

19.
3.8
6.9.)26.2.2
−207
552
−552
0

20.
49.8
1.7.)84.6.6
−68
166
−153
136
−136
0

21.
6.32 ≈ 6.3
8.8.)55.6.20
−528
282
−264
180
−176
4

22.
4.70 ≈ 4.7
5.4.)25.4.30
−216
383
−378
50
− 0
50

23. $0.57 \approx 0.6$
9.5.)5.4.27
−475
677
−665
12

24. $1.31 \approx 1.3$
1.4.)1.8.37
−14
43
−42
17
−14
3

25. $2.52 \approx 2.5$
7.3.)18.4.00
−146
380
−365
150
−146
4

26. $6.53 \approx 6.5$
8.1.)52.9.00
−486
430
−405
250
−243
7

27. $1.07 \approx 1.1$
0.17.)0.18.30
−17
13
−0
130
−119
11

28. $0.81 \approx 0.8$
0.47.)0.38.10
−376
50
−47
3

29. $130.64 \approx 130.6$
0.053.)6.924.00
−53
162
−159
34
−0
340
−318
220
−212
8

30. $0.301 \approx 0.30$
16)4.817
−48
01
−0
17
−16
1

31. $0.808 \approx 0.81$
8)6.467
−64
06
−0
67
−64
3

32. $0.078 \approx 0.08$
0.53.)0.04.180
−371
470
−424
46

33. $0.089 \approx 0.09$
0.72.)0.06.470
−576
710
−648
62

34. $12.727 \approx 12.73$
0.55.)7.00.00
−55
150
−110
400
−385
150
−110
400
−385
15

35. 40.70
0.95.)38.66.5
−380
66
−0
665
−665
0

36. 0.55
25.4.)13.9.70
−1270
1270
−1270
0

37. $0.456 \approx 0.46$
60.8.)27.7.380
−2432
3418
−3040
3780
−3648
132

38. $0.069 \approx 0.07$
45.6.)3.1.710
−2736
4350
−4104
246

39. $0.0190 \approx 0.019$
54)1.0280
−54
488
−486
20
−0
0

40. $0.2492 \approx 0.249$
27)6.7290
−54
132
−108
249
−243
60
−54
6

41. $0.0874 \approx 0.087$
0.5.)0.0.4370
−40
37
−35
20
−20
0

42. 0.9700 ≈ 0.970
77.8)75.4.6900
−7002
5449
−5446
30
−0
300
−0
300

43. 0.3600 ≈ 0.360
95.3)34.3.1000
−2859
5720
−5718
20
−0
200
−0
200

44. 0.1009 ≈ 0.101
2.67)0.26.9500
−267
25
−0
250
−0
2500
−2403
97

45. 0.1031 ≈ 0.103
4.72)0.48.7100
−472
151
−0
1510
−1416
940
−472
468

46. 0.0066 ≈ 0.007
17.2)0.1.1420
−1032
1100
−1032
78

47. 0.0086 ≈ 0.009
26.7)0.2.3070
−2136
1710
−1602
108

48. 4.1 ≈ 4
4)16.5
−16
05
−4
1

49. 0.9 ≈ 1
90)89.76
−810
87

50. 6.4 ≈ 6
0.3)1.9.4
−18
14
−12
2

51. 2.5 ≈ 3
0.413)1.047.8
−826
2218
−2065
153

52. 4.1 ≈ 4
0.519)2.148.0
−2076
720
−519
201

53. 1.0 ≈ 1
0.778)0.790.0
−778
120

54. 41.2 ≈ 41
0.075)3.092.0
−300
92
−75
170
−150
20

55. 56.8 ≈ 57
6.9)392.0.0
−345
470
−414
560
−552
8

56. 116.3 ≈ 116
0.075)8.729.0
−75
122
−75
479
−450
290
−225
65

57. $4.07 \div 10 = 0.407$

58. $0.039 \div 10 = 0.0039$

59. $42.67 \div 10 = 4.267$

60. $389.7 \div 100 = 3.897$

61. $1.037 \div 100 = 0.01037$

62. $237.835 \div 100 = 2.37835$

63. $8.295 \div 1000 = 0.008295$

64. $82{,}547 \div 1000 = 82.547$

65. $825.37 \div 1000 = 0.82537$

66. $8.35 \div 10^1 = 0.835$

67. $0.32 \div 10^1 = 0.032$

68. $87.65 \div 10^1 = 8.765$

69. $23.627 \div 10^2 = 0.23627$

70. $2.954 \div 10^2 = 0.02954$

71. $0.0053 \div 10^2 = 0.000053$

72. $289.32 \div 10^3 = 0.28932$

73. $1.8932 \div 10^3 = 0.0018932$

74. $0.139 \div 10^3 = 0.000139$

75. 18.42
2.4)44.2.08
−24
202
−192
100
−96
48
−48
0

76. 0.106
0.44)0.04.664
−44
26
−0
264
−264
0

77.

16.07
45)723.15
−45
273
−270
31
− 0
315
−315
0

78.

1.09
3.07.)3.34.63
−307
276
− 0
2763
−2763
0

79. $13.5 \div 10^3 = 0.0135$

80. $0.045 \div 10^5 = 0.00000045$

81. $23.678 \div 1000 = 0.023678$

82. $7.005 \div 10{,}000 = 0.0007005$

83.

0.112
0.05.)0.00.560
−5
06
− 5
10
−10
0

84.

6190.
0.02.)123.80.
−12
03
− 2
18
−18
00
− 0
0

85. Cal.: $42.42 \div 3.8 = 11.1632$
Est.: $40 \div 4 = 10$

86. Cal.: $69.8 \div 7.2 = 9.6944$
Est.: $70 \div 7 = 10$

87. Cal.: $389 \div 0.44 = 884.0909$
Est.: $400 \div 0.4 = 1000$

88. Cal.: $642 \div 0.83 = 773.4940$
Est.: $600 \div 0.8 = 750$

89. Cal.: $6.394 \div 3.5 = 1.8269$
Est.: $6 \div 4 = 1.5$

90. Cal.: $8.429 \div 4.2 = 2.0069$
Est.: $8 \div 4 = 2$

91. Cal.: $1.235 \div 0.021 = 58.8095$
Est.: $1 \div 0.02 = 50$

92. Cal.: $7.456 \div 0.072 = 103.5556$
Est.: $7 \div 0.07 = 100$

93. Cal.: $95.443 \div 1.32 = 72.3053$
Est.: $100 \div 1 = 100$

94. Cal.: $423.0925 \div 4.0927 = 103.3774$
Est.: $400 \div 4 = 100$

95. Cal.: $1.000523 \div 429.07 = 0.0023$
Est.: $1 \div 400 = 0.0025$

96. Cal.: $0.03629 \div 0.00054 = 67.2037$
Est.: $0.04 \div 0.0005 = 80$

Objective B Exercises

97. Strategy To find the number of yards per carry, divide the total number of yards (162) by the number of carries (26).

Solution

6.230 ≈ 6.23
26)162.000
−156
60
−52
80
−78
20
− 0
0

6.23 yards are gained per carry.

98. Strategy To find the mileage per gallon:

- Subtract 17,814.2 from 18,130.4 to find the number of miles driven.
- Divide the number of miles driven by the amount of gas used (12.4 gallons).

Solution

18,130.4
−17,814.2
316.2

25.5
12.4.)316.2.0
−248
682
−620
620
−620
0

The car can travel 25.5 miles on 1 gallon of gasoline.

99. Strategy To find the cost per can, divide the cost of a case ($6.79) by the number of cans in a case (24).

Solution

$$\begin{array}{r} \$.282 \approx \$.28 \\ 24\overline{)\$6.79} \\ -48 \\ 199 \\ -192 \\ 70 \\ -48 \\ 22 \end{array}$$

The cost per can is $.28.

100. Strategy To find the number of complete shelves, divide the board length (12 feet) by the length of a shelf (3.4 feet). The answer is the whole-number part of the quotient.

Solution

$$\begin{array}{r} 3. \\ 3.4\overline{)12.0} \\ -102 \\ 18 \end{array}$$

The board can be cut into 3 shelves.

101. Strategy To find the cost per mile, divide the toll ($5.60) by the number of miles (136 miles).

Solution $5.60 \div 136 = 0.041$
$0.041 \approx 0.04$
The cost per mile is $.04.

102. Strategy To find the dividend for each share, divide the total dividends ($6,090,990,120) by the number of shares (3,541,221,500).

Solution $6{,}090{,}990{,}120 \div 3{,}541{,}221{,}500 = 1.72$
The dividend for each share is $1.72.

103. Strategy To find the monthly payment, divide the yearly premium ($703.80) by 12.

Solution

$$\begin{array}{r} \$58.65 \\ 12\overline{)\$703.80} \\ -60 \\ 103 \\ -96 \\ 78 \\ -72 \\ 60 \\ -60 \\ 0 \end{array}$$

The monthly payment is $58.65.

104. Strategy To find how many times greater the number of spam messages sent daily in 2004 is than in 2000, divide the 2004 number of spam messages (8.8 billion) by the 2000 number of spam messages (2.3 billion).

Solution $8.8 \div 2.3 \approx 3.8$
The number of spam messages sent daily in 2004 is 3.8 times greater than in 2000.

105. Strategy To find how many more women than men will be enrolled at institutions of higher learning in 2010, subtract the expected number of men (7.3 million) from the expected number of women (10.2 million).

Solution

$$\begin{array}{rl} 10.2 & \text{million} \\ -\ 7.3 & \text{million} \\ \hline 2.9 & \text{million} \end{array}$$

2.9 million more women are expected to be attending institutions of higher learning in 2010.

106. Strategy To find the difference between the Army's advertising budget and the Marines' advertising budget, subtract the Marines' budget ($15.9 million) from the Army's budget ($85.3 million)

Solution

$$\begin{array}{rl} \$85.3 & \text{million} \\ -15.9 & \text{million} \\ \hline \$69.4 & \text{million} \end{array}$$

The difference is 69.4 million.

107. Strategy To find how many times greater the Army's advertising budget is than the Navy's advertising budget, divide the Army's budget ($85.3 million) by the Navy's budget ($20.5 million).

Solution $85.3 \div 20.5 \approx 4.2$
The Army's advertising budget was 4.2 times greater than the Navy's.

108. Strategy To find the total advertising budget for the four branches of the service, add the four numbers given in the table.

Solution Values given in millions.
$85.3 + 41.1 + 20.5 + 15.9 = 162.8$
The total of the advertising budgets was $162.8 million.

109. Strategy To find how many times greater the population of 85 and over is expected to be in 2030 than in 2000, divide the expected population in 2030 (8.9 million) by the population in 2000 (4.2 million).

Solution $8.9 \div 4.2 \approx 2.1$
The population of this segment is expected to be 2.1 times greater in 2030 than in 2000.

110. Strategy To find the increase in cigarette consumption from 1950 to 1990, subtract the consumption in 1950 (1.7 trillion) from the consumption in 1990 (5.4 trillion).

Solution
$$\begin{array}{rl} 5.4 & \text{trillion} \\ \underline{-1.7} & \text{trillion} \\ 3.7 & \text{trillion} \end{array}$$
The increase in consumption from 1950 to 1990 was 3.7 trillion cigarettes.

111. Strategy To find how many times greater the cigarette consumption was in 2000 then in 1960, divide the 2000 consumption (5.5 trillion) by the 1960 consumption (2.2 trillion).

Solution $5.5 \div 2.2 = 2.5$
The cigarette consumption in 2000 was 2.5 times greater than in 1960.

112. Strategy To find between which 10-year period the increase in cigarette consumption was (a) greatest (b) least, find the difference for each 10-year period and determine the appropriate 10-year period.

Solution
$2.2 - 1.7 = 0.5$ Increase from 1950 to 1960
$3.1 - 2.2 = 0.9$ Increase from 1960 to 1970
$4.4 - 3.1 = 1.3$ Increase from 1970 to 1980
$5.4 - 4.4 = 1.0$ Increase from 1980 to 1990
$5.5 - 5.4 = 0.1$ Increase from 1990 to 2000
a. The increase was greatest from 1970 to 1980.
b. The increase was least from 1990 to 2000.

113. Strategy To find the total number of acres burned in the 4 years, add the numbers given in the table.

Solution
$$\begin{array}{rl} 2.9 & \text{million} \\ 1.5 & \text{million} \\ 3.8 & \text{million} \\ \underline{1.5} & \text{million} \\ 9.7 & \text{million} \end{array}$$
A total of 9.7 million acres was burned.

114. Strategy To find how many more acres was burned in 2002 and 2003 than in 2000 and 2001:
- Add the values in the table for 2002 and 2003.
- Add the values in the table for 2000 and 2001.
- Subtract the value for 2000 and 2001 from the value for 2002 and 2003.

Solution

2002 and 2003	2000 and 2001	
3.8 million	2.9 million	5.3 million
1.5 million	1.5 million	−4.4 million
5.3 million	4.4 million	0.9 million

0.9 million more acres were burned in 2002 and 2003 than in 2000 and 2001.

Applying the Concepts

115. When a number is divided by 10, 100, 1000, 10,000, etc., the decimal point is moved as many places to the left as there are zeros in the power of 10. For example, the decimal point in a number divided by 1000 would be moved three places to the left.

116. To calculate a batting average, divide the number of hits by the number of times at bat. Round to the nearest thousandth. Nomar Garciaparra's batting average $= 190 \div 532 = 0.357$.

117. To determine where a decimal point is placed in a quotient, first move the decimal point in the divisor to make it a whole number. Then move the decimal point in the dividend the same number of places to the right. The decimal point in the quotient lines up vertically with the decimal point in the dividend.

118. $3.45 \div 0.5 = 6.9$

119. $3.46 \times 0.24 = 0.8304$

120. $6.009 - 4.68 = 1.329$

121. $0.064 \times 1.6 = 0.1024$

122. $9.876 + 23.12 = 32.996$

123. $3.0381 \div 1.23 = 2.47$

124. 5.217

125. 2.53

126. 0.025

Section 3.6

Objective A Exercises

1. $\begin{array}{r} 0.625 \\ 8\overline{)5.000} \end{array}$

2. $\begin{array}{r} 0.5833 \approx 0.583 \\ 12\overline{)7.0000} \end{array}$

3. $\begin{array}{r} 0.6666 \approx 0.667 \\ 3\overline{)2.0000} \end{array}$

4. $\begin{array}{r} 0.8333 \approx 0.833 \\ 6\overline{)5.0000} \end{array}$

5. $\begin{array}{r} 0.1666 \approx 0.167 \\ 6\overline{)1.0000} \end{array}$

6. $\begin{array}{r} 0.875 \\ 8\overline{)7.000} \end{array}$

7. $\begin{array}{r} 0.4166 \approx 0.417 \\ 12\overline{)5.0000} \end{array}$

8. $\begin{array}{r} 0.5625 \approx 0.563 \\ 16\overline{)9.0000} \end{array}$

9. $\begin{array}{r} 1.750 \\ 4\overline{)7.000} \end{array}$

10. $\begin{array}{r} 1.6666 \approx 1.667 \\ 3\overline{)5.0000} \end{array}$

11. $1\frac{1}{2} = \frac{3}{2}; \begin{array}{r} 1.500 \\ 2\overline{)3.000} \end{array}$

12. $2\frac{1}{3} = \frac{7}{3}; \begin{array}{r} 2.3333 \approx 2.333 \\ 3\overline{)7.0000} \end{array}$

13. $\begin{array}{r} 4.000 \\ 4\overline{)16.000} \end{array}$

14. $\begin{array}{r} 4.000 \\ 9\overline{)36.000} \end{array}$

15. $\begin{array}{r} 0.003 \\ 1000\overline{)3.000} \end{array}$

16. $\begin{array}{r} 0.500 \\ 10\overline{)5.000} \end{array}$

17. $7\frac{2}{25} = \frac{177}{25}; \begin{array}{r} 7.080 \\ 25\overline{)177.000} \end{array}$

18. $16\frac{7}{9} = \frac{151}{9}; \begin{array}{r} 16.7777 \approx 16.778 \\ 9\overline{)151.0000} \end{array}$

19. $37\frac{1}{2} = \frac{75}{2}; \begin{array}{r} 37.500 \\ 2\overline{)75.000} \end{array}$

20. $\begin{array}{r} 0.2083 \approx 0.208 \\ 24\overline{)5.0000} \end{array}$

21. $\begin{array}{r} 0.160 \\ 25\overline{)4.000} \end{array}$

22. $3\frac{1}{3} = \frac{10}{3}; \begin{array}{r} 3.3333 \approx 3.333 \\ 3\overline{)10.0000} \end{array}$

23. $8\frac{2}{5} = \frac{42}{5}; \begin{array}{r} 8.400 \\ 5\overline{)42.000} \end{array}$

24. $5\frac{4}{9} = \frac{49}{9}; \begin{array}{r} 5.4444 \approx 5.444 \\ 9\overline{)49.0000} \end{array}$

Objective B Exercises

25. $0.8 = \frac{8}{10} = \frac{4}{5}$

26. $0.4 = \frac{4}{10} = \frac{2}{5}$

27. $0.32 = \frac{32}{100} = \frac{8}{25}$

28. $0.48 = \frac{48}{100} = \frac{12}{25}$

29. $0.125 = \frac{125}{1000} = \frac{1}{8}$

30. $0.485 = \frac{485}{1000} = \frac{97}{200}$

31. $1.25 = 1\frac{25}{100} = 1\frac{1}{4}$

32. $3.75 = 3\frac{75}{100} = 3\frac{3}{4}$

33. $16.9 = 16\frac{9}{10}$

34. $17.5 = 17\frac{5}{10} = 17\frac{1}{2}$

35. $8.4 = 8\frac{4}{10} = 8\frac{2}{5}$

36. $10.7 = 10\frac{7}{10}$

37. $8.437 = 8\frac{437}{1000}$

38. $9.279 = 9\frac{279}{1000}$

39. $2.25 = 2\frac{25}{100} = 2\frac{1}{4}$

40. $7.75 = 7\frac{75}{100} = 7\frac{3}{4}$

41. $0.15\frac{1}{3} = \frac{15\frac{1}{3}}{100} = 15\frac{1}{3} \div 100 = \frac{46}{3} \times \frac{1}{100}$
$= \frac{46}{300} = \frac{23}{150}$

42. $0.17\frac{2}{3} = \frac{17\frac{2}{3}}{100} = 17\frac{2}{3} \div 100 = \frac{53}{3} \times \frac{1}{100} = \frac{53}{300}$

43. $0.87\frac{7}{8} = \frac{87\frac{7}{8}}{100} = 87\frac{7}{8} \div 100 = \frac{703}{8} \times \frac{1}{100} = \frac{703}{800}$

44. $0.12\frac{5}{9} = \frac{12\frac{5}{9}}{100} = 12\frac{5}{9} \div 100 = \frac{113}{9} \times \frac{1}{100} = \frac{113}{900}$

45. $7.38 = 7\frac{38}{100} = 7\frac{19}{50}$

46. $0.33 = \frac{33}{100}$

47. $0.57 = \frac{57}{100}$

48. $0.33\frac{1}{3} = \frac{33\frac{1}{3}}{100} = 33\frac{1}{3} \div 100 = \frac{100}{3} \times \frac{1}{100} = \frac{1}{3}$

49. $0.66\frac{2}{3} = \frac{66\frac{2}{3}}{100} = 66\frac{2}{3} \div 100 = \frac{200}{3} \times \frac{1}{100} = \frac{2}{3}$

Objective C Exercises

50. $0.15 < 0.5$

51. $0.6 > 0.45$

52. $6.65 > 6.56$

53. $3.89 < 3.98$

54. $2.504 > 2.054$

55. $0.025 < 0.105$

56. $\frac{3}{8} = 0.375$
$0.375 > 0.365$
$\frac{3}{8} > 0.365$

57. $\frac{4}{5} = 0.8$
$0.8 < 0.802$
$\frac{4}{5} < 0.802$

58. $\frac{2}{3} \approx 0.67$
$0.67 > 0.65$
$\frac{2}{3} > 0.65$

59. $\frac{7}{8} = 0.875$
$0.85 < 0.875$
$0.85 < \frac{7}{8}$

60. $\frac{5}{9} \approx 0.556$
$0.556 > 0.55$
$\frac{5}{9} > 0.55$

61. $\frac{7}{12} \approx 0.583$
$0.583 > 0.58$
$\frac{7}{12} > 0.58$

62. $\frac{7}{15} \approx 0.467$
$0.62 > 0.467$
$0.62 > \frac{7}{15}$

63. $\frac{11}{12} \approx 0.9167$
$0.9167 < 0.92$
$\frac{11}{12} < 0.92$

64. $\frac{1}{7} \approx 0.14$
$0.161 > 0.14$
$0.161 > \frac{1}{7}$

65. $0.623 > 0.6023$

66. $0.86 > 0.855$

67. $0.87 > 0.087$

68. $1.005 > 0.5$

69. $0.033 < 0.3$

Applying the Concepts

70. Strategy To find whether there are more individuals ages 0 to 39 or ages 40 and over:
- Add the values given on the graph for 0–19 and 20–39.
- Add the values given on the graph for 40–59, 60–79, and 80–up.
- Compare the values of there sums to determine which is larger.

Solution

80.5	million (0–19)	73.6	million (40–59)
81.6	million (20–39)	36.6	million (60–79)
162.1	million	9.2	million (80–up)
		119.4	

162.1 million > 119.4 million
There are more individuals ages 0 to 39.

71. Strategy To find whether the population ages 0 to 19 is more or less than $\frac{1}{4}$ the total population, compare the population ages 0 to 19 (80.5 million) with $\frac{1}{4}$ of the sum of the population in all the classes.

Solution

80.5 million (0–19)
81.6 million (20–39)
73.6 million (40–59)
36.6 million (60–79)
9.2 million (80–up)
281.5 million

$\frac{1}{4} \times 281.5 \text{ million} \approx 70.4 \text{ million}$

80.5 million > 70.4 million
The population ages 0 to 19 is more than $\frac{1}{4}$ of the total population.

72. Strategy To compare the population 0 to 39 with $\frac{1}{2}$ of the total population:
- Add the populations from 0 to 19 and from 20 to 39.
- Compare this number with $\frac{1}{2}$ the total population. (*Note:* The total population using the information on the graph was found to be 281.5 million in Exercise 71.)

Solution

80.5 million (0–19) $\quad \frac{1}{2}(281.5 \text{ million}) \approx 141 \text{ million}$
+81.6 million (20–39)
162.1 million
162.1 million > 141 million
The population ages 0 to 39 is more than $\frac{1}{2}$ of the total population.

73. $\frac{7}{13} = 0.538461538461\ldots$

Yes, the digits 538461 repeat.

74. No, 0.0402 rounded to hundredths is 0.04; to thousandths it is 0.040.

75. A terminating decimal ends, or stops. For example, 3.25 and 9.762104 are terminating decimals.
A repeating decimal never ends. One or more digits to the right of the decimal point repeat without end. The decimals in the Optional Student Activity for Objective 3.6C are examples of repeating decimals: 0.111..., 0.222..., 0.333..., 0.444..., etc.
A nonrepeating decimal never ends nor does it have any digits to the right of the decimal point that repeat. For example, 1.20200200020000200000... is a nonrepeating decimal.

Chapter 3 Review Exercises

1. $\begin{array}{r} 54.5 \\ 0.067\overline{)3.651.5} \\ -335 \\ 301 \\ -268 \\ 335 \\ -335 \\ 0 \end{array}$

2. $\begin{array}{r} 369.41 \\ 88.3 \\ 9.774 \\ +366.474 \\ \hline 833.958 \end{array}$

3. $0.055 < 0.1$

4. Twenty-two and ninety-two ten-thousandths

5. Given place value
0.05678235
$2 < 5$
0.05678

6. $2\frac{1}{3} = \frac{7}{3}$; $\quad 3\overline{)7.000}$ $2.333 \approx 2.33$

7. $0.375 = \frac{375}{1000} = \frac{3}{8}$

8. $\begin{array}{r} 3.42 \\ 0.794 \\ +32.5 \\ \hline 36.714 \end{array}$

9. 34.025

10. $\frac{5}{8} = 0.625,\ \frac{5}{8} > 0.62$

11. $9\overline{)7.0000}$ $0.7777 \approx 0.778$

12. $0.66\frac{2}{3} = \frac{66\frac{2}{3}}{100} = 66\frac{2}{3} \div 100 = \frac{200}{3} \div 100$
$= \frac{200}{3} \times \frac{1}{100} = \frac{2}{3}$

13. $\begin{array}{r} 27.3100 \\ -4.4465 \\ \hline 22.8635 \end{array}$

14. Given place value
7.93704
$7 > 5$
7.94

15. $\begin{array}{r} 3.08 \\ \times\ 2.9 \\ \hline 2772 \\ 616 \\ \hline 8.932 \end{array}$

16. Three hundred forty-two and thirty-seven hundredths

17. 3.06753

18. $\begin{array}{r} 34.79 \\ \times\ 0.74 \\ \hline 13916 \\ 24353 \\ \hline 25.7446 \end{array}$

19. $\begin{array}{r} 6.594 \\ 0.053\overline{)0.349.482} \\ -318 \\ 314 \\ -265 \\ 498 \\ -477 \\ 212 \\ -212 \\ 0 \end{array}$

20. $\begin{array}{r} 7.7960 \\ -2.9175 \\ \hline 4.8785 \end{array}$

21. **Strategy** To find the new balance in your checking account:
• Find the total amount of the checks by adding the check amounts ($145.72 and $88.45).
• Subtract the total check amounts from the original balance ($895.68).

Solution $\begin{array}{r} \$145.72 \\ +\ 88.45 \\ \hline \$234.17 \end{array}$ $\quad \begin{array}{r} \$895.68 \\ -\ 234.17 \\ \hline \$661.51 \end{array}$

The new balance in your account is $661.51.

22. **Strategy** To find the total number of children, add the number of children in public school (46.353 million), in private school (5.863 million), and in home-schooling (1.23 million).

Solution $\begin{array}{r} 46.353 \\ 5.863 \\ +\ 1.23 \\ \hline 53.446 \end{array}$

There are 53.446 million children in grades K–12.

23. Strategy To find the difference in the number of children, subtract the number of children in private school (5.863 million) from the number of children in public school (46.353 million).

Solution

$$\begin{array}{r} 46.353 \\ -\ 5.863 \\ \hline 40.490 \end{array}$$

There are 40.49 million more children in public school than in private school.

24. Strategy To find the amount of milk served during a 5-day school week, multiply the amount of milk served daily (1.9 million gallons) by 5 days.

Solution

$$\begin{array}{r} 1.9 \\ \times 5 \\ \hline 9.5 \end{array}$$

During a 5-day school week, 9.5 million gallons of milk are served.

25. Strategy To find how many times greater the number who drove (30.6 million) was than the number who flew (4.8 million), divide the number who drove by the number who flew.

Solution $30.6 \div 4.8 \approx 6.4$

The number who drove is 6.4 times greater than the number who flew.

Chapter 3 Test

1. $0.66 < 0.666$

2. $$\begin{array}{r} \scriptstyle 2\ 10\ 12 \\ 13.027 \\ -\ 8.940 \\ \hline 4.087 \end{array}$$

3. Forty-five and three hundred two ten-thousandths

4. $\frac{9}{13} = \quad 13\overline{)9.0000}$ $\quad 0.6923 \approx 0.692$

5. $0.825 = \frac{825}{1000} = \frac{33}{40}$

6. Given place value: 0.07395
   $5 = 5$
   0.0740

7. $0.037\overline{)0.056.9000}$ $\quad 1.5378 \approx 1.538$

$$\begin{array}{r} -37 \\ \hline 199 \\ -185 \\ \hline 140 \\ -111 \\ \hline 290 \\ -259 \\ \hline 310 \\ -296 \\ \hline 14 \end{array}$$

8. $$\begin{array}{r} 37.00300 \\ -9.23674 \\ \hline 27.76626 \end{array}$$

9. Given place value: 7.0954625
   $4 < 5$
   7.095

10. $0.006.\overline{)1.392.}$ $\quad 232.$

$$\begin{array}{r} -12 \\ \hline 19 \\ -18 \\ \hline 12 \\ -12 \\ \hline 0 \end{array}$$

11. $$\begin{array}{r} 270.93 \\ 97. \\ 1.976 \\ +\ 88.675 \\ \hline 458.581 \end{array}$$

12. **Strategy** To find the missing dimension, subtract the given length (4.86 inches) from the total length (6.23 inches).

Solution

$$\begin{array}{r} 6.23 \\ -\ 4.86 \\ \hline 1.37 \end{array}$$

The missing dimension is 1.37 inches.

13. $$\begin{array}{r} 1.37 \\ \times\ 0.004 \\ \hline 0.00548 \end{array}$$

14. $$\begin{array}{r} 62.3 \\ 4.007 \\ +189.65 \\ \hline 255.957 \end{array}$$

15. 209.07086

16. Strategy To find the amount of each payment:
- Find the total amount to be paid by subtracting the down payment ($2500) from the cost of the car ($16,734.40).
- Divide the amount remaining to be paid by the number of payments (36).

Solution

$$\begin{array}{r} \$16,734.40 \\ -\ \ 2,500.00 \\ \hline \$14,234.40 \end{array}$$

$$\begin{array}{r} \$395.40 \\ 36\overline{)\$14,234.40} \\ -108 \\ \hline 343 \\ -324 \\ \hline 194 \\ -180 \\ \hline 144 \\ -144 \\ \hline 00 \\ -\ 0 \\ \hline 0 \end{array}$$

Each payment is $395.40.

17. Strategy To find your total income, add the salary ($727.50), commission ($1909.64), and bonus ($450).

Solution

$$\begin{array}{r} \$\ 727.50 \\ 1909.64 \\ +\ \ 450.00 \\ \hline \$3087.14 \end{array}$$

Your total income is $3087.14.

18. Strategy To find the cost of the 12-minute call:
- Find the number of additional minutes charged above the 3-minute base by subtracting the base (3 minutes) from the total call length (12 minutes).
- Multiply the number of additional minutes by the rate ($.42).
- Add the charge for additional minutes to the base rate ($.85).

Solution $12 - 3 = 9$

$$\begin{array}{r} \$.42 \\ \times\ \ 9 \\ \hline \$3.78 \end{array} \qquad \begin{array}{r} \$3.78 \\ +\ .85 \\ \hline \$4.63 \end{array}$$

The cost of the call is $4.63.

19. Strategy To find average hours per year, multiply the weekly computer use by a 10th-grade student (6.7 hours) by 52 weeks.

Solution

$$\begin{array}{r} 6.7 \\ \times\ 52 \\ \hline 134 \\ 335\ \\ \hline 348.4 \end{array}$$

The yearly average computer use by a 10th-grade student is 348.4 hours.

20. Strategy To find how many more hours a 2nd-grade student uses a computer than a 5th-grade student:
- Subtract the number of hours the 5th-grade student uses the computer (4.2) from the number of hours the 2nd-grade student uses the computer (4.9).
- Multiply the difference by 52 weeks.

Solution

$$\begin{array}{r} 4.9 \\ -4.2 \\ \hline 0.7 \end{array} \qquad \begin{array}{r} 52 \\ \times\ 0.7 \\ \hline 36.4 \end{array}$$

On average a 2nd-grade student uses the computer 36.4 hours more per year than a 5th-grade student.

Cumulative Review Exercises

1.
$$\begin{array}{r} 235\ \text{r}17 \\ 89\overline{)20932} \\ -178\ \ \\ \hline 313\ \\ -267\ \\ \hline 462 \\ -445 \\ \hline 17 \end{array}$$

2. $2^3 \cdot 4^2 = 8 \cdot 16 = 128$

3. $2^2 - (7 - 3) \div 2 + 1$
$4 - 4 \div 2 + 1$
$4 - 2 + 1$
3

4.

	2	3
9 =		(3 · 3)
12 =	2 · 2	3
24 =	(2 · 2 · 2)	3

LCM = $2 \cdot 2 \cdot 2 \cdot 3 \cdot 3 = 72$

5. $\frac{22}{5} = \begin{array}{r} 4\ \text{r}2 \\ 5\overline{)22} \\ -20 \\ \hline 2 \end{array} = 4\frac{2}{5}$

6. $4\frac{5}{8} = \frac{32 + 5}{8} = \frac{37}{8}$

7. $\frac{5 \cdot 5}{12 \cdot 5} = \frac{25}{60}$

8.
$$\begin{array}{r} \frac{3}{8} = \frac{18}{48} \\ \frac{5}{12} = \frac{20}{48} \\ +\frac{9}{16} = \frac{27}{48} \\ \hline \frac{65}{48} = 1\frac{17}{48} \end{array}$$

9.
$$\begin{array}{r} 5\frac{7}{12} = 5\frac{21}{36} \\ +3\frac{7}{18} = 3\frac{14}{36} \\ \hline 8\frac{35}{36} \end{array}$$

10.
$$\begin{array}{r} 9\frac{5}{9} = 9\frac{20}{36} = 8\frac{56}{36} \\ -3\frac{11}{12} = 3\frac{33}{36} = 3\frac{33}{36} \\ \hline 5\frac{23}{36} \end{array}$$

11. $\frac{9}{16} \times \frac{4}{27} = \frac{9 \times 4}{16 \times 27} = \frac{\overset{1}{\cancel{3}} \cdot \overset{1}{\cancel{3}} \cdot \overset{1}{\cancel{2}} \cdot \overset{1}{\cancel{2}}}{\underset{1}{\cancel{2}} \cdot \underset{1}{\cancel{2}} \cdot 2 \cdot 2 \cdot \underset{1}{\cancel{3}} \cdot \underset{1}{\cancel{3}} \cdot 3} = \frac{1}{12}$

12. $2\frac{1}{8} \times 4\frac{5}{17} = \frac{17}{8} \times \frac{73}{17} = \frac{17 \cdot 73}{8 \cdot 17} = \frac{73}{8} = 9\frac{1}{8}$

13. $\frac{11}{12} \div \frac{3}{4} = \frac{11}{12} \times \frac{4}{3} = \frac{11 \cdot 4}{12 \cdot 3} = \frac{11 \cdot \overset{1}{\cancel{2}} \cdot \overset{1}{\cancel{2}}}{\underset{1}{\cancel{2}} \cdot \underset{1}{\cancel{2}} \cdot 3 \cdot 3} = \frac{11}{9} = 1\frac{2}{9}$

14. $2\frac{3}{8} \div 2\frac{1}{2} = \frac{19}{8} \div \frac{5}{2} = \frac{19}{8} \times \frac{2}{5} = \frac{19 \cdot 2}{8 \cdot 5}$

$= \frac{19 \cdot \overset{1}{\cancel{2}}}{2 \cdot 2 \cdot \underset{1}{\cancel{2}} \cdot 5} = \frac{19}{20}$

15. $\left(\frac{2}{3}\right)^2 \left(\frac{3}{4}\right)^3 = \left(\frac{2}{3} \cdot \frac{2}{3}\right)\left(\frac{3}{4} \cdot \frac{3}{4} \cdot \frac{3}{4}\right)$

$= \frac{\overset{1}{\cancel{2}} \cdot \overset{1}{\cancel{2}} \cdot \overset{1}{\cancel{3}} \cdot \overset{1}{\cancel{3}} \cdot 3}{\underset{1}{\cancel{3}} \cdot \underset{1}{\cancel{3}} \cdot \underset{1}{\cancel{2}} \cdot \underset{1}{\cancel{2}} \cdot 2 \cdot 2 \cdot 2 \cdot 2} = \frac{3}{16}$

16. $\left(\frac{2}{3}\right)^2 - \left(\frac{2}{3} - \frac{1}{2}\right) + 2$

$= \left(\frac{2}{3} \cdot \frac{2}{3}\right) - \left(\frac{4}{6} - \frac{3}{6}\right) + 2$

$= \frac{4}{9} - \frac{1}{6} + 2$

$= \frac{8}{18} - \frac{3}{18} + \frac{36}{18}$

$= \frac{41}{18} = 2\frac{5}{18}$

17. Sixty-five and three hundred nine ten-thousandths

18.
$$\begin{array}{r} {\scriptstyle 231\ 111} \\ 379.006 \\ 27.523 \\ 9.8707 \\ +\ 88.2994 \\ \hline 504.6991 \end{array}$$

19.
$$\begin{array}{r} {\scriptstyle 9\ 9\ 14} \\ {\scriptstyle 8\ 10\,10\ 4\ 10} \\ 2\cancel{9}.\cancel{0}\cancel{0}\cancel{5}\cancel{0} \\ -\ 7.9286 \\ \hline 21.0764 \end{array}$$

20.
$$\begin{array}{r} 9.074 \\ \times\ 6.09 \\ \hline 81666 \\ 544440 \\ \hline 55.26066 \end{array}$$

21.
$$\begin{array}{r} 2.1544 \approx 2.154 \\ 8.09\overline{)17.42.9630} \\ -1618 \\ \hline 1249 \\ -809 \\ \hline 4406 \\ -4045 \\ \hline 3613 \\ -3236 \\ \hline 3770 \\ -3236 \\ \hline 534 \end{array}$$

22. $\frac{11}{15} = 15\overline{)11.000}$ $\quad 0.7333 \approx 0.733$

23. $0.16\frac{2}{3} = \frac{16\frac{2}{3}}{100} = \frac{\frac{50}{3}}{100} = \frac{50}{3} \div 100 = \frac{50}{3} \times \frac{1}{100}$

$= \frac{50}{300} = \frac{1}{6}$

24. $\frac{8}{9} \approx 0.89, \frac{8}{9} < 0.98$

25. **Strategy** To find how many more vacation days are mandated in Sweden than in Germany, subtract the number of days mandated in Germany (18) from the number of days mandated in Sweden (32).

Solution
$$\begin{array}{r} 32 \\ -18 \\ \hline 14 \end{array}$$

Sweden mandates 14 days more vacation than Germany.

26. **Strategy** To find the loss needed the third month:

- Add the losses for the first two months.
- Subtract this sum from the goal (24 pounds).

Solution $9\frac{1}{2} + 6\frac{3}{4} = 9\frac{2}{4} + 6\frac{3}{4} = 15\frac{5}{4} = 16\frac{1}{4}$

pounds lost first two months

$24 - 16\frac{1}{4} = 23\frac{4}{4} - 16\frac{1}{4} = 7\frac{3}{4}$ pounds

The patient must lose $7\frac{3}{4}$ pounds the third month to achieve the goal.

27. Strategy To find your balance after you write the checks:

- Find the total of the checks written by adding the amounts of the checks ($42.98, $16.43, and $137.56).
- Subtract the total of the checks written from the original balance ($814.35).

Solution

```
 $ 42.98      $814.35
   16.43      -196.97
 +137.56      $617.38
 $196.97
```

Your checking account balance is $617.38.

28. Strategy To find the resulting thickness, subtract the amount removed (0.017 inch) from the original thickness (1.412 inches).

Solution

```
  1.412
 -0.017
  1.395
```

The resulting thickness is 1.395 inches.

29. Strategy To find the amount of income tax you paid:

- Find the amount of tax paid on profit by multiplying the profit ($64,860) by the rate (0.08).
- Add the amount of tax paid on profit to the base tax ($820).

Solution

```
 $64,860      $5188.80
 ×  0.08      + 820.00
 $5188.80     $6008.80
```

You paid $6008.80 in income tax last year.

30. Strategy To find the amount of the monthly payment:

- Find the amount to be paid in payments by subtracting the down payment ($20) from the cost ($210.96).
- Divide the amount to be paid in payments by the number of payments (8).

Solution

```
 $210.96
 -20.00
 $190.96

     $23.87
  8)$190.96
    -16
      30
    - 24
       69
     - 64
        56
       -56
         0
```

The amount of each payment is $23.87.

Chapter 4: Ratio and Proportion

Prep Test

1. $\frac{8}{10} = \frac{\overset{1}{\cancel{2}} \cdot 2 \cdot 2}{\underset{1}{\cancel{2}} \cdot 5} = \frac{4}{5}$

2. $\frac{450}{650 + 250} = \frac{450}{900} = \frac{\overset{1}{\cancel{450}}}{2 \cdot \underset{1}{\cancel{450}}} = \frac{1}{2}$

3. $15\overline{)372.0}$ = 24.8

4. $4 \times 33 = 132$
$62 \times 2 = 124$
$132 > 124$
4×33 is greater.

5. $5\overline{)20}$ = 4

Go Figure

From the third statement, we know that the order of three of the four men is either Luis, Kim, and Reggie or Reggie, Kim, and Luis. From the fourth statement, Luis is standing between Dave and Kim. So building from what we already know, the order is either Dave, Luis, Kim, and Reggie or Reggie, Kim, Luis, and Dave. From the second statement, we know that Dave is not first. Therefore, the order is Reggie, Kim, Luis, and Dave.

Section 4.1

Objective A Exercises

1. $\frac{3 \text{ pints}}{15 \text{ pints}} = \frac{3}{15} = \frac{1}{5}$
3 pints:15 pints = 3:15 = 1:5
3 pints to 15 pints = 3 to 15 = 1 to 5

2. $\frac{6 \text{ pounds}}{8 \text{ pounds}} = \frac{6}{8} = \frac{3}{4}$
6 pounds:8 pounds = 6:8 = 3:4
6 pounds to 8 pounds = 6 to 8 = 3 to 4

3. $\frac{\$40}{\$20} = \frac{40}{20} = \frac{2}{1}$
\$40:\$20 = 40:20 = 2:1
\$40 to \$20 = 40 to 20 = 2 to 1

4. $\frac{10 \text{ feet}}{2 \text{ feet}} = \frac{10}{2} = \frac{5}{1}$
10 feet:2 feet = 10:2 = 5:1
10 feet to 2 feet = 10 to 2 = 5 to 1

5. $\frac{3 \text{ miles}}{8 \text{ miles}} = \frac{3}{8}$
3 miles:8 miles = 3:8
3 miles to 8 miles = 3 to 8

6. $\frac{2 \text{ hours}}{3 \text{ hours}} = \frac{2}{3}$
2 hours:3 hours = 2:3
2 hours to 3 hours = 2 to 3

7. $\frac{37 \text{ hours}}{24 \text{ hours}} = \frac{37}{24}$
37 hours:24 hours = 37:24
37 hours to 24 hours = 37 to 24

8. $\frac{29 \text{ inches}}{12 \text{ inches}} = \frac{29}{12}$
29 inches:12 inches = 29:12
29 inches to 12 inches = 29 to 12

9. $\frac{6 \text{ minutes}}{6 \text{ minutes}} = \frac{6}{6} = \frac{1}{1}$
6 minutes:6 minutes = 6:6 = 1:1
6 minutes to 6 minutes = 6 to 6 = 1 to 1

10. $\frac{8 \text{ days}}{12 \text{ days}} = \frac{8}{12} = \frac{2}{3}$
8 days:12 days = 8:12 = 2:3
8 days to 12 days = 8 to 12 = 2 to 3

11. $\frac{35 \text{ cents}}{50 \text{ cents}} = \frac{35}{50} = \frac{7}{10}$
35 cents:50 cents = 35:50 = 7:10
35 cents to 50 cents = 35 to 50 = 7 to 10

12. $\frac{28 \text{ inches}}{36 \text{ inches}} = \frac{28}{36} = \frac{7}{9}$
28 inches:36 inches = 28:36 = 7:9
28 inches to 36 inches = 28 to 36 = 7 to 9

13. $\frac{30 \text{ minutes}}{60 \text{ minutes}} = \frac{30}{60} = \frac{1}{2}$
30 minutes:60 minutes = 30:60 = 1:2
30 minutes to 60 minutes = 30 to 60 = 1 to 2

14. $\frac{25 \text{ cents}}{100 \text{ cents}} = \frac{25}{100} = \frac{1}{4}$
25 cents:100 cents = 25:100 = 1:4
25 cents to 100 cents = 25 to 100 = 1 to 4

15. $\frac{32 \text{ ounces}}{16 \text{ ounces}} = \frac{32}{16} = \frac{2}{1}$
32 ounces:16 ounces = 32:16 = 2:1
32 ounces to 16 ounces = 32 to 16 = 2 to 1

16. $\frac{12 \text{ quarts}}{4 \text{ quarts}} = \frac{12}{4} = \frac{3}{1}$
12 quarts:4 quarts = 12:4 = 3:1
12 quarts to 4 quarts = 12 to 4 = 3 to 1

17. $\frac{3 \text{ cups}}{4 \text{ cups}} = \frac{3}{4}$
3 cups:4 cups = 3:4
3 cups to 4 cups = 3 to 4

18. $\frac{6\text{ years}}{7\text{ years}} = \frac{6}{7}$
6 years:7 years = 6:7
6 years to 7 years = 6 to 7

19. $\frac{\$5}{\$3} = \frac{5}{3}$
\$5:\$3 = 5:3
\$5 to \$3 = 5 to 3

20. $\frac{30\text{ yards}}{12\text{ yards}} = \frac{30}{12} = \frac{5}{2}$
30 yards:12 yards = 30:12 = 5:2
30 yards to 12 yards = 30 to 12 = 5 to 2

21. $\frac{12\text{ quarts}}{18\text{ quarts}} = \frac{12}{18} = \frac{2}{3}$
12 quarts:18 quarts = 12:18 = 2:3
12 quarts to 18 quarts = 12 to 18 = 2 to 3

22. $\frac{20\text{ gallons}}{28\text{ gallons}} = \frac{20}{28} = \frac{5}{7}$
20 gallons:28 gallons = 20:28 = 5:7
20 gallons to 28 gallons = 20 to 28 = 5 to 7

23. $\frac{14\text{ days}}{7\text{ days}} = \frac{14}{7} = \frac{2}{1}$
14 days:7 days = 14:7 = 2:1
14 days to 7 days = 14 to 7 = 2 to 1

24. $\frac{9\text{ feet}}{3\text{ feet}} = \frac{9}{3} = \frac{3}{1}$
9 feet to 3 feet = 9:3 = 3:1
9 feet to 3 feet = 9 to 3 = 3 to 1

Objective B Exercises

25. Strategy To find the ratio, write the ratio of housing (\$1600) to total expenses (\$4800) in simplest form.

Solution $\frac{\$1600}{\$4800} = \frac{1600}{4800} = \frac{1}{3}$

The ratio is $\frac{1}{3}$.

26. Strategy To find the ratio, write the ratio of food (\$800) to total expenses (\$4800) in simplest form.

Solution $\frac{\$800}{\$4800} = \frac{800}{4800} = \frac{1}{6}$

The ratio is $\frac{1}{6}$.

27. Strategy To find the ratio, write the ratio of utilities (\$300) to food (\$800) in simplest form.

Solution $\frac{\$300}{\$800} = \frac{300}{800} = \frac{3}{8}$

The ratio is $\frac{3}{8}$.

28. Strategy To find the ratio, write the ratio of transportation (\$600) to housing (\$1600) in simplest form.

Solution $\frac{\$600}{\$1600} = \frac{600}{1600} = \frac{3}{8}$

The ratio is $\frac{3}{8}$.

29. Strategy To find the ratio, write in simplest form the number of college freshmen playing basketball over the number of high school seniors playing basketball.

Solution $\frac{4000}{154{,}000} = \frac{2}{77}$

The ratio is $\frac{2}{77}$.

30. Strategy To find the ratio, write in simplest form the number of National Basketball Association rookies over the number of college seniors playing basketball.

Solution $\frac{50}{2800} = \frac{1}{56}$

The ratio is $\frac{1}{56}$.

31. Strategy To find the ratio, write the ratio of turns in the primary coil (40) to the number of turns in the secondary coil (480) in simplest form.

Solution $\frac{40}{480} = \frac{1}{12}$

The ratio is $\frac{1}{12}$.

32. Strategy To find the ratio, write in simplest form the ratio of the amount received for the computer (\$900) to the cost of the computer (\$2400).

Solution $\frac{\$900}{\$2400} = \frac{900}{2400} = \frac{3}{8}$

The ratio is $\frac{3}{8}$.

33a. Strategy To find the amount of the increase, subtract the original value (\$90,000) from the increased value (\$110,000).

Solution
$$\begin{array}{r} \$110{,}000 \\ -\ \ 90{,}000 \\ \hline \$20{,}000 \end{array}$$

The amount of the increase is \$20,000.

b. Strategy To find the ratio, write the ratio of the increase ($20,000) to the original value ($90,000) in simplest form.

Solution $\frac{\$20{,}000}{\$90{,}000} = \frac{20{,}000}{90{,}000} = \frac{2}{9}$

The ratio is $\frac{2}{9}$.

34a. Strategy To find the increase in cost of gasoline, subtract the lower cost ($1.35 per gallon) from the higher cost ($1.62 per gallon).

Solution

$$\begin{array}{r} \$1.62 \\ +\ 1.35 \\ \hline \$.27 \end{array}$$

The increase in price per gallon was $.27.

b. Strategy To find the ratio, write the ratio of the increase ($.27) to the original price ($1.35) in simplest form.

Solution $\frac{\$.27}{\$1.35} = \frac{27}{135} = \frac{1}{5}$

The ratio is $\frac{1}{5}$.

Applying the Concepts

35. Income = $5500 + $450 + $250 = $6200
Debts = $1200 + $300 + $450 + $250 = $2200
$\frac{\$2200}{\$6200} = \frac{11}{31}$
The ratio is $\frac{11}{31}$.

36. No, $\frac{11}{31} \approx 0.3548$, which is greater than $\frac{1}{3}$ (0.3333).

37. Income = $3400 + $83 + $650 + $34 = $4167
Debts = $1800 + $104 + $35 + $120 + $234 + $197 = $2490
No, the ratio $= \frac{\$2490}{\$4167} = \frac{830}{1389} \approx 0.5976$,
which is greater than $\frac{2}{5}$ (0.4).

38. No, the value of a ratio is not always less than 1. For example, a ratio of $8 to $4 is 2 to $1 = \frac{2}{1} = 2$, which is greater than 1.

Section 4.2

Objective A Exercises

1. $\frac{3 \text{ pounds}}{4 \text{ people}}$

2. $\frac{30 \text{ ounces}}{24 \text{ glasses}} = \frac{5 \text{ ounces}}{4 \text{ glasses}}$

3. $\frac{\$80}{12 \text{ boards}} = \frac{\$20}{3 \text{ boards}}$

4. $\frac{84 \text{ cents}}{3 \text{ bars}} = \frac{28 \text{ cents}}{1 \text{ bar}}$

5. $\frac{300 \text{ miles}}{15 \text{ gallons}} = \frac{20 \text{ miles}}{1 \text{ gallon}}$

6. $\frac{88 \text{ feet}}{8 \text{ seconds}} = \frac{11 \text{ feet}}{1 \text{ second}}$

7. $\frac{20 \text{ children}}{8 \text{ families}} = \frac{5 \text{ children}}{2 \text{ families}}$

8. $\frac{48 \text{ leaves}}{9 \text{ plants}} = \frac{16 \text{ leaves}}{3 \text{ plants}}$

9. $\frac{16 \text{ gallons}}{2 \text{ hours}} = \frac{8 \text{ gallons}}{1 \text{ hour}}$

10. $\frac{25 \text{ ounces}}{5 \text{ minutes}} = \frac{5 \text{ ounces}}{1 \text{ minute}}$

Objective B Exercises

11. $\frac{10 \text{ feet}}{4 \text{ seconds}} = 2.5 \text{ feet/second}$

12. $\frac{816 \text{ miles}}{6 \text{ days}} = 136 \text{ miles/day}$

13. $\frac{\$3900}{4 \text{ weeks}} = \$975\text{/week}$

14. $\frac{\$51{,}000}{12 \text{ months}} = \$4250\text{/month}$

15. $\frac{1100 \text{ trees}}{10 \text{ acres}} = 110 \text{ trees/acre}$

16. $\frac{3750 \text{ words}}{15 \text{ pages}} = 250 \text{ words/page}$

17. $\frac{\$131.88}{7 \text{ hours}} = \$18.84\text{/hour}$

18. $\frac{\$315.70}{22 \text{ hours}} = \$14.35\text{/hour}$

19. $\frac{628.8 \text{ miles}}{12 \text{ hours}} = 52.4 \text{ miles/hour}$

20. $\frac{388.8 \text{ miles}}{8 \text{ hours}} = 48.6 \text{ miles/hour}$

21. $\frac{344.4 \text{ miles}}{12.3 \text{ gallons}} = 28 \text{ miles/gallon}$

22. $\frac{409.4 \text{ miles}}{11.5 \text{ gallons}} = 35.6 \text{ miles/gallon}$

23. $\frac{\$349.80}{212 \text{ pounds}} = \$1.65\text{/pound}$

24. $\frac{\$11.05}{3.4 \text{ pounds}} = \$3.25\text{/pound}$

Objective C Exercises

25. Strategy To find the number of miles driven per gallon of gas, divide the total number of miles (326.6) by the total number of gallons (11.5).

Solution $11.5\overline{)326.6}$ = 28.4

The gas mileage was 28.4 miles/gallon.

26. Strategy To find the number of miles driven per hour, divide the total number of miles driven (246.6) by the number of hours (4.5).

Solution $4.5\overline{)246.6}$ = 54.8

You drove 54.8 miles/hour.

27. Strategy To find how much fuel the rocket uses in 1 minute, divide the total fuel (534,000 gallons) by the number of minutes (2.5).

Solution $2.5\overline{)534{,}000}$ = 213,600

The rocket uses 213,600 gallons/minute.

28a. Strategy To find how many Zip disks met company standards, subtract the number that did not meet company standards (122) from the total (5000).

Solution $5000 - 122 = 4878$

4878 disks met company standards.

b. Strategy To find the cost per disk of those disks that met company standards, divide the total cost ($26,536.32) by the number of disks that met company standards (4878).

Solution $4878\overline{)\$26{,}536.32}$ = $5.44

The cost was $5.44/disk.

29a. Strategy To find how many pounds of beef were packaged, subtract the waste (75 pounds) from the original weight (250 pounds).

Solution $250 - 75 = 175$

175 pounds of beef was packaged.

b. Strategy To find the cost per pound of the packaged beef, divide the total cost ($365.75) by the weight of the packaged beef (175 pounds).

Solution $175\overline{)\$365.75}$ = $2.09

The beef cost $2.09/pound.

30. Strategy To find the price per second, divide the price for a 30-second commercial ($455,700) by 30 seconds.

Solution $30\overline{)455{,}700}$ = 15,190

The price was $15,190 per second.

31a. Strategy To find the rate per minute, multiply the rate (5.6 feet per second) by 60 seconds per minute.

Solution $\frac{5.6 \text{ ft}}{1 \text{ sec}} \times \frac{60 \text{ sec}}{1 \text{ min}} = 336 \text{ ft/min}$

The camera goes through film at the rate of 336 feet/minute.

b. Strategy To find how fast the camera uses a 500-foot roll, divide the length of the roll (500 feet) by the rate that it is used (5.6 feet per second).

Solution $5.6\overline{)500}$ = 89.2

$89.2 \approx 89$

The camera uses the film at a rate of 89 seconds/roll.

32a. Strategy To find which country has the least population density, find the population density for each country by dividing the population of each country by the area of that country.

Solution $2{,}968{,}000\overline{)19{,}547{,}000}$ = 6.59

$1{,}269{,}000\overline{)1{,}045{,}845{,}000}$ = 824.15

$3{,}619{,}000\overline{)291{,}929{,}000}$ = 80.67

Australia has a population density of 6.59 people per square mile. India has a population density of 824.15 people per square mile. The United States has a population density of 80.67 people per square mile. Australia is the country with the least population density.

b. Strategy To find how many more people per square mile, use the results rounded to the nearest whole number from part a to subtract the population density of the United States (81) from the population density of India (824).

Solution

$$\begin{array}{r} 824 \\ -\ 81 \\ \hline 743 \end{array}$$

There are 743 more people per square mile in India than in the United States.

33a. Strategy To find the price of the computer hardware in euros, multiply the price ($120,000) by the euro exchange rate (0.9103 euros per U.S. dollar).

Solution $\frac{\$120{,}000}{1} \times \frac{0.9103 \text{ euros}}{\$1} = 109{,}236 \text{ euros}$

The price of the computer hardware would be 109,236 euros.

b. Strategy To find the price of a car in yen, multiply the price ($34,000) by the Japanese yen exchange rate (117 yen per U.S. dollar).

Solution $\frac{\$34{,}000}{1} \times \frac{117 \text{ yen}}{\$1} = 3{,}978{,}000 \text{ yen}$

The price of the car would be 3,978,000 yen.

Applying the Concepts

34. $34,000 per year
$2840 × 12 = 34,080
$650 × 52 = $33,800
$18 × 40 × 52 = $37,440
The job that pays $18/hour has the highest yearly income.

35. The price–earnings ratio of a company's stock is computed by dividing the current price per share of the stock by the annual earnings per share. For example, if the price–earnings ratio of a company's stock is 8.5, the price of the stock is 8.5 times the earnings per share of the stock.

Section 4.3

Objective A Exercises

1. $\frac{4}{8}$ $\frac{10}{20}$ $\quad 10 \to 8 \times 10 = 80$; $\ 20 \to 4 \times 20 = 80$
The proportion is true.

2. $\frac{39}{48}$ $\frac{13}{16}$ $\quad 13 \to 48 \times 13 = 624$; $\ 16 \to 39 \times 16 = 624$
The proportion is true.

3. $\frac{7}{8}$ $\frac{11}{12}$ $\quad 11 \to 8 \times 11 = 88$; $\ 12 \to 7 \times 12 = 84$
The proportion is not true.

4. $\frac{15}{7}$ $\frac{17}{8}$ $\quad 17 \to 7 \times 17 = 119$; $\ 8 \to 15 \times 8 = 120$
The proportion is not true.

5. $\frac{27}{8}$ $\frac{9}{4}$ $\quad 9 \to 8 \times 9 = 72$; $\ 4 \to 27 \times 4 = 108$
The proportion is not true.

6. $\frac{3}{18}$ $\frac{4}{19}$ $\quad 4 \to 18 \times 4 = 72$; $\ 19 \to 3 \times 19 = 57$
The proportion is not true.

7. $\frac{45}{135}$ $\frac{3}{9}$ $\quad 3 \to 135 \times 3 = 405$; $\ 9 \to 45 \times 9 = 405$
The proportion is true.

8. $\frac{3}{4}$ $\frac{54}{72}$ $\quad 54 \to 4 \times 54 = 216$; $\ 72 \to 3 \times 72 = 216$
The proportion is true.

9. $\frac{16}{3}$ $\frac{48}{9}$ $\quad 48 \to 3 \times 48 = 144$; $\ 9 \to 16 \times 9 = 144$
The proportion is true.

10. $\frac{15}{5}$ $\frac{3}{1}$ $\quad 3 \to 5 \times 3 = 15$; $\ 1 \to 15 \times 1 = 15$
The proportion is true.

11. $\frac{7}{40}$ $\frac{7}{8}$ $\quad 7 \to 40 \times 7 = 280$; $\ 8 \to 7 \times 8 = 56$
The proportion is not true.

12. $\frac{9}{7}$ $\frac{6}{5}$ $\quad 6 \to 7 \times 6 = 42$; $\ 5 \to 9 \times 5 = 45$
The proportion is not true.

13. $\frac{50}{2}$ $\frac{25}{1}$ $\quad 25 \to 2 \times 25 = 50$; $\ 1 \to 50 \times 1 = 50$
The proportion is true.

14. $\frac{16}{10}$ $\frac{24}{15}$ $\quad 24 \to 10 \times 24 = 240$; $\ 15 \to 16 \times 15 = 240$
The proportion is true.

15. $\frac{6}{5}$ $\frac{30}{25}$ $\quad 30 \to 5 \times 30 = 150$; $\ 25 \to 6 \times 25 = 150$
The proportion is true.

16. $\frac{16}{12}$ $\frac{20}{14}$ $\quad 20 \to 12 \times 20 = 240$; $\ 14 \to 16 \times 14 = 224$
The proportion is not true.

17. $\frac{15}{4}$ $\frac{45}{12}$ $\quad 45 \to 4 \times 45 = 180$; $\ 12 \to 15 \times 12 = 180$
The proportion is true.

18. $\frac{270}{6}$ $\frac{90}{2}$ $\quad 90 \to 6 \times 90 = 540$; $\ 2 \to 270 \times 2 = 540$
The proportion is true.

19. $\dfrac{300}{4} \quad \dfrac{450}{7}$ $\rightarrow 4 \times 450 = 1800$; $\rightarrow 300 \times 7 = 2100$
The proportion is not true.

20. $\dfrac{1}{4} \quad \dfrac{7}{28}$ $\rightarrow 4 \times 7 = 28$; $\rightarrow 1 \times 28 = 28$
The proportion is true.

21. $\dfrac{65}{5} \quad \dfrac{26}{2}$ $\rightarrow 5 \times 26 = 130$; $\rightarrow 65 \times 2 = 130$
The proportion is true.

22. $\dfrac{80}{2} \quad \dfrac{110}{3}$ $\rightarrow 2 \times 110 = 220$; $\rightarrow 80 \times 3 = 240$
The proportion is not true.

23. $\dfrac{7}{4} \quad \dfrac{42}{20}$ $\rightarrow 4 \times 42 = 168$; $\rightarrow 7 \times 20 = 140$
The proportion is not true.

24. $\dfrac{15}{3} \quad \dfrac{90}{18}$ $\rightarrow 3 \times 90 = 270$; $\rightarrow 15 \times 18 = 270$
The proportion is true.

Objective B Exercises

25.
$n \times 8 = 4 \times 6$
$n \times 8 = 24$
$n = 24 \div 8$
$n = 3$

26.
$n \times 21 = 7 \times 9$
$n \times 21 = 63$
$n = 63 \div 21$
$n = 3$

27.
$12 \times 9 = 18 \times n$
$108 = 18 \times n$
$108 \div 18 = n$
$6 = n$

28.
$7 \times n = 21 \times 35$
$7 \times n = 735$
$n = 735 \div 7$
$n = 105$

29.
$6 \times 36 = n \times 24$
$216 = n \times 24$
$216 \div 24 = n$
$9 = n$

30.
$3 \times 10 = n \times 15$
$30 = n \times 15$
$30 \div 15 = n$
$2 = n$

31.
$n \times 135 = 45 \times 17$
$n \times 135 = 765$
$n = 765 \div 135$
$n \approx 5.67$

32.
$9 \times n = 4 \times 18$
$9 \times n = 72$
$n = 72 \div 9$
$n = 8$

33.
$n \times 3 = 6 \times 2$
$n \times 3 = 12$
$n = 12 \div 3$
$n = 4$

34.
$5 \times 144 = 12 \times n$
$720 = 12 \times n$
$720 \div 12 = n$
$60 = n$

35.
$n \times 8 = 5 \times 7$
$n \times 8 = 35$
$n = 35 \div 8$
$n \approx 4.38$

36.
$4 \times 5 = n \times 9$
$20 = n \times 9$
$20 \div 9 = n$
$2.22 \approx n$

37.
$n \times 4 = 11 \times 32$
$n \times 4 = 352$
$n = 352 \div 4$
$n = 88$

38.
$3 \times n = 4 \times 8$
$3 \times n = 32$
$n = 32 \div 3$
$n \approx 10.67$

39.
$5 \times 8 = 12 \times n$
$40 = 12 \times n$
$40 \div 12 = n$
$3.33 \approx n$

40.
$36 \times n = 20 \times 12$
$36 \times n = 240$
$n = 240 \div 36$
$n \approx 6.67$

41.
$n \times 12 = 15 \times 21$
$n \times 12 = 315$
$n = 315 \div 12$
$n = 26.25$

42.
$40 \times 8 = n \times 15$
$320 = n \times 15$
$320 \div 15 = n$
$21.33 \approx n$

43.
$32 \times 3 = n \times 1$
$96 = n \times 1$
$96 \div 1 = n$
$96 = n$

44.
$5 \times n = 8 \times 42$
$5 \times n = 336$
$n = 336 \div 5$
$n = 67.2$

45. $18 \times n = 11 \times 16$
$18 \times n = 176$
$n = 176 \div 18$
$n \approx 9.78$

46. $25 \times 12 = 4 \times n$
$300 = 4 \times n$
$300 \div 4 = n$
$75 = n$

47. $28 \times n = 8 \times 12$
$28 \times n = 96$
$n = 96 \div 28$
$n \approx 3.43$

48. $n \times 120 = 30 \times 65$
$n \times 120 = 1950$
$n = 1950 \div 120$
$n = 16.25$

49. $0.3 \times 25 = 5.6 \times n$
$7.5 = 5.6 \times n$
$7.5 \div 5.6 = n$
$1.34 \approx n$

50. $1.3 \times 30 = 16 \times n$
$39 = 16 \times n$
$39 \div 16 = n$
$2.44 \approx n$

51. $0.7 \times n = 9.8 \times 3.6$
$0.7 \times n = 35.28$
$n = 35.28 \div 0.7$
$n = 50.4$

52. $1.9 \times n = 7 \times 13$
$1.9 \times n = 91$
$n = 91 \div 1.9$
$n \approx 47.89$

Objective C Exercises

53. **Strategy** To find out how many calories are in a 0.5-ounce serving of cereal, write and solve a proportion using n to represent the calories.

Solution $\frac{6 \text{ ounces}}{600 \text{ calories}} = \frac{0.5 \text{ ounces}}{n \text{ calories}}$
$6 \times n = 600 \times 0.5$
$6 \times n = 300$
$n = 300 \div 6$
$n = 50$
A 0.5-ounce serving contains 50 calories.

54. **Strategy** To find the number of miles a car will travel on 14 gallons of gas, write and solve a proportion using n to represent the number of miles.

Solution $\frac{70.5 \text{ miles}}{3 \text{ gallons}} = \frac{n \text{ miles}}{14 \text{ gallons}}$
$70.5 \times 14 = 3 \times n$
$987 = 3 \times n$
$987 \div 3 = n$
$329 = n$
The car can travel 329 miles on 14 gallons of gas.

55. **Strategy** To find out how many pounds of fertilizer are used, write and solve a proportion using n to represent the pounds of fertilizer.

Solution $\frac{2 \text{ pounds}}{100 \text{ square feet}} = \frac{n \text{ pounds}}{3500 \text{ square feet}}$
$2 \times 3500 = 100 \times n$
$7000 = 100 \times n$
$7000 \div 100 = n$
$70 = n$
Ron used 70 pounds of fertilizer.

56. **Strategy** To find out how gallons of water are required, write and solve a proportion using n to represent the gallons of water.

Solution $\frac{1 \text{ gallon}}{2 \text{ ounces}} = \frac{n \text{ gallons}}{25 \text{ ounces}}$
$1 \times 25 = 2 \times n$
$25 = 2 \times n$
$25 \div 2 = n$
$12.5 = n$
12.5 gallons of water are required.

57. **Strategy** To find the number of wooden bats produced, write and solve a proportion using n to represent the number of wooden bats.

Solution $\frac{4 \text{ alum. bats}}{15 \text{ wooden bats}} = \frac{100 \text{ alum. bats}}{n \text{ wooden bats}}$
$4 \times n = 15 \times 100$
$4 \times n = 1500$
$n = 1500 \div 4$
$n = 375$
There were 375 wooden bats produced.

58. **Strategy** To find out how many bricks it would take to build a wall 48 feet long, write and solve a proportion using n to represent the number of bricks.

Solution $\frac{20 \text{ feet}}{1040 \text{ bricks}} = \frac{48 \text{ feet}}{n \text{ bricks}}$
$20 \times n = 1040 \times 48$
$20 \times n = 49{,}920$
$n = 49{,}920 \div 20$
$n = 2496$
It would take 2496 bricks to build the 48-foot-long wall.

59. Strategy To find the distance between two cities that are 2 inches apart on the map, write and solve a proportion using n to represent the number of miles.

Solution $\frac{1.25 \text{ inches}}{10 \text{ miles}} = \frac{2 \text{ inches}}{n \text{ miles}}$

$1.25 \times n = 10 \times 2$

$1.25 \times n = 20$

$n = 20 \div 1.25$

$n = 16$

The distance is 16 miles.

60. Strategy To find the length and width on the drawing, where 1 inch equals 3 feet:

- Find the length by writing and solving a proportion using l for length.
- Find the width by writing and solving a proportion using w for width.

Solution $\frac{l}{8 \text{ inches}} = \frac{3 \text{ feet}}{1 \text{ inch}}$

$3 \times 8 = l \times 1$

$24 = l$

$\frac{w}{5 \text{ inches}} = \frac{3 \text{ feet}}{1 \text{ inch}}$

$3 \times 5 = w \times 1$

$15 = w$

a. The length is 24 feet.
b. The width is 15 feet.

61. Strategy To find the dosage for a person who weighs 150 pounds, write and solve a proportion using n to represent the number of ounces.

Solution $\frac{n}{150 \text{ pounds}} = \frac{\frac{1}{3} \text{ ounce}}{40 \text{ pounds}}$

$40 \times n = \frac{1}{3} \times 150$

$40 \times n = 50$

$n = 50 \div 40$

$n = 1.25$

1.25 ounces are required.

62. Strategy To find the monthly payment, write and solve a proportion using n to represent the monthly payment.

Solution $\frac{\$33.45}{\$2500} = \frac{n}{\$10{,}000}$

$33.45 \times 10{,}000 = 2500 \times n$

$334{,}500 = 2500 \times n$

$334{,}500 \div 2500 = n$

$133.80 = n$

The payment is $133.80 per month.

63. Strategy To find how many people in a county of 240,000 eligible voters would vote in the election, write and solve a proportion using n to represent the number of voters.

Solution $\frac{n}{240{,}000} = \frac{2}{3}$

$2 \times 240{,}000 = 3 \times n$

$480{,}000 = 3 \times n$

$480{,}000 \div 3 = n$

$160{,}000 = n$

160,000 people would vote.

64. Strategy To find how many gallons of paint would be required for a room that has 1400 square feet of wall, write and solve a proportion using n to represent the number of gallons.

Solution $\frac{n}{1400 \text{ square feet}} = \frac{1 \text{ gallon}}{400 \text{ square feet}}$

$1 \times 1400 = 400 \times n$

$1400 \div 400 = n$

$3.5 = n$

3.5 gallons would be required.

65. Strategy To find the monthly payment, write and solve a proportion using n to represent the monthly payment.

Solution $\frac{\$35.35}{\$10{,}000} = \frac{n}{\$50{,}000}$

$35.35 \times 50{,}000 = 10{,}000 \times n$

$1{,}767{,}500 = 10{,}000 \times n$

$1{,}767{,}500 \div 10{,}000 = n$

$176.75 = n$

The monthly payment is $176.75.

66. Strategy To find how many defects would be expected from a run of 25,000 circuit boards, write and solve a proportion using n to represent the number of defective circuit boards.

Solution $\frac{60 \text{ defective}}{2000 \text{ boards}} = \frac{n}{25{,}000 \text{ boards}}$

$60 \times 25{,}000 = 2000 \times n$

$1{,}500{,}000 = 2000 \times n$

$1{,}500{,}000 \div 2000 = n$

$750 = n$

750 defective boards can be expected.

67. Strategy To find how many shares of stock you own after a split, write and solve a proportion using n to represent the number of shares.

Solution

$$\frac{5}{3} = \frac{n}{240}$$
$$5 \times 240 = n \times 3$$
$$1200 = n \times 3$$
$$1200 \div 3 = n$$
$$400 = n$$

You will own 400 shares.

68. Strategy To find how many hours the students used when the administration used 200 hours, write and solve a proportion using n to represent the student hours.

Solution

$$\frac{3}{2} = \frac{n}{200}$$
$$3 \times 200 = n \times 2$$
$$600 = n \times 2$$
$$600 \div 2 = n$$
$$300 = n$$

The students used the computer 300 hours.

69. Strategy To find how much a bowling ball weighs on the moon, write and solve a proportion using n to represent the weight on the moon.

Solution

$$\frac{1}{6} = \frac{n}{16}$$
$$1 \times 16 = n \times 6$$
$$16 = n \times 6$$
$$16 \div 6 = n$$
$$2.67 = n$$

The bowling ball would weigh 2.67 pounds on the moon.

70. Strategy To find the length of the actual size door, write and solve a proportion using n to represent the length of the car door.

Solution

$$\frac{2}{5} = \frac{1.3}{n}$$
$$2 \times n = 5 \times 1.3$$
$$2 \times n = 6.5$$
$$n = 6.5 \div 2$$
$$n = 3.25$$

The length of the actual size car door would be 3.25 feet.

71. Strategy To find what dividend Carlos would receive after purchasing additional shares:

- Find the total number of shares owned by adding the original number (50) to the number purchased (300).
- Find the dividend by writing and solving a proportion using n to represent the dividend.

Solution

$$\begin{array}{r} 300 \\ +\ 50 \\ \hline 350 \text{ shares} \end{array}$$

$$\frac{n}{350 \text{ shares}} = \frac{\$153}{50 \text{ shares}}$$
$$153 \times 350 = n \times 50$$
$$53{,}550 = n \times 50$$
$$53{,}550 \div 50 = n$$
$$\$1071 = n$$

The dividend would be \$1071.

Applying the Concepts

72. From the given information, we can write the ratio of the number of Atkins books sold to the number of Grisham books sold: $\frac{100}{7.3}$. Let the unknown number of Atkins books sold be n. We'll use 20,000 for the number of Grisham books sold. The ratio $\frac{100}{7.3}$ is equal to $\frac{n}{20{,}000}$, and we can write the proportion $\frac{100}{7.3} = \frac{n}{20{,}000}$. Solve this proportion for n to determine the number of copies of Atkins book sold.

73. The fact that the number of workers per retiree is decreasing means that for each retiree drawing money out of Social Security, there are fewer and fewer workers paying into the Social Security system. In other words, fewer workers are supporting each retiree. Therefore, unless the amount paid into the system by each worker is increased or other radical changes are made, the funds to pay the Social Security benefits will be depleted.

74. To determine the average pay of a CEO in 2000, you would need to know the pay of the average factory worker in 2000. Suppose the average factory worker's pay in 2000 was \$50,000 and we let S be the average pay of a CEO in 2000. Then we can use the ratio $\frac{531}{1}$ and write the proportion $\frac{531}{1} = \frac{S}{50{,}000}$. Solve this proportion for S to determine the average pay of a CEO in 2000.

75. No, it is not possible. The sum of the fractions is $\frac{2}{5}+\frac{3}{4}=\frac{23}{20}=1\frac{3}{20}$, which is greater than 1. In order for the responses to be possible, the sum of the fractions must be 1.

76. Answers will vary. Here's an example: One 200-pound bag of fertilizer will cover 5000 square feet of lawn. How many pounds of fertilizer are required for 18,000 square feet of lawn?

Chapter 4 Review Exercises

1. $\frac{2}{9} \;\; \frac{10}{45}$ $10 \rightarrow 9 \times 10 = 90$; $45 \rightarrow 2 \times 45 = 90$
The proportion is true.

2. $\frac{\$32}{\$80}=\frac{32}{80}=\frac{2}{5}$
$32:$80 = 32:80 = 2:5
$32 to $80 = 32 to 80 = 2 to 5

3. $\frac{250 \text{ miles}}{4 \text{ hours}} = 62.5$ miles/hour

4. $\frac{8}{15} \;\; \frac{32}{60}$ $32 \rightarrow 15 \times 32 = 480$; $60 \rightarrow 8 \times 60 = 480$
The proportion is true.

5. $\frac{16}{n}=\frac{4}{17}$
$16 \times 17 = n \times 4$
$272 = n \times 4$
$272 \div 4 = n$
$68 = n$

6. $\frac{\$300}{40 \text{ hours}} = \$7.50/\text{hour}$

7. $\frac{\$8.75}{5 \text{ pounds}} = \$1.75/\text{pound}$

8. $\frac{8 \text{ feet}}{28 \text{ feet}}=\frac{8}{28}=\frac{2}{7}$
8 feet:28 feet = 8:28 = 2:7
8 feet to 28 feet = 8 to 28 = 2 to 7

9. $\frac{n}{8}=\frac{9}{2}$
$n \times 2 = 8 \times 9$
$n \times 2 = 72$
$n = 72 \div 2$
$n = 36$

10. $\frac{18}{35}=\frac{10}{n}$
$n \times 18 = 35 \times 10$
$n \times 18 = 350$
$n = 350 \div 18$
$n \approx 19.44$

11. $\frac{6 \text{ inches}}{15 \text{ inches}}=\frac{6}{15}=\frac{2}{5}$
6 inches:15 inches = 6:15 = 2:5
6 inches to 15 inches = 6 to 15 = 2 to 5

12. $\frac{3}{8} \;\; \frac{10}{24}$ $10 \rightarrow 8 \times 10 = 80$; $24 \rightarrow 3 \times 24 = 72$
The proportion is not true.

13. $\frac{\$15}{4 \text{ hours}}$

14. $\frac{326.4 \text{ miles}}{12 \text{ gallons}} = 27.2$ miles/gallon

15. $\frac{12 \text{ days}}{12 \text{ days}}=\frac{12}{12}=\frac{1}{1}$
12 days:12 days = 12:12 = 1:1
12 days to 12 days = 12 to 12 = 1 to 1

16. $\frac{5}{7} \;\; \frac{25}{35}$ $25 \rightarrow 7 \times 25 = 175$; $35 \rightarrow 5 \times 35 = 175$
The proportion is true.

17. $\frac{24}{11}=\frac{n}{30}$
$24 \times 30 = n \times 11$
$720 = n \times 11$
$720 \div 11 = n$
$65.45 \approx n$

18. $\frac{100 \text{ miles}}{3 \text{ hours}}$

19. **Strategy** To find the ratio:
- Find the amount of the decrease by subtracting the current price ($24) from the original price ($40).
- Write the ratio between the decrease and the original price.

Solution $40
−24
$16

$\frac{\$16}{\$40}=\frac{16}{40}=\frac{2}{5}$

The ratio is $\frac{2}{5}$.

20. **Strategy** To find the property tax on a home valued at $320,000, write and solve a proportion using n to represent the property tax.

Solution $\frac{n}{\$320{,}000}=\frac{\$4900}{\$245{,}000}$
$4900 \times 320{,}000 = 245{,}000 \times n$
$1{,}568{,}000{,}000 = 245{,}000 \times n$
$1{,}568{,}000{,}000 \div 245{,}000 = n$
$6400 = n$

The property tax is $6400.

21. **Strategy** To find the ratio, write the ratio of the high temperature (84 degrees) to the low temperature (42 degrees).

Solution $\frac{84 \text{ degrees}}{42 \text{ degrees}}=\frac{84}{42}=\frac{2}{1}$

The ratio is $\frac{2}{1}$.

22. Strategy To find the cost per phone of the phones that did pass inspection:
- Find the number of phones that did pass inspection by subtracting the number that did not pass inspection (24) from the total (1000).
- Divide the total manufacturing cost ($36,600) by the number of phones that did pass inspection.

Solution

$$\begin{array}{r} 1000 \\ -\ 24 \\ \hline 976 \end{array}$$

$$976\overline{)\$36{,}600}\quad \$37.50$$

The cost per phone was \$37.50.

23. Strategy To find how many concrete blocks would be needed to build a wall 120 feet long, write and solve a proportion using n to represent the number of concrete blocks.

Solution

$$\frac{n}{120\text{ feet}} = \frac{448\text{ concrete blocks}}{40\text{ feet}}$$
$$n \times 40 = 120 \times 448$$
$$n \times 40 = 53{,}760$$
$$n = 53{,}760 \div 40$$
$$n = 1344$$

1344 blocks would be needed.

24. Strategy To find the ratio, write a ratio of radio advertising (\$30,000) to newspaper advertising (\$12,000).

Solution $\frac{\$30{,}000}{\$12{,}000} = \frac{30{,}000}{12{,}000} = \frac{5}{2}$

The ratio is $\frac{5}{2}$.

25. Strategy To find the cost per pound, divide the total cost (\$13.95) by the number of pounds (15).

Solution $15\overline{)\$13.95}\quad \$.93$

The turkey costs \$.93/pound.

26. Strategy To find the average number of miles driven per hour, divide the total number of miles driven (198.8) by the number of hours (3.5).

Solution $3.5\overline{)198.8}\quad 56.8$

The average was 56.8 miles/hour.

27. Strategy To find the cost of \$50,000 of insurance, write and solve a proportion using n to represent the cost.

Solution

$$\frac{n}{\$50{,}000} = \frac{\$9.87}{\$1000}$$
$$n \times 1000 = 9.87 \times 50{,}000$$
$$n \times 1000 = 493{,}500$$
$$n = 493{,}500 \div 1000$$
$$n = 493.50$$

The cost is \$493.50.

28. Strategy To find the cost per share, divide the total cost (\$3580) by the number of shares (80).

Solution $80\overline{)\$3580}\quad \$44.75$

The cost is \$44.75/share.

29. Strategy To find how many pounds of fertilizer are used on a lawn that measures 3000 square feet, write and solve a proportion using n to represent the number of pounds of fertilizer.

Solution

$$\frac{n}{3000\text{ square feet}} = \frac{1.5\text{ pounds}}{200\text{ square feet}}$$
$$n \times 200 = 1.5 \times 3000$$
$$n \times 200 = 4500$$
$$n = 4500 \div 200$$
$$n = 22.5$$

22.5 pounds of fertilizer will be used.

30. Strategy To find the ratio:
- Find the amount of the increase by subtracting the original value (\$80,000) from the increased value (\$120,000).
- Write the ratio of the amount of the increase to the original value (\$80,000).

Solution

$$\begin{array}{r} \$120{,}000 \\ -\ 80{,}000 \\ \hline \$40{,}000 \end{array}$$

$$\frac{\$40{,}000}{\$80{,}000} = \frac{40{,}000}{80{,}000} = \frac{1}{2}$$

The ratio is $\frac{1}{2}$.

Chapter 4 Test

1. $\frac{46{,}036.80}{12\text{ months}} = \$3836.40/\text{month}$

2. $\frac{40\text{ miles}}{240\text{ miles}} = \frac{40}{240} = \frac{1}{6}$

   40 miles:240 miles = 40:240 = 1:6
   40 miles to 240 miles = 40 to 240 = 1 to 6

3. $\frac{18\text{ supports}}{8\text{ feet}} = \frac{9\text{ supports}}{4\text{ feet}}$

4. $\frac{40}{125} \times \frac{5}{25}$ $\rightarrow 125 \times 5 = 625$; $\rightarrow 40 \times 25 = 1000$
The proportion is not true.

5. $\frac{12 \text{ days}}{8 \text{ days}} = \frac{12}{8} = \frac{3}{2}$
12 days:8 days = 12:8 = 3:2
12 days to 8 days = 12 to 8 = 3 to 2

6. $\frac{5}{12} = \frac{60}{n}$
$n \times 5 = 12 \times 60$
$n \times 5 = 720$
$n = 720 \div 5$
$n = 144$

7. $\frac{256.2 \text{ miles}}{8.4 \text{ gallons}} = 30.5 \text{ miles/gallon}$

8. $\frac{\$27}{\$81} = \frac{27}{81} = \frac{1}{3}$
\$27:\$81 = 27:81 = 1:3
\$27 to \$81 = 27 to 81 = 1 to 3

9. $\frac{5}{14} \times \frac{25}{70}$ $\rightarrow 14 \times 25 = 350$; $\rightarrow 5 \times 70 = 350$
The proportion is true.

10. $\frac{n}{18} = \frac{9}{4}$
$n \times 4 = 9 \times 18$
$n \times 4 = 162$
$n = 162 \div 4$
$n = 40.5$

11. $\frac{\$81}{12 \text{ boards}} = \frac{\$27}{4 \text{ boards}}$

12. $\frac{18 \text{ feet}}{30 \text{ feet}} = \frac{18}{30} = \frac{3}{5}$
18 feet:30 feet = 18:30 = 3:5
18 feet to 30 feet = 18 to 30 = 3 to 5

13. Strategy To find the dividend on 500 shares of the utility stock, write and solve a proportion using n to represent the dividend.

Solution $\frac{n}{500 \text{ shares}} = \frac{\$62.50}{50 \text{ shares}}$
$n \times 50 = 500 \times \$62.50$
$n \times 50 = 31{,}250$
$n = 31{,}250 \div 50$
$n = 625$
The dividend is \$625.

14. Strategy To find the ratio, write the ratio of the city temperature (86°) to the desert temperature (112°).

Solution $\frac{86 \text{ degrees}}{112 \text{ degrees}} = \frac{86}{112} = \frac{43}{56}$
The ratio is $\frac{43}{56}$.

15. $\frac{2421 \text{ miles}}{4.5 \text{ hours}} = 538 \text{ miles/hour}$
The plane's speed is 538 miles/hour.

16. Strategy To estimate the number of pounds of water in a college student weighing 150 pounds, write and solve a proportion using n to represent the number of pounds of water.

Solution $\frac{88 \text{ pounds water}}{100 \text{ pounds body weight}} = \frac{n}{150 \text{ pounds body weight}}$
$88 \times 150 = n \times 100$
$13{,}200 = n \times 100$
$13{,}200 \div 100 = n$
$132 = n$
The college student's body contains 132 pounds of water.

17. $\frac{\$69.20}{40 \text{ feet}} = \$1.73/\text{foot}$
The cost of the umber is \$1.73/foot.

18. Strategy To find how many ounces of medication are required for a person who weighs 175 pounds, write and solve a proportion using n to represent the ounces of medication.

Solution $\frac{\frac{1}{4} \text{ ounce}}{50 \text{ pounds}} = \frac{n}{175 \text{ pounds}}$
$\frac{1}{4} \times 175 = n \times 50$
$43.75 = n \times 50$
$43.75 \div 50 = n$
$0.875 = n$
The amount of medication required is 0.875 ounce.

19. Strategy To find the ratio of the number of games won to the total number of games played, add the number of games won (20) to the number of games lost (5) to determine the number of games played. Then write the ratio of the number of games won to the number of games played.

Solution $20 + 5 = 25$ games played
$\frac{20}{25} = \frac{4}{5}$
The ratio of the number of games won to the total number of games played is $\frac{4}{5}$.

20. Strategy To find the number of defective hard drives in the production of 1200 hard drives, write and solve a proportion using n to represent the number of defective hard drives.

Solution

$$\frac{n}{1200} = \frac{3}{100}$$
$$n \times 100 = 1200 \times 3$$
$$n \times 100 = 3600$$
$$n = 3600 \div 100$$
$$n = 36$$

36 defective hard drives are expected to be found in the production of 1200 hard drives.

Cumulative Review Exercises

1.
$$\begin{array}{r} 20{,}095 \\ -10{,}937 \\ \hline 9{,}158 \end{array}$$

2. $2 \cdot 2 \cdot 2 \cdot 2 \cdot 3 \cdot 3 \cdot 3 = 2^4 \cdot 3^3$

3.
$$\begin{aligned} 4-(5-2)^2 \div 3+2 &= 4-(-3)^2 \div 3+2 \\ &= 4-9 \div 3+2 \\ &= 4-3+2 \\ &= 1+2=3 \end{aligned}$$

4. $160 = 2 \cdot 2 \cdot 2 \cdot 2 \cdot 2 \cdot 5$

	160
2	80
2	40
2	20
2	10
2	5
5	1

5.

	2	3
9 =		3 · 3
12 =	(2 · 2)	3
18 =	2	(3 · 3)

LCM = $2 \cdot 2 \cdot 3 \cdot 3 = 36$

6.

	2	3	7
28 =	2 · 2		(7)
42 =	(2)	3	7

GCF = $2 \cdot 7 = 14$

7. $\dfrac{40}{64} = \dfrac{2 \cdot 2 \cdot 2 \cdot 5}{2 \cdot 2 \cdot 2 \cdot 2 \cdot 2 \cdot 2} = \dfrac{5}{8}$

8.
$$\begin{array}{r} 3\frac{5}{6} = 3\frac{25}{30} \\ +4\frac{7}{15} = 4\frac{14}{30} \\ \hline 7\frac{39}{30} = 8\frac{9}{30} = 8\frac{3}{10} \end{array}$$

9.
$$\begin{array}{r} 10\frac{1}{6} = 10\frac{3}{18} = 9\frac{21}{18} \\ -4\frac{5}{9} = 4\frac{10}{18} = 4\frac{10}{18} \\ \hline 5\frac{11}{18} \end{array}$$

10.
$$\begin{aligned} \frac{11}{12} \times 3\frac{1}{11} &= \frac{11}{12} \times \frac{34}{11} \\ &= \frac{11 \times 34}{12 \times 11} \\ &= \frac{\overset{1}{\cancel{11}} \cdot \overset{1}{\cancel{2}} \cdot 17}{2 \cdot \underset{1}{\cancel{2}} \cdot 3 \cdot \underset{1}{\cancel{11}}} = \frac{17}{6} = 2\frac{5}{6} \end{aligned}$$

11.
$$\begin{aligned} 3\frac{1}{3} \div \frac{5}{7} &= \frac{10}{3} \div \frac{5}{7} \\ &= \frac{10}{3} \times \frac{7}{5} \\ &= \frac{10 \cdot 7}{3 \cdot 5} = \frac{2 \cdot \overset{1}{\cancel{5}} \cdot 7}{3 \cdot \underset{1}{\cancel{5}}} = \frac{14}{3} = 4\frac{2}{3} \end{aligned}$$

12.
$$\begin{aligned} \left(\frac{2}{5}+\frac{3}{4}\right) \div \frac{3}{2} &= \left(\frac{8}{20}+\frac{15}{20}\right) \div \frac{3}{2} \\ &= \frac{23}{20} \times \frac{2}{3} \\ &= \frac{23 \times 2}{20 \times 3} = \frac{23 \cdot \overset{1}{\cancel{2}}}{2 \cdot \underset{1}{\cancel{2}} \cdot 5 \cdot 3} = \frac{23}{30} \end{aligned}$$

13. Four and seven hundred nine ten-thousandths

14. 2.09762 — *Given place value* (the 9); $7 > 5$

2.10

15. $1.9898 \approx 1.990$

$$\begin{array}{r} 1.9898 \\ 8.09)\overline{16.09.7600} \\ -\ 809 \\ \hline 8007 \\ -7281 \\ \hline 7266 \\ -6472 \\ \hline 7940 \\ -7281 \\ \hline 6590 \\ -6472 \\ \hline 118 \end{array}$$

16. $$0.06\frac{2}{3} = \frac{6\frac{2}{3}}{100} = 6\frac{2}{3} \div 100 = \frac{20}{3} \div 100$$
$$= \frac{20}{3} \times \frac{1}{100}$$
$$= \frac{20 \cdot 1}{3 \cdot 100} = \frac{1}{15}$$

17. $$\frac{25 \text{ miles}}{200 \text{ miles}} = \frac{25}{200} = \frac{1}{8}$$

18. $$\frac{87¢}{6 \text{ pencils}} = \frac{29¢}{2 \text{ pencils}}$$

19. $$\frac{250.5 \text{ miles}}{7.5 \text{ gallons of gas}} = 33.4 \text{ miles/gallon}$$

20. $$\frac{40}{n} = \frac{160}{17}$$
$$40 \times 17 = n \times 160$$
$$680 = n \times 160$$
$$680 \div 160 = n$$
$$4.25 = n$$

21. $$\frac{457.6 \text{ miles}}{8 \text{ hours}} = 57.2 \text{ miles/hour}$$
The car's speed is 57.2 miles/hour.

22. $$\frac{12}{5} = \frac{n}{15}$$
$$12 \times 15 = n \times 5$$
$$180 = n \times 5$$
$$180 \div 5 = n$$
$$36 = n$$

23. Strategy To find your new checking account balance:
- Find the total of the checks written by adding the two checks ($192 and $88).
- Subtract the total of the checks written from the original balance ($1024).

Solution
$$\begin{array}{r} \$192 \\ +\ 88 \\ \hline \$280 \end{array} \qquad \begin{array}{r} \$1024 \\ -\ 280 \\ \hline \$744 \end{array}$$
Your new balance is $744.

24. Strategy To find the monthly payment:
- Find the amount to be paid by subtracting the down payment ($5000) from the original cost ($32,360).
- Divide the amount remaining to be paid by the number of payments (48).

Solution
$$\begin{array}{r} \$32{,}360 \\ -\ 5{,}000 \\ \hline \$27{,}360 \end{array} \qquad 48\overline{)\$27{,}360}\ = \$570$$

The monthly payment is $570.

25. Strategy To find how many pages remain to be read:
- Find the number read during vacation by multiplying the total (175 pages) by $\frac{2}{5}$.
- Subtract the number of pages read during vacation from the total (175 pages).

Solution $\frac{2}{5} \times 175 = \frac{2}{5} \times \frac{175}{1} = 70$
$175 - 70 = 105$
105 pages remain to be read.

26. Strategy To find the cost per acre, divide the total cost ($84,000) by the number of acres $\left(2\frac{1}{3}\right)$.

Solution $$\$84{,}000 \div 2\frac{1}{3} = 84{,}000 \div \frac{7}{3}$$
$$= 84{,}000 \times \frac{3}{7} = \$36{,}000$$
The cost per acre was $36,000.

27. Strategy To find the amount of change:
- Find the total amount of the purchases by adding the two purchases ($22.79 and $9.59).
- Subtract the total amount of the purchases from $50.

Solution
$$\begin{array}{r} \$22.79 \\ +\ 9.59 \\ \hline \$32.38 \end{array} \qquad \begin{array}{r} \$50.00 \\ -32.38 \\ \hline \$17.62 \end{array}$$
The change was $17.62.

28. Strategy To find your monthly salary, divide your annual salary ($41,691) by 12 months.

Solution
$$\begin{array}{r} 3468.25 \\ 12\overline{)41{,}619.00} \\ \underline{-36}\phantom{{,}619.00} \\ 56 \\ \underline{-48} \\ 81 \\ \underline{-72} \\ 99 \\ \underline{-96} \\ 30 \\ \underline{-24} \\ 60 \\ \underline{-60} \\ 0 \end{array}$$
Your monthly salary is $3468.25.

29. Strategy To find how many inches will be eroded in 50 months, write and solve a proportion using n to represent the number of inches.

Solution

$$\frac{3 \text{ inches}}{6 \text{ months}} = \frac{n}{50 \text{ months}}$$
$$3 \times 50 = n \times 6$$
$$150 = n \times 6$$
$$150 \div 6 = n$$
$$25 = n$$

25 inches will erode in 50 months.

30. Strategy To find how many ounces of medication are required for a person who weighs 160 pounds, write and solve a proportion using n to represent the number of ounces.

Solution

$$\frac{n}{160} = \frac{\frac{1}{2} \text{ ounce}}{50 \text{ pounds}}$$
$$n \times 50 = \frac{1}{2} \times 160$$
$$n \times 50 = 80$$
$$n = 80 \div 50$$
$$n = 1.6$$

1.6 ounces of medication are required.

Chapter 5: Percents

Prep Test

1. $\frac{19}{100}$

2. 0.23

3. 47

4. 2850

5.
$$\begin{array}{r} 4000. \\ 0.015.\overline{)60.000.} \\ -60 \\ \hline 00 \\ -0 \\ \hline 00 \\ -0 \\ \hline 0 \end{array}$$

6. $8 \div \frac{1}{4} = \frac{8}{1} \times \frac{4}{1} = 32$

7. $\frac{5}{8} \times \frac{100}{1} = \frac{5 \cdot \overset{1}{\cancel{2}} \cdot \overset{1}{\cancel{2}} \cdot 5 \cdot 5}{\underset{1}{\cancel{2}} \cdot \underset{1}{\cancel{2}} \cdot 2} = \frac{125}{2} = 62\frac{1}{2} = 62.5$

8. $66\frac{2}{3}$

9.
$$\begin{array}{r} 1.75 \\ 16\overline{)28.00} \end{array}$$

Go Figure

a. The smallest three-digit palindrome is 101. However, any number that ends in 1 is not divisible by 2, and hence not by 6. So the numbers 111, 121, and 191 are also eliminated. The next smallest three-digit palindrome is 202, which is not divisible by 3, and neither is 212. However, 222 is divisible by 2 and 3, which means that it is a multiple of 6. So 222 is the smallest three-digit multiple of 6 that is a palindrome.

b. To use the process, add 874 and 478.
$$\begin{array}{r} 478 \\ +\ 874 \\ \hline 1352 \end{array}$$
Then add 1352 and 2531.
$$\begin{array}{r} 1352 \\ +\ 2531 \\ \hline 3883 \end{array}$$
The number 3883 is a palindrome.

Section 5.1

Objective A Exercises

1. $25\% = 25 \times \frac{1}{100} = \frac{25}{100} = \frac{1}{4}$
$25\% = 25 \times 0.01 = 0.25$

2. $40\% = 40 \times \frac{1}{100} = \frac{40}{100} = \frac{2}{5}$
$40\% = 40 \times 0.01 = 0.40$

3. $130\% = 130 \times \frac{1}{100} = \frac{130}{100} = 1\frac{3}{10}$
$130\% = 130 \times 0.01 = 1.30$

4. $150\% = 150 \times \frac{1}{100} = \frac{150}{100} = 1\frac{1}{2}$
$150\% = 150 \times 0.01 = 1.50$

5. $100\% = 100 \times \frac{1}{100} = \frac{100}{100} = 1$
$100\% = 100 \times 0.01 = 1.00$

6. $87\% = 87 \times \frac{1}{100} = \frac{87}{100}$
$87\% = 87 \times 0.01 = 0.87$

7. $73\% = 73 \times \frac{1}{100} = \frac{73}{100}$
$73\% = 73 \times 0.01 = 0.73$

8. $45\% = 45 \times \frac{1}{100} = \frac{45}{100} = \frac{9}{20}$
$45\% = 45 \times 0.01 = 0.45$

9. $383\% = 383 \times \frac{1}{100} = \frac{383}{100} = 3\frac{83}{100}$
$383\% = 383 \times 0.01 = 3.83$

10. $425\% = 425 \times \frac{1}{100} = \frac{425}{100} = 4\frac{1}{4}$
$425\% = 425 \times 0.01 = 4.25$

11. $70\% = 70 \times \frac{1}{100} = \frac{70}{100} = \frac{7}{10}$
$70\% = 70 \times 0.01 = 0.70$

12. $55\% = 55 \times \frac{1}{100} = \frac{55}{100} = \frac{11}{20}$
$55\% = 55 \times 0.01 = 0.55$

13. $88\% = 88 \times \frac{1}{100} = \frac{88}{100} = \frac{22}{25}$
$88\% = 88 \times 0.01 = 0.88$

14. $64\% = 64 \times \frac{1}{100} = \frac{64}{100} = \frac{16}{25}$
$64\% = 64 \times 0.01 = 0.64$

15. $32\% = 32 \times \frac{1}{100} = \frac{32}{100} = \frac{8}{25}$
$32\% = 32 \times 0.01 = 0.32$

16. $18\% = 18 \times \frac{1}{100} = \frac{18}{100} = \frac{9}{50}$
$18\% = 18 \times 0.01 = 0.18$

17. $66\frac{2}{3}\% = 66\frac{2}{3} \times \frac{1}{100} = \frac{200}{3} \times \frac{1}{100}$
$= \frac{200}{300} = \frac{2}{3}$

18. $12\frac{1}{2}\% = 12\frac{1}{2} \times \frac{1}{100} = \frac{25}{2} \times \frac{1}{100}$
$= \frac{25}{200} = \frac{1}{8}$

19. $83\frac{1}{3}\% = 83\frac{1}{3} \times \frac{1}{100} = \frac{250}{3} \times \frac{1}{100}$
$= \frac{250}{300} = \frac{5}{6}$

20. $3\frac{1}{8}\% = 3\frac{1}{8} \times \frac{1}{100} = \frac{25}{8} \times \frac{1}{100}$
$= \frac{25}{800} = \frac{1}{32}$

21. $11\frac{1}{9}\% = 11\frac{1}{9} \times \frac{1}{100} = \frac{100}{9} \times \frac{1}{100}$
$= \frac{100}{900} = \frac{1}{9}$

22. $\frac{3}{8}\% = \frac{3}{8} \times \frac{1}{100} = \frac{3}{800}$

23. $45\frac{5}{11}\% = 45\frac{5}{11} \times \frac{1}{100} = \frac{500}{11} \times \frac{1}{100}$
$= \frac{500}{1100} = \frac{5}{11}$

24. $15\frac{3}{8}\% = 15\frac{3}{8} \times \frac{1}{100} = \frac{123}{8} \times \frac{1}{100} = \frac{123}{800}$

25. $4\frac{2}{7}\% = 4\frac{2}{7} \times \frac{1}{100} = \frac{30}{7} \times \frac{1}{100}$
$= \frac{30}{700} = \frac{3}{70}$

26. $5\frac{3}{4}\% = 5\frac{3}{4} \times \frac{1}{100} = \frac{23}{4} \times \frac{1}{100} = \frac{23}{400}$

27. $6\frac{2}{3}\% = 6\frac{2}{3} \times \frac{1}{100} = \frac{20}{3} \times \frac{1}{100} = \frac{20}{300} = \frac{1}{15}$

28. $8\frac{2}{3}\% = 8\frac{2}{3} \times \frac{1}{100} = \frac{26}{3} \times \frac{1}{100} = \frac{26}{300} = \frac{13}{150}$

29. $6.5\% = 6.5 \times 0.01 = 0.065$

30. $9.4\% = 9.4 \times 0.01 = 0.094$

31. $12.3\% = 12.3 \times 0.01 = 0.123$

32. $16.7\% = 16.7 \times 0.01 = 0.167$

33. $0.55\% = 0.55 \times 0.01 = 0.0055$

34. $0.45\% = 0.45 \times 0.01 = 0.0045$

35. $8.25\% = 8.25 \times 0.01 = 0.0825$

36. $6.75\% = 6.75 \times 0.01 = 0.0675$

37. $5.05\% = 5.05 \times 0.01 = 0.0505$

38. $3.08\% = 3.08 \times 0.01 = 0.0308$

39. $2\% = 2 \times 0.01 = 0.02$

40. $7\% = 7 \times 0.01 = 0.07$

41. $80.4\% = 80.4 \times 0.01 = 0.804$

42. $36.2\% = 36.2 \times 0.01 = 0.362$

43. $4.9\% = 4.9 \times 0.01 = 0.049$

Objective B Exercises

44. $0.16 = 0.16 \times 100\% = 16\%$

45. $0.73 = 0.73 \times 100\% = 73\%$

46. $0.05 = 0.05 \times 100\% = 5\%$

47. $0.01 = 0.01 \times 100\% = 1\%$

48. $1.07 = 1.07 \times 100\% = 107\%$

49. $2.94 = 2.94 \times 100\% = 294\%$

50. $0.004 = 0.004 \times 100\% = 0.4\%$

51. $0.006 = 0.006 \times 100\% = 0.6\%$

52. $1.012 = 1.012 \times 100\% = 101.2\%$

53. $3.106 = 3.106 \times 100\% = 310.6\%$

54. $0.80 = 0.80 \times 100\% = 80\%$

55. $0.70 = 0.70 \times 100\% = 70\%$

56. $\frac{27}{50} = \frac{27}{50} \times 100\% = \frac{2700}{50}\% = 54\%$

57. $\frac{37}{100} = \frac{37}{100} \times 100\% = \frac{3700}{100}\% = 37\%$

58. $\frac{1}{3} = \frac{1}{3} \times 100\% = \frac{100}{3}\% \approx 33.3\%$

59. $\frac{2}{5} = \frac{2}{5} \times 100\% = \frac{200}{5}\% = 40\%$

60. $\frac{5}{8} = \frac{5}{8} \times 100\% = \frac{500}{8}\% = 62.5\%$

61. $\frac{1}{8} = \frac{1}{8} \times 100\% = \frac{100}{8}\% = 12.5\%$

62. $\frac{1}{6} = \frac{1}{6} \times 100\% = \frac{100}{6}\% \approx 16.7\%$

63. $1\frac{1}{2} = 1\frac{1}{2} \times 100\% = \frac{3}{2} \times 100\% = \frac{300}{2}\% = 150\%$

64. $\frac{7}{40} = \frac{7}{40} \times 100\% = \frac{700}{40}\% = 17.5\%$

65. $1\frac{2}{3} = 1\frac{2}{3} \times 100\% = \frac{5}{3} \times 100\% = \frac{500}{3}\% \approx 166.7\%$

66. $1\frac{7}{9} = 1\frac{7}{9} \times 100\% = \frac{1600}{9}\% \approx 177.8\%$

67. $\frac{7}{8} = \frac{7}{8} \times 100\% = \frac{700}{8}\% = 87.5\%$

68. $\frac{15}{50} = \frac{15}{50} \times 100\% = \frac{1500}{50}\% = 30\%$

69. $\frac{12}{25} = \frac{12}{25} \times 100\% = \frac{1200}{25}\% = 48\%$

70. $\frac{7}{30} = \frac{7}{30} \times 100\% = \frac{700}{30}\% = 23\frac{1}{3}\%$

71. $\frac{1}{3} = \frac{1}{3} \times 100\% = \frac{100}{3}\% = 33\frac{1}{3}\%$

72. $2\frac{3}{8} = 2\frac{3}{8} \times 100\% = \frac{19}{8} \times 100\%$
$= \frac{1900}{8}\% = 237\frac{1}{2}\%$

73. $1\frac{2}{3} = 1\frac{2}{3} \times 100\% = \frac{5}{3} \times 100\% = \frac{500}{3}\% = 166\frac{2}{3}\%$

74. $2\frac{1}{6} = 2\frac{1}{6} \times 100\% = \frac{13}{6} \times 100\%$
$= \frac{1300}{6}\% = 216\frac{2}{3}\%$

75. $\frac{7}{8} = \frac{7}{8} \times 100\% = \frac{700}{8}\% = 87\frac{1}{2}\%$

76. $\frac{1}{4}$, 0.25, 25%, $\frac{3}{4}$, 0.75, 75%

Applying the Concepts

77. **Strategy** To find the percent of those surveyed that did not name corn, cole slow, corn bread, or fries, add the percents representing these four side dishes and subtract the sum from 100%

Solution
38% Corn on the Cob
35% Cole slaw
11% Corn bread
10% Fries
94%
100% − 94% = 6%
6% of those surveyed named something other than corn on the cob, cole slaw, corn bread, or fries.

78. $\frac{1}{3} \times 100\% = 33\frac{1}{3}\%$; this represents $33\frac{1}{3}\%$ off the regular price.

79. $50\% = \frac{50}{100} = \frac{1}{2}$; this represents $\frac{1}{2}$ off the regular price.

80. $1 - \frac{2}{5} = \frac{5}{5} - \frac{2}{5} = \frac{3}{5}$
$\frac{3}{5} \times 100\% = 60\%$; 60% of the population did not vote.

81. **a.** False **b.** For example, 200% × 4 = 2 × 4 = 8

Section 5.2

Objective A Exercises

1. $0.08 \times 100 = n$
$8 = n$

2. $0.16 \times 50 = n$
$8 = n$

3. $0.27 \times 40 = n$
$10.8 = n$

4. $0.52 \times 95 = n$
$49.4 = n$

5. $0.0005 \times 150 = n$
$0.075 = n$

6. $0.00075 \times 625 = n$
$0.46875 = n$

7. $1.25 \times 64 = n$
$80 = n$

8. $2.10 \times 12 = n$
$25.2 = n$

9. $0.107 \times 485 = n$
$51.895 = n$

10. $0.128 \times 625 = n$
$80 = n$

11. $0.0025 \times 3000 = n$
$7.5 = n$

12. $0.0006 \times 250 = n$
$0.15 = n$

13. $0.80 \times 16.25 = n$
$13 = n$

14. $0.26 \times 19.5 = n$
$5.07 = n$

15. $0.015 \times 250 = n$
$3.75 = n$

16. $n = 0.0575 \times 65$
$n = 3.7375$

17. $\frac{1}{6} \times 120 = n$
$20 = n$

18. $\frac{5}{6} \times 246 = n$
$205 = n$

19. $\frac{1}{3} \times 630 = n$
$210 = n$

20. $n = \frac{2}{3} \times 891$
$n = 594$

21. $0.05 \times 95 = n$ or $0.75 \times 6 = n$
$4.75 = n$ $4.5 = n$
Because 4.75 > 4.5, 5% of 95 is larger.

22. $1.12 \times 5 = n$ or $0.0045 \times 800 = n$
$5.6 = n$ $3.6 = n$
Because 5.6 > 3.6, 112% of 5 is larger.

23. $0.79 \times 16 = n$ or $0.20 \times 65 = n$
$12.64 = n$ $13 = n$
Because 12.64 < 13, 79% of 16 is smaller.

24. $0.15 \times 80 = n$ or $0.95 \times 15 = n$
$12 = n$ $14.25 = n$
Because 12 < 14.25, 15% of 80 is smaller.

25. $0.02 \times 1500 = n$ or $0.72 \times 40 = n$
$30 = n$ $28.8 = n$
Because 28.8 < 30, 72% of 40 is smaller.

26. $0.22 \times 120 = n$ or $0.84 \times 32 = n$
$26.4 = n$ $26.88 = n$
Because $26.88 > 26.4$, 84% of 32 is larger.

27. $0.31294 \times 82{,}460 = n$
$25{,}805.0324 = n$

28. $1.2394 \times 275{,}976 = n$
$342{,}044.6544 = n$

Objective B Exercises

29. **Strategy** To find the number of people who do not have health insurance, write and solve the basic percent equation using n to represent the number of people between ages 18 and 24 who do not have health insurance.The percent is 30% and the base is 44.

Solution $30\% \times 44 = n$
$0.30 \times 44 = n$
$13.2 = n$
About 13.2 million people aged 18 to 24 do not have health insurance.

30. **Strategy** To find how many new student pilots are flying single-engine planes this year, write and solve the basic percent equation using n to represent the new student pilots. The percent is 106% and the base is 55,422.

Solution $106\% \times 55{,}422 = n$
$1.06 \times 55{,}422 = n$
$58{,}747.32 = n$
58,747 new student pilots are flying single-engine planes this year.

31. **Strategy** To find how many more faculty members described their political views as liberal than described their views as far left:
• Find the number that described their views as liberal by writing and solving the basic percent equation using n to represent the number with liberal views. The percent is 42.3% and the base is 32,840.
• Find the number that described their views as far left by writing and solving the basic percent equation using n to represent the number with far left views. The percent is 5.3% and the base is 32,840.
• Subtract the number with far left views from the number with liberal views.

Solution

Liberal	Far left
$42.3\% \times 32{,}840 = n$	$5.3\% \times 32{,}840 = n$
$0.423 \times 32{,}840 = n$	$0.053 \times 32{,}840 = n$
$13{,}891.32 = n$	$1740.52 = n$

$13{,}891.32 - 1740.52 = 12{,}150.8$
12,151 more faculty members described their political views as liberal than described their views as far left.

32. **Strategy** To find how many fewer faculty members described their political views as conservative than described their views as middle of the road:
• Find the number that described their views as conservative by writing and solving the basic percent equation using n to represent the number with conservative views. The percent is 17.7% and the base is 32,840.
• Find the number that described their views as middle of the road by writing and solving the basic percent equation using n to represent the number with middle of the road views. The percent is 34.3% and the base is 32,840.
• Subtract the number with conservative views from the number with middle of the road views.

Solution

Conservative	Middle of the Road
$17.7\% \times 32{,}840 = n$	$34.3\% \times 32{,}840 = n$
$0.177 \times 32{,}840 = n$	$0.343 \times 32{,}840 = n$
$5812.68 = n$	$11{,}264.12 = n$

$11{,}264.12 - 5812.68 = 5451.44$
5451 fewer faculty members described their political views as conservative than described their views as middle of the road.

33a. **Strategy** To find the sales tax, write and solve the basic percent equation using n as the sales tax. The percent is 6% and the base is \$29,500.

Solution $6\% \times \$29{,}500 = n$
$0.06 \times 29{,}500 = n$
$1770 = n$
The sales tax is \$1770.

b. **Strategy** To find the total cost of the car, add the sales tax (\$1770) to the purchase price of the car (\$29,500).

Solution
$$\begin{array}{r} \$29{,}500 \\ +\quad 1{,}770 \\ \hline \$31{,}270 \end{array}$$
The total cost of the car is \$31,270.

34a. Strategy To find how many pounds of oranges were spoiled, write and solve the basic percent equation using n to represent the spoiled oranges.The percent is 4.8% and the base is 20,000.

Solution
$4.8\% \times 20{,}000 = n$
$0.048 \times 20{,}000 = n$
$960 = n$

960 pounds of oranges were spoiled.

b. Strategy To find how many pounds of oranges were not spoiled, subtract the number of pounds spoiled (960 pounds) from the total (20,000 pounds).

Solution
$$\begin{array}{r} 20{,}000 \\ -\quad 960 \\ \hline 19{,}040 \end{array}$$

19,040 pounds of oranges were unspoiled.

35. Strategy To find the number of respondents that did not answer yes to the question:
- Find the number that did answer yes by writing and solving the basic percent equation using n to represent the number that said yes. The percent is 29.8% and the base is 8878.
- Subtract the number of yes answers from the total number polled (8878).

Solution
$29.8\% \times 8878 = n$
$0.298 \times 8878 = n$
$2646 \approx n$
$8878 - 2646 = 6232$

6232 respondents did not answer yes to the question.

36. Strategy To find the number of employees needed for the vacation season:
- Find the number of additional employees needed for the vacation season by writing and solving the basic percent equation using n to represent the number of additional employees. The percent is 22% and the base is 550.
- Add the number of additional employees to those already hired (550).

Solution
$22\% \times 550 = n$
$0.22 \times 550 = n$
$121 = n$

$$\begin{array}{r} 550 \\ +121 \\ \hline 671 \end{array}$$

671 employees are needed for the vacation season.

Applying the Concepts

37. $43\% \times 112 = 48.16$
Employees spent 48.2 hours with family and friends.

38. $112 \times 30\% = 33.6$
Employees would prefer to spend 33.6 hours on job/career.

39. Actual time: $112 \times 20\% = 22.4$
Preferred time: $112 \times 23\% = 25.76$
$25.76 - 22.4 = 3.36$
There are approximately 3.4 hours difference between the actual and preferred amounts of time the employees spent on self.

Section 5.3

Objective A Exercises

1. $n \times 75 = 24$
$n = 24 \div 75$
$n = 0.32$
$n = 32\%$

2. $n \times 80 = 20$
$n = 20 \div 80$
$n = 0.25$
$n = 25\%$

3. $n \times 90 = 15$
$n = 15 \div 90$
$n = 0.16\frac{2}{3}$
$n = 16\frac{2}{3}\%$

4. $n \times 60 = 24$
$n = 24 \div 60$
$n = 0.4$
$n = 40\%$

5. $n \times 12 = 24$
$n = 24 \div 12$
$n = 2$
$n = 200\%$

6. $n \times 6 = 9$
$n = 9 \div 6$
$n = 1.5$
$n = 150\%$

7. $n \times 16 = 6$
$n = 6 \div 16$
$n = 0.375$
$n = 37.5\%$

8. $n \times 24 = 18$
$n = 18 \div 24$
$n = 0.75$
$n = 75\%$

9. $n \times 100 = 18$
$n = 18 \div 100$
$n = 0.18$
$n = 18\%$

10. $n \times 100 = 54$
$n = 54 \div 100$
$n = 0.54$
$n = 54\%$

11. $n \times 2000 = 5$
$n = 5 \div 2000$
$n = 0.0025$
$n = 0.25\%$

12. $n \times 2500 = 8$
$n = 8 \div 2500$
$n = 0.0032$
$n = 0.32\%$

13. $n \times 6 = 1.2$
$n = 1.2 \div 6$
$n = 0.2$
$n = 20\%$

14. $n \times 2.4 = 0.6$
$n = 0.6 \div 2.4$
$n = 0.25$
$n = 25\%$

15. $n \times 4.1 = 16.4$
$n = 16.4 \div 4.1$
$n = 4$
$n = 400\%$

16. $n \times 50 = 5.3$
$n = 5.3 \div 50$
$n = 0.106$
$n = 10.6\%$

17. $n \times 40 = 1$
$n = 1 \div 40$
$n = 0.025$
$n = 2.5\%$

18. $n \times 20 = 0.3$
$n = 0.3 \div 20$
$n = 0.015$
$n = 1.5\%$

19. $n \times 48 = 18$
$n = 18 \div 48$
$n = 0.375$
$n = 37.5\%$

20. $n \times 11 = 88$
$n = 88 \div 11$
$n = 8$
$n = 800\%$

21. $n \times 2800 = 7$
$n = 7 \div 2800$
$n = 0.0025$
$n = 0.25\%$

22. $n \times 400 = 12$
$n = 12 \div 400$
$n = 0.03$
$n = 3\%$

23. $n \times 175 = 4.2$
$n = 4.2 \div 175$
$n = 0.024$
$n = 2.4\%$

24. $n \times 99.5 = 41.79$
$n = 41.79 \div 99.5$
$n = 0.42$
$n = 42\%$

25. $n \times 86.5 = 8.304$
$n = 8.304 \div 86.5$
$n = 0.096$
$n = 9.6\%$

26. $n \times 1282.5 = 2.565$
$n = 2.565 \div 1282.5$
$n = 0.002$
$n = 0.2\%$

Objective B Exercises

27. Strategy To find what percent of couples disagree about financial matters, write and solve the basic percent equation using n to represent the unknown percent. The base is 10 and the amount is 7.

Solution $n \times 10 = 7$
$n = 7 \div 10$
$n = 0.70$
70% of couples disagree about financial matters.

28. Strategy To find what percent were most irked by tailgaters, write and solve the basic percent equation using n to represent the unknown percent.The base is 1236 and the amount is 293.

Solution $n \times 1236 = 293$
$n = 293 \div 1236$
$n \approx 0.237$
Approximately 23.7% of those surveyed were most irked by tailgaters.

29. Strategy To find what percent of the vegetables was wasted, write and solve the basic percent equation using n to represent the unknown percent. The base is 63 billion and the amount is 16 billion.

Solution $n \times 63 \text{ billion} = 16 \text{ billion}$

$n = 16 \text{ billion} \div 63 \text{ billion}$

$n \approx 0.254$

Approximately 25.4% of the vegetables were wasted.

30. Strategy To find what percent of the cranberries grown were produced in Wisconsin, write and solve the basic percent equation using n to represent the unknown percent.The base is 572 million and the amount is 281.72 million.

Solution $n \times 572 \text{ million} = 281.72 \text{ million}$

$n = 281.72 \text{ million} \div 572 \text{ million}$

$n \approx 0.49$

49% of the total cranberry crop was produced in Wisconsin.

31. Strategy To find what percent of the total amount spent on energy utilities is spent on lighting, write and solve the basic percent equation using n to represent the unknown percent. The base is \$1355 and the amount is \$81.30.

Solution $n \times \$1355 = \$81.30$

$n = 81.30 \div 1355$

$n = 0.06$

The typical American household spends 6% of its total energy utilities on lighting.

32. Strategy To find out whether the number of questions was enough to pass the test:

- Find what percent of the questions were answered correctly by writing and solving the basic percent equation using n to represent the unknown percent. The base is 250 and the amount is 177.
- Compare the unknown percent with 70%.

Solution $n \times 250 = 177$

$n = 177 \div 250$

$n = 0.708 = 70.8\%$

$70.8\% > 70\%$

Yes, it was enough to pass the test.

33. Strategy To find what percent of food produced in the United States is wasted:

- Find the amount wasted by subtracting the amount not wasted (260 billion pounds) from the total (356 billion pounds).
- Find the percent by writing and solving the basic percent equation using n to represent the unknown percent. The base is 356 billion and the amount is (356 billion − 260 billion).

Solution

$$\begin{array}{r} 356 \text{ billion} \\ -260 \text{ billion} \\ \hline 96 \text{ billion} \end{array} \qquad \begin{aligned} n \times 356 \text{ billion} &= 96 \text{ billion} \\ n &= 96 \text{ billion} \div 356 \text{ billion} \\ n &\approx 0.27 \end{aligned}$$

27% of the food produced in United States is wasted.

34. Strategy To find what percent of the slabs did meet safety requirements:

- Find how many slabs did meet safety requirements by subtracting the number that did not pass (3) from the total (200).
- Find the percent by writing and solving the basic percent equation using n to represent the unknown percent. The number that did pass (200 − 3 = 197) is the amount and the total (200) is the base.

Solution

$$\begin{array}{r} 200 \\ -\ \ 3 \\ \hline 197 \end{array} \qquad \begin{aligned} n \times 200 &= 197 \\ n &= 197 \div 200 \\ n &= 0.985 = 98.5\% \end{aligned}$$

The percent of the slabs that did meet safety requirements was 98.5%.

Applying the Concepts

35.

$$\begin{array}{r} \$1,400 \\ 1,200 \\ 4,000 \\ 3,900 \\ 3,000 \\ +\ 1,100 \\ \hline 14,600 \end{array}$$

\$14,600 is the total amount spent.
\$4000 is spent for food.

$$\frac{\$4,000}{\$14,600} \approx 0.274$$

Approximately 27.4% of the total expenses is spent for food.

36. $1,400
1,200
4,000
3,900
3,000
+1,100
$14,600

$14,600 is the total amount spent.

$3900 is spent for veterinary care.

$\frac{\$3,900}{\$14,600} \approx 0.267$

Approximately 26.7% of the total was spent for veterinary care.

37. $1,400
1,200
4,000
3,900
3,000
+1,100
$14,600

$14,600 is the total amount spent.

$14,600
−1,200
$13,400 total spent on all categories except training.

$\frac{\$13,400}{\$14,600} \approx 0.918$

91.8% of the total is spent on all categories except training.

38. The sum of the percents in the percent column is 113%. In order for the responses to be possible, the sum of the percents must be 100%.

Section 5.4

Objective A Exercises

1. $0.12 \times n = 9$
$n = 9 \div 0.12$
$n = 75$

2. $0.38 \times n = 171$
$n = 171 \div 0.38$
$n = 450$

3. $0.16 \times n = 8$
$n = 8 \div 0.16$
$n = 50$

4. $0.90 \times n = 54$
$n = 54 \div 0.90$
$n = 60$

5. $0.10 \times n = 10$
$n = 10 \div 0.10$
$n = 100$

6. $0.37 \times n = 37$
$n = 37 \div 0.37$
$n = 100$

7. $0.30 \times n = 25.5$
$n = 25.5 \div 0.30$
$n = 85$

8. $0.25 \times n = 21.5$
$n = 21.5 \div 0.25$
$n = 86$

9. $0.025 \times n = 30$
$n = 30 \div 0.025$
$n = 1200$

10. $0.104 \times n = 52$
$n = 52 \div 0.104$
$n = 500$

11. $1.25 \times n = 24$
$n = 24 \div 1.25$
$n = 19.2$

12. $1.80 \times n = 21.6$
$n = 21.6 \div 1.80$
$n = 12$

13. $2.4 \times n = 18$
$n = 18 \div 2.4$
$n = 7.5$

14. $3.2 \times n = 24$
$n = 24 \div 3.2$
$n = 7.5$

15. $0.15 \times n = 4.8$
$n = 4.8 \div 0.15$
$n = 32$

16. $0.50 \times n = 87.5$
$n = 87.5 \div 0.50$
$n = 175$

17. $0.128 \times n = 25.6$
$n = 25.6 \div 0.128$
$n = 200$

18. $0.634 \times n = 45.014$
$n = 45.014 \div 0.634$
$n = 71$

19. $0.007 \times n = 0.56$
$n = 0.56 \div 0.007$
$n = 80$

20. $0.0025 \times n = 1$
$n = 1 \div 0.0025$
$n = 400$

21. $0.30 \times n = 2.7$
$n = 2.7 \div 0.30$
$n = 9$

22. $0.78 \times n = 3.9$
$n = 3.9 \div 0.78$
$n = 5$

23. $\frac{1}{6} \times n = 84$
$n = 84 \div \frac{1}{6}$
$n = 504$

24. $\frac{1}{3} \times n = 120$
$n = 120 \div \frac{1}{3}$
$n = 360$

25. $\frac{2}{3} \times n = 72$
$n = 72 \div \frac{2}{3}$
$n = 108$

26. $\frac{5}{6} \times n = 13.5$
$n = 13.5 \div \frac{5}{6}$
$n = 16.2$

Objective B Exercises

27. **Strategy** To find the number of travelers who allowed their children to miss school, write and solve the basic percent equation using n to represent the number of travelers. The percent is 11% and the amount is 1.738 million.

Solution $11\% \times n = 1.738$
$0.11 \times n = 1.738$
$n = 1.738 \div 0.11$
$n = 15.8$
There were 15.8 million travelers who allowed their children to miss school to go along on a trip.

28. The percent is given but an amount is not. There is insufficient information to solve this exercise.

29. **Strategy** To find how many people responded to the survey, write and solve the basic percent equation using n to represent the number of people that responded. The percent is 22% and the amount is 740 people.

Solution $22\% \times n = 740$
$0.22 \times n = 740$
$n = 740 \div 0.22$
$n \approx 3363.6$
3364 people responded to the survey.

30. **Strategy** To find the amount of medical expenses claimed in the over-$200,000 bracket,write and solve the basic percent equation using n to represent the unknown amount of medical expenses. The percent is 26% and the known amount is $4500.

Solution $26\% \times n = \$4,500$
$0.26 \times n = \$4,500$
$n = \$4,500 \div 0.26$
$n \approx \$17,000$
Medical expenses claimed by the people earning over $200,000 will average approximately $17,000.

31a. **Strategy** To find the number of computer boards tested, write and solve the basic percent equation using n to represent the number of computer boards tested. The percent is 0.8% and the amount is 24.

Solution $0.8\% \times n = 24$
$0.008 \times n = 24$
$n = 24 \div 0.008$
$n = 3000$
3000 boards were tested.

b. **Strategy** To find the number of boards that were tested as not defective, subtract the number of defective boards (24) from the total tested (3000).

Solution
$$\begin{array}{r} 3000 \\ -\ \ 24 \\ \hline 2976 \end{array}$$
2976 boards were tested as not defective.

32a. **Strategy** To find how many calls the operator received, write and solve the basic percent equation using n to represent the total number of calls received. The percent is 98% and the amount is 441.

Solution $98\% \times n = 441$
$0.98 \times n = 441$
$n = 441 \div 0.98$
$n = 450$
450 calls were received.

b. **Strategy** To find how many telephone numbers were not listed, subtract the numbers that were listed (441) from the total requested (450).

Solution
$$\begin{array}{r} 450 \\ -441 \\ \hline 9 \end{array}$$
9 numbers were not listed.

Applying the Concepts

33. Strategy To find the number of people in the United States that were age 20 and older:

- Find the number that are under the age of 20 by using the basic percent equation using n to represent the number of people under 20. The percent is 28.6% and the base is 281,422,000.
- Subtract the number under 20 from the base (281,422,000).

Solution

$$28.6\% \times 281{,}422{,}000 = n$$
$$0.286 \times 281{,}422{,}000 = n$$
$$80{,}486{,}692 = n$$

$$\begin{array}{r} 281{,}422{,}000 \\ -\ 80{,}486{,}692 \\ \hline 200{,}935{,}308 \end{array}$$

200,935,308 people in the United States were age 20 and older in 2000.

34. $30\% \times n = 0.45$ milligrams
$n = 0.45 \div 0.30$
$n = 1.5$ milligrams
The recommended daily amount of thiamin for an adult is 1.5 milligrams.

35. $0.08 \div 0.04 = 2$ milligrams
The recommended daily amount of copper for an adult is 2 milligrams.

36. Suppose we increase 100 by 10%.
$100 + 0.10(100) = 100 + 10 = 110$
Now we decrease 110 by 10%.
$110 - 0.10(110) = 110 - 11 = 99$
No, the new number is not the original number. The 10% increase applied to the number 100, but the 10% decrease applied to 110. Therefore, the decrease was greater than the increase.

Section 5.5

Objective A Exercises

1.
$$\frac{26}{100} = \frac{n}{250}$$
$26 \times 250 = n \times 100$
$6500 = n \times 100$
$6500 \div 100 = n$
$65 = n$

2.
$$\frac{18}{100} = \frac{n}{150}$$
$18 \times 150 = 100 \times n$
$2700 = 100 \times n$
$2700 \div 100 = n$
$27 = n$

3.
$$\frac{n}{100} = \frac{37}{148}$$
$148 \times n = 37 \times 100$
$148 \times n = 3700$
$n = 3700 \div 148$
$n = 25$
37 is 25% of 148.

4.
$$\frac{n}{100} = \frac{33}{150}$$
$100 \times 33 = n \times 150$
$3300 = n \times 150$
$3300 \div 150 = n$
$22 = n$
22% of 150 is 33.

5.
$$\frac{68}{100} = \frac{51}{n}$$
$68 \times n = 100 \times 51$
$68 \times n = 5100$
$n = 5100 \div 68$
$n = 75$

6.
$$\frac{84}{100} = \frac{126}{n}$$
$84 \times n = 126 \times 100$
$84 \times n = 12{,}600$
$n = 12{,}600 \div 84$
$n = 150$

7.
$$\frac{n}{100} = \frac{43}{344}$$
$n \times 344 = 100 \times 43$
$n \times 344 = 4300$
$n = 4300 \div 344$
$n = 12.5$
12.5% of 344 is 43.

8.
$$\frac{n}{100} = \frac{750}{50}$$
$50 \times n = 750 \times 100$
$50 \times n = 75{,}000$
$n = 75{,}000 \div 50$
$n = 1500$
750 is 1500% of 50.

9.
$$\frac{20.5}{100} = \frac{82}{n}$$
$n \times 20.5 = 82 \times 100$
$n \times 20.5 = 8200$
$n = 8200 \div 20.5$
$n = 400$

10.
$$\frac{2.4}{100} = \frac{21}{n}$$
$2.4 \times n = 100 \times 21$
$2.4 \times n = 2100$
$n = 2100 \div 2.4$
$n = 875$

11. $\dfrac{6.5}{100} = \dfrac{n}{300}$
$300 \times 6.5 = n \times 100$
$1950 = n \times 100$
$1950 \div 100 = n$
$19.5 = n$

12. $\dfrac{96}{100} = \dfrac{n}{75}$
$96 \times 75 = 100 \times n$
$7200 = 100 \times n$
$7200 \div 100 = n$
$72 = n$

13. $\dfrac{n}{100} = \dfrac{7.4}{50}$
$50 \times n = 7.4 \times 100$
$50 \times n = 740$
$n = 740 \div 50$
$n = 14.8$
7.4 is 14.8% of 50.

14. $\dfrac{n}{100} = \dfrac{693}{1500}$
$n \times 1500 = 100 \times 693$
$n \times 1500 = 69{,}300$
$n = 69{,}300 \div 1500$
$n = 46.2$
46.2% of 1500 is 693.

15. $\dfrac{50.5}{100} = \dfrac{n}{124}$
$50.5 \times 124 = n \times 100$
$6262 = n \times 100$
$6262 \div 100 = n$
$62.62 = n$

16. $\dfrac{87.4}{100} = \dfrac{n}{255}$
$255 \times 87.4 = n \times 100$
$22{,}287 = n \times 100$
$22{,}287 \div 100 = n$
$222.87 = n$

17. $\dfrac{120}{100} = \dfrac{6}{n}$
$120 \times n = 6 \times 100$
$120 \times n = 600$
$n = 600 \div 120$
$n = 5$

18. $\dfrac{175}{100} = \dfrac{14}{n}$
$n \times 175 = 14 \times 100$
$n \times 175 = 1400$
$n = 1400 \div 175$
$n = 8$

19. $\dfrac{250}{100} = \dfrac{n}{18}$
$250 \times 18 = n \times 100$
$4500 = n \times 100$
$4500 \div 100 = n$
$45 = n$

20. $\dfrac{325}{100} = \dfrac{n}{4.4}$
$325 \times 4.4 = n \times 100$
$1430 = n \times 100$
$1430 \div 100 = n$
$14.3 = n$

21. $\dfrac{220}{100} = \dfrac{33}{n}$
$n \times 220 = 33 \times 100$
$n \times 220 = 3300$
$n = 3300 \div 220$
$n = 15$

22. $\dfrac{160}{100} = \dfrac{40}{n}$
$160 \times n = 40 \times 100$
$160 \times n = 4000$
$n = 4000 \div 160$
$n = 25$

Objective B Exercises

23. Strategy To find the total amount the charity organization collected, write and solve a proportion using n to represent the total collected (base). The percent is 12% and the amount is \$2940.

Solution $\dfrac{12}{100} = \dfrac{2940}{n}$
$12 \times n = 2940 \times 100$
$12 \times n = 294{,}000$
$n = 294{,}000 \div 12$
$n = 24{,}500$
The total amount collected was \$24,500.

24. Strategy To find the length of time the drug will be effective as determined by the testing service, write and solve a proportion using n to represent the length of time determined by the testing service. The percent is 80% and the base is 6 hours.

Solution $\dfrac{80}{100} = \dfrac{n}{6}$
$100 \times n = 80 \times 6$
$100 \times n = 480$
$n = 480 \div 100$
$n = 4.8$
The length of time that the drug will be effective, as determined by the testing service, is 4.8 hours.

25. Strategy To find the total land area, write and solve a proportion using n to represent the total land area (base). The percent is 16% and the amount is 9,400,000 square miles.

Solution

$$\frac{16}{100} = \frac{9{,}400{,}000}{n}$$
$$16 \times n = 9{,}400{,}000 \times 100$$
$$16 \times n = 940{,}000{,}000$$
$$n = 940{,}000{,}000 \div 16$$
$$n = 58{,}750{,}000$$

The world's total land area is 58,750,000 square miles.

26. Strategy To find what percent of the alarms were false alarms, write and solve a proportion using n to represent the percent. The base is 200 and the amount is 24.

Solution

$$\frac{n}{100} = \frac{24}{200}$$
$$n \times 200 = 24 \times 100$$
$$n \times 200 = 2400$$
$$n = 2400 \div 200$$
$$n = 12$$

12% of the alarms received were false alarms.

27. Strategy To find the number of hotels in the United States that are located along highways, write and solve a proportion using n to represent the number along highways. The percent is 42.2% and the base is 53,500.

Solution

$$\frac{42.2}{100} = \frac{n}{53{,}500}$$
$$42.2 \times 53{,}500 = 100 \times n$$
$$2{,}257{,}700 = 100 \times n$$
$$2{,}257{,}700 \div 100 = n$$
$$22{,}577 = n$$

22,577 hotels in the United States are located along highways.

28. Strategy To find the total turkey production, write and solve a proportion using n to represent the total turkey production. The percent is 18.6% and the amount is 1,300,000,000 pounds.

Solution

$$\frac{18.6}{100} = \frac{1{,}300{,}000{,}000}{n}$$
$$18.6 \times n = 1{,}300{,}000{,}000 \times 100$$
$$18.6 \times n = 130{,}000{,}000{,}000$$
$$n = 130{,}000{,}000{,}000 \div 18.6$$
$$n \approx 7{,}000{,}000{,}000$$

The total turkey production was 7 billion pounds.

29. Strategy To find the number of ounces of gold mined in the United States that year, write and solve a proportion using n to represent that the total number of ounces mined. The percent is 16%, and the amount is 2,240,000 ounces.

Solution

$$\frac{16}{100} = \frac{\$2{,}240{,}000}{n}$$
$$16 \times n = 100 \times 2{,}240{,}000$$
$$16 \times n = 224{,}000{,}000$$
$$n = 224{,}000{,}000 \div 16$$
$$n = 14{,}000{,}000$$

14,000,000 ounces of gold were mined in the United States that year.

30a. Strategy To find what percent of the 2000 population of Sacramento County is the increase in population, write and solve a proportion using n to represent the percent. The base is 1,200,000 and the amount is 900,000.

Solution

$$\frac{n}{100} = \frac{900{,}000}{1{,}200{,}000}$$
$$n \times 1{,}200{,}000 = 100 \times 900{,}000$$
$$n \times 1{,}200{,}000 = 90{,}000{,}000$$
$$n = 90{,}000{,}000 \div 1{,}200{,}000$$
$$n = 75$$

75% of the 2000 population of Sacramento County is the increase in population.

b. Strategy To find what percent of the 2000 population of Kern County is the increase in population, write and solve a proportion using n to represent the percent. The base is 651,700 and the amount is 948,300.

Solution

$$\frac{n}{100} = \frac{948{,}300}{651{,}700}$$
$$n \times 651{,}700 = 100 \times 948{,}300$$
$$n \times 651{,}700 = 94{,}830{,}000$$
$$n = 94{,}830{,}000 \div 651{,}700$$
$$n \approx 145.5$$

Approximately 145.5% of the 2000 population of Kern County is the increase in population.

31. Strategy To find the percent of the deaths due to traffic accidents:

- Find the total number of deaths.
- Write and solve a proportion using n to represent the percent. The base is the total deaths (156) and the amount is 73.

Solution

$$\begin{array}{r} 19 \\ 6 \\ 58 \\ +\ 73 \\ \hline 156 \end{array}$$

$$\frac{n}{100} = \frac{73}{156}$$
$$n \times 156 = 100 \times 73$$
$$n \times 156 = 7300$$
$$n = 7300 \div 156$$
$$n \approx 46.8$$

46.8% of the deaths were due to traffic accidents.

Applying the Concepts

32. The percents are given but a base is not. There is insufficient information to solve the exercise.

33. 108th Senate $\frac{51}{100} = \frac{n}{100}$, $n = 51\%$ 108th House of Representatives $\frac{229}{435} = \frac{n}{100}$, $n \approx 52.6\%$ Republicans

The 108th House of Representatives had the larger percent of Republicans.

Chapter 5 Review Exercises

1. $0.30 \times 200 = n$
$60 = n$

2. $n \times 80 = 16$
$n = 16 \div 80$
$n = 0.2$
$n = 20\%$

3. $1\frac{3}{4} \times 100\% = 1.75 \times 100\% = 175\%$

4. $0.20 \times n = 15$
$n = 15 \div 0.20$
$n = 75$

5. $12\% = 12 \times \frac{1}{100} = \frac{12}{100} = \frac{3}{25}$

6. $0.22 \times 88 = n$
$19.36 = n$

7. $n \times 20 = 30$
$n = 30 \div 20$
$n = 1.5$
$n = 150\%$

8. $0.16\frac{2}{3} \times n = 84$
$\frac{1}{6} \times n = 84$
$n = 84 \div \frac{1}{6}$
$n = 84 \times 6$
$n = 504$

9. $42\% = 42 \times 0.01 = 0.42$

10. $0.075 \times 72 = n$
$5.4 = n$

11. $0.66\frac{2}{3} \times n = 105$
$\frac{2}{3} \times n = 105$
$n = 105 \div \frac{2}{3}$
$n = 105 \times \frac{3}{2}$
$n = 157.5$

12. $7.6\% = 7.6 \times 0.01 = 0.076$

13. $1.25 \times 62 = n$
$77.5 = n$

14. $16\frac{2}{3}\% = 16\frac{2}{3} \times \frac{1}{100} = \frac{50}{3} \times \frac{1}{100} = \frac{50}{300} = \frac{1}{6}$

15. $\frac{n}{100} = \frac{40}{25}$
$n \times 25 = 40 \times 100$
$n \times 25 = 4000$
$n = 4000 \div 25$
$n = 160$
160% of 25 is 40.

16. $\frac{20}{100} = \frac{15}{n}$
$20 \times n = 100 \times 15$
$20 \times n = 1{,}500$
$n = 1{,}500 \div 20$
$n = 75$

17. $0.38 \times 100\% = 38\%$

18. $0.78 \times n = 8.5$
$n = 8.5 \div 0.78$
$n \approx 10.89 \approx 10.9$

19. $n \times 30 = 2.2$
$n = 2.2 \div 30$
$n \approx 0.073$
$n \approx 7.3\%$

20. $n \times 15 = 92$
$n = 92 \div 15$
$n \approx 6.133$
$n \approx 613.3\%$

21. Strategy To find the percent of the questions answered correctly:

- Find the number of questions answered correctly by subtracting the number missed (9) from the total number of questions (60).
- Write and solve a proportion using n to represent the percent. The base is 60 and the amount is the number of questions answered correctly.

Solution

$60 - 9 = 51$

$\frac{n}{100} = \frac{51}{60}$

$n \times 60 = 51 \times 100$

$n \times 60 = 5100$

$n = 5100 \div 60$

$n = 85$

The student answered 85% of the questions correctly.

22. Strategy To find how much of the budget was spent for newspaper advertising, write and solve the basic percent equation using n to represent the newspaper advertising. The percent is 7.5% and the base is \$60,000.

Solution

$7.5\% \times \$60{,}000 = n$

$0.075 \times 60{,}000 = n$

$4500 = n$

The company spent \$4500 for newspaper advertising.

23. Strategy To find what percent of total energy use is electricity:

- Find the total of the costs given on the graph. This sum is the base.
- Write and solve the basic percent equation using n as the unknown percent. The cost for electricity is the amount.

Solution

910	Electricity
1492	Motor gasoline
383	Natural gas
+ 83	Fuel oil, kerosene
2868	

$n \times 2868 = 910$

$n = 910 \div 2868$

$n \approx 0.317$

31.7% of the cost is for electricity.

24. Strategy To find the total cost of the video camera:

- Find the amount of the sales tax by writing and solving the basic percent equation using n to represent the sales tax. The percent is 6.25% and the base is \$980.
- Add the sales tax to the cost of the camera (\$980).

Solution

$6.25\% \times \$980 = n$

$0.0625 \times 980 = n$

$61.25 = n$

$$\begin{array}{r} \$980.00 \\ +\ 61.25 \\ \hline \$1041.25 \end{array}$$

The total cost of the video camera is \$1041.25.

25. Strategy To find the percent of women who wore sunscreen often, write and solve the basic percent equation using n to represent the unknown percent.The base is 350 women and the amount is 275 women.

Solution

$n \times 350 = 275$

$n = 275 \div 350$

$n \approx 0.7857$

Approximately 78.6% of the women wore sunscreen often.

26. Strategy To find the world's population in 2000, write and solve the basic percent equation using n to represent the population in 2000.The percent is 149% and the amount is 9,100,000,000 people.

Solution

$149\% \times n = 9{,}100{,}000{,}000$

$1.49 \times n = 9{,}100{,}000{,}000$

$n = 9{,}100{,}000{,}000 \div 1.49$

$n \approx 6{,}100{,}000{,}000$

The world's population in 2000 was approximately 6,100,000,000 people.

27. Strategy To find the cost of the computer 4 years ago, write and solve a proportion using n to represent the cost 4 years ago. The percent is 60% and the amount is \$1800.

Solution

$\frac{60}{100} = \frac{1800}{n}$

$60 \times n = 1800 \times 100$

$60 \times n = 180{,}000$

$n = 180{,}000 \div 60$

$n = 3000$

The cost of the computer 4 years ago was \$3000.

28. **Strategy** To find the dollar value of all online transactions, write and solve the basic percent equation using n to represent the dollar value of all online transactions. The percent is 50.4% and the amount is \$25.96 billion.

Solution
$$0.504 \times n = \$25.96 \text{ billion}$$
$$n = 25.96 \text{ billion} \div 0.504$$
$$n \approx 51.5 \text{ billion}$$
The dollar value of all the online transactions made that year was \$52 billion.

Chapter 5 Test

1. $97.3\% = 97.3 \times 0.01 = 0.973$

2. $83\frac{1}{3}\% = 83\frac{1}{3} \times \frac{1}{100} = \frac{250}{3} \times \frac{1}{100} = \frac{250}{300} = \frac{5}{6}$

3. $0.3 \times 100\% = 30\%$

4. $1.63 \times 100\% = 163\%$

5. $\frac{3}{2} \times 100\% = 1.5 \times 100\% = 150\%$

6. $\frac{2}{3} \times 100\% = \frac{200}{3}\% = 66\frac{2}{3}\%$

7. $77\% \times 65 = n$
$0.77 \times 65 = n$
$50.05 = n$

8. $47.2\% \times 130 = n$
$0.472 \times 130 = n$
$61.36 = n$

9. 7% of $120 = n$ or 76% of $13 = n$
$0.07 \times 120 = n$ $\quad$ $0.76 \times 13 = n$
$8.4 = n$ $\quad$ $9.88 = n$
$9.88 > 8.4$, so 76% of 13 is larger.

10. 13% of $200 = n$ or 212% of $12 = n$
$0.13 \times 200 = n$ $\quad$ $2.12 \times 12 = n$
$26 = n$ $\quad$ $25.44 = n$
$25.44 < 26$, so 212% of 12 is smaller.

11. **Strategy** To find the amount spent for advertising, write and solve the basic percent equation using n to represent the amount spent for advertising. The percent is 6% and the base is \$75,000.

Solution
$6\% \times \$75{,}000 = n$
$0.06 \times 75{,}000 = n$
$4500 = n$
The amount spent for advertising is \$4500.

12. **Strategy** To find how many pounds of vegetables were not spoiled:
- Write and solve the basic percent equation using n to represent the number of pounds that were spoiled. The percent is 6.4% and the base is 1250.
- Find the number of pounds that were not spoiled by subtracting the number of pounds of spoiled vegetables from the total (1250 pounds).

Solution
$6.4\% \times 1250 = n$ $\quad$ 1250
$0.064 \times 1250 = n$ $\quad$ $-\ 80$
$80 = n$ $\quad$ 1170

1170 pounds of vegetables were not spoiled.

13. $\frac{440}{3000} \approx 0.147 = 14.7\%$
14.7% of the daily recommended amount of potassium is provided.

14. Total number of calories $= 180 + 20 = 200$.
The percent provided $= \frac{200}{2200} = 9.1\%$.
9.1% of the daily recommended number of calories is provided.

15. **Strategy** To find what percent of the permanent employees is hired as temporary employees, write and solve the basic percent using n to represent the percent of the permanent employees. The base is 125 and the amount is 20.

Solution
$n \times 125 = 20$
$n = 20 \div 125$
$n = 0.16$
$n = 16\%$
16% of the permanent employees are hired.

16. Strategy To find what percent of the questions the student answered correctly:
- Find how many questions the student answered correctly by subtracting the number missed (7) from the total number of questions (80).
- Write and solve the basic percent equation using n to represent the percent of questions answered correctly. The base is 80 and the amount is the number of questions answered correctly.

Solution $80 - 7 = 73$

$n \times 80 = 73$

$n = 73 \div 80$

$n = 0.9125$

$n \approx 91.3\%$

The student answered approximately 91.3% of the questions correctly.

17. $15\% \times n = 12$

$0.15 \times n = 12$

$n = 12 \div 0.15$

$n = 80$

18. $150\% \times n = 42.5$

$1.5 \times n = 42.5$

$n = 42.5 \div 1.5$

$n \approx 28.3$

19. Strategy To find the number of PDAs tested, write and solve the basic percent equation using n to represent the number of PDAs tested. The percent is 1.2% and the amount is 384.

Solution $1.2\% \times n = 384$

$0.012 \times n = 384$

$n = 384 \div 0.012$

$n = 32{,}000$

32,000 PDAs were tested.

20. Strategy To find what percent the increase is of the original price:
- Find the amount of the increase by subtracting the original value ($95,000) from the price 5 years later ($152,000).
- Write and solve the basic percent equation using n to represent the percent. The base is the original price ($95,000) and the amount is the amount of the increase.

Solution

$$\begin{array}{r} \$152{,}000 \\ -\ 95{,}000 \\ \hline \$57{,}000 \end{array}$$

$n \times \$95{,}000 = \$57{,}000$

$n = 57{,}000 \div 95{,}000$

$n = 0.60$

$n = 60\%$

The increase is 60% of the original price.

21. $\frac{86}{100} = \frac{123}{n}$

$86 \times n = 123 \times 100$

$86 \times n = 12{,}300$

$n = 12{,}300 \div 86$

$n \approx 143.02$

$n \approx 143.0$

22. $\frac{n}{100} = \frac{120}{12}$

$12 \times n = 100 \times 120$

$12 \times n = 12{,}000$

$n = 12{,}000 \div 12$

$n = 1000$

1000% of 12 is 120.

23. Strategy To find the dollar increase in the hourly wage:
- Write and solve a proportion to find the hourly wage last year. Let n represent last year's wage. The amount is $16.24 and the percent is 112%.
- Subtract last year's wage from this year's wage ($16.24).

Solution $\frac{112}{100} = \frac{16.24}{n}$

$112 \times n = 16.24 \times 100$

$112 \times n = 1624$

$n = 1624 \div 112$

$n = 14.5$

$$\begin{array}{r} \$16.24 \\ -\ 14.50 \\ \hline \$1.74 \end{array}$$

The dollar increase is $1.74.

24. Strategy To find what percent the population now is of the population 10 years ago, write and solve a proportion using n to represent the percent. The base is 32,500 and the amount is 71,500.

Solution

$$\frac{n}{100} = \frac{71{,}500}{32{,}500}$$
$$32{,}500 \times n = 71{,}500 \times 100$$
$$32{,}500 \times n = 7{,}150{,}000$$
$$n = 7{,}150{,}000 \div 32{,}500$$
$$n = 220$$

The population now is 220% of what it was 10 years ago.

25. Strategy To find the value of the car, write and solve a proportion using n to represent the value of the car. The percent is 1.4% and the amount is \$175.

Solution

$$\frac{1.4}{100} = \frac{175}{n}$$
$$1.4 \times n = 175 \times 100$$
$$1.4 \times n = 17{,}500$$
$$n = 17{,}500 \div 1.4$$
$$n = 12{,}500$$

The value of the car is \$12,500.

Cumulative Review Exercises

1. $18 \div (7-4)^2 + 2 = 18 \div (3)^2 + 2$
$= 18 \div 9 + 2$
$= 2 + 2 = 4$

2.

	2	3	5
16 =	(2·2·2·2)		
24 =	2·2·2	(3)	
30 =	2	3	(5)

GCF = 2·2·2·2·3·5 = 240

3.
$$2\frac{1}{3} = 2\frac{8}{24}$$
$$3\frac{1}{2} = 3\frac{12}{24}$$
$$+4\frac{5}{8} = 4\frac{15}{24}$$
$$9\frac{35}{24} = 10\frac{11}{24}$$

4.
$$25\frac{5}{12} = 27\frac{20}{48} = 26\frac{68}{48}$$
$$-14\frac{9}{16} = 14\frac{27}{48} = 14\frac{27}{48}$$
$$12\frac{41}{48}$$

5.
$$7\frac{1}{3} \times 1\frac{5}{7} = \frac{22}{3} \times \frac{12}{7}$$
$$= \frac{22 \times 12}{3 \times 7}$$
$$= \frac{2 \cdot 11 \cdot 2 \cdot 2 \cdot \overset{1}{\cancel{3}}}{\underset{1}{\cancel{3}} \cdot 7}$$
$$= \frac{88}{7} = 12\frac{4}{7}$$

6.
$$\frac{14}{27} \div 1\frac{7}{9} = \frac{14}{27} \div \frac{16}{9}$$
$$= \frac{14}{27} \times \frac{9}{16}$$
$$= \frac{14 \times 9}{27 \times 16}$$
$$= \frac{\overset{1}{\cancel{2}} \cdot 7 \cdot \overset{1}{\cancel{3}} \cdot \overset{1}{\cancel{3}}}{3 \cdot \underset{1}{\cancel{3}} \cdot \underset{1}{\cancel{3}} \cdot \underset{1}{\cancel{2}} \cdot 2 \cdot 2 \cdot 2}$$
$$= \frac{7}{24}$$

7.
$$\left(\frac{3}{4}\right)^3 \left(\frac{8}{9}\right)^2 = \left(\frac{3}{4} \cdot \frac{3}{4} \cdot \frac{3}{4}\right)\left(\frac{8}{9} \cdot \frac{8}{9}\right)$$
$$= \frac{27}{64} \cdot \frac{64}{81}$$
$$= \frac{1}{3}$$

8.
$$\left(\frac{2}{3}\right)^2 - \left(\frac{3}{8} - \frac{1}{3}\right) \div \frac{1}{2} = \frac{4}{9} - \left(\frac{9}{24} - \frac{8}{24}\right) \div \frac{1}{2}$$
$$= \frac{4}{9} - \frac{1}{24} \div \frac{1}{2}$$
$$= \frac{4}{9} - \left(\frac{1}{24} \times \frac{2}{1}\right)$$
$$= \frac{4}{9} - \frac{1}{12}$$
$$= \frac{16}{36} - \frac{3}{36} = \frac{13}{36}$$

9. 3.07973 — Given place value (the 7 in the hundredths place); 9 > 5

3.08

10.

```
  2 10 8 10 12   (9 above second 10)
  3.0 9 0 2
 -1.9 7 0 6
  1.1 1 9 6
```

11. $0.032\overline{)1.097.00000}$ = 34.28125 ≈ 34.2813

$$\begin{array}{r} 34.28125 \\ 0.032.\overline{)1.097.00000} \\ \underline{-96} \\ 137 \\ \underline{-128} \\ 90 \\ \underline{-64} \\ 260 \\ \underline{-256} \\ 40 \\ \underline{-32} \\ 80 \\ \underline{-64} \\ 160 \\ \underline{-160} \\ 0 \end{array} \approx 34.2813$$

12. $3\frac{5}{8} = \frac{29}{8}$

$$\begin{array}{r} 3.625 \\ 8\overline{)29.000} \\ \underline{-24} \\ 50 \\ \underline{-48} \\ 20 \\ \underline{-16} \\ 40 \\ \underline{-40} \\ 0 \end{array}$$

13. $1.75 = \frac{175}{100} = \frac{7}{4} = 1\frac{3}{4}$

14. $\frac{3}{8} = 0.375$

$\frac{3}{8} < 0.87$

15. $\frac{3}{8} = \frac{20}{n}$

$3 \times n = 8 \times 20$

$3 \times n = 160$

$n = 160 \div 3$

$n \approx 53.3$

16. $\frac{\$76.80}{8 \text{ hours}} = \$9.60/\text{hour}$

17. $18\frac{1}{3}\% = 18\frac{1}{3} \times \frac{1}{100} = \frac{55}{3} \times \frac{1}{100} = \frac{55}{300} = \frac{11}{60}$

18. $\frac{5}{6} \times 100\% = \frac{500}{6}\% = 83\frac{1}{3}\%$

19. $16.3\% \times 120 = n$

$0.163 \times 120 = n$

$19.56 = n$

20. $n \times 18 = 24$

$n = 24 \div 18$

$n = 1.33\ldots.$

$n = 133\frac{1}{3}\%$

21. $125\% \times n = 12.4$

$1.25 \times n = 12.4$

$n = 12.4 \div 1.25$

$n = 9.92$

22. $n \times 35 = 120$

$n = 120 \div 35$

$n \approx 3.4285$

$n \approx 342.9\%$

23. Strategy To find Sergio's take-home pay:
- Find the amount deducted by multiplying the income ($740) by $\frac{1}{5}$.
- Subtract the amount deducted from the income.

Solution $\frac{1}{5} \times \$740 = \$148$

$\$740 - \$148 = \$592$

Sergio's take-home pay is $592.

24. Strategy To find the amount of the monthly payment:
- Find the amount that will be paid by payments by subtracting the down payment ($1000) from the price of the car ($8353).
- Divide the total amount remaining to be paid by the number of payments (36).

Solution $\begin{array}{r} \$8353 \\ \underline{-1000} \\ \$7353 \end{array}$ $\quad \begin{array}{r} \$204.25 \\ 36\overline{)\$7353.00} \end{array}$

Each monthly payment is $204.25.

25. Strategy To find the number of gallons of gasoline used during the month, divide the total paid in taxes ($79.80) by the tax paid per gallon ($.19).

Solution $\$79.80 \div \$.19 = 420$

420 gallons were used during the month.

26. Strategy To find the real estate tax on a house valued at $250,000, write and solve a proportion using n to represent the tax.

Solution $\frac{3440}{172{,}000} = \frac{n}{250{,}000}$

$3440 \times 250{,}000 = 172{,}000 \times n$

$860{,}000{,}000 = 172{,}000 \times n$

$860{,}000{,}000 \div 172{,}000 = n$

$5000 = n$

The real estate tax is $5000.

27. Strategy To find what percent of the purchase price the sales tax is, write and solve the basic percent equation using n to represent the percent. The base is \$490 and the amount is \$29.40.

Solution

$$n \times \$490 = \$29.40$$
$$n = 29.40 \div 490$$
$$n = 0.06$$
$$n = 6\%$$

The sales tax is 6% of the purchase price.

28. Strategy To find what percent of the people did not favor the candidate:

- Find the number of people who did not favor the candidate by subtracting the number of people who did favor the candidate (165) from the total surveyed (300).
- Write and solve the basic percent equation using n to represent the percent of people who did not favor the candidate. The base is 300 and the amount is the number of people who did not favor the candidate.

Solution

$$\begin{array}{r} 300 \\ -165 \\ \hline 135 \end{array}$$

$$n \times 300 = 135$$
$$n = 135 \div 300$$
$$n = 0.45$$
$$n = 45\%$$

45% of the people did not favor the candidate.

29. Strategy To find the average hours:

- Find the number of hours in a week by multiplying the number of hours in a day (24) by the number of days in a week (7).
- Write and solve the basic percent equation using n to represent the number of hours spent watching TV. The percent is 36.5% and the base is 168.

Solution

$$\begin{array}{r} 24 \\ \times\ 7 \\ \hline 168 \end{array}$$

$$36.5\% \times 168 = n$$
$$0.365 \times 168 = n$$
$$61.3 \approx n$$

The approximate average number of hours spent watching TV in a week is 61.3 hours.

30. Strategy To find what percent of the children tested had levels of lead that exceeded federal standards, write and solve a proportion using n to represent the percent who had levels of lead that exceeded federal standards. The base is 5500 and the amount is 990.

Solution

$$\frac{n}{100} = \frac{990}{5500}$$
$$n \times 5500 = 990 \times 100$$
$$n \times 5500 = 99{,}000$$
$$n = 99{,}000 \div 5500$$
$$n = 18$$

18% of the children tested had levels of lead that exceeded federal standards.

Chapter 6: Applications for Business and Consumers

Prep Test

1. 0.75
2. 52.05
3. 504.51
4. 9750
5. $1500 \times 0.06 \times 0.5 = 90 \times 0.5 = 45$
6. 1417.24
7.
```
     3.33
  3)10.00
    -9
     10
     -9
      10
      -9
       1
```
8.
```
         0.605
  570)345.000
      -3420
         300
        -  0
        3000
       -2850
         150
```
9. $0.379 < 0.397$

Go Figure

To find the price of the earrings including sales tax, note that multiplying 1.04 by the price before the sales tax is added (in dollars and cents) must yield a whole number. To solve for the number in dollars and cents, divide both sides by 1.04. So we want to find a whole number that when divided by 1.04 results in a terminating decimal with no more than 2 decimal places. To anticipate a solution, the factors of 104 are 2, 2, 2, and 13. Therefore, 2, 4, or 8 divided by 104 results in a terminating decimal; 13, 26, 52, or 104 divided by 104 results in a nonterminating decimal. So the whole number cannot be 2, 4, or 8 since the result would be a nonterminating decimal.

Using trial and error,

$1 \div 1.04 = 0.961538\ldots$ (nonterminating decimal)
$2 \div 1.04 = 1.923076\ldots$ (nonterminating decimal)
$3 \div 1.04 = 2.884615\ldots$ (nonterminating decimal)
$4 \div 1.04 = 3.846153\ldots$ (nonterminating decimal)

⋮

$12 \div 1.04 = 11.53846\ldots$ (nonterminating decimal)
$13 \div 1.04 = 12.5$

The earrings sold for \$12.50 plus 4% tax (\$.50). So a customer paid \$13, including 4% tax for the pair of earrings.

Section 6.1

Objective A Exercises

1. **Strategy** To find the unit cost, divide the total cost (\$.99) by the number of units (18).

   Solution $.99 \div 18 = 0.055$
   The unit cost is \$.055 per ounce.

2. **Strategy** To find the unit cost, divide the total cost (\$18.75) by the number of units (6).

   Solution $18.75 \div 6 = 3.125$
   The unit cost is \$3.125 per foot.

3. **Strategy** To find the unit cost, divide the total cost (\$2.99) by the number of units (8).

   Solution $2.99 \div 8 \approx 0.3737$
   The unit cost is \$.374 per ounce.

4. **Strategy** To find the unit cost, divide the total cost (\$2.99) by the number of units (6).

   Solution $2.99 \div 6 \approx 0.4983$
   The unit cost is \$.498 per can.

5. **Strategy** To find the unit cost, divide the total cost (\$3.99) by the number of units (50).

   Solution $3.99 \div 50 = 0.0798$
   The unit cost is \$.080 per tablet.

6. **Strategy** To find the unit cost, divide the total cost (\$3.89) by the number of units (0.5).

   Solution $3.89 \div 0.5 = 7.78$
   The unit cost is \$7.780 per ounce.

7. **Strategy** To find the unit cost, divide the total cost (\$13.95) by the number of units (2).

   Solution $13.95 \div 2 = 6.975$
   The unit price is \$6.975 per clamp.

8. **Strategy** To find the unit cost, divide the total cost (\$1.85) by the number of units (6).

   Solution $1.85 \div 6 \approx 0.3083$
   The unit price is \$.308 per ear.

9. Strategy To find the unit cost, divide the total cost ($2.99) by the number of units (15).

Solution $2.99 \div 15 \approx 0.1993$
The unit cost is $.199 per ounce.

10. Strategy To find the unit cost, divide the total cost ($2.99) by the number of units (14.5).

Solution $2.99 \div 14.5 \approx 0.2062$
The unit cost is $.206 per ounce.

11. Strategy To find the unit cost, divide the total cost ($.95) by the number of units (8).

Solution $0.95 \div 8 \approx 0.1187$
The unit cost is $.119 per screw.

12. Strategy To find the unit cost, divide the total cost ($4.79) by the number of units (11.5).

Solution $4.79 \div 11.5 \approx 0.4165$
The unit cost is $.417 per ounce.

Objective B Exercises

13. Strategy To find the more economical purchase, compare the unit costs.

Solution Sutter Home: $3.29 \div 25.5 \approx 0.1290$
Muir Glen: $3.79 \div 26 \approx 0.1458$
$0.1290 < 0.1458$
The Sutter Home pasta sauce is the more economical purchase.

14. Strategy To find the more economical purchase, compare the unit costs.

Solution Kraft: $2.98 \div 40 = 0.0745$
Springfield: $2.39 \div 32 \approx 0.0747$
$0.0745 < 0.0747$
The Kraft mayonnaise is the more economical purchase.

15. Strategy To find the more economical purchase, compare the unit costs.

Solution 20 ounces: $3.29 \div 20 = 0.1645$
12 ounces: $1.99 \div 12 \approx 0.1658$
$0.1645 < 0.1648$
20 ounces is the more economical purchase.

16. Strategy To find the more economical purchase, compare the unit costs.

Solution L'Oréal shampoo: $4.69 \div 13 \approx 0.3608$
Cortexx shampoo: $3.99 \div 12 = 0.3325$
$0.3325 < 0.3608$
Cortexx shampoo is the more economical purchase.

17. Strategy To find the more economical purchase, compare the unit costs.

Solution 200 tablets: $7.39 \div 200 \approx 0.0370$
400 tablets: $12.99 \div 400 \approx 0.0325$
$0.0325 < 0.0370$
400 tablets is the more economical purchase.

18. Strategy To find the more economical purchase, compare the unit costs.

Solution Ultra Mr. Clean: $2.67 \div 20 = 0.1335$
Ultra Spic and Span: $2.19 \div 14$
≈ 0.1564
$0.1335 < 0.1564$
Ultra Mr. Clean is the more economical purchase.

19. Strategy To find the more economical purchase, compare the unit costs.

Solution Kraft: $4.37 \div 16 \approx 0.2731$
Land O' Lakes: $2.29 \div 9 \approx 0.2544$
$0.2544 < 0.2731$
Land O' Lakes cheddar cheese is the more economical purchase.

20. Strategy To find the more economical purchase, compare the unit costs.

Solution Bertolli: $9.49 \div 34 \approx 0.2791$
Pompeian: $2.39 \div 8 \approx 0.2988$
$0.2791 < 0.2988$
Bertolli olive oil is the more economical purchase.

21. Strategy To find the more economical purchase, compare the unit costs.

Solution Maxwell House: $3.99 \div 4 = 0.9975$
Sanka: $2.39 \div 2 = 1.195$
$0.9975 < 1.195$
Maxwell House coffee is the more economical purchase.

22. Strategy To find the more economical purchase, compare the unit costs.

Solution Wagner's: $3.29 \div 1.5 \approx 2.1933$
Durkee: $2.74 \div 1 = 2.74$
$2.1933 < 2.74$
Wagner's vanilla extract is the more economical purchase.

23. Strategy To find the more economical purchase, compare the unit costs.

Solution Purina: $4.19 \div 56 \approx 0.0748$
Friskies: $3.37 \div 50.4 \approx 0.0669$
$0.0669 < 0.0748$
Friskies Chef's Blend is the more economical purchase.

24. Strategy To find the more economical purchase, compare the unit costs.

Solution Kleenex: $1.73 \div 250 \approx 0.0069$
Puffs: $1.23 \div 175 \approx 0.0070$
$0.0069 < 0.0070$
Kleenex is the more economical purchase.

Objective C Exercises

25. Strategy To find the total cost, multiply the unit cost ($4.59) by the number of units (3).

Solution $4.59 \times 3 = 13.77$
The total cost is $13.77.

26. Strategy To find the total cost, multiply the unit cost ($.98) by the number of units (75).

Solution $0.98 \times 75 = 73.50$
The total cost is $73.50.

27. Strategy To find the total cost, multiply the unit cost ($.23) by the number of units (8).

Solution $0.23 \times 8 = 1.84$
The total cost is $1.84.

28. Strategy To find the total cost, multiply the unit cost ($4.69) by the number of units (3.6).

Solution $4.69 \times 3.6 = 16.884$
The total cost is $16.88.

29. Strategy To find the total cost, multiply the unit cost ($.98) by the number of units (6.5).

Solution $0.98 \times 6.5 = 6.37$
The total cost is $6.37.

30. Strategy To find the total cost, multiply the unit cost ($5.99) by the number of units (0.65).

Solution $5.99 \times 0.65 \approx 3.893$
The total cost is $3.89.

31. Strategy To find the total cost, multiply the unit cost ($1.29) by the number of units (2.1).

Solution $1.29 \times 2.1 = 2.709$
The total cost is $2.71.

32. Strategy To find the total cost, multiply the unit cost ($8.49) by the number of units (2.8).

Solution $8.49 \times 2.8 = 23.772$
The total cost is $23.77.

33. Strategy To find the total cost, multiply the unit cost ($7.95) by the number of units $\left(\frac{3}{4}\right)$.

Solution $7.95 \times \frac{3}{4} = 7.95 \times 0.75 \approx 5.962$
The total cost is $5.96.

34. Strategy To find the total cost, multiply the unit cost ($.89) by the number of units (120).

Solution $0.89 \times 120 = 106.80.$
The total cost is $106.80.

Applying the Concepts

35. Students might explain that unit pricing is used in grocery stores. The unit price of a product is the total price divided by the number of units the product contains. Consumers can use this information to determine which size of a product is the more economical purchase.

36. The Universal Product Code, or UPC, is a series of lines, bars, and numbers found on the packages of consumer products. The UPC is used with an optical scanning device that "reads" the UPC and signals the computer to search its memory for the price of the item.

Section 6.2

Objective A Exercises

1. Strategy To find the percent increase:
- Find the amount of the increase by subtracting the enrollment for 1988 (45.4 million) from the projected enrollment for 2008 (54.3 million).
- Write and solve the basic percent equation for percent. The base is 45.4 and the amount is the amount of the increase.

Solution $54.3 - 45.4 = 8.9$

Percent × base = amount

$n \times 45.4 = 8.9$

$n = 8.9 \div 45.4$

$n \approx 0.196$

The percent increase is 19.6%.

2. Strategy To find the percent increase:
- Find the amount of the increase by subtracting the miles per gallon before the increase (17.5) from the miles per gallon after the increase (18.2).
- Write and solve the basic percent equation for percent. The base is 17.5 and the amount is the amount of the increase.

Solution $18.2 - 17.5 = 0.7$

Percent × base = amount

$n \times 17.5 = 0.7$

$n = 0.7 \div 17.5$

$n = 0.04$

The percent increase is 4%.

3. Strategy To find the percent increase:
- Subtract the number of stores before the increase (420) from the number of stores after the increase (914).
- Write and solve the basic percent equation for percent. The base is 420 and the amount is the amount of the increase.

Solution $914 - 420 = 494$

Percent × base = amount

$n \times 420 = 494$

$n = 494 \div 420$

$n \approx 1.176$

The percent increase is 117.6%.

4. Strategy To find the percent increase:
- Find the amount of the increase by subtracting the number of unmarried couples in 1980 (1.6 million) from the number of unmarried couples in 2000 (4.7 million).
- Write and solve the basic percent equation for percent. The base is 1.6 and the amount is the amount of the increase.

Solution $4.7 - 1.6 = 3.1$

Percent × base = amount

$n \times 1.6 = 3.1$

$n = 3.1 \div 1.6$

$n = 1.9375$

The percent increase is 193.8%.

5. Strategy To find the percent increase:
- Find the amount of the increase by subtracting the number of events in 1924 (14) from the number of events in 2002 (78).
- Write and solve the basic percent equation for percent. The base is 14 and the amount is the amount of the increase.

Solution $78 - 14 = 64$

Percent × base = amount

$n \times 14 = 64$

$n = 64 \div 14$

$n \approx 4.571$

The percent increase is 457.1%.

6. Strategy To find the percent increase:
- Find the amount of the increase by subtracting the number of households in 1975 (350,000) from the number of households in 2005 (5,600,000).
- Write and solve the basic percent equation for percent. The base is 350,000 and the amount is the amount of the increase.

Solution $5{,}600{,}000 - 350{,}000 = 5{,}250{,}000$

Percent × base = amount

$n \times 350{,}000 = 5{,}250{,}000$

$n = 5{,}250{,}000 \div 350{,}000$

$n = 15$

The percent increase is 1500%.

7. **Strategy** To find the population 8 years later:
• Write and solve the basic percent equation for the amount of increase. The percent is 24.3% and the base is 127,000.
• Add the increase to initial population (127,000).

Solution
Percent × base = amount
$24.3\% \times 127{,}000 = n$
$0.243 \times 127{,}000 = n$
$30{,}861 = n$
$30{,}861 + 127{,}000 = 157{,}861$
The population 8 years later was 157,861 people.

8. **Strategy** To find the number of subscribers:
• Write and solve the basic percent equation for the amount of increase. The percent is 87% and the base is 2.3 million.
• Add the increase to number of subscribers at the beginning of the year (2.3 million).

Solution
Percent × base = amount
$87\% \times 2.3 = n$
$0.87 \times 2.3 = n$
$2.001 = n$
$2.001 + 2.3 = 4.301$
There were 4.301 million subscribers at the end of the year.

9. **Strategy** To find the average age of American mothers giving birth to their first child:
• Find the increase by writing and solving the basic percent equation for amount of increase. The percent is 16.4% and the base is 21.4 years.
• Add the increase to the 1970 age (21.4)

Solution
Percent × base = amount
$16.4\% \times 21.4 = n$
$0.164 \times 21.4 = n$
$3.5096 = n$
$21.4 + 3.5 = 24.9$ years
The average age of American mothers giving birth in 2000 was 24.9 years.

Objective B Exercises

10. **Strategy** To find the markup, solve the basic percent equation for amount.

Solution
Percent × base = amount
$25\% \times 285 = n$
$0.25 \times 285 = n$
$71.25 = n$
The markup is $71.25.

11. **Strategy** To find the markup, solve the basic percent equation for amount.

Solution
Percent × base = amount
$42\% \times 85 = n$
$0.42 \times 85 = n$
$35.70 = n$
The markup is $35.70.

12. **Strategy** To find the markup, solve the basic percent equation for amount.

Solution
Percent × base = amount
$38\% \times 45 = n$
$0.38 \times 45 = n$
$17.10 = n$
The markup is $17.10.

13. **Strategy** To find the markup rate, solve the basic percent equation for percent. The base is $3250 and the amount is $975.

Solution
Percent × base = amount
$n \times 3250 = 975$
$n = 975 \div 3250$
$n = 0.30 = 30\%$
The markup rate is 30%.

14. **Strategy** To find the markup rate, solve the basic percent equation for percent. The base is $20 and the amount is $12.

Solution
Percent × base = amount
$n \times 20 = 12$
$n = 12 \div 20$
$n = 0.60 = 60\%$
The markup rate is 60%.

15a. **Strategy** To find the markup, solve the basic percent equation for amount.

Solution
Percent × base = amount
$48\% \times 162 = n$
$0.48 \times 162 = n$
$77.76 = n$
The markup is $77.76.

b. **Strategy** To find the selling price, add the markup to the cost.

Solution
$77.76 + 162 = 239.76$
The selling price is $239.76.

16a. **Strategy** To find the markup, solve the basic percent equation for amount.

Solution
Percent × base = amount
$45\% \times 210 = n$
$0.45 \times 210 = n$
$94.50 = n$
The markup is $94.50.

b. Strategy To find the selling price, add the markup to the cost.

Solution $94.50 + 210 = 304.50$
The selling price is \$304.50.

17a. Strategy To find the markup, solve the basic percent equation for amount.

Solution Percent × base = amount
$55\% \times 2 = n$
$0.55 \times 2 = n$
$1.1 = n$
The markup is \$1.10.

b. Strategy To find the selling price, add the markup to the cost.

Solution $2.00 + 1.10 = 3.10$
The selling price is \$3.10.

18. Strategy To find the selling price:
- Solve the basic percent equation for amount to find the amount of the markup.
- Add the amount of the markup to the cost (\$160).

Solution Percent × base = amount
$42\% \times 160 = n$
$0.42 \times 160 = n$
$67.2 = n$
$67.2 + 160 = 227.20$
The selling price is \$227.20.

19. Strategy To find the selling price:
- Solve the basic percent equation for amount to find the amount of the markup.
- Add the amount of the markup to the cost (\$50).

Solution Percent × base = amount
$48\% \times 50 = n$
$0.48 \times 50 = n$
$24 = n$
$50 + 24 = 74$
The selling price is \$74.

Objective C Exercises

20. Strategy To find the percent decrease, solve the basic percent equation for percent. The base is 45 and the amount is 18.

Solution Percent × base = amount
$n \times 45 = 18$
$n = 18 \div 45$
$n = 0.40 = 40\%$
The amount represents a decrease of 40%.

21. Strategy To find the percent decrease, solve the basic percent equation for percent. The base is \$800 and the amount is \$320.

Solution Percent × base = amount
$n \times 800 = 320$
$n = 320 \div 800$
$n = 0.40 = 40\%$
The amount represents a decrease of 40%.

22. Strategy To find how much value the car loses, solve the basic percent equation for amount. The base is \$18,200 and the percent is 30%.

Solution Percent × base = amount
$30\% \times 18{,}200 = n$
$0.30 \times 18{,}200 = n$
$5460 = n$
The car loses \$5460 in value after 1 year.

23. Strategy To find the decrease in the number of employees, solve the percent equation for amount. The base is 1200 and the percent is 45%.

Solution Percent × base = amount
$45\% \times 1200 = n$
$0.45 \times 1200 = n$
$540 = n$
There is decrease of 540 employees.

24a. Strategy To find the amount of the decrease, subtract the new value (8) from the earlier value (20).

Solution $20 - 8 = 12$
The amount of the decrease is 12 cameras.

b. Strategy To find the percent decrease, solve the percent equation for percent. The base is 20 and the amount is 12.

Solution Percent × base = amount
$n \times 20 = 12$
$n = 12 \div 20$
$n = 0.60 = 60\%$
The amount represents a decrease of 60%.

25a. Strategy To find the amount of decrease, subtract the new value (39) from the original value (52).

Solution $52 - 39 = 13$
The amount of the decrease is 13 minutes.

b. Strategy To find the percent decrease, solve the basic percent equation for percent. The base is 52 and the amount is 13.

Solution Percent × base = amount

$n \times 52 = 13$

$n = 13 \div 52$

$n = 0.25 = 25\%$

The amount represents a decrease of 25%.

26a. Strategy To find the amount of decrease, solve the basic percent equation for amount. The base is $76 and the percent is 20%.

Solution Percent × base = amount

$20\% \times 76 = n$

$0.20 \times 76 = n$

$15.2 = n$

The amount of the decrease was $15.20.

b. Strategy To find the average monthly gasoline bill now, subtract the amount of the decrease ($15.20) from the original amount ($76).

Solution $76 - 15.20 = 60.80$

The average monthly gasoline bill now is $60.80.

27a. Strategy To find the amount of decrease, solve the basic percent equation for amount. The base is $1.60 and the percent is 37.5%.

Solution Percent × base = amount

$37.5\% \times 1.60 = n$

$0.375 \times 1.60 = n$

$0.60 = n$

The amount of decrease is $.60.

b. Strategy To find the dividend this year, subtract the amount of the decrease ($0.60) from the dividend last year ($1.60).

Solution $1.60 - 0.60 = 1.00$

The dividend this year is $1.00.

28. Strategy To find the percent decrease:

- Find the amount of the decrease by subtracting the new value (2.8) from the original value (3.5).
- Solve the basic percent equation for percent. The amount is the amount of the decrease and the base is 3.5.

Solution $3.5 - 2.8 = 0.7$

Percent × base = amount

$n \times 3.5 = 0.7$

$n = 0.7 \div 3.5$

$n = 0.20 = 20\%$

The amount represents a decrease of 20%.

29. Strategy To find the percent decrease, solve the basic percent equation for percent. The amount is the amount of the decrease (26) and the base is 394.

Solution Percent × base = amount

$n \times 394 = 26$

$n = 26 \div 394$

$n \approx 0.066 = 6.6\%$

The amount represents a decrease of 6.6%.

30. Strategy To find the percent decrease:

- Find the amount of the decrease by subtracting the new value (36,940) from the original value (54,246).
- Solve the basic percent equation for percent. The amount is the amount of the decrease and the base is 54,246.

Solution $54{,}246 - 36{,}940 = 17{,}306$

Percent × base = amount

$n \times 54{,}246 = 17{,}306$

$n = 17{,}306 \div 54{,}246$

$n \approx 0.319 = 31.9\%$

The amount represents a decrease of 31.9%.

Objective D Exercises

31. Strategy To find the discount rate, solve the basic percent equation for percent. The base is $24 and the amount is $8.

Solution Percent × base = amount

$n \times 24 = 8$

$n = 8 \div 24$

$n = 0.333\ldots = 33\frac{1}{3}\%$

The discount rate is $33\frac{1}{3}\%$.

32. Strategy To find the discount rate, solve the basic percent equation for percent. The base is $72 and the amount is $24.

Solution Percent × base = amount

$n \times 72 = 24$

$n = 24 \div 72$

$n = 0.333\ldots = 33\frac{1}{3}\%$

The discount rate is $33\frac{1}{3}\%$.

33. Strategy To find the discount, solve the basic percent equation for amount. The percent is 20% and the base is \$340.

Solution Percent × base = amount

$20\% \times 340 = n$

$0.20 \times 340 = n$

$68 = n$

The discount is \$68.

34. Strategy To find the discount, solve the basic percent equation for amount. The percent is 15% and the base is \$450.

Solution Percent × base = amount

$15\% \times 450 = n$

$0.15 \times 450 = n$

$67.5 = n$

The discount is \$67.50.

35. Strategy To find the discount rate, solve the basic percent equation for percent. The base is \$140 and the amount is \$42.

Solution Percent × base = amount

$n \times 140 = 42$

$n = 42 \div 140$

$n = 0.30 = 30\%$

The discount rate is 30%.

36a. Strategy To find the discount, solve the basic percent equation for amount. The percent is 16% and the base is \$45.

Solution Percent × base = amount

$16\% \times 45 = n$

$0.16 \times 45 = n$

$7.2 = n$

The discount is \$7.20.

b. Strategy To find the sale price, subtract the discount (\$7.20) from the original price (\$45).

Solution $45 - 7.20 = 37.80$

The sale price is \$37.80.

37a. Strategy To find the discount, solve the basic percent equation for amount. The percent is 20% and the base is \$1.25.

Solution Percent × base = amount

$20\% \times 1.25 = n$

$0.20 \times 1.25 = n$

$0.25 = n$

The discount is \$.25 per pound.

b. Strategy To find the sale price, subtract the discount (\$.25) from the original price (\$1.25).

Solution $1.25 - 0.25 = 1.00$

The sale price is \$1.00 per pound.

38a. Strategy To find the discount, subtract the sale price (\$120) from the original price (\$160).

Solution $160 - 120 = 40$

The discount is \$40.

b. Strategy To find the discount rate, solve the basic percent equation for percent. The base is \$160 and the amount is \$40.

Solution Percent × base = amount

$n \times 160 = 40$

$n = 40 \div 160$

$n = 0.25 = 25\%$

The discount rate is 25%.

39a. Strategy To find the discount, subtract the sale price (\$16) from the original cost (\$20).

Solution $20 - 16 = 4$

The amount of the discount is \$4.

b. Strategy To find the discount rate, solve the basic percent equation for percent. The base is \$20 and the amount is \$4.

Solution Percent × base = amount

$n \times 20 = 4$

$n = 4 \div 20$

$n = 0.20 = 20\%$

The discount rate is 20%.

40. Strategy To find the greatest percent decrease:
- Find the amount of each decrease by subtracting the new value for each branch from the original value.
- Solve the basic percent equation for percent. The amount is the amount of the decrease and the base is number of personnel in 1990 for each branch.
- Compare the results to find the greatest percent decrease.

Solution
$751 - 480 = 271$ Army
$n \times 751 = 271$
$n = 271 \div 751$
$n \approx 0.361 = 36.1\%$
$583 - 372 = 211$ Navy
$n \times 583 = 211$
$n = 211 \div 583$
$n \approx 0.362 = 36.2\%$
$539 - 361 = 178$ Air Force
$n \times 539 = 178$
$n = 178 \div 539$
$n \approx 0.330 = 33.0\%$
$197 - 172 = 25$ Marines
$n \times 197 = 25$
$n = 25 \div 197$
$n \approx 0.127 = 12.7\%$

a. The Navy had the greatest percent decrease.
b. The amount represents a decrease of 36.2%.

Applying the Concepts

41. $\$12 \times 0.10 + \$12 = \$1.20 + \$12 = \$13.20$
$\$12(1.10) = \$13.20$
Yes

42a. Total cost $= 200 \times \$.86 = \$172$

b. Total selling price $= \$172(1.50)$
$= \$258$

c. Number of salable roses $= (1 - .07) \times 200$
$= 186$ roses

d. Selling price $= \$258 \div 186 = \$1.39$ per rose

43. No. Suppose the regular price is \$100. Then the sale price is \$75 because $100 - 0.25(100) = 100 - 25 = 75$. The promotional sale offers 25% off the sale price of \$75, so the price is lowered to \$56.25 because $75 - 0.25(75) = 75 - 18.75 = 56.25$. A sale that offers 50% off the regular price of \$100 offers the product for \$50. Because \$50 < \$56.25, the better price is the one that is 50% off the regular price.

Section 6.3

Objective A Exercises

1a. \$10,000

b. \$850

c. 4.25%

d. 2 years

2a. \$80,000

b. \$5850

c. 9.75%

d. 9 months

3. Strategy To find the simple interest, multiply the principal by the annual interest rate by the time (in years).

Solution $8000 \times 0.06 \times 2 = 960$
The simple interest owed is \$960.

4. Strategy To find the simple interest, multiply the principal by the annual interest rate by the time (in years).

Solution $1500 \times 0.075 \times 1\frac{1}{2} = 168.75$
The simple interest owed is \$168.75.

5. Strategy To find the simple interest, multiply the principal by the annual interest rate by the time (in years).

Solution $100{,}000 \times 0.045 \times \frac{9}{12} = 3375$
The simple interest due is \$3375.

6. Strategy To find the simple interest, multiply the principal by the annual interest rate by the time (in years).

Solution $50{,}000 \times 0.095 \times \frac{8}{12} \approx 3166.67$
The simple interest due is \$3166.67.

7. Strategy To find the simple interest, multiply the principal by the annual interest rate by the time (in years).

Solution $20{,}000 \times 0.088 \times \frac{9}{12} = 1320$
The simple interest due is \$1320.

8. Strategy To find the simple interest, multiply the principal by the annual interest rate by the time (in years).

Solution $4500 \times 0.062 \times \frac{8}{12} = 186$
The simple interest owed is \$186.

9. Strategy To find the simple interest, multiply the principal by the annual interest rate by the time (in years).

Solution $5000 \times 0.075 \times \frac{90}{365} \approx 92.47$

The simple interest due is $92.47.

10. Strategy To find the simple interest, multiply the principal by the annual interest rate by the time (in years).

Solution $8500 \times 0.0925 \times \frac{180}{365} \approx 387.74$

The simple interest due is $387.74.

11. Strategy To find the simple interest, multiply the principal by the annual interest rate by the time (in years).

Solution $7500 \times 0.055 \times \frac{75}{365} \approx 84.76$

The simple interest due is $84.76.

12. Strategy To find the simple interest, multiply the principal by the annual interest rate by the time (in years).

Solution $15{,}000 \times 0.074 \times \frac{90}{365} \approx 273.70$

The simple interest due is $273.70.

13. Strategy To find the maturity value of the loan, add the principal and the simple interest.

Solution $4800 + 320 = 5120$

The maturity value of the loan is $5120.

14. Strategy To find the maturity value of the loan, add the principal and the simple interest.

Solution $6500 + 80.14 = 6580.14$

The maturity value of the loan is $6580.14.

15. Strategy To find the maturity value:

- Find the simple interest due by multiplying the principal by the annual interest rate by the time (in years).
- Find the maturity value by adding the principal and the simple interest.

Solution $150{,}000 \times 0.095 \times 1 = 14{,}250$

$150{,}000 + 14{,}250 = 164{,}250$

The maturity value is $164,250.

16. Strategy To find the maturity value:

- Find the simple interest due by multiplying the principal by the annual interest rate by the time (in years).
- Find the maturity value by adding the principal and the simple interest.

Solution $25{,}000 \times 0.082 \times 1 = 2050$

$25{,}000 + 2050 = 27{,}050$

The maturity value is $27,050.

17. Strategy To find the total amount due:

- Find the simple interest due by multiplying the principal by the annual interest rate by the time (in years).
- Find the total amount due by adding the principal and the simple interest.

Solution $12{,}500 \times 0.045 \times \frac{8}{12} \approx 375$

$12{,}500 + 375 = 12{,}875$

The total amount due on the loan is $12,875.

18. Strategy To find the total amount due:

- Find the simple interest due by multiplying the principal by the annual interest rate by the time (in years).
- Find the total amount due by adding the principal and the simple interest.

Solution $9000 \times 0.085 \times \frac{9}{12} = 573.75$

$9000 + 573.75 = 9573.75$

The total amount you repay to the bank is $9573.75.

19. Strategy To find the maturity value:

- Find the simple interest due by multiplying the principal by the annual interest rate by the time (in years).
- Find the maturity value by adding the principal and the simple interest.

Solution $14{,}000 \times 0.0525 \times \frac{270}{365} \approx 543.70$

$14{,}000 + 543.70 = 14{,}543.70$

The maturity value is $14,543.70.

20. Strategy To find the maturity value:
- Find the simple interest due by multiplying the principal by the annual interest rate by the time (in years).
- Find the maturity value by adding the principal and the simple interest.

Solution $5000 \times 0.069 \times \frac{18}{12} = 517.5$
$5000 + 517.5 = 5517.5$
The maturity value is $5517.50.

21. Strategy To find the monthly payment, divide the sum of the loan amount ($225,000) and the interest ($72,000) by the number of payments (48).

Solution $\frac{225{,}000 + 72{,}000}{48} = 6187.50$
The monthly payment is $6187.50.

22. Strategy To find the monthly payment, divide the sum of the loan amount ($1900) and the interest ($357.20) by the number of payments (24).

Solution $\frac{1900 + 357.20}{24} = 94.05$
The monthly payment is $94.05.

23a. Strategy To find the simple interest charged, multiply the principal ($12,000) by the annual interest rate by the time (in years).

Solution $12{,}000 \times 0.045 \times 2 = 1080$
The interest charged is $1080.

b. Strategy To find the monthly payment, divide the sum of the loan amount ($12,000) and the interest ($1080) by the number of payments (24).

Solution $\frac{12{,}000 + 1080}{24} = 545$
The monthly payment is $545.

24a. Strategy To find the simple interest due, multiply the principal by the annual interest rate by the time (in years).

Solution $57{,}000 \times 0.09 \times 5 = 25{,}650$
The interest due on the loan is $25,650.

b. Strategy To find the monthly payment, divide the sum of the loan amount ($57,000) and the interest ($25,650) by the number of payments (60).

Solution $\frac{57{,}000 + 25{,}650}{60} = 1377.50$
The monthly payment is $1377.50.

25. Strategy To find the monthly payment:
- Find the simple interest due by multiplying the principal by the annual interest rate by the time (in years).
- Find the monthly payment by adding the interest due to the loan amount ($42,000) and dividing that sum by the number of payments (42).

Solution $42{,}000 \times 0.095 \times 3.5 = 13{,}965$
The monthly payment is
$\frac{42{,}000 + 13{,}965}{42} = \$1332.50.$

26. Strategy To find the monthly payment:
- Find the simple interest due by multiplying the principal by the annual interest rate by the time (in years).
- Find the monthly payment by adding the interest due to the loan amount ($12,000) and dividing that sum by the number of payments (6).

Solution $12{,}000 \times 0.085 \times \frac{6}{12} = 510$
The monthly payment is
$\frac{12{,}000 + 510}{6} = \$2085.$

Objective B Exercises

27. Strategy To find the finance charge, multiply the unpaid balance by the monthly interest rate by the number of months.

Solution $118.72 \times 0.0125 \times 1 = 1.48$
The finance charge is $1.48.

28. Strategy To find the finance charge, multiply the unpaid balance by the monthly interest rate by the number of months.

Solution $391.64 \times 0.0175 \times 1 = 6.85$
The finance charge is $6.85.

29. Strategy To find the finance charge, multiply the unpaid balance by the monthly interest rate by the number of months.

Solution $12{,}368.92 \times 0.015 \times 1 = 185.53$
The finance charge is $185.53.

30. Strategy To find the finance charge, multiply the unpaid balance by the monthly interest rate by the number of months.

Solution $995.04 \times 0.012 \times 1 \approx 11.94$
The finance charge is $11.94.

31. Strategy To find the difference in finance charges:
- Find the difference in monthly interest rates by subtracting the smaller rate (1.15%) from the larger rate (1.85%).
- To find the difference in finance charges, multiply the unpaid balance by the difference in monthly interest rates by the number of months.

Solution $0.0185 - 0.0115 = 0.007 = 0.7\%$
$1438.20 \times 0.007 \times 1 \approx 10.07$
The difference in finance charges is $10.07.

32. Strategy To find the difference in finance charges:
- Find the difference in monthly interest rates by subtracting the smaller rate (1.25%) from the larger rate (1.75%).
- To find the difference in finance charges, multiply the unpaid balance by the difference in monthly interest rates by the number of months.

Solution $0.0175 - 0.0125 = 0.005 = 0.5\%$
$687.45 \times 0.005 \times 1 \approx 3.44$
The difference in finance charges is $3.44.

Objective C Exercises

33. Strategy To find the value of the investment in 1 year, multiply the original investment by the compound interest factor.

Solution $750 \times 1.04080 = 780.60$
The value of the investment after 1 year is $780.60.

34. Strategy To find the value of the investment after 20 years, multiply the original investment by the compound interest factor.

Solution $2500 \times 4.95217 \approx 12,380.43$
The value of the investment after 20 years is $12,380.43.

35. Strategy To find the value of the investment after 15 years, multiply the original investment by the compound interest factor.

Solution $3000 \times 2.42726 = 7281.78$
The value of the investment after 15 years is $7281.78.

36. Strategy To find the value of the investment after 5 years, multiply the original investment by the compound interest factor.

Solution $20,000 \times 1.417625 = 28,352.50$
The value of the investment after 5 years is $28,352.50.

37a. Strategy To find the value of the investment in 5 years, multiply the original investment by the compound interest factor.

Solution $75,000 \times 1.48595 = 111,446.25$
The value of the investment in 5 years will be $111,446.25.

b. Strategy To find the amount of interest that will be earned, subtract the original investment from the new value of the investment.

Solution $111,446.25 - 75,000 = 36,446.25$
The amount of interest earned will be $36,446.25.

38a. Strategy To find the value of the investment in 10 years, multiply the original investment by the compound interest factor.

Solution $3000 \times 2.01362 = 6040.86$
The value of the investment in 10 years will be $6040.86.

b. Strategy To find how much interest will be earned, subtract the original investment from the new value of the investment.

Solution $6040.86 - 3000 = 3040.86$
The amount of interest earned in 10 years will be $3040.86.

39. Strategy To find the amount of interest earned over a 20-year period:
- Find the value of the investment after 20 years by multiplying the original investment by the compound interest factor.
- Subtract the original value of the investment ($2500) from the new value of the investment.

Solution $2500 \times 3.31979 = 8299.48$
$8299.48 - 2500 = 5799.48$
The amount of interest earned is $5799.48.

40. Strategy To find the amount of interest earned over a 2-year period:
- Find the value of the investment after 1 year by multiplying the original investment by the compound interest factor.
- Find the value of the investment after the second year by multiplying the new investment (4245.44) by the compound interest factor.
- Subtract the original value of the investment ($4000) from the value of the investment after 2 years.

Solution $4000 \times 1.06136 = 4245.44$
$4245.44 \times 1.06136 \approx 4505.94$
$4505.94 - 4000 = 505.94$
The amount of interest earned is $505.94.

Applying the Concepts

41. Strategy To find the simple interest owed to the credit union, multiply the principal by the monthly interest rate by the time (in months).

Solution $800 \times 0.02 \times 1 = 16$
The interest owed is $16.

42a. $100 \times 0.06 \times \frac{1}{12} = 0.5 = \$.50$
$100 + 0.50 + 100 = 200.50$
The value of the account after the deposit is $200.50.

b. $200.50 \times 0.06 \times \frac{1}{12} = 1.0025 \approx \$1.00$
$200.50 + 1.00 + 100 = 301.50$
The value of the account after the deposit is $301.50.

43. You received less interest during the second month because there are fewer days in the month of September (30 days) than in the month of August (31 days). Using the simple interest formula:
$500 \times 0.05 \times \frac{31}{365} \approx 2.12$
$502.12 \times 0.05 \times \frac{30}{365} \approx 2.06$
Even though the principal is greater during the second month, the interest earned is less because there are fewer days in the month.

Section 6.4

Objective A Exercises

1. Strategy To find the mortgage, subtract the down payment from the purchase price.

Solution $97,000 - 14,550 = 82,450$
The mortgage is $82,450.

2. Strategy To find the mortgage, subtract the down payment from the purchase price.

Solution $173,000 - 34,600 = 138,400$
The mortgage is $138,400.

3. Strategy To find the down payment, solve the basic percent equation for amount. The base is $25,000 and the percent is 30%.

Solution Percent × base = amount
$0.30 \times 25,000 = 7500$
The down payment is $7500.

4. Strategy To find the down payment, solve the basic percent equation for amount. The base is $188,500 and the percent is 20%.

Solution Percent × base = amount
$0.20 \times 188,500 = 37,700$
The down payment is $37,700.

5. Strategy To find the down payment, solve the basic percent equation for amount. The base is $850,000 and the percent is 25%.

Solution Percent × base = amount
$0.25 \times 850,000 = 212,500$
The down payment is $212,500.

6. Strategy To find the down payment, solve the basic percent equation for amount. The base is $125,000 and the percent is 25%.

Solution Percent × base = amount
$0.25 \times 125,000 = 31,250$
The down payment is $31,250.

7. Strategy To find the loan origination fee, solve the basic percent equation for amount. The base is \$150,000 and the percent is $2\frac{1}{2}\%$.

Solution Percent × base = amount
0.025 × 150,000 = 3750
The loan origination fee is \$3750.

8. Strategy To find the loan origination fee, solve the basic percent equation for amount. The base is \$90,000 and the percent is $3\frac{1}{2}\%$.

Solution Percent × base = amount
0.035 × 90,000 = 3150
The loan origination fee is \$3150.

9a. Strategy To find the down payment, solve the basic percent equation for amount. The base is \$150,000 and the percent is 5%.

Solution Percent × base = amount
0.05 × 150,000 = 7,500
The down payment is \$7,500.

b. Strategy To find the mortgage, subtract the down payment from the purchase price.

Solution 150,000 – 7,500 = 142,500
The mortgage is \$142,500.

10a. Strategy To find the down payment, solve the basic percent equation for amount. The base is \$240,000 and the percent is 15%.

Solution Percent × base = amount
0.15 × 240,000 = 36,000
The down payment is \$36,000.

b. Strategy To find the mortgage, subtract the down payment from the purchase price.

Solution 240,000 – 36,000 = 204,000
The mortgage is \$204,000.

11. Strategy To find the mortgage:
- Find the down payment by solving the basic percent equation for amount. The percent is 10% and the base is \$210,000.
- Subtract the down payment from the purchase price.

Solution Percent × base = amount
0.10 × 210,000 = 21,000
210,000 – 21,000 = 189,000
The mortgage is \$189,000.

12. Strategy To find the mortgage:
- Find the down payment by solving the basic percent equation for amount. The percent is 5% and the base is \$80,000.
- Subtract the down payment from the purchase price.

Solution Percent × base = amount
0.05 × 80,000 = 4,000
80,000 – 4,000 = 76,000
The mortgage is \$76,000.

Objective B Exercises

13. Strategy To find the monthly mortgage payment, multiply the mortgage by the monthly mortgage factor.

Solution 150,000 × 0.0077182 = 1157.73
The monthly mortgage payment is \$1157.73.

14. Strategy To find the monthly mortgage payment, multiply the mortgage by the monthly mortgage factor.

Solution 90,000 × 0.0071643 ≈ 644.79
The monthly mortgage payment is \$644.79.

15. Strategy To determine whether the couple can afford to buy the house:
- Find the monthly mortgage payment by multiplying the mortgage amount by the monthly mortgage factor.
- Compare the monthly mortgage payment with \$800.

Solution 110,000 × 0.0073376 ≈ 807.14
\$800 < \$807.14
No, the couple cannot afford to buy the house.

16. Strategy To determine whether the lawyer can afford the monthly mortgage payment:
- Find the monthly mortgage payment by multiplying the mortgage by the monthly mortgage factor.
- Compare the monthly mortgage payment with \$3500.

Solution 400,000 × 0.0084386 = 3375.44
\$3375.44 < \$3500
Yes, the lawyer can afford the monthly mortgage payment.

17. Strategy To find the monthly property tax payment, divide the annual property tax by 12.

Solution $1348.20 \div 12 = 112.35$
The monthly property tax is $112.35.

18. Strategy To find the monthly property tax payment, divide the annual property tax by 12.

Solution $1992 \div 12 = 166$
The monthly property tax is $166.

19a. Strategy To find the monthly mortgage payment, multiply the mortgage by the monthly mortgage factor.

Solution $200{,}000 \times 0.0083920 = 1678.40$
The monthly mortgage payment is $1678.40.

b. Strategy To find how much of the monthly mortgage payment is interest, subtract the amount that is principal ($941.72) from the monthly mortgage payment.

Solution $1678.40 - 941.72 = 736.68$
The interest payment is $736.68.

20a. Strategy To find the monthly mortgage payment, multiply the mortgage by the monthly mortgage factor.

Solution $135{,}000 \times 0.0066530 \approx 898.16$
The monthly mortgage payment is $898.16.

b. Strategy To find how much of the monthly mortgage payment is interest, subtract the amount that is principal ($392.47) from the monthly mortgage payment.

Solution $898.16 - 392.47 = 505.69$
The interest payment is $505.69.

21. Strategy To find the monthly payment for property tax and home mortgage:
- Find the monthly tax payment by dividing the annual property tax by 12.
- Find the monthly mortgage payment by dividing the annual mortgage payment by 12.
- Add the monthly tax payment to the monthly mortgage payment.

Solution $948 \div 12 = 79$ = monthly tax payment
$10{,}844.40 \div 12 = 903.70$
$903.70 + 79 = 982.70$
The total monthly payment for the property tax and home mortgage is $982.70.

22. Strategy To find the total monthly payment for the mortgage and property tax:
- Find the monthly property tax payment by dividing the annual tax ($792) by 12.
- Add the monthly property tax to the monthly mortgage payment ($716.40).

Solution $792 \div 12 = 66$
$66 + 716.40 = 782.40$
The total monthly payment for the mortgage and property tax is $782.40.

23. Strategy To find the monthly mortgage payment:
- Find the mortgage amount by subtracting the down payment from the purchase price.
- Multiply the mortgage amount by the monthly mortgage factor.

Solution $210{,}000 - 15{,}000 = 195{,}000$
$195{,}000 \times 0.0084386 \approx 1645.53$
The monthly mortgage payment is $1645.53.

24. Strategy To find the monthly mortgage payment:
- Find the mortgage amount by subtracting the down payment from the purchase price.
- Multiply the mortgage amount by the monthly mortgage factor.

Solution $185{,}000 - 20{,}000 = 165{,}000$
$165{,}000 \times 0.0066530 \approx 1097.75$
The monthly mortgage payment is $1097.75.

Applying the Concepts

25. Choice 1: 8% for 20 years
$100,000 \times 0.0083644 = 836.44$/month
Payback $= 836.44 \times 240$ months $= \$200,745.60$, or 100,745.60 in interest
Choice 2: 8% for 30 years
$100,000 \times 0.0073376 = 733.76$
Payback $= 733.76 \times 360$ months $= \$264,153.60$ or 164,153.60 in interest
$\$164,153.60 - 100,745.60 = \$63,408$
By using the 20-year loan, the couple will save $63,408.

26. In a fixed-rate mortgage, a fixed interest rate is charged, and fixed payments are made on the loan throughout the term of the loan. This means that the interest rate of the loan never changes and that the amount of the monthly payment remains the same throughout the life of the loan. An adjustable-rate mortgage (ARM) does not have a fixed interest rate throughout the term of the mortgage. Instead, the interest rate charged is adjusted periodically to more closely reflect current interest rates. In return for taking a risk that interest rates may rise, borrowers usually get a lower interest rate at the beginning of the ARM than they would have if they had taken out a fixed-rate mortgage for the same term.

Section 6.5

Objective A Exercises

1. Strategy To determine whether Amanda has enough money for the down payment:
- Find the down payment by solving the basic percent equation for amount. The base is $7100 and the percent is 12%.
- Compare the required down payment with $780.

Solution Percent × base = amount
$0.12 \times 7100 = 852$ down payment
$\$852 > \$780$
No, Amanda does not have enough for the down payment.

2. Strategy To find the down payment, solve the basic percent equation for amount. The base is $23,500 and the percent is 15%.

Solution Percent × base = amount
$0.15 \times 23,500 = 3,525$
The down payment is $3525.

3. Strategy To find how much sales tax is paid, solve the basic percent equation for amount. The base is $26,500 and the percent is 4.5%.

Solution $0.045 \times 26,500 = 1192.5$
The sales tax is $1192.50.

4. Strategy To find the sales tax, solve the basic percent equation for amount. The base is $28,500 and the percent is 4%.

Solution Percent × base = amount
$0.04 \times 28,500 = 1140$
The sales tax is $1140.

5. Strategy To find the state license fee, solve the basic percent equation for amount. The base is $22,500 and the percent is 2%.

Solution Percent × base = amount
$0.02 \times 22,500 = 450$
The license fee is $450.

6. Strategy To find the state license fee, solve the basic percent equation for amount. The base is $16,998 and the percent is 1.5%.

Solution Percent × base = amount
$0.015 \times 16,998 = 254.97$
The state license fee is $254.97.

7a. Strategy To find the sales tax, solve the basic percent equation for amount. The base is $32,000 and the percent is 3.5%.

Solution Percent × base = amount
$0.035 \times 32,000 = 1120$
The sales tax is $1120.

b. Strategy To find the total cost of the sales tax and license fee, add the sales tax ($1120) and the license fee ($275).

Solution $1120 + 275 = 1395$
The total cost of the sales tax and license fee is $1395.

8a. Strategy To find the sales tax, solve the basic percent equation for amount. The base is $9375 and the percent is 5%.

Solution Percent × base = amount
$0.05 \times 9375 = 468.75$
The sales tax is $468.75.

b. Strategy To find the total of the down payment and the sales tax, add the sales tax to the down payment.

Solution $1875 + 468.57 = 2343.75$
The total cost of the down payment and sales tax is $2343.75.

9a. Strategy To find the down payment, solve the basic percent equation for amount. The base is $16,200 and the percent is 25%.

Solution Percent × base = amount
$0.25 \times 16{,}200 = 4050$
The down payment is $4050.

b. Strategy To find the amount financed, subtract the down payment from the purchase price.

Solution $16{,}200 - 4050 = 12{,}150$
The amount financed is $12,150.

10a. Strategy To find the down payment, solve the basic percent equation for amount. The base is $24,900 and the percent is 15%.

Solution Percent × base = amount
$0.15 \times 24{,}900 = 3735$
The down payment is $3735.

b. Strategy To find the amount financed, subtract the down payment from the purchase price.

Solution $24{,}900 - 3735 = 21{,}165$
The amount financed is $21,165.

11. Strategy To find the amount financed:
- Find the amount of the down payment by solving the basic percent equation for amount. The base is $35,000 and the percent is 20%.
- Subtract the down payment from the purchase price ($35,000).

Solution Percent × base = amount
$0.20 \times 35{,}000 = 7000$
$35{,}000 - 7000 = 28{,}000$
The amount financed is $28,000.

12. Strategy To find the amount financed:
- Find the down payment by solving the basic percent equation for amount. The base is $13,500 and the percent is 25%.
- Subtract the down payment from the purchase price.

Solution Percent × base = amount
$0.25 \times 13{,}500 = 3375$
$13{,}500 - 3375 = 10{,}125$
The amount financed is $10,125.

Objective B Exercises

13. Strategy To find the monthly truck payment, multiply the amount financed by the monthly payment factor.

Solution $24{,}000 \times 0.0230293 \approx 552.70$
The monthly truck payment is $552.70.

14. Strategy To find the monthly car payment, multiply the amount financed by the monthly payment factor.

Solution $18{,}000 \times 0.0295240 \approx 531.43$
The monthly car payment is $531.43.

15. Strategy To find how much it costs to operate a car, multiply the number of miles (16,000) by the cost per mile ($.32).

Solution $0.32 \times 16{,}000 = 5120$
The cost is $5120.

16. Strategy To find the cost for the care and maintenance of tires for 14,000 miles, multiply the cost per mile by the number of miles.

Solution $0.015 \times 14{,}000 = 210$
The cost is $210.

17. Strategy To find the cost per mile, divide the total cost by the number of miles.

Solution $1600 \div 14{,}000 \approx 0.11$
The cost is about $.11 per mile.

18. Strategy To find the cost per mile for gasoline, divide the total cost by the number of miles.

Solution $2100 \div 15{,}000 = 0.14$
The cost was $.14 per mile.

19. Strategy To find the amount of interest, subtract the amount of principal from the monthly car payment.

Solution $143.50 - 68.75 = 74.75$
The amount of interest is $74.75.

20. Strategy To find the total cost for the truck, find the sum of the payments ($2868), gasoline ($2400), and insurance ($675).

Solution $2868 + 2400 + 675 = 5943$
The total cost is $5943.

21a. Strategy To find the amount financed, subtract the down payment ($10,800) from the purchase price ($164,000).

Solution $164{,}000 - 10{,}800 = 153{,}200$
The amount financed is $153,200.

b. Strategy To find the monthly truck payment, multiply the amount financed by the monthly payment factor.

Solution $153{,}200 \times 0.0193328 = 2961.78$
The monthly payment is $2961.78.

22a. Strategy To find the amount financed, subtract the down payment from the purchase price.

Solution $14{,}999 - 2999 = 12{,}000$
The amount financed is $12,000.

b. Strategy To find the monthly payment, multiply the amount financed by the monthly payment factor.

Solution $12{,}000 \times 0.0299709 \approx 359.65$.
The monthly car payment is $359.65.

23. Strategy To find the monthly car payment:
- Find the amount financed by subtracting the down payment from the purchase price.
- Multiply the amount financed by the monthly payment factor.

Solution $27{,}500 - 5500 = 22{,}000$
$22{,}000 \times 0.0295240 \approx 649.53$
The monthly payment is $649.53.

24. Strategy To find the monthly car payment:
- Find the amount financed by subtracting the down payment from the purchase price.
- Multiply the amount financed by the monthly payment factor.

Solution $39{,}500 - 5000 = 34{,}500$
$34{,}500 \times 0.0234850 \approx 810.23$
The monthly payment is $810.23.

Applying the Concepts

25. The total loan cost for the 7% loan plus application fee = $5800 × 0.0239462 × 48 + $45 − $5800 = $911.62
The total loan cost for the 8% loan with no fee = $5800 × 0.0244129 × 48 − $5800 = $996.55
The 7% loan has the lesser loan cost.

26. The monthly payment is 9000 × 0.0207584 = $186.8256. The total interest repaid is $186.8256(12 × 5) − $9000 ≈ $2209.54.

Section 6.6

Objective A Exercises

1. Strategy To find the earnings, multiply the hourly wage by the number of hours.

Solution $9.50 \times 40 = 380$
Lewis earns $380.

2. Strategy To find the payment, multiply the hourly wage by the number of hours.

Solution $11 \times 25 = 275$
She pays the gardener $275.

3. Strategy To find the commission, solve the basic percent equation for amount. The base is $131,000 and the percent is 3%.

Solution Percent × base = amount
$0.03 \times 131{,}000 = 3930$
The real estate agent's commission is $3930.

4. Strategy To find the commission, solve the basic percent equation for amount. The base is $1050 and the percent is 40%.

Solution Percent × base = amount
$0.40 \times 1050 = 420$
Ron's commission is $420.

5. Strategy To find the commission, solve the basic percent equation for amount. The base is $5600 and the percent is 1.5%.

Solution Percent × base = amount
$0.015 \times 5600 = 84$
The stockbroker's commission is $84.

6. **Strategy** To find the commission, solve the basic percent equation for amount. The base is $22,500 and the percent is 20%.

Solution Percent × base = amount
0.20 × 22,500 = 4500
The owner's commission is $4500.

7. **Strategy** To find the monthly salary, divide the annual salary by 12.

Solution 38,928 ÷ 12 = 3244
Keisha receives $3244 a month.

8. **Strategy** To find the monthly salary, divide the annual salary by 12.

Solution 27,900 ÷ 12 = 2325
The plumber receives $2325 a month.

9. **Strategy** To find the electrician's hourly wage for overtime, multiply the regular hourly wage by 2 (double time).

Solution 25.80 × 2 = 51.60
The overtime wage is $51.60/hour.

10. **Strategy** To find the commission, solve the basic percent equation for amount. The base is $4500 and the percent is 12%.

Solution Percent × base = amount
0.12 × 4500 = 540
Carlos's commission was $540.

11. **Strategy** To find the commission, solve the basic percent equation for amount. The base is $450 and the percent is 25%.

Solution Percent × base = amount
0.25 × 450 = 112.5
The golf pro's commission was $112.50.

12. **Strategy** To find the earnings, multiply the earnings per square yard by the number of square yards.

Solution 3.75 × 160 = 600
Steven receives $600.

13. **Strategy** To find the earnings, multiply the earnings per page by the number of pages.

Solution 2.75 × 225 = 618.75
The typist earns $618.75.

14. **Strategy** To find the chemist's hourly wage, divide the total wage by the number of hours.

Solution 15,000 ÷ 120 = 125
The chemist's hourly wage is $125.

15. **Strategy** To find the hourly wage, divide the total wage by the number of hours.

Solution 3400 ÷ 40 = 85
Maxine's hourly wage is $85.

16a. **Strategy** To find the hourly wage for overtime, multiply the regular wage by 2 (double time).

Solution 10.78 × 2 = 21.56
Gil's overtime hourly wage is $21.56.

b. **Strategy** To find the earnings, multiply the overtime hourly wage by the number of hours.

Solution 21.56 × 16 = 344.96
Gil earns $344.96 for overtime.

17a. **Strategy** To find the hourly wage on Saturday, multiply the regular hourly wage by 1.5 (time and a half).

Solution 15.90 × 1.5 = 23.85
Mark's hourly wage on Saturday is $23.85.

b. **Strategy** To find the earnings for Saturday, multiply the hourly wage by the number of hours.

Solution 23.85 × 8 = 190.8
Mark earns $190.80.

18a. **Strategy** To find the increase in pay for the evening shift, solve the basic percent equation for amount. The base is $8.20 and the percent is 15%.

Solution Percent × base = amount
0.15 × 8.20 = 1.23
The increase in pay is $1.23.

b. **Strategy** To find the hourly wage for the evening shift, add the increase in pay to the regular hourly wage

Solution 8.20 + 1.23 = 9.43
The clerk's hourly wage for the evening shift is $9.43.

19a. Strategy To find the increase in pay, solve the basic percent equation for amount. The base is \$21.50 and the percent is 10%.

Solution Percent × base = amount
$0.10 \times 21.50 = \$2.15.$
The nurse's increase in pay is \$2.15.

b. Strategy To find the hourly wage for the night shift, add the increase in pay to the regular hourly wage.

Solution $21.50 + 2.15 = 23.65$
The nurse's hourly pay is \$23.65.

20. Strategy To find the hourly wage for working the night shift:
- Find the amount of the increase by solving the basic percent equation for amount. The base is \$9.40 and the percent is 25%.
- Add the amount of the increase to the original pay (\$9.40).

Solution Percent × base = amount
$0.25 \times 9.40 = 2.35$
$2.35 + 9.40 = 11.75$
Tony's hourly wage for working the night shift is \$11.75.

21. Strategy To find the earnings for the week:
- Find the amount of sales over \$1500 by subtracting \$1500 from the total sales (\$3000).
- Find the commission by solving the basic percent equation for amount. The base is the sales over \$1500 and the percent is 15%.
- Add the commission to the weekly salary (\$250).

Solution $3000 - 1500 = 1500$ sales over 1500
Percent × base = amount
$0.15 \times 1500 = 225$ commission
$250 + 225 = 475$
Nicole's earnings were \$475.

Applying the Concepts

22. Let n represent the previous year's salary.
Percent × base = amount
$1.026 \times n = 41{,}360$
$n = 41{,}360 \div 1.026$
$n \approx 40{,}312$
The starting salary in the previous year for an accountant was \$40,312.

23. Let n represent the previous year's salary.
Percent × base = amount
$1.018 \times n = 52{,}169$
$n = 52{,}169 \div 1.018$
$n \approx 51{,}247$
Increase in salary: $52{,}169 - 51{,}247 = \$922$
The amount of increase in the starting salary for a chemical engineer from the previous year was \$922.

24. Let n represent the previous year's salary.
Percent × base = amount
$0.924 \times n = 46{,}536$
$n = 46{,}536 \div 0.924$
$n \approx 50{,}364$
The starting salary in the previous year for a computer science major was \$50,364.

25. Let n represent the previous year's salary.
Percent × base = amount
$0.874 \times n = 28{,}546$
$n = 28{,}546 \div 0.874$
$n \approx 32{,}661$
Decrease in salary: $32{,}661 - 28{,}546 = 4115$
The amount of decrease in the starting salary for a political science major from the previous year was \$4115.

Section 6.7

Objective A Exercises

1. Strategy To find your current checking balance, add the deposit to the old balance.

Solution $342.51 + 143.81 = 486.32$
Your current checking account balance is \$486.32.

2. Strategy To find the current checking account balance, subtract the amount of the check from the old balance.

Solution $493.26 - 48.39 = 444.87$
Carmen's current checking account balance is \$444.87.

3. Strategy To find the current checking account balance, subtract the amount of the check from the old balance.

Solution $2431.76 - 1209.29 = 1222.47$
The real estate firm's current checking account balance is \$1222.47.

4. Strategy To find the current checking account balance, add the deposit to the old balance.

Solution $1536.97 + 439.21 = 1976.18$
The tire store's current checking balance is \$1976.18.

5. Strategy To find the current checking account balance, subtract the amount of each check from the original balance.

Solution

```
  1204.63
−  119.27
  1085.36
−  260.09
   825.27
```

The nutritionist's current balance is $825.27.

6. Strategy To find Sam's current checkbook balance, subtract the amount of the check and add the deposit to the original balance.

Solution

```
  3046.93
− 1027.33
  2019.60
+  150.00
  2169.60
```

Sam's current checkbook balance is $2169.60.

7. Strategy To find the current checking account balance, add the amount of the deposit to the old balance. Then subtract the amount of each check.

Solution

```
  3476.85
+ 1048.53
  4525.38
−  848.37
  3677.01
−  676.19
  3000.82
```

The current checking account balance is $3000.82.

8. Strategy To find the current checking account balance, add the amount of the deposit to the old balance. Then subtract the amount of each check.

Solution

```
  427.38
+ 127.29
  554.67
−  43.52
  511.15
− 249.78
  261.37
```

The current checking account balance is $261.37.

9. Strategy To determine whether there is enough money in the account, compare $675 with the current balance after finding the current checking account balance.

Solution

```
  404.96
+ 350.00
  754.96
−  71.29
  683.67
```

$\$683.67 > \$675$

Yes, there is enough money in the carpenter's account to purchase the refrigerator.

10. Strategy To determine whether there is enough money in the account, compare the amount of the check with the current balance after making the deposit.

Solution $149.85 + 245 = 394.85$ current balance

$\$387.68 < \$394.85$

Yes, there is enough money in the taxi driver's account to pay the check.

11. Strategy To determine whether there is enough money in the account to make the two purchases, add the amounts of the two purchases and compare the total with the current checking account balance.

Solution $3500 + 2050 = 5550$ total of purchases

$\$5550 < \$5625.42$

Yes, there is enough money in the account to make the two purchases.

12. Strategy To determine whether there is enough money in the account to make the two purchases, add the amounts of the two purchases and compare the total with the current checking account balance.

Solution $525 + 650 = 1175$ total of purchases

$\$1175 > \$1143.42$

No, there is not enough money in the lathe operator's account to make the two purchases.

13. Solution

Current checkbook balance:		989.86
Checks:	228	419.32
	233	166.40
	235	+288.39
		1863.97
Interest:		+13.22
		1877.19
Service charge:		−0.00
		1877.19
Deposits:		−0.00
Checkbook balance:		1877.19

Current bank balance from bank statement: $1877.19.

Checkbook balance: $1877.19.

The bank statement and checkbook balance.

14. Solution

Current checkbook balance:	1306.26
Checks: 520	22.50
522	313.44
526	144.16
528	+877.42
	2663.78
Interest:	+7.82
	2671.60
Service charge:	−0.00
	2671.60
Deposits:	−0.00
Checkbook balance:	2671.60

Current checkbook balance from bank statement: $2671.60.
Checkbook balance: $2671.60.
The bank statement and checkbook balance.

15. Solution

Current checkbook balance:	1051.92
Checks: 223	414.83
224	113.37
Interest:	+5.15
	1585.27
Service charge:	−0.00
	1585.27
Deposits:	−0.00
Checkbook balance:	1585.27

Current bank balance from bank statement: $1585.27.
Checkbook balance: $1585.27.
The bank statement and checkbook balance.

Applying the Concepts

16. subtracted

17. added

18. add

19. subtract

20. When applied to a checking account, a credit is a deposit into the account. A debit is a payment or withdrawal from the account.

Chapter 6 Review Exercises

1. **Strategy** To find the unit cost, divide the total cost ($3.90) by the number of units (20).

   Solution $3.90 \div 20 = 0.195$
   The unit cost is $.195 per ounce or 19.5¢ per ounce.

2. **Strategy** To find the cost per mile:
   - Find the total cost by adding the amounts spent ($1025.58, $605.82, $37.92, and $188.27).
   - Divide the total cost by the number of miles (11,320).

   Solution $1025.58 + 605.82 + 37.92 + 188.27 = 1857.59$
   $1857.59 \div 11{,}320 \approx 0.164$
   The cost is $.164 or 16.4¢ per mile.

3. **Strategy** To find the percent increase:
   - Find the amount of the increase by subtracting the original price ($42.375) from the increased price ($55.25).
   - Solve the basic percent equation for percent. The base is $42.375 and the amount is the amount of the increase.

   Solution $\$55.25 - 42.375 = 12.875$
   $n \times 42.375 = 12.875$
   $n = 12.875 \div 42.375 \approx 0.304$
   $= 30.4\%$
   The percent increase is 30.4%.

4. **Strategy** To find the markup, solve the basic percent equation for amount. The base is $180 and the percent is 40%.

   Solution $0.40 \times 180 = n$
   $72 = n$
   The markup is $72.

5. **Strategy** To find the simple interest, multiply the principal by the annual interest rate by the time (in years).

   Solution $100{,}000 \times 0.04 \times \frac{9}{12} = 3000$
   The simple interest due is $3000.

6. **Strategy** To find the value of the investment in 10 years, multiply the original investment by the compound interest factor.

   Solution $25{,}000 \times 1.82203 = 45{,}550.75$
   The value of the investment after 10 years is $45,550.75.

7. **Strategy** To find the percent increase:
   - Find the amount of the increase by subtracting the original amount ($4.12) from the increased amount ($4.73).
   - Solve the basic percent equation for percent. The base is $4.12 and the amount is the increased amount.

   Solution $4.73 - 4.12 = 0.61$
   $n \times 4.12 = 0.61$
   $n = 0.61 \div 4.12 \approx 0.15 = 15\%$
   The percent increase is 15%.

8. Strategy To find the total monthly payment:
- Find the monthly property tax by dividing the annual tax ($658.32) by 12.
- Add the monthly property tax payment to the monthly mortgage payment ($523.67).

Solution
$658.32 \div 12 = 54.86$
$54.86 + 523.67 = 578.53$
The total monthly payment for the mortgage and property tax is $578.53.

9. Strategy To find the monthly payment:
- Find the down payment by solving the basic percent equation for amount. The percent is 8% and the base is $24,450.
- Find the amount financed by subtracting the down payment from the purchase price ($24,450).
- Multiply the amount financed by the monthly payment factor.

Solution
$0.08 \times 24{,}450 = 1956$
$24{,}450 - 1956 = 22{,}494$
$22{,}494 \times 0.0230293 \approx 518.02$
The monthly payment is $518.02.

10. Strategy To find the value of the investment in 1 year, multiply the original investment by the compound interest factor.

Solution $50{,}000 \times 1.07186 = 53{,}593$
The value of the investment will be $53,593.

11. Strategy To find the down payment, solve the basic percent equation for amount. The base is $125,000 and the percent is 15%.

Solution $0.15 \times 125{,}000 = 18{,}750$
The down payment is $18,750.

12. Strategy To find the total cost of the sales tax and license fee:
- Find the sales tax by solving the basic percent equation for amount. The base is $18,500 and the percent is 6.25%.
- Add the sales tax and the license fee ($315).

Solution
$0.0625 \times 18{,}500 = 1156.25$
$1156.25 + 315 = 1471.25$
The total cost of the sales tax and license fee is $1471.25.

13. Strategy To find the selling price:
- Find the markup by solving the basic percent equation for amount. The percent is 35% and the base is $1540.
- Find the selling price by adding the markup to the cost.

Solution
$0.35 \times 1540 = 539$
$539 + 1540 = 2079$
The selling price is $2079.

14. Strategy To find how much of the payment is interest, subtract the principal ($25.45) from the total payment ($122.78).

Solution $122.78 - 25.45 = 97.33$
The interest paid is $97.33.

15. Strategy To find the commission, solve the basic percent equation for amount. The base is $108,000 and the percent is 3%.

Solution
$0.03 \times 108{,}000 = n$
$3240 = n$
The commission was $3240.

16. Strategy To find the sale price:
- Find the amount of the discount by solving the basic percent equation for amount. The base is $235 and the percent is 40%.
- Subtract the discount from the original price.

Solution
$0.40 \times 235 = n$
$94 = n$
$235 - 94 = 141$
The discount price is $141.

17. Strategy To find the current checkbook balance, subtract the amount of each check and add the amount of the deposit.

Solution
1568.45
−123.76
1444.69
−756.45
688.24
−88.77
599.47
+344.21
943.68

The current checkbook balance is $943.68.

18. Strategy To find the maturity value:
- Find the simple interest due by multiplying the principal by the annual interest rate by the time (in years).
- Find the maturity value by adding the principal and the simple interest.

Solution $30{,}000 \times 0.08 \times \frac{6}{12} = 1200$

$30{,}000 + 1200 = 31{,}200$

The maturity value is \$31,200.

19. Strategy To find the origination fee, solve the basic percent equation for amount. The base is \$75,000 and the percent is $2\frac{1}{2}\%$.

Solution $0.025 \times 75{,}000 = 1875$

The origination fee is \$1875.

20. Strategy To find the more economical purchase, compare the unit costs.

Solution $3.49 \div 16 \approx 0.218$

$6.99 \div 33 \approx 0.212$

The more economical purchase is 33 ounces for \$6.99.

21. Strategy To find the monthly mortgage payment:
- Find the down payment by solving the basic percent equation for amount. The base is \$156,000 and the percent is 10%.
- Find the amount financed by subtracting the down payment from the purchase price.
- Find the monthly mortgage payment by multiplying the amount financed by the monthly mortgage factor.

Solution $0.10 \times 156{,}000 = 15{,}600$

$156{,}000 - 15{,}600 = 140{,}400$

$140{,}400 \times 0.006653 = 934.08$

The monthly mortgage payment is \$934.08.

22. Strategy To find the total income:
- Find the overtime wage by multiplying the regular wage by 1.5 (time and half).
- Find the number of overtime hours worked by subtracting the regular weekly schedule (40) from the total hours worked (48).
- Find the wages earned for overtime by multiplying the overtime wage by the number of overtime hours worked.
- Find the wages for the 40-hour week by multiplying the hourly rate (\$12.60) by 40.
- Add the pay from the overtime hours to the pay from the regular week.

Solution $1.5 \times 12.60 = 18.90$

$48 - 40 = 8; 8 \times 18.90 = 151.20$

$40 \times 12.60 = 504$

$504 + 151.20 = 655.20$

The total income was \$655.20.

23. Strategy To find the donut shop's current checkbook balance, subtract the amount of each check and add the amount of each deposit.

Solution

$$\begin{array}{r} 9567.44 \\ -\ 1023.55 \\ \hline 8543.89 \\ -\ 345.44 \\ \hline 8198.45 \\ -\ 23.67 \\ \hline 8174.78 \\ +\ 555.89 \\ \hline 8730.67 \\ +\ 135.91 \\ \hline 8866.58 \end{array}$$

The donut shop's checkbook balance is \$8866.58.

24. Strategy To find the monthly payment, divide the sum of the loan amount (\$55,000) and the interest (\$1375) by the number of payments (4).

Solution $\frac{55{,}000 + 1375}{4} = 14{,}093.75$

The monthly payment is \$14,093.75.

25. Strategy To find the finance charge, multiply the unpaid balance by the monthly interest rate by the number of months.

Solution $576 \times 0.0125 \times 1 = 7.2$

The finance charge is \$7.20.

Chapter 6 Test

1. Strategy To find the cost per foot, divide the total cost (\$138.40) by the number of feet (20).

Solution $138.40 \div 20 = 6.92$

The cost per foot is \$6.92.

2. Strategy To find the more economical purchase, compare the unit prices of the items.

Solution $7.49 \div 3$ or $12.59 \div 5$

$7.49 \div 3 \approx 2.50$; $12.59 \div 5 \approx 2.52$

The more economical purchase is 3 pounds for \$7.49.

3. **Strategy** To find the total cost, multiply the cost per pound ($4.15) by the number of pounds (3.5).

Solution $4.15 \times 3.5 \approx 14.53$
The total cost is $14.53.

4. **Strategy** To find the percent increase:
• Find the amount of the increase by subtracting the original price ($415) from the increased price ($498).
• Solve the basic percent equation for percent. The base is $415 and the amount is the amount of the increase.

Solution $498 - 415 = 83$
$n \times 415 = 83$
$n = 83 \div 415$
$n = 0.20 = 20\%$
The percent increase in the cost of the exercise bicycle is 20%.

5. **Strategy** To find the selling price:
• Find the amount of the markup by solving the basic percent equation for amount. The percent is 40% and the base is $215.
• Add the markup to the cost ($215).

Solution $0.40 \times 215 = 86$
$215 + 86 = 301$
The selling price of a compact disc player is $301.

6. **Strategy** To find the percent decrease:
• Find the amount of the decrease by subtracting the decreased value ($360) from the original value ($390).
• Solve the basic percent equation for percent. The base is ($390) and the amount is the amount of the decrease.

Solution $390 - 360 = 30$
$n \times 390 = 30$
$n = 30 \div 390$
$n \approx 0.077 = 7.7\%$
The percent decrease is 7.7%.

7. **Strategy** To find the percent decrease:
• Find the amount of the decrease by subtracting the decreased value ($896) from the original value ($1120).
• Solve the basic percent equation for percent. The base is $1120 and the amount is the amount of the decrease.

Solution $1120 - 896 = 224$
$n \times 1120 = 224$
$n = 224 \div 1120 = 0.20 = 20\%$
The percent decrease is 20%.

8. **Strategy** To find the sale price:
• Find the amount of the discount by solving the basic percent equation for amount. The base is $299 and the percent is 30%.
• Subtract the amount of the discount from the regular price ($299).

Solution $0.30 \times 299 = n$
$89.7 = n$
$299 - 89.70 = 209.30$
The sale price of the corner hutch is $209.30.

9. **Strategy** To find the discount rate:
• Find the amount of the discount by subtracting the sale price ($5.70) from the regular price ($9.50).
• Solve the basic percent equation for percent. The base is $9.50 and the amount is the amount of the discount.

Solution $9.50 - 5.70 = 3.80$
$n \times 9.50 = 3.80$
$n = 3.80 \div 9.50 = 0.40 = 40\%$
The discount rate is 40%.

10. **Strategy** To find the simple interest due, multiply the principal by the annual interest rate by the time in years.

Solution $75{,}000 \times 0.08 \times \frac{4}{12} = 2000$
The simple interest due is $2000.

11. **Strategy** To find the maturity value:
• Find the simple interest due by multiplying the principal by the annual interest rate by the time (in years).
• Find the maturity value by adding the principal and the simple interest.

Solution $25{,}000 \times 0.092 \times \frac{9}{12} = 1725$
$25{,}000 + 1725 = 26{,}725$
The maturity value is $26,725.

12. **Strategy** To find the finance charge, multiply the unpaid balance by the monthly interest rate by the number of months.

Solution $374.95 \times 0.012 \times 1 = 4.50$
The finance charge is $4.50.

13. Strategy To find the interest earned:
- Find the value of the investment in 10 years by multiplying the original investment by the compound interest factor.
- Find the interest earned by subtracting the original investment from the new value of the investment.

Solution $30{,}000 \times 1.81402 = 54{,}420.6$
$54{,}420.60 - 30{,}000 = 24{,}420.60$
The amount of interest earned in 10 years will be $24,420.60.

14. Strategy To find the loan origination fee, solve the basic percent equation for amount. The base is $134,000 and the percent is $2\frac{1}{2}\%$.

Solution $0.025 \times 134{,}000 = 3350$
The origination fee is $3350.

15. Strategy To find the monthly mortgage payment, multiply the mortgage amount by the monthly mortgage factor.

Solution $222{,}000 \times 0.0077182 \approx 1713.44$
The monthly mortgage payment is $1713.44.

16. Strategy To find the amount financed:
- Find the amount of the down payment by solving the basic percent equation for amount. The base is $23,750 and the percent is 20%.
- Subtract the down payment from the purchase price.

Solution $0.20 \times 23{,}750 = 4{,}750$
$23{,}750 - 4{,}750 = 19{,}000$
The amount financed is $19,000.

17. Strategy To find the monthly car payment:
- Find the amount of the down payment by solving the basic percent equation for amount. The base is $23,714 and the percent is 15%.
- Find the amount financed by subtracting the down payment from the purchase price ($23,714).
- Multiply the amount financed by the monthly mortgage factor.

Solution $0.15 \times 23{,}714 = 3{,}557.10$
$23{,}714 - 3{,}557.10 = 20{,}156.90$
$20{,}156.90 \times 0.0239462 \approx 482.681$
The monthly car payment is $482.68.

18. Strategy To find Shaney's total weekly earnings:
- Find the hourly overtime wage for multiplying the hourly wage ($20.40) by 1.5 (time and a half).
- Find the earnings for overtime by multiplying the number of overtime hours (15) by the hourly overtime wage.
- Find the earnings for the normal hours worked by multiplying the number of hours worked (30) by the hourly rate ($20.40).
- Add the earnings from the night hours to the salary from the normal hours.

Solution $20.40 \times 1.5 = 30.60$
$15 \times 30.60 = 459$
$30 \times 20.40 = 612$
$459 + 612 = 1071$
Shaney earns $1071.

19. Strategy Find the current checkbook balance by subtracting the checks written and adding the deposit to the original balance.

Solution

	7349.44
−	1349.67
	5999.77
−	344.12
	5655.65
+	956.60
	6612.25

The current checkbook balance is $6612.25.

20. Solution

Current checkbook balance:	1106.31
Checks:	322.37
	413.45
	+78.20
	1920.33
Service charge:	−0.00
	1920.33
Deposits:	−0.00
Checkbook balance:	1920.33

Current bank balance from bank statement: $1920.33.
Checkbook balance: $1920.33.
The bank statement and checkbook balance.

Cumulative Review Exercises

1. $12 - (10 - 8)^2 \div 2 + 3$
$12 - 2^2 \div 2 + 3$
$12 - 4 \div 2 + 3$
$12 - 2 + 3$
$10 + 3 = 13$

2. $3\frac{1}{3} = 3\frac{8}{24}$

$4\frac{1}{8} = 4\frac{3}{24}$

$+1\frac{1}{12} = 1\frac{2}{24}$

$8\frac{13}{24}$

3. $12\frac{3}{16} = 12\frac{9}{48} = 11\frac{57}{48}$

$-9\frac{5}{12} = 9\frac{20}{48} = 9\frac{20}{48}$

$2\frac{37}{48}$

4. $5\frac{5}{8} \times 1\frac{9}{15} = \frac{45}{8} \times \frac{24}{15}$

$= \frac{45 \times 24}{8 \times 15}$

$= \frac{\overset{1}{\cancel{3}} \cdot 3 \cdot \overset{1}{\cancel{5}} \cdot \overset{1}{\cancel{2}} \cdot \overset{1}{\cancel{2}} \cdot \overset{1}{\cancel{2}} \cdot 3}{\underset{1}{\cancel{2}} \cdot \underset{1}{\cancel{2}} \cdot \underset{1}{\cancel{2}} \cdot \underset{1}{\cancel{3}} \cdot \underset{1}{\cancel{5}}} = 9$

5. $3\frac{1}{2} \div 1\frac{3}{4} = \frac{7}{2} \div \frac{7}{4} = \frac{7}{2} \times \frac{4}{7} = \frac{\overset{1}{\cancel{7}} \cdot \overset{1}{\cancel{2}} \cdot 2}{\underset{1}{\cancel{2}} \cdot \underset{1}{\cancel{7}}} = 2$

6. $\left(\frac{3}{4}\right)^2 \div \left(\frac{3}{8} - \frac{1}{4}\right) + \frac{1}{2}$

$\left(\frac{3}{4} \cdot \frac{3}{4}\right) \div \left(\frac{3}{8} - \frac{2}{8}\right) + \frac{1}{2}$

$\frac{9}{16} \div \frac{1}{8} + \frac{1}{2}$

$\frac{9}{16} \times \frac{8}{1} + \frac{1}{2}$

$\frac{9}{2} + \frac{1}{2} = \frac{10}{2} = 5$

7.
```
          52.18 ≈ 52.2
0.059.)3.079.20
       -295
         129
        -118
         112
         -59
         530
        -472
          58
```

8. $\frac{17}{12} = 17 \div 12$

```
     1.4166 ≈ 1.417
12)17.0000
  -12
    50
   -48
    20
   -12
    80
   -72
    80
   -72
     8
```

9. $\frac{\$410}{8 \text{ hours}} = \$51.25/\text{hour}$

10. $\frac{5}{n} = \frac{16}{35}$

$5 \times 35 = n \times 16$

$175 = n \times 16$

$175 \div 16 = n$

$10.9375 = n$

$10.94 \approx n$

11. $\frac{5}{8} \times 100\% = \frac{500}{8}\% = 62.5\%$

12. $6.5\% \text{ of } 420 = 0.065 \times 420 = 27.3$

13. $18.2 \times 0.01 = 0.182$

14. $n \times 20 = 8.4$

$n = 8.4 \div 20 = 0.42 = 42\%$

15. $0.12 \times n = 30$

$n = 30 \div 0.12 = 250$

16. $0.42 \times n = 65$

$n = 65 \div 0.42 \approx 154.76$

17. Strategy To find the total rainfall for the 3 weeks, add the 3 weekly amounts $\left(3\frac{3}{4}, 8\frac{1}{2}, \text{ and } 1\frac{2}{3} \text{ inches}\right)$.

Solution $3\frac{3}{4} = 3\frac{9}{12}$

$8\frac{1}{2} = 8\frac{6}{12}$

$+1\frac{2}{3} = 1\frac{8}{12}$

$12\frac{23}{12} = 13\frac{11}{12}$

The total rainfall is $13\frac{11}{12}$ inches.

18. Strategy Find the amount paid in taxes by multiplying the total monthly income ($4850) by the portion paid in taxes $\left(\frac{1}{5}\right)$.

Solution $4850 \times \frac{1}{5} = 970$

The amount paid in taxes is $970.

19. Strategy To find the ratio:

- Find the amount of the decrease by subtracting the decreased price ($30) from the original price ($75).
- Write in simplest form the ratio of the decrease to the original price.

Solution $75 - 30 = 45$

$\frac{45}{75} = \frac{3}{5}$

The ratio is $\frac{3}{5}$.

20. Strategy To find the number of miles driven per gallon of gasoline, divide the number of miles driven (417.5) by the number of gallons used (12.5).

Solution $417.5 \div 12.5 = 33.4$
The mileage was 33.4 miles per gallon.

21. Strategy To find the unit cost, divide the total cost ($12.96) by the number of pounds (14).

Solution $12.96 \div 14 \approx 0.93$
The cost is $.93 per pound.

22. Strategy To find the dividend on 200 shares, write and solve a proportion.

Solution
$$\frac{80}{112} = \frac{200}{n}$$
$$80 \times n = 112 \times 200$$
$$80 \times n = 22{,}400$$
$$n = 22{,}400 \div 80$$
$$n = 280$$
The dividend is $280.

23. Strategy To find the sale price:
- Solve the basic percent equation for amount to find the amount of the discount. The base is $900 and the percent is 20%.
- Subtract the discount from the regular price.

Solution $0.20 \times 900 = 180$
$900 - 180 = 720$
The sale price is $720.

24. Strategy To find the selling price:
- Find the amount of markup by solving the basic percent equation for amount. The base is $85 and the percent is 40%.
- Add the markup to the cost.

Solution $0.40 \times 85 = 34$
$85 + 34 = 119$
The selling price of the disc player is $119.

25. Strategy To find the percent increase:
- Find the amount of the increase by subtracting the original value from the value after the increase.
- Solve the basic percent equation for the percent. The base is $2800 and the amount is the amount of the increase.

Solution $3024 - 2800 = 224$
$n \times 2800 = 224$
$n = 224 \div 2800 = 0.08 = 8\%$
The percent increase in Sook Kim's salary is 8%.

26. Strategy To find the simple interest due, multiply the principal by the annual rate by the time (in years).

Solution $120{,}000 \times 0.045 \times \frac{6}{12} = 2700$
The simple interest due is $2700.

27. Strategy To find the monthly payment:
- Find the amount financed by subtracting the down payment from the purchase price.
- Multiply the amount financed by the monthly mortgage factor.

Solution $26{,}900 - 2{,}000 = 24{,}900$
$24{,}900 \times 0.0317997 \approx 791.812$
The monthly car payment is $791.81.

28. Strategy To find the new checking account balance, add the deposit to the original balance and subtract the check amounts.

Solution
```
 1846.78
+568.30
 2415.08
−123.98
 2291.10
 −47.33
 2243.77
```
The family's new checking account balance is $2243.77.

29. Strategy To find the cost per mile:
- Find the total cost by adding the expenses ($840, $520, $185, and $432).
- Divide the total cost by the number of miles driven (10,000).

Solution
```
  840
  520
  185
 +432
 1977
```
$1977 \div 10{,}000 = 0.1977$
The cost per mile is about $.20.

30. Strategy To find the monthly mortgage payment, multiply the mortgage amount by the monthly mortgage factor.

Solution $172{,}000 \times 0.0071643 \approx 1232.26$
The monthly mortgage payment is $1232.26.

Chapter 7: Statistics and Probability

Prep Test

1. $\frac{49 \text{ billion}}{102 \text{ billion}} \approx 0.480 = 48.0\%$ was bill-related mail.

2. Between 2005 and 2006
$74,418 – 70,206 = $4212
Between 2006 and 2007
$78,883 – 74,418 = $4465
Between 2007 and 2008
$83,616 – 78,883 = $4733
Between 2008 and 2009
$88,633 – $83,616 = $5017
Between 2009 and 2010
$93,951 – 88,633 = $5318
a. The greatest cost increase is between 2009 and 2010.
b. Between those years, there was an increase of $5318.

3a. $\frac{45 \text{ gold}}{27 \text{ silver}} = \frac{45}{27} = \frac{5}{3}$

b. 27 silver : 27 bronze = 27 : 27 = 1 : 1.

4a. 3.9, 3.9, 4.2, 4.5, 5.2, 5.5, 7.1

b. $\frac{3.9 + 4.5 + 4.2 + 3.9 + 5.2 + 7.1 + 5.5}{7} = 4.9$ million

5a. $5\% \times 90{,}000 = 0.05 \times 90{,}000$
$= 4500$ women are in the Marine Corps.

b. $5\% = 0.05 = \frac{5}{100} = \frac{1}{20}$
or $\frac{4500}{90{,}000} = \frac{1}{20}$ of the women in the military are in the Marine Corps.

Go Figure

If my father's parents have 10 grandchildren, and I have 2 brothers and 1 sister, then my siblings and I account for 4 out of the 10 grandchildren. We have 6 first cousins on my father's side.
If my mother's parents have 11 grandchildren, and I have 2 brothers and 1 sister, then my siblings and I account for 4 out of the 11 grandchildren. We have 7 first cousins on my mother's side.
Adding the 6 first cousins on my father's side to the 7 first cousins on my mother's side, results in my having 13 first cousins.

Section 7.1

Objective A Exercises

1. **Strategy** To find the gross revenue:
• Read the pictograph to determine the gross revenue of the four movies.
• Add the four numbers.

Solution
150 million
300 million
200 million
+ 100 million
750 million
The gross revenue is $750 million.

2. **Strategy** To find the ratio:
• Read the pictograph to find the gross revenue for *Beauty and the Beast* and *The Hunchback of Notre Dame.*
• Write in simplest form the ratio of the revenues from *Beauty and the Beast* and *The Hunchback of Notre Dame*.

Solution Revenue from *Beauty and the Beast*: 150 million
Revenue from *The Hunchback of Notre Dame*: 100 million
$\frac{150 \text{ million}}{100 \text{ million}} = \frac{3}{2}$
The ratio is $\frac{3}{2}$.

3. **Strategy** To find the percent, solve the basic percent equation for percent. The base is 750 million (from Exercise 1) and the amount is the revenue from *The Lion King* (300 million).

Solution Percent × base = amount
$n \times 750 \text{ million} = 300 \text{ million}$
$n = 300 \div 750$
$n = 0.40$
The percent is 40%.

4. Strategy To find the ratio:
- Read the pictograph to find the number of people who agreed that space exploration impacts daily life and the number of people who agreed that space will be colonized in their lifetime.
- Write in simplest form the ratio of the number of people who agreed that space exploration impacts daily life to the number of people who agreed that space will be colonized in their lifetime.

Solution Number of people who agreed that space exploration impacts daily life: 600
Number of people who agreed that space will be colonized in their lifetime: 200

$\frac{600}{200} = \frac{3}{1}$

The ratio is $\frac{3}{1}$.

5. Strategy To find how many more people agreed that humanity should explore planets than agreed that space exploration impacts daily life, subtract the number that agreed that space exploration impacts daily life (600) from the number that agreed that humanity should explore planets (650).

Solution $650 - 600 = 50$
50 more people agreed that humanity should explore space than agreed that space exploration impacts daily life.

6. Strategy To find whether the number of people who agreed that they would travel in space is more than twice the number of those who agreed that space will be colonized in their lifetime, read the pictograph and determine whether the number of people who agreed that they would travel in space (350) is more than twice those who agreed that space would be colonized in their lifetime (200).

Solution $2 \times 200 = 400$
$350 < 400$
No, the number of people who agreed that they would travel in space is not more than twice the number who agreed that space will be colonized in their lifetime.

7. Strategy To find the number of children who said they hid vegetables under a napkin, write and solve the basic percent equation for amount. The percent is 30% and the base is 500.

Solution Percent × base = amount
$0.30 \times 500 = 150$
150 children said they hid their vegetables under a napkin.

8. Strategy To find the difference:
- Use the basic percent equation to find the number of children who fed vegetables to the dog and the number who dropped the vegetables on the floor.
- Subtract the number of children who fed them to the dog from the number who dropped them on the floor.

Solution Percent × base = amount
$0.25 \times 500 = 125$ children who fed the vegetables to the dog.
$0.10 \times 500 = 50$ children who dropped the vegetables on the floor.
$125 - 50 = 75$
75 more children fed the vegetables to the dog.

9. No, the sum of the percents given in the graph is only 80%, not 100%.

Objective B Exercises

10. Strategy To find the units required:
- Read the circle graph to determine the units needed.
- Add the units.

Solution

Accounting =	45
Humanities =	15
Math =	12
Science =	8
English =	9
Finance =	15
Others =	24
Total =	128

128 units are required to graduate.

11. Strategy To find the ratio:
- Read the circle graph to determine the units in Finance and Accounting.
- Write in the simplest form the ratio of the number of units in Finance to the number of units in Accounting.

Solution Number of units in Finance: 15
Number of units in Accounting: 45

$\frac{15}{45} = \frac{1}{3}$

The ratio is $\frac{1}{3}$.

12. Strategy To find the percent, solve the basic percent equation for percent. The base is the total number of units needed (128 units) and the amount is the number of units in Accounting (45 units).

Solution Percent × base = amount

$n \times 128 = 45$

$n = 45 \div 128 \approx 0.352 = 35.2\%$

The percent is 35.2%.

13. Strategy To find the percent, solve the basic percent equation for percent. The base is the total number of units needed (128 units) and the amount is the number of units in math (12 units).

Solution Percent × base = amount

$n \times 128 = 12$

$n = 12 \div 128 = 0.094 = 9.4\%$

The percent is 9.4%.

14a. People talking was the complaint mentioned the most often.

b. Uncomfortable seats was the complaint mentioned the least often.

15. Strategy To find the number of people surveyed:
- Read the circle graph to determine the number of responses.
- Add the five numbers.

Solution

High ticket prices:	33
People talking:	42
Uncomfortable seats:	17
Dirty floors:	27
High food prices :	+31
	150

The number of people surveyed is 150 people.

16. Strategy To find the ratio:
- Read the circle graph to determine the number of people responding "dirty floors" and "high ticket prices."
- Write in simplest form the ratio of the number of people responding "dirty floors" to the number of people responding "high ticket prices."

Solution Dirty floors: 27 people
High ticket prices: 33 people

$\frac{27}{33} = \frac{9}{11}$

The ratio is $\frac{9}{11}$.

17. Strategy To find the percent, solve the basic percent equation for percent. The base is the total number of responses (150) and the amount is the number of "people talking" responses (42).

Solution Percent × base = amount

$n \times 150 = 42$

$n = 42 \div 150 = 0.28 = 28\%$

The percent is 28%.

18. Strategy To find the amount of money spent:
- Read the circle graph to find the percent of money spent on TV game machines
- Use the basic percent equation to find the amount.

Solution 35% is spent on TV game machines.

Percent × base = amount

$0.35 \times 3{,}100{,}000{,}000 = n$

$1{,}085{,}000{,}000 = n$

Americans spend $1,085,000,000 on TV game machines.

19. Strategy To find the amount of money spent:
- Read the circle graph to find the percent of money spent on portable game machines.
- Use the basic percent equation to find the amount.

Solution 9% is spent on portable game machines.

Percent × base = amount

$0.09 \times 3{,}100{,}000{,}000 = n$

$279{,}000{,}000 = n$

Americans spend $279,000,000 on portable game machines.

20. Strategy To find the fractional amount spent on accessories:
- Use the basic percent equation to find the amount spent on accessories.
- Write the ratio of the amount spent on accessories to the total amount spent in simplest form.

Solution Percent × base = amount

$0.08 \times 3{,}100{,}000{,}000 = 248{,}000{,}000$

$\frac{248{,}000{,}000}{3{,}100{,}000{,}000} = \frac{2}{25}$

The fractional amount is $\frac{2}{25}$.

21. Strategy To determine whether the amount spent for TV game machines is more than three times the amount spent for portable game machines:
• Multiply by 3 the amount spent for portable game machines (Use amount from Exercise 19).
• Compare the result with the amount spent for TV game machines. (Use amount from Exercise 18).

Solution $3 \times 279{,}000{,}000 = 837{,}000{,}000$
$837{,}000{,}000 < 1{,}085{,}000{,}000$
Yes, the amount spent for TV game machines is more than three times the amount spent for portable game machines.

22. The age group 35 to 44 represents the largest segment.

23. Strategy To find whether the number of homeless who are aged 25 to 34 is more or less than twice the number of homeless under the age of 25, read the pictograph and determine whether the number of homeless aged 25 to 34 (25%) is more or less than twice the number of homeless under 25 (12%).

Solution $2 \times 12\% = 24\%$
$25\% > 24\%$
The number of homeless aged 25 to 34 is more than twice the number of homeless under the age of 25.

24. Strategy To find the percent of the homeless population under 35, add the percent of homeless under 25 (12%) and the percent of homeless aged 25 to 34 (25%).

Solution $12\% + 25\% = 37\%$
The percent of the homeless population under age 35 is 37%.

25. Strategy To find how many of every 100,000 homeless people are over age 54:
• Locate the percent of homeless over age 54.
• Solve the basic percent equation for amount. The base is 100,000.

Solution Percent homeless over age 54: 8%
Percent × base = amount
$0.08 \times 100{,}000 = n$
$8{,}000 = n$
Out of every 100,000 homeless people, there are 8000 people over age 54.

26. Strategy To find the total land area of the seven continents:
• Read the circle graph to determine the land area of the seven continents.
• Add the seven numbers.

Solution

2,970,000	Australia
4,060,000	Europe
5,100,000	Antarctica
6,870,000	South America
9,420,000	North America
11,670,000	Africa
+ 17,150,000	Asia
57,240,000	

The total land area is 57,240,000 square miles.

27. Strategy To find the difference, subtract the area of South America (6,870,000 square miles) from the area of North America (9,420,000 square miles).

Solution

9,420,000	North America
− 8,870,000	South America
2,550,000	

North America is 2,550,000 square miles larger than South America.

28. Strategy To find the percent:
• Read the circle graph to determine the land area of Asia.
• Write and solve the basic percent equation for percent. The amount is the land area of Asia and the base is the total land area of the seven continents. (57,240,000 square miles).

Solution The area of Asia is 17,150,000 square miles.
Percent × base = amount
$n \times 57{,}240{,}000 = 17{,}150{,}000$
$n = 17{,}150{,}000 \div 57{,}240{,}000$
$n \approx 0.300$
Asia is 30.0% of the total land area.

29. **Strategy** To find the percent:
- Read the circle graph to determine the land area of Australia.
- Write and solve the basic percent equation for percent. The amount is the land area of Australia and the base is the total land area of the seven continents. (57,240,000 square miles).

Solution The area of Australia is 2,970,000 square miles.

Percent × base = amount
$n \times 57{,}240{,}000 = 2{,}970{,}000$
$n = 2{,}970{,}000 \div 57{,}240{,}000$
≈ 0.052
Australia is 5.2% of the total land area.

30. **Strategy** To find the amount spent on food:
- Locate the percent of the after-tax income that is spent on food.
- Solve the basic percent equation for amount.

Solution Spent on food: 14%

Percent × base = amount
$0.14 \times 40{,}550 = 5677$
\$5677 is spent on food.

31. **Strategy** To find the amount spent on health care:
- Locate the percent of the after-tax income that is spent on health care.
- Solve the basic percent equation for amount.

Solution Spent on health care: 5%

Percent × base = amount
$0.05 \times 40{,}550 = 2027.5$
\$2027.50 is spent on health care.

32. **Strategy** To find how much more is spent on clothing than is spent on entertainment:
- Find the amount spent on each by using the percents given in the circle graph.
- Find the difference in these amounts.

Solution Spent on clothing: 6%

$0.06 \times 40{,}550 = \$2433$ on clothing
Spent on entertainment: 5%
$0.05 \times 40{,}550 = \$2027.50$
on entertainment

$\$2433 - 2027.50 = \$405.50$
\$405.50 more is spent on clothing than on entertainment.

33. **Strategy** To find whether the amount for housing is more than twice the amount spent on transportation, since the base is the same (\$40,550) in each case, compare the percents.

Solution Spent on housing: 32%
Spent on transportation: 17%
$32\% < 2 \times 17\% = 34\%$
No, the amount spent on housing is not more than twice the amount spent on transportation.

Applying the Concepts

34a. You might have students supply examples of pictographs with their explanations. Students can use the reference section at the library to find copies of *USA Today* or some other source for pictographs. In that case, it will be necessary for them to photocopy any examples they submit to you with their explanations.
Students may state that pictographs are more dramatic or visually appealing than some other type of graph. Presenting data in the form of a pictograph gives an overall picture of the relationship of each category to the whole and illustrates the relationship between categories.

b. A disadvantage is that the pictograph usually sacrifices some degree of accuracy.

35. Answers will vary. For example: The couple's largest single expense was rent.
Food represents approximately one-quarter of the month's expenditures.
Rent represents approximately one-third of the month's expenditures.
The expenditure for food is approximately the same as the expenditures for entertainment and transportation.
The couple spent more for transportation than for entertainment.

Section 7.2

Objective A Exercises

1. **Strategy** To find the total passenger cars produced worldwide:
   • Read the bar graph to determine the number of cars produced (in millions) in each region.
   • Add the five numbers

   Solution
   15 Western Europe
   11 Asia
   8 Eastern Europe/Russia
   3 North America
   +2 Latin America
   39
   39 million passenger cars were produced worldwide.

2. **Strategy** To find the difference:
   • Read the bar graph to find the number of passenger cars produced in Western Europe (15 million) and the number of cars produced in North America (3 million).
   • Subtract the two numbers.

   Solution
   15 million Western Europe
   − 3 million North America
   12 million
   The difference is 12 million passenger cars.

3. **Strategy** To find the percent, solve the basic percent equation for percent. The base is the total number of cars produced (39 million, from Exercise 1) and the amount is the number of cars produced in Asia (11 million)

   Solution Percent × base = amount
   $n \times 39 = 11$
   $n = 11 \div 39 \approx 0.28 = 28\%$
   The percent is 28%.

4. **Strategy** To find which is greater, fuel efficiency of the Toyota Prius on the highway or in city driving, read the double bar graph and compare the highway MPG and city MPG.

   Solution Fuel efficiency for the Toyota Prius is greater in city driving.

5. **Strategy** To find the difference:
   • Read the double bar graph for the Mini Cooper to find the fuel efficiency in the city (28 MPG) and the fuel efficiency on the highway (38 MPG).
   • Subtract the two numbers.

   Solution
   38 Highway
   − 28 City
   10
   The difference is approximately 10 miles per gallon.

6. **Strategy** To find the difference:
   • Read the double bar graph for Honda Insight to find the fuel efficiency in the city (approximately 60 MPG) and the fuel efficiency in the city for the VW New Beetle (approximately 40 MPG).
   • Subtract the two numbers.

   Solution
   60 Honda Insight
   − 40 VW New Beetle
   20
   The difference is approximately 20 miles per gallon.

7. **Strategy** To estimate the difference between the maximum salaries in New York:
   • Read the double-bar graph for the maximum salaries for city and suburb police officers.
   • Subtract to find the difference between the two salaries.

   Solution
   Suburb salary: 60,000
   City salary: − 44,000
   16,000
   The maximum salary of police officers in the suburbs is $16,000 higher than the maximum salary of police officers in the city.

8. **Strategy** Read the double-bar graph to determine if the maximum salary of any police officer in a city is greater than the maximum salary of a police officer in the suburb.

   Solution No, the maximum salary of the police officers in the city is lower than the maximum salary of a police officer in the suburb.

9. Strategy To find which city has the greatest difference between the maximum salary in the city and in the suburb:
- Read the double-bar graph to find maximum salaries for in the city and the suburb.
- Subtract the maximum salary in the city from the maximum salary in the suburb.

Solution Washington, D.C.:
51,000 – 41,000 = 10,000
Detroit:
46,000 – 38,000 = 8,000
New York:
60,000 – 44,000 = 16,000
Philadelphia:
56,000 – 38,000 = 18,000
Los Angeles:
52,000 – 49,000 = 3,000
The greatest difference in salaries is in Philadelphia.

10. Strategy To find which city has the lowest maximum salary for police officers in the suburbs, read the double-bar graph to find the shortest bar that represents salaries in the suburb.

Solution Detroit has the lowest maximum salary for police officers in the suburbs.

Objective B Exercises

11. Strategy To find the amount of snowfall during January, read the broken-line graph for January.

Solution The amount of snowfall during January was 20 inches.

12. Strategy To find the month in which the snowfall amount was greatest, read the broken-line graph and select the month beneath the highest point.

Solution The month with the greatest snowfall amount was January.

13. Strategy To find the total snowfall during March and April:
- Read the broken-line graph to find the snowfall amounts for March and April.
- Add the two amounts.

Solution

March	17
April	+8
	25

The snowfall during March and April was 25 inches.

14. Strategy To find the ratio:
- Read the broken-line graph to find the amount of snowfall in November and December.
- Write in simplest form the ratio of the amount in November to the amount in December.

Solution $\frac{12 \text{ in.}}{18 \text{ in.}} = \frac{2}{3}$

The ratio is $\frac{2}{3}$.

15. Strategy To find the difference:
- Read the broken-line graph to find the number of Calories recommended for men and the number recommended for women 19–22 years of age.
- Subtract the number recommended for women from the number recommended for men.

Solution

For men:	2900
For women:	– 2100
	800

The difference is 800 Calories.

16. Strategy To find what age and gender has the lowest number of recommended Calories, read the double broken-line graph and select the age and gender beneath the lowest point.

Solution The age and gender that has the lowest number of recommended Calories is for women age 75+.

17. Strategy To find the ratio:
- Read the double broken-line graph to find the number of Calories recommended for women 15–18 years old and the number recommended for women 51–74 years old.
- Write in simplest form the ratio of the number of Calories recommended for women 15–18 years old to the number recommended for women 51–74 years old.

Solution Women 15–18 years old: 2100
Women 51–74 years old: 1800

$\frac{2100}{1800} = \frac{7}{6}$

The ratio is $\frac{7}{6}$.

Applying the Concepts

18. Strategy To create each entry of the table, read the values (in billions of dollars) from the graph of the foreign aid and domestic aid, and find the sum.

Solution For 1991, the total aid:
$2.1 + 0.8 = $2.9 billion
For 1992, the total aid:
$1.9 + 0.8 = $2.7 billion
For 1993, the total aid:
$1.7 + 0.7 = $2.4 billion
For 1994, the total aid:
$1.5 + 0.6 = $2.1 billion
For 1995, the total aid:
$1.3 + 0.5 = $1.8 billion
For 1996, the total aid:
$1.3 + 0.5 = $1.8 billion
For 1997, the total aid:
$1.8 + 0.7 = $2.5 billion
For 1998, the total aid:
$1.7 + 0.8 = $2.5 billion
For 1999, the total aid:
$2.3 + 1.3 = $3.6 billion

Year	Total
1991	$2.9 billion
1992	$2.7 billion
1993	$2.4 billion
1994	$2.1 billion
1995	$1.8 billion
1996	$1.8 billion
1997	$2.5 billion
1998	$2.5 billion
1999	$3.6 billion

19. Strategy To create each entry of the table, read the values (in billions of dollars) from the graph of the foreign aid and domestic aid, and find the difference.

Solution For 1991, the total aid:
$2.1 – 0.8 = $1.3 billion
For 1992, the total aid:
$1.9 – 0.8 = $1.1 billion
For 1993, the total aid:
$1.7 – 0.7 = $1.0 billion
For 1994, the total aid:
$1.5 – 0.6 = $0.9 billion
For 1995, the total aid:
$1.3 – 0.5 = $0.8 billion
For 1996, the total aid:
$1.3 – 0.5 = $0.8 billion
For 1997, the total aid:
$1.8 – 0.7 = $1.1 billion
For 1998, the total aid:
$1.7 – 0.8 = $0.9 billion
For 1999, the total aid:
$2.3 – 1.3 = $1.0 billion

Year	Difference
1991	$1.3 billion
1992	$1.1 billion
1993	$1.0 billion
1994	$0.9 billion
1995	$0.8 billion
1996	$0.8 billion
1997	$1.1 billion
1998	$0.9 billion
1999	$1.0 billion

Section 7.3

Objective A Exercises

1. Strategy Read the histogram to find the number of students who have a tuition between $3000 and $6000.

Solution 44 students have a tuition that is between $3000 and $6000.

2. Strategy To find the ratio:
- Find the number of students whose tuition is between $9000 and $12,000 per year.
- Write in simplest form the ratio of the number of students whose tuition is between $9000 and $12,000 to the total number of students (120).

Solution Number of students whose tuition is between $9000 and $12,000: 12

$\frac{12}{120} = \frac{1}{10}$

The ratio is $\frac{1}{10}$.

3. **Strategy** To find the number of students who pay more than \$12,000 for tuition:
- Read the histogram to find the number of students whose tuition is between \$12,000 and \$15,000 and the number whose tuition is between \$15,000 and \$18,000.
- Add the two numbers.

Solution

\$12,000 – \$15,000	10 students
\$15,000 – \$18,000	+ 8 students
	18 students

18 students paid more than \$12,000.

4. **Strategy** To find the percent:
- Read the histogram to find the number of students who pay between \$0 and \$3000 and the number of students who pay between \$3000 and \$6000.
- Add the two numbers to find the number of students who paid less than \$6000 in tuition.
- Solve the basic percent equation for percent. The base is 120 and the amount is the total number of students who paid less than \$6000 in tuition.

Solution

\$0 – \$3000	40 students
\$3000 – \$6000	+ 44 students
	84 students

Percent × base = amount

$$n \times 120 = 84$$
$$n = 84 \div 120$$
$$n = 0.7$$

The percent is 70%.

5. **Strategy** To find the number of cars between 6 and 12 years old:
- Read the histogram to find the number of cars between 6 and 9 years old and the number between 9 and 12 years old.
- Add the two numbers.

Solution

6 to 9 years:	220 cars
9 to 12 years:	+ 190 cars
	410 cars

There are 410 cars between 6 and 12 years old.

6. **Strategy** To find the ratio:
- Read the histogram to find the number of cars between 12 and 15 years old.
- Write in simplest form the ratio of the number of cars between 12 and 15 years old and the total number of cars (1000).

Solution Number of cars between 12 and 15 years old: 90

$$\frac{90}{1000} = \frac{9}{100}$$

The ratio is $\frac{9}{100}$.

7. **Strategy** To find the number of cars more than 12 years old:
- Read the histogram to find the number of cars 12 to 15 years old and the number 15 to 18 years old.
- Add the two numbers.

Solution

12 to 15 years:	90 cars
15 to 18 years:	+ 140 cars
	230 cars

230 cars are more than 12 years old.

8. **Strategy** To find the percent:
- Read the histogram to find the number of cars 0 to 3 years old, the number 3 to 6 years old, and the number 6 to 9 years old.
- Add the three numbers.
- Solve the basic percent equation for percent. The base is the total number of cars sold and the amount is the number of cars less than 9 years old.

Solution

0 to 3 years:	170 cars
3 to 6 years:	190 cars
6 to 9 years:	+ 220 cars
	580 cars

Percent × base = amount

$$n \times 1000 = 580$$
$$n = 580 \div 1000$$
$$n = 0.58$$

58% of the cars are less than 9 years old.

9. **Strategy** To find the number of adults who spend between 1 and 2 hours at the mall, read the histogram.

Solution 54 adults spend between 1 and 2 hours at the mall.

10. **Strategy** To find the number of adults who spend between 3 and 4 hours at the mall, read the histogram.

Solution 18 adults spend between 3 and 4 hours at the mall.

11. Strategy To find the percent:
- Read the histogram to find the number of adults who spend less than 1 hour at the mall.
- Solve the basic percent equation for percent. The base is 100 and the amount is the number of adults who spend less than one hour at the mall.

Solution Number of adults who spend less then one hour at the mall: 22

Percent × base = amount
$n \times 100 = 22$
$n = 22 \div 100$
$n = 0.22$

The percent is 22%.

12. Strategy To find the percent:
- Read the histogram to find the number of adults who spend 5 or more hours at the mall.
- Solve the basic percent equation for percent. The base is 100 and the amount is the number of adults who spend 5 or more hours at the mall.

Solution Number of adults who spend 5 or more hours at the mall: 6

Percent × base = amount
$n \times 100 = 6$
$n = 6 \div 100$
$n = 0.06$

The percent is 6%.

Objective B Exercises

13. Strategy To find how many entrants were in the discus finals:
- Read the number of entrants for each of the points on the frequency polygon.
- Add the five numbers.

Solution
8 between 150 and 160 feet
9 between 160 and 170 feet
4 between 170 and 180 feet
2 between 180 and 190 feet
+1 between 190 and 200 feet
24

There were 24 entrants in the discus finals.

14. Strategy To find the number of entrants with distances of more than 170 feet:
- Read the number of entrants associated with distances of between 170 and 180 feet, between 180 and 190 feet, and between 190 and 200 feet.
- Add the three numbers.

Solution
4 between 170 and 180 feet
2 between 180 and 190 feet
+1 between 190 and 200 feet
7

There were 7 entrants with distances of more than 170 feet.

15. Strategy To find the percent:
- Read the frequency polygon to find the number of entrants that had distances between 160 feet and 170 feet (9).
- Solve the basic percent equation for percent. The base is the total number of entrants (24) and the amount is the number of entrants that had distances between 160 and 170 feet (9).

Solution Percent × base = amount
$n \times 24 = 9$
$n = 9 \div 24$
$n = 0.375$

37.5% of the entrants had distances between 160 feet and 170 feet.

16. Strategy To find the number of people who purchased 0 and 10 tickets, read the frequency polygon.

Solution There were 44 people who purchased between 0 and 10 tickets.

17. Strategy To find the percent:
- Read the frequency polygon to find how many people purchased between 20 and 30 tickets.
- Solve the basic percent equation for percent. The base is 74 and the amount is the number of people who purchased between 20 and 30 tickets.

Solution Between 20 and 30 tickets: 8

Percent × base = amount
$n \times 74 = 8$
$n = 8 \div 74$
$n \approx 0.108$

The percent is 10.8%.

18. Strategy To find the percent:
- Read the frequency polygon to find how many people purchased between 10 and 20 tickets, between 20 and 30 tickets, and between 30 and 40 tickets.
- Add the three numbers.
- Solve the basic percent equation for percent. The base is 74, and the amount is the sum of the three numbers.

Solution

Between 10 and 20:	16 tickets
Between 20 and 30:	8 tickets
Between 30 and 40:	+ 6 tickets
	30 tickets

Percent × base = amount

$n \times 74 = 30$

$n = 30 \div 74$

$n \approx 0.405$

The percent is 40.5%.

19. No, a frequency polygon shows only the number of occurrences in a class. It does not show the number of occurrences for any particular value.

20. Strategy To find the number of students who scored between 1200 and 1400 on the exam, read the frequency polygon.

Solution 170,000 students scored between 1200 and 1400.

21. Strategy To find the percent:
- Read the frequency polygon to find the number of students that scored between 800 and 1000.
- Solve the basic percent equation for percent. The base is 1,080,000 and the amount is the number of students scoring between 800 and 1000.

Solution Number of student scoring between 800 and 1000: 350,000

Percent × base = amount

$n \times 1{,}080{,}000 = 350{,}000$

$n = 350{,}000 \div 1{,}080{,}000$

$n \approx 0.324$

The percent is 32.4%.

22. Strategy To find the number of students:
- Read the frequency polygon to find the number of students who scored between 400 and 600, between 600 and 800, and between 800 and 1,000.
- Add the three numbers.

Solution

Between 400 and 600:	30,000
Between 600 and 800:	150,000
Between 800 and 1000:	+ 350,000
	530,000

530,000 students scored below 1000.

23. Strategy To find the number of students:
- Read the frequency polygon to find the number of students who scored between 800 and 1000, between 1000 and 1200, between 1200 and 1400, and between 1400 and 1600.
- Add the four numbers.

Solution

Between 800 and 1000:	350,000
Between 1000 and 1200:	350,000
Between 1200 and 1400:	170,000
Between 1400 and 1600:	+ 30,000
	900,000

900,000 students scored above 800.

Applying the Concepts

24. A bar graph represents categorical data, whereas a histogram breaks the range of values of a set of data into intervals of equal width and displays the number of values that fall into each interval.

25. A frequency table is another method of organizing data. In a frequency table, or a frequency distribution, data are combined into categories called classes, and the frequency, which is the number of pieces of data in each class, is shown.

Section 7.4

Objective A Exercises

1a. Median

b. Mean

c. Mode

d. Median

e. Mode

f. Mean

2. **Strategy** To find the mean value of the monthly television sales:
- Find the sum of the monthly sales.
- Divide the sum by the number of months (12).

Solution

15
12
20
20
19
17
22
24
17
20
15
+ 27
228

$$12\overline{)228} = 19$$

The mean value of the monthly sales is 19 TVs.

Strategy To find the median value of the monthly television sales, arrange the sales in order from smallest to largest. The median is the mean of the two middle numbers.

Solution

12, 15, 15, 17, 17 } 5 numbers
19, 20 } middle numbers
20, 20, 22, 24, 27 } 5 numbers

$$\frac{19 + 20}{2} = 19.5$$

The median of the monthly sales is 19.5 TVs.

Strategy To find the mode, look at the monthly sales record and identify the number that occurs most frequently.

Solution The mode is 20 TVs as that is the number that occurs most frequently.

3. **Strategy** To find the mean value of the number of seats occupied:
- Find the sum of the number of seats occupied.
- Divide the sum by the number of flights (16).

Solution

309
422
389
412
401
352
367
319
410
391
330
408
399
387
411
+398
6,105

$$16\overline{)6,105} = 381.5625$$

The mean of the number of seats filled is 381.5625 seats.

Strategy To find the median value of the number of seats occupied, arrange the numbers in order from smallest to largest. The median is the mean of the two middle numbers.

Solution

309, 319, 330, 352, 367, 387, 389 } 7 numbers
391, 398 } Middle numbers
399, 401, 408, 410, 411, 412, 422 } 7 numbers

$$\frac{391 + 398}{2} = 394.5$$

The median of the number of seats filled is 394.5 seats.

Strategy To find the mode, look at the number of seats occupied and locate the number that occurs most frequently.

Solution Since each number occurs only once, there is no mode.

4. **Strategy** To find the mean time:
- Find the sum of the times.
- Divide the sum by the number of times (10).

Solution

```
  10.45
  10.23
  10.57
  11.01
  10.26
  10.90          10.61
  10.74      10)106.10
  10.64
  10.52
+ 10.78
 106.10
```

The mean time is 10.61 seconds.

Strategy To find the median time, arrange the times in order from smallest to largest. The median is the mean of the two middle numbers.

Solution

```
10.23 ┐
10.26 │
10.45 ├ 4 numbers
10.52 ┘
10.57 ┐
10.64 ┘ middle numbers
10.74 ┐
10.78 │
10.90 ├ 4 numbers
11.01 ┘
```

$$\frac{10.57 + 10.64}{2} = 10.605$$

The median time is 10.605 seconds.

5. **Strategy** To find the mean cost:
- Find the sum of the costs.
- Divide the total costs by the number of purchases (8).

Solution

```
  $45.89
  $52.12
  $41.43
  $40.67
  $48.73        45.615
  $42.45     8)364.920
  $47.81
+ $45.82
 $364.92
```

The mean cost is $45.615.

Strategy To find the median cost, arrange the costs in order from smallest to largest. The median is the mean of the two middle numbers.

Solution

```
$40.67 ┐
$41.43 ├ 3 numbers
$42.45 ┘
$45.82 ┐
$45.89 ┘ middle numbers
$47.81 ┐
$48.73 ├ 3 numbers
$52.12 ┘
```

$$\frac{\$45.82 + 45.88}{2} = \$45.855$$

The median cost is $45.855.

6. **Strategy** To find the mean hard drive speed:
- Find the sum of the hard drive speeds.
- Divide the sums by the number of speeds.

Solution

```
   5
   4.5
   4
   4.5
   5
   5.5         4.727
   6       11)52.000
   5.5
   3
   4.5
 + 4.5
  52
```

The mean is 4.7 milliseconds.

Strategy To find the median hard-drive speed, write the speeds in order from smallest to largest. The median is the middle number.

Solution

```
3   ┐
4   │
4.5 ├ 5 numbers
4.5 │
4.5 ┘
4.5 } middle number
5   ┐
5   │
5.5 ├ 5 numbers
5.5 │
6   ┘
```

The median is 4.5 milliseconds.

7. Strategy To find the mean monthly rate:

- Find the sum of the monthly rates.
- Divide the sum by the number of plans (8).

Solution

$$\begin{array}{r} \$423 \\ \$390 \\ \$405 \\ \$396 \\ \$426 \\ \$355 \\ \$404 \\ +\ \$430 \\ \hline \$3{,}229 \end{array} \qquad \begin{array}{r} \$403.625 \\ 8\overline{)\$3{,}229.000} \end{array}$$

The mean monthly rate is \$403.625.

Strategy To find the median monthly rate, write the rates in order from smallest to largest. The median is the mean of the two middle terms.

Solution

$$\left.\begin{array}{r} \$355 \\ \$390 \\ \$396 \end{array}\right\} \text{3 numbers}$$
$$\left.\begin{array}{r} \$404 \\ \$405 \end{array}\right\} \text{middle numbers}$$
$$\left.\begin{array}{r} \$423 \\ \$426 \\ \$430 \end{array}\right\} \text{3 numbers}$$

$$\frac{\$404 + 405}{2} = \$404.50$$

The median monthly rate is \$404.50.

8. Strategy To find the mean length of tenure for the chief justices:

- Find the sum of the years served.
- Divide the sum by the number of chief justices (15).

Solution

$$\begin{array}{r} 5 \\ 0 \\ 4 \\ 34 \\ 28 \\ 8 \\ 14 \\ 21 \\ 10 \\ 8 \\ 11 \\ 4 \\ 7 \\ 15 \\ +17 \\ \hline 186 \end{array} \qquad \begin{array}{r} 12.4 \\ 15\overline{)186.0} \end{array}$$

The mean number of years of service is 12.4 years.

Strategy To find the median length of tenure for the chief justices, write the years in order from smallest to largest. The median is the middle number.

Solution

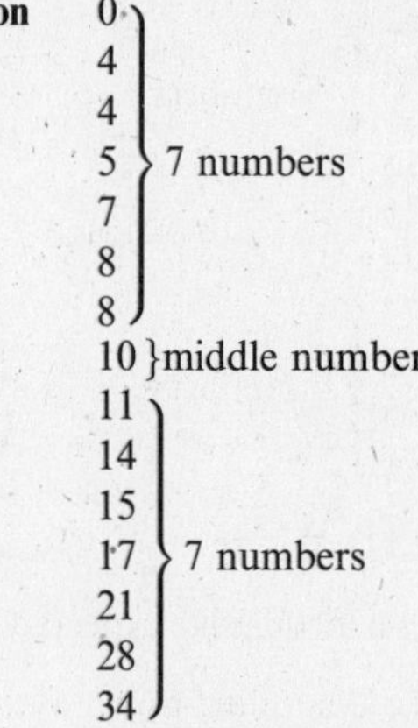

The median number of years of service is 10 years.

9. Strategy To find the mean life expectancy:

- Find the sum of the years.
- Divide the sum by the number of countries (10).

Solution

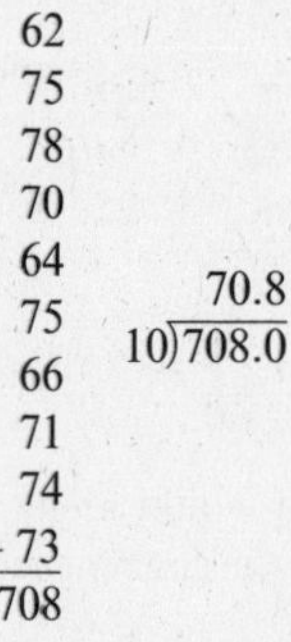

$$\begin{array}{r} 70.8 \\ 10\overline{)708.0} \end{array}$$

The mean life expectancy is 70.8 years.

Strategy To find the median life expectancy, write the years in order from lowest to highest. The median is the mean of the two middle numbers.

Solution
62, 64, 66, 70 } 4 numbers
71, 73 } middle numbers
74, 75, 75, 78 } 4 numbers

$$\frac{71+73}{2}=72$$

The median life expectancy is 72 years.

10. Strategy To determine which average you would prefer:
- Find the mean of the test scores.
- Find the median of the test scores.
- Choose the higher score.

Solution

Mean	Median	
78	77	2 numbers
92	78	
95	88	middle numbers
77	92	
94	94	2 numbers
+ 88	95	
524		

$524.0 \div 6 = 87.3$ $\qquad \frac{88+92}{2}=90$

You would prefer that the instructor use the higher median score 90.

11. No, the mean scores of the two students are not the same. The mean score of the second student is 5 points higher than the mean score of the first student.

12a. Strategy To find the mean annual expenditures:
- Find the sum of the expenditures.
- Divide the sum by the number of years (9).

Solution
$49.6
56.8
70.1
80.5
81.2
80.3
77.7
78.3
+ 76.0
$650.5

$650.5 \div 9 = 72.3$

The mean annual defense expenditures is $72.3 billion.

b. Strategy To find the median annual defense expenditure, write the expenditures in order from smallest to largest. The median is the middle number.

Solution
49.6, 56.8, 70.1, 76.0 } 4 numbers
77.7} middle number
78.3, 80.3, 80.5, 81.2 } 4 numbers

The median is $77.7 billion.

c. If the year 1965 were eliminated from the data, the mean would increase and the median would increase, because the expenditures for 1965 are the lowest in the set of data.

Objective B Exercises

13a. 25%

b. 75%

c. 75%

d. 25%

14a–e. Strategy Read the youngest age, the oldest age, the first quartile, the third quartile, the median directly from the box-and-whiskers plot.

Solution Youngest is 42 years.
Oldest is 69 years.
$Q_1 = 51$ years
$Q_3 = 58$ years
Median = 55 years

f. Strategy Find the range by subtracting the youngest from the oldest.

Solution Range: 69 – 42 = 27 years

g. Strategy Interquartile range = $Q_3 - Q_1$.

Solution Interquartile range = 58 – 51 = 7 years

15. Strategy
- Read the lowest value, the highest value, the first quartile, the third quartile, the median directly from the box-and-whiskers plot.
- Find the range by subtracting the lowest from the highest.
- Interquartile range = $Q_3 - Q_1$.

Solution Lowest is \$46,596.
Highest is \$82,879.
Q_1 = \$56,067
Q_3 = \$66,507
Median = \$61,036
Range: 82,879 – 46,596 = \$36,283
Interquartile range:
66,507 – 56,067 = \$10,440

16a. Strategy To find the number of students who scored over 88, the third quartile, solve the basic percent equation for the amount, where the base is 200 and the percent is 25%.

Solution Percent × base = amount
0.25 × 200 = 50
There were 50 students who scored over 88.

b. Strategy To find the number of students who scored below 72, the median, solve the basic percent equation for the amount, where the base is 200 and the percent is 50%.

Solution Percent × base = amount
0.50 × 200 = 100
There were 100 students who scored below 72.

c. Strategy To find the number of scores represented in each quartile, solve the basic percent equation for the amount, where the base is 200 and the percent is 25%.

Solution Percent × base = amount
0.25 × 200 = 50
There are 50 scores in each quartile.

d. The first quartile is at 54. There are 25% of the scores below the first quartile. So 75% of the scores were above the first quartile.

17a. Strategy To find the number of adults who had a cholesterol level above 217, the median, solve the basic percent equation for the amount, where the base is 80 and the percent is 50%.

Solution Percent × base = amount
0.50 × 80 = 40
There were 40 adults who had cholesterol levels above 217.

b. Strategy To find the number of adults who had a cholesterol level below 254, the third quartile, solve the basic percent equation for the amount, where the base is 80 and the percent is 75%.

Solution Percent × base = amount
0.75 × 80 = 60
There were 60 adults who had cholesterol levels below 254.

c. Strategy To find the number of cholesterol levels represented in each quartile, solve the basic percent equation for the amount, where the base is 80 and the percent is 25%.

Solution Percent × base = amount
0.25 × 80 = 20
There are 20 cholesterol levels in each quartile.

d. The first quartile is at 198. So 25% of the adults had cholesterol levels not more than 198.

18a. Strategy
- Arrange the data from smallest to largest.
- Find the range.
- Find Q_1, the median of the lower half of the data.
- Find Q_3, the median of the upper half of the data.
- Interquartile range = $Q_3 - Q_1$.

Solution

16	17	19	20	20	21	21	22	24	25
26	26	28	30	30	31	31	32	33	

Range: 33 – 16 = 17 mpg
Q_1 = 20 mpg
Q_3 = 30 mpg
Interquartile range = $Q_3 - Q_1$
= 30 – 20
= 10 mpg

b.

16 20 25 30 33

c. Yes, 21 is between Q_1 and Q_3.

19a. Strategy
- Arrange the data from smallest to largest.
- Find the range.
- Find Q_1, the median of the lower half of the data.
- Find Q_3, the median of the upper half of the data.
- Interquartile range $= Q_3 - Q_1$.

Solution

0.41	0.41	0.56	0.61	0.76
0.87	1.06	2.10	2.60	4.80

Range: $4.80 - 0.41 = 4.39$ million metric tons

$Q_1 = 0.56$ million metric tons

$Q_3 = 2.10$ million metric tons

Interquartile range $= Q_3 - Q_1$

$= 2.10 - 0.56$

$= 1.54$ million metric tons

b. 

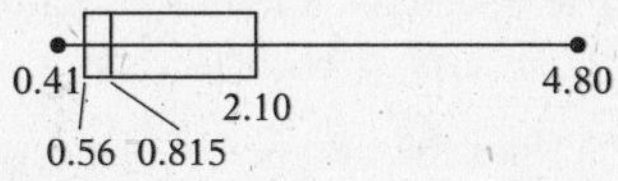

c. 4.80

20a. Strategy To determine whether the difference in means is greater than 1 inch:
- Find the sum of the rainfall in Seattle.
- Divide the sum by the number of months (12) to find the mean.
- Find the sum of the rainfall in Houston.
- Divide the sum by the number of months (12) to find the mean.
- Find the difference in the means.

Solution

Seattle		Houston	
6.0		3.2	
4.2		3.3	
3.6		2.7	
2.4		4.2	
1.6		4.7	
1.4	3.2	4.1	3.7
0.7	$12\overline{)38.5}$	3.3	$12\overline{)44.9}$
1.3		3.7	
2.0		4.9	
3.4		3.7	
5.6		3.4	
+6.3		+3.7	
38.5		44.9	

$3.7 - 3.1 = 0.6$

No, the difference in the means is not greater than 1 inch.

b. Strategy To find the median the difference in the medians, write the rainfall in order from lowest to highest. The median is the mean of the two middle numbers. Find the difference between the Seattle median and Houston median.

Solution

Seattle		Houston	
0.7, 1.3, 1.4, 1.6, 2.0	5 numbers	2.7, 3.2, 3.3, 3.3, 3.4	5 numbers
2.4, 3.4	middle	3.7, 3.7	middle
3.6, 4.2, 5.6, 6.0, 6.3	5 numbers	3.7, 4.1, 4.2, 4.7, 4.9	5 numbers

For Seattle, $\dfrac{2.4 + 3.4}{2} = 2.9$

For Houston, $\dfrac{3.7 + 3.7}{2} = 3.7$

$3.7 - 2.9 = 0.8$

The difference in medians is 0.8 inch.

c. Strategy To draw the box-and-whiskers plot:
- Find Q_1 and Q_3 in Seattle.
- Find Q_1 and Q_3 in Houston.

Solution For Seattle, $Q_1 = \dfrac{1.4 + 1.6}{2} = 1.5$,

$Q_3 = \dfrac{4.2 + 5.6}{2} = 4.9$

For Houston, $Q_1 = \dfrac{3.3 + 3.3}{2} = 3.3$,

$Q_3 = \dfrac{4.1 + 4.2}{2} = 4.15$

0.7 1.5 2.9 4.9 6.3

2.7 3.3 4.15 4.9 3.7

d. Answers will vary. For example, Seattle has months that average less rainfall than any month in Houston, and it has months that average more rainfall than any month in Houston. The range of the Seattle data is wider than the range of the Houston data. Almost all of the Houston data lie between the median and the third quartile of the Seattle data. The average amount of rain per month in Houston varies relatively little compared to the average amount of rain per month in Seattle.

21a. Strategy To determine whether the difference in means is greater than 1 inch:

- Find the sum of the rainfall in Orlando.
- Divide the sum by the number of months (12) to find the mean.
- Find the sum of the rainfall in Portland.
- Divide the sum by the number of months (12) to find the mean.
- Find the difference in the means.

Solution

Orlando		Portland	
2.1		6.2	
2.8		3.9	
3.2		3.6	
2.2		2.3	
4.0		2.1	
7.4	$12\overline{)47.8}$ = 4.0	1.5	$12\overline{)37.5}$ = 3.1
7.8		0.5	
6.3		1.1	
5.6		1.6	
2.8		3.1	
1.8		5.2	
+ 1.8		+ 6.4	
47.8		37.5	

$4.0 - 3.1 = 0.9$

No, the difference in the means is not greater than 1 inch.

b. Strategy To find the difference between the medians, write the rainfall in order from lowest to highest. The median is the mean of the two middle numbers. Find the difference between the Orlando median and Portland median.

Solution

Orlando		Portland	
1.8	5 numbers	0.5	5 numbers
1.8		1.1	
2.1		1.5	
2.2		1.6	
2.8		2.1	
2.8	middle	2.3	middle
3.2		3.1	
4.0	5 numbers	3.6	5 numbers
5.6		3.9	
6.3		5.2	
7.4		6.2	
7.8		6.4	

For Orlando, $\dfrac{2.8 + 3.2}{2} = 3.0$

For Portland, $\dfrac{2.3 + 3.1}{2} = 2.7$

$3.0 - 2.7 = 0.3$

The difference in medians is 0.3 inch.

c. Strategy To draw box-and-whiskers:

- Find Q_1 and Q_3 in Orlando.
- Find Q_1 and Q_3 in Portland.

Solution For Orlando, $Q_1 = \dfrac{2.1 + 2.2}{2} = 2.15$, $Q_3 = \dfrac{5.6 + 6.3}{2} = 5.95$

For Portland, $Q_1 = \dfrac{1.5 + 1.6}{2} = 1.55$, $Q_3 = \dfrac{3.9 + 5.2}{2} = 4.55$

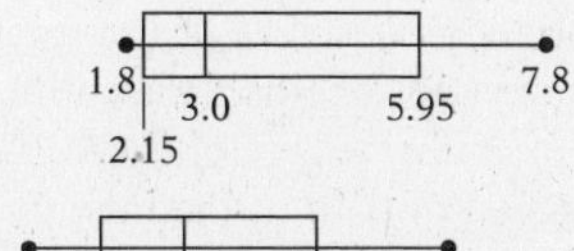

0.5 6.4
1.55 2.7 4.55

d. Answers will vary. For example, the distribution of the data is relatively similar for the two cities. However, the value of each of the 5 points on the boxplot for the Portland data is less than the corresponding value on the boxplot for the Orlando data. The average monthly rainfall in Portland is less than the average monthly rainfall in Orlando.

Applying the Concepts

22a. To determine the mean, find the sum of the numbers in the set of data. Divide by the number of numbers in the set.

b. To find the median, arrange the numbers from smallest to largest. If there are an *odd* number of values in the set of data, the median is the middle number.If there are an *even* number of values in the set of data, the median is the mean of the two middle numbers.

c. To find the mode, find the number in the set of data that occurs more often than any other number in the set.

23. Answers will vary. For example, 55, 55, 55, 55, 55, or 50, 55, 55, 55, 60

24. The mode must be a value in the data because it is the number that occurs most often in a set of data.

25a. Q_1 is the number that one-quarter of the data lie below.

b. Q_3 is the number that one-quarter of the data lie above.

c. $\bar{x}$ is the symbol for the mean of a set of data.

26. A box-and-whiskers plot displays the following values in a set of data: the lowest value, Q_1, the median, Q_3, and the highest value. The lowest value is shown at the far left of the plot (at the end of the left whisker). The highest value is shown at the far right of the plot (at the end of the right whisker). Q_1 is shown at the left end of the box, and Q_3 is shown at the right end of the box. The median is represented by the vertical line within the box.

27. The box does represent 50% of the data, but it provides a picture of the spread of the data. The box is not one-half the entire length of the box-and-whiskers plot because there is a greater spread of data in the interquartile range than in the first quarter or fourth quarter of the data.

28. Answers will vary. For example, 20, 21, 22, 24, 26, 27, 29, 31, 31, 32, 32, 33, 33, 36, 37, 37, 39, 40, 41, 43, 45, 46, 50, 54, 57

Section 7.5

Objective A Exercises

1. The possible outcomes of tossing a coin four times: {(HHHH), (HHHT), (HHTT), (HHTH), (HTTT), (HTHH), (HTTH), (HTHT), (TTTT), (TTTH), (TTHH), (THHH), (TTHT), (THHT), (THTT), (THTH)}

2. The possible outcomes of having three colors: RGB, RBG, GRB, GBR, BRG, BGR

3. The possible outcomes of tossing two tetrahedral dice: {(1, 1), (1, 2), (1, 3), (1, 4), (2, 1), (2, 2), (2, 3), (2, 4), (3, 1), (3, 2), (3, 3), (3, 4), (4, 1), (4, 2), (4, 3), (4, 4)}

4. The possible outcomes of tossing a coin and then a die: {(H, 1), (H, 2), (H, 3), (H, 4), (H, 5), (H, 6), (T, 1), (T, 2), (T, 3), (T, 4), (T, 5), (T, 6)}

5a. The sample space is {1, 2, 3, 4, 5, 6, 7, 8}.

b. The outcomes in the event the number is less than 4 is {1, 2, 3}.

6a. Strategy To calculate the probability:
- Count the number of possible outcomes. Refer to Exercise 1.
- Count the number of favorable outcomes.
- Use the probability formula.

Solution There are 16 possible outcomes.
There is 1 favorable outcome: HHTT.

$\text{Probability} = \frac{1}{16}$

The probability of HHTT is $\frac{1}{16}$.

b. Strategy To calculate the probability:
- Count the number of possible outcomes. Refer to Exercise 1.
- Count the number of favorable outcomes.
- Use the probability formula.

Solution There are 16 possible outcomes.
There are 6 favorable outcomes: HHTT, HTTH, TTHH, HTHT, THTH, THHT.

$\text{Probability} = \frac{6}{16} = \frac{3}{8}$

The probability of two heads and two tails is $\frac{3}{8}$.

c. Strategy To calculate the probability:
- Count the number of possible outcomes. Refer to Exercise 1.
- Count the number of favorable outcomes.
- Use the probability formula.

Solution There are 16 possible outcomes.
There are 4 favorable outcomes: HTTT, TTTH, TTHT, THTT.

$\text{Probability} = \frac{4}{16} = \frac{1}{4}$

The probability of one head and three tails is $\frac{1}{4}$.

7a. Strategy To calculate the probability:
- Count the number of possible outcomes. See the table on p. 323.
- Count the number of favorable outcomes.
- Use the probability formula.

Solution There are 36 possible outcomes.
There are 4 favorable outcomes: (1, 4), (4, 1), (2, 3), (3, 2).

$\text{Probability} = \frac{4}{36} = \frac{1}{9}$

The probability that the sum is 5 is $\frac{1}{9}$.

b. Strategy To calculate the probability:
- Count the number of possible outcomes. See the table on p. 323.
- Count the number of favorable outcomes.
- Use the probability formula.

Solution There are 36 possible outcomes.
There are 0 favorable outcomes.

$\text{Probability} = \frac{0}{36} = 0$

The probability that the sum is 15 is 0.

c. Strategy To calculate the probability:
- Count the number of possible outcomes. See the table on p. 323.
- Count the number of favorable outcomes.
- Use the probability formula.

Solution There are 36 possible outcomes.
There are 36 favorable outcomes.

Probability $= \frac{36}{36} = 1$

The probability that the sum is less than 15 is 1.

d. Strategy To calculate the probability:
- Count the number of possible outcomes. See the table on p. 323.
- Count the number of favorable outcomes.
- Use the probability formula.

Solution There are 36 possible outcomes.
There is 1 favorable outcome: (1, 1).

Probability $= \frac{1}{36}$

The probability that the sum is 2 is $\frac{1}{36}$.

8a. Strategy To calculate the probability:
- Count the number of possible outcomes.
- Count the number of favorable outcomes.
- Use the probability formula.

Solution A dodecahedral die has 12 sides.
There is 1 favorable outcome: 11.

Probability $= \frac{1}{12}$

The probability that the number is 11 is $\frac{1}{12}$.

b. Strategy To calculate the probability:
- Count the number of possible outcomes.
- Count the number of favorable outcomes.
- Use the probability formula.

Solution A dodecahedral die has 12 sides.
There is 1 favorable outcome: 5.

Probability $= \frac{1}{12}$

The probability that the number is 5 is $\frac{1}{12}$.

9a. Strategy To calculate the probability:
- Count the number of possible outcomes.
- Count the number of favorable outcomes.
- Use the probability formula.

Solution A dodecahedral die has 12 sides.
There are 3 favorable outcomes: 4, 8, 12.

Probability $= \frac{3}{12} = \frac{1}{4}$

The probability that the number is divisible by 4 is $\frac{1}{4}$.

b. Strategy To calculate the probability:
- Count the number of possible outcomes.
- Count the number of favorable outcomes.
- Use the probability formula.

Solution A dodecahedral die has 12 sides.
There are 4 favorable outcomes: 3, 6, 9, 12.

Probability $= \frac{4}{12} = \frac{1}{3}$

The probability that the number is a multiple of 3 is $\frac{1}{3}$.

10a. Strategy To calculate the probability:
- Count the number of possible outcomes. Refer to Exercise 3.
- Count the number of favorable outcomes.
- Use the probability formula.

Solution There are 16 possible outcomes.
There are 3 favorable outcomes: (1, 3), (3, 1), (2, 2).

Probability $= \frac{3}{16}$

The probability is $\frac{3}{16}$ that the sum of the dots on the two dice is 4.

b. Strategy To calculate the probability:
- Count the number of possible outcomes. Refer to Exercise 3.
- Count the number of favorable outcomes.
- Use the probability formula.

Solution There are 16 possible outcomes.
There are 3 favorable outcomes: (2, 4), (4, 2), (3, 3).

Probability $= \frac{3}{16}$

The probability is $\frac{3}{16}$ that the sum of the dots on the two dice is 6.

11. Strategy To calculate the probability:
- Count the number of possible outcomes. See the table on p. 323.
- Count the number of favorable outcomes.
- Use the probability formula.
- Compare the probabilities.

Solution There are 36 possible outcomes.
For a sum of 10, there are 3 favorable outcomes: (5, 5), (4, 6), (6, 4).

Probability $= \frac{3}{36}$

For a sum of 5, there are 4 favorable outcomes:
(1, 4), (4, 1), (2, 3), (3, 2).

Probability $= \frac{4}{36}$

$\frac{4}{36} > \frac{3}{36}$

The probability of throwing a sum of 5 is greater.

12. Strategy To calculate the probability:
- Count the number of possible outcomes. See the table on p. 323.
- Count the number of favorable outcomes.
- Use the probability formula.

Solution There are 36 possible outcomes.
There are 6 favorable outcomes:
(1, 1), (2, 2), (3, 3), (4, 4), (5, 5), (6, 6).

Probability $= \frac{6}{36} = \frac{1}{6}$

The probability that numbers are equal is $\frac{1}{6}$.

13a. Strategy To calculate the probability:
- Count the number of possible outcomes.
- Count the number of favorable outcomes.
- Use the probability formula.

Solution There are 11 possible outcomes.
There are 4 favorable outcomes.

Probability $= \frac{4}{11}$

The probability is $\frac{4}{11}$ that the letter I is drawn.

b. Strategy To calculate the probability:
- Count the number of possible outcomes.
- Count the number of favorable outcomes.
- Use the probability formula.
- Compare the probabilities.

Solution There are 11 possible outcomes.
There are 4 favorable outcomes of choosing an S.

Probability $= \frac{4}{11}$

There are 2 favorable outcomes of choosing a P.

Probability $= \frac{2}{11}$

$\frac{4}{11} > \frac{2}{11}$.

The probability of choosing an S is greater.

14. Strategy To calculate the probability:
- Count the number of possible outcomes.
- Count the number of favorable outcomes.
- Use the probability formula.

Solution There are 5 possible outcomes.
There is 1 favorable outcome: the correct answer.

Probability $= \frac{1}{5}$

The probability of choosing the correct answer by just guessing is $\frac{1}{5}$.

15a. Strategy To calculate the probability:
- Count the number of possible outcomes.
- Count the number of favorable outcomes.
- Use the probability formula.

Solution There are 12 possible outcomes (3 blue + 4 green + 5 red).
There are 4 favorable outcomes.

$\text{Probability} = \frac{4}{12} = \frac{1}{3}$

The probability is $\frac{1}{3}$ that the marble chosen is green.

b. Strategy To calculate the probability:
- Count the number of possible outcomes.
- Count the number of favorable outcomes.
- Use the probability formula.
- Compare the probabilities.

Solution There are 12 possible outcomes.
There are 3 favorable outcomes of choosing a blue marble.

$\text{Probability} = \frac{3}{12} = \frac{1}{4}$

There are 5 favorable outcomes of choosing a red marble.

$\text{Probability} = \frac{5}{12}$

$\frac{5}{12} > \frac{3}{12}$

The probability of choosing a red marble is greater.

16. Strategy To calculate the probability:
- Count the number of possible outcomes.
- Count the number of favorable outcomes.
- Use the probability formula.
- Compare the probabilities.

Solution There are 52 possible outcomes.
There are 12 favorable outcomes of drawing a jack, queen, or king.

$\text{Probability} = \frac{12}{52} = \frac{3}{13}$

There are 13 favorable outcomes of drawing a spade.

$\text{Probability} = \frac{13}{52} = \frac{1}{4}$

$\frac{13}{52} > \frac{12}{52}$

The probability of drawing a spade is greater.

17. Strategy To calculate the probability:
- Count the number of possible outcomes.
- Count the number of favorable outcomes.
- Use the probability formula.

Solution There are 47 possible outcomes $(4 + 8 + 22 + 10 + 3)$.
There are 8 favorable outcomes.

$\text{Probability} = \frac{8}{47}$

The probability is $\frac{8}{47}$ that the paper has a B grade.

18. Strategy To calculate the empirical probability, use the probability formula and divide the number of observations (37) by the total number of observations (95).

Solution $\text{Probability} = \frac{37}{95} \approx 0.39$

The probability is 0.39 that a person prefers a cash discount.

19. Strategy To calculate the empirical probability, use the probability formula and divide the number of observations (587) by the total number of observations (725).

Solution $\text{Probability} = \frac{587}{725} \approx 0.81$

The probability is 0.81 that an employee has a group health insurance plan.

20. Strategy To calculate the probability:
- Count the number of possible outcomes.
- Count the number of favorable outcomes.
- Use the probability formula.

Solution There are 377 $(98 + 87 + 129 + 42 + 21)$ possible outcomes.
There are 185 $(98 + 87)$ favorable outcomes.

$\text{Probability} = \frac{185}{377}$

The probability is $\frac{185}{377}$ that the customer rated the cable service satisfactory or excellent.

Applying the Concepts

21. No, the numbers 1 through 5 are not equally likely because the sizes of the sectors are different.

22. The probability of tossing a fair coin and having it land heads up is $\frac{1}{2}$. This does not mean that if the coin is tossed 100 times, it will land heads up 50 times. Theoretical probabilities are obtained from logical reasoning, not from experimental data.

23. The mathematical probability of an event is a number from 0 to 1. Because $\frac{5}{3} = 1\frac{2}{3}, \frac{5}{3} > 1$. The probability of an even cannot be $\frac{5}{3}$ because the probability cannot be greater than 1.

Chapter 7 Review Exercises

1. **Strategy** To find the amount of money:
   - Read the circle graph to determine the amounts of money spent.
   - Add the amounts.

   Solution

Defense:	\$148 million
Agriculture:	\$15 million
EPA:	\$24 million
Commerce:	\$27 million
NASA:	\$31 million
Other:	+ 104 million
	\$349 million

   The agencies spent \$349 million in maintaining websites.

2. **Strategy** To find the ratio:
   - Read the circle graph to find the amount spent by the Department of Commerce and by the EPA.
   - Write, in simplest form, the ratio of the amount spent by the Department of Commerce to the amount spent by the EPA.

   Solution Commerce: \$27 million
   EPA: \$24 million

   $$\frac{\$27 \text{ million}}{\$24 \text{ million}} = \frac{9}{8}$$

   The ratio is $\frac{9}{8}$.

3. **Strategy** To find the percent, solve the basic percent equation for percent. The base is the total amount spent (\$349 million) and the amount is the amount spent by NASA (\$31 million)

   Solution Percent × base = amount
   $n \times \$349 \text{ million} = \$31 \text{ million}$
   $n = \$31 \text{ million} \div \$349 \text{ million}$
   $n \approx 0.0888$
   8.9% of the total mount of money was spent by NASA.

4. Texas had the larger population.

5. **Strategy** To find the difference in populations:
   - Read the double broken-line graph to find the Texas population and the California population in 2000.
   - Subtract the population of Texas from the population of California.

   Solution

California:	32.5
Texas:	− 20.0
	12.5

   The population of California is 12.5 million people more than the population of Texas.

6. **Strategy** To find which 25-year period Texas had the smallest increase in population.
   - Read the double-line graph to find the population for each 25-year period.
   - Subtract the two numbers.

   Solution 1900 to 1925:
   $6 - 2.5 = 3.5$ million
   1925 to 1950:
   $8 - 6 = 2$ million
   1950 to 1975:
   $12 - 8 = 4$ million
   1975 to 2000:
   $21 - 12 = 9$ million
   The Texas population increased the least from 1925 to 1950.

7. **Strategy** To find the number of games in which the Knicks scored fewer than 100 points:
   - Read the frequency polygon to find the number of games in which the Knicks scored 60–70 points, 70–80 points, 80–90 points, and 90–100 points.
   - Add the four numbers.

   Solution

60–70 points:	1 game
70–80 points:	7 games
80–90 points:	15 games
90–100 points:	+ 31 games
	54

   There were 54 games in which the Knicks scored fewer than 100 points.

8. Strategy To find the ratio:
- Read the frequency polygon to find the number of games in which the Knicks scored between 90 and 100 points and between 110 and 120 points.
- Write in simplest form the ratio of the number of games in which the Knicks scored between 90 and 100 points to the number of games in which they scored between 110 and 120 points.

Solution 90 to 100 points: 31 games
110 to 120 points: 8 games

$$\frac{31 \text{ games}}{8 \text{ games}} = \frac{31}{8}$$

The ratio is $\frac{31}{8}$.

9. Strategy To find the percent:
- Read the frequency polygon to find the number of games in which the Knicks scored 110 to 120 points and 120 to 130 points.
- Add the two numbers.
- Solve the basic percent equation for percent. The base is 80 and the amount is the number of games in which more than 110 points were scored.

Solution 110–120 points: 8 games
120–130 points: + 1 game
9 games

Percent × base = amount
$n \times 80 = 9$
$n = 9 \div 80$
$n = 0.1125$

The percent is 11.3%.

10. From the pictograph, O'Hare airport has 10 million more passengers than Los Angeles airport.

11. Strategy To find the ratio:
- Read the pictograph to find the number of passengers going through San Francisco airport and the number of passengers going through Dallas/Ft. Worth airport.
- Write in simplest form the ratio of the number of passengers going through San Francisco airport to the number of passengers going through Dallas/Ft. Worth airport.

Solution San Francisco: 40
Dallas/Ft. Worth: 60

$$\frac{40}{60} = \frac{2}{3} = 2:3$$

The ratio is 2 : 3.

12. Strategy To find the difference between the total days of operation and days of full operation of the Midwest ski areas:
- Read the double-bar graph for the number of days that the resorts were open and the days of full operation.
- Subtract the two numbers.

Solution Days open: 90
Days of full operation: − 40
50

The difference was 50 days.

13. Strategy To find the percent:
- Read the double-bar graph to find the number of days that the Rocky Mountain ski areas were open and the number of days of full operation.
- Solve the basic percent equation for percent. The base is the number of days open and the amount is the number of days of full operation.

Solution Days open: 140
Days of full operation: 70

Percent × base = amount
$n \times 140 = 70$
$n = 70 \div 140$
$n = 0.5$

The percent is 50%.

14a. Strategy To determine which region has the lowest number of days of full operation, read the bar graph and select the lowest graph that shows days of full operation.

Solution The Southeast had the lowest number of days of full operation.

b. Strategy Read the number of days from the lowest graph.

Solution This region had 30 days of full operation.

15. Strategy To calculate the probability:
- Count the number of possible outcomes.
- Count the number of favorable outcomes.
- Use the probability formula.

Solution There are 16 possible outcomes.
There are 4 favorable outcomes:
THHH, HHHT, HHTH, HTHH.

$\text{Probability} = \frac{4}{16} = \frac{1}{4}$

The probability of one tail and three heads is $\frac{1}{4}$.

16. Strategy To find the number of people who slept 8 hours or more:
- Read the histogram to find the number of people who slept 8 hours, 9 hours, or more than 9 hours.
- Add the three numbers.

Solution

Slept 8 hours:	12
Slept 9 hours:	2
Slept more than 9 hours:	+ 1
	15

There were 15 people who slept 8 or more hours.

17. Strategy To find the percent:
- Read the histogram to find the number of people who slept 7 hours.
- Solve the basic percent equation for percent. The base is 46 and the amount is the number of people who slept 7 hours.

Solution Slept 7 hours: 13

$$\begin{aligned} \text{Percent} \times \text{base} &= \text{amount} \\ n \times 46 &= 13 \\ n &= 13 \div 46 \\ n &\approx 0.2826 \end{aligned}$$

The percent is 28.3%.

18a. Strategy To find the mean heart rates:
- Find the sum of the heart rates.
- Divide the sum by the number of women.

Solution

80
82
99
91
93
87
103
94
73
96
86
80
97
94
108
81
100
109
91
84
78
96
96
+ 100
2198

The mean heart rate is 91.6 heartbeats per minute.

Strategy To find the median heart rate: write the heart rates in order from smallest to largest. The median is the mean of the two middle numbers.

Solution
73, 78, 80, 80, 81, 82, 84, 86, 87, 91, 91 } 11 numbers
93, 94 } middle numbers
94, 96, 96, 96, 97, 99, 100, 100, 103, 108, 109 } 11 numbers

$$\frac{93+94}{2} = 93.5$$

The median heart rate is 93.5 heartbeats per minute.

Strategy To find the mode, look at the heart rates and identify the number that occurs most frequently.

Solution The mode is 96 heartbeats per minute, the number that occurs most frequently.

b. Strategy
- Arrange the data from smallest to largest. Then find the range.
- Find Q_1, the median of the lower half of the data.
- Find Q_3, the median of the upper half of the data.
- Interquartile range $= Q_3 - Q_1$.

Solution Use the list in part a.
Range $= 109 - 73 = 36$
The range is 36 heartbeats per minute.

$$Q_1 = \frac{82+84}{2} = 83$$

$$Q_3 = \frac{97+99}{2} = 98$$

$$Q_3 - Q_1 = 98 - 83 = 15$$

The interquartile range is 15 heartbeats per minute.

Chapter 7 Test

1. Strategy To find the number of students who spent between \$15 and \$25 each week:
- Read the frequency polygon to find the number of students who spent between \$15 and \$20 and the number who spent between \$20 and \$25.
- Add the two numbers.

Solution

Number between \$15–\$20:	12
Number between \$20–\$25:	+ 7
	19

19 students spent between \$15 and \$25 each week.

2. Strategy To find the ratio:
- Read the frequency polygon to find the number of students who spent between \$10 and \$15 and the number who spent between \$15 and \$20.
- Write in simplest form the ratio of the number of students who spent between \$10 and \$15 to the number of students who spent between \$15 and \$20.

Solution

Between \$10 and \$15:	8 students
Between \$15 and \$20:	12 students

$$\frac{8 \text{ students}}{12 \text{ students}} = \frac{2}{3}$$

The ratio is $\frac{2}{3}$.

3. Strategy To find the percent:
- Read the frequency polygon to find the number of students who spent between \$0 to \$5, between \$5 and \$10, and between \$10 and \$15 each week.
- Add the three numbers.
- Solve the basic percent equation for percent. The base is 40 and the amount is the number of students who spent less than \$15 per week.

Solution

Between \$0 and \$5:	4 students
Between \$5 and \$10:	6 students
Between \$10 and \$15:	+ 8 students
	18 students

Percent × base = amount

$$n \times 40 = 18$$
$$n = 18 \div 40$$
$$n = 0.45$$

The percent is 45%.

4. Strategy To find the number of people surveyed:
- Read the pictograph to determine the number of people for each letter grade.
- Add the four numbers.

Solution

Number of A grades:	21
Number of B grades:	10
Number of C grades:	4
Number of D grades:	+ 1
	36

There were 36 people that were surveyed for the Gallup poll.

5. Strategy To find the ratio:
- Read the pictograph to find the number of people who gave their marriage a B grade and the number who gave their marriage a C grade.
- Write in simplest form the ratio of the number of people who gave their marriage a B grade to the number of people who gave their marriage a C grade.

Solution Number of B grades: 10 people
Number of C grades: 4 people

$$\frac{10 \text{ people}}{4 \text{ people}} = \frac{5}{2}$$

The ratio is $\frac{5}{2}$.

6. Strategy To find the percent:
- Read the pictograph to find the number of people who gave their marriage an A grade.
- Solve the basic percent equation for percent. The base is 36 (from Exercise 4) and the amount is the number of people who gave their marriage an A grade.

Solution Number of A grades: 21 people

$$\begin{aligned} \text{Percent} \times \text{base} &= \text{amount} \\ n \times 36 &= 21 \\ n &= 21 \div 36 \\ n &\approx 0.583 \end{aligned}$$

The percent is 58.3%.

7. Strategy Read the bar graph to find the two consecutive years that the number of fatalities were the same.

Solution During 1995 and 1996, the number of fatalities was the same.

8. Strategy To find the total fatalities on amusement rides during 1991 to 1999:
- Read the bar graph to determine the number of fatalities for each year.
- Add the nine numbers.

Solution

3	1991
2	1992
4	1993
2	1994
3	1995
3	1996
4	1997
5	1998
+ 6	1999
32	

There were 32 fatal accidents from 1991 to 1999.

9. Strategy To find how many more fatalities in 1995 to 1998 than 1991 to 1994:
- Add the number of fatalities for 1995 to 1998.
- Add the number of fatalities for 1991 to 1994.
- Subtract the two numbers.

Solution

3	1995	3	1991
3	1996	2	1992
4	1997	4	1993
+ 5	1998	+ 2	1994
15		11	

$15 - 11 = 4$

There were 4 more fatalities from 1995 to 1998.

10. Strategy To find how many more R-rated films than PG:
- Read the circle graph to find the number of films rated R and PG.
- Subtract the two numbers.

Solution

R:	427
PG:	− 72
	355

There were 355 more films rated R.

11. Strategy To find how many times more PG-13 films were released than NC-17:
- Read the circle graph to find the number of films rated PG-13 and NC-17.
- Divide the two numbers.

Solution PG-13: 112
NC-17: 7

$$7\overline{)112} = 16$$

There were 16 times more films rated PG-13.

12. Strategy To find the percent of films rated G:
- Read the circle graph to find the number of G-rated films.
- Write and solve the basic percent equation for the percent. The base is the total number of films (655) and the amount is the number of G-rated films.

Solution G: 37

Percent × base = amount

$n \times 655 = 37$

$n = 37 \div 655$

$n \approx 0.056$

The percent of films rated G was 5.6%.

13. Strategy To find the number of states with median income between \$40,000 and \$60,000.
- Read the histogram to find the number of states with per capita income between \$40,000 and \$50,000 and between \$50,000 and \$60,000.
- Add the two numbers.

Solution

\$40,000 to \$50,000:	5 states
\$50,000 to \$60,000:	+ 19 states
	24 states

There are 24 states that have a median income between \$40,000 and \$60,000.

14. Strategy To find the percent of the states with a median income between \$50,000 and \$70,000:
- Read the histogram to find the number of states with median incomes between \$50,000 and \$60,000 and between \$60,000 and \$70,000.
- Add the two numbers.
- Solve the basic percent equation for percent. The base is 50 and the amount is the number of states with a median income between \$50,000 and \$70,000.

Solution

\$50,000 to \$60,000:	19 states
\$60,000 to \$70,000:	+ 17 states
	36 states

Percent × base = amount

$n \times 50 = 36$

$n = 36 \div 50$

$n = 0.72$

The percent is 72%.

15. Strategy To find the percent:
- Read the histogram to find the number of states that have a median income between \$70,000 and \$80,000 and between \$80,000 and \$90,000.
- Add the two numbers.
- Solve the basic percent equation for percent. The base is 50 and the amount is the number of states with a median income above \$70,000.

Solution

\$70,000–\$80,000:	5 states
\$80,000–\$90,000:	+ 4 states
	9 states

Percent × base = amount

$n \times 50 = 9$

$n = 9 \div 50$

$n = 0.18$

The percent is 18%.

16. Strategy To calculate the probability:
- Count the number of possible outcomes.
- Count the number of favorable outcomes.
- Use the probability formula.

Solution There are 50 possible outcomes. There are 15 favorable outcomes.

$\text{Probability} = \frac{15}{50} = \frac{3}{10}$

The probability is $\frac{3}{10}$ that the ball chosen is red.

17. Strategy To find which decade had the smallest increase in enrollment.
- Read the line graph to find the enrollment for each decade.
- Subtract the two numbers.

Solution 1960 to 1970:
$8 - 4 = 4$ million
1970 to 1980:
$12 - 8 = 4$ million
1980 to 1990:
$14 - 12 = 2$ million
1990 to 2000:
$15 - 14 = 1$ million
The student enrollment increased the least during the 1990s.

18. Strategy To approximate the increase in enrollment:
- Read the enrollment for 1960 and 2000.
- Subtract the two numbers.

Solution

$$\begin{array}{lr} 2000: & 15 \text{ million} \\ 1960: & \underline{-\ 4 \text{ million}} \\ & 11 \text{ million} \end{array}$$

The increase in enrollment was 11 million students.

19a. Strategy To find the mean lifetime of the batteries:
- Find the sum of the times.
- Divide the sum by the number of batteries tested (20).

Solution

$$\begin{array}{r} 2.9 \\ 2.4 \\ 3.1 \\ 2.5 \\ 2.6 \\ 2.0 \\ 3.0 \\ 2.3 \\ 2.4 \\ 2.7 \\ 2.0 \\ 2.4 \\ 2.6 \\ 2.7 \\ 2.1 \\ 2.9 \\ 2.8 \\ 2.4 \\ 2.0 \\ \underline{+\ 2.8} \\ 50.6 \end{array} \qquad 20\overline{)50.60} = 2.53$$

The mean time is 2.53 days.

b. Strategy To find the median lifetime of the batteries, write times in order from lowest to highest. The median is the mean of the two middle numbers.

Solution

$$\left.\begin{array}{l} 2.0 \\ 2.0 \\ 2.0 \\ 2.1 \\ 2.3 \\ 2.4 \\ 2.4 \\ 2.4 \\ 2.4 \end{array}\right\} \text{9 numbers}$$

$$\left.\begin{array}{l} 2.5 \\ 2.6 \end{array}\right\} \text{middle numbers}$$

$$\left.\begin{array}{l} 2.6 \\ 2.7 \\ 2.7 \\ 2.8 \\ 2.8 \\ 2.9 \\ 2.9 \\ 3.0 \\ 3.1 \end{array}\right\} \text{9 numbers}$$

$$\frac{2.5 + 2.6}{2} = 2.55$$

The median time is 2.55 days.

c. Strategy The data is arranged from smallest to largest in part b.
- Find Q_1, the median of the lower half of the data.
- Find Q_3, the median of the upper half of the data.
- Draw the box-and-whiskers plot.

Solution

$$Q_1 = \frac{2.3 + 2.4}{2} = 2.35$$

$$Q_3 = \frac{2.8 + 2.8}{2} = 2.8$$

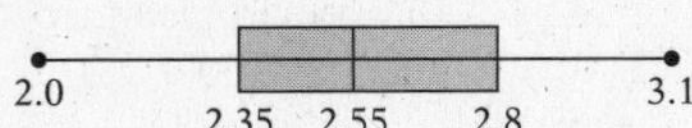

Cumulative Review Exercises

1. $2^2 \cdot 3^3 \cdot 5 = (2 \cdot 2) \cdot (3 \cdot 3 \cdot 3) \cdot (5)$
$= 4 \cdot 27 \cdot 5 = 540$

2. $3^2 \cdot (5-2) \div 3 + 5$
$9 \cdot (3) \div 3 + 5$
$27 \div 3 + 5$
$9 + 5$
14

3.

	2	3	5
24 =	(2·2·2)	(3)	
40 =	2·2·2		(5)

LCM = 2 · 2 · 2 · 3 · 5 = 120

4. $\dfrac{60}{144} = \dfrac{\overset{1}{\cancel{2}}\cdot\overset{1}{\cancel{2}}\cdot\overset{1}{\cancel{3}}\cdot 5}{\underset{1}{\cancel{2}}\cdot\underset{1}{\cancel{2}}\cdot 2\cdot 2\cdot\underset{1}{\cancel{3}}\cdot 3} = \dfrac{5}{12}$

5.
$$\begin{aligned} 4\tfrac{1}{2} &= 4\tfrac{20}{40} \\ 2\tfrac{3}{8} &= 2\tfrac{15}{40} \\ +5\tfrac{1}{5} &= 5\tfrac{8}{40} \\ \hline & 11\tfrac{43}{40} = 12\tfrac{3}{40} \end{aligned}$$

6.
$$\begin{aligned} 12\tfrac{5}{8} &= 12\tfrac{15}{24} = 11\tfrac{39}{24} \\ -7\tfrac{11}{12} &= 7\tfrac{22}{24} = 7\tfrac{22}{24} \\ \hline & \qquad\qquad 4\tfrac{17}{24} \end{aligned}$$

7. $\dfrac{5}{8} \times 3\dfrac{1}{5} = \dfrac{5}{8} \times \dfrac{16}{5}$
$= \dfrac{5 \cdot 16}{8 \cdot 5}$
$= \dfrac{\overset{1}{\cancel{5}}\cdot\overset{1}{\cancel{2}}\cdot\overset{1}{\cancel{2}}\cdot\overset{1}{\cancel{2}}\cdot 2}{\underset{1}{\cancel{2}}\cdot\underset{1}{\cancel{2}}\cdot\underset{1}{\cancel{2}}\cdot\underset{1}{\cancel{5}}} = 2$

8. $3\dfrac{1}{5} \div 4\dfrac{1}{4} = \dfrac{16}{5} \div \dfrac{17}{4} = \dfrac{16}{5} \times \dfrac{4}{17} = \dfrac{16 \cdot 4}{5 \cdot 17} = \dfrac{64}{85}$

9. $\dfrac{5}{8} \div \left(\dfrac{3}{4} - \dfrac{2}{3}\right) + \dfrac{3}{4} = \dfrac{5}{8} \div \left(\dfrac{9}{12} - \dfrac{8}{12}\right) + \dfrac{3}{4}$
$= \dfrac{5}{8} \div \dfrac{1}{12} + \dfrac{3}{4}$
$= \dfrac{5}{8} \times \dfrac{12}{1} + \dfrac{3}{4}$
$= \dfrac{5 \cdot \overset{1}{\cancel{2}} \cdot \overset{1}{\cancel{2}} \cdot 3}{\underset{1}{\cancel{2}} \cdot \underset{1}{\cancel{2}} \cdot 2} + \dfrac{3}{4}$
$= \dfrac{15}{2} + \dfrac{3}{4} = \dfrac{30}{4} + \dfrac{3}{4} = \dfrac{33}{4} = 8\dfrac{1}{4}$

10. 209.305

11.
$$\begin{array}{r} 4.092 \\ \times\ 0.69 \\ \hline 36828 \\ 24552 \\ \hline 2.82348 \end{array}$$

12. $16\dfrac{2}{3} = \dfrac{50}{3}$

$$\begin{array}{r} 16.666 \approx 16.67 \\ 3\overline{)50.000} \\ -3 \\ \hline 20 \\ -18 \\ \hline 20 \\ -18 \\ \hline 20 \\ -18 \\ \hline 20 \\ -18 \\ \hline 20 \end{array}$$

13. $\dfrac{330 \text{ miles}}{12.5 \text{ gal}} = 26.4 \text{ mpg}$

14. $\dfrac{n}{5} = \dfrac{16}{25}$
$n \times 25 = 5 \times 16$
$n \times 25 = 80$
$n = 80 \div 25 = 3.2$

15. $\dfrac{4}{5} \times 100\% = 80\%$

16. $10\% \times n = 8$
$0.10 \times n = 8$
$n = 8 \div 0.10 = 80$

17. $38\% \times 43 = n$
$0.38 \times 43 = n$
$16.34 = n$

18. $n \times 75 = 30$
$n = 30 \div 75 = 0.40 = 40\%$

19. **Strategy** To find the income for the week:
- Find the commission earned on sales by solving the basic percent equation for amount. The base is \$27,500 and the percent is 2%.
- Find the total income by adding the base salary (\$100) to the commission.

Solution $2\% \times 27{,}500 = n$
$0.02 \times 27{,}500 = n$
$550 = n$
$100 + 550 = 650$
The salesperson's income for the week was \$650.

20. Strategy To find the cost, write and solve a proportion.

Solution

$$\frac{8.15}{1000} = \frac{n}{50{,}000}$$
$$8.15 \times 50{,}000 = n \times 1000$$
$$407{,}500 = n \times 1000$$
$$407{,}500 \div 1000 = n$$
$$407.50 = n$$

The cost is \$407.50.

21. Strategy To find the interest due, multiply the principal by the annual interest rate and the time (in years).

Solution $125{,}000 \times 0.06 \times \frac{6}{12} = 3750$

The interest due is \$3750.

22. Strategy To find the markup rate of the compact disc player:

- Find the markup amount by subtracting the cost (\$180) from the selling price (\$279).
- Solve the basic percent equation for percent. The base is \$180 and the amount is the amount of the markup.

Solution

$$279 - 180 = 99$$
$$\text{Percent} \times \text{base} = \text{amount}$$
$$n \times 180 = 99$$
$$n = 99 \div 180 = 0.55 = 55\%$$

The markup rate is 55%.

23. Strategy To find how much is budgeted for food:

- Read the circle graph to find what percent of the budget is spent on food.
- Solve the basic percent equation for amount. The base is \$3000 and the rate is the percent of the budget that is spent on food.

Solution Amount spent on food: 19%

$$\text{Percent} \times \text{base} = \text{amount}$$
$$19\% \times 3000 = \text{amount}$$
$$0.19 \times 3000 = 570$$

The amount budgeted for food is \$570.

24. Strategy To find the difference:

- Read the double-broken-line graph to find the number of problems student 1 answered correctly on test 1 and the number of problems student 2 answered correctly on test 1.
- Subtract the student 1 total from the student 2 total to find the difference.

Solution

student 2: 27 answered correctly
student 1: −15 answered correctly
12 answered correctly

The difference in the number answered correctly is 12 problems.

25. Strategy To find the mean high temperature:

- Find the sum of the high temperatures.
- Divide the sum of the high temperatures by the number of temperatures (7).

Solution

$$\begin{array}{r} 56^\circ \\ 72^\circ \\ 80^\circ \\ 75^\circ \\ 68^\circ \\ 62^\circ \\ +\,74^\circ \\ \hline 487^\circ \end{array}$$ sum of high temperatures

$$7\overline{)487.00} = 69.57$$

The mean high temperatures is 69.6°F.

26. Strategy To calculate the probability:

- Count the number of possible outcomes.
- Count the number of favorable outcomes.
- Use the probability formula.

Solution There are 36 possible outcomes. There are 5 favorable outcomes: (2, 6), (6, 2), (3, 5), (5, 3), (4, 4).

$$\text{Probability} = \frac{5}{36}$$

The probability is $\frac{5}{36}$ that the sum of the dots on the two dice is 8.

Chapter 8: U.S. Customary Units of Measurement

Prep Test

1. 702

2. 58

3. 4

4. $\frac{5}{3} \times 6 = \frac{5 \cdot 2 \cdot \overset{1}{\cancel{3}}}{\underset{1}{\cancel{3}}} = 10$

5. $400 \times \frac{1}{8} \times \frac{1}{2} = \frac{\overset{1}{\cancel{2}} \cdot \overset{1}{\cancel{2}} \cdot \overset{1}{\cancel{2}} \cdot \overset{1}{\cancel{2}} \cdot 5 \cdot 5}{\underset{1}{\cancel{2}} \cdot \underset{1}{\cancel{2}} \cdot \underset{1}{\cancel{2}} \cdot \underset{1}{\cancel{2}}} = 25$

6. $5\frac{3}{4} \times 8 = \frac{23}{4} \times 8 = \frac{23 \cdot \overset{1}{\cancel{2}} \cdot \overset{1}{\cancel{2}} \cdot 2}{\underset{1}{\cancel{2}} \cdot \underset{1}{\cancel{2}}} = 46$

7. $3\overline{)714}$ = 238

8. $12\overline{)18.0}$ = 1.5

Go Figure

To go from the bank to the bookstore takes 10 minutes. She goes a distance of $\frac{3}{4} - \frac{1}{3} = \frac{9}{12} - \frac{4}{12} = \frac{5}{12}$.
We want to find how long it takes her to reach the halfway mark on her way to work. The distance between the bank and the halfway point is $\frac{1}{2} - \frac{1}{3} = \frac{3}{6} - \frac{2}{6} = \frac{1}{6} = \frac{2}{12}$.

We can say that $\frac{1}{12} = 1$ unit. This is similar to the inches and foot relationship. Using a proportion: it takes 10 minutes to go 5 units, how many minutes does it take to go 2 units?

$$\frac{10 \text{ min}}{5 \text{ units}} = \frac{n \text{ min}}{2 \text{ units}}$$
$$10 \times 2 = 5 \times n$$
$$20 = 5 \times n$$
$$20 \div 5 = n$$
$$4 = n$$

It takes Mandy 4 minutes to go 2 units. It takes 4 minutes to go from the bank to the halfway point. 7:52 A.M. + 4 minute = 7:56 A.M.
She reaches the halfway point at 7:56 A.M.

Section 8.1

Objective A Exercises

1. $6 \text{ ft} = 6 \cancel{\text{ft}} \times \frac{12 \text{ in.}}{1 \cancel{\text{ft}}} = 72 \text{ in.}$

2. $9 \text{ ft} = 9 \cancel{\text{ft}} \times \frac{12 \text{ in.}}{1 \cancel{\text{ft}}} = 108 \text{ in.}$

3. $30 \text{ in.} = 30 \cancel{\text{in.}} \times \frac{1 \text{ ft}}{12 \cancel{\text{in.}}} = 2\frac{1}{2} \text{ ft}$

4. $64 \text{ in.} = 64 \cancel{\text{in.}} \times \frac{1 \text{ ft}}{12 \cancel{\text{in.}}} = 5\frac{1}{3} \text{ ft}$

5. $13 \text{ yd} = 13 \cancel{\text{yd}} \times \frac{3 \text{ ft}}{1 \cancel{\text{yd}}} = 39 \text{ ft}$

6. $4\frac{1}{2} \text{ yd} = 4\frac{1}{2} \cancel{\text{yd}} \times \frac{3 \text{ ft}}{1 \cancel{\text{yd}}} = 13\frac{1}{2} \text{ ft}$

7. $16 \text{ ft} = 16 \cancel{\text{ft}} \times \frac{1 \text{ yd}}{3 \cancel{\text{ft}}} = 5\frac{1}{3} \text{ yd}$

8. $4\frac{1}{2} \text{ ft} = 4\frac{1}{2} \cancel{\text{ft}} \times \frac{1 \text{ yd}}{3 \cancel{\text{ft}}} = 1\frac{1}{2} \text{ yd}$

9. $2\frac{1}{3} \text{ yd} = 2\frac{1}{3} \cancel{\text{yd}} \times \frac{36 \text{ in.}}{1 \cancel{\text{yd}}} = 84 \text{ in.}$

10. $5 \text{ yd} = 5 \cancel{\text{yd}} \times \frac{36 \text{ in.}}{1 \cancel{\text{yd}}} = 180 \text{ in.}$

11. $120 \text{ in.} = 120 \cancel{\text{in.}} \times \frac{1 \text{ yd}}{36 \cancel{\text{in.}}} = 3\frac{1}{3} \text{ yd}$

12. $66 \text{ in.} = 66 \cancel{\text{in.}} \times \frac{1 \text{ yd}}{36 \cancel{\text{in.}}} = 1\frac{5}{6} \text{ yd}$

13. $2 \text{ mi} = 2 \cancel{\text{mi}} \times \frac{5280 \text{ ft}}{1 \cancel{\text{mi}}} = 10{,}560 \text{ ft}$

14. $1\frac{1}{2} \text{ mi} = 1\frac{1}{2} \cancel{\text{mi}} \times \frac{5280 \text{ ft}}{1 \cancel{\text{mi}}} = 7920 \text{ ft}$

15. $7\frac{1}{2} \text{ in.} = 7\frac{1}{2} \cancel{\text{in.}} \times \frac{1 \text{ ft}}{12 \cancel{\text{in.}}} = \frac{5}{8} \text{ ft}$

Objective B Exercises

16. $12\overline{)100}$ = 8 ft 4 in.
-96
4
100 in. = 8 ft 4 in.

17. $5280\overline{)6400}$ = 1 mi 1120 ft
-5280
1120
6400 ft = 1 mi 1120 ft

18. $12\overline{)15}$ = 1ft 3 in.
-12
3
15 in. = 1 ft 3 in.

19.
$$\begin{array}{r} 6\text{ ft } 7\text{ in.} \\ +\ 3\text{ ft } 4\text{ in.} \\ \hline 9\text{ ft } 11\text{ in.} \end{array}$$

20.
$$\begin{array}{l} \ \ 9\text{ ft } 11\text{ in.} \\ +\ 3\text{ ft } 6\text{ in.} \\ \hline 12\text{ ft } 17\text{ in.} = 13\text{ ft } 5\text{ in.} \end{array}$$

21.
$$\begin{array}{r} 4\text{ ft } 15\text{ in.} \\ \not{5}\text{ ft } \not{3}\text{ in.} \\ -\ 2\text{ ft } 6\text{ in.} \\ \hline 2\text{ ft } 9\text{ in.} \end{array}$$

22.
$$\begin{array}{r} 8\text{ yd } 4\text{ ft} \\ 9\text{ yd } 1\text{ ft} \\ -\ 3\text{ yd } 2\text{ ft} \\ \hline 5\text{ yd } 2\text{ ft} \end{array}$$

23.
$$\begin{array}{l} \ \ 2\text{ ft } \ 5\text{ in.} \\ \times \qquad\quad 6 \\ \hline 12\text{ ft } 30\text{ in.} = 14\text{ ft } 6\text{ in.} \end{array}$$

24.
$$\begin{aligned} 3\frac{2}{3}\text{ ft} \times 4 &= \frac{11}{3}\text{ ft} \times 4 \\ &= \frac{44}{3}\text{ ft} \\ &= 14\frac{2}{3}\text{ ft} \end{aligned}$$

25.
$$\begin{array}{l} \qquad 2\text{ ft } 8\text{ in.} \\ 2\overline{)5\text{ ft } 4\text{ in.}} \\ \ \underline{-4\text{ ft}} \\ \ \ 1\text{ ft} = \underline{12\text{ in.}} \\ \qquad\qquad 16\text{ in.} \\ \qquad\quad \underline{-16\text{ in.}} \\ \qquad\qquad\quad 0 \end{array}$$

26.
$$\begin{aligned} 12\frac{1}{2}\text{ in.} \div 3 &= 12\frac{1}{2}\text{ in.} \times \frac{1}{3} \\ &= \frac{25}{2}\text{ in.} \times \frac{1}{3} \\ &= \frac{25}{6}\text{ in.} \\ &= 4\frac{1}{6}\text{ in.} \end{aligned}$$

27.
$$\begin{aligned} 4\frac{2}{3}\text{ ft} + 6\frac{1}{2}\text{ ft} &= 4\frac{4}{6}\text{ ft} + 6\frac{3}{6}\text{ ft} \\ &= 10\frac{7}{6}\text{ ft} \\ &= 11\frac{1}{6}\text{ ft} \end{aligned}$$

28.
$$\begin{array}{l} \ \ 3\text{ yd } 2\text{ ft} \\ +\ 6\text{ yd } 2\text{ ft} \\ \hline \ \ 9\text{ yd } 4\text{ ft} = 10\text{ yd } 1\text{ ft} \end{array}$$

29.
$$\begin{array}{l} \ \ 1\text{ mi } \ 4200\text{ ft} \\ +\ 2\text{ mi } \ 3600\text{ ft} \\ \hline \ \ 3\text{ mi } \ 7800\text{ ft} = 4\text{ mi } 2520\text{ ft} \end{array}$$

30.
$$\begin{array}{r} 4\text{ yd } 4\text{ ft} \\ 5\text{ yd } 1\text{ ft} \\ -2\text{ yd } 2\text{ ft} \\ \hline 2\text{ yd } 2\text{ ft} \end{array}$$

Objective C Exercises

31. Strategy To find how many 4-inch tiles can be placed along the counter:
- Convert the length (4 ft 8 in.) to inches.
- Divide the total length by the length of one tile (4 in.).

Solution $4\text{ ft} = 4\text{ ft} \times \dfrac{12\text{ in.}}{1\text{ ft}} = 48\text{ in.}$

$4\text{ ft } 8\text{ in.} = 48\text{ in.} + 8\text{ in.} = 56\text{ in.}$

$56 \div 4 = 14$

14 tiles can be placed along one row.

32. Strategy To find the number of feet of material used, convert the number of yards of material used (32) to feet.

Solution $32\text{ yd} = 32\text{ yd} \times \dfrac{3\text{ ft}}{1\text{ yd}} = 96\text{ ft}$

96 ft of materials were used.

33. Strategy To find the missing dimension:
- Find the total of the two given dimensions by adding the two lengths $\left(1\frac{1}{3}\text{ ft and } 1\frac{1}{3}\text{ ft}\right)$.
- Subtract the total of the two given dimensions from the entire length $\left(4\frac{1}{2}\text{ ft}\right)$.

Solution $1\frac{1}{3}\text{ ft} + 1\frac{1}{3}\text{ ft} = 2\frac{2}{3}\text{ ft}$

$$\begin{array}{r} 4\frac{1}{2}\text{ ft} = 4\frac{3}{6} = 3\frac{9}{6} \\ -2\frac{2}{3}\text{ ft} = 2\frac{4}{6} = 2\frac{4}{6} \\ \hline 1\frac{5}{6} \end{array}$$

The missing dimension is $1\frac{5}{6}$ ft.

34. Strategy To find the total length of the shaft, add the three lengths (6 in., 1 ft 5 in., 1 ft 2 in.).

Solution
$$\begin{array}{l} \qquad 6\text{ in.} \\ \ \ 1\text{ ft } 5\text{ in.} \\ +1\text{ ft } 2\text{ in.} \\ \hline \ \ 2\text{ ft } 13\text{ in.} = 3\text{ ft } 1\text{ in.} \end{array}$$

The total length is 3 ft 1 in.

35. Strategy To find the length of material needed, add the diameters of the two holes (3 in. each) and the lengths of the three spaces left in between.

Solution

$$\begin{array}{l} 3\text{ in.} \\ 3\text{ in.} \\ \frac{1}{2}\text{ in.} \\ \frac{1}{2}\text{ in.} \\ +\frac{1}{2}\text{ in.} \\ \hline 6\frac{3}{2}\text{ in.} = 7\frac{1}{2}\text{ in.} \end{array}$$

The length of material needed is $7\frac{1}{2}$ in.

36. Strategy To find the missing dimension:

- Find the sum of the four given dimensions $\left(\frac{1}{2}, \frac{3}{4}, \frac{3}{4}, \text{ and } \frac{1}{2}\text{ in.}\right)$.
- Subtract the sum of the four given dimensions from the total length (4 in.).

Solution

$$\begin{array}{l} \frac{1}{2}\text{ in.} = \frac{2}{4}\text{ in.} \\ \frac{3}{4}\text{ in.} = \frac{3}{4}\text{ in.} \\ \frac{3}{4}\text{ in.} = \frac{3}{4}\text{ in.} \\ +\frac{1}{2}\text{ in.} = \frac{2}{4}\text{ in.} \\ \hline \frac{10}{4}\text{ in.} = \frac{5}{2}\text{ in.} = 2\frac{1}{2}\text{ in.} \end{array}$$

$$\begin{array}{l} 4\text{ in.} = 3\frac{2}{2}\text{ in.} \\ -2\frac{1}{2}\text{ in.} = 2\frac{1}{2}\text{ in.} \\ \hline 1\frac{1}{2}\text{ in.} \end{array}$$

The missing dimension is $1\frac{1}{2}$ in.

37. Strategy To find the length of each piece, divide the total length $\left(6\frac{2}{3}\text{ ft}\right)$ by the number of equal pieces (4).

Solution

$$\begin{aligned} 6\frac{2}{3}\text{ ft} \div 4 &= \frac{20}{3} \div 4 \\ &= \frac{20}{3} \times \frac{1}{4} = \frac{\not{2}\cdot\not{2}\cdot 5}{3\cdot\not{2}\cdot\not{2}} \\ &= \frac{5}{3}\text{ ft} = 1\frac{2}{3}\text{ ft} \end{aligned}$$

The length of each piece is $1\frac{2}{3}$ ft

38. Strategy To find the total length of the board, multiply the length of each cut piece (3 ft 4 in.) by the number of equal pieces (4).

Solution

$$\begin{array}{r} 3\text{ ft } \ 4\text{ in.} \\ \times \qquad\quad 4 \\ \hline 12\text{ ft } 16\text{ in.} = 13\text{ ft } 4\text{ in.} \end{array}$$

The board must be 13 ft 4 in. long.

39. Strategy To find the length of framing needed, add the lengths of the four sides of the frame (1 ft 9 in., 1 ft 6 in., 1 ft 9 in., and 1 ft 6 in.).

Solution

$$\begin{array}{l} 1\text{ ft } \ 9\text{ in.} \\ 1\text{ ft } \ 6\text{ in.} \\ 1\text{ ft } \ 9\text{ in.} \\ +1\text{ ft } \ 6\text{ in.} \\ \hline 4\text{ ft } 30\text{ in.} = 6\text{ ft } 6\text{ in.} \end{array}$$

The length of framing needed is 6 ft 6 in.

40. Strategy To find the number of inches of baseboard you purchased, convert the number of feet of baseboard (32) to inches.

Solution $32\text{ ft} = 32\text{ }\not{\text{ft}} \times \frac{12\text{ in.}}{1\text{ }\not{\text{ft}}} = 384\text{ in.}$

You purchased 384 in. of baseboard.

41. Strategy To find the total length of the wall in feet:

- Multiply the length of each brick (9 in.) by the number of bricks (45) to find the total length in inches.
- Convert the total length in inches to feet.

Solution

$$\begin{array}{r} 9\text{ in.} \\ \times \ \ 45 \\ \hline 405\text{ in.} \end{array} \qquad 405\text{ }\not{\text{in.}} \times \frac{1\text{ ft}}{12\text{ }\not{\text{in.}}} = 33\frac{3}{4}\text{ ft}$$

The total length of the wall is $33\frac{3}{4}$ ft.

42. Strategy To find the total number of feet of material needed to build the rafters:

- Multiply the length of each rafter (8 ft 4 in.) by the number of rafters (9) to find the total length.
- Convert the length in inches to feet.

Solution

$$\begin{array}{r} 8\text{ ft } \ 4\text{ in.} \\ \times \qquad\quad 9 \\ \hline 72\text{ ft } 36\text{ in.} = 75\text{ ft} \end{array}$$

The total length of material needed is 75 ft.

Applying the Concepts

43. $\frac{19\text{ in.}}{1} \times \frac{1\text{ ft}}{12\text{ in.}} \times \frac{1\text{ mi}}{5280\text{ ft}} \times 200{,}000{,}000$

$\approx 59{,}975$ mi

Yes, since 59,975 > 25,000 the line would reach around the Earth at the equator.

44. Answers will vary.

Section 8.2

Objective A Exercises

1. $64\text{ oz} = 64\ \cancel{\text{oz}} \times \frac{1\text{ lb}}{16\ \cancel{\text{oz}}} = 4\text{ lb}$
2. $36\text{ oz} = 36\ \cancel{\text{oz}} \times \frac{1\text{ lb}}{16\ \cancel{\text{oz}}} = 2\frac{1}{4}\text{ lb}$
3. $8\text{ lb} = 8\ \cancel{\text{lb}} \times \frac{16\text{ oz}}{1\ \cancel{\text{lb}}} = 128\text{ oz}$
4. $7\text{ lb} = 7\ \cancel{\text{lb}} \times \frac{16\text{ oz}}{1\ \cancel{\text{lb}}} = 112\text{ oz}$
5. $3200\text{ lb} = 3200\ \cancel{\text{lb}} \times \frac{1\text{ ton}}{2000\ \cancel{\text{lb}}} = 1\frac{3}{5}\text{ tons}$
6. $9000\text{ lb} = 9000\ \cancel{\text{lb}} \times \frac{1\text{ ton}}{2000\ \cancel{\text{lb}}} = 4\frac{1}{2}\text{ tons}$
7. $6\text{ tons} = 6\ \cancel{\text{tons}} \times \frac{2000\text{ lb}}{1\ \cancel{\text{ton}}} = 12{,}000\text{ lb}$
8. $1\frac{1}{4}\text{ tons} = 1\frac{1}{4}\ \cancel{\text{tons}} \times \frac{2000\text{ lb}}{1\ \cancel{\text{ton}}} = 2500\text{ lb}$
9. $66\text{ oz} = 66\ \cancel{\text{oz}} \times \frac{1\text{ lb}}{16\ \cancel{\text{oz}}} = 4\frac{1}{8}\text{ lb}$
10. $90\text{ oz} = 90\ \cancel{\text{oz}} \times \frac{1\text{ lb}}{16\ \cancel{\text{oz}}} = 5\frac{5}{8}\text{ lb}$
11. $1\frac{1}{2}\text{ lb} = 1\frac{1}{2}\ \cancel{\text{lb}} \times \frac{16\text{ oz}}{1\ \cancel{\text{lb}}} = 24\text{ oz}$
12. $2\frac{5}{8}\text{ lb} = 2\frac{5}{8}\ \cancel{\text{lb}} \times \frac{16\text{ oz}}{1\ \cancel{\text{lb}}} = 42\text{ oz}$
13. $1\frac{3}{10}\text{ tons} = 1\frac{3}{10}\ \cancel{\text{tons}} \times \frac{2000\text{ lb}}{1\ \cancel{\text{ton}}} = 2600\text{ lb}$
14. $\frac{4}{5}\text{ ton} = \frac{4}{5}\ \cancel{\text{ton}} \times \frac{2000\text{ lb}}{1\ \cancel{\text{ton}}} = 1600\text{ lb}$
15. $500\text{ lb} = 500\ \cancel{\text{lb}} \times \frac{1\text{ ton}}{2000\ \cancel{\text{lb}}} = \frac{1}{4}\text{ ton}$
16. $5000\text{ lb} = 5000\ \cancel{\text{lb}} \times \frac{1\text{ ton}}{2000\ \cancel{\text{lb}}} = 2\frac{1}{2}\text{ tons}$
17. $180\text{ oz} = 180\ \cancel{\text{oz}} \times \frac{1\text{ lb}}{16\ \cancel{\text{oz}}} = 11\frac{1}{4}\text{ lb}$
18. $12\text{ oz} = 12\ \cancel{\text{oz}} \times \frac{1\text{ lb}}{16\ \cancel{\text{oz}}} = \frac{3}{4}\text{ lb}$

Objective B Exercises

19.

$$\begin{array}{r} 4\text{ tons } 1000\text{ lb} \\ 2000\overline{)9000} \\ \underline{-8000} \\ 1000 \end{array}$$

9000 lb = 4 tons 1000 lb

20.

$$\begin{array}{r} 5\text{ lb } 5\text{ oz} \\ 16\overline{)85} \\ \underline{-80} \\ 5 \end{array}$$

85 oz = 5 lb 5 oz

21.

$$\begin{array}{r} 2\text{ lb } 8\text{ oz} \\ 16\overline{)40} \\ \underline{-32} \\ 8 \end{array}$$

40 oz = 2 lb 8 oz

22.

$$\begin{array}{r} 4\text{ lb } \ 7\text{ oz} \\ \underline{+3\text{ lb } 12\text{ oz}} \\ 7\text{ lb } 19\text{ oz} = 8\text{ lb } 3\text{ oz} \end{array}$$

23.

$$\begin{array}{r} 1\text{ ton } \ 800\text{ lb} \\ \underline{+3\text{ tons } 1600\text{ lb}} \\ 4\text{ tons } 2400\text{ lb} = 5\text{ tons } 400\text{ lb} \end{array}$$

24.

$$\begin{array}{r} \overset{6}{\cancel{7}}\text{ lb } \overset{21}{\cancel{5}}\text{ oz} \\ \underline{-3\text{ lb } \ 8\text{ oz}} \\ 3\text{ lb } 13\text{ oz} \end{array}$$

25.

$$\begin{array}{r} \overset{2}{\cancel{3}}\text{ tons } \overset{2500}{\cancel{500}}\text{ lb} \\ \underline{-1\text{ ton } \ 800\text{ lb}} \\ 1\text{ ton } 1700\text{ lb} \end{array}$$

26.

$$\begin{array}{r} 3\text{ lb } \ 6\text{ oz} \\ \underline{\times \qquad\quad 4} \\ 12\text{ lb } 24\text{ oz} = 13\text{ lb } 8\text{ oz} \end{array}$$

27. $5\frac{1}{2}\text{ lb} \times 6 = \frac{11}{2}\text{ lb} \times 6$

$= \frac{66}{2}\text{ lb}$

$= 33\text{ lb}$

28.

$$\begin{array}{r} 1\text{ lb } 12\text{ oz} \\ 2\overline{)3\text{ lb } 8\text{ oz}} \\ \underline{-2\text{ lb}} \qquad \\ 1\text{ lb} = \underline{16\text{ oz}} \\ 24\text{ oz} \\ \underline{-24\text{ oz}} \\ 0 \end{array}$$

29. $4\frac{2}{3}\text{ lb} \times 3 = \frac{14}{3}\text{ lb} \times 3$

$= \frac{42}{3}\text{ lb}$

$= 14\text{ lb}$

30.

$$\begin{array}{r} 7\text{ lb}\ \ 7\text{ oz} \\ +\ 6\text{ lb}\ \ 9\text{ oz} \\ \hline 13\text{ lb}\ 16\text{ oz} = 14\text{ lb} \end{array}$$

31.

$$\begin{array}{r} 6\frac{1}{2}\text{ oz} \\ +2\frac{1}{2}\text{ oz} \\ \hline 8\frac{2}{2}\text{ oz} = 9\text{ oz} \end{array}$$

32.

$$\begin{array}{r} 6\frac{3}{8}\text{ lb} = 6\frac{9}{24}\text{ lb} = 5\frac{33}{24}\text{ lb} \\ -2\frac{5}{6}\text{ lb} = 2\frac{20}{24}\text{ lb} = 2\frac{20}{24}\text{ lb} \\ \hline 3\frac{13}{24}\text{ lb} \end{array}$$

33.

$$\begin{array}{r} 1\text{ lb}\ 7\text{ oz} \\ 4\overline{)\,5\text{ lb}\ \ 12\text{ oz}} \\ -4\text{ lb}\qquad\quad \\ 1\text{ lb} = \underline{16\text{ oz}} \\ 28\text{ oz} \\ \underline{-28\text{ oz}} \\ 0 \end{array}$$

Objective C Exercises

34. Strategy To find the total weight of the iron rods:
- Multiply the number of rods (25) by the weight of each rod (20 oz).
- Convert the number of ounces to pounds.

Solution

$$\begin{array}{r} 25 \\ \times\ 20\text{ oz} \\ \hline 500\text{ oz} \end{array}$$

$$500\ \cancel{\text{oz}} \times \frac{1\text{ lb}}{16\ \cancel{\text{oz}}} = 31\frac{1}{4}\text{ lb}$$

The iron rods weigh $31\frac{1}{4}$ lb.

35. Strategy To find the weight of the load, multiply the number of bricks (800) by the weight of one brick $\left(2\frac{1}{2}\text{ lb}\right)$.

Solution

$$\begin{aligned} 800 \times 2\frac{1}{2}\text{ lb} &= 800 \times \frac{5}{2}\text{ lb} \\ &= \frac{4000}{2}\text{ lb} \\ &= 2000\text{ lb} \end{aligned}$$

The load of bricks weighs 2000 lb.

36. Strategy To find the total weight of the textbooks:
- Multiply the number of textbooks (1200) by the weight of one textbook (9 oz).
- Convert the number of ounces to pounds.

Solution

$$\begin{array}{r} 1200 \\ \times\quad 9\text{ oz} \\ \hline 10{,}800\text{ oz} \end{array}$$

$$10{,}800\ \cancel{\text{oz}} \times \frac{1\text{ lb}}{16\ \cancel{\text{oz}}} = 675\text{ lb}$$

The total weight of the textbooks is 675 lb.

37. Strategy To find the weight of the package in pounds:
- Multiply the number of tiles (144) by the weight of one tile (7 oz).
- Convert the number of ounces to pounds.

Solution

$$\begin{array}{r} 144 \\ \times\quad 7\text{ oz} \\ \hline 1008\text{ oz} \end{array}$$

$$1008\ \cancel{\text{oz}} \times \frac{1\text{ lb}}{16\ \cancel{\text{oz}}} = 63\text{ lb}$$

The package of tiles weighs 63 lb.

38. Strategy To find how many pounds of feed each cow has eaten per day:
- Find the total amount of feed eaten during the 15 days by subtracting the amount of feed left (5 tons) from the original amount (20 tons).
- Find the amount of feed eaten per day by dividing the total amount eaten by the number of days (15).
- Convert the feed eaten per day to pounds.
- Divide the feed eaten per day (in pounds) by the number of cattle eating (100).

Solution

20 tons − 5 tons = 15 tons

$$\frac{15\text{ tons}}{15\text{ days}} = 1\text{ ton/day}$$

$$1\ \cancel{\text{ton}} \times \frac{2000\text{ lb}}{1\ \cancel{\text{ton}}} = 2000\text{ lb/day}$$

2000 lb/day ÷ 100 cattle = 20 lb/day/cow

Each cow has eaten 20 lb/day.

39. Strategy To find the weight of the case in pounds:
- Find the weight in ounces by multiplying the weight of each can (6 oz) by the number of cans (24).
- Convert the weight in ounces to pounds.

Solution
$$\begin{array}{r} 6 \text{ oz} \\ \times \quad 24 \\ \hline 144 \text{ oz} \end{array}$$

$144\ \cancel{\text{oz}} \times \dfrac{1 \text{ lb}}{16\ \cancel{\text{oz}}} = 9 \text{ lb}$

The weight of the case of soft drinks is 9 lb.

40. Strategy To find the increase in the baby's weight, subtract the weight at birth (7 lb 8 oz) from the weight 6 months later (15 lb 13 oz).

Solution
$$\begin{array}{r} 15 \text{ lb } 13 \text{ oz} \\ -\ 7 \text{ lb } \ 8 \text{ oz} \\ \hline 8 \text{ lb } \ 5 \text{ oz} \end{array}$$

The increase in the baby's weight was 8 lb 5 oz.

41. Strategy To find how much shampoo is in each container, divide the total weight of the shampoo (5 lb 4 oz) by the number of containers (4).

Solution
$$\begin{array}{rl} & 1 \text{ lb} \quad 5 \text{ oz} \\ 4 \overline{)} & 5 \text{ lb} \quad 4 \text{ oz} \\ & \underline{-4 \text{ lb}} \\ & 1 \text{ lb} = \underline{16 \text{ oz}} \\ & \qquad 20 \text{ oz} \\ & \qquad \underline{-20 \text{ oz}} \\ & \qquad 0 \end{array}$$

Each container holds 1 lb 5 oz of shampoo.

42. Strategy To find the weight of each piece, divide the total weight (16 lb 11 oz) by the number of pieces (3).

Solution
$$\begin{array}{rl} & 5 \text{ lb} \quad 9 \text{ oz} \\ 3 \overline{)} & 16 \text{ lb} \quad 11 \text{ oz} \\ & \underline{-15 \text{ lb}} \\ & 1 \text{ lb} = \underline{16 \text{ oz}} \\ & \qquad 27 \text{ oz} \\ & \qquad \underline{-27 \text{ oz}} \\ & \qquad 0 \end{array}$$

Each piece of steel rod weighs 5 lb 9 oz.

43. Strategy To find the cost of the ham roast:
- Convert 5 lb 10 oz to pounds.
- Multiply the number of pounds by the price per pound ($4.80).

Solution $5 \text{ lb } 10 \text{ oz} = 5\frac{5}{8} \text{ lb} = 5.625 \text{ lb}$
$$\begin{array}{r} \$\ 4.80 \\ \times \quad 5.625 \\ \hline \$\ 27.00000 \end{array}$$

The ham roast costs $27.

44. Strategy To find the markup on the candy:
- Convert 12 lb to ounces.
- Divide the number of ounces by 6 to find the number of packages.
- Multiply the number of packages by $1.15 to find the total income.
- Subtract the original cost of the candy ($14.40) from the total income to find the markup.

Solution $12\ \cancel{\text{lb}} \times \dfrac{16 \text{ oz}}{1\ \cancel{\text{lb}}} = 192 \text{ oz}$

$$\begin{array}{r} 32 \text{ packages} \\ 6 \overline{)192 \text{ oz}} \end{array}$$

$$\begin{array}{r} \$1.15 \\ \times \quad 32 \\ \hline \$36.80 \end{array} \text{ total income}$$

$$\begin{array}{r} \$36.80 \\ -14.40 \\ \hline \$22.40 \end{array}$$

The markup on the 12 lb of candy is $22.40.

45. Strategy To find the cost of mailing the manuscript:
- Convert 2 lb 3 oz to ounces.
- Multiply the number of ounces by the postage rate per ounce ($.25)

Solution 2 lb 3 oz = 35 oz
$$\begin{array}{r} \$0.25 \\ \times \quad 35 \\ \hline \$8.75 \end{array}$$

The cost of mailing the manuscript is $8.75.

Applying the Concepts

46. Student essays should describe the increase in technology in society as civilization has progressed. Some might discuss the increased dependence on and sophistication of trade in the world.
With respect to the need for precision in space, students might describe lunar landings, landings on Mars, or orbiting satellites (the position of which is crucial for everything from cellular phones to television broadcasts).

47. Answers will vary.

Section 8.3

Objective A Exercises

1. $60 \text{ fl oz} = 60 \cancel{\text{fl oz}} \times \frac{1 \text{ c}}{8 \cancel{\text{fl oz}}} = 7\frac{1}{2} \text{ c}$

2. $48 \text{ fl oz} = 48 \cancel{\text{fl oz}} \times \frac{1 \text{ c}}{8 \cancel{\text{fl oz}}} = 6 \text{ c}$

3. $3 \text{ c} = 3 \cancel{\text{c}} \times \frac{8 \text{ fl oz}}{1 \cancel{\text{c}}} = 24 \text{ fl oz}$

4. $2\frac{1}{2} \text{ c} = 2\frac{1}{2} \cancel{\text{c}} \times \frac{8 \text{ fl oz}}{1 \cancel{\text{c}}} = 20 \text{ fl oz}$

5. $8 \text{ c} = 8 \cancel{\text{c}} \times \frac{1 \text{ pt}}{2 \cancel{\text{c}}} = 4 \text{ pt}$

6. $5 \text{ c} = 5 \cancel{\text{c}} \times \frac{1 \text{ pt}}{2 \cancel{\text{c}}} = 2\frac{1}{2} \text{ pt}$

7. $3\frac{1}{2} \text{ pt} = 3\frac{1}{2} \cancel{\text{pt}} \times \frac{2 \text{ c}}{1 \cancel{\text{pt}}} = 7 \text{ c}$

8. $12 \text{ pt} = 12 \cancel{\text{pt}} \times \frac{1 \text{ qt}}{2 \cancel{\text{pt}}} = 6 \text{ qt}$

9. $22 \text{ qt} = 22 \cancel{\text{qt}} \times \frac{1 \text{ gal}}{4 \cancel{\text{qt}}} = 5\frac{1}{2} \text{ gal}$

10. $10 \text{ qt} = 10 \cancel{\text{qt}} \times \frac{1 \text{ gal}}{4 \cancel{\text{qt}}} = 2\frac{1}{2} \text{ gal}$

11. $2\frac{1}{4} \text{ gal} = 2\frac{1}{4} \cancel{\text{gal}} \times \frac{4 \text{ qt}}{1 \cancel{\text{gal}}} = 9 \text{ qt}$

12. $7 \text{ gal} = 7 \cancel{\text{gal}} \times \frac{4 \text{ qt}}{1 \cancel{\text{gal}}} = 28 \text{ qt}$

13. $7\frac{1}{2} \text{ pt} = 7\frac{1}{2} \cancel{\text{pt}} \times \frac{1 \text{ qt}}{2 \cancel{\text{pt}}} = 3\frac{3}{4} \text{ qt}$

14. $3\frac{1}{2} \text{ qt} = 3\frac{1}{2} \cancel{\text{qt}} \times \frac{2 \text{ pt}}{1 \cancel{\text{qt}}} = 7 \text{ pt}$

15. $20 \text{ fl oz} = 20 \cancel{\text{fl oz}} \times \frac{1 \cancel{\text{c}}}{8 \cancel{\text{fl oz}}} \times \frac{1 \text{ pt}}{2 \cancel{\text{c}}} = \frac{5}{4} \text{ pt} = 1\frac{1}{4} \text{ pt}$

16. $1\frac{1}{2} \text{ pt} = 1\frac{1}{2} \cancel{\text{pt}} \times \frac{2 \cancel{\text{c}}}{1 \cancel{\text{pt}}} \times \frac{8 \text{ fl oz}}{1 \cancel{\text{c}}} = 24 \text{ fl oz}$

17. $17 \text{ c} = 17 \cancel{\text{c}} \times \frac{1 \cancel{\text{pt}}}{2 \cancel{\text{c}}} \times \frac{1 \text{ qt}}{2 \cancel{\text{pt}}} = 4\frac{1}{4} \text{ qt}$

18. $1\frac{1}{2} \text{ qt} = 1\frac{1}{2} \cancel{\text{qt}} \times \frac{2 \cancel{\text{pt}}}{1 \cancel{\text{qt}}} \times \frac{2 \text{ c}}{1 \cancel{\text{pt}}} = \frac{12}{2} \text{ c} = 6 \text{ c}$

Objective B Exercises

19.
$$\begin{array}{r} 3 \text{ gal } 2 \text{ qt} \\ 4\overline{)14} \\ \underline{-12} \\ 2 \end{array}$$
14 qt = 3 gal 2 qt

20.
$$\begin{array}{r} 4 \text{ qt } 1 \text{ pt} \\ 2\overline{)9} \\ \underline{-8} \\ 1 \end{array}$$
9 pt = 4 qt 1 pt

21.
$$\begin{array}{r} 2 \text{ qt } 1 \text{ pt} \\ 2\overline{)5} \\ \underline{-4} \\ 1 \end{array}$$
5 pt = 2 qt 1 pt

22.
$$\begin{array}{r} 3 \text{ gal } 2 \text{ qt} \\ \underline{+\ 4 \text{ gal } 3 \text{ qt}} \\ 7 \text{ gal } 5 \text{ qt} \end{array} = 8 \text{ gal } 1 \text{ qt}$$

23.
$$\begin{array}{r} 4 \text{ qt } 1 \text{ pt} \\ \underline{+\ 2 \text{ qt } 1 \text{ pt}} \\ 6 \text{ qt } 2 \text{ pt} \end{array} = 7 \text{ qt}$$

24.
$$\begin{array}{r} 2 \text{ gal } 5 \text{ qt} \\ \cancel{3 \text{ gal } 1 \text{ qt}} \\ \underline{-1 \text{ gal } 2 \text{ qt}} \\ 1 \text{ gal } 3 \text{ qt} \end{array}$$

25.
$$\begin{array}{r} 2 \text{ c } 11 \text{ fl oz} \\ \cancel{3 \text{ c}}\ \cancel{3 \text{ fl oz}} \\ \underline{-2 \text{ c } 5 \text{ fl oz}} \\ 6 \text{ fl oz} \end{array}$$

26.
$$\begin{array}{r} 2 \text{ qt } 1 \text{ pt} \\ \underline{\times \qquad 5} \\ 10 \text{ qt } 5 \text{ pt} \end{array} = 12 \text{ qt } 1 \text{ pt}$$

27. $3\frac{1}{2} \text{ pt} \times 5 = \frac{7}{2} \text{ pt} \times 5 = \frac{35}{2} \text{ pt} = 17\frac{1}{2} \text{ pt}$

28.
$$\begin{array}{r} 1 \text{ gal} \quad 1 \text{ qt} \\ 5\overline{)6 \text{ gal} \quad 1 \text{ qt}} \\ \underline{-5 \text{ gal}} \quad\quad\ \\ 1 \text{ gal} = 4 \text{ qt} \\ \underline{5 \text{ qt}} \\ \underline{-5 \text{ qt}} \\ 0 \end{array}$$

29.
$$\begin{aligned} 3\frac{1}{2} \text{ gal} \div 4 &= 3\frac{1}{2} \text{ gal} \times \frac{1}{4} \\ &= \frac{7}{2} \text{ gal} \times \frac{1}{4} \\ &= \frac{7}{8} \text{ gal} \end{aligned}$$

30.
$$\begin{array}{r} 5 \text{ c } 3 \text{ fl oz} \\ \underline{+\ 3 \text{ c } 6 \text{ fl oz}} \\ 8 \text{ c } 9 \text{ fl oz} \end{array} = 9 \text{ c } 1 \text{ fl oz}$$

31. $\begin{array}{r} 3\text{ gal } 3\text{ qt} \\ +\ 1\text{ gal } 2\text{ qt} \\ \hline 4\text{ gal } 5\text{ qt} \end{array} = 5\text{ gal } 1\text{ qt}$

32. $\begin{array}{r} 3\text{ c } 14\text{ fl oz} \\ \cancel{4\text{ c}}\ \ \cancel{6\text{ fl oz}} \\ -2\text{ c }\ 7\text{ fl oz} \\ \hline 1\text{ c }\ 7\text{ fl oz} \end{array}$

33. $\begin{array}{r} 2\text{ gal } 4\text{ qt} \\ \cancel{3\text{ gal}} \\ -1\text{ gal } 2\text{ qt} \\ \hline 1\text{ gal } 2\text{ qt} \end{array}$

34. $1\frac{1}{2}\text{ pt} + 2\frac{2}{3}\text{ pt} = 1\frac{3}{6}\text{ pt} + 2\frac{4}{6}\text{ pt}$
$= 3\frac{7}{6}\text{ pt}$
$= 4\frac{1}{6}\text{ pt}$

35. $4\frac{1}{2}\text{ gal} - 1\frac{3}{4}\text{ gal} = 4\frac{2}{4}\text{ gal} - 1\frac{3}{4}\text{ gal}$
$= 3\frac{6}{4}\text{ gal} - 1\frac{3}{4}\text{ gal}$
$= 2\frac{3}{4}\text{ gal}$

36. $\begin{array}{r} 1\text{ gal}\quad 3\text{ qt} \\ 2)\overline{3\text{ gal}\quad 2\text{ qt}} \\ -2\text{ gal}\qquad\quad \\ \hline 1\text{ gal} = 4\text{ qt} \\ 6\text{ qt} \\ -6\text{ qt} \\ \hline 0 \end{array}$

Objective C Exercises

37. Strategy To find how many gallons of coffee should be prepared:
- Find how many cups of coffee should be prepared by multiplying the number of adults attending (60) by the number of cups each adult will drink (2).
- Convert the number of cups to gallons.

Solution $2\text{ c} \times 60 = 120\text{ c}$

$120\,\cancel{\text{c}} \times \frac{1\,\cancel{\text{pt}}}{2\,\cancel{\text{c}}} \times \frac{1\,\cancel{\text{qt}}}{2\,\cancel{\text{pt}}} \times \frac{1\text{ gal}}{4\,\cancel{\text{qt}}} = \frac{120\text{ gal}}{16}$
$= 7\frac{1}{2}\text{ gal}$

$7\frac{1}{2}$ gal of coffee should be prepared.

38. Strategy To find the number of gallons of punch, convert 200 c to gallons.

Solution $200\text{ c} = 200\,\cancel{\text{c}} \times \frac{1\,\cancel{\text{pt}}}{2\,\cancel{\text{c}}} \times \frac{1\,\cancel{\text{qt}}}{2\,\cancel{\text{pt}}} \times \frac{1\text{ gal}}{4\,\cancel{\text{qt}}}$
$= \frac{200}{16}\text{ gal} = 12.5\text{ gal}$

12.5 gal of punch should be ordered.

39. Strategy To find the number of quarts of final solution:
- Find the total number of ounces in the solution by adding the number of ounces in the three components (72, 16, and 48 oz).
- Convert the number of ounces to quarts.

Solution $\begin{array}{r} 72\text{ fl oz} \\ 16\text{ fl oz} \\ +\ 48\text{ fl oz} \\ \hline 136\text{ fl oz} \end{array}$

$136\,\cancel{\text{fl oz}} \times \frac{1\,\cancel{\text{c}}}{8\,\cancel{\text{fl oz}}} \times \frac{1\,\cancel{\text{pt}}}{2\,\cancel{\text{c}}} \times \frac{1\text{ qt}}{2\,\cancel{\text{pt}}} = \frac{136}{32}\text{ qt}$
$= 4\frac{1}{4}\text{ qt}$

There are $4\frac{1}{4}$ qt of final solution.

40. Strategy To find the number of quarts of milk sold, convert 124 c to quarts.

Solution $124\text{ c} = 124\,\cancel{\text{c}} \times \frac{1\,\cancel{\text{pt}}}{2\,\cancel{\text{c}}} \times \frac{1\text{ qt}}{2\,\cancel{\text{pt}}} = \frac{124}{4}\text{ qt}$
$= 31\text{ qt}$

31 qt of milk were sold that day.

41. Strategy To find the number of gallons of oil the farmer used:
- Multiply 5 qt by 7 to find the number of quarts used.
- Convert the number of quarts to gallons.

Solution $\begin{array}{r} 5\text{ qt} \\ \times\ 7\qquad \\ \hline 35\text{ qt of oil} \end{array}$

$35\text{ qt} = 35\,\cancel{\text{qt}} \times \frac{1\text{ gal}}{4\,\cancel{\text{qt}}} = 8\frac{3}{4}\text{ gal}$

The farmer used $8\frac{3}{4}$ gal of oil.

42. Strategy To find the number of 1-cup servings:
- Multiply 10 oz by 24 to find the number of ounces of tomato juice.
- Convert the number of ounces to cups.

Solution

$$\begin{array}{r} 10 \text{ fl oz} \\ \times \quad 24 \\ \hline 240 \text{ fl oz} \end{array}$$

$240 \cancel{\text{fl oz}} \times \frac{1 \text{ c}}{8 \cancel{\text{fl oz}}} = 30 \text{ c}$

There are 30 servings.

43. Strategy To find the more economical purchase:
- Convert 1 qt to ounces.
- Compare the price per ounce of each brand of tomato juice.

Solution $1 \text{ qt} = 1 \cancel{\text{qt}} \times \frac{2 \cancel{\text{pt}}}{1 \cancel{\text{qt}}} \times \frac{2 \cancel{\text{c}}}{1 \cancel{\text{pt}}} \times \frac{8 \text{ oz}}{1 \cancel{\text{c}}} = 32 \text{ oz}$

First brand: $32\overline{)\$1.5900}$ = \$0.0497

Second brand: $24\overline{)\$1.250}$ = \$0.052

$\$0.0497 < \$0.052$

The more economical purchase is 1 qt for \$1.59 (the first brand).

44. Strategy To find the weight of the water:
- Find the number of gallons carried by converting the number of quarts (12) to gallons.
- Multiply the number of gallons by the weight per gallon $\left(8\frac{1}{3} \text{ lb}\right)$.

Solution $12 \cancel{\text{qt}} \times \frac{1 \text{ gal}}{4 \cancel{\text{qt}}} = \frac{12}{4} \text{ gal} = 3 \text{ gal}$

$3 \cancel{\text{gal}} \times \frac{8\frac{1}{3} \text{ lb}}{1 \cancel{\text{gal}}} = 3 \times \frac{25}{3} = 25 \text{ lb}$

The weight of the water is 25 lb.

45. Strategy To find the profit:
- Convert 5 qt to fluid ounces.
- Divide the number of fluid ounces by 8 to find the number of bottles.
- Multiply the number of bottles by \$8.25 to find the total income.
- Subtract the original cost (\$81.50) from the total income to find the profit.

Solution $5 \text{ qt} = 5 \cancel{\text{qt}} \times \frac{2 \cancel{\text{pt}}}{1 \cancel{\text{qt}}} \times \frac{2 \cancel{\text{c}}}{1 \cancel{\text{pt}}} \times \frac{8 \text{ oz}}{1 \cancel{\text{c}}}$

$= 160 \text{ fl oz}$

$8\overline{)160 \text{ fl oz}}$ = 20 number of bottles

$$\begin{array}{r} \$8.25 \\ \times \quad 20 \\ \hline \$165.00 \end{array}$$ total income

$$\begin{array}{r} \$165.00 \\ -\ 81.50 \\ \hline \$\ 83.50 \end{array}$$

The profit made was \$83.50.

46. Strategy To find the profit Orlando makes:
- Convert 50 gallons to quarts.
- Multiply the number of quarts by the customer's cost per quart (\$2.10) to find the total income.
- Subtract Orlando's cost (\$240) from the total income to find the profit.

Solution $50 \cancel{\text{gal}} \times \frac{4 \text{ qt}}{1 \cancel{\text{gal}}} = 200 \text{ qt}$

$200 \times \$2.10 = \$420$

$\$420 - \$240 = \$180$

Orlando's profit was \$180.

Applying the Concepts

47. Grain: A unit of weight in the U.S. Customary System; an avoirdupois unit equal to 0.002286 ounce, or 0.036 dram
Dram: A unit of weight in the U.S. Customary System; an avoirdupois unit equal to 0.0625 ounce, or 27.344 grains
Furlong: A unit of measuring distance, equal to 0.125 mile, or 220 yards
Rod: A linear measure equal to 5.5 yards, to 16.5 feet, and to 5.03 meters
Examples will vary.

48. Students may enjoy exercising the creativity required to answer this question. However, they should note that a standard unit of measurement must be developed first. Related units can then be developed using equivalences that allow for conversion of units.

Section 8.4

Objective A Exercises

1. $98 \text{ days} = 98 \cancel{\text{days}} \times \frac{1 \text{ week}}{7 \cancel{\text{days}}} = 14 \text{ weeks}$

2. $12 \text{ weeks} = 12 \cancel{\text{weeks}} \times \frac{7 \text{ days}}{1 \cancel{\text{week}}} = 84 \text{ days}$

3. $6\frac{1}{4} \text{ days} = \frac{25}{4} \cancel{\text{days}} \times \frac{24 \text{ h}}{1 \cancel{\text{day}}} = 150 \text{ h}$

4. $114 \text{ h} = 114 \cancel{\text{h}} \times \frac{1 \text{ day}}{24 \cancel{\text{h}}} = 4\frac{3}{4} \text{ days}$

5. $555 \text{ min} = 555 \cancel{\text{min}} \times \frac{1 \text{ h}}{60 \cancel{\text{min}}} = 9\frac{1}{4} \text{ h}$

6. $7\frac{3}{4} \text{ h} = 7\frac{3}{4} \cancel{\text{h}} \times \frac{60 \text{ min}}{1 \cancel{\text{h}}} = 465 \text{ min}$

7. $18\frac{1}{2} \text{ min} = 18\frac{1}{2} \cancel{\text{min}} \times \frac{60 \text{ s}}{1 \cancel{\text{min}}} = 1110 \text{ s}$

8. $750 \text{ s} = 750 \cancel{\text{s}} \times \frac{1 \text{ min}}{60 \cancel{\text{s}}} = 12\frac{1}{2} \text{ min}$

9. $12{,}600 \text{ s} = 12{,}600 \cancel{\text{s}} \times \frac{1 \cancel{\text{min}}}{60 \cancel{\text{s}}} \times \frac{1 \text{ h}}{60 \cancel{\text{min}}} = 3\frac{1}{2} \text{ h}$

10. $15{,}300 \text{ s} = 15{,}300 \cancel{\text{s}} \times \frac{1 \cancel{\text{min}}}{60 \cancel{\text{s}}} \times \frac{1 \text{ h}}{60 \cancel{\text{min}}} = 4\frac{1}{4} \text{ h}$

11. $6\frac{1}{2} \text{ h} = 6\frac{1}{2} \cancel{\text{h}} \times \frac{60 \cancel{\text{min}}}{1 \cancel{\text{h}}} \times \frac{60 \text{ s}}{1 \cancel{\text{min}}} = 23{,}400 \text{ s}$

12. $5\frac{3}{4} \text{ h} = 5\frac{3}{4} \cancel{\text{h}} \times \frac{60 \cancel{\text{min}}}{1 \cancel{\text{h}}} \times \frac{60 \text{ s}}{1 \cancel{\text{min}}} = 20{,}700 \text{ s}$

13. $5040 \text{ min} = 5040 \cancel{\text{min}} \times \frac{1 \cancel{\text{h}}}{60 \cancel{\text{min}}} \times \frac{1 \text{ day}}{24 \cancel{\text{h}}} = 3\frac{1}{2} \text{ days}$

14. $6840 \text{ min} = 6840 \cancel{\text{min}} \times \frac{1 \cancel{\text{h}}}{60 \cancel{\text{min}}} \times \frac{1 \text{ day}}{24 \cancel{\text{h}}} = 4\frac{3}{4} \text{ days}$

15. $2\frac{1}{2} \text{ days} = 2\frac{1}{2} \cancel{\text{days}} \times \frac{24 \cancel{\text{h}}}{1 \cancel{\text{day}}} \times \frac{60 \text{ min}}{1 \cancel{\text{h}}} = 3600 \text{ min}$

16. $6\frac{1}{4} \text{ days} = 6\frac{1}{4} \cancel{\text{days}} \times \frac{24 \cancel{\text{h}}}{1 \cancel{\text{day}}} \times \frac{60 \text{ min}}{1 \cancel{\text{h}}} = 9000 \text{ min}$

17. $672 \text{ h} = 672 \cancel{\text{h}} \times \frac{1 \cancel{\text{day}}}{24 \cancel{\text{h}}} \times \frac{1 \text{ week}}{7 \cancel{\text{days}}} = 4 \text{ weeks}$

18. $588 \text{ h} = 588 \cancel{\text{h}} \times \frac{1 \cancel{\text{day}}}{24 \cancel{\text{h}}} \times \frac{1 \text{ week}}{7 \cancel{\text{days}}} = 3\frac{1}{2} \text{ weeks}$

19. $3 \text{ weeks} = 3 \cancel{\text{weeks}} \times \frac{7 \cancel{\text{days}}}{1 \cancel{\text{week}}} \times \frac{24 \text{ h}}{1 \cancel{\text{day}}} = 504 \text{ h}$

20. $5\frac{1}{2} \text{ weeks} = 5\frac{1}{2} \cancel{\text{weeks}} \times \frac{7 \cancel{\text{days}}}{1 \cancel{\text{week}}} \times \frac{24 \text{ h}}{1 \cancel{\text{day}}} = 924 \text{ h}$

21. $172{,}800 \text{ s} = 172{,}800 \cancel{\text{s}} \times \frac{1 \cancel{\text{min}}}{60 \cancel{\text{s}}} \times \frac{1 \cancel{\text{h}}}{60 \cancel{\text{min}}} \times \frac{1 \text{ day}}{24 \cancel{\text{h}}} = 2 \text{ days}$

22. $20{,}160 \text{ min} = 20{,}160 \cancel{\text{min}} \times \frac{1 \cancel{\text{h}}}{60 \cancel{\text{min}}} \times \frac{1 \cancel{\text{day}}}{24 \cancel{\text{h}}} \times \frac{1 \text{ week}}{7 \cancel{\text{days}}} = 2 \text{ weeks}$

23. $3 \text{ days} = 3 \cancel{\text{days}} \times \frac{24 \cancel{\text{h}}}{1 \cancel{\text{day}}} \times \frac{60 \cancel{\text{min}}}{1 \cancel{\text{h}}} \times \frac{60 \text{ s}}{1 \cancel{\text{min}}} = 259{,}200 \text{ s}$

24. $3 \text{ weeks} = 3 \cancel{\text{weeks}} \times \frac{7 \cancel{\text{days}}}{1 \cancel{\text{week}}} \times \frac{24 \cancel{\text{h}}}{1 \cancel{\text{day}}} \times \frac{60 \text{ min}}{1 \cancel{\text{h}}} = 30{,}240 \text{ min}$

Applying the Concepts

25. Yes, the year 1984 is divisible by 4.

26. No, the year 1994 is not divisible by 4.

27. Yes, the year 2144 is divisible by 4.

28. $1825 \text{ days} = 1825 \cancel{\text{days}} \times \dfrac{1 \text{ year}}{365 \cancel{\text{days}}} = 5 \text{ years}$

29. $2555 \text{ days} = 2555 \cancel{\text{days}} \times \dfrac{1 \text{ year}}{365 \cancel{\text{days}}} = 7 \text{ years}$

30. $4 \text{ years} = 4 \cancel{\text{years}} \times \dfrac{365 \text{ days}}{1 \cancel{\text{year}}} = 1460 \text{ days}$

31. $6 \text{ years} = 6 \cancel{\text{years}} \times \dfrac{365 \text{ days}}{1 \cancel{\text{year}}} = 2190 \text{ days}$

32. $2 \text{ years} = 2 \cancel{\text{years}} \times \dfrac{365 \cancel{\text{days}}}{1 \cancel{\text{year}}} \times \dfrac{24 \text{ h}}{1 \cancel{\text{day}}} = 17{,}520 \text{ h}$

33. $3\frac{1}{2} \text{ years} = 3\frac{1}{2} \cancel{\text{years}} \times \dfrac{365 \cancel{\text{days}}}{1 \cancel{\text{year}}} \times \dfrac{24 \text{ h}}{1 \cancel{\text{day}}} = 30{,}660 \text{ h}$

Section 8.5

Objective A Exercises

1. $25 \text{ Btu} = 25 \cancel{\text{Btu}} \times \dfrac{778 \text{ ft}\cdot\text{lb}}{1 \cancel{\text{Btu}}}$
$= 19{,}450 \text{ ft}\cdot\text{lb}$

2. $6000 \text{ Btu} = 6000 \cancel{\text{Btu}} \times \dfrac{778 \text{ ft}\cdot\text{lb}}{1 \cancel{\text{Btu}}}$
$= 4{,}668{,}000 \text{ ft}\cdot\text{lb}$

3. $25{,}000 \text{ Btu} = 25{,}000 \cancel{\text{Btu}} \times \dfrac{778 \text{ ft}\cdot\text{lb}}{1 \cancel{\text{Btu}}}$
$= 19{,}450{,}000 \text{ ft}\cdot\text{lb}$

4. $40{,}000 \text{ Btu} = 40{,}000 \cancel{\text{Btu}} \times \dfrac{778 \text{ ft}\cdot\text{lb}}{1 \cancel{\text{Btu}}}$
$= 31{,}120{,}000 \text{ ft}\cdot\text{lb}$

5. Energy $= 150 \text{ lb} \times 10 \text{ ft}$
$= 1500 \text{ ft}\cdot\text{lb}$

6. Energy $= 300 \text{ lb} \times 16 \text{ ft}$
$= 4800 \text{ ft}\cdot\text{lb}$

7. Energy $= 3300 \text{ lb} \times 9 \text{ ft}$
$= 29{,}700 \text{ ft}\cdot\text{lb}$

8. Energy $= 3680 \text{ lb} \times 325 \text{ ft}$
$= 1{,}196{,}000 \text{ ft}\cdot\text{lb}$

9. 3 tons $= 6000 \text{ lb}$
Energy $= 6000 \text{ lb} \times 5 \text{ ft}$
$= 30{,}000 \text{ ft}\cdot\text{lb}$

10. 7 tons $= 14{,}000 \text{ lb}$
Energy $= 14{,}000 \text{ lb} \times 12 \text{ ft}$
$= 168{,}000 \text{ ft}\cdot\text{lb}$

11. $850 \times 3 \text{ lb} = 2550 \text{ lb}$
Energy $= 2550 \text{ lb} \times 10 \text{ ft} = 25{,}500 \text{ ft}\cdot\text{lb}$

12. Energy $= 1800 \text{ lb} \times 36 \text{ ft}$
$= 64{,}800 \text{ ft}\cdot\text{lb}$

13. $45{,}000 \text{ Btu} = 45{,}000 \cancel{\text{Btu}} \times \dfrac{778 \text{ ft}\cdot\text{lb}}{1 \cancel{\text{Btu}}}$
$= 35{,}010{,}000 \text{ ft}\cdot\text{lb}$

14. $22{,}500 \text{ Btu} = 22{,}500 \cancel{\text{Btu}} \times \dfrac{778 \text{ ft}\cdot\text{lb}}{1 \cancel{\text{Btu}}}$
$= 17{,}505{,}000 \text{ ft}\cdot\text{lb}$

15. $12{,}000 \text{ Btu} = 12{,}000 \cancel{\text{Btu}} \times \dfrac{778 \text{ ft}\cdot\text{lb}}{1 \cancel{\text{Btu}}}$
$= 9{,}336{,}000 \text{ ft}\cdot\text{lb}$

16. $21{,}000 \text{ Btu} = 21{,}000 \cancel{\text{Btu}} \times \dfrac{778 \text{ ft}\cdot\text{lb}}{1 \cancel{\text{Btu}}}$
$= 16{,}338{,}000 \text{ ft}\cdot\text{lb}$

Objective B Exercises

17. $\dfrac{1100}{550} = 2 \text{ hp}$

18. $\dfrac{6050}{550} = 11 \text{ hp}$

19. $\dfrac{4400}{550} = 8 \text{ hp}$

20. $\dfrac{1650}{550} = 3 \text{ hp}$

21. $9 \times 550 \dfrac{\text{ft}\cdot\text{lb}}{\text{s}} = 4950 \dfrac{\text{ft}\cdot\text{lb}}{\text{s}}$

22. $4 \times 550 \dfrac{\text{ft}\cdot\text{lb}}{\text{s}} = 2200 \dfrac{\text{ft}\cdot\text{lb}}{\text{s}}$

23. $7 \times 550 \dfrac{\text{ft}\cdot\text{lb}}{\text{s}} = 3850 \dfrac{\text{ft}\cdot\text{lb}}{\text{s}}$

24. $8 \times 550 \dfrac{\text{ft}\cdot\text{lb}}{\text{s}} = 4400 \dfrac{\text{ft}\cdot\text{lb}}{\text{s}}$

25. Power $= \dfrac{125 \text{ lb} \times 12 \text{ ft}}{3 \text{ s}}$
$= 500 \dfrac{\text{ft}\cdot\text{lb}}{\text{s}}$

26. Power $= \dfrac{500 \text{ lb} \times 60 \text{ ft}}{8 \text{ s}}$
$= 3750 \dfrac{\text{ft}\cdot\text{lb}}{\text{s}}$

27. Power $= \dfrac{3000 \text{ lb} \times 40 \text{ ft}}{25 \text{ s}} = 4800 \dfrac{\text{ft}\cdot\text{lb}}{\text{s}}$

28. Power $= \dfrac{12{,}000 \text{ lb} \times 40 \text{ ft}}{60 \text{ s}} = 8000 \dfrac{\text{ft}\cdot\text{lb}}{\text{s}}$

29. Power $= \dfrac{180 \text{ lb} \times 40 \text{ ft}}{5 \text{ s}} = 1440 \dfrac{\text{ft}\cdot\text{lb}}{\text{s}}$

30. Power $= \dfrac{1200 \text{ lb} \times 18 \text{ ft}}{30 \text{ s}} = 720 \dfrac{\text{ft}\cdot\text{lb}}{\text{s}}$

31. $\frac{4950}{550} = 9$ hp

32. $\frac{16{,}500}{550} = 30$ hp

33. $\frac{6600}{550} = 12$ hp

Applying the Concepts

34. Students can select from a number of energy sources: natural gas, coal, wood, oil, nuclear power, hydroelectric power, or solar energy. Research will be required to answer the questions concerning sources, possible pollution problems, and future prospects associated with the form of energy.

Chapter 8 Review Exercises

1. $4 \text{ ft} = 4 \cancel{\text{ft}} \times \frac{12 \text{ in.}}{1 \cancel{\text{ft}}} = 48 \text{ in.}$

2.
$$\begin{array}{r} 2 \text{ ft } 6 \text{ in.} \\ 3\overline{)7 \text{ ft} \quad 6 \text{ in.}} \\ \underline{-6 \text{ ft}} \qquad\quad \\ 1 \text{ ft} = \underline{12 \text{ in.}} \\ 18 \text{ in.} \\ \underline{-18 \text{ in.}} \\ 0 \end{array}$$

3. Energy = 200 lb × 8 ft = 1600 ft · lb

4. $2\frac{1}{2} \text{ pt} = 2\frac{1}{2} \cancel{\text{pt}} \times \frac{2 \cancel{\text{c}}}{1 \cancel{\text{pt}}} \times \frac{8 \text{ fl oz}}{1 \cancel{\text{c}}}$
$= 2\frac{1}{2} \times 16 \text{ fl oz}$
$= \frac{5}{2} \times 16 \text{ fl oz}$
$= 40 \text{ fl oz}$

5. $14 \text{ ft} = 14 \cancel{\text{ft}} \times \frac{1 \text{ yd}}{3 \cancel{\text{ft}}}$
$= \frac{14}{3} \text{ yd}$
$= 4\frac{2}{3} \text{ yd}$

6. $2400 \text{ lb} = 2400 \cancel{\text{lb}} \times \frac{1 \text{ ton}}{2000 \cancel{\text{lb}}}$
$= \frac{2400}{2000} \text{ tons} = 1\frac{1}{5} \text{ tons}$

7.
$$\begin{array}{r} 2 \text{ lb} \quad 7 \text{ oz} \\ 3\overline{)7 \text{ lb} \quad 5 \text{ oz}} \\ \underline{-6 \text{ lb}} \qquad\quad \\ 1 \text{ lb} = \underline{16 \text{ oz}} \\ 21 \text{ oz} \\ \underline{-21 \text{ oz}} \\ 0 \end{array}$$

8. $3\frac{3}{8} \text{ lb} = 3\frac{3}{8} \cancel{\text{lb}} \times \frac{16 \text{ oz}}{1 \cancel{\text{lb}}}$
$= 3\frac{3}{8} \times 16 \text{ oz}$
$= \frac{27}{8} \times 16 \text{ oz} = 54 \text{ oz}$

9.
$$\begin{array}{r} 3 \text{ ft} \quad 9 \text{ in.} \\ \underline{+\,5 \text{ ft} \quad 6 \text{ in.}} \\ 8 \text{ ft} \quad 15 \text{ in.} \end{array} = 9 \text{ ft } 3 \text{ in.}$$

10.
$$\begin{array}{r} \overset{2}{3} \text{ tons} \quad \overset{2500}{500} \text{ lb} \\ \underline{-1 \text{ ton} \quad 1500 \text{ lb}} \\ 1 \text{ ton} \quad 1000 \text{ lb} \end{array}$$

11.
$$\begin{array}{r} 4 \text{ c} \quad 7 \text{ fl oz} \\ \underline{+2 \text{ c} \quad 3 \text{ fl oz}} \\ 6 \text{ c} \quad 10 \text{ fl oz} \end{array} = 7 \text{ c } 2 \text{ fl oz}$$

12.
$$\begin{array}{r} \overset{4}{5} \text{ yd} \quad \overset{4}{1} \text{ ft} \\ \underline{-3 \text{ yd} \quad 2 \text{ ft}} \\ 1 \text{ yd} \quad 2 \text{ ft} \end{array}$$

13. $12 \cancel{\text{c}} \times \frac{1 \cancel{\text{pt}}}{2 \cancel{\text{c}}} \times \frac{1 \text{ qt}}{2 \cancel{\text{pt}}} = \frac{12}{4} \text{ qt} = 3 \text{ qt}$

14. $375 \text{ min} \times \frac{1 \text{ h}}{60 \text{ min}} = 6\frac{1}{4} \text{ h}$

15. $2.5 \text{ hp} \times 550 \frac{\text{ft} \cdot \text{lb}}{\text{s}} = 1375 \frac{\text{ft} \cdot \text{lb}}{\text{s}}$

16.
$$\begin{array}{r} 5 \text{ lb} \quad 8 \text{ oz} \\ \underline{\times \qquad\quad 8} \\ 40 \text{ lb} \quad 64 \text{ oz} \end{array} = 44 \text{ lb}$$

17. $50 \text{ Btu} = 50 \cancel{\text{Btu}} \times \frac{778 \text{ ft} \cdot \text{lb}}{1 \cancel{\text{Btu}}} = 38{,}900 \text{ ft} \cdot \text{lb}$

18. $\frac{3850}{550} = 7$ hp

19. **Strategy** To find the length of the remaining piece of board, subtract the length of the piece cut (6 ft 11 in.) from the total length (10 ft 5 in.).

Solution
$$\begin{array}{r} \overset{9}{10} \text{ ft} \quad \overset{17}{5} \text{ in.} \\ \underline{-\quad 6 \text{ ft} \quad 11 \text{ in.}} \\ 3 \text{ ft} \quad 6 \text{ in.} \end{array}$$
The length of the remaining piece is 3 ft 6 in.

20. Strategy To find the cost of mailing the book:
- Find the weight of the book in ounces.
- Multiply the weight of the book in ounces by the price per ounce for postage ($0.24).

Solution 2 lb 3 oz = 35 oz

$$\begin{array}{r} \$0.24 \\ \times \quad 35 \\ \hline \$8.40 \end{array}$$

The cost of mailing the book is $8.40.

21. Strategy To find the number of quarts in a case:
- Find the number of ounces in a case by multiplying the number of ounces in a can (18 fl oz) by the number of cans in a case (24).
- Convert the number of ounces to quarts.

Solution

$$\begin{array}{r} 18 \text{ fl oz} \\ \times \quad 24 \\ \hline 432 \text{ fl oz} \end{array}$$

$$432 \not{\text{fl oz}} \times \frac{1 \not{c}}{8 \not{\text{fl oz}}} \times \frac{1 \not{\text{pt}}}{2 \not{c}} \times \frac{1 \text{ qt}}{2 \not{\text{pt}}}$$

$$= \frac{432}{32} \text{ qt} = 13\frac{1}{2} \text{ qt}$$

There are $13\frac{1}{2}$ qt in a case.

22. Strategy To find how many gallons of milk were sold:
- Find the number of cups sold by multiplying the number of cartons (256) by the number of cups per carton (1).
- Convert the number of cups to gallons.

Solution 256 cartons × 1 c = 256 c

$$256 \text{ c} = 256 \not{c} \times \frac{1 \not{\text{pt}}}{2 \not{c}} \times \frac{1 \not{\text{qt}}}{2 \not{\text{pt}}} \times \frac{1 \text{ gal}}{4 \not{\text{qt}}}$$

$$= \frac{256}{16} \text{ gal} = 16 \text{ gal}$$

16 gal of milk were sold that day.

23. $35{,}0000 \text{ Btu} = 35{,}000 \not{\text{Btu}} \times \frac{778 \text{ ft} \cdot \text{lb}}{1 \not{\text{Btu}}}$

$= 27{,}230{,}000 \text{ ft} \cdot \text{lb}$

24. $\text{Power} = \frac{800 \text{ lb} \times 15 \text{ ft}}{25 \text{ s}} = 480 \frac{\text{ft} \cdot \text{lb}}{\text{s}}$

Chapter 8 Test

1. $2\frac{1}{2} \text{ ft} = 2\frac{1}{2} \not{\text{ft}} \times \frac{12 \text{ in.}}{1 \not{\text{ft}}} = 2\frac{1}{2} \times 12 \text{ in.}$

$= \frac{5}{2} \times 12 \text{ in.}$

$= 30 \text{ in.}$

2.

$$\begin{array}{r} \overset{3}{\not{4}} \text{ ft } \overset{14}{2} \text{ in.} \\ -1 \text{ ft } 9 \text{ in.} \\ \hline 2 \text{ ft } 5 \text{ in.} \end{array}$$

3. Strategy To find the length of each equal piece, divide the total length $\left(6\frac{2}{3} \text{ ft}\right)$ by the number of pieces (5).

Solution $6\frac{2}{3} \text{ ft} \div 5 = \frac{20}{3} \text{ ft} \div 5$

$= \frac{20}{3} \text{ ft} \times \frac{1}{5}$

$= \frac{4}{3} \text{ ft} = 1\frac{1}{3} \text{ ft}$

4. Strategy To find the length of the wall in feet:
- Find the length of the wall in inches by multiplying the length of one brick (8 in.) by the number of bricks (72).
- Convert the length in inches to feet.

Solution

$$\begin{array}{r} 8 \text{ in.} \\ \times \quad 72 \\ \hline 576 \text{ in.} \end{array}$$

$576 \text{ in.} = 576 \not{\text{in.}} \times \frac{1 \text{ ft}}{12 \not{\text{in.}}}$

$= 48 \text{ ft}$

The wall is 48 ft long.

5. $2\frac{7}{8} \text{ lb} = 2\frac{7}{8} \text{ lb} \times \frac{16 \text{ oz}}{1 \text{ lb}}$

$= 2\frac{7}{8} \times 16 \text{ oz} = \frac{23}{8} \times 16 \text{ oz}$

$= 46 \text{ oz}$

6.

$$\begin{array}{r} 2 \text{ lb } 8 \text{ oz} \\ 16\overline{)40} \\ -32 \\ \hline 8 \end{array}$$

40 oz = 2 lb 8 oz

7.

$$\begin{array}{r} 9 \text{ lb } \ 6 \text{ oz} \\ +\ 7 \text{ lb } 11 \text{ oz} \\ \hline 16 \text{ lb } 17 \text{ oz} \end{array} = 17 \text{ lb } 1 \text{ oz}$$

8.

$$\begin{array}{rr} 1 \text{ lb} & 11 \text{ oz} \\ 4\overline{)6 \text{ lb}} & 12 \text{ oz} \\ -4 \text{ lb} & \\ \hline 2 \text{ lb} = & \underline{32 \text{ oz}} \\ & 44 \text{ oz} \\ & -44 \text{ oz} \\ \hline & 0 \end{array}$$

9. **Strategy** To find the total weight of the workbooks in pounds:
- Find the total weight of the workbooks in ounces by multiplying the number of workbooks (1000) by the weight per workbook (12 oz).
- Convert the weight in ounces to pounds.

Solution $1000 \times 12 \text{ oz} = 12{,}000 \text{ oz}$

$12{,}000 \text{ oz} = 12{,}000 \cancel{\text{oz}} \times \frac{1 \text{ lb}}{16 \cancel{\text{oz}}} = 750 \text{ lb}$

The total weight of the workbooks is 750 lb.

10. **Strategy** To find the amount received for recycling the cans:
- Find the weight in ounces of the cans by solving a proportion.
- Convert the weight in ounces to pounds.
- Multiply the weight in pounds by the price paid per pound.

Solution $\frac{4 \text{ cans}}{3 \text{ oz}} = \frac{800 \text{ cans}}{n}$

$4 \times n = 3 \times 800$

$4 \times n = 2400$

$n = 2400 \div 4 = 600$

The cans weigh 600 oz.

$600 \text{ oz} = 600 \cancel{\text{oz}} \times \frac{1 \text{ lb}}{16 \cancel{\text{oz}}} = 37.5 \text{ lb}$

$37.5 \text{ lb} \times \$0.75 = \$28.13$

The amount the class received for recycling was $28.13.

11. $13 \text{ qt} = 13 \cancel{\text{qt}} \times \frac{1 \text{ gal}}{4 \cancel{\text{qt}}} = \frac{13}{4} \text{ gal} = 3\frac{1}{4} \text{ gal}$

12. $3\frac{1}{2} \text{ gal} = 3\frac{1}{2} \cancel{\text{gal}} \times \frac{4 \cancel{\text{qt}}}{1 \cancel{\text{gal}}} \times \frac{2 \text{ pt}}{1 \cancel{\text{qt}}}$

$= 3\frac{1}{2} \times 8 \text{ pt} = 28 \text{ pt}$

13. $1\frac{3}{4} \text{ gal} \times 7 = \frac{7}{4} \text{ gal} \times 7 = \frac{49}{4} \text{ gal}$

$= 12\frac{1}{4} \text{ gal}$

14.
$$\begin{array}{r} 5 \text{ gal } 2 \text{ qt} \\ +\ 2 \text{ gal } 3 \text{ qt} \\ \hline 7 \text{ gal } 5 \text{ qt} \end{array} = 8 \text{ gal } 1 \text{ qt}$$

15. $756 \text{ h} = 756 \cancel{\text{h}} \times \frac{1 \cancel{\text{day}}}{24 \cancel{\text{h}}} \times \frac{1 \text{ week}}{7 \cancel{\text{days}}} = 4\frac{1}{2} \text{ weeks}$

16. $3\frac{1}{4} \text{ days} = 3\frac{1}{4} \cancel{\text{days}} \times \frac{24 \cancel{\text{h}}}{1 \cancel{\text{day}}} \times \frac{60 \text{ min}}{1 \cancel{\text{h}}} = 4680 \text{ min}$

17. **Strategy** To find the number of cups of grapefruit juice in a case:
- Find the number of ounces of juice in a case by multiplying the number of cans in a case (24) by the number of ounces in a can (20).
- Convert the number of ounces to cups.

Solution $24 \times 20 \text{ oz} = 480 \text{ oz}$

$480 \text{ oz} = 480 \cancel{\text{oz}} \times \frac{1 \text{ c}}{8 \cancel{\text{oz}}} = 60 \text{ c}$

There are 60 c in a case.

18. **Strategy** To find the profit:
- Convert 40 gal to quarts.
- To find the total income for the sale of the oil, multiply the number of quarts by the sale price per quart ($2.15).
- To find the profit, subtract the price the mechanic pays for the oil ($200) from the total income.

Solution $40 \text{ gal} = 40 \cancel{\text{gal}} \times \frac{4 \text{ qt}}{1 \cancel{\text{gal}}} = 160 \text{ qt}$

$160 \text{ qt} \times \$2.15 = \$344$ total income

$\$344 - \$200 = \$144$

Nick's profit is $144.

19. $\text{Energy} = 250 \text{ lb} \times 15 \text{ ft} = 3750 \text{ ft} \cdot \text{lb}$

20. $40{,}000 \text{ Btu} = 40{,}000 \cancel{\text{Btu}} \times \frac{778 \text{ ft} \cdot \text{lb}}{1 \cancel{\text{Btu}}}$

$= 31{,}120{,}000 \text{ ft} \cdot \text{lb}$

21. $\text{Power} = \frac{200 \text{ lb} \times 20 \text{ ft}}{25 \text{ s}} = 160 \frac{\text{ft} \cdot \text{lb}}{\text{s}}$

22. $\frac{2200}{550} = 4 \text{ hp}$

Cumulative Review Exercises

1.

	2	3	5
9 =		(3 · 3)	
12 =	(2 · 2)	3	
15 =		3	(5)

$\text{LCM} = 2 \cdot 2 \cdot 3 \cdot 3 \cdot 5 = 180$

2. $\frac{43}{8} = \begin{array}{r} 5\frac{3}{8} \\ 8\overline{)43} \\ -40 \\ \hline 3 \end{array}$

3. $5\frac{7}{8} = 5\frac{21}{24}$

$-2\frac{7}{12} = 2\frac{14}{24}$

$3\frac{7}{24}$

4. $5\frac{1}{3} \div 2\frac{2}{3} = \frac{16}{3} \div \frac{8}{3} = \frac{16}{3} \times \frac{3}{8} = 2$

5. $\frac{5}{8} \div \left(\frac{3}{8} - \frac{1}{4}\right) - \frac{5}{8}$

$\frac{5}{8} \div \left(\frac{3}{8} - \frac{2}{8}\right) - \frac{5}{8}$

$\frac{5}{8} \div \frac{1}{8} - \frac{5}{8}$

$\frac{5}{8} \times \frac{8}{1} - \frac{5}{8}$

$5 - \frac{5}{8}$

$4\frac{8}{8} - \frac{5}{8} = 4\frac{3}{8}$

6. Given place value

2.0972

$7 > 5$

2.10

7.

$$\begin{array}{r} 0.0792 \\ \times \quad 0.49 \\ \hline 7128 \\ 3168 \\ \hline 0.038808 \end{array}$$

8. $\frac{n}{12} = \frac{44}{60}$

$n \times 60 = 12 \times 44$

$n \times 60 = 528$

$n = 528 \div 60 = 8.8$

9. $2\frac{1}{2}\% \times 50 = n$

$0.025 \times 50 = n$

$1.25 = n$

10. $42\% \times n = 18$

$0.42 \times n = 18$

$n = 18 \div 0.42$

$n \approx 42.86$

11. $37.08 ÷ 7.2 lb = $5.15/lb

12. $3\frac{2}{5}$ in. $= 3\frac{6}{15}$ in.

$+5\frac{1}{3}$ in. $= 5\frac{5}{15}$ in.

$8\frac{11}{15}$ in.

13.

$$\begin{array}{r} 1 \text{ lb } 8 \text{ oz} \\ 16\overline{)24} \\ -16 \\ \hline 8 \end{array}$$

24 oz = 1 lb 8 oz

14.

$$\begin{array}{r} 3 \text{ lb } \ 8 \text{ oz} \\ \times \qquad 9 \\ \hline 27 \text{ lb } 72 \text{ oz} \end{array} = 31 \text{ lb } 8 \text{ oz}$$

15. $4\frac{1}{3}$ qt $= 4\frac{2}{6}$ qt $= 3\frac{8}{6}$ qt

$-1\frac{5}{6}$ qt $= 1\frac{5}{6}$ qt $= 1\frac{5}{6}$ qt

$2\frac{3}{6}$ qt $= 2\frac{1}{2}$ qt

16.

$$\begin{array}{r} \overset{3}{4} \text{ lb } \ \overset{22}{6} \text{ oz} \\ -2 \text{ lb } 10 \text{ oz} \\ \hline 1 \text{ lb } 12 \text{ oz} \end{array}$$

17. Strategy To find the dividend, solve a proportion.

Solution $\frac{\$56}{40 \text{ shares}} = \frac{n}{200 \text{ shares}}$

$56 \times 200 = 40 \times n$

$11{,}200 = 40 \times n$

$11{,}200 \div 40 = n$

$280 = n$

The dividend would be $280.

18. Strategy To find Anna's checking balance, subtract the amounts of the checks and add the deposit.

Solution

$$\begin{array}{r} 578.56 \\ -216.98 \\ \hline 361.58 \\ -\ 34.12 \\ \hline 327.46 \\ +315.33 \\ \hline 642.79 \end{array}$$

Anna's balance is $642.79.

19. Strategy To find the executive's total monthly income:
- Find the amount of sales over \$25,000 by subtracting \$25,000 from the total sales (\$140,000).
- Find the amount of the commission by solving the basic percent equation for amount. The base is the amount of sales over \$25,000 and the percent is 2%.
- Add the amount of commission to the salary (\$1800).

Solution \$140,000 – \$25,000 = \$115,000
Percent × base = amount
$2\% \times 115{,}000 = n$
$0.02 \times 115{,}000 = n$
$2300 = n$
\$2300 + \$1800 = \$4100
The executive's monthly income is \$4100.

20. Strategy To find the amount of carrots that could be sold:
- Find the amount of spoiled carrots by solving the basic percent equation for the amount. The percent is 3% and the base is 2500.
- Subtract the amount of spoiled carrots from the total amount of the shipment (2500 lb).

Solution Percent × base = amount
$3\% \times 2500 = n$
$0.03 \times 2500 = n$
$75 = n$
2500 lb – 75 lb = 2425 lb
The amount of carrots that could be sold is 2425 lb.

21. Strategy To find the percent:
- Find the total number of students who took the final exam by reading the histogram and adding the frequencies.
- Find the number of students who received a score between 80% and 90% by reading the histogram.
- Solve the basic percent equation for percent. The base is the total number of students who took the exam and the amount is the number of students with scores between 80% and 90%.

Solution

Score:	
40–50:	2 students
50–60:	1 student
60–70:	5 students
70–80:	7 students
80–90:	4 students
90–100:	3 students
Total number of students:	22

Percent × base = amount
$n \times 22 = 4$
$n = 4 \div 22 \approx 0.18 = 18\%$
The percent is 18%.

22. Strategy To find the selling price:
- Find the amount of the markup by solving the basic percent equation for amount. The base is \$220 and the percent is 40%.
- Add the markup to the cost (\$220).

Solution Percent × base = amount
$40\% \times 220 = n$
$0.40 \times 220 = n$
$88 = n$
\$220 + \$88 = \$308
The selling price of a compact disc player is \$308.

23. Strategy To find the interest paid, multiply the principal (\$200,000) by the annual interest rate (6%) by the time (8 months) in years.

Solution $200{,}000 \times 0.06 \times \frac{8}{12} = 8000$
The interest paid on the loan is \$8000.

24. Strategy To find how much each student received:
- Convert 1 lb 3 oz to ounces.
- Find the total value of the gold by multiplying the number of ounces by the price per ounce (\$200).
- Divide the total value by the number of students (6).

Solution 1 lb 3 oz = 19 oz
19 × \$200 = \$3800 total value
\$3800 ÷ 6 ≈ \$633
Each student received \$633.

25. Strategy To find the cost of mailing the books:
- Find the total weight of the books by adding the 4 weights (1 lb 3 oz, 13 oz, 1 lb 8 oz, and 1 lb).
- Convert the total weight to ounces.
- Find the cost by multiplying the total number of ounces by the price per ounce ($.28).

Solution

```
  1 lb   3 oz
        13 oz
  1 lb   8 oz
+ 1 lb
  3 lb  24 oz = 72 oz

  $ 0.28
×     72
  $20.16
```

The cost of mailing the books is $20.16.

26. Strategy To find the better buy:
- Find the unit price for each brand.
- Compare unit prices.

Solution $.79 for 8 oz $2.98 for 36 oz

$\frac{0.79}{8} = 0.09875$ $\frac{2.98}{36} \approx 0.08278$

$\$0.08278 < \$0.09875$

The better buy is 36 oz for $2.98.

27. Strategy To calculate the probability:
- Count the number of possible outcomes.
- Count the number of favorable outcomes.
- Use the probability formula.

Solution There are 36 possible outcomes. There are 4 favorable outcomes: (3, 6), (4, 5), (5, 4), (6, 3).

$\text{Probability} = \frac{4}{36} = \frac{1}{9}$

The probability is $\frac{1}{9}$ that the sum of the dots on the two dice is 9.

28. $\text{Energy} = 400 \text{ lb} \times 8 \text{ ft} = 3200 \text{ ft} \cdot \text{lb}$

29. $\text{Power} = \frac{600 \text{ lb} \times 8 \text{ ft}}{12 \text{ s}} = 400 \frac{\text{ft} \cdot \text{lb}}{\text{s}}$

Chapter 9: The Metric System of Measurement

Prep Test

1. 37,320
2. 659,000
3. 0.04107
4. $28{,}496 \div 10^3 = 28{,}496 \div 1000 = 28.496$
5. 5.125
6. 5.96
7. 0.13
8. $35 \times \frac{1.61}{1} = 35 \times 1.61 = 56.35$
9. $1.67 \times \frac{1}{3.34} = 1.67 \div 3.34$

   $$3.34\overline{)1.670}\quad 0.5$$
10. $4\frac{1}{2} \times 150 = \frac{9}{2} \times 150$

   $$= \frac{3 \cdot 3 \cdot \overset{1}{\cancel{2}} \cdot 3 \cdot 5 \cdot 5}{\underset{1}{\cancel{2}}} = 675$$

Go Figure

Adding an even amount (6) of odd numbers results in an even number. Using that rule eliminates 15, 29, and 31 as possible solutions. Also, 4 cannot be a solution because the lowest possible score is 6. The highest possible score is 54, so 58 can also be eliminated as a solution. A possible score is 28. One possible combination is 9, 7, 5, 5, 1, 1. Another is 7, 7, 5, 5, 3, 1.

Section 9.1

Objective A Exercises

1. 42 cm = 420 mm
2. 62 cm = 620 mm
3. 81 mm = 8.1 cm
4. 68.2 mm = 6.82 cm
5. 6804 m = 6.804 km
6. 3750 m = 3.750 km
7. 2.109 km = 2109 m
8. 32.5 km = 32,500 m
9. 432 cm = 4.32 m
10. 61.7 cm = 0.617 m
11. 0.88 m = 88 cm
12. 3.21 m = 321 cm
13. 7038 m = 7.038 km
14. 2589 m = 2.589 km
15. 3.5 km = 3500 m
16. 9.75 km = 9750 m
17. 260 cm = 2.60 m
18. 705 cm = 7.05 m
19. 1.685 m = 168.5 cm
20. 0.975 m = 97.5 cm
21. 14.8 cm = 148 mm
22. 6 m 42 cm = 6 m + 0.42 m = 6.42 m
23. 62 m 7 cm = 62 m + 0.07 m = 62.07 m
24. 42 cm 6 mm = 42 cm + 0.6 cm = 42.6 cm
25. 31 cm 9 mm = 31 cm + 0.9 cm = 31.9 cm
26. 62 km 482 m = 62 km + 0.482 km = 62.482 km
27. 8 km 75 m = 8 km + 0.075 km = 8.075 km

Objective B Exercises

28. **Strategy** To find how many shelves can be cut:
    - Convert the length of each shelf (140 cm) to meters.
    - Divide the total length (4.20 m) by the length, in meters, of each shelf.

    Solution 140 cm = 1.40 m

    $$1.40\overline{)4.20}\quad 3$$

    The remainder is 0. No length is remaining.
    Three shelves can be cut, with no length remaining.

29. Strategy To find the missing dimension:
- Convert 40 mm to centimeters.
- Find the sum of the given dimensions.
- Subtract the sum of the given dimensions from the entire length (27.4 cm).

Solution 40 mm = 4 cm

4 cm
+ 15.6 cm
19.6 cm

27.4 cm
− 19.6 cm
7.8 cm

The missing dimension is 7.8 cm.

30. Strategy To find the distance of the walk-a-thon:
- Convert the distances to kilometers.
- Add the three distances.

Solution 1400 m = 1.4 km
1200 m = 1.2 km
1800 m = + 1.8 km
4.4 km

The distance of the walk-a-thon was 4.4 km.

31. Strategy To find the distance between the rivets, convert 3.4 m to centimeters and then divide the total length of the plate by the number of spaces between the rivets (19).

Solution 3.4 m = 340 cm

$340 \div 19 = 17.89 \approx 17.9$

The distance between the rivets is 17.9 cm.

32. Strategy To find the total length, convert 1.21 m to centimeters and then add the given dimensions.

Solution 1.21 m = 121 cm

42 cm
18 cm
+ 121 cm
181 cm

The total length is 181 cm.

33. Strategy To find how much fencing is left on the roll:
- Convert the length and width of the dog run to meters.
- Add the four lengths of fencing to make the dog run.
- Subtract the total fencing used from the length of the full roll (50 m).

Solution

340 cm	3.40 m
1380 cm	13.80 m
340 cm	3.40 m
1380 cm	+ 13.80 m
	34.40 m

50 − 34.40 = 15.6

The amount of fencing left on the roll is 15.6 m.

34. Strategy To find the average distance cleaned up each day:
- Convert the distance cleaned up each day to km.
- Add the 5 distances.
- Divide the sum by 5.

Solution

2500 m	2.5 km
1500 m	1.5 km
1200 m	1.2 km
1300 m	1.3 km
1400 m	+ 1.4 km
	7.9 km

$7.90 \div 5 = 1.58$

The average distance cleaned up each day was 1.58 km.

35. Strategy To find the time for light to travel to Earth from the sun:
- Convert the distance light travels in 1 s (300,000,000 m) to kilometers.
- Divide the distance from the sun to Earth (150,000,000 km) by the distance light travels in 1 s.

Solution 300,000,000 m = 300,000 km
150,000,000 km ÷ 300,000 km/s
= 500 s

It takes 500 s for light to travel from the sun to Earth.

36. Strategy To find the time to travel around Earth, divide the distance around Earth (40,000 km) by the speed of travel (85 km/h).

Solution 40,000 km ÷ 85 km/h ≈ 470.6 h

It would take 470.6 h to travel around Earth.

37. Strategy To find the distance that light travels in 1 day:
• Find the number of seconds in 1 day.
• Multiply the distance that light travels in 1 s (300,000 km) by the number of seconds in 1 day.

Solution 1 day

$= 1\,\cancel{\text{day}} \times \frac{24\,\cancel{\text{h}}}{1\,\cancel{\text{day}}} \times \frac{60\,\cancel{\text{min}}}{1\,\cancel{\text{h}}} \times \frac{60\text{ s}}{1\,\cancel{\text{min}}}$

= 86,400 s (in 1 day).

300,000 × 86,400

= 25,920,000,000 km

Light travels 25,920,000,000 km in 1 day.

Applying the Concepts

38. tera: trillion, giga: billion, mega: million, micro, millionth, nano: billionth, pico: trillionth

39. A very brief history of the metric system appears on page 373. You might decide whether you want students to write about its early development at the end of the 18th century or about its more recent history. For example, in 1975, Congress passed the Metric Conversion Act, which encourages voluntary use of the metric system in the United States.

Section 9.2

Objective A Exercises

1. 420 g = 0.420 kg

2. 7421 g = 7.421 kg

3. 127 mg = 0.127 g

4. 43 mg = 0.043 g

5. 4.2 kg = 4200 g

6. 0.027 kg = 27 g

7. 0.45 g = 450 mg

8. 325 g = 325,000 mg

9. 1856 g = 1.856 kg

10. 8900 g = 8.900 kg

11. 4057 mg = 4.057 g

12. 1970 mg = 1.970 g

13. 1.37 kg = 1370 g

14. 5.1 kg = 5100 g

15. 0.0456 g = 45.6 mg

16. 0.2 g = 200 mg

17. 18,000 g = 18.000 kg

18. 0.87 kg = 870 g

19. 3 kg 922 g = 3 kg + 0.922 kg = 3.922 kg

20. 1 kg 47 g = 1 kg + 0.047 kg = 1.047 kg

21. 7 g 891 mg = 7 g + 0.891 g = 7.891 g

22. 209 g 42 mg = 209 g + 0.042 g = 209.042 g

23. 4 kg 63 g = 4 kg + 0.063 kg = 4.063 kg

24. 18 g 5 mg = 18 g + 0.005 g = 18.005 g

Objective B Exercises

25. Strategy To find the number of grams in one serving of Quaker Oats:
• Convert the amount of Quaker Oats (1.19 kg) to grams.
• Divide the amount of Quaker Oats by the number of servings (30).

Solution 1.19 kg = 1190 g

$30\overline{)1190.0}$ = 39.67

There are 40 g in 1 serving.

26. Strategy To find the number of tablets to take:
• Convert the amount of the supplement (2 g) to milligrams.
• Divide the amount of the supplement by the amount of calcium in one tablet (500 mg).

Solution 2 g = 2000 mg

$500\overline{)2000}$ = 4

The patient should take 4 tablets per day.

27a. Strategy To find the number of grams of cholesterol in one dozen eggs:
• Convert the amount of cholesterol that one egg contains (274 mg) to grams.
• Multiply the number of grams of cholesterol in one egg by the number of eggs (12).

Solution 274 mg = 0.274 g

12 × 0.274 = 3.288 g

There are 3.288 g of cholesterol in 12 eggs.

b. Strategy To find the number of grams of cholesterol in 4 glasses of milk:
- Convert the amount of cholesterol in one glass of milk (33 mg) to grams.
- Multiply the number of grams in one glass of milk by the number of glasses of milk (4).

Solution 33 mg = 0.033 g
$4 \times 0.033 = 0.132$
There are 0.132 g of cholesterol in four glasses of milk.

28. Strategy To find the weight of the precious stone in grams:
- Convert the weight of a carat (200 mg) to grams.
- Multiply the weight of the stone in carats (10) by the weight of one carat in grams.

Solution 200 mg = 0.2 g
$10 \times 0.2 = 2$
The weight of the precious stone is 2 g.

29a. Strategy To find the weight of the package in kilograms:
- Convert the weight of one serving (31 g) to kilograms.
- Multiply the weight of one serving by the number of servings (6).

Solution 31 g = 0.031 kg
$0.031 \times 6 = 0.186$
There are 0.186 kg of mix in the package.

b. Strategy To find the number of grams of sodium contained in two servings:
- Convert the weight of sodium in one servings (210 mg) to grams.
- Multiply the weight of sodium in one servings by the number of servings (2).

Solution 210 mg = 0.210 g
$0.210 \times 2 = 0.420$
There are 0.42 g of sodium in two servings.

30. Strategy To find the cost of the three packages of ground meat:
- Convert the weight of the three packages to kilograms.
- Add the three weights.
- Multiply the sum by $8.40.

Solution

470 g	0.470 kg
680 g	0.680 kg
590 g	+ 0.590 kg
	1.740 kg

$1.74 \times 8.40 = 14.616$
The three packages of meat cost $14.62.

31. Strategy To find the amount of grass seed:
- Convert 80 g to kilograms.
- Write and solve a proportion.

Solution 80 g = 0.08 kg

$$\frac{0.08\text{ kg}}{100\text{ m}^2} = \frac{n}{2000\text{ m}^2}$$
$$0.08 \times 2000 = 100 \times n$$
$$160 = 100 \times n$$
$$160 \div 100 = n$$
$$1.6 = n$$

The amount of seed needed is 1.6 kg.

32. Strategy To find the extra charge for the luggage:
- Convert the weights of the three pieces of luggage to kilograms.
- Add the three weights.
- Find the amount of weight over 15 kg by subtracting 15 kg from the total weight.
- Round up the next whole number and multiply by the charge per kilogram ($9.95).

Solution

6450 g	6.450 kg
5850 g	5.850 kg
7500 g	+ 7.500 kg
	19.800 kg

$19.8 - 15 = 4.8$
Round 4.8 to 5.
$5 \times 9.95 = 49.75$
An extra $49.75 must be paid for the luggage.

33. Strategy To find the profit:
- Convert the weight of a 10-kilogram container to grams.
- Find the number of bags of nuts in a 10-kilogram container by dividing the total weight in grams by the weight of one bag (200 g).
- Find the cost of the bags by multiplying the number of bags by \$.04.
- Add the cost of the bags to the cost of a 10-kilogram container (\$75) to find the total cost.
- Multiply the number of bags by \$3.89 to find the total revenue.
- Subtract the total cost from the revenue to find the profit.

Solution 10 kg = 10,000 g
10,000 g ÷ 200 g = 50 bags of nuts
50 × \$0.04 = \$2 cost of the bags
\$75 + \$2 = \$77 total cost
50 × \$3.89 = \$194.50 total revenue
\$194.50 – \$77.00 = \$117.50 profit
The profit from repackaging the nuts is \$117.50.

34. Strategy To find the total weight, multiply the number of cars (9) by the weight per car (1405 kg).

Solution 1405 kg × 9 = 12,645 kg.
The total weight of the cars is 12,645 kg.

35. Strategy To find the percent of corn:
- Add the amount of exports of wheat (37,141 million kg), rice (2,680 million kg), and corn (40,365 million kg).
- Solve the basic percent equation for percent. The base is the total amount of exports and the amount is the amount of corn (40,365 million kg).

Solution

$$\begin{array}{r} 37{,}141 \text{ million kg} \\ 2{,}680 \text{ million kg} \\ +\ 40{,}365 \text{ million kg} \\ \hline 80{,}186 \text{ million kg} \end{array}$$

Percent × base = amount

$$\begin{aligned} n \times 80{,}186 &= 40{,}365 \\ n &= 40{,}365 \div 80{,}186 \\ n &\approx 0.503 \end{aligned}$$

Corn was 50.3% of the total exports.

Applying the Concepts

36. 1 metric ton = 1000 kg

$$\begin{aligned} 37{,}141 \text{ million kg} &= 37{,}141{,}000{,}000 \text{ kg} \\ &= 37{,}141{,}000 \text{ metric tons} \\ 2{,}680 \text{ million kg} &= 2{,}680{,}000{,}000 \text{ kg} \\ &= 2{,}680{,}000 \text{ metric tons} \\ 40{,}365 \text{ million kg} &= 40{,}365{,}000{,}000 \text{ kg} \\ &= 40{,}365{,}000 \text{ metric tons} \end{aligned}$$

37. Students might list familiarity among the advantages of the U.S. Customary System and difficulty in converting units among the disadvantages. They might list ease of conversion among the advantages of the metric system, as well as the fact that international trade is based on the metric system.
A disadvantage for Americans is that they are unfamiliar with metric units. Another disadvantage is related to American industry: If forced to change to the metric system, companies would face the difficulty and expense of altering the present dimensions of machinery, tools, and products.

Section 9.3

Objective A Exercises

1. 4200 ml = 4.2 L

2. 7.5 ml = 0.0075 L

3. 3.42 L = 3420 ml

4. 0.037 L = 37 ml

5. 423 ml = 423 cm^3

6. 0.32 ml = 0.32 cm^3

7. 642 cm^3 = 642 ml

8. 0.083 cm^3 = 0.083 ml

9. 42 cm^3 = 42 ml = 0.042 L

10. 3075 cm^3 = 3075 ml = 3.075 L

11. 0.435 L = 435 ml = 435 cm^3

12. 2.57 L = 2570 ml = 2570 cm^3

13. 4.62 kl = 4620 L

14. 0.035 kl = 35 L

15. 1423 L = 1.423 kl

16. 897 L = 0.897 kl

17. 1.267 L = 1267 cm^3

18. 4.105 L = 4105 cm^3

19. 3 L 42 ml = 3 L + 0.042 L = 3.042 L

20. 1 L 127 ml = 1 L + 0.127 L = 1.127 L

21. 3 kl 4 L = 3 kl + 0.004 kl = 3.004 kl

22. 6 kl 32 L = 6 kl + 0.032 kl = 6.032 kl

23. 8 L 200 ml = 8 L + 0.200 L = 8.200 L

24. 9 kl 505 L = 9 kl + 0.505 kl = 9.505 kl

Objective B Exercises

25a. Strategy To determine whether the amount of oxygen in 50 L of air is more or less than 25 L, note the percent of air that is oxygen.

Solution Because oxygen makes up only 21% of air, which is much less than $\frac{1}{2}$, there could not be 25 L of oxygen in 50 L of air.

b. Strategy To find the amount of oxygen, solve the basic percent equation for the amount. The percent is 21% and the base is 50 L.

Solution Percent × base = amount

$21\% \times 50 = n$
$0.21 \times 50 = n$
$10.5 = n$

There are 10.5 L of oxygen in 50 L of air.

26. Strategy To find the number of servings:
- Convert the amount of tomato juice (1.36 L) to milliliters.
- Divide the number of milliliters of tomato juice by the amount of tomato juice per serving (170).

Solution 1.36 L = 1360 ml
$1360 \div 170 = 8$
There are 8 servings in the can of tomato juice.

27. Strategy To find the amount of chlorine used in a month:
- Convert 800 ml to liters.
- Multiply the amount of chlorine used in a day by the number of days in a month (30).

Solution 800 ml = 0.8 L
$0.8 \times 30 = 24$ L
24 L of chlorine were used in a month.

28. Strategy To find the number of servings:
- Convert the amount of milk (3.78 L) to milliliters.
- Divide the amount of milk by the amount of milk in one serving (230 ml).

Solution 3.78 L = 3780 ml
$3780 \div 230 \approx 16.43$
There are 16 servings in the container of milk.

29. Strategy To find how many patients can be immunized:
- Convert 3 cm^3 to liters.
- Divide the total number of liters of flu vaccine (12) by the number of liters of vaccine each person receives.

Solution 3 cm^3 = 3 ml = 0.003 L
$12 \div 0.003 = 4000$
4000 patients can be immunized.

30. Strategy To find the number of liters to be ordered:
- Find the number of milliliters of acid needed by multiplying the number of classes (4) by the number of students per class (90) by the number of milliliters of acid required by each student (12).
- Convert milliliters to liters.
- Round up to the nearest whole number.

Solution $4 \times 90 \times 12 = 4320$ ml
4320 ml = 4.320 L
4.32 rounded up to the nearest whole number is 5.
The experiment requires 5 L of acid.

31. Strategy To determine the better buy:
- Find the unit cost (cost per liter) of the 12 one-liter bottles by dividing the cost ($19.80) by the amount of apple juice (12 L).
- Find the unit cost (cost per liter) of the 24 cans by converting the amount to liters and then dividing $14.50 by the amount of juice.

Solution The cost of 12 one-liter bottles:
$19.80 \div 12 = 1.65$
The unit cost is $1.65 per liter.
The cost of 24 cans:
24×340 ml = 8160 ml = 8.16 L
$14.50 \div 8.16 \approx 1.78$
The unit cost is $1.78 per liter.
Since $1.65 < $1.78, the 12 one-liter bottles are the better buy.

32. **Strategy** To find the profit:
- Convert the volume of 5 L of cough syrup to milliliters.
- Find the number of bottles of cough syrup by dividing the total volume in milliliters by the volume of the 250-ml bottles.
- Find the cost of the bottles by multiplying the number of bottles by the cost per bottle ($.55).
- Add the cost of the bottles to the cost of the 5 L of cough syrup ($195) to find the total cost.
- Multiply the number of bottles by $23.89 to find the total revenue.
- Subtract the total cost from the revenue to find the profit.

Solution 5 L = 5000 ml
5000 ÷ 250 = 20 (Bottles of cough syrup)
20 × $.55 = $11 (Cost of the bottles)
$11 + $195 = $206 (Total cost)
20 × $23.89 = $477.80 (Revenue)
$477.80 − $206 = $271.80 (Profit)
The profit was $271.80.

33. **Strategy** To find the profit:
- Convert 85 kl to liters.
- Find the income by multiplying the price per liter ($.379) by the number of liters sold.
- Subtract the cost ($23,750) from the total income.

Solution 85 kl = 85,000 L

85,000 L	$32,215
× $.379	− 23,750
Income: $32,215	$8,465

The profit on the gasoline was $8465.

34. **Strategy** To find the profit:
- Convert the 32 kl of cooking oil to liters.
- Find the number of bottles of cooking oil by dividing the amount of cooking oil by the volume of one bottle (1.25 L)
- Find the cost of the bottles by multiplying the number of bottles by the cost of one bottle ($.21)
- Add the cost of the bottles to the cost of the cooking oil ($44,480) to find the total cost.
- Multiply the number of bottles by $2.97 to find the total revenue.
- Subtract the total cost from the total revenue to find the profit.

Solution 32 kl = 32,000 L
32,000 ÷ 1.25 = 25,600 bottles of cooking oil
25,600 × $.21 = $5,376 cost of the bottles
$5376 + $44,480 = $49,856 total cost
25,600 × $2.97 = $76,032 revenue
$76,032 − 49,856 = $26,176 profit
The total profit was $26,176.

Applying the Concepts

35. 3 L − 280 ml = 3 L − 0.280 L = 2.72 L
2.72 L = 2720 ml
2.72 L = 2 L 720 ml

36. Students may discuss any number of difficulties. For example, comparing unit costs or prices is more difficult. Parts are not interchangeable within similar products. Different dimensions of machinery and tools limit trade between the United States and the European countries.

Section 9.4

Objective A Exercises

1. **Strategy** To find the number of Calories that can be omitted from your diet, multiply the number of Calories omitted each day (110) by the number of days (30).

Solution 110 × 30 = 3300
3300 Calories can be omitted from your diet.

2. **Strategy** To find the number of Calories that can be omitted from your diet, multiply the number of Calories omitted each day (400) by the number of days (14).

Solution 400 × 14 = 5,600
5600 Calories can be omitted from your diet.

3a. **Strategy**
- From the nutrition label find the number of Calories per serving.
- Multiply the number of Calories per serving by $1\frac{1}{2}$.

Solution There are 60 Calories per serving.
$60 \times 1\frac{1}{2} = 90$
There are 90 Calories in $1\frac{1}{2}$ servings.

b. Strategy • From the nutrition label find the serving size and the number of Calories from fat.
• Determine how many servings are in 6 slices of bread.
• Multiply the number of fat Calories in a serving by the number of servings.

Solution 2 slices of bread is one serving.
10 fat Calories are in one serving.
$6 \div 2 = 3$ number of servings
$10 \times 3 = 30$
There are 30 fat Calories in 6 slices of bread.

4. Strategy To find the number of Calories per day that a 150-lb person needs to maintain body weight, multiply the weight (150 lb) by the number of Calories needed per pound (20).

Solution $150 \times 20 = 3000$
3000 Calories would be needed to maintain the weight.

5. Strategy To find how many Calories a 135-lb person would need to maintain body weight, multiply the body weight (135 lb) by the number of Calories per pound needed (15).

Solution $135 \times 15 = 2025$
2025 Calories would be needed.

6. Strategy Find the daily intake of Calories from carbohydrates by solving the basic percent equation for amount. The percent is 55% and the base is 1600.

Solution Percent × base = amount

$$55\% \times 1600 = n$$
$$0.55 \times 1600 = n$$
$$880 = n$$

880 Calories from carbohydrates would be the daily intake.

7. Strategy To find how many Calories you burn up playing tennis:
• Convert 45 min to hours.
• Find how many hours of tennis are played by multiplying the number of days (30) by the time per day in hours.
• Multiply the number of hours played by the Calories burned per hour (450).

Solution $45 \text{ min} = 45 \cancel{\text{min}} \times \dfrac{1 \text{ h}}{60 \cancel{\text{min}}} = \dfrac{3}{4} \text{ h}$

$$30 \times \frac{3}{4} \text{ h} = \frac{90}{4} \text{ h} = 22.5 \text{ h}$$

$450 \text{ Calories} \times 22.5 = 10{,}125 \text{ Calories}$

You burn 10,125 Calories.

8a. Strategy To estimate whether Ruben lost or gained Calories:
• Estimate the number of Calories lost by playing golf.
• Compare this number with 550 (the number of Calories in the banana split).

Solution $3 \times 300 = 900$
Approximately 900 Calories were lost playing golf. The banana split contained fewer Calories than were burned.

b. Strategy To find how many Calories Ruben gained or lost:
• Find the number of Calories used by multiplying the Calories used per hour (320) by the number of hours played (3).
• Subtract the number of Calories gained (550) from the total used.

Solution $320 \times 3 = 960$
$960 - 550 = 410$
There was a loss of 410 Calories.

9. Strategy To find how many hours you would have to hike:
• Add to find the total number of Calories consumed (375 + 150 + 280).
• Divide the sum by the number of Calories used in 1 h (315).

Solution

$$\begin{array}{r} 375 \\ 150 \\ +280 \\ \hline 805 \end{array}$$

805 number of Calories consumed

$805 \div 315 \approx 2.6$

You would have to hike for 2.6 h.

10. Strategy To find how many hours of bicycling Shawna would need:
- Add to find the total number of Calories consumed (320 + 310 + 150).
- Divide the sum by the number of Calories used in 1 h (265).

Solution
$$\begin{array}{r} 320 \\ 310 \\ +150 \\ \hline 780 \end{array} \quad \text{number of Calories consumed}$$
$$\frac{780}{265} \approx 2.9$$
Shawna would have to ride a bicycle for 2.9 h.

11. Strategy To find the energy used, multiply the number of watts (500) by the number of hours $\left(2\frac{1}{2}\right)$.

Solution $500 \times 2\frac{1}{2} = 1250$ Wh

1250 Wh are used.

12. Strategy To find the number of kilowatt-hours:
- Find the number of hours spent by multiplying the number of hours per day $\left(3\frac{1}{2}\right)$ by the number of days (7).
- Find the number of watt-hours by multiplying the number of watts (90) by the number of hours.
- Convert watt-hours to kilowatt-hours.

Solution $3\frac{1}{2}$ h × 7 = 24.5 h

24.5 h × 90 W = 2205 Wh

2,205 Wh = 2.205 kWh

2.205 kWh are used.

13. Strategy To find the number of kilowatt-hours used:
- Find the number of watt-hours used in standby mode.
- Find the number of watt-hours used in operation.
- Add the two numbers.
- Convert watt-hours to kilowatt hours.

Solution
$$\begin{array}{rr} 30 \times 9 = & 351 \\ 6 \times 36 = & +216 \\ \hline & 567 \text{ Wh} \end{array}$$

567 W = 0.567 kWh

The fax machine used 0.567 kWh.

14. Strategy To find the cost:
- Find the number of hours used by multiplying the number of hours used per day (2) by the number of days (14).
- Find the number of watt-hours by multiplying the number of watts used (120) by the number of hours.
- Convert watt-hours to kilowatt-hours.
- Multiply the number of kilowatt-hours by the cost per kilowatt-hour (9.4¢).

Solution 2 h × 14 = 28 h

28 h × 120 W = 3360 Wh

3360 Wh = 3.360 kWh

3.360 kWh × $.094

= $.31584 ≈ $.32

The cost of listening to the CD player is $.32.

15. Strategy To find the cost:
- Multiply the watts by the number of hours (8) to find the number of watt-hours.
- Convert the watt-hours to kilowatt-hours.
- Multiply the number of kilowatt-hours by the price per kilowatt-hour ($.09).

Solution 2200 W × 8 h = 17,600 Wh

17,600 Wh = 17.6 kWh

17.6 kWh × $.09 = $1.584 ≈ $1.58

The cost of running an air conditioner is $1.58.

16. Strategy To find the cost:
- Find the number of watt-hours by multiplying the number of watts used per hour (1400) by the number of hours (3).
- Convert the watt-hours to kilowatt-hours.
- Multiply the number of kilowatt-hours by the price per kilowatt-hour (11.1¢).

Solution 1400 W × 3 h = 4200 Wh

4200 Wh = 4.2 kWh

4.2 kWh × $.111 = $.4662 ≈ $.47

The cost of using the heater is $.47.

17a. Strategy To determine if the light output of the Energy Saver Bulb is more or less than half the energy of the Long Life Soft White bulb, compare the light output of each bulb.

Solution Energy Saver—400 lumens
Soft White—835 lumens
400 lumens is less than half the output of the Soft White bulb.

b. Strategy To find the cost for each bulb:
- Find the number of watt-hours by multiplying the number of watts by the number of hours.
- Convert watt-hours to kilowatt-hours.
- Multiply the number of kilowatt-hours by the cost per kilowatt hour.
- Find the difference in cost.

Solution Sylvania Long Life Bulb:
$60 \times 150 = 9000$ Wh
9000 Wh $= 9$ kWh
$9 \times \$.108 = \$.972$
Energy Saver Soft White Bulb:
$34 \times 150 = 5100$ Wh
5100 Wh $= 5.1$ kWh
$5.1 \times \$.108 = \$.5508$
$\$.972 - \$.5508 = \$.4212$
The energy saver bulb costs \$.42 less to operate.

18. Strategy To find the percent decrease, solve the basic percent equation for percent. The base is 265 and the amount is 45.

Solution Percent × base = amount

$$n \times 265 = 45$$
$$n = 45 \div 265$$
$$n \approx 0.170 = 17.5\%$$

The percent decrease is 17.0%.

19. Strategy To find the cost:
- Multiply to find the total number of hours the welder is used.
- Multiply the number of hours by the number of kilowatts used each hour.
- Multiply the number of kilowatt-hours by the cost per kilowatt-hour.

Solution $30 \times 6 = 180$ h
$180 \times 6.5 = 1170$ kWh
$1170 \times 0.094 = \$109.98$
The cost of using the welder is \$109.98.

Applying the Concepts

20. The energy efficiency of a home can be improved in a number of ways. Students might mention increasing the amount or thickness of insulation, using weather stripping around doors and windows, using window treatments that help to retain heat or cool air in the home, and insulating the hot water heater. Also, repairing a cracked foundation or reproofing an older home can be beneficial.

21. Answers will vary. For example,

Age	Weight	Calories per Day to Maintain Weight	Calories per Day to Lose 1 Lb/Week
Men 11–14	99	2500	2000
15–18	145	3000	2500
19–24	160	2900	2400
25–50	174	2900	2400
51+	170	2300	1800
Women 11–14	101	2200	1700
15–18	120	2200	1700
19–24	128	2200	1700
25–50	138	2200	1700
51+	143	1900	1400

Section 9.5

Objective A Exercises

1. $100 \text{ yd} \approx 100 \cancel{\text{yd}} \times \dfrac{1 \text{ m}}{1.09 \cancel{\text{yd}}} = 91.74 \text{ m}$

2. $145 \text{ lb} \approx 145 \cancel{\text{lb}} \times \dfrac{1 \text{ kg}}{2.2 \cancel{\text{lb}}} \approx 65.91 \text{ kg}$

3. $5 \text{ ft } 8 \text{ in.} = 5\dfrac{8}{12} \text{ ft} = 5\dfrac{2}{3} \text{ ft} \approx \dfrac{17}{3} \cancel{\text{ft}} \times \dfrac{1 \text{ m}}{3.28 \cancel{\text{ft}}} \approx 1.73 \text{ m}$

4. $2 \text{ c} \approx 2\cancel{\text{c}} \times \dfrac{1 \cancel{\text{pt}}}{2\cancel{\text{c}}} \times \dfrac{1 \cancel{\text{qt}}}{2 \cancel{\text{pt}}} \times \dfrac{1 \text{ L}}{1.06 \cancel{\text{qt}}} \approx 0.47 \text{ L}$

5. $15 \text{ lb} \approx 15 \cancel{\text{lb}} \times \dfrac{1 \text{ kg}}{2.2 \cancel{\text{lb}}} \approx 6.82 \text{ kg}$

6. $14.3 \text{ gal} \approx 14.3 \cancel{\text{gal}} \times \dfrac{3.79 \text{ L}}{1 \cancel{\text{gal}}} \approx 54.20 \text{ L}$

7. $1 \text{ c} \approx 1 \cancel{\text{c}} \times \dfrac{1 \cancel{\text{pt}}}{2\cancel{\text{c}}} \times \dfrac{1 \cancel{\text{qt}}}{2 \cancel{\text{pt}}} \times \dfrac{1 \text{ L}}{1.06 \cancel{\text{qt}}}$
$\approx 0.23585 \text{ L} \approx 235.85 \text{ ml}$

8. $29 \text{ ft } 2 \text{ in.} \approx 29.17 \text{ ft}$
$29.17 \text{ ft} = 29.17 \cancel{\text{ft}} \times \dfrac{1 \text{ m}}{3.28 \cancel{\text{ft}}} \approx 8.89 \text{ m}$

9. $65 \dfrac{\text{mi}}{\text{h}} = 65 \dfrac{\cancel{\text{mi}}}{\text{h}} \times \dfrac{1.61 \text{ km}}{1 \cancel{\text{mi}}} = 104.65 \dfrac{\text{km}}{\text{h}}$

10. $30\frac{\text{mi}}{\text{h}} \approx 30\frac{\cancel{\text{mi}}}{\text{h}} \times \frac{1.61\text{ km}}{1\cancel{\text{ mi}}} = 48.3\frac{\text{km}}{\text{h}}$

11. $\frac{\$3.49}{\text{lb}} \approx \frac{\$3.49}{\cancel{\text{lb}}} \times \frac{2.2\cancel{\text{ lb}}}{1\text{ kg}} \approx \$7.68/\text{kg}$

12. $\frac{\$.59}{\text{lb}} \approx \frac{\$.59}{\cancel{\text{lb}}} \times \frac{2.2\cancel{\text{ lb}}}{1\text{ kg}} \approx \$1.30/\text{kg}$

13. $\frac{\$1.47}{\text{gal}} \approx \frac{\$1.47}{\cancel{\text{gal}}} \times \frac{1\cancel{\text{ gal}}}{3.79\text{ L}} \approx \$.39/\text{L}$

14. $\frac{\$24.99}{\text{gal}} \approx \frac{\$24.99}{\cancel{\text{gal}}} \times \frac{1\cancel{\text{ gal}}}{3.79\text{ L}} \approx \$6.59/\text{L}$

15. $24{,}887\text{ mi} \approx 24{,}887\cancel{\text{ mi}} \times \frac{1.61\text{ km}}{1\cancel{\text{ mi}}}$
$= 40{,}068.07\text{ km}$

16. $93{,}000{,}000\text{ mi} = 93{,}000{,}000\cancel{\text{ mi}} \times \frac{1.61\text{ km}}{1\cancel{\text{ mi}}}$
$= 149{,}730{,}000\text{ km}$

Objective B Exercises

17. $100\text{ m} \approx 100\cancel{\text{ m}} \times \frac{3.28\text{ ft}}{1\cancel{\text{ m}}} = 328\text{ ft}$

18. $86\text{ kg} \approx 86\cancel{\text{ kg}} \times \frac{2.2\text{ lb}}{1\cancel{\text{ kg}}} = 189.2\text{ lb}$

19. $6\text{ L} \approx 6\cancel{\text{ L}} \times \frac{1\text{ gal}}{3.79\cancel{\text{ L}}} \approx 1.58\text{ gal}$

20. $1.85\text{ m} \approx 1.85\cancel{\text{ m}} \times \frac{3.28\cancel{\text{ ft}}}{1\cancel{\text{ m}}} \times \frac{12\text{ in.}}{1\cancel{\text{ ft}}} \approx 72.82\text{ in.}$

21. $1500\text{ m} \approx 1500\cancel{\text{ m}} \times \frac{3.28\text{ ft}}{1\cancel{\text{ m}}} = 4920\text{ ft}$

22. $327\text{ g} \approx 327\cancel{\text{ g}} \times \frac{1\text{ oz}}{28.35\cancel{\text{ g}}} \approx 11.53\text{ oz}$

23. $24\text{ L} \approx 24\cancel{\text{ L}} \times \frac{1\text{ gal}}{3.79\cancel{\text{ L}}} \approx 6.33\text{ gal}$

24. $35\text{ mm} = 35\cancel{\text{ mm}} \times \frac{1\cancel{\text{ cm}}}{10\cancel{\text{ mm}}} \times \frac{1\text{ in.}}{2.54\cancel{\text{ cm}}} \approx 1.38\text{ in.}$

25. $\frac{80\text{ km}}{\text{h}} \approx \frac{80\cancel{\text{ km}}}{\text{h}} \times \frac{1\text{ mi}}{1.61\cancel{\text{ km}}} \approx 49.69\text{ mph}$

26. $30\text{ m/s} \approx \frac{30\cancel{\text{ m}}}{\text{s}} \times \frac{3.28\text{ ft}}{\cancel{\text{m}}} = 98.4\text{ ft/s}$

27. $\frac{\$.385}{\text{L}} \approx \frac{\$.385}{\cancel{\text{L}}} \times \frac{3.79\cancel{\text{ L}}}{\text{gal}} \approx \$1.46/\text{gal}$

28. $\frac{\$10}{\text{kg}} \approx \frac{\$10}{\cancel{\text{kg}}} \times \frac{1\cancel{\text{ kg}}}{2.2\text{ lb}} \approx \$4.55/\text{lb}$

29. $2.1\text{ kg} \approx 2.1\cancel{\text{ kg}} \times \frac{2.2\text{ lb}}{\cancel{\text{kg}}} = 4.62\text{ lb}$

30. $\frac{\$7.89}{2.5\text{ kg}} \approx \frac{\$7.89}{2.5\cancel{\text{ kg}}} \times \frac{1\cancel{\text{ kg}}}{2.2\text{ lb}} \approx \$1.43/\text{lb}$

31. **Strategy** To find the number of pounds lost:
- Multiply to find the number of hours spent hiking.
- Multiply the number of hours spent hiking by the number of extra Calories used in hiking to find the total number of extra Calories used.
- Multiply the number of extra Calories consumed each day by the number of days.
- Subtract to find the difference between the number of Calories used in hiking and the number of extra Calories consumed.
- Divide the difference by 3500.

Solution $5 \times 5 = 25\text{ h}$
$25 \times 320 = 8000$ Calories
$5 \times 900 = 4500$ Calories
$8000 - 4500 = 3500$
$\frac{3500}{3500} = 1\text{ lb}$
Gary will lose 1 lb.

32. **Strategy** To find the number of pounds that could be lost:
- Multiply to find the number of hours spent swimming.
- Multiply the total number of hours spent swimming by the number of Calories used per hour.
- Divide the total number of Calories by 3500.

Solution $5 \times 1\frac{1}{2} = 5 \times \frac{3}{2} = \frac{15}{2} = 7\frac{1}{2}\text{ h}$

$7\frac{1}{2} \times 550 = 4125$ Calories

$\frac{4125}{3500} = 1.18\text{ lb}$

1.18 lb could be lost.

33. $\frac{300{,}000\text{ km}}{\text{s}} \approx \frac{300{,}000\cancel{\text{ km}}}{\text{s}} \times \frac{1\text{ mi}}{1.61\cancel{\text{ km}}}$
$\approx 186{,}335.40\text{ mi/s}$

Applying the Concepts

34. 60 mph = 96.6 km/h
120 lb = 54.5 kg
6 ft = 183 cm
1 mi = 1.61 km
1 gal = 3.79 L
1 quarter mile = 402 m

35a. False

b. False

c. True

d. True

e. False

36. This is an "opinion paper." Answers will vary.

Chapter 9 Review Exercises

1. 1.25 km = 1250 m

2. 0.450 g = 450 mg

3. 0.0056 L = 5.6 ml

4. $1000 \text{ m} \approx 1000 \cancel{\text{m}} \times \dfrac{1.09 \text{ yd}}{1 \cancel{\text{m}}} = 1090 \text{ yd}$

5. 79 mm = 7.9 cm

6. 5 m 34 cm = 5 m + 0.34 m = 5.34 m

7. 990 g = 0.990 kg

8. 2550 ml = 2.550 L

9. 4870 m = 4.870 km

10. 0.37 cm = 3.7 mm

11. 6 g 829 mg = 6 g + 0.829 g = 6.829 g

12. 1.2 L = 1200 cm^3

13. 4.050 kg = 4050 g

14. 8.7 m = 870 cm

15. 192 ml = 192 cm^3

16. 356 mg = 0.356 g

17. 372 cm = 3.72 m

18. 8.3 kl = 8300 L

19. 2 L 89 ml = 2 L + 0.089 L = 2.089 L

20. 5410 cm^3 = 5.410 L

21. 3792 L = 3.792 kl

22. 468 cm^3 = 468 ml

23. Strategy To find the amount of the wire left on the roll:
- Convert the lengths of the three pieces cut from the roll to meters.
- Add the three numbers.
- Subtract the sum from the length of the original roll (50 m).

Solution

$$\begin{aligned} 240 \text{ cm} &= 2.40 \text{ m} \\ 560 \text{ cm} &= 5.60 \text{ m} \\ 480 \text{ cm} &= \underline{+\ 4.80 \text{ m}} \\ & 12.80 \text{ m} \end{aligned}$$

$$\begin{array}{r} 50.0 \text{ m} \\ \underline{-\ 12.8 \text{ m}} \\ 37.2 \text{ m} \end{array}$$

There are 37.2 m of wire left on the roll.

24. Strategy To find the total cost:
- Convert the weights of the packages to kilograms.
- Add the weights.
- Multiply the total weight by the cost per kilogram ($5.59).

Solution

$$\begin{aligned} 790 \text{ g} &= 0.790 \text{ kg} \\ 830 \text{ g} &= 0.830 \text{ kg} \\ 655 \text{ g} &= \underline{+\ 0.655 \text{ kg}} \\ & 2.275 \text{ kg} \end{aligned}$$

2.275 × $5.59 = $12.71725
The total cost of the chicken is $12.72.

25. $\dfrac{\$3.40}{\text{lb}} \approx \dfrac{\$3.40}{\cancel{\text{lb}}} \times \dfrac{2.2 \cancel{\text{lb}}}{1 \text{ kg}} = \$7.48/\text{kg}$

26. Strategy To find how many liters of coffee should be prepared:
- Convert 400 ml to liters.
- Multiply the number of guests expected to attend (125) by the number of liters per guest.

Solution 400 ml = 0.4 L
0.4 L × 125 = 50 L
The amount of coffee that should be prepared is 50 L.

27. Strategy To find the number of Calories that can be eliminated, multiply the number of Calories in one egg (90) by the number of days it is eliminated (30).

Solution 90 Cal × 30 = 2700 Cal
You can eliminate 2700 Calories.

28. Strategy To find the cost of running the TV set:
- Find the number of hours the TV is used each month by multiplying the number of hours per day (5) by the number of days (30).
- Find the number of watt-hours by multiplying the number of watts per hour (240) by the total number of hours.
- Convert watt-hours to kilowatt-hours.
- Multiply the number of kilowatt-hours by the cost per kilowatt-hour (9.5¢).

Solution $5 \text{ h} \times 30 = 150 \text{ h}$
$150 \text{ h} \times 240 \text{ W} = 36{,}000 \text{ Wh}$
$36{,}000 \text{ Wh} = 36 \text{ kWh}$
$36 \text{ kWh} \times (\$.095) = \$3.42$
The cost of running the TV set is \$3.42.

29. $1.90 \text{ kg} = 1.90 \cancel{\text{kg}} \times \dfrac{2.2 \text{ lb}}{1 \cancel{\text{kg}}} = 4.18 \text{ lb}$

30. Strategy To find how many hours of cycling are necessary to lose 1 lb, divide 1 lb (3500 Calories) by the number of Calories cycling burns per hour (400).

Solution $400\overline{)3500.00}$ = 8.75

8.75 hours of cycling are needed.

31. Strategy To find the profit:
- Convert the amount of soap purchased (6 L) to milliliters.
- Divide the volume of one plastic container (150 ml) into the amount of soap purchased to determine the number of containers of soap for sale.
- Multiply the number of containers by the cost per container (\$.26) to find the cost of the containers.
- Multiply the number of liters of soap (6) by the cost per liter (\$11.40) to find the cost of the soap.
- Add the cost of the soap and the cost of the containers to find the total cost.
- Multiply the number of containers by \$3.29 to find the total revenue.
- Subtract the total cost from the total revenue to find the profit.

Solution $6 \text{ L} = 6000 \text{ ml}$ amount of soap
$6000 \div 150 = 40$ number of containers
$40 \times \$.26 = \$10.40$ cost of containers
$6 \times \$11.40 = \$68.40$ cost of soap
$\$10.40 + \$68.40 = \$78.80$ total cost
$40 \times \$3.29 = \$131.60$ revenue
$\$131.60 - \$78.80 = \$52.80$
The profit was \$52.80.

32. Strategy To find the number of kilowatt-hours of energy used:
- Multiply 80 W times 2 h times 7 days to find the number of watt-hours used.
- Convert the watt-hours to kilowatt-hours.

Solution $80 \times 2 \times 7 = 1120 \text{ Wh}$
$1120 \text{ Wh} = 1.120 \text{ kWh}$
The color TV used 1.120 kWh of electricity.

33. Strategy To find the amount of fertilizer:
- Multiply the number of trees (500) by the amount of fertilizer per tree (250 g).
- Convert the grams to kilograms.

Solution $500 \times 250 = 125{,}000 \text{ g}$
$125{,}000 \text{ g} = 125 \text{ kg}$
The amount of fertilizer used was 125 kg.

Chapter 9 Test

1. $2.96 \text{ km} = 2960 \text{ m}$
2. $0.378 \text{ g} = 378 \text{ mg}$
3. $0.046 \text{ L} = 46 \text{ ml}$
4. $919 \text{ cm}^3 = 919 \text{ ml}$
5. $42.6 \text{ mm} = 4.26 \text{ cm}$
6. $7 \text{ m } 96 \text{ cm} = 7 \text{ m} + 0.96 \text{ m} = 7.96 \text{ m}$
7. $847 \text{ g} = 0.847 \text{ kg}$
8. $3920 \text{ ml} = 3.920 \text{ L}$
9. $5885 \text{ m} = 5.885 \text{ km}$
10. $1.5 \text{ cm} = 15 \text{ mm}$
11. $3 \text{ g } 89 \text{ mg} = 3 \text{ g} + 0.089 \text{ g} = 3.089 \text{ g}$
12. $1.6 \text{ L} = 1600 \text{ cm}^3$
13. $3.29 \text{ kg} = 3290 \text{ g}$
14. $4.2 \text{ m} = 420 \text{ cm}$

15. 96 ml = 96 cm^3

16. 1375 mg = 1.375 g

17. 402 cm = 4.02 m

18. 8.92 kl = 8920 L

19. **Strategy** To find the number of Calories needed to maintain the weight of a 140-pound sedentary person, multiply the weight (140 pounds) by the number of Calories per pound a sedentary person needs (15) to maintain weight.

Solution 140 × 15 = 2100
A 140-pound sedentary person should consume 2100 Calories per day to maintain that weight.

20. **Strategy** To find the number of kilowatt-hours of energy used:
- Multiply 100 W times $4\frac{1}{2}$ h times 7 days to find the number of watt-hours used.
- Convert the watt-hours to kilowatt-hours.

Solution $100 \times 4\frac{1}{2} \times 7 = 3150$ Wh
3150 Wh = 3.15 kWh.
3.15 kWh of energy are used during the week for operating the television.

21. **Strategy** To find the total length of the rafters:
- Multiply the number of rafters (30) by the length of each rafter (380 cm).
- Convert the length in centimeters to meters.

Solution 30 × 380 = 11,400 cm
11,400 = 114 m
The total length of the rafters is 114 m.

22. **Strategy** To find the weight of the box of tiles, multiply the weight of one tile (250 g) by the number of tiles in the box (144).

Solution
$$\begin{array}{r} 250\text{ g} \\ \underline{\times\ 144} \\ 36{,}000\text{ g} = 36\text{ kg} \end{array}$$
The weight of the box is 36 kg.

23. **Strategy** To find how many liters of vaccine are needed:
- Multiply the number of people (2600) by the amount of vaccine per flu shot (2 cm^3).
- Convert the total amount of vaccine to liters.

Solution
$$\begin{array}{r} 2600 \\ \underline{\times\quad 2\text{ cm}^3} \\ 5200\ \text{cm}^3 = 5.2\text{ L} \end{array}$$
The amount of vaccine needed is 5.2 L.

24. $35 \text{ mph} \approx \frac{35 \text{ mi}}{\text{h}} \times \frac{1.61 \text{ km}}{1 \text{ mi}} \approx 56.4 \text{ km/h}$

25. **Strategy** To find the distance between the rivets:
- Convert the length of the plate (4.20 m) to centimeters.
- Divide the length of the plate by the number of spaces (24).

Solution 4.20 m = 420 cm
420 ÷ 24 = 17.5 cm
The distance between the rivets is 17.5 cm.

26. **Strategy** To find how much it costs to fertilize the orchard:
- Find out how much fertilizer is needed by multiplying the number of trees in the orchard (1200) by the amount of fertilizer for each tree (200 g).
- Convert the total amount of fertilizer to kilograms.
- Multiply the number of kilograms of fertilizer by the cost per kilogram ($2.75).

Solution 1200 × 200 = 240,000 g
240,000 g = 240 kg
240 × $2.75 = $660
The cost to fertilize the trees is $660.

27. **Strategy** To find the cost of the electricity:
- Determine the amount of electricity used by multiplying 1600 W times the hours used per day (4) times the number of days (30).
- Convert the watt-hours to kilowatt-hours.
- Multiply the kilowatt-hours by the cost per kilowatt hour ($.085).

Solution 1600 × 4 × 30 = 192,000 Wh
192,000 Wh = 192 kWh
192 × $.085 = $16.32
The total cost is $16.32.

28. **Strategy** To find how much acid should be ordered:
- Find the amount of acid needed by multiplying the number of classes (3) times the number of students in each class (40) times the amount of acid needed by each student (90).
- Convert the amount to liters.

Solution 3 × 40 × 90 = 10,800 ml
10.8 L
The assistant should order 11 L of acid.

29. Strategy Convert the measure of the large hill (120 m) to feet.

Solution $120 \text{ m} = 120\text{m} \times \frac{3.28 \text{ ft}}{1 \text{ m}} = 393.6 \text{ ft}$

The measure of the large hill is 393.6 ft.

30. Strategy Convert the measure of the diameter of the bulls eye (4.8 in.) to centimeters.

Solution $4.8 \text{ in.} = 4.8 \text{ in.} \times \frac{2.54 \text{ cm}}{1 \text{ in.}} = 12.192 \text{ cm}$

4.8 in. is approximately 12.2 cm.

Cumulative Review Exercises

1. $$\begin{aligned} 12 - 8 \div (6-4)^2 \cdot 3 &= 12 - 8 \div 2^2 \cdot 3 \\ &= 12 - 8 \div 4 \cdot 3 \\ &= 12 - 2 \cdot 3 \\ &= 12 - 6 \\ &= 6 \end{aligned}$$

2. $$\begin{aligned} 5\tfrac{3}{4} &= 5\tfrac{27}{36} \\ 1\tfrac{5}{6} &= 1\tfrac{30}{36} \\ +\ 4\tfrac{7}{9} &= 4\tfrac{28}{36} \\ \hline 10\tfrac{85}{36} &= 12\tfrac{13}{36} \end{aligned}$$

3. $$\begin{aligned} 4\tfrac{2}{9} &= 4\tfrac{8}{36} = 3\tfrac{44}{36} \\ -\ 3\tfrac{5}{12} &= 3\tfrac{15}{36} = 3\tfrac{15}{36} \\ \hline & \qquad\qquad \tfrac{29}{36} \end{aligned}$$

4. $$\begin{aligned} 5\tfrac{3}{8} \div 1\tfrac{3}{4} &= \frac{43}{8} \div \frac{7}{4} \\ &= \frac{43}{8} \times \frac{4}{7} \\ &= \frac{43 \cdot \overset{1}{\cancel{2}} \cdot \overset{1}{\cancel{2}}}{\underset{1}{\cancel{2}} \cdot \underset{1}{\cancel{2}} \cdot 2 \cdot 7} = \frac{43}{14} = 3\frac{1}{14} \end{aligned}$$

5. $$\left(\frac{2}{3}\right)^4 \cdot \left(\frac{9}{4}\right)^2 = \left(\frac{2}{3} \cdot \frac{2}{3} \cdot \frac{2}{3} \cdot \frac{2}{3}\right)\left(\frac{9}{4} \cdot \frac{9}{4}\right) = \frac{16}{81} \cdot \frac{81}{16} = 1$$

6. $$\begin{array}{r} 12.0072 \\ -\ 9.937 \\ \hline 2.0702 \end{array}$$

7. $$\begin{aligned} \frac{5}{8} &= \frac{n}{50} \\ 5 \times 50 &= 8 \times n \\ 250 &= 8 \times n \\ 250 \div 8 &= n \\ n &= 31.3 \end{aligned}$$

8. $1\frac{3}{4} = \frac{7}{4} \times 100\% = \frac{700}{4}\% = 175\%$

9. $$\begin{aligned} 4.2\% \times n &= 6.09 \\ 0.042 \times n &= 6.09 \\ n &= 6.09 \div 0.042 = 145 \end{aligned}$$

10. $18 \text{ pt} \times \frac{1 \text{ qt}}{2 \text{ pt}} \times \frac{1 \text{ gal}}{4 \text{ qt}} = \frac{18}{8} \text{ gal} = 2.25 \text{ gal}$

11. 875 cm = 8.75 m

12. 3420 m = 3.420 km

13. 5.05 kg = 5050 g

14. 3 g 672 mg = 3 g + 0.672 g = 3.672 g

15. 6 L = 6000 ml

16. 2.4 kl = 2400 L

17. Strategy To find how much money is left after the rent is paid:
- Find the amount that is paid in rent by multiplying $\frac{1}{4}$ by the total monthly income ($5244).
- Subtract the amount paid in rent from the total monthly income.

Solution $\frac{1}{4} \times \$5244 = \frac{\$5244}{4} = \$1311$

$$\begin{array}{r} \$5244 \\ -\ 1311 \\ \hline \$3933 \end{array}$$

$3933 is left after the rent is paid.

18. Strategy To find the amount of income tax paid:
- Find the amount of income tax paid on the profit by multiplying 0.08 by the profit ($82,340).
- Add $620 to the amount of income tax paid on the profit.

Solution $0.08 \times \$82{,}340 = \$6587.20$

$$\begin{array}{r} \$6587.20 \\ +\ 620.00 \\ \hline \$7207.20 \end{array}$$

The business paid $7207.20 in income tax.

19. Strategy To find the property tax, solve a proportion.

Solution
$$\begin{aligned} \frac{\$4900}{\$245{,}000} &= \frac{n}{\$275{,}000} \\ 4900 \times 275{,}000 &= 245{,}000 \times n \\ 1{,}347{,}500{,}000 &= 245{,}000 \times n \\ 1{,}347{,}500{,}000 \div 245{,}000 &= n \\ 5500 &= n \end{aligned}$$

The property tax is $5500.

20. Strategy To find the rebate, solve the basic percent equation for amount. The base is \$23,500 and the rate is 12%.

Solution Percent × base = amount

$12\% \times 23{,}500 = n$
$0.12 \times 23{,}500 = n$
$2820 = n$

The car buyer will receive a rebate of \$2820.

21. Strategy To find the percent, solve the basic percent equation for percent. The base is \$8200 and the amount is \$533.

Solution Percent × base = amount

$n \times 8200 = 533$
$n = 533 \div 8200$
$n = 0.065 = 6.5\%$

The percent is 6.5%.

22. Strategy To find your mean grade, find the sum of the grades and divide the sum by the number of grades (5).

Solution

$$\begin{array}{r} 78 \\ 92 \\ 45 \\ 80 \\ +85 \\ \hline 380 \end{array} \text{ sum of grades} \qquad 5\overline{)380} = 76$$

Your average grade is 76.

23. Strategy To find what the salary will be next year, find the amount of the increase by solving the basic percent equation for amount. The base is \$22,500 and the percent is 12%.

Solution Percent × base = amount

$12\% \times 22{,}500 = n$
$0.12 \times 22{,}500 = n$
$2700 = n$

$$\begin{array}{r} \$22{,}500 \\ +\ 2{,}700 \\ \hline \$25{,}200 \end{array}$$

Karla's salary next year will be \$25,200.

24. Strategy To find the discount rate:
- Find the amount of the discount by subtracting the sale price (\$140.40) from the original price (\$180).
- Solve the basic percent equation for percent. The base is the original price (\$180) and the amount is the amount of the discount.

Solution

$$\begin{array}{r} \$180.00 \\ -\ 140.40 \\ \hline \$\ 39.60 \end{array}$$

Percent × base = amount

$n \times 180 = 39.60$
$n = 39.60 \div 180$
$n = 0.22 = 22\%$

The discount rate is 22%.

25. Strategy To find the length of the wall:
- Convert 9 in. to feet.
- Multiply the length, in feet, of one brick by the number of bricks (48).

Solution $9 \text{ in.} = 9 \cancel{\text{in.}} \times \frac{1 \text{ ft}}{12 \cancel{\text{in.}}} = \frac{9}{12} \text{ ft} = 0.75 \text{ ft}$

$$\begin{array}{r} 48 \\ \times\ 0.75 \text{ ft} \\ \hline 36 \text{ ft} \end{array}$$

The length of the wall is 36 ft.

26. Strategy To find the number of quarts:
- Find the total amount of juice by multiplying the amount in a jar (24 oz) by the number of jars in a case (16).
- Convert the ounce amount of juice to quarts.

Solution

$$\begin{array}{r} 24 \text{ oz} \\ \times\ 16 \\ \hline 384 \text{ oz} \end{array}$$

$384 \cancel{\text{oz}} \times \frac{1 \cancel{\text{c}}}{8 \cancel{\text{oz}}} \times \frac{1 \cancel{\text{pt}}}{2 \cancel{\text{c}}} \times \frac{1 \text{ qt}}{2 \cancel{\text{pt}}}$

$= \frac{384}{32} \text{ qt} = 12 \text{ qt}$

There are 12 qt of apple juice in the case.

27. Strategy To find the profit:
- Convert the amount of oil to quarts.
- Find the cost by multiplying the number of gallons (40) by the cost per gallon (\$4.88).
- Find the revenue by multiplying the number of quarts by the selling price per quart (\$1.99).
- Subtract the cost from the revenue.

Solution $40 \text{ gal} = 40 \cancel{\text{gal}} \times \frac{4 \text{ qt}}{1 \cancel{\text{gal}}} = 160 \text{ quarts}$

$40 \times \$4.88 = \$195.20$ cost

$160 \times \$1.99 = \$318.40$ revenue

$\$318.40 - \$195.20 = \$123.20$

The profit was \$123.20.

28. Strategy To find the amount of chlorine used:
- Convert the amount of chlorine used to liters.
- Multiply the amount used each day by the number of days (20).

Solution 1200 ml = 1.2 L
1.2 L × 20 = 24 L
24 L of chlorine was used.

29. Strategy To find how much it costs to operate the hairdryer:
- Find how many hours the hair dryer is used by multiplying the amount used each day $\left(\frac{1}{2}\text{ h}\right)$ by the number of days (30).
- Find the watt-hours by multiplying the number of watts (1200) by the number of hours.
- Convert watt-hours to kilowatt-hours.
- Multiply the number of kilowatt-hours by the cost per kilowatt-hour (10.5¢).

Solution $30 \times \frac{1}{2}\text{ h} = 15\text{ h}$
1200 W × 15 h = 18,000 Wh
18,000 Wh = 18 kWh
18 kWh × \$0.105 = \$1.89
The total cost of operating the hair dryer is \$1.89.

30. $\frac{60\text{ mi}}{1\text{ h}} = \frac{60\text{ }\cancel{\text{mi}}}{1\text{ h}} \times \frac{1.61\text{ km}}{1\text{ }\cancel{\text{mi}}} = 96.6\text{ km/h}$

Chapter 10: Rational Numbers

Prep Test

1. $54 > 45$
2. 4
3. 15,847
4. 3779
5. 26,432
6. $\dfrac{144}{24} = \dfrac{2 \cdot \overset{1}{\cancel{2}} \cdot \overset{1}{\cancel{2}} \cdot \overset{1}{\cancel{2}} \cdot 3 \cdot \overset{1}{\cancel{3}}}{\underset{1}{\cancel{2}} \cdot \underset{1}{\cancel{2}} \cdot \underset{1}{\cancel{2}} \cdot \underset{1}{\cancel{3}}} = 6$
7. $\dfrac{2}{3} + \dfrac{3}{5} = \dfrac{10}{15} + \dfrac{9}{15}$
   $= \dfrac{19}{15} = 1\dfrac{4}{15}$
8. $\dfrac{3}{4} - \dfrac{5}{16} = \dfrac{12}{16} - \dfrac{5}{16}$
   $= \dfrac{7}{16}$
9. 11.058
10. 3.781
11. $\dfrac{3}{4} \times \dfrac{8}{15} = \dfrac{\overset{1}{\cancel{3}} \cdot \overset{1}{\cancel{2}} \cdot \overset{1}{\cancel{2}} \cdot 2}{\underset{1}{\cancel{2}} \cdot \underset{1}{\cancel{2}} \cdot \underset{1}{\cancel{3}} \cdot 5} = \dfrac{2}{5}$
12. $\dfrac{5}{12} \div \dfrac{3}{4} = \dfrac{5}{12} \cdot \dfrac{4}{3}$
    $= \dfrac{5 \cdot \overset{1}{\cancel{2}} \cdot \overset{1}{\cancel{2}}}{\underset{1}{\cancel{2}} \cdot \underset{1}{\cancel{2}} \cdot 3 \cdot 3} = \dfrac{5}{9}$
13. 9.4
14. $2.4\overline{)0.96}$ = 0.4
15. $(8-6)^2 + 12 \div 4 \cdot 3^2 = 2^2 + 12 \div 4 \cdot 9$
    $= 4 + 3 \cdot 9$
    $= 4 + 27$
    $= 31$

Go Figure

If it takes one loaf 30 minutes to fill the oven, doubling in volume each minute, then at 29 minutes, the oven would be half filled. At 28 minutes, the oven would be one-quarter filled with one loaf. So for the oven to be half filled with two loaves of bread, it would take 28 minutes.

Section 10.1

Objective A Exercises

1. −120 ft
2. −15°
3. +2 dollars
4. −324 dollars
5. −6 −5 −4 −3 −2 −1 0 1 2 3 4 5 6
6. −6 −5 −4 −3 −2 −1 0 1 2 3 4 5 6
7. −6 −5 −4 −3 −2 −1 0 1 2 3 4 5 6
8. −6 −5 −4 −3 −2 −1 0 1 2 3 4 5 6
9. 1
10. 2
11. −1
12. −3
13. 3
14. 0
15. **a.** *A* is −4. **b.** *C* is −2.
16. **a.** *B* is −4. **b.** *D* is −2.
17. **a.** *A* is −7. **b.** *D* is −4.
18. **a.** *B* is −3. **b.** *E* is 0.
19. $-2 > -5$
20. $-6 < -1$
21. $-16 < 1$
22. $-2 < 13$
23. $3 > -7$
24. $5 > -6$
25. $-11 < -8$
26. $-4 > -10$
27. $35 > 28$
28. $42 > 19$
29. $-42 < 27$
30. $-36 < 49$
31. $21 > -34$
32. $53 > -46$

33. $-27 > -39$
34. $-51 < -20$
35. $-87 < 63$
36. $-75 < 92$
37. $86 > -79$
38. $95 > -71$
39. $-62 > -84$
40. $-91 < -70$
41. $-131 < 101$
42. $127 > -150$
43. −7, −2, 0, 3
44. −4, −1, 6, 8
45. −5, −3, 1, 4
46. −8, −6, 2, 7
47. −4, 0, 5, 9
48. −12, −9, 6, 8
49. −10, −7, −5, 4, 12
50. −8, −6, −1, 7, 11
51. −11, −7, −2, 5, 10

Objective B Exercises

52. −4
53. −16
54. 2
55. 3
56. −22
57. −45
58. 31
59. 59
60. −70
61. 88
62. 4
63. 4
64. 7
65. 9
66. 1
67. 11
68. 10
69. 12
70. $|2| = 2$
71. $|-2| = 2$
72. $|-6| = 6$
73. $|6| = 6$
74. $|8| = 8$
75. $|5| = 5$
76. $|-9| = 9$
77. $|-1| = 1$
78. $-|-1| = -1$
79. $-|-5| = -5$
80. $-|0| = 0$
81. $|16| = 16$
82. $|19| = 19$
83. $|-12| = 12$
84. $|-22| = 22$
85. $-|29| = -29$
86. $-|20| = -20$
87. $-|-14| = -14$
88. $-|-18| = -18$
89. $|-15| = 15$
90. $|-23| = 23$
91. $-|33| = -33$
92. $-|27| = -27$
93. $|32| = 32$
94. $|25| = 25$
95. $-|-42| = -42$
96. $|-74| = 74$
97. $|-61| = 61$
98. $-|88| = -88$
99. $-|52| = -52$
100. $|7| < |-9|$
101. $|-12| > |8|$
102. $|-5| > |-2|$
103. $|6| < |13|$
104. $|-8| > |3|$
105. $|-1| < |-17|$
106. $|-14| = |14|$
107. $|17| = |-17|$
108. $-|-5|, -3, |2|, |-8|$
109. $-9, -|6|, -4, |-7|$
110. $-|3|, -1, |0|, |-6|$
111. $-9, -|-7|, |4|, 5$
112. $-8, -|2|, |1|, 6$
113. $-|10|, -|-8|, -3, |5|$

Applying the Concepts

114. New York has the lowest recorded temperature.
115a. 8 and −2 are 5 units from 3.
b. 2 and −4 are 3 units from −1.
116a. −6 is halfway between −7 and −5.
b. −8 is halfway between −10 and −6.
c. −9 and −6 are both one-third of the way between −12 and −3.
117. −12 min and counting is closer to blastoff.
118. Stock B showed the least net change.
119. The loss was greater during the first quarter.
120. 7, −7
121. 11, −11

122a. Students might describe the opposite of a number as the number with the sign changed, or they might rephrase the definition that states that opposite numbers are two numbers that are the same distance from zero on the number line but on opposite sides of zero.

b. Students might rephrase the definition that states that the absolute value of a number is its distance from zero on the number line. You might check that students include in their description that the absolute value of a number cannot be negative (or that the absolute value of a number is either a positive number or zero).

Section 10.2

Objective A Exercises

1. $-14, -364$

2. $-37, -561$

3. $3 + (-5) = -2$

4. $-4 + 2 = -2$

5. $8 + 12 = 20$

6. $16 + 23 = 39$

7. $-3 + (-8) = -11$

8. $-12 + (-1) = -13$

9. $-4 + (-5) = -9$

10. $-12 + (-12) = -24$

11. $6 + (-9) = -3$

12. $4 + (-9) = -5$

13. $-6 + 7 = 1$

14. $-12 + 6 = -6$

15. $2 + (-3) + (-4) = -1 + (-4) = -5$

16. $7 + (-2) + (-8) = 5 + (-8) = -3$

17. $-3 + (-12) + (-15) = -15 + (-15) = -30$

18. $9 + (-6) + (-16) = 3 + (-16) = -13$

19. $-17 + (-3) + 29 = -20 + 29 = 9$

20. $13 + 62 + (-38) = 75 + (-38) = 37$

21. $-3 + (-8) + 12 = -11 + 12 = 1$

22. $-27 + (-42) + (-18) = -69 + (-18) = -87$

23. $13 + (-22) + 4 + (-5) = -9 + 4 + (-5)$
$= -5 + (-5) = -10$

24. $-14 + (-3) + 7 + (-6) = -17 + 7 + (-6)$
$= -10 + (-6) = -16$

25. $-22 + 10 + 2 + (-18) = -12 + 2 + (-18)$
$= -10 + (-18) = -28$

26. $-6 + (-8) + 13 + (-4) = -14 + 13 + (-4)$
$= -1 + (-4) = -5$

27. $-16 + (-17) + (-18) + 10 = -33 + (-18) + 10$
$= -51 + 10 = -41$

28. $-25 + (-31) + 24 + 19 = -56 + 24 + 19$
$= -32 + 19 = -13$

29. $-126 + (-247) + (-358) + 339$
$= -373 + (-358) + 339$
$= -731 + 339$
$= -392$

30. $-651 + (-239) + 524 + 487$
$= -890 + 524 + 487$
$= -366 + 487$
$= 121$

31. $-12 + (-8) = -20$

32. $3 + (-5) = -2$

33. $-7 + (-16) = -23$

34. $7 + (-25) = -18$

35. $-4 + 2 = -2$

36. $-22 + (-17) = -39$

37. $-2 + 8 + (-12) = 6 + (-12) = -6$

38. $4 + (-4) + (-6) = 0 + (-6) = -6$

39. $2 + (-3) + 8 + (-13) = -1 + 8 + (-13)$
$= 7 + (-13) = -6$

40. $-6 + (-8) + 13 + (-2) = -14 + 13 + (-2)$
$= -1 + (-2) = -3$

Objective B Exercises

41. Negative six minus positive four

42. Negative six minus negative four

43. Positive six minus negative four

44. Positive six minus positive four

45. $9 + 5$

46. $-3 + (-7)$

47. $1 + (-8)$

48. $-2 + 10$

49. $16 - 8 = 16 + (-8) = 8$

50. $12 - 3 = 12 + (-3) = 9$

51. $7 - 14 = 7 + (-14) = -7$

52. $6 - 9 = 6 + (-9) = -3$

53. $-7 - 2 = -7 + (-2) = -9$

54. $-9 - 4 = -9 + (-4) = -13$

55. $7 - (-29) = 7 + 29 = 36$

56. $3 - (-4) = 3 + 4 = 7$

57. $-6 - (-3) = -6 + 3 = -3$

58. $-4 - (-2) = -4 + 2 = -2$

59. $6 - (-12) = 6 + 12 = 18$

60. $-12 - 16 = -12 + (-16) = -28$

61. $-4 - 3 - 2 = -4 + (-3) + (-2)$
$= -7 + (-2) = -9$

62. $4 - 5 - 12 = 4 + (-5) + (-12)$
$= -1 + (-12) = -13$

63. $12 - (-7) - 8 = 12 + 7 + (-8)$
$= 19 + (-8) = 11$

64. $-12 - (-3) - (-15) = -12 + 3 + 15$
$= -9 + 15 = 6$

65. $4 - 12 - (-8) = 4 + (-12) + 8$
$= -8 + 8 = 0$

66. $13 - 7 - 15 = 13 + (-7) + (-15)$
$= 6 + (-15) = -9$

67. $-6 - (-8) - (-9) = -6 + 8 + 9$
$= 2 + 9 = 11$

68. $7 - 8 - (-1) = 7 + (-8) + 1$
$= -1 + 1 = 0$

69. $-30 - (-65) - 29 - 4 = -30 + 65 + (-29) + (-4)$
$= 35 + (-29) + (-4)$
$= 6 + (-4) = 2$

70. $42 - (-82) - 65 - 7 = 42 + 82 + (-65) + (-7)$
$= 124 + (-65) + (-7)$
$= 59 + (-7) = 52$

71. $-16 - 47 - 63 - 12 = -16 + (-47) + (-63) + (-12)$
$= -63 + (-63) + (-12)$
$= -126 + (-12)$
$= -138$

72. $42 - (-30) - 65 - (-11) = 42 + 30 + (-65) + 11$
$= 72 + (-65) + 11$
$= 7 + 11 = 18$

73. $47 - (-67) - 13 - 15 = 47 + 67 + (-13) + (-15)$
$= 114 + (-13) + (-15)$
$= 101 + (-15) = 86$

74. $-18 - 49 - (-84) - 27 = -18 + (-49) + 84 + (-27)$
$= -67 + 84 + (-27)$
$= 17 + (-27) = -10$

75. $167 - 432 - (-287) - 359$
$= 167 + (-432) + 287 + (-359)$
$= -265 + 287 + (-359)$
$= 22 + (-359)$
$= -337$

76. $-521 - (-350) - 164 - (-299)$
$= -521 + 350 + (-164) + 299$
$= -171 + (-164) + 299$
$= -335 + 299$
$= -36$

77. $-4 - (-8) = -4 + 8 = 4$

78. $3 - (-12) = 3 + 12 = 15$

79. $-8 - 4 = -8 + (-4) = -12$

80. $8 - (-3) = 8 + 3 = 11$

81. $-4 - 8 = -4 + (-8) = -12$

82. $-13 - 9 = -13 + (-9) = -22$

83. $1 - (-2) = 1 + 2 = 3$

84. $-5 - (-3) = -5 + 3 = -2$

Objective C Exercises

85. **Strategy** To find the temperature, add the increase (7°C) to the previous temperature (−8°C).

Solution $-8 + 7 = -1$
The temperature is −1°C.

86. **Strategy** To find the temperature, add the increase (5°C) to the previous temperature (−19°C).

Solution $-19 + 5 = -14$
The temperature is −14°C.

87. **Strategy** To find Nick's score, subtract 26 points from his original score (11).

Solution $11 - 26 = 11 + (-26) = -15$
Nick's score was −15 points after his opponent shot the moon.

88. **Strategy** To find Monique's score, add 26 points to her original score (−19).

Solution $-19 + 26 = 7$
Monique's score was 7 points after she shot the moon.

89. Strategy To find the price of Byplex stock add the change in price for each day of the week.

Solution $-2 + (-3) + (-1) + (-2) + (-1)$
$= -5 + (-1) + (-2) + (-1)$
$= -6 + (-2) + (-1)$
$= (-8) + (-1)$
$= -9$
The change in the price of the stock is -9 dollars.

90. Strategy To find the temperature, subtract the nighttime temperature (−292°F) from the daytime temperature (266°F).

Solution $266 - (-292) = 266 + 292 = 558$
The difference in temperature is 558°F.

91. Strategy To find the difference in temperature, subtract the temperature in Earth's stratosphere (−70°F) from the temperature of Earth's surface (45°F).

Solution $45 - (-70) = 45 + 70 = 115$
The difference is 115°F.

92. Strategy To find the difference in elevation, subtract the elevation of Lake Assal (−156 m) from the elevation of Mt. Kilimanjaro (5895 m).

Solution $5895 - (-156) = 5895 + 156$
$= 6051$
The difference in elevation is 6051 m.

93. Strategy To find the difference in elevation, subtract the elevation of Valdes Peninsula (−86 m) from the elevation of Mt. Aconcagua (6960 m).

Solution $6960 - (-86) = 6960 + 86$
$= 7046$
The difference in elevation is 7046 m.

94. Strategy To find in which continent the difference in elevation is greatest:
- Find the difference in elevation for each continent.
- Determine the greatest difference in elevation.

Solution Africa:
$5895 - (-156) = 5895 + 156$
$= 6051$
Asia:
$8850 - (-411) = 8850 + 411$
$= 9261$
North America:
$5642 - (-28) = 5642 + 28$
$= 5670$
South America:
$6960 - (-86) = 6960 + 86$
$= 7046$
The greatest difference in elevation is found in Asia.

95. Strategy To find the difference between the highest and lowest temperatures in Africa, subtract the lowest temperature (−24°C) from the highest temperature (58°C).

Solution $58 - (-24) = 58 + 24 = 82$
The difference is 82°C.

96. Strategy To find the difference between the highest and lowest temperatures in South America, subtract the lowest temperature (−33°C) from the highest temperature (49°C).

Solution $49 - (-33) = 49 + 33 = 82$
The difference is 82°C.

97. Strategy To find the difference, subtract the lowest temperature in Asia (−68°C) from the lowest temperature in Europe (−55°C).

Solution $-55 - (-68) = -55 + 68 = 13$
The difference in temperature is 13°C.

Applying the Concepts

98. The largest difference: $13 - (-9) = 22$
The smallest positive difference: $-7 - (-9) = 2$ or $-5 - (-7) = -5 + 7 = 2$

99.

−3	2	1
4	0	−4
−1	−2	3

100. $-7 + (-1) = -8$
$-6 + (-2) = -8$
$-5 + (-3) = -8$
$-4 + (-4) = -8$

101. Students should include in their description the fact that *minus* refers to the operation of subtraction, whereas *negative* refers to the sign of a number.

Section 10.3

Objective A Exercises

1. Subtraction
2. Multiplication
3. Multiplication
4. Addition
5. $14 \times 3 = 42$
6. $62 \times 9 = 558$
7. $-4 \cdot 6 = -24$
8. $-7 \cdot 3 = -21$
9. $-2 \cdot (-3) = 6$
10. $-5 \cdot (-1) = 5$
11. $(9)(2) = 18$
12. $(3)(8) = 24$
13. $5(-4) = -20$
14. $4(-7) = -28$
15. $-8(2) = -16$
16. $-9(3) = -27$
17. $(-5)(-5) = 25$
18. $(-3)(-6) = 18$
19. $(-7)(0) = 0$
20. $-32 \times 4 = -128$
21. $-24 \times 3 = -72$
22. $19(-7) = -133$
23. $6(-17) = -102$
24. $-8(-26) = 208$
25. $-4(-35) = 140$
26. $-5(23) = -115$
27. $-6 \cdot (38) = -228$
28. $9(-27) = -243$
29. $8(-40) = -320$
30. $-7(-34) = 238$
31. $-4(39) = -156$
32. $4 \cdot (-8) \cdot 3 = -32 \cdot 3 = -96$
33. $5 \times 7 \times (-2) = 35 \times (-2) = -70$
34. $8 \cdot (-6) \cdot (-1) = -48 \cdot (-1) = 48$
35. $(-9)(-9)(2) = 81(2) = 162$
36. $-8(-7)(-4) = 56(-4) = -224$
37. $-5(8)(-3) = -40(-3) = 120$
38. $(-6)(5)(7) = -30(7) = -210$
39. $-1(4)(-9) = -4(-9) = 36$
40. $6(-3)(-2) = -18(-2) = 36$
41. $4(-4) \cdot 6(-2) = -16 \cdot 6(-2) = -96(-2) = 192$
42. $-5 \cdot 9(-7) \cdot 3 = -45(-7) \cdot 3 = 315 \cdot 3 = 945$
43. $-9(4) \cdot 3(1) = -36 \cdot 3(1) = -108(1) = -108$
44. $8(8)(-5)(-4) = 64(-5)(-4) = -320(-4) = 1280$
45. $$\begin{aligned}(-6) \cdot 7 \cdot (-10)(-5) &= -42 \cdot (-10)(-5) \\ &= 420(-5) \\ &= -2100\end{aligned}$$
46. $$\begin{aligned}-9(-6)(11)(-2) &= 54(11)(-2) \\ &= 594(-2) \\ &= -1188\end{aligned}$$
47. $-5(-4) = 20$
48. $6(-5) = -30$
49. $-8(6) = -48$
50. $-8(-7) = 56$
51. $-4(7)(-5) = -28(-5) = 140$
52. $-2(-4)(-7) = 8(-7) = -56$

Objective B Exercises

53. $3(-12) = -36$
54. $-4(-7) = 28$
55. $-5(11) = -55$
56. $2(-10) = -20$
57. $12 \div (-6) = -2$
58. $18 \div (-3) = -6$
59. $(-72) \div (-9) = 8$
60. $(-64) \div (-8) = 8$
61. $0 \div (-6) = 0$
62. $-49 \div 7 = -7$
63. $45 \div (-5) = -9$
64. $-24 \div 4 = -6$
65. $-36 \div 4 = -9$
66. $-56 \div 7 = -8$
67. $-81 \div (-9) = 9$
68. $-40 \div (-5) = 8$
69. $72 \div (-3) = -24$

70. $44 \div (-4) = -11$

71. $(-60) \div 5 = -12$

72. $-66 \div 6 = -11$

73. $-93 \div (-3) = 31$

74. $-98 \div (-7) = 14$

75. $(-85) \div (-5) = 17$

76. $(-60) \div (-4) = 15$

77. $120 \div 8 = 15$

78. $144 \div 9 = 16$

79. $78 \div (-6) = -13$

80. $84 \div (-7) = -12$

81. $-72 \div 4 = -18$

82. $-80 \div 5 = -16$

83. $-114 \div (-6) = 19$

84. $-91 \div (-7) = 13$

85. $-104 \div (-8) = 13$

86. $-126 \div (-9) = 14$

87. $57 \div (-3) = -19$

88. $162 \div (-9) = -18$

89. $-136 \div (-8) = 17$

90. $-128 \div 4 = -32$

91. $-130 \div (-5) = 26$

92. $(-280) \div 8 = -35$

93. $(-92) \div (-4) = 23$

94. $-196 \div (-7) = 28$

95. $-150 \div (-6) = 25$

96. $(-261) \div 9 = -29$

97. $204 \div (-6) = -34$

98. $165 \div (-5) = -33$

99. $-132 \div (-12) = 11$

100. $-156 \div (-13) = 12$

101. $-182 \div 14 = -13$

102. $-144 \div 12 = -12$

103. $143 \div 11 = 13$

104. $168 \div 14 = 12$

105. $-180 \div (-15) = 12$

106. $-169 \div (-13) = 13$

107. $154 \div (-11) = -14$

108. $\frac{-132}{-11} = 12$

109. $\frac{182}{-13} = -14$

110. $\frac{-60}{-15} = 4$

111. $\frac{144}{-24} = -6$

112. $\frac{-135}{15} = -9$

113. $\frac{-88}{22} = -4$

Objective C Exercises

114. Strategy To find the average daily low temperature:
- Add the seven temperature readings.
- Divide by 7.

Solution
$$4 + (-5) + 8 + (-1) + (-12) + (-14) + (-8)$$
$$= -1 + 8 + (-1) + (-12) + (-14) + (-8)$$
$$= 7 + (-1) + (-12) + (-14) + (-8)$$
$$= 6 + (-12) + (-14) + (-8)$$
$$= -6 + (-14) + (-8)$$
$$= -20 + (-8)$$
$$= -28$$
$$-28 \div 7 = -4$$
The average daily low temperature was −4°F.

115. Strategy To find the average daily high temperature:
- Add the seven temperature readings.
- Divide by 7.

Solution
$$-6 + (-11) + 1 + 5 + (-3) + (-9) + (-5)$$
$$= -17 + 1 + 5 + (-3) + (-9) + (-5)$$
$$= -16 + 5 + (-3) + (-9) + (-5)$$
$$= -11 + (-3) + (-9) + (-5)$$
$$= -14 + (-9) + (-5)$$
$$= -23 + (-5)$$
$$= -28$$
$$-28 \div 7 = -4$$
The average high temperature was −4°F.

116a. Strategy To determine whether the boiling point of neon is above or below 0°C, note whether the product of 7 and the highest boiling point on the graph is positive or negative.

Solution $7 \times (-35)$ is a negative number. The boiling point of neon is below 0°C.

b. Strategy To find the boiling point of neon, multiply the highest boiling point on the graph (−35°C) by 7.

Solution $-35 \times 7 = -245$
The boiling point of neon is −245°C.

117. Strategy To find the average score, divide the combined scores (−20) by the number of golfers (10).

Solution $-20 \div 10 = -2$
The average score was −2.

118. Strategy To find the average score, divide the combined scores (−12) by the number of golfers (4).

Solution $-12 \div 4 = -3$
The average score was −3.

119. Strategy To find the wind chill factor, multiply the wind chill factor at 10°F with a 20 mph wind (−9°F) by 5.

Solution $-9 \times 5 = -45$
The wind chill factor is −45°F.

120. Strategy To find the student's score:
- Multiply the number of questions answered correctly (20) by 5. Multiply the number of questions left blank (2) by −2. Multiply the number of questions answered incorrectly (5) by −5.
- Add the three products.

Solution $20 \times 5 = 100$
$2 \times (-2) = -4$
$5 \times (-5) = -25$
$100 + (-4) + (-25) = 96 + (-25) = 71$
The student's score was 71.

Applying the Concepts

121a. The greatest possible product is that of (−5) and (−5). $(-5)(-5) = 25$
All other contributions, (−1) and (−9), (−2) and (−8), (−3) and (−7), and (−4) and (−6) have a product less than 25.

b. The least possible sum is −17.
$(-1) + (-16) = -17$(the sum)
$-1(-16) = 16$(the product)
Other combinations are (−2) and (−8), and (−4) and (−4), which have a product of 16 and a sum greater than −17.

122. Answers will vary. For example, −5(3) is the same as $(-5) + (-5) + (-5) = -15$.

123a. True

b. True

124. Students should rephrase the rules for multiplying two integers and for dividing two integers:

To multiply two integers with the same sign, multiply the absolute values of the factors; the product is positive. To multiply two integers with different signs, multiply the absolute values of the factors; the product is negative.

To divide two integers with the same sign, divide the absolute values of the numbers; the quotient is positive. To divide two integers with different signs, divide the absolute values of the numbers; the quotient is negative.

• Be sure that students are describing both the signs of the numbers being multiplied or divided and the sign of the resulting product or quotient.

Section 10.4

Objective A Exercises

1. $$\frac{5}{8} - \frac{5}{6} = \frac{15}{24} - \frac{20}{24} = \frac{15}{24} + \frac{(-20)}{24} = \frac{15 + (-20)}{24} = -\frac{5}{24}$$

2. $$\frac{1}{9} - \frac{5}{27} = \frac{3}{27} - \frac{5}{27} = \frac{3}{27} + \frac{(-5)}{27} = \frac{3 + (-5)}{27} = \frac{-2}{27} = -\frac{2}{27}$$

3. $$-\frac{5}{12}-\frac{3}{8}=\frac{-10}{24}-\frac{9}{24}$$
$$=\frac{-10}{24}+\frac{(-9)}{24}$$
$$=\frac{-10+(-9)}{24}=\frac{-19}{24}=-\frac{19}{24}$$

4. $$-\frac{5}{6}-\frac{5}{9}=\frac{-15}{18}-\frac{10}{18}$$
$$=\frac{-15}{18}+\frac{(-10)}{18}$$
$$=\frac{-15+(-10)}{18}=\frac{-25}{18}=-1\frac{7}{18}$$

5. $$-\frac{6}{13}+\frac{17}{26}=\frac{-12}{26}+\frac{17}{26}$$
$$=\frac{-12+17}{26}=\frac{5}{26}$$

6. $$-\frac{7}{12}+\frac{5}{8}=\frac{-14}{24}+\frac{15}{24}=\frac{-14+15}{24}=\frac{1}{24}$$

7. $$-\frac{5}{8}-\left(-\frac{11}{12}\right)=\frac{-15}{24}-\left(\frac{-22}{24}\right)$$
$$=\frac{-15}{24}+\frac{22}{24}=\frac{-15+22}{24}=\frac{7}{24}$$

8. $$-\frac{7}{12}-\left(-\frac{7}{8}\right)=\frac{-14}{24}-\left(\frac{-21}{24}\right)$$
$$=\frac{-14}{24}+\frac{21}{24}=\frac{-14+21}{24}=\frac{7}{24}$$

9. $$\frac{5}{12}-\frac{11}{15}=\frac{25}{60}-\frac{44}{60}$$
$$=\frac{25}{60}+\frac{(-44)}{60}=\frac{25+(-44)}{60}=\frac{-19}{60}=-\frac{19}{60}$$

10. $$\frac{2}{5}-\frac{14}{15}=\frac{6}{15}-\frac{14}{15}$$
$$=\frac{6}{15}+\frac{(-14)}{15}$$
$$=\frac{6+(-14)}{15}=\frac{-8}{15}=-\frac{8}{15}$$

11. $$-\frac{3}{4}-\frac{5}{8}=\frac{-6}{8}-\frac{5}{8}$$
$$=\frac{-6}{8}+\frac{(-5)}{8}$$
$$=\frac{-6+(-5)}{8}=\frac{-11}{8}=-1\frac{3}{8}$$

12. $$-\frac{2}{3}-\frac{5}{8}=\frac{-16}{24}-\frac{15}{24}$$
$$=\frac{-16}{25}+\frac{(-15)}{24}$$
$$=\frac{-16+(-15)}{24}=\frac{-31}{24}=-1\frac{7}{24}$$

13. $$-\frac{5}{2}-\left(-\frac{13}{4}\right)=\frac{-10}{4}-\left(\frac{-13}{4}\right)$$
$$=\frac{-10}{4}+\frac{13}{4}=\frac{-10+13}{4}=\frac{3}{4}$$

14. $$-\frac{7}{3}-\left(-\frac{3}{2}\right)=\frac{-14}{6}-\left(-\frac{9}{6}\right)$$
$$=\frac{-14}{6}+\frac{9}{6}$$
$$=\frac{-14+9}{6}=\frac{-5}{6}=-\frac{5}{6}$$

15. $$-\frac{3}{8}-\frac{5}{12}-\frac{3}{16}=\frac{-18}{48}-\frac{20}{48}-\frac{9}{48}$$
$$=\frac{-18}{48}+\frac{(-20)}{48}+\frac{(-9)}{48}$$
$$=\frac{-18+(-20)+(-9)}{48}=\frac{-47}{48}=-\frac{47}{48}$$

16. $$-\frac{5}{16}+\frac{3}{4}-\frac{7}{8}=\frac{-5}{16}+\frac{12}{16}-\frac{14}{16}$$
$$=\frac{-5}{16}+\frac{12}{16}+\frac{(-14)}{16}$$
$$=\frac{-5+12+(-14)}{16}=-\frac{7}{16}=-\frac{7}{16}$$

17. $$\frac{1}{2}-\frac{3}{8}-\left(-\frac{1}{4}\right)=\frac{4}{8}-\frac{3}{8}-\left(\frac{-2}{8}\right)$$
$$=\frac{4}{8}+\frac{(-3)}{8}+\frac{2}{8}$$
$$=\frac{4+(-3)+2}{8}=\frac{3}{8}$$

18. $$\frac{3}{4}-\left(-\frac{7}{12}\right)-\frac{7}{8}=\frac{18}{24}-\left(\frac{-14}{24}\right)-\frac{21}{24}$$
$$=\frac{18}{24}+\frac{14}{24}+\frac{(-21)}{24}$$
$$=\frac{18+14+(-21)}{24}=\frac{11}{24}$$

19. $$\frac{1}{3}-\frac{1}{4}-\frac{1}{5}=\frac{20}{60}-\frac{15}{60}-\frac{12}{60}$$
$$=\frac{20}{60}+\frac{(-15)}{60}+\frac{(-12)}{60}$$
$$=\frac{20+(-15)+(-12)}{60}=\frac{-7}{60}=-\frac{7}{60}$$

20. $$\frac{5}{16}+\frac{1}{8}-\frac{1}{2}=\frac{5}{16}+\frac{2}{16}-\frac{8}{16}$$
$$=\frac{5}{16}+\frac{2}{16}+\frac{(-8)}{16}$$
$$=\frac{5+2+(-8)}{16}=\frac{-1}{16}=-\frac{1}{16}$$

21. $\frac{1}{2}+\left(-\frac{3}{8}\right)+\frac{5}{12}=\frac{12}{24}+\frac{(-9)}{24}+\frac{10}{24}$
$=\frac{12+(-9)+10}{24}=\frac{13}{24}$

22. $-\frac{3}{8}+\frac{3}{4}-\left(-\frac{3}{16}\right)=\frac{-6}{16}+\frac{12}{16}-\left(\frac{-3}{16}\right)$
$=\frac{-6}{16}+\frac{12}{16}+\frac{3}{16}$
$=\frac{-6+12+3}{16}=\frac{9}{16}$

23. $3.4+(-6.8)=-3.4$

24. $-4.9+3.27=-1.63$

25. $-8.32+(-0.57)=-8.89$

26. $-3.5+7=3.5$

27. $-4.8+(-3.2)=-8.0$

28. $6.2+(-4.29)=1.91$

29. $-4.6+3.92=-0.68$

30. $7.2+(-8.42)=-1.22$

31. $-45.71+(-135.8)=-181.51$

32. $-35.274+12.47=-22.804$

33. $4.2+(-6.8)+5.3=-2.6+5.3=2.7$

34. $6.7+3.2+(-10.5)=9.9+(-10.5)=-0.6$

35. $-4.5+3.2+(-19.4)=-1.3+(-19.4)=-20.7$

36. $2.09-6.72-5.4=2.09+(-6.72)+(-5.4)$
$=-4.63+(-5.4)=-10.03$

37. $-18.39+4.9-23.7=-18.39+4.9+(-23.7)$
$=-13.49+(-23.7)=-37.19$

38. $19-(-3.72)-82.75=19+3.72+(-82.75)$
$=22.72+(-82.75)=-60.03$

39. $-3.09-4.6-27.3=-3.09+(-4.6)+(-27.3)$
$=-7.69+(-27.3)=-34.99$

40. $-3.89+(-2.9)+4.723+0.2$
$=-6.79+4.723+0.2$
$=-2.067+0.2=-1.867$

41. $-4.02+6.809-(-3.57)-(-0.419)$
$=-4.02+6.809+3.57+0.419$
$=2.789+3.57+0.419$
$=6.359+0.419=6.778$

42. $0.0153+(-1.0294)+(-1.0726)$
$=-1.0141+(-1.0726)$
$=-2.0867$

43. $0.27+(-3.5)-(-0.27)+(-5.44)$
$=0.27+(-3.5)+0.27+(-5.44)$
$=-3.23+0.27+(-5.44)$
$=-2.96+(-5.44)$
$=-8.4$

Objective B Exercises

44. $\frac{1}{2}\times\left(-\frac{3}{4}\right)=-\left(\frac{1\cdot 3}{2\cdot 4}\right)=-\frac{3}{8}$

45. $-\frac{2}{9}\times\left(-\frac{3}{14}\right)=\frac{2\cdot 3}{9\cdot 14}=\frac{1}{21}$

46. $\left(-\frac{3}{8}\right)\left(-\frac{4}{15}\right)=\frac{3\cdot 4}{8\cdot 15}=\frac{1}{10}$

47. $\left(-\frac{3}{4}\right)\left(-\frac{8}{27}\right)=\frac{3\cdot 8}{4\cdot 27}=\frac{2}{9}$

48. $-\frac{1}{2}\times\frac{8}{9}=-\left(\frac{1\cdot 8}{2\cdot 9}\right)=-\frac{4}{9}$

49. $\frac{5}{12}\times\left(-\frac{8}{15}\right)=-\left(\frac{5\cdot 8}{12\cdot 15}\right)=-\frac{2}{9}$

50. $\left(-\frac{5}{12}\right)\left(\frac{42}{65}\right)=-\left(\frac{5\cdot 42}{12\cdot 65}\right)=-\frac{7}{26}$

51. $\left(\frac{3}{8}\right)\left(-\frac{15}{41}\right)=-\left(\frac{3\cdot 15}{8\cdot 41}\right)=-\frac{45}{328}$

52. $\left(-\frac{15}{8}\right)\left(-\frac{16}{3}\right)=\frac{15\cdot 16}{8\cdot 3}=10$

53. $\left(-\frac{5}{7}\right)\left(-\frac{14}{15}\right)=\frac{5\cdot 14}{7\cdot 15}=\frac{2}{3}$

54. $\frac{5}{8}\times\left(-\frac{7}{12}\right)\times\frac{16}{25}=-\left(\frac{5\cdot 7\cdot 16}{8\cdot 12\cdot 25}\right)=-\frac{7}{30}$

55. $\left(\frac{1}{2}\right)\left(-\frac{3}{4}\right)\left(-\frac{5}{8}\right)=\frac{1\cdot 3\cdot 5}{2\cdot 4\cdot 8}=\frac{15}{64}$

56. $\frac{1}{3}\div\left(-\frac{1}{2}\right)=\frac{1}{3}\times -\frac{2}{1}=-\left(\frac{1\cdot 2}{3\cdot 1}\right)=-\frac{2}{3}$

57. $-\frac{3}{8}\div\frac{7}{8}=-\frac{3}{8}\times\frac{8}{7}=-\frac{3}{7}$

58. $\left(-\frac{3}{4}\right)\div\left(-\frac{7}{40}\right)=-\frac{3}{4}\times\left(-\frac{40}{7}\right)$
$=\frac{3\cdot 40}{4\cdot 7}$
$=\frac{30}{7}=4\frac{2}{7}$

59. $\frac{5}{6}\div\left(-\frac{3}{4}\right)=\frac{5}{6}\times\left(-\frac{4}{3}\right)$
$=-\left(\frac{5\cdot 4}{6\cdot 3}\right)=-\frac{10}{9}=-1\frac{1}{9}$

60. $-\frac{5}{12} \div \frac{15}{32} = -\frac{5}{12} \times \frac{32}{15}$

$= -\left(\frac{5 \cdot 32}{12 \cdot 15}\right) = -\frac{8}{9}$

61. $-\frac{5}{16} \div \left(-\frac{3}{8}\right) = -\frac{5}{16} \times -\frac{8}{3} = \frac{5 \cdot 8}{16 \cdot 3} = \frac{5}{6}$

62. $\left(-\frac{3}{8}\right) \div \left(-\frac{5}{12}\right) = -\frac{3}{8} \times -\frac{12}{5} = \frac{3 \cdot 12}{8 \cdot 5} = \frac{9}{10}$

63. $-\frac{8}{19} \div \frac{7}{38} = -\frac{8}{19} \times \frac{38}{7}$

$= -\left(\frac{8 \cdot 38}{19 \cdot 7}\right) = -\frac{16}{7} = -2\frac{2}{7}$

64. $-\frac{2}{3} \div 4 = -\frac{2}{3} \times \frac{1}{4} = -\left(\frac{2 \cdot 1}{3 \cdot 4}\right) = -\frac{1}{6}$

65. $-6 \div \frac{4}{9} = -\frac{6}{1} \times \frac{9}{4}$

$= -\left(\frac{6 \cdot 9}{1 \cdot 4}\right) = -\frac{27}{2} = -13\frac{1}{2}$

66. $-6.7 \times (-4.2) = 28.14$

$$\begin{array}{r} 4.2 \\ \times\, 6.7 \\ \hline 294 \\ 252 \\ \hline 28.14 \end{array}$$

67. $-8.9 \times (-3.5) = 8.9 \times 3.5 = 31.15$

$$\begin{array}{r} 8.9 \\ \times\, 3.5 \\ \hline 445 \\ 267 \\ \hline 31.15 \end{array}$$

68. $-1.6 \times 4.9 = -(1.6 \times 4.9) = -7.84$

$$\begin{array}{r} 4.9 \\ \times\, 1.6 \\ \hline 294 \\ 49 \\ \hline 7.84 \end{array}$$

69. $-14.3 \times 7.9 = -(14.3 \times 7.9) = -112.97$

$$\begin{array}{r} 14.3 \\ \times\, 7.9 \\ \hline 1287 \\ 1001 \\ \hline 112.97 \end{array}$$

70. $(-0.78)(-0.15) = (0.78)(0.15) = 0.117$

$$\begin{array}{r} 0.78 \\ \times\, 0.15 \\ \hline 390 \\ 78 \\ \hline 0.1170 \end{array}$$

71. $(-1.21)(-0.03) = (1.21)(0.03) = 0.0363$

$$\begin{array}{r} 1.21 \\ \times\, 0.03 \\ \hline 0.0363 \end{array}$$

72. $(-8.919) \div (-0.9) = 8.919 \div 0.9 = 9.91$

$$\begin{array}{r} 9.91 \\ 0.9\overline{)8.9.19} \\ \underline{81} \\ 81 \\ \underline{81} \\ 09 \\ \underline{-\ 9} \\ 0 \end{array}$$

73. $-77.6 \div (-0.8) = 77.6 \div 0.8 = 97$

$$\begin{array}{r} 97. \\ 0.8\overline{)77.6.} \\ \underline{72} \\ 56 \\ \underline{-56} \\ 0 \end{array}$$

74. $59.01 \div (-0.7) = -(59.01 \div 0.7) = -84.3$

$$\begin{array}{r} 84.3 \\ 0.7\overline{)59.0.1} \\ \underline{-56} \\ 30 \\ \underline{-28} \\ 21 \\ \underline{-21} \\ 0 \end{array}$$

75. $(-7.04) \div (-3.2) = 7.04 \div 3.2 = 2.2$

$$\begin{array}{r} 2.2 \\ 3.2\overline{)7.0.4} \\ \underline{-64} \\ 64 \\ \underline{-64} \\ 0 \end{array}$$

76. $(-84.66) \div 1.7 = -(84.66 \div 1.7) = -49.8$

$$\begin{array}{r} 49.8 \\ 1.7\overline{)84.6.6} \\ \underline{-68} \\ 166 \\ \underline{-153} \\ 136 \\ \underline{-136} \\ 0 \end{array}$$

77. $-3.312 \div (0.8) = -(3.312 \div 0.8) = -4.14$

$$\begin{array}{r} 4.14 \\ 0.8\overline{)3.3.12} \\ \underline{-32} \\ 11 \\ \underline{-8} \\ 32 \\ \underline{-32} \\ 0 \end{array}$$

78. $1.003 \div (-0.59) = -(1.003 \div 0.59) = -1.7$

$$\begin{array}{r} 1.7 \\ 0.59\overline{)1.00.3} \\ -59 \\ \hline 413 \\ -413 \\ \hline 0 \end{array}$$

79. $26.22 \div (-6.9) = -(26.22 \div 6.9) = -3.8$

$$\begin{array}{r} 3.8 \\ 6.9\overline{)26.2.3} \\ -207 \\ \hline 552 \\ -552 \\ \hline 0 \end{array}$$

80. $-19.08 \div 0.45 = -(19.08 \div 0.45) = -42.40$

81. $21.792 \div (-0.96) = -(21.792 \div 0.96) = -22.70$

82. $-38.665 \div (-9.5) = 38.665 \div 9.5 = 4.07$

83. $-3.171 \div (-45.3) = 3.171 \div 45.3 = 0.07$

84. $27.738 \div (-60.3) = -(27.738 \div 60.3) = -0.46$

85. $(-13.97) \div (-25.4) = 13.97 \div 25.4 = 0.55$

Objective C Exercises

86. Strategy To find the difference in temperature, subtract the temperature on January 24 (−48.9°C) from the temperature on January 23 (6.67°C).

Solution $6.67 - (-48.9) = 55.57$
The difference in temperature from January 23 to January 24 was 55.57°C.

87. Strategy To find the amount the temperature fell from 9:00 A.M. subtract the temperature at 9:27 A.M. from the temperature at 9:00 A.M.

Solution $12.22 - (-20) = 32.22$
The temperature fell 32.22°C in 27 min.

88. Strategy To find the difference, subtract the melting point of nitrogen (−209.86°C) from its boiling point (−195.8°C).

Solution $-195.8 - (-209.86) = -195.8 + 209.86$
$= 14.06$
The difference between the boiling point of nitrogen and its melting point is 14.06°C.

89. Strategy To find the difference, subtract the melting point of oxygen (−218.4°C) from its boiling point (−182.962°C).

Solution $-182.962 - (-218.4)$
$= -182.962 + 218.4$
$= 35.438$
The difference between the boiling point of oxygen and its melting point is 35.438°C.

90a. Strategy To find the closing price on the previous day, subtract the change in price (−\$.11) from the closing price on September 15, 2003 (\$47.10).

Solution $47.10 - (-0.11) = 47.10 + 0.11 = 47.21$
The closing price the previous day for General Mills was \$47.21.

b. Strategy To find the closing price on the previous day, subtract the change in price (−\$.08) from the closing price on September 15, 2003 (\$22.42).

Solution $22.42 - (-0.08) = 22.42 + 0.08 = 22.50$
The closing price the previous day for Hormel Foods was \$22.50.

91a. Strategy To find the closing price on the previous day, subtract the change in price (−0.21) from the closing price on September 15, 2003 (19.18).

Solution $19.18 - (-0.21) = 19.18 + 0.21 = 19.39$
The closing price the previous day for Sara Lee Corp. was \$19.39.

b. Strategy To find the closing price on the previous day, subtract the change in price (+\$.11) from the closing price on September 15, 2003 (\$72.57).

Solution $72.57 - (+0.11) = 72.57 - 0.11 = 72.46$
The closing price the previous day for Hershey Foods, Inc., was \$72.46.

Applying the Concepts

92a. True

b. True

c. False

d. False

93. $-\frac{17}{24}$ is one example.

94a. Answers will vary. For example, 0.15.

b. Answers will vary. For example, 1.05.

c. Answers will vary. For example, 0.001.

95. Given any two different rational numbers, it is always possible to find a rational number between them. One method is to add the two numbers and divide by 2.
Another method is to add the numerators and add the denominators. For example, given the fractions $\frac{2}{5}$ and $\frac{3}{4}$, $\frac{2+3}{5+4}=\frac{5}{9}$ and $\frac{2}{5}<\frac{5}{9}<\frac{3}{4}$.

Section 10.5

Objective A Exercises

1. Since the number is greater than 10, move the decimal point 6 places to the left. The exponent on 10 is 6.

$2,370,000 = 2.37 \times 10^6$

2. Since the number is greater than 10, move the decimal point 4 places to the left. The exponent on 10 is 4.

$75,000 = 7.5 \times 10^4$

3. Since the number is less than 1, move the decimal point 4 places to the right. The exponent on 10 is −4.

$0.00045 = 4.5 \times 10^{-4}$

4. Since the number is less than 1, move the decimal point 5 places to the right. The exponent is −5.

$0.000076 = 7.6 \times 10^{-5}$

5. Since the number is greater than 10, move the decimal point 5 places to the left. The exponent on 10 is 5.

$309,000 = 3.09 \times 10^5$

6. Since the number is greater than 10, move the decimal point 8 places to the left. The exponent on 10 is 8.

$819,000,000 = 8.19 \times 10^8$

7. Since the number is less than 1, move the decimal point 7 places to the right. The exponent on 10 is −7.

$0.000000601 = 6.01 \times 10^{-7}$

8. Since the number is less than 1, move the decimal point 10 places to the right. The exponent on 10 is −10.

$0.00000000096 = 9.6 \times 10^{-10}$

9. Since the number is greater than 10, move the decimal point 10 places to the left. The exponent on 10 is 10.

$57,000,000,000 = 5.7 \times 10^{10}$

10. Since the number is greater than 10, move the decimal point 11 places to the left. The exponent on 10 is 11.

$934,800,000,000 = 9.348 \times 10^{11}$

11. Since the number is less than 1, move the decimal point 8 places to the right. The exponent on 10 is −8.

$0.000000017 = 1.7 \times 10^{-8}$

12. Since the number is less than 1, move the decimal point 7 places to the right. The exponent on 10 is −7.

$0.0000009217 = 9.217 \times 10^{-7}$

13. The exponent on 10 is positive. Move the decimal point 5 places to the right.

$7.1 \times 10^5 = 710,000$

14. The exponent on 10 is positive. Move the decimal point 7 places to the right.

$2.3 \times 10^7 = 23,000,000$

15. The exponent on 10 is negative. Move the decimal point 5 places to the left.

$4.3 \times 10^{-5} = 0.000043$

16. The exponent on 10 is negative. Move the decimal point 7 places to the left.

$9.21 \times 10^{-7} = 0.000000921$

17. The exponent on 10 is positive. Move the decimal point 8 places to the right.

$6.71 \times 10^8 = 671,000,000$

18. The exponent on 10 is positive. Move the decimal point 9 places to the right.

$5.75 \times 10^9 = 5,750,000,000$

19. The exponent on 10 is negative. Move the decimal point 6 places to the left.

$7.13 \times 10^{-6} = 0.00000713$

20. The exponent on 10 is negative. Move the decimal point 8 places to the left.

$3.54 \times 10^{-8} = 0.0000000354$

21. The exponent on 10 is positive. Move the decimal point 12 places to the right.

$5 \times 10^{12} = 5,000,000,000,000$

22. The exponent on 10 is positive. Move the decimal point 11 places to the right.

$1.0987 \times 10^{11} = 109,870,000,000$

23. The exponent on 10 is negative. Move the decimal point 3 places to the left.

$8.01 \times 10^{-3} = 0.00801$

24. The exponent on 10 is negative. Move the decimal point 9 places to the left.

$4.0162 \times 10^{-9} = 0.0000000040162$

25. The number is greater than 10. Move the decimal point 10 places to the left. The exponent on 10 is 10.

$16{,}000{,}000{,}000$ mi $= 1.6 \times 10^{10}$ mi

26. The number is greater than 10. Move the decimal point 24 places to the left. The exponent on 10 is 24.
$5{,}980{,}000{,}000{,}000{,}000{,}000{,}000{,}000$ kg
$= 5.98 \times 10^{24}$ kg

27. The monetary cost is \$3.1 trillion. The exponent on 10 is 12.

$\$3.1 \times 10^{12}$

28. The number is less than 1. Move the decimal point 19 places to the right. The exponent on 10 is −19.

0.00000000000000000016 coulomb
$= 1.6 \times 10^{-19}$ coulomb

29. The number is less than 1. Move the decimal point 6 places to the right. The exponent on 10 is −6.

0.0000037 m $= 3.7 \times 10^{-6}$ m

30. The number is less than 1. Move the decimal point 12 places to the right. The exponent on 10 is −12.

$0.000000000001 = 1 \times 10^{-12}$

Objective B Exercises

31. $8 \div 4 + 2 = 2 + 2 = 4$

32. $3 - 12 \div 2 = 3 - 6 = 3 + (-6) = -3$

33. $4 + (-7) + 3 = -3 + 3 = 0$

34. $-16 \div 2 + 8 = -8 + 8 = 0$

35. $4^2 - 4 = 16 - 4 = 16 + (-4) = 12$

36. $6 - 2^2 = 6 - 4 = 6 + (-4) = 2$

37. $2 \times (3 - 5) - 2 = 2 \times [3 + (-5)] - 2$
$= 2 \times (-2) - 2$
$= 4 - 2$
$= -4 + (-2) = -6$

38. $2 - (8 - 10) \div 2 = 2 - [8 + (-10)] \div 2$
$= 2 - (-2) \div 2$
$= 2 - (-1) = 2 + 1 = 3$

39. $4 - (-3)^2 = 4 - 9 = 4 + (-9) = -5$

40. $(-2)^2 - 6 = 4 - 6 = 4 + (-6) = -2$

41. $4 - (-3) - 5 = 4 + 3 + (-5)$
$= 7 + (-5) = 2$

42. $6 + (-8) - (-3) = 6 + (-8) + 3$
$= -2 + 3 = 1$

43. $4 - (-2)^2 + (-3) = 4 - 4 + (-3)$
$= 4 + (-4) + (-3)$
$= 0 + (-3) = -3$

44. $-3 + (-6)^2 - 1 = -3 + 36 - 1$
$= -3 + 36 + (-1)$
$= 33 + (-1) = 32$

45. $3^2 - 4 \times 2 = 9 - 4 \times 2$
$= 9 - 8 = 9 + (-8) = 1$

46. $9 \div 3 - (-3)^2 = 9 \div 3 - 9$
$= 3 - 9 = 3 + (-9) = -6$

47. $3 \times (6 - 2) \div 6 = 3 \times [6 + (-2)] \div 6$
$= 3 \times 4 \div 6 = 12 \div 6 = 2$

48. $4 \times (2 - 7) \div 5 = 4 \times [2 + (-7)] \div 5$
$= 4 \times (-5) \div 5 = -20 \div 5 = -4$

49. $2^2 - (-3)^2 + 2 = 4 - 9 + 2$
$= 4 + (-9) + 2$
$= -5 + 2 = -3$

50. $3 \times (8 - 5) + 4 = 3 \times [8 + (-5)] + 4$
$= 3 \times 3 + 4 = 9 + 4 = 13$

51. $6 - 2 \times (1 - 5) = 6 - 2 \times [1 + (-5)]$
$= 6 - 2 \times (-4)$
$= 6 - (-8) = 6 + 8 = 14$

52. $4 \times 2 \times (3 - 6) = 4 \times 2 \times [3 + (-6)]$
$= 4 \times 2 \times (-3)$
$= 8 \times (-3) = -24$

53. $(-2)^2 - (-3)^2 + 1 = 4 - 9 + 1$
$= 4 + (-9) + 1$
$= -5 + 1 = -4$

54. $4^2 - 3^2 - 4 = 16 - 9 - 4$
$= 16 + (-9) + (-4)$
$= 7 + (-4) = 3$

55. $6 - (-3) \times (-3)^2 = 6 - (-3) \times 9$
$= 6 - (-27) = 6 + 27 = 33$

56. $4 - (-5) \times (-2)^2 = 4 - (-5) \times 4$
$= 4 - (-20) = 4 + 20 = 24$

57. $4 \times 2 - 3 \times 7 = 8 - 3 \times 7$
$= 8 - 21 = 8 + (-21) = -13$

58. $16 \div 2 - 9 \div 3 = 8 - 9 \div 3$
$= 8 - 3 = 8 + (-3) = 5$

59. $(-2)^2 - 5 \times 3 - 1 = 4 - 5 \times 3 - 1$
$= 4 - 15 - 1$
$= 4 + (-15) + (-1)$
$= -11 + (-1) = -12$

60. $4 - 2 \times 7 - 3^2 = 4 - 2 \times 7 - 9$
$= 4 - 14 - 9$
$= 4 + (-14) + (-9)$
$= -10 + (-9) = -19$

61. $7 \times 6 - 5 \times 6 + 3 \times 2 - 2 + 1$
$= 42 - 5 \times 6 + 3 \times 2 - 2 + 1$
$= 42 - 30 + 3 \times 2 - 2 + 1$
$= 42 - 30 + 6 - 2 + 1$
$= 42 + (-30) + 6 + (-2) + 1$
$= 12 + 6 + (-2) + 1$
$= 18 + (-2) + 1$
$= 16 + 1 = 17$

62. $3 \times 2^2 + 5 \times (3 + 2) - 17$
$= 3 \times 2^2 + 5 \times 5 - 17$
$= 3 \times 4 + 5 \times 5 - 17$
$= 12 + 5 \times 5 - 17$
$= 12 + 25 - 17$
$= 12 + 25 + (-17)$
$= 37 + (-17) = 20$

63. $-4 \times 3 \times (-2) + 12 \times (3 - 4) + (-12)$
$= -4 \times 3 \times (-2) + 12 \times [3 + (-4)] + (-12)$
$= -4 \times 3 \times (-2) + 12 \times (-1) + (-12)$
$= -12 \times (-2) + 12 \times (-1) + (-12)$
$= 24 + 12 \times (-1) + (-12)$
$= 24 + (-12) + (-12)$
$= 12 + (-12) = 0$

64. $3 \times 4^2 - 16 - 4 + 3 - (1 - 2)^2$
$= 3 \times 4^2 - 16 - 4 + 3 - [1 + (-2)]^2$
$= 3 \times 4^2 - 16 - 4 + 3 - (-1)^2$
$= 3 \times 16 - 16 - 4 + 3 - 1$
$= 48 - 16 - 4 + 3 - 1$
$= 48 + (-16) + (-4) + 3 + (-1)$
$= 32 + (-4) + 3 + (-1)$
$= 28 + 3 + (-1)$
$= 31 + (-1) = 30$

65. $-12 \times (6 - 8) + 1^2 \times 3^2 \times 2 - 6 \times 2$
$= -12 \times [6 + (-8)] + 1^2 \times 3^2 \times 2 - 6 \times 2$
$= -12 \times (-2) + 1^2 \times 3^2 \times 2 - 6 \times 2$
$= -12 \times (-2) + 1 \times 9 \times 2 - 6 \times 2$
$= 24 + 1 \times 9 \times 2 - 6 \times 2$
$= 24 + 18 - 6 \times 2$
$= 24 + 18 - 12$
$= 24 + 18 + (-12)$
$= 42 + (-12) = 30$

66. $-3 \times (-2)^2 \times 4 \div 8 - (-12)$
$= -3 \times 4 \times 4 \div 8 - (-12)$
$= -12 \times 4 \div 8 - (-12)$
$= -48 \div 8 - (-12)$
$= -6 - (-12)$
$= -6 + 12 = 6$

67. $10 \times 9 - (8 + 7) \div 5 + 6 - 7 + 8$
$= 10 \times 9 - 15 \div 5 + 6 - 7 + 8$
$= 90 - 15 \div 5 + 6 - 7 + 8$
$= 90 - 3 + 6 - 7 + 8$
$= 90 + (-3) + 6 + (-7) + 8$
$= 87 + 6 + (-7) + 8$
$= 93 + (-7) + 8$
$= 86 + 8 = 94$

68. $-27 - (-3)^2 - 2 - 7 + 6 \times 3$
$= -27 - 9 - 2 - 7 + 6 \times 3$
$= -27 - 9 - 2 - 7 + 18$
$= -27 + (-9) + (-2) + (-7) + 18$
$= -36 + (-2) + (-7) + 18$
$= -38 + (-7) + 18$
$= -45 + 18 = -27$

69. $3^2 \times (4 - 7) \div 9 + 6 - 3 - 4 \times 2$
$= 3^2 \times [4 + (-7)] \div 9 + 6 - 3 - 4 \times 2$
$= 3^2 \times (-3) \div 9 + 6 - 3 - 4 \times 2$
$= 9 \times (-3) \div 9 + 6 - 3 - 4 \times 2$
$= -27 \div 9 + 6 - 3 - 4 \times 2$
$= -3 + 6 - 3 - 4 \times 2$
$= -3 + 6 - 3 - 8$
$= -3 + 6 + (-3) + (-8)$
$= 3 + (-3) + (-8)$
$= 0 + (-8) = -8$

70. $16 - 4 \times 8 + 4^2 - (-18) \div (-9)$
$= 16 - 4 \times 8 + 16 - (-18) \div (-9)$
$= 16 - 32 + 16 - (-18) \div (-9)$
$= 16 - 32 + 16 - 2$
$= 16 + (-32) + 16 + (-2)$
$= -16 + 16 + (-2)$
$= 0 + (-2) = -2$

71. $(-3)^2 \times (5 - 7)^2 - (-9) \div 3$
$= (-3)^2 \times [5 + (-7)]^2 - (-9) \div 3$
$= (-3)^2 \times (-2)^2 - (-9) \div 3$
$= 9 \times 4 - (-9) \div 3$
$= 36 - (-9 \div 3)$
$= 36 - (-3)$
$= 36 + 3 = 39$

72. $-2 \times 4^2 - 3 \times (2 - 8) - 3$
$= -2 \times 4^2 - 3 \times [2 + (-8)] - 3$
$= -2 \times 4^2 - 3 \times (-6) - 3$
$= -2 \times 16 - 3 \times (-6) - 3$
$= -32 - 3 \times (-6) - 3$
$= -32 - (-18) - 3$
$= -32 + 18 - 3$
$= -14 - 3 = -14 + (-3) = -17$

73. $4 - 6(2 - 5)^3 \div (17 - 8)$
$= 4 - 6[2 + (-5)]^3 \div [17 + (-8)]$
$= 4 - 6(-3)^3 \div 9$
$= 4 - 6(-27) \div 9$
$= 4 - (-162) \div 9$
$= 4 - (-18) = 4 + 18 = 22$

74. $5 + 7(3 - 8)^2 \div (-14 + 9)$
$= 5 + 7[3 + (-8)]^2 \div (-14 + 9)$
$= 5 + 7(-5)^2 \div (-5)$
$= 5 + 7(25) \div (-5)$
$= 5 + 175 \div (-5)$
$= 5 + (-35) = -30$

75. $(1.2)^2 - 4.1 \times 0.3 = 1.44 - 4.1 \times 0.3$
$= 1.44 - 1.23$
$= 1.44 + (-1.23) = 0.21$

76. $2.4 \times (-3) - 2.5 = -7.2 - 2.5$
$= -7.2 + (-2.5) = -9.7$

77. $1.6 - (-1.6)^2 = 1.6 - 2.56$
$= 1.6 + (-2.56) = -0.96$

78. $4.1 \times 8 \div (-4.1) = 32.8 \div (-4.1) = -8$

79. $(4.1 - 3.9) - 0.7^2 = [4.1 + (-3.9)] - 0.7^2$
$= 0.2 - 0.7^2$
$= 0.2 - 0.49$
$= 0.2 + (-0.49) = -0.29$

80. $1.8 \times (-2.3) - 2 = -4.14 - 2$
$= -4.14 + (-2) = -6.14$

81. $(-0.4)^2 \times 1.5 - 2 = 0.16 \times 1.5 - 2$
$= 0.24 - 2$
$= 0.24 + (-2) = -1.76$

82. $(6.2 - 1.3) \times (-3) = [6.2 + (-1.3)] \times (-3)$
$= 4.9 \times (-3) = -14.7$

83. $4.2 - (-3.9) - 6 = 4.2 + 3.9 + (-6)$
$= 8.1 + (-6) = 2.1$

84. $-\frac{1}{2} + \frac{3}{8} \div \left(-\frac{3}{4}\right) = -\frac{1}{2} + \left(\frac{3}{8} \times -\frac{4}{3}\right)$
$= -\frac{1}{2} + \left(-\frac{1}{2}\right) = -\frac{2}{2} = -1$

85. $\left(\frac{3}{4}\right)^2 - \frac{3}{8} = \frac{9}{16} - \frac{3}{8}$
$= \frac{9}{16} - \frac{6}{16} = \frac{3}{16}$

86. $\left(\frac{1}{2}\right)^2 - \left(-\frac{1}{2}\right)^2 = \frac{1}{4} - \frac{1}{4} = 0$

87. $\frac{5}{16} - \frac{3}{8} + \frac{1}{2} = \frac{5}{16} - \frac{6}{16} + \frac{1}{2}$
$= \frac{5}{16} + \left(-\frac{6}{16}\right) + \frac{1}{2}$
$= -\frac{1}{16} + \frac{1}{2} = -\frac{1}{16} + \frac{8}{16} = \frac{7}{16}$

88. $\frac{2}{7} \div \frac{5}{7} - \frac{3}{14} = \frac{2}{7} \times \frac{7}{5} - \frac{3}{14}$
$= \frac{2}{5} - \frac{3}{14}$
$= \frac{28}{70} - \frac{15}{70} = \frac{13}{70}$

89. $\frac{1}{2} \times \frac{1}{4} \times \frac{1}{2} - \frac{3}{8} = \frac{1}{8} \times \frac{1}{2} - \frac{3}{8}$
$= \frac{1}{16} - \frac{3}{8}$
$= \frac{1}{16} + \left(-\frac{3}{8}\right) = \frac{1}{16} + \left(-\frac{6}{16}\right) = -\frac{5}{16}$

90. $\frac{2}{3} \times \frac{5}{8} \div \frac{2}{7} = \frac{5}{12} \div \frac{2}{7}$
$= \frac{5}{12} \times \frac{7}{2} = \frac{35}{24} = 1\frac{11}{24}$

91. $\frac{1}{2} - \left(\frac{3}{4} - \frac{3}{8}\right) \div \frac{1}{3} = \frac{1}{2} - \left(\frac{6}{8} - \frac{3}{8}\right) \div \frac{1}{3}$
$= \frac{1}{2} - \frac{3}{8} \div \frac{1}{3} = \frac{1}{2} - \frac{3}{8} \times \frac{3}{1}$
$= \frac{1}{2} - \frac{9}{8} = \frac{4}{8} + \left(-\frac{9}{8}\right) = -\frac{5}{8}$

92. $\frac{3}{8} \div \left(-\frac{1}{2}\right)^2 + 2 = \frac{3}{8} \div \frac{1}{4} + 2$
$= \frac{3}{8} \times \frac{4}{1} + 2$
$= \frac{3}{2} + 2 = 1\frac{1}{2} + 2 = 3\frac{1}{2}$

Applying the Concepts

93a. $3.45 \times 10^{-14} > 3.45 \times 10^{-15}$

b. $5.23 \times 10^{18} > 5.23 \times 10^{17}$

c. $3.12 \times 10^{12} > 3.12 \times 10^{11}$

94. $\frac{3 \times 10^8}{\text{s}} \times \frac{3600 \text{ s}}{\text{h}} \times \frac{24 \text{ h}}{\text{day}} \times \frac{365 \text{ days}}{\text{yr}}$
$= 9.4608 \times 10^{15}\text{m}$

95a. $1^3 + 2^3 + 3^3 + 4^3 = 1 + 8 + 27 + 64 = 100$

b. $(-1)^3 + (-2)^3 + (-3)^3 + (-4)^3$
$= -1 + (-8) + (-27) + (-64)$
$= -100$

c. $1^3 + 2^3 + 3^3 + 4^3 + 5^3$
$= 1 + 8 + 27 + 64 + 125$
$= 225$

d. $(-1)^3 + (-2)^3 + (-3)^3 + (-4)^3 + (-5)^3 = -225$

96. $2^{(3^2)} = 2^9 = 512$
$(2^3)^2 = 8^2 = 64$
No. $2^{(3^2)}$ is larger.

97. Because the first statement is false (it was either Becky or Diana), neither Becky nor Diana could have done it. Therefore, it was either Abdul or Carl. Because the second statement is false, (it was neither Becky nor Carl), either Becky or Carl did it. Because the first statement ensured that it was Abdul or Carl, it must have been Carl.

98. Check that students state that, for a number to be written in scientific notation, it must be the product of a number between 1 and 10 and a power of 10, where the exponent on 10 is an integer.

99a. 1.99×10^{30} kg

b. 1.67×10^{-27} kg

Chapter 10 Review Exercises

1. -22

2. $-8-(-2)-(-10)-3 = -8+2+10-3$
$= -6+10-3 = 4-3 = 1$

3. $\frac{5}{8}-\frac{5}{6} = \frac{15}{24}-\frac{20}{24}$
$= \frac{15}{24}+\frac{(-20)}{24} = \frac{15+(-20)}{24} = \frac{-5}{24} = -\frac{5}{24}$

4. $-0.33+1.98-1.44 = -0.33+1.98+(-1.44)$
$= 1.65+(-1.44) = 0.21$

5. $\left(-\frac{2}{3}\right)\left(\frac{6}{11}\right)\left(-\frac{22}{25}\right) = \frac{2\cdot 6\cdot 22}{3\cdot 11\cdot 25} = \frac{8}{25}$

6. $-0.08 \times 16 = -(0.08 \times 16) = -1.28$

$$\begin{array}{r} 16 \\ \times .08 \\ \hline 1.28 \end{array}$$

7. $12-6\div 3 = 12-2 = 12+(-2) = 10$

8. $\left(\frac{2}{3}\right)^2-\frac{5}{6} = \left(\frac{2}{3}\cdot\frac{2}{3}\right)-\frac{5}{6}$
$= \frac{4}{9}-\frac{5}{6} = \frac{8}{18}-\frac{15}{18}$
$= \frac{8}{18}+\left(-\frac{15}{18}\right) = \frac{8+(-15)}{18} = -\frac{7}{18}$

9. 4

10. $0 > -3$

11. $-|-6| = -6$

12. $-18\div(-3) = 18\div 3 = 6$

13. $-\frac{3}{8}+\frac{5}{12}+\frac{2}{3} = \frac{-9}{24}+\frac{10}{24}+\frac{16}{24}$
$= \frac{-9+10+16}{24} = \frac{17}{24}$

14. $\frac{1}{3}\times\left(-\frac{3}{4}\right) = -\left(\frac{1}{3}\times\frac{3}{4}\right) = -\frac{1}{4}$

15. $-\frac{7}{12}\div\left(-\frac{14}{39}\right) = -\frac{7}{12}\times\left(-\frac{39}{14}\right)$
$= \frac{7\cdot 39}{12\cdot 14} = \frac{13}{8} = 1\frac{5}{8}$

16. $16\div 4(8-2) = 16\div 4[8+(-2)]$
$= 16\div 4(6) = 4(6) = 24$

17. $-22+14+(-18) = -8+(-18) = -26$

18. $3^2-9+2 = 9-9+2$
$= 9+(-9)+2$
$= 0+2 = 2$

19. The number is less than 1. Move the decimal point 5 places to the right. The exponent on 10 is -5.

$0.0000397 = 3.97 \times 10^{-5}$

20. $-1.464\div 18.3 = -(1.464\div 18.3) = -0.08$

$$\begin{array}{r} 0.08 \\ 18.3\overline{)1.4.64} \\ -1464 \\ \hline 0 \end{array}$$

21. $-\frac{5}{12}+\frac{7}{9}-\frac{1}{3} = \frac{-15}{36}+\frac{28}{36}-\frac{12}{36}$
$= \frac{-15}{36}+\frac{28}{36}+\frac{(-12)}{36}$
$= \frac{-15+28+(-12)}{36} = \frac{1}{36}$

22. $\frac{6}{34}\times\frac{17}{40} = \frac{6\cdot 17}{34\cdot 40} = \frac{3}{40}$

23. $1.2\times(-0.035) = -(1.2\times 0.035) = -0.042$

$$\begin{array}{r} 0.035 \\ \times 1.2 \\ \hline 70 \\ 35 \\ \hline 0.042 \end{array}$$

24. $-\frac{1}{2}+\frac{3}{8}\div\frac{9}{20} = -\frac{1}{2}+\frac{3}{8}\times\frac{20}{9}$
$= -\frac{1}{2}+\frac{3\cdot 20}{8\cdot 9}$
$= -\frac{1}{2}+\frac{5}{6} = -\frac{3}{6}+\frac{5}{6} = \frac{2}{6} = \frac{1}{3}$

25. $|-5| = 5$

26. $-2 > -40$

27. $2\times(-13) = -(2\times 13) = -26$

28. $-0.4\times 5-(-3.33) = -2-(-3.33)$
$= -2+3.33 = 1.33$

29. $\frac{5}{12}+\left(-\frac{2}{3}\right) = \frac{5}{12}+\frac{(-8)}{12}$
$= \frac{5+(-8)}{12} = \frac{-3}{12} = \frac{-1}{4} = -\frac{1}{4}$

30. $-33.4+9.8-(-16.2) = -33.4+9.8+16.2$
$= -23.6+16.2 = -7.4$

31. $\left(-\frac{3}{8}\right)\div\left(-\frac{4}{5}\right) = -\frac{3}{8}\times\left(-\frac{5}{4}\right) = \frac{3\cdot 5}{8\cdot 4} = \frac{15}{32}$

32. The exponent on 10 is positive. Move the decimal point 5 places to the right.

$2.4 \times 10^5 = 240{,}000$

33. Strategy To find the temperature, add the increase (18°) to the original temperature (−22°).

Solution $-22 + 18 = -4$
The temperature is −4°.

34. Strategy To find the student's score:
- Multiply the number of questions answered correctly (38) by 3.
Multiply the number of questions left blank (8) by −1.
Multiply the number of questions answered incorrectly (4) by −2.
- Add the three products.

Solution $38 \times 3 = 114$
$8 \times -1 = -8$
$4 \times -2 = -8$
$114 + (-8) + (-8) = 106 + (-8) = 98$
The student's score was 98.

35. Strategy To find the difference between the boiling point and the melting point of mercury, subtract the melting point (−38.87°C) from the boiling point (356.58°C).

Solution $356.58 - (-38.87) = 395.45$
The difference between the boiling and melting points is 395.45°C.

Chapter 10 Test

1. $-5 - (-8) = -5 + 8 = 3$

2. $-|-2| = -2$

3. $-\frac{2}{5} + \frac{7}{15} = \frac{-6}{15} + \frac{7}{15} = \frac{-6+7}{15} = \frac{1}{15}$

4. $0.032 \times (-1.9) = -(0.032 \times 1.9) = -0.0608$

$$\begin{array}{r} 0.032 \\ \times\ 1.9 \\ \hline 288 \\ 32 \\ \hline 0.0608 \end{array}$$

5. $-8 > -10$

6. $1.22 + (-3.1) = -1.88$

7. $4 \times (4 - 7) \div (-2) - 4 \times 8$
$= 4 \times [4 + (-7)] \div (-2) - 4 \times 8$
$= 4 \times (-3) \div (-2) - 4 \times 8$
$= -12 \div (-2) - 4 \times 8$
$= 6 - 4 \times 8$
$= 6 - 32$
$= 6 + (-32) = -26$

8. $-5 \times (-6) \times 3 = 5 \times 6 \times 3 = 30 \times 3 = 90$

9. $-1.004 - 3.01 = -1.004 + (-3.01) = -4.014$

10. $-72 \div 8 = -(72 \div 8) = -9$

11. $-2 + 3 + (-8) = 1 + (-8) = -7$

12. $-\frac{3}{8} + \frac{2}{3} = \frac{-9}{24} + \frac{16}{24} = \frac{-9+16}{24} = \frac{7}{24}$

13. The number is greater than 10. Move the decimal point 10 places to the left. The exponent on 10 is 10.

$87{,}600{,}000{,}000 = 8.76 \times 10^{10}$

14. $-4 \times 12 = -(4 \times 12) = -48$

15. $\frac{0}{-17} = 0$

16. $16 - 4 - (-5) - 7 = 16 + (-4) + 5 + (-7)$
$= 12 + 5 + (-7)$
$= 17 + (-7) = 10$

17. $-\frac{2}{3} \div \frac{5}{6} = -\frac{2}{3} \times \frac{6}{5} = -\left(\frac{2 \cdot 6}{3 \cdot 5}\right) = -\frac{4}{5}$

18. $0 > -4$

19. $16 + (-10) + (-20) = 6 + (-20) = -14$

20. $(-2)^2 - (-3)^2 \div (1 - 4)^2 \times 2 - 6$
$= (-2)^2 - (-3)^2 \div [1 + (-4)]^2 \times 2 - 6$
$= (-2)^2 - (-3)^2 \div (-3)^2 \times 2 - 6$
$= 4 - 9 \div 9 \times 2 - 6$
$= 4 - 1 \times 2 - 6$
$= 4 - 2 - 6$
$= 4 + (-2) + (-6)$
$= 2 + (-6) = -4$

21. $-\frac{2}{5} - \left(\frac{-7}{10}\right) = \frac{-4}{10} - \left(-\frac{7}{10}\right)$
$= \frac{-4}{10} + \frac{7}{10} = \frac{-4+7}{10} = \frac{3}{10}$

22. The exponent on 10 is negative. Move the decimal point 8 places to the left.

$9.601 \times 10^{-8} = 0.00000009601$

23. $-15.64 \div (-4.6) = (15.64 \div 4.6) = 3.4$

$$\begin{array}{r} 3.4 \\ 4.6\overline{)15.64} \\ -13\,8 \\ \hline 1\,84 \\ -1\,84 \\ \hline 0 \end{array}$$

24. $-\frac{1}{2}+\frac{1}{3}+\frac{1}{4}=\frac{-6}{12}+\frac{4}{12}+\frac{3}{12}$
$=\frac{-6+4+3}{12}=\frac{1}{12}$

25. $\frac{3}{8}\times\left(-\frac{5}{6}\right)\times\left(-\frac{4}{15}\right)=\frac{3}{8}\times\frac{5}{6}\times\frac{4}{15}$
$=\frac{3\cdot5\cdot4}{8\cdot6\cdot15}=\frac{1}{12}$

26. $2.113-(-1.1)=2.113+1.1=3.213$

27. **Strategy** To find the temperature, add the increase (11°C) to the previous temperature (−4°C).

Solution $-4+11=7$
The temperature is 7°C.

28. **Strategy** To find the melting point of oxygen, multiply the melting point of radon (−71°C) by 3.

Solution $-71\times3=-213$
The melting point of oxygen is −213°C.

29. **Strategy** To find the amount the temperature fell, subtract the temperature at midnight (−29.4°C) from the temperature at noon (17.22°C).

Solution $17.22-(-29.4)=46.62$
The temperature fell 46.62°C.

30. **Strategy** To find the average daily low temperature:
- Add the three temperature readings.
- Divide by 3.

Solution $-7+9+(-8)=2+(-8)=-6$
$-6\div3=-2$
The average low temperature was −2°F.

Cumulative Review Exercises

1. $16-4\cdot(3-2)^2\cdot4=16-4\cdot(1)^2\cdot4$
$=16-4\cdot(1)\cdot4=16-16=0$

2. $8\frac{1}{2}=8\frac{7}{14}=7\frac{21}{14}$
$-3\frac{4}{7}=3\frac{8}{14}=3\frac{8}{14}$
$4\frac{13}{14}$

3. $3\frac{7}{8}\div1\frac{1}{2}=\frac{31}{8}\div\frac{3}{2}$
$=\frac{31}{8}\times\frac{2}{3}$
$=\frac{31}{12}=2\frac{7}{12}$

4. $\frac{3}{8}\div\left(\frac{3}{8}-\frac{1}{4}\right)\div\frac{7}{3}=\frac{3}{8}\div\left(\frac{3}{8}-\frac{2}{8}\right)\div\frac{7}{3}$
$=\frac{3}{8}\div\left(\frac{1}{8}\right)\div\frac{7}{3}=\frac{3}{8}\times\frac{8}{1}\div\frac{7}{3}$
$=3\div\frac{7}{3}=3\times\frac{3}{7}=\frac{3\cdot3}{7}=\frac{9}{7}=1\frac{2}{7}$

5.
$$\begin{array}{r}2.90700\\-1.09761\\\hline1.80939\end{array}$$

6. $\frac{7}{12}=\frac{n}{32}$
$7\cdot32=12\times n$
$224=12\times n$
$224\div12=n$
$18.67\approx n$

7. $160\%\times n=22$
$1.6\times n=22$
$n=22\div1.6$
$n=13.75$

8. 7 qt = 1 gal 3 qt

9. 6692 ml = 6.692 L

10. $4.2\text{ ft}=4.2\text{ ft}\times\frac{1\text{ m}}{3.28\text{ ft}}=\frac{4.2}{3.28}\text{ m}\approx1.28\text{ m}$

11. Percent × base = amount
$0.32\times180=n$
$57.6=n$

12. $3\frac{2}{5}\times100\%=\frac{1700}{5}\%=340\%$

13. $-8+5=-3$

14. $3\frac{1}{4}+\left(-6\frac{5}{8}\right)=\frac{13}{4}+\left(\frac{-53}{8}\right)=\frac{26}{8}+\frac{(-53)}{8}$
$=\frac{26+(-53)}{8}=\frac{-27}{8}=-3\frac{3}{8}$

15. $-6\frac{1}{8}-4\frac{5}{12}=\frac{-49}{8}-\frac{53}{12}$
$=\frac{-147}{24}-\frac{106}{24}=\frac{-147}{24}+\frac{(-106)}{24}$
$=\frac{-147+(-106)}{24}=\frac{-253}{24}=-10\frac{13}{24}$

16. $-12-(-7)-3(-8)=-12+7+24=-5+24=19$

17. $-3.2\times-1.09=3.2\times1.09=3.488$
$$\begin{array}{r}1.09\\\times3.2\\\hline218\\327\\\hline3.488\end{array}$$

18. $-6\times7\times\left(-\frac{3}{4}\right)=6\times7\times\frac{3}{4}$
$=\frac{6\cdot7\cdot3}{4}=\frac{126}{4}=\frac{63}{2}=31\frac{1}{2}$

19. $42\div(-6)=-(42\div6)=-7$

20. $-2\frac{1}{7} \div \left(-3\frac{3}{5}\right) = \frac{15}{7} \div \left(\frac{18}{5}\right)$

$= \frac{15}{7} \times \left(\frac{5}{18}\right) = \frac{25}{42}$

21. $3 \times (3-7) \div 6 - 2 = 3 \times [3 + (-7)] \div 6 - 2$

$= 3 \times (-4) \div 6 - 2$

$= -12 \div 6 - 2$

$= -2 + (-2) = -4$

22. $4 - (-2)^2 \div (1-2)^2 \times 3 + 4$

$= 4 - (-2)^2 \div [1 + (-2)]^2 \times 3 + 4$

$= 4 - (-2)^2 \div (-1)^2 \times 3 + 4$

$= 4 - 4 \div 1 \times 3 + 4$

$= 4 - 4 \times 3 + 4$

$= 4 - 12 + 4$

$= 4 + (-12) + 4$

$= -8 + 4 = -4$

23. Strategy To find the length of the remaining board, subtract the length cut $\left(5\frac{2}{3}\text{ ft}\right)$ from the original length (8 ft).

Solution

$8 \text{ ft} = 7\frac{3}{3} \text{ ft}$

$-5\frac{2}{3} \text{ ft} = 5\frac{2}{3} \text{ ft}$

$2\frac{1}{3} \text{ ft}$

The length remaining is $2\frac{1}{3}$ ft.

24. Strategy To find Nimisha's new balance:

- Subtract the amounts of the checks written.
- Add the amount of the deposit.

Solution

$763.56

– 135.88

627.68

– 47.81

579.87

+ 223.44

$803.31

Nimisha's new balance is $803.31.

25. Strategy To find the percent:

- Subtract the sale price ($120) from the original price ($165) to find the amount of the decrease.
- Solve the basic percent equation for percent. The base is $165 and the amount is the amount of the decrease.

Solution $165 – $120 = $45

Percent × base = amount

$n \times 165 = 45$

$n = 45 \div 165$

$n \approx 0.273 = 27.3\%$

The percent decrease is 27.3%.

26. Strategy To find how many gallons of coffee must be prepared:

- Multiply the number of guests (80) by the amount of coffee each guest is expected to drink (2 c) to find the number of cups of coffee to prepare.
- Convert cups to gallons.

Solution $80 \times 2 \text{ c} = 160 \text{ c}$

$160 \text{ c} = 160 \cancel{\text{c}} \times \frac{1 \cancel{\text{pt}}}{2 \cancel{\text{c}}} \times \frac{1 \cancel{\text{qt}}}{2 \cancel{\text{pt}}} \times \frac{1 \text{ gal}}{4 \cancel{\text{qt}}}$

$= \frac{160}{16} \text{ gal} = 10 \text{ gal}$

The amount of coffee that should be prepared is 10 gal.

27. Strategy To find the dividend per share:

- Solve the basic percent equation for amount to find the amount of the increase. The base amount is $1.50 and the percent is 12%.
- Add the amount of the increase to the dividend ($1.50).

Solution

$12\% \times 1.50 = n$

$0.12 \times 1.50 = n$

$0.18 = n$

1.50

+ 0.18

1.68

The dividend per share after the increase was $1.68.

28. Strategy To find the median:

- Arrange the hourly wages in order from least to greatest.
- Pick the middle number.

Solution $9.32; $10.73; <u>$11.40</u>; $13.10; $15.25

The median hourly pay is $11.40.

29. Strategy To find the number of voters, write and solve a proportion.

Solution

$\frac{5}{8} = \frac{n}{960{,}000}$

$5 \times 960{,}000 = 8 \times n$

$4{,}800{,}000 = 8 \times n$

$4{,}800{,}000 \div 8 = n$

$600{,}000 = n$

600,000 people would vote.

30. Strategy To find the average high temperature, add the daily high temperatures (−19°, −7°, 1°, and 9°) and divide that sum by the number of temperatures (4).

Solution $(-19) + (-7) + (1) + (9)$

$= -26 + 1 + 9$

$= -25 + 9$

$= -16$ = sum of temperatures

$-16 \div 4 = -4$

The average high temperature is −4°.

Chapter 11: Introduction to Algebra

Prep Test

1. -7

2. -20

3. 0

4. 1

5. 1

6. $\left(\frac{3}{5}\right)^3 \cdot \left(\frac{5}{9}\right)^2 = \frac{3}{5} \cdot \frac{3}{5} \cdot \frac{3}{5} \cdot \frac{5}{9} \cdot \frac{5}{9} = \frac{\overset{1}{\cancel{3}} \cdot \overset{1}{\cancel{3}} \cdot \overset{1}{\cancel{3}} \cdot \overset{1}{\cancel{5}} \cdot \overset{1}{\cancel{5}}}{\underset{1}{\cancel{5}} \cdot \underset{1}{\cancel{5}} \cdot 5 \cdot \underset{1}{\cancel{3}} \cdot \underset{1}{\cancel{3}} \cdot \underset{1}{\cancel{3}} \cdot 3} = \frac{1}{15}$

7. $\frac{2}{3} + \left(\frac{3}{4}\right)^2 \cdot \frac{2}{9} = \frac{2}{3} + \frac{9}{16} \cdot \frac{2}{9}$
$= \frac{2}{3} + \frac{1}{8}$
$= \frac{16}{24} + \frac{3}{24}$
$= \frac{19}{24}$

8. $-8 \div (-2)^2 + 6 = -8 \div 4 + 6$
$= -2 + 6$
$= 4$

9. $4 + 5(2-7)^2 \div (-8+3)$
$= 4 + 5(-5)^2 \div (-5)$
$= 4 + 5(25) \div (-5)$
$= 4 + 125 \div (-5)$
$= 4 + (-25) = -21$

Go Figure

Replacing the known values,

$$\begin{array}{r} 271 \\ 51 \\ +3HE \\ \hline S71 \end{array}$$

In the first column,
$1 + 1 + E = 11$
$2 + E = 11$
$E = 9$
In the second column,
$1 + 7 + 5 + H = 17$
$13 + H = 17$
$H = 4$
So then, the third column,
$1 + 2 + 3 = S$
$S = 6$

Section 11.1

Objective A Exercises

1. $5a - 3b = 5(-3) - 3(6)$
$= -15 - 18$
$= -15 + (-18)$
$= -33$

2. $4c - 2b = 4(-2) - 2(6)$
$= -8 - 12$
$= -8 + (-12) = -20$

3. $2a + 3c = 2(-3) + 3(-2)$
$= -6 + (-6) = -12$

4. $2c + 4a = 2(-2) + 4(-3)$
$= -4 + (-12) = -16$

5. $-c^2 = -(-2)^2 = -4$

6. $-a^2 = -(-3)^2 = -9$

7. $b - a^2 = 6 - (-3)^2 = 6 - 9 = 6 + (-9) = -3$

8. $b - c^2 = 6 - (-2)^2 = 6 - 4 = 6 + (-4) = 2$

9. $ab - c^2 = (-3)(6) - (-2)^2$
$= -18 - 4$
$= -18 + (-4) = -22$

10. $bc - a^2 = 6(-2) - (-3)^2$
$= -12 - 9$
$= -12 + (-9) = -21$

11. $2ab - c^2 = 2(-3)6 - (-2)^2$
$= -36 - 4$
$= -36 + (-4) = -40$

12. $3bc - a^2 = 3(6)(-2) - (-3)^2$
$= -36 - 9$
$= -36 + (-9) = -45$

13. $a - (b \div a) = -3 - [6 \div (-3)]$
$= -3 - (-2)$
$= -3 + 2 = -1$

14. $c - (b \div c) = -2 - [6 \div (-2)]$
$= -2 - (-3)$
$= -2 + 3 = 1$

15. $2ac - (b \div a) = 2(-3)(-2) - [6 \div (-3)]$
$= 12 - (-2)$
$= 12 + 2 = 14$

16. $4ac \div (b \div a) = 4(-3)(-2) \div [6 \div (-3)]$
$= 24 \div (-2) = -12$

17. $b^2 - c^2 = (6)^2 - (-2)^2$
$= 36 - 4$
$= 36 + (-4) = 32$

18. $b^2 - a^2 = (6)^2 - (-3)^2$
$= 36 - 9$
$= 36 + (-9) = 27$

19. $b^2 \div (ac) = (6)^2 \div (-3)(-2)$
$= 36 \div 6 = 6$

20. $3c^2 \div (ab) = 3(-2)^2 \div (-3)(6)$
$= 3 \cdot 4 \div (-18)$
$= 12 \div (-18) = -\frac{2}{3}$

21. $c^2 - (b \div c) = (-2)^2 - [6 \div (-2)]$
$= 4 - (-3)$
$= 4 + 3 = 7$

22. $a^2 - (b \div a) = (-3)^2 - [6 \div (-3)]$
$= 9 - (-2)$
$= 9 + 2 = 11$

23. $a^2 + b^2 + c^2 = (-3)^2 + 6^2 + (-2)^2$
$= 9 + 36 + 4$
$= 45 + 4 = 49$

24. $a^2 - b^2 - c^2 = (-3)^2 - 6^2 - (-2)^2$
$= 9 - 36 - 4$
$= 9 + (-36) + (-4)$
$= -27 + (-4) = -31$

25. $ac + bc + ab = (-3)(-2) + 6(-2) + (-3)(6)$
$= 6 + (-12) + (-18)$
$= -6 + (-18) = -24$

26. $ac - bc - ab = (-3)(-2) - 6(-2) - (-3)(6)$
$= 6 - (-12) - (-18)$
$= 6 + 12 + 18$
$= 18 + 18 = 36$

27. $a^2 + b^2 - ab = (-3)^2 + 6^2 - (-3)(6)$
$= 9 + 36 - (-3)(6)$
$= 9 + 36 - (-18)$
$= 9 + 36 + 18$
$= 45 + 18 = 63$

28. $b^2 + c^2 - bc = 6^2 + (-2)^2 - 6(-2)$
$= 36 + 4 - (-12)$
$= 36 + 4 + 12$
$= 40 + 12 = 52$

29. $2b - (3c + a^2) = 2(6) - [3(-2) + (-3)^2]$
$= 2(6) - [3(-2) + 9]$
$= 2(6) - (-6 + 9)$
$= 2(6) - 3$
$= 12 - 3$
$= 12 + (-3) = 9$

30. $\frac{2}{3}b + \left(\frac{1}{2}c - a\right) = \frac{2}{3} \cdot 6 + \left[\frac{1}{2}(-2) - (-3)\right]$
$= \frac{2}{3} \cdot 6 + (-1 + 3)$
$= \frac{2}{3} \cdot 6 + 2 = 4 + 2 = 6$

31. $\frac{1}{3}a + \left(\frac{1}{2}b - \frac{2}{3}a\right) = \frac{1}{3}(-3) + \left[\frac{1}{2} \cdot 6 - \frac{2}{3}(-3)\right]$
$= \frac{1}{3}(-3) + [3 - (-2)]$
$= \frac{1}{3}(-3) + (3 + 2) = -1 + 5 = 4$

32. $-\frac{2}{3}b - \left(\frac{1}{2}c + a\right) = -\frac{2}{3} \cdot 6 - \left[\frac{1}{2}(-2) + (-3)\right]$
$= -\frac{2}{3} \cdot 6 - [-1 + (-3)]$
$= -4 - (-4) = -4 + 4 = 0$

33. $\frac{1}{6}b + \frac{1}{3}(c + a) = \frac{1}{6} \cdot 6 + \frac{1}{3}[-2 + (-3)]$
$= \frac{1}{6} \cdot 6 + \frac{1}{3}(-5)$
$= 1 + \left(-\frac{5}{3}\right) = \frac{3}{3} + \left(-\frac{5}{3}\right) = -\frac{2}{3}$

34. $\frac{1}{2}c + \left(\frac{1}{3}b - a\right) = \frac{1}{2}(-2) + \left[\frac{1}{3} \cdot 6 - (-3)\right]$
$= \frac{1}{2}(-2) + (2 + 3) = -1 + 5 = 4$

35. $4a + (3b - c) = 4\left(-\frac{1}{2}\right) + \left[3\left(\frac{3}{4}\right) - \frac{1}{4}\right]$
$= 4\left(-\frac{1}{2}\right) + \left[\frac{9}{4} - \frac{1}{4}\right]$
$= 4\left(-\frac{1}{2}\right) + \frac{8}{4}$
$= -2 + 2 = 0$

36. $2b + (c - 3a) = 2\left(\frac{3}{4}\right) + \left[\frac{1}{4} - 3\left(-\frac{1}{2}\right)\right]$
$= \frac{6}{4} + \left(\frac{1}{4} + \frac{3}{2}\right)$
$= \frac{6}{4} + \left(\frac{1}{4} + \frac{6}{4}\right) = \frac{6}{4} + \frac{7}{4} = \frac{13}{4} = 3\frac{1}{4}$

37. $2a - b^2 \div c = 2\left(-\frac{1}{2}\right) - \left(\frac{3}{4}\right)^2 \div \frac{1}{4}$
$= 2\left(-\frac{1}{2}\right) - \frac{9}{16} \div \frac{1}{4}$
$= -1 - \frac{9}{16} \div \frac{1}{4}$
$= -1 - \frac{9}{16} \times \frac{4}{1}$
$= -1 - \frac{9}{4}$
$= -1 + \left(-\frac{9}{4}\right) = -3\frac{1}{4}$

38. $b \div (-c) + 2a = \frac{3}{4} \div \left(-\frac{1}{4}\right) + 2\left(-\frac{1}{2}\right)$
$= -\left(\frac{3}{4} \cdot \frac{4}{1}\right) + 2\left(-\frac{1}{2}\right)$
$= -3 + (-1) = -4$

39. $\begin{aligned} a^2 - b^2 &= (3.72)^2 - (-2.31)^2 \\ &= 13.8384 - 5.3361 = 8.5023 \end{aligned}$

40. $\begin{aligned} a^2 - b \cdot c &= (3.72)^2 - (-2.31)(-1.74) \\ &= 13.8384 - 4.0194 = 9.819 \end{aligned}$

41. $\begin{aligned} 3ac - (c \div a) &= 3(3.72)(-1.74) - (-1.74 \div 3.72) \\ &\approx -18.950658 \end{aligned}$

42. $\begin{aligned} 2c + (b^2 - c) &= 2(-1.74) + [(-2.31)^2 - (-1.74)] \\ &= 2(-1.74) + (5.3361 + 1.74) \\ &= -3.48 + 7.0761 \\ &= 3.5961 \end{aligned}$

Objective B Exercises

43. $2x^2, 3x, \underline{-4}$

44. $-4y^2, \underline{5}$

45. $3a^2, -4a, \underline{8}$

46. $-b, \underline{7}$

47. $\underline{3}x^2, \underline{-4}x$

48. $\underline{-5}a^2, \underline{1}a$

49. $\underline{1}y^2, \underline{6}a$

50. $\underline{-1}c$

51. $16z$

52. $11x$

53. $12m - 3m = 12m + (-3)m = 9m$

54. $5y - 12y = 5y + (-12)y = -7y$

55. $12at$

56. $23mn$

57. $3yt$

58. $-7yt$

59. Unlike terms

60. $-12y - 7y = -12y + (-7)y = -19y$

61. $3t^2 - 5t^2 = 3t^2 + (-5)t^2 = -2t^2$

62. $15t^2$

63. $6c - 5 + 7c = 6c + 7c - 5 = 13c - 5$

64. $7x - 5 + 3x = 7x + 3x - 5 = 10x - 5$

65. $2t + 3t - 7t = 2t + 3t + (-7)t = 5t + (-7)t = -2t$

66. $\begin{aligned} 9x^2 - 5 - 3x^2 &= 9x^2 + (-5) + (-3)x^2 \\ &= 9x^2 + (-3)x^2 + (-5) \\ &= 6x^2 - 5 \end{aligned}$

67. $\begin{aligned} 7y^2 - 2 - 4y^2 &= 7y^2 + (-2) + (-4)y^2 \\ &= 7y^2 + (-4)y^2 + (-2) \\ &= 3y^2 - 2 \end{aligned}$

68. $\begin{aligned} 3w - 7u + 4w &= 3w + (-7)u + 4w \\ &= 3w + 4w + (-7)u \\ &= 7w - 7u \end{aligned}$

69. $\begin{aligned} 6w - 8u + 8w &= 6w + (-8)u + 8w \\ &= 6w + 8w + (-8)u \\ &= 14w - 8u \end{aligned}$

70. $\begin{aligned} 4 - 6xy - 7xy &= 4 + (-6)xy + (-7)xy \\ &= 4 + (-13)xy \\ &= 4 - 13xy = -13xy + 4 \end{aligned}$

71. $\begin{aligned} 10 - 11xy - 12xy &= 10 + (-11)xy + (-12)xy \\ &= 10 + (-23)xy \\ &= 10 - 23xy = -23xy + 10 \end{aligned}$

72. $\begin{aligned} 7t^2 - 5t^2 - 4t^2 &= 7t^2 + (-5)t^2 + (-4)t^2 \\ &= 2t^2 + (-4)t^2 \\ &= -2t^2 \end{aligned}$

73. $\begin{aligned} 3v^2 - 6v^2 - 8v^2 &= 3v^2 + (-6)v^2 + (-8)v^2 \\ &= -3v^2 + (-8)v^2 \\ &= -11v^2 \end{aligned}$

74. $\begin{aligned} 5ab - 7a - 10ab &= 5ab + (-7)a + (-10)ab \\ &= 5ab + (-10)ab + (-7)a \\ &= -5ab - 7a \end{aligned}$

75. $\begin{aligned} -10ab - 3a + 2ab &= -10ab + 2ab - 3a \\ &= -8ab - 3a \end{aligned}$

76. $\begin{aligned} -4x^2 - x + 2x^2 &= -4x^2 + 2x^2 - x \\ &= -2x^2 - x \end{aligned}$

77. $\begin{aligned} -3y^2 - y + 7y^2 &= -3y^2 + 7y^2 - y \\ &= 4y^2 - y \end{aligned}$

78. $\begin{aligned} 4x^2 - 8y - x^2 + y &= 4x^2 + (-8)y + (-x^2) + y \\ &= 4x^2 + (-x^2) + (-8)y + y \\ &= 3x^2 - 7y \end{aligned}$

79. $\begin{aligned} 2a - 3b^2 - 5a + b^2 &= 2a + (-3)b^2 + (-5)a + b^2 \\ &= 2a + (-5)a + (-3)b^2 + b^2 \\ &= -3a - 2b^2 \end{aligned}$

80. $\begin{aligned} 8y - 4z - y + 2z &= 8y + (-4)z + (-y) + 2z \\ &= 8y + (-y) + (-4)z + 2z \\ &= 7y - 2z \end{aligned}$

81. $\begin{aligned} 3x^2 - 7x + 4x^2 - x &= 3x^2 + (-7)x + 4x^2 + (-1)x \\ &= 3x^2 + 4x^2 + (-7)x + (-1)x \\ &= 7x^2 - 8x \end{aligned}$

82. $\begin{aligned} 5y^2 - y + 6y^2 - 5y &= 5y^2 + (-1)y + 6y^2 + (-5)y \\ &= 5y^2 + 6y^2 + (-1)y + (-5)y \\ &= 11y^2 - 6y \end{aligned}$

83. $\begin{aligned} 6s - t - 9s + 7t &= 6s + (-1)t + (-9)s + 7t \\ &= 6s + (-9)s + (-1)t + 7t \\ &= -3s + 6t \end{aligned}$

84. $\begin{aligned} 5w - 2v - 9w + 5v &= 5w + (-2)v + (-9)w + 5v \\ &= 5w + (-9)w + (-2)v + 5v \\ &= -4w + 3v \end{aligned}$

85. $4m + 8n - 7m + 2n = 4m + 8n + (-7)m + 2n$
$= 4m + (-7)m + 8n + 2n$
$= -3m + 10n$

86. $z + 9y - 4z + 3y = z + 9y + (-4)z + 3y$
$= z + (-4)z + 9y + 3y$
$= -3z + 12y$

87. $-5ab + 7ac + 10ab - 3ac$
$= -5ab + 7ac + 10ab + (-3)ac$
$= -5ab + 10ab + 7ac + (-3)ac$
$= 5ab + 4ac$

88. $-2x^2 - 3x - 11x^2 + 14x$
$= -2x^2 + (-3)x + (-11)x^2 + 14x$
$= -2x^2 + (-11)x^2 + (-3)x + 14x$
$= -13x^2 + 11x$

89. $\frac{4}{9}a^2 - \frac{1}{5}b^2 + \frac{2}{9}a^2 + \frac{4}{5}b^2$
$= \frac{4}{9}a^2 + \left(-\frac{1}{5}\right)b^2 + \frac{2}{9}a^2 + \frac{4}{5}b^2$
$= \frac{4}{9}a^2 + \frac{2}{9}a^2 + \left(-\frac{1}{5}\right)b^2 + \frac{4}{5}b^2$
$= \frac{6}{9}a^2 + \frac{3}{5}b^2$
$= \frac{2}{3}a^2 + \frac{3}{5}b^2$

90. $\frac{6}{7}x^2 + \frac{2}{5}x - \frac{3}{7}x^2 - \frac{4}{5}x$
$= \frac{6}{7}x^2 + \frac{2}{5}x + \left(-\frac{3}{7}\right)x^2 + \left(-\frac{4}{5}\right)x$
$= \frac{6}{7}x^2 + \left(-\frac{3}{7}\right)x^2 + \frac{2}{5}x + \left(-\frac{4}{5}\right)x$
$= \frac{3}{7}x^2 - \frac{2}{5}x$

91. $6.994x$

92. $5.0757y$

93. $1.56m - 3.77n$

94. $2.27y^2 - 9.6y$

Objective C Exercises

95. $5(x + 4) = 5x + 5 \cdot 4 = 5x + 20$

96. $3(m + 6) = 3m + 3 \cdot 6 = 3m + 18$

97. $(y - 3)4 = [y + (-3)]4$
$= y \cdot 4 + (-3)4$
$= 4y + (-12)$
$= 4y - 12$

98. $(z - 3)7 = [z + (-3)]7$
$= z \cdot 7 + (-3)(7)$
$= 7z + (-21)$
$= 7z - 21$

99. $-2(a + 4) = -2(a) + (-2)(4)$
$= -2a + (-8)$
$= -2a - 8$

100. $-5(b + 3) = -5(b) + (-5)(3)$
$= -5b + (-15)$
$= -5b - 15$

101. $3(5x + 10) = 3(5x) + 3(10) = 15x + 30$

102. $2(4m - 7) = 2[4m + (-7)]$
$= 2(4m) + 2(-7)$
$= 8m + (-14)$
$= 8m - 14$

103. $5(3c - 5) = 5[3c + (-5)]$
$= 5(3c) + 5(-5)$
$= 15c + (-25)$
$= 15c - 25$

104. $-4(w - 3) = -4[w + (-3)]$
$= -4w + (-4)(-3)$
$= -4w + 12$

105. $-3(y - 6) = -3[y + (-6)]$
$= -3y + (-3)(-6)$
$= -3y + 18$

106. $3m + 4(m + z) = 3m + 4m + 4z$
$= 7m + 4z$

107. $5x + 2(x + 7) = 5x + 2x + 2(7) = 7x + 14$

108. $6z - 3(z + 4) = 6z + (-3)(z + 4)$
$= 6z + (-3)(z) + (-3)(4)$
$= 6z + (-3z) + (-12)$
$= 3z - 12$

109. $8y - 4(y + 2) = 8y + (-4)(y + 2)$
$= 8y + (-4)y + (-4)(2)$
$= 8y + (-4y) + (-8)$
$= 4y - 8$

110. $7w - 2(w - 3) = 7w + (-2)[w + (-3)]$
$= 7w + (-2)(w) + (-2)(-3)$
$= 7w + (-2w) + 6$
$= 5w + 6$

111. $9x - 4(x - 6) = 9x + (-4)[x + (-6)]$
$= 9x + (-4)(x) + (-4)(-6)$
$= 9x + (-4)x + 24$
$= 5x + 24$

112. $-5m + 3(m + 4) = -5m + 3m + 3(4)$
$= -5m + 3m + 12$
$= -2m + 12$

113. $-2y + 3(y - 2) = -2y + 3[y + (-2)]$
$= -2y + 3y + 3(-2)$
$= -2y + 3y + (-6)$
$= y - 6$

114. $$\begin{aligned} 5m + 3(m+4) - 6 &= 5m + 3(m+4) + (-6) \\ &= 5m + 3m + 3(4) + (-6) \\ &= 5m + 3m + 12 + (-6) \\ &= 8m + 6 \end{aligned}$$

115. $$\begin{aligned} 4n + 2(n+1) - 5 &= 4n + 2(n+1) + (-5) \\ &= 4n + 2n + 2(1) + (-5) \\ &= 4n + 2n + 2 + (-5) \\ &= 6n - 3 \end{aligned}$$

116. $$\begin{aligned} 8z - 2(z-3) + 8 &= 8z + (-2)[z + (-3)] + 8 \\ &= 8z + (-2)(z) + (-2)(-3) + 8 \\ &= 8z + (-2)z + 6 + 8 \\ &= 6z + 14 \end{aligned}$$

117. $$\begin{aligned} 9y - 3(y-4) + 8 &= 9y + (-3)[y + (-4)] + 8 \\ &= 9y + (-3)(y) + (-3)(-4) + 8 \\ &= 9y + (-3)y + 12 + 8 \\ &= 6y + 20 \end{aligned}$$

118. $$\begin{aligned} 6 - 4(a+4) + 6a &= 6 + (-4)(a+4) + 6a \\ &= 6 + (-4)(a) + (-4)(4) + 6a \\ &= 6 + (-4)a + (-16) + 6a \\ &= 6 + (-16) + (-4)a + 6a \\ &= -10 + 2a = 2a - 10 \end{aligned}$$

119. $$\begin{aligned} 3x + 2(x+2) + 5x &= 3x + 2x + 2(2) + 5x \\ &= 3x + 2x + 4 + 5x \\ &= 3x + 2x + 5x + 4 \\ &= 5x + 5x + 4 \\ &= 10x + 4 \end{aligned}$$

120. $$\begin{aligned} 7x + 4(x+1) + 3x &= 7x + 4x + 4(1) + 3x \\ &= 7x + 4x + 4 + 3x \\ &= 7x + 4x + 3x + 4 \\ &= 11x + 3x + 4 \\ &= 14x + 4 \end{aligned}$$

121. $$\begin{aligned} -7t + 2(t-3) - t &= -7t + 2[t + (-3)] + (-1)t \\ &= -7t + 2t + 2(-3) + (-1)t \\ &= -7t + 2t + (-6) + (-1)t \\ &= -7t + 2t + (-1)t + (-6) \\ &= -5t + (-1)t + (-6) \\ &= -6t - 6 \end{aligned}$$

122. $$\begin{aligned} -3y + 2(y-4) - y &= -3y + 2[y + (-4)] + (-1)y \\ &= -3y + 2y + 2(-4) + (-1)y \\ &= -3y + 2y + (-8) + (-1)y \\ &= -3y + 2y + (-1)y + (-8) \\ &= -y + (-1)y + (-8) \\ &= -2y - 8 \end{aligned}$$

123. $$\begin{aligned} z - 2(1-z) - 2z &= z + (-2)[1 + (-z)] + (-2)z \\ &= z + (-2)(1) + (-2)(-z) + (-2)z \\ &= z + (-2) + 2z + (-2)z \\ &= z + 2z + (-2)z + (-2) \\ &= 3z + (-2)z + (-2) \\ &= z - 2 \end{aligned}$$

124. $$\begin{aligned} 2y - 3(2-y) + 4y &= 2y + (-3)[2 + (-y)] + 4y \\ &= 2y + (-3)(2) + (-3)(-y) + 4y \\ &= 2y + (-6) + 3y + 4y \\ &= 2y + 3y + 4y + (-6) \\ &= 5y + 4y + (-6) \\ &= 9y - 6 \end{aligned}$$

125. $$\begin{aligned} 3(y-2) - 2(y-6) &= 3[y + (-2)] + (-2)[y + (-6)] \\ &= 3y + 3(-2) + (-2)y + (-2)(-6) \\ &= 3y + (-6) + (-2)y + 12 \\ &= 3y + (-2)y + (-6) + 12 \\ &= y + 6 \end{aligned}$$

126. $$\begin{aligned} 7(x+2) + 3(x-4) &= 7(x+2) + 3[x + (-4)] \\ &= 7x + 7(2) + 3x + 3(-4) \\ &= 7x + 14 + 3x + (-12) \\ &= 7x + 3x + 14 + (-12) \\ &= 10x + 2 \end{aligned}$$

127. $$\begin{aligned} 2(t-3) + 7(t+3) &= 2[t + (-3)] + 7(t+3) \\ &= 2t + 2(-3) + 7t + 7(3) \\ &= 2t + (-6) + 7t + 21 \\ &= 2t + 7t + (-6) + 21 \\ &= 9t + 15 \end{aligned}$$

128. $$\begin{aligned} 3(y-4) - 2(y-3) &= 3[y + (-4)] + (-2)[y + (-3)] \\ &= 3y + 3(-4) + (-2)y + (-2)(-3) \\ &= 3y + (-12) + (-2)y + 6 \\ &= 3y + (-2)y + (-12) + 6 \\ &= y + (-6) \\ &= y - 6 \end{aligned}$$

129. $$\begin{aligned} 3t - 6(t-4) + 8t &= 3t + (-6)[t + (-4)] + 8t \\ &= 3t + (-6)(t) + (-6)(-4) + 8t \\ &= 3t + (-6)t + 24 + 8t \\ &= 3t + (-6)t + 8t + 24 \\ &= -3t + 8t + 24 \\ &= 5t + 24 \end{aligned}$$

130. $$\begin{aligned} 5x + 3(x-7) - 9x &= 5x + 3[x + (-7)] - 9x \\ &= 5x + 3x + 3(-7) - 9x \\ &= 5x + 3x - 21 - 9x \\ &= 5x + 3x - 9x - 21 \\ &= 8x - 9x - 21 \\ &= -x - 21 \end{aligned}$$

Applying the Concepts

131a. $3 + 2x$

1	1	1	x	x

b. $4x + 6$

x	x	x	x	1	1	1	1	1	1

c. $3x + 2$

x	x	x	1	1

d. $2x + 4$

x	x	1	1	1	1

e. $3x + 3$

x	x	x	1	1	1

f. $3x + 3$

132a. $2 + 3x$

1	1	x	x	x

b. $2(2 + 3x)$

1	1	x	x	x	1	1	x	x	x

c. $4x+3$

x	x	x	x	1	1	1

d. $4x+6$

x	x	x	x	1	1	1	1	1	1

e. Yes. $2(2x+3)=4x+6$. This equivalence shows that the Distributive Property preserves the quantity. $2(2x+3)$ and $4x+6$ differ in arrangement only.

f. No. $2+3x \neq 5x$. Because 2 and $3x$ are *not* like terms, 2 and $3x$ cannot be combined.

133a. Answers will vary. Combining like terms is like sorting things out: apples with apples, oranges with oranges.

b. Answers will vary. 4 ft measures distance from one point to the other, whereas 4 square feet measures an area of 2 ft × 2 ft. Therefore, 4 ft and 4 square feet are not to be combined.

134. The simplification is incorrect because, by the Order of Operations Agreement, we multiply first and then add. The correct simplification is

$$\begin{aligned} & 2+3(2x+4) \\ &= 2+6x+12 \\ &= 6x+2+12 \\ &= 6x+14 \end{aligned}$$

Section 11.2

Objective A Exercises

1.
$$\begin{array}{r|l} \multicolumn{2}{c}{2x+9=3} \\ \hline 2(-3)+9 & 3 \\ -6+9 & 3 \\ \multicolumn{2}{c}{3=3} \end{array}$$
Yes, -3 is a solution.

2.
$$\begin{array}{r|l} \multicolumn{2}{c}{5x+7=12} \\ \hline 5(-2)+7 & 12 \\ -10+7 & 12 \\ \multicolumn{2}{c}{-3 \neq 12} \end{array}$$
No, -2 is not a solution.

3.
$$\begin{array}{r|l} \multicolumn{2}{c}{4-2x=8} \\ \hline 4-2(2) & 8 \\ 4-4 & 8 \\ \multicolumn{2}{c}{0 \neq 8} \end{array}$$
No, 2 is not a solution.

4.
$$\begin{array}{r|l} \multicolumn{2}{c}{5-2x=4x} \\ \hline 5-2(4) & 4(4) \\ 5-8 & 16 \\ \multicolumn{2}{c}{-3 \neq 16} \end{array}$$
No, 4 is not a solution.

5.
$$\begin{array}{r|l} \multicolumn{2}{c}{3x-2=x+4} \\ \hline 3(3)-2 & 3+4 \\ 9-2 & 7 \\ \multicolumn{2}{c}{7=7} \end{array}$$
Yes, 3 is a solution.

6.
$$\begin{array}{r|l} \multicolumn{2}{c}{4x+8=4-2x} \\ \hline 4(2)+8 & 4-2(2) \\ 8+8 & 4-4 \\ \multicolumn{2}{c}{16 \neq 0} \end{array}$$
No, 2 is not a solution.

7.
$$\begin{array}{r|l} \multicolumn{2}{c}{x^2-5x+1=10-5x} \\ \hline 3^2-5(3)+1 & 10-5(3) \\ 9-15+1 & 10-15 \\ \multicolumn{2}{c}{-5=-5} \end{array}$$
Yes, 3 is a solution.

8.
$$\begin{array}{r|l} \multicolumn{2}{c}{x^2-3x-1=9-6x} \\ \hline (-5)^2-3(-5)-1 & 9-6(-5) \\ 25-(-15)-1 & 9-(-30) \\ 25+15-1 & 9+30 \\ \multicolumn{2}{c}{39=39} \end{array}$$
Yes, -5 is a solution.

9.
$$\begin{array}{r|l} \multicolumn{2}{c}{2x(x-1)=3-x} \\ \hline 2(-1)(-1-1) & 3-(-1) \\ -2(-2) & 3+1 \\ \multicolumn{2}{c}{4=4} \end{array}$$
Yes, -1 is a solution.

10.
$$\begin{array}{r|l} \multicolumn{2}{c}{3x(x-3)=x-8} \\ \hline 3(2)(2-3) & 2-8 \\ 6(-1) & -6 \\ \multicolumn{2}{c}{-6=-6} \end{array}$$
Yes, 2 is a solution.

11.
$$\begin{array}{r|l} \multicolumn{2}{c}{x(x-2)=x^2-4} \\ \hline 2(2-2) & 2^2-4 \\ 2(0) & 4-4 \\ \multicolumn{2}{c}{0=0} \end{array}$$
Yes, 2 is a solution.

12.
$$\begin{array}{r|l} \multicolumn{2}{c}{x(x+4)=x^2+16} \\ \hline -4(-4+4) & (-4)^2+16 \\ -4(0) & 16+16 \\ \multicolumn{2}{c}{0 \neq 32} \end{array}$$
No, -4 is not a solution.

13.
$$\begin{array}{r|l} \multicolumn{2}{c}{3x+6=4} \\ \hline 3\left(-\frac{2}{3}\right)+6 & 4 \\ -2+6 & 4 \\ \multicolumn{2}{c}{4=4} \end{array}$$
Yes, $-\frac{2}{3}$ is a solution.

14.
$$\begin{array}{c|c} \multicolumn{2}{c}{2x-7=-3} \\ \hline 2\left(\frac{1}{2}\right)-7 & -3 \\ 1-7 & -3 \\ \multicolumn{2}{c}{-6 \neq -3} \end{array}$$

No, $\frac{1}{2}$ is not a solution.

15.
$$\begin{array}{c|c} \multicolumn{2}{c}{2x-3=1-14x} \\ \hline 2\left(\frac{1}{4}\right)-3 & 1-14\left(\frac{1}{4}\right) \\ \frac{2}{4}-3 & 1-\frac{14}{4} \\ \frac{1}{2}-3 & 1-\frac{7}{2} \\ \multicolumn{2}{c}{-2\frac{1}{2}=-2\frac{1}{2}} \end{array}$$

Yes, $\frac{1}{4}$ is a solution.

16.
$$\begin{array}{c|c} \multicolumn{2}{c}{5x-2=1-2x} \\ \hline 5\left(-\frac{1}{3}\right)-2 & 1-2\left(-\frac{1}{3}\right) \\ -\frac{5}{3}-2 & 1+\frac{2}{3} \\ \multicolumn{2}{c}{-3\frac{2}{3} \neq 1\frac{2}{3}} \end{array}$$

No, $-\frac{1}{3}$ is not a solution.

17.
$$\begin{array}{c|c} \multicolumn{2}{c}{3x(x-2)=x-4} \\ \hline 3\left(\frac{3}{4}\right)\left(\frac{3}{4}-2\right) & \frac{3}{4}-4 \\ \frac{9}{4}\left(-\frac{5}{4}\right) & \frac{3}{4}-\frac{16}{4} \\ \multicolumn{2}{c}{-\frac{45}{16} \neq -\frac{13}{4}} \end{array}$$

No, $\frac{3}{4}$ is not a solution.

18.
$$\begin{array}{c|c} \multicolumn{2}{c}{5x(x+1)=x+3} \\ \hline 5\left(\frac{2}{5}\right)\left(\frac{2}{5}+1\right) & \frac{2}{5}+3 \\ 2\left(\frac{7}{5}\right) & \frac{2}{5}+\frac{15}{5} \\ \multicolumn{2}{c}{\frac{14}{5} \neq \frac{17}{5}} \end{array}$$

No, $\frac{2}{5}$ is not a solution.

19.
$$\begin{array}{c|c} \multicolumn{2}{c}{x^2-3x=-0.8776-x} \\ \hline (1.32)^2-3(1.32) & -0.8776-1.32 \\ 1.7424-3.96 & -2.1976 \\ \multicolumn{2}{c}{-2.2176 \neq -2.1976} \end{array}$$

No, 1.32 is not a solution.

20.
$$\begin{array}{c|c} \multicolumn{2}{c}{x^2-3x=x+3.8} \\ \hline (-1.9)^2-3(-1.9) & -1.9+3.8 \\ 3.61+5.7 & 1.9 \\ \multicolumn{2}{c}{9.31 \neq 1.9} \end{array}$$

No, −1.9 is not a solution.

21.
$$\begin{array}{c|c} \multicolumn{2}{c}{x^2+3x=x(x+3)} \\ \hline (1.05)^2+3(1.05) & 1.05(1.05+3) \\ 1.1025+3.15 & 4.2525 \\ \multicolumn{2}{c}{4.2525=4.2525} \end{array}$$

Yes, 1.05 is a solution.

Objective B Exercises

22.
$$\begin{aligned} x+3&=9 \\ x+3-3&=9-3 \\ x+0&=6 \\ x&=6 \end{aligned}$$

23.
$$\begin{aligned} x+7&=5 \\ x+7-7&=5-7 \\ x+0&=-2 \\ x&=-2 \end{aligned}$$

24.
$$\begin{aligned} y-6&=16 \\ y-6+6&=16+6 \\ y+0&=22 \\ y&=22 \end{aligned}$$

25.
$$\begin{aligned} z-4&=10 \\ z-4+4&=10+4 \\ z+0&=14 \\ z&=14 \end{aligned}$$

26.
$$\begin{aligned} 3+n&=4 \\ 3-3+n&=4-3 \\ 0+n&=1 \\ n&=1 \end{aligned}$$

27.
$$\begin{aligned} 6+x&=8 \\ 6-6+x&=8-6 \\ 0+x&=2 \\ x&=2 \end{aligned}$$

28.
$$\begin{aligned} z+7&=2 \\ z+7-7&=2-7 \\ z+0&=-5 \\ z&=-5 \end{aligned}$$

29.
$$\begin{aligned} w+9&=5 \\ w+9-9&=5-9 \\ w+0&=-4 \\ w&=-4 \end{aligned}$$

30.
$$\begin{aligned} x-3&=-7 \\ x-3+3&=-7+3 \\ x+0&=-4 \\ x&=-4 \end{aligned}$$

31.
$$\begin{aligned} m-4&=-9 \\ m-4+4&=-9+4 \\ m+0&=-5 \\ m&=-5 \end{aligned}$$

32.
$$\begin{aligned} y+6&=6\\ y+6-6&=6-6\\ y+0&=0\\ y&=0 \end{aligned}$$

33.
$$\begin{aligned} t-3&=-3\\ t-3+3&=-3+3\\ t+0&=0\\ t&=0 \end{aligned}$$

34.
$$\begin{aligned} v-7&=-4\\ v-7+7&=-4+7\\ v+0&=3\\ v&=3 \end{aligned}$$

35.
$$\begin{aligned} x-3&=-1\\ x-3+3&=-1+3\\ x+0&=2\\ x&=2 \end{aligned}$$

36.
$$\begin{aligned} 1+x&=0\\ 1-1+x&=0-1\\ 0+x&=0+(-1)\\ 0+x&=-1\\ x&=-1 \end{aligned}$$

37.
$$\begin{aligned} 3+y&=0\\ 3-3+y&=0-3\\ 0+y&=0+(-3)\\ 0+y&=-3\\ y&=-3 \end{aligned}$$

38.
$$\begin{aligned} x-10&=5\\ x-10+10&=5+10\\ x+0&=15\\ x&=15 \end{aligned}$$

39.
$$\begin{aligned} y-7&=3\\ y-7+7&=3+7\\ y+0&=10\\ y&=10 \end{aligned}$$

40.
$$\begin{aligned} x+4&=-7\\ x+4-4&=-7-4\\ x+0&=-7+(-4)\\ x+0&=-11\\ x&=-11 \end{aligned}$$

41.
$$\begin{aligned} t-3&=-8\\ t-3+3&=-8+3\\ t+0&=-5\\ t&=-5 \end{aligned}$$

42.
$$\begin{aligned} w+5&=-5\\ w+5-5&=-5-5\\ w+0&=-5+(-5)\\ w+0&=-10\\ w&=-10 \end{aligned}$$

43.
$$\begin{aligned} z+6&=-6\\ z+6-6&=-6-6\\ z+0&=-6+(-6)\\ z+0&=-12\\ z&=-12 \end{aligned}$$

44.
$$\begin{aligned} x+7&=-8\\ x+7-7&=-8-7\\ x+0&=-8+(-7)\\ x&=-15 \end{aligned}$$

45.
$$\begin{aligned} x+2&=-5\\ x+2-2&=-5-2\\ x+0&=-5+(-2)\\ x&=-7 \end{aligned}$$

46.
$$\begin{aligned} x+\frac{1}{2}&=-\frac{1}{2}\\ x+\frac{1}{2}-\frac{1}{2}&=-\frac{1}{2}-\frac{1}{2}\\ x+0&=-\frac{1}{2}+\left(-\frac{1}{2}\right)\\ x&=-1 \end{aligned}$$

47.
$$\begin{aligned} x-\frac{5}{6}&=-\frac{1}{6}\\ x-\frac{5}{6}+\frac{5}{6}&=-\frac{1}{6}+\frac{5}{6}\\ x+0&=\frac{4}{6}\\ x&=\frac{4}{6}=\frac{2}{3} \end{aligned}$$

48.
$$\begin{aligned} y+\frac{7}{11}&=-\frac{3}{11}\\ y+\frac{7}{11}-\frac{7}{11}&=-\frac{3}{11}-\frac{7}{11}\\ y+0&=-\frac{3}{11}+\left(-\frac{7}{11}\right)\\ y&=-\frac{10}{11} \end{aligned}$$

49.
$$\begin{aligned} \frac{2}{5}+x&=-\frac{3}{5}\\ \frac{2}{5}-\frac{2}{5}+x&=-\frac{3}{5}-\frac{2}{5}\\ 0+x&=-\frac{3}{5}+\left(-\frac{2}{5}\right)\\ x&=-\frac{5}{5}\\ x&=-1 \end{aligned}$$

50. $\frac{7}{8} + y = -\frac{1}{8}$
$\frac{7}{8} - \frac{7}{8} + y = -\frac{1}{8} - \frac{7}{8}$
$0 + y = -\frac{1}{8} + \left(-\frac{7}{8}\right)$
$y = -\frac{8}{8}$
$y = -1$

51. $\frac{1}{3} + x = \frac{2}{3}$
$\frac{1}{3} - \frac{1}{3} + x = \frac{2}{3} - \frac{1}{3}$
$0 + x = \frac{2}{3} + \left(-\frac{1}{3}\right)$
$x = \frac{1}{3}$

52. $x + \frac{1}{2} = -\frac{1}{3}$
$x + \frac{1}{2} - \frac{1}{2} = -\frac{1}{3} - \frac{1}{2}$
$x + 0 = -\frac{1}{3} + \left(-\frac{1}{2}\right)$
$x = -\frac{5}{6}$

53. $y + \frac{3}{8} = \frac{1}{4}$
$y + \frac{3}{8} - \frac{3}{8} = \frac{1}{4} - \frac{3}{8}$
$y + 0 = \frac{1}{4} + \left(-\frac{3}{8}\right)$
$y = -\frac{1}{8}$

54. $y + \frac{2}{3} = -\frac{3}{8}$
$y + \frac{2}{3} - \frac{2}{3} = -\frac{3}{8} - \frac{2}{3}$
$y + 0 = -\frac{3}{8} + \left(-\frac{2}{3}\right)$
$y = -\frac{25}{24}$
$y = -1\frac{1}{24}$

55. $t + \frac{1}{4} = -\frac{1}{2}$
$t + \frac{1}{4} - \frac{1}{4} = -\frac{1}{2} - \frac{1}{4}$
$t + 0 = -\frac{1}{2} + \left(-\frac{1}{4}\right)$
$t = -\frac{3}{4}$

56. $x + \frac{1}{3} = \frac{5}{12}$
$x + \frac{1}{3} - \frac{1}{3} = \frac{5}{12} - \frac{1}{3}$
$x + 0 = \frac{5}{12} + \left(-\frac{1}{3}\right)$
$x = \frac{1}{12}$

57. $y + \frac{2}{3} = -\frac{5}{12}$
$y + \frac{2}{3} - \frac{2}{3} = -\frac{5}{12} - \frac{2}{3}$
$y + 0 = -\frac{5}{12} + \left(-\frac{2}{3}\right)$
$y = -\frac{13}{12}$
$y = -1\frac{1}{12}$

Objective C Exercises

58. $3y = 12$
$\frac{3y}{3} = \frac{12}{3}$
$1y = 4$
$y = 4$

59. $5x = 30$
$\frac{5x}{5} = \frac{30}{5}$
$1x = 6$
$x = 6$

60. $5z = -20$
$\frac{5z}{5} = \frac{-20}{5}$
$1z = -4$
$z = -4$

61. $3z = -27$
$\frac{3z}{3} = \frac{-27}{3}$
$1z = -9$
$z = -9$

62. $-2x = 6$
$\frac{-2x}{-2} = \frac{6}{-2}$
$1x = -3$
$x = -3$

63. $-4t = 20$
$\frac{-4t}{-4} = \frac{20}{-4}$
$1t = -5$
$t = -5$

64. $-5x = -40$
$\frac{-5x}{-5} = \frac{-40}{-5}$
$1x = 8$
$x = 8$

65. $-2y = -28$
$\frac{-2y}{-2} = \frac{-28}{-2}$
$1y = 14$
$y = 14$

66. $40 = 8x$
$\frac{40}{8} = \frac{8x}{8}$
$5 = 1x$
$5 = x$

67. $24 = 3y$
$\frac{24}{3} = \frac{3y}{3}$
$8 = 1y$
$8 = y$

68. $-24 = 4x$
$\frac{-24}{4} = \frac{4x}{4}$
$-6 = 1x$
$-6 = x$

69. $-21 = 7y$
$\frac{-21}{7} = \frac{7y}{7}$
$-3 = 1y$
$-3 = y$

70. $\frac{x}{3} = 5$
$\frac{1}{3}x = 5$
$3\left(\frac{1}{3}x\right) = 3(5)$
$1x = 15$
$x = 15$

71. $\frac{y}{2} = 10$
$\frac{1}{2}y = 10$
$2\left(\frac{1}{2}y\right) = 2(10)$
$1y = 20$
$y = 20$

72. $\frac{n}{4} = -2$

$\frac{1}{4}n = -2$

$4\left(\frac{1}{4}n\right) = 4(-2)$

$1n = -8$

$n = -8$

73. $\frac{y}{7} = -3$

$\frac{1}{7}y = -3$

$7\left(\frac{1}{7}y\right) = 7(-3)$

$1y = -21$

$y = -21$

74. $-\frac{x}{4} = 1$

$-\frac{1}{4}x = 1$

$-4\left(-\frac{1}{4}x\right) = -4(1)$

$1x = -4$

$x = -4$

75. $\frac{-y}{3} = 5$

$-\frac{1}{3}y = 5$

$-3\left(-\frac{1}{3}y\right) = -3(5)$

$1y = -15$

$y = -15$

76. $\frac{2}{3}w = 4$

$\frac{3}{2}\left(\frac{2}{3}w\right) = \frac{3}{2}(4)$

$1w = 6$

$w = 6$

77. $\frac{5}{8}x = 10$

$\frac{8}{5}\left(\frac{5}{8}x\right) = \frac{8}{5}(10)$

$1x = 16$

$x = 16$

78. $\frac{3}{4}v = -3$

$\frac{4}{3}\left(\frac{3}{4}v\right) = \frac{4}{3}(-3)$

$1v = -4$

$v = -4$

79. $\frac{2}{7}x = -12$

$\frac{7}{2}\left(\frac{2}{7}x\right) = \frac{7}{2}(-12)$

$1x = -42$

$x = -42$

80. $-\frac{1}{3}x = -2$

$-3\left(-\frac{1}{3}x\right) = -3(-2)$

$1x = 6$

$x = 6$

81. $-\frac{1}{5}y = -3$

$-5\left(-\frac{1}{5}y\right) = -5(-3)$

$1y = 15$

$y = 15$

82. $\frac{3}{8}x = -24$

$\frac{8}{3}\left(\frac{3}{8}x\right) = \frac{8}{3}(-24)$

$1x = -64$

$x = -64$

83. $\frac{5}{12}y = -16$

$\frac{12}{5}\left(\frac{5}{12}y\right) = \frac{12}{5}(-16)$

$1y = -\frac{192}{5}$

$y = -38\frac{2}{5}$

84. $-4 = -\frac{2}{3}z$

$-\frac{3}{2}(-4) = -\frac{3}{2}\left(-\frac{2}{3}z\right)$

$6 = 1z$

$6 = z$

85. $-8 = -\frac{5}{6}x$

$\left(-\frac{6}{5}\right)(-8) = \left(-\frac{6}{5}\right)\left(-\frac{5}{6}\right)x$

$\frac{48}{5} = 1x$

$9\frac{3}{5} = x$

86. $-12 = -\frac{3}{8}y$

$\left(-\frac{8}{3}\right)(-12) = \left(-\frac{8}{3}\right)\left(-\frac{3}{8}\right)y$

$32 = 1y$

$32 = y$

87. $-9 = \frac{5}{6}t$

$\frac{6}{5}(-9) = \left(\frac{6}{5}\right)\left(\frac{5}{6}\right)t$

$-\frac{54}{5} = 1t$

$-10\frac{4}{5} = t$

88. $\frac{2}{3}x = -\frac{2}{7}$

$\frac{3}{2}\left(\frac{2}{3}x\right) = \frac{3}{2}\left(-\frac{2}{7}\right)$

$1x = -\frac{3}{7}$

$x = -\frac{3}{7}$

89. $\frac{3}{7}y = \frac{5}{6}$

$\frac{7}{3}\left(\frac{3}{7}\right)y = \frac{7}{3}\left(\frac{5}{6}\right)$

$1y = \frac{35}{18}$

$y = 1\frac{17}{18}$

90. $4x - 2x = 7$

$2x = 7$

$\frac{2x}{2} = \frac{7}{2}$

$1x = \frac{7}{2}$

$x = 3\frac{1}{2}$

91. $3a - 6a = 8$

$-3a = 8$

$\frac{-3a}{-3} = \frac{8}{-3}$

$1a = -\frac{8}{3}$

$a = -2\frac{2}{3}$

92. $\frac{4}{5}m - \frac{1}{5}m = 9$

$\frac{3}{5}m = 9$

$\frac{5}{3}\left(\frac{3}{5}m\right) = \frac{5}{3}(9)$

$1m = 15$

$m = 15$

93. $\frac{1}{3}b - \frac{2}{3}b = -1$

$-\frac{1}{3}b = -1$

$(-3)\left(-\frac{1}{3}b\right) = (-3)(-1)$

$1b = 3$

$b = 3$

Objective D Exercises

94. **Strategy** To find the amount of the original investment, replace the variables A and I by the given values and solve for P.

Solution

$$A = P + I$$
$$17{,}700 = P + 2700$$
$$17{,}700 - 2700 = P + 2700 - 2700$$
$$17{,}700 + (-2700) = P + 0$$
$$15{,}000 = P$$

The original investment was $15,000.

95. **Strategy** To find the value of the original investment, replace the variables A and I by the given values and solve for P.

Solution

$$A = P + I$$
$$26{,}440 = P + 2830$$
$$26{,}440 - 2830 = P + 2830 - 2830$$
$$26{,}440 + (-2830) = P + 0$$
$$23{,}610 = P$$

The original investment was $23,610.

96. **Strategy** To find the increase in value of the investment, replace the variables A and P in the formula by the given values and solve for I.

Solution

$$A = P + I$$
$$11{,}420 = 8000 + I$$
$$11{,}420 - 8000 = 8000 - 8000 + I$$
$$11{,}420 + (-8000) = 0 + I$$
$$3420 = I$$

The increase is $3420.

97. **Strategy** To find the increase in the value of the investment, replace the variables A and P by the given values and solve for I.

Solution

$$A = P + I$$
$$8690 = 7500 + I$$
$$8690 - 7500 = 7500 - 7500 + I$$
$$8690 + (-7500) = 0 + I$$
$$1190 = I$$

The value of the fund increased by $1190.

98. **Strategy** To find the number of gallons of gasoline used, replace the variables D and M in the formula by the given values and solve for G.

Solution

$$D = M \cdot G$$
$$621 = 28 \cdot G$$
$$\frac{621}{28} = \frac{28G}{28}$$
$$22.2 \approx G$$

22.2 gal of gasoline was used.

99. **Strategy** To find the number of gallons of gasoline used, replace the variables D and M in the formula by the given values and solve for G.

Solution

$$D = M \cdot G$$
$$592 = 32 \cdot G$$
$$\frac{592}{32} = \frac{32G}{32}$$
$$18.5 = G$$

18.5 gal of gasoline was used.

100. **Strategy** To find the number of miles per gallon, replace the variables D and G in the formula by the given values and solve for M.

Solution

$$D = M \cdot G$$
$$560 = M \cdot 15$$
$$\frac{560}{15} = \frac{15M}{15}$$
$$37.3 \approx M$$

The car gets 37.3 mi/gal.

101. **Strategy** To find the number of miles per gallon, replace the variables D and G in the formula by the given values and solve for M.

Solution

$$D = M \cdot G$$
$$410 = M \cdot 12$$
$$\frac{410}{12} = \frac{12M}{12}$$
$$34.2 \approx M$$

The car gets 34.2 mi/gal.

102. Strategy To find the cost, replace the variables S and M in the formula by the given values and solve for C.

Solution
$$\begin{aligned} S &= C + M \\ 2240 &= C + 420 \\ 2240 - 420 &= C + 420 - 420 \\ 2240 + (-420) &= C + 0 \\ 1820 &= C \end{aligned}$$
The cost of the computer is \$1820.

103. Strategy To find the markup, replace the variables S and C in the formula by the given values and solve for M.

Solution
$$\begin{aligned} S &= C + M \\ 39.80 &= 23.50 + M \\ 39.80 - 23.50 &= 23.50 - 23.50 + M \\ 39.80 + (-23.50) &= 0 + M \\ 16.30 &= M \end{aligned}$$
The markup on each stuffed animal is \$16.30.

104. Strategy To find the cost of a blender, replace the variables S and R in the formula by the given values and solve for C.

Solution
$$\begin{aligned} S &= C + RC \\ 77.50 &= C + 0.24C \\ 77.50 &= 1.24C \\ \frac{77.50}{1.24} &= \frac{1.24C}{1.24} \\ 62.50 &= C \end{aligned}$$
The blender costs \$62.50.

105. Strategy To find the cost of a compact disc, replace the variables S and R in the formula by the given values and solve for C.

Solution
$$\begin{aligned} S &= C + RC \\ 18.85 &= C + 0.30C \\ 18.85 &= 1.30C \\ \frac{18.85}{1.30} &= \frac{1.30C}{1.30} \\ 14.50 &= C \end{aligned}$$
The compact disc costs \$14.50.

Applying the Concepts

106.
$$x - 3 = -5$$
$$x - 3 + 3 = -5 + 3 \text{ Addition Property of Equations}$$
$$x + 0 = -2$$
$$x = -2 \text{ Addition Property of Zero}$$

107.
$$\frac{3}{4}x = 6$$
$$\frac{4}{3}\left(\frac{3}{4}x\right) = \frac{4}{3}(6) \text{ Multiplication Property of Equations}$$
$$1x = 8 \text{ Multiplication Property of Reciprocals}$$
$$x = 8 \text{ Multiplication Property of One}$$

108. No, none of the numbers 2, −2, 0, 3, 6, or 10 is a solution of the equation. There is no solution of the equation because there is no number that is equal to itself plus 4.

109. Answers will vary. For example, $x + 5 = 1$.

110. Answers will vary. For example, $3 - x = 5$.

111a. Students should rephrase the Addition Property of Equations (the same number or variable expression can be added to each side of an equation without changing the solution of the equation).

b. Students should rephrase the Multiplication Property of Equations (each side of an equation can be multiplied by the same nonzero number without changing the solution of the equation).

Section 11.3

Objective A Exercises

1.
$$\begin{aligned} 3x + 5 &= 14 \\ 3x + 5 - 5 &= 14 - 5 \\ 3x &= 9 \\ \frac{3x}{3} &= \frac{9}{3} \\ x &= 3 \end{aligned}$$

2.
$$\begin{aligned} 5z + 6 &= 31 \\ 5z + 6 - 6 &= 31 - 6 \\ 5z &= 25 \\ \frac{5z}{5} &= \frac{25}{5} \\ z &= 5 \end{aligned}$$

3.
$$\begin{aligned}2n-3&=7\\2n-3+3&=7+3\\2n&=10\\\frac{2n}{2}&=\frac{10}{2}\\n&=5\end{aligned}$$

4.
$$\begin{aligned}4y-4&=20\\4y-4+4&=20+4\\4y&=24\\\frac{4y}{4}&=\frac{24}{4}\\y&=6\end{aligned}$$

5.
$$\begin{aligned}5w+8&=3\\5w+8-8&=3-8\\5w&=-5\\\frac{5w}{5}&=\frac{-5}{5}\\w&=-1\end{aligned}$$

6.
$$\begin{aligned}3x+10&=1\\3x+10-10&=1-10\\3x&=-9\\\frac{3x}{3}&=\frac{-9}{3}\\x&=-3\end{aligned}$$

7.
$$\begin{aligned}3z-4&=-16\\3z-4+4&=-16+4\\3z&=-12\\\frac{3z}{3}&=\frac{-12}{3}\\z&=-4\end{aligned}$$

8.
$$\begin{aligned}6x-1&=-13\\6x-1+1&=-13+1\\6x&=-12\\\frac{6x}{6}&=\frac{-12}{6}\\x&=-2\end{aligned}$$

9.
$$\begin{aligned}5+2x&=7\\5-5+2x&=7-5\\2x&=2\\\frac{2x}{2}&=\frac{2}{2}\\x&=1\end{aligned}$$

10.
$$\begin{aligned}12+7x&=33\\12-12+7x&=33-12\\7x&=21\\\frac{7x}{7}&=\frac{21}{7}\\x&=3\end{aligned}$$

11.
$$\begin{aligned}6-x&=3\\6+(-1)x&=3\\6-6+(-1)x&=3-6\\(-1)x&=-3\\(-1)(-1)x&=(-1)(-3)\\x&=3\end{aligned}$$

12.
$$\begin{aligned}4-x&=-2\\4+(-1)x&=-2\\4-4+(-1)x&=-2-4\\(-1)x&=-6\\(-1)(-1)x&=(-1)(-6)\\x&=6\end{aligned}$$

13.
$$\begin{aligned}3-4x&=11\\3-3-4x&=11-3\\-4x&=8\\\frac{-4x}{-4}&=\frac{8}{-4}\\x&=-2\end{aligned}$$

14.
$$\begin{aligned}2-3x&=11\\2-2-3x&=11-2\\-3x&=9\\\frac{-3x}{-3}&=\frac{9}{-3}\\x&=-3\end{aligned}$$

15.
$$\begin{aligned}5-4x&=17\\5-5-4x&=17-5\\-4x&=12\\\frac{-4x}{-4}&=\frac{12}{-4}\\x&=-3\end{aligned}$$

16.
$$\begin{aligned}8-6x&=14\\8-8-6x&=14-8\\-6x&=6\\\frac{-6x}{-6}&=\frac{6}{-6}\\x&=-1\end{aligned}$$

17.
$$\begin{aligned}3x+6&=0\\3x+6-6&=0-6\\3x&=-6\\\frac{3x}{3}&=\frac{-6}{3}\\x&=-2\end{aligned}$$

18.
$$\begin{aligned}5x-20&=0\\5x-20+20&=0+20\\5x&=20\\\frac{5x}{5}&=\frac{20}{5}\\x&=4\end{aligned}$$

19.
$$\begin{aligned}-3x-4&=-1\\-3x-4+4&=-1+4\\-3x&=3\\\frac{-3x}{-3}&=\frac{3}{-3}\\x&=-1\end{aligned}$$

20.
$$\begin{aligned}-7x-22&=-1\\-7x-22+22&=-1+22\\-7x&=21\\\frac{-7x}{-7}&=\frac{21}{-7}\\x&=-3\end{aligned}$$

21.
$$\begin{aligned}12y-30&=6\\12y-30+30&=6+30\\12y&=36\\\frac{12y}{12}&=\frac{36}{12}\\y&=3\end{aligned}$$

22.
$$\begin{aligned}9b-7&=2\\9b-7+7&=2+7\\9b&=9\\\frac{9b}{9}&=\frac{9}{9}\\b&=1\end{aligned}$$

23.
$$\begin{aligned}3c+7&=4\\3c+7-7&=4-7\\3c&=-3\\\frac{3c}{3}&=\frac{-3}{3}\\c&=-1\end{aligned}$$

24.
$$\begin{aligned}8t+13&=5\\8t+13-13&=5-13\\8t&=-8\\\frac{8t}{8}&=\frac{-8}{8}\\t&=-1\end{aligned}$$

25.
$$\begin{aligned}-2x+11&=-3\\-2x+11-11&=-3-11\\-2x&=-14\\\frac{-2x}{-2}&=\frac{-14}{-2}\\x&=7\end{aligned}$$

26.
$$\begin{aligned}-4x+15&=-1\\-4x+15-15&=-1-15\\-4x&=-16\\\frac{-4x}{-4}&=\frac{-16}{-4}\\x&=4\end{aligned}$$

27.
$$\begin{aligned} 14-5x&=4\\ 14-14-5x&=4-14\\ -5x&=-10\\ \frac{-5x}{-5}&=\frac{-10}{-5}\\ x&=2 \end{aligned}$$

28.
$$\begin{aligned} 7-3x&=4\\ 7-7-3x&=4-7\\ -3x&=-3\\ \frac{-3x}{-3}&=\frac{-3}{-3}\\ x&=1 \end{aligned}$$

29.
$$\begin{aligned} -8x+7&=-9\\ -8x+7-7&=-9-7\\ -8x&=-16\\ \frac{-8x}{-8}&=\frac{-16}{-8}\\ x&=2 \end{aligned}$$

30.
$$\begin{aligned} -7x+13&=-8\\ -7x+13-13&=-8-13\\ -7x&=-21\\ \frac{-7x}{-7}&=\frac{-21}{-7}\\ x&=3 \end{aligned}$$

31.
$$\begin{aligned} 9x+13&=13\\ 9x+13-13&=13-13\\ 9x&=0\\ \frac{9x}{9}&=\frac{0}{9}\\ x&=0 \end{aligned}$$

32.
$$\begin{aligned} -2x+7&=7\\ -2x+7-7&=7-7\\ -2x&=0\\ \frac{-2x}{-2}&=\frac{0}{-2}\\ x&=0 \end{aligned}$$

33.
$$\begin{aligned} 7d-14&=0\\ 7d-14+14&=0+14\\ 7d&=14\\ \frac{7d}{7}&=\frac{14}{7}\\ d&=2 \end{aligned}$$

34.
$$\begin{aligned} 5z+10&=0\\ 5z+10-10&=0-10\\ 5z&=-10\\ \frac{5z}{5}&=\frac{-10}{5}\\ z&=-2 \end{aligned}$$

35.
$$\begin{aligned} 4n-4&=-4\\ 4n-4+4&=-4+4\\ 4n&=0\\ \frac{4n}{4}&=\frac{0}{4}\\ n&=0 \end{aligned}$$

36.
$$\begin{aligned} -13m-1&=-1\\ -13m-1+1&=-1+1\\ -13m&=0\\ \frac{-13m}{-13}&=\frac{0}{-13}\\ m&=0 \end{aligned}$$

37.
$$\begin{aligned} 3x+5&=7\\ 3x+5-5&=7-5\\ 3x&=2\\ \frac{3x}{3}&=\frac{2}{3}\\ x&=\frac{2}{3} \end{aligned}$$

38.
$$\begin{aligned} 4x+6&=9\\ 4x+6-6&=9-6\\ 4x&=3\\ \frac{4x}{4}&=\frac{3}{4}\\ x&=\frac{3}{4} \end{aligned}$$

39.
$$\begin{aligned} 6x-1&=16\\ 6x-1+1&=16+1\\ 6x&=17\\ \frac{6x}{6}&=\frac{17}{6}\\ x&=2\frac{5}{6} \end{aligned}$$

40.
$$\begin{aligned} 12x-3&=7\\ 12x-3+3&=7+3\\ 12x&=10\\ \frac{12x}{12}&=\frac{10}{12}\\ x&=\frac{5}{6} \end{aligned}$$

41.
$$\begin{aligned} 2x-3&=-8\\ 2x-3+3&=-8+3\\ 2x&=-5\\ \frac{2x}{2}&=\frac{-5}{2}\\ x&=-2\frac{1}{2} \end{aligned}$$

42.
$$\begin{aligned} 5x-3&=-12\\ 5x-3+3&=-12+3\\ 5x&=-9\\ \frac{5x}{5}&=\frac{-9}{5}\\ x&=-1\frac{4}{5} \end{aligned}$$

43.
$$\begin{aligned} -6x+2&=-7\\ -6x+2-2&=-7-2\\ -6x&=-9\\ \frac{-6x}{-6}&=\frac{-9}{-6}\\ x&=1\frac{1}{2} \end{aligned}$$

44.
$$\begin{aligned} -3x+9&=-1\\ -3x+9-9&=-1-9\\ -3x&=-10\\ \frac{-3x}{-3}&=\frac{-10}{-3}\\ x&=3\frac{1}{3} \end{aligned}$$

45.
$$\begin{aligned} -2x-3&=-7\\ -2x-3+3&=-7+3\\ -2x&=-4\\ \frac{-2x}{-2}&=\frac{-4}{-2}\\ x&=2 \end{aligned}$$

46.
$$\begin{aligned} -5x-7&=-4\\ -5x-7+7&=-4+7\\ -5x&=3\\ \frac{-5x}{-5}&=\frac{3}{-5}\\ x&=-\frac{3}{5} \end{aligned}$$

47.
$$\begin{aligned} 3x+8&=2\\ 3x+8-8&=2-8\\ 3x&=-6\\ \frac{3x}{3}&=\frac{-6}{3}\\ x&=-2 \end{aligned}$$

48.
$$\begin{aligned} 2x-9&=8\\ 2x-9+9&=8+9\\ 2x&=17\\ \frac{2x}{2}&=\frac{17}{2}\\ x&=8\frac{1}{2} \end{aligned}$$

49.
$$\begin{aligned} 3w - 7 &= 0 \\ 3w - 7 + 7 &= 0 + 7 \\ 3w &= 7 \\ \frac{3w}{3} &= \frac{7}{3} \\ w &= 2\frac{1}{3} \end{aligned}$$

50.
$$\begin{aligned} 7b - 2 &= 0 \\ 7b - 2 + 2 &= 0 + 2 \\ 7b &= 2 \\ \frac{7b}{7} &= \frac{2}{7} \\ b &= \frac{2}{7} \end{aligned}$$

51.
$$\begin{aligned} -2d + 9 &= 12 \\ -2d + 9 - 9 &= 12 - 9 \\ -2d &= 3 \\ \frac{-2d}{-2} &= \frac{3}{-2} \\ d &= -1\frac{1}{2} \end{aligned}$$

52.
$$\begin{aligned} -7c + 3 &= 1 \\ -7c + 3 - 3 &= 1 - 3 \\ -7c &= -2 \\ \frac{-7c}{-7} &= \frac{-2}{-7} \\ c &= \frac{2}{7} \end{aligned}$$

53.
$$\begin{aligned} \frac{1}{2}x - 2 &= 3 \\ \frac{1}{2}x - 2 + 2 &= 3 + 2 \\ \frac{1}{2}x &= 5 \\ 2\left(\frac{1}{2}x\right) &= 5 \cdot 2 \\ x &= 10 \end{aligned}$$

54.
$$\begin{aligned} \frac{1}{3}x + 1 &= 4 \\ \frac{1}{3}x + 1 - 1 &= 4 - 1 \\ \frac{1}{3}x &= 3 \\ 3 \cdot \left(\frac{1}{3}x\right) &= 3 \cdot 3 \\ x &= 9 \end{aligned}$$

55.
$$\begin{aligned} \frac{3}{5}w - 1 &= 2 \\ \frac{3}{5}w - 1 + 1 &= 2 + 1 \\ \frac{3}{5}w &= 3 \\ \frac{5}{3} \cdot \frac{3}{5}w &= 3 \cdot \frac{5}{3} \\ w &= 5 \end{aligned}$$

56.
$$\begin{aligned} \frac{2}{5}w + 5 &= 6 \\ \frac{2}{5}w + 5 - 5 &= 6 - 5 \\ \frac{2}{5}w &= 1 \\ \frac{5}{2} \cdot \frac{2}{5}w &= 1 \cdot \frac{5}{2} \\ w &= \frac{5}{2} = 2\frac{1}{2} \end{aligned}$$

57.
$$\begin{aligned} \frac{2}{9}t - 3 &= 5 \\ \frac{2}{9}t - 3 + 3 &= 5 + 3 \\ \frac{2}{9}t &= 8 \\ \frac{9}{2} \cdot \frac{2}{9}t &= 8 \cdot \frac{9}{2} \\ t &= 36 \end{aligned}$$

58.
$$\begin{aligned} \frac{5}{9}t - 3 &= 2 \\ \frac{5}{9}t - 3 + 3 &= 2 + 3 \\ \frac{5}{9}t &= 5 \\ \frac{9}{5} \cdot \frac{5}{9}t &= \frac{9}{5} \cdot 5 \\ t &= 9 \end{aligned}$$

59.
$$\begin{aligned} \frac{y}{3} - 6 &= -8 \\ \frac{y}{3} - 6 + 6 &= -8 + 6 \\ \frac{y}{3} &= -2 \\ 3 \cdot \frac{y}{3} &= 3(-2) \\ y &= -6 \end{aligned}$$

60.
$$\begin{aligned} \frac{y}{2} - 2 &= 3 \\ \frac{y}{2} - 2 + 2 &= 3 + 2 \\ \frac{y}{2} &= 5 \\ 2 \cdot \frac{y}{2} &= 2 \cdot 5 \\ y &= 10 \end{aligned}$$

61.
$$\begin{aligned} \frac{x}{3} - 2 &= -5 \\ \frac{x}{3} - 2 + 2 &= -5 + 2 \\ \frac{x}{3} &= -3 \\ 3 \cdot \frac{x}{3} &= 3(-3) \\ x &= -9 \end{aligned}$$

62.
$$\begin{aligned} \frac{x}{4} - 3 &= 5 \\ \frac{x}{4} - 3 + 3 &= 5 + 3 \\ \frac{x}{4} &= 8 \\ 4 \cdot \frac{x}{4} &= 8 \cdot 4 \\ x &= 32 \end{aligned}$$

63.
$$\begin{aligned} \frac{5}{8}v + 6 &= 3 \\ \frac{5}{8}v + 6 - 6 &= 3 - 6 \\ \frac{5}{8}v &= -3 \\ \frac{8}{5} \cdot \frac{5}{8}v &= \frac{8}{5} \cdot (-3) \\ v &= -\frac{24}{5} = -4\frac{4}{5} \end{aligned}$$

64.
$$\begin{aligned} \frac{2}{3}v - 4 &= 3 \\ \frac{2}{3}v - 4 + 4 &= 3 + 4 \\ \frac{2}{3}v &= 7 \\ \frac{3}{2} \cdot \frac{2}{3}v &= \frac{3}{2} \cdot 7 \\ v &= \frac{21}{2} \\ v &= 10\frac{1}{2} \end{aligned}$$

65. $\frac{4}{7}z + 10 = 5$

$\frac{4}{7}z + 10 - 10 = 5 - 10$

$\frac{4}{7}z = -5$

$\frac{7}{4} \cdot \frac{4}{7}z = \frac{7}{4} \cdot (-5)$

$z = -\frac{35}{4} = -8\frac{3}{4}$

66. $\frac{3}{8}v - 3 = 4$

$\frac{3}{8}v - 3 + 3 = 4 + 3$

$\frac{3}{8}v = 7$

$\frac{8}{3} \cdot \frac{3}{8}v = \frac{8}{3} \cdot 7$

$v = \frac{56}{3} = 18\frac{2}{3}$

67. $\frac{2}{9}x - 3 = 5$

$\frac{2}{9}x - 3 + 3 = 5 + 3$

$\frac{2}{9}x = 8$

$\frac{9}{2} \cdot \frac{2}{9}x = \frac{9}{2} \cdot 8$

$x = 36$

68. $\frac{1}{2}x + 3 = -8$

$\frac{1}{2}x + 3 - 3 = -8 - 3$

$\frac{1}{2}x = -11$

$2 \cdot \left(\frac{1}{2}\right)x = 2 \cdot (-11)$

$x = -22$

69. $\frac{3}{4}x - 5 = -4$

$\frac{3}{4}x - 5 + 5 = -4 + 5$

$\frac{3}{4}x = 1$

$\frac{4}{3} \cdot \frac{3}{4}x = \frac{4}{3} \cdot 1$

$x = \frac{4}{3} = 1\frac{1}{3}$

70. $\frac{2}{3}x - 5 = -8$

$\frac{2}{3}x - 5 + 5 = -8 + 5$

$\frac{2}{3}x = -3$

$\frac{3}{2} \cdot \frac{2}{3}x = \frac{3}{2} \cdot -3$

$x = -\frac{9}{2} = -4\frac{1}{2}$

71. $1.5x - 0.5 = 2.5$

$1.5x - 0.5x + 0.5 = 2.5 + 0.5$

$1.5x = 3$

$\frac{1.5x}{1.5} = \frac{3}{1.5}$

$x = 2$

72. $2.5w - 1.3 = 3.7$

$2.5w - 1.3 + 1.3 = 3.7 + 1.3$

$2.5w = 5$

$\frac{2.5w}{2.5} = \frac{5}{2.5}$

$w = 2$

73. $0.8t + 1.1 = 4.3$

$0.8t + 1.1 - 1.1 = 4.3 - 1.1$

$0.8t = 3.2$

$\frac{0.8t}{0.8} = \frac{3.2}{0.8}$

$t = 4$

74. $0.3v + 2.4 = 1.5$

$0.3v + 2.4 - 2.4 = 1.5 - 2.4$

$0.3v = -0.9$

$\frac{0.3v}{0.3} = \frac{-0.9}{0.3}$

$v = -3$

75. $0.4x - 2.3 = 1.3$

$0.4x - 2.3 + 2.3 = 1.3 + 2.3$

$0.4x = 3.6$

$\frac{0.4x}{0.4} = \frac{3.6}{0.4}$

$x = 9$

76. $1.2t + 6.5 = 2.9$

$1.2t + 6.5 - 6.5 = 2.9 - 6.5$

$1.2t = -3.6$

$\frac{1.2t}{1.2} = \frac{-3.6}{1.2}$

$t = -3$

77. $3.5y - 3.5 = 10.5$

$3.5y - 3.5 + 3.5 = 10.5 + 3.5$

$3.5y = 14$

$\frac{3.5y}{3.5} = \frac{14}{3.5}$

$y = 4$

78. $1.9x - 1.9 = -1.9$

$1.9x - 1.9 + 1.9 = -1.9 + 1.9$

$1.9x = 0$

$\frac{1.9x}{1.9} = \frac{0}{1.9}$

$x = 0$

79. $0.32x + 4.2 = 3.2$

$0.32x + 4.2 - 4.2 = 3.2 - 4.2$

$0.32x = -1$

$\frac{0.32x}{0.32} = \frac{-1}{0.32}$

$x = -3.125$

80. $5x - 3x + 2 = 8$

$2x + 2 = 8$

$2x + 2 - 2 = 8 - 2$

$2x = 6$

$\frac{2x}{2} = \frac{6}{2}$

$x = 3$

81. $6m + 2m - 2 = 5$

$8m - 3 = 5$

$8m - 3 + 3 = 5 + 3$

$8m = 8$

$\frac{8m}{8} = \frac{8}{8}$

$m = 1$

82. $4a - 7a - 8 = 4$

$-3a - 8 = 4$

$-3a - 8 + 8 = 4 + 8$

$-3a = 12$

$\frac{-3a}{-3} = \frac{12}{-3}$

$a = -4$

83. $3y - 8y - 9 = 6$

$-5y - 9 = 6$

$-5y - 9 + 9 = 6 + 9$

$-5y = 15$

$\frac{-5y}{-5} = \frac{15}{-5}$

$y = -3$

84. $x - 4x + 5 = 11$

$-3x + 5 = 11$

$-3x + 5 - 5 = 11 - 5$

$-3x = 6$

$\frac{-3x}{-3} = \frac{6}{-3}$

$x = -2$

85. $-2y + y - 3 = 6$

$-y - 3 = 6$

$-y - 3 + 3 = 6 + 3$

$-y = 9$

$(-1)(-y) = (-1)9$

$y = -9$

86.
$$\begin{aligned} -4y - y - 8 &= 12 \\ -5y - 8 &= 12 \\ -5y - 8 + 8 &= 12 + 8 \\ \frac{-5y}{-5} &= \frac{20}{-5} \\ y &= -4 \end{aligned}$$

87.
$$\begin{aligned} 0.032x - 0.0194 &= 0.139 \\ 0.032x - 0.0194 + 0.0194 &= 0.139 + 0.0194 \\ 0.032x &= 0.1584 \\ \frac{0.032x}{0.032} &= \frac{0.1584}{0.032} \\ x &= 4.95 \end{aligned}$$

88.
$$\begin{aligned} -3.256x + 42.38 &= -16.9 \\ -3.256x + 42.38 - 42.38 &= -16.9 - 42.38 \\ -3.256x &= -59.28 \\ \frac{-3.256x}{-3.256} &= \frac{-59.28}{-3.256} \\ x &\approx 18.206388 \end{aligned}$$

89.
$$\begin{aligned} 6.09x + 17.33 &= 16.805 \\ 6.09x + 17.33 - 17.33 &= 16.805 - 17.33 \\ 6.09x &= -0.525 \\ \frac{6.09x}{6.09} &= \frac{-0.525}{6.09} \\ x &\approx -0.0862069 \end{aligned}$$

90.
$$\begin{aligned} 1.925x + 32.87 &= -16.994 \\ 1.925x + 32.87 - 32.87 &= -16.994 - 32.87 \\ 1.925x &= -49.864 \\ \frac{1.925x}{1.925} &= \frac{-49.864}{1.925} \\ x &\approx -25.903377 \end{aligned}$$

Objective B Exercises

91. Strategy To find the Celsius temperature, replace the variable F in the formula by the given value and solve for C.

Solution
$$\begin{aligned} F &= 1.8C + 32 \\ -40 &= 1.8C + 32 \\ -40 - 32 &= 1.8C + 32 - 32 \\ -72 &= 1.8C \\ \frac{-72}{1.8} &= \frac{1.8C}{1.8} \\ -40 &= C \end{aligned}$$

The temperature is -40°C.

92. Strategy To find the Celsius temperature, replace the variable F in the formula by the given value and solve for C.

Solution
$$\begin{aligned} F &= 1.8C + 32 \\ 72 &= 1.8C + 32 \\ 72 - 32 &= 1.8C + 32 - 32 \\ 40 &= 1.8C \\ \frac{40}{1.8} &= \frac{1.8C}{1.8} \\ 22.2 &\approx C \end{aligned}$$

The temperature is 22.2°C.

93. Strategy To find the time required, replace the variables V and V_0 in the formula by the given values and solve for t.

Solution
$$\begin{aligned} V &= V_0 + 32t \\ 472 &= 8 + 32t \\ 472 - 8 &= 8 - 8 + 32t \\ 464 &= 32t \\ \frac{464}{32} &= \frac{32t}{32} \\ 14.5 &= t \end{aligned}$$

The time is 14.5 s.

94. Strategy To find the time required, replace the variables V and V_0 in the formula by the given values and solve for t.

Solution
$$\begin{aligned} V &= V_0 + 32t \\ 128 &= 16 + 32t \\ 128 - 16 &= 16 - 16 + 32t \\ 112 &= 32t \\ \frac{112}{32} &= \frac{32t}{32} \\ 3.5 &= t \end{aligned}$$

The time is 3.5 s.

95. Strategy To find the number of units made, replace the variables T, U, and F in the formula by the given values and solve for N.

Solution
$$\begin{aligned} T &= U \cdot N + F \\ 25{,}000 &= 8 \cdot N + 5000 \\ 25{,}000 - 5000 &= 8N + 5000 - 5000 \\ 20{,}000 &= 8N \\ \frac{20{,}000}{8} &= \frac{8N}{8} \\ 2500 &= N \end{aligned}$$

2500 units were made.

96. Strategy To find the cost per unit, replace the variables T, N, and F in the formula by the given values and solve for U.

Solution
$$\begin{aligned} T &= U \cdot N + F \\ 80{,}000 &= U \cdot 500 + 15{,}000 \\ 80{,}000 - 15{,}000 &= U \cdot 500 + 15{,}000 - 15{,}000 \\ 65{,}000 &= U \cdot 500 \\ \frac{65{,}000}{500} &= \frac{U \cdot 500}{500} \\ 130 &= U \end{aligned}$$
The cost per unit was \$130.

97. Strategy To find the monthly income, replace the variables T, R, and B in the formula by the given values and solve for I.

Solution
$$\begin{aligned} T &= I \cdot R + B \\ 476 &= I \cdot 0.22 + 80 \\ 476 - 80 &= 0.22I + 80 - 80 \\ 396 &= 0.22I \\ \frac{396}{0.22} &= \frac{0.22I}{0.22} \\ 1800 &= I \end{aligned}$$
The clerk's monthly income is \$1800.

98. Strategy To find the income tax rate, replace the variables T, I, and B in the formula by the given values and solve for R.

Solution
$$\begin{aligned} T &= I \cdot R + B \\ 770 &= 3100R + 150 \\ 770 - 150 &= 3100R + 150 - 150 \\ 620 &= 3100R \\ \frac{620}{3100} &= \frac{3100R}{3100} \\ 0.20 &= R \\ 20\% &= R \end{aligned}$$
Marcy's income tax rate is 20%.

99. Strategy To find the total sales, replace the variables M, R, and B in the formula by the given values and solve for S.

Solution
$$\begin{aligned} M &= S \cdot R + B \\ 3480 &= S \cdot 0.09 + 600 \\ 3480 - 600 &= 0.09S + 600 - 600 \\ 2880 &= 0.09S \\ \frac{2880}{0.09} &= \frac{0.09S}{0.09} \\ 32{,}000 &= S \end{aligned}$$
The total sales were \$32,000.

100. Strategy To find the total sales, replace the variables M, R, and B in the formula by the given values and solve for S.

Solution
$$\begin{aligned} M &= S \cdot R + B \\ 2800 &= S \cdot 0.05 + 1000 \\ 2800 - 1000 &= 0.05S + 1000 - 1000 \\ 1800 &= 0.05S \\ \frac{1800}{0.05} &= \frac{0.05S}{0.05} \\ 36{,}000 &= S \end{aligned}$$
The total sales were \$36,000.

101. Strategy To find the commission rate, replace the variables M, S, and B in the formula by the given values and solve for R.

Solution
$$\begin{aligned} M &= S \cdot R + B \\ 2640 &= 42{,}000R + 750 \\ 2640 - 750 &= 42{,}000R + 750 - 750 \\ 1890 &= 42{,}000R \\ \frac{1890}{42{,}000} &= \frac{42{,}000R}{42{,}000} \\ 0.045 &= R \\ 4.5\% &= R \end{aligned}$$
Miguel's commission rate was 4.5%.

102. Strategy To find the commission rate, replace the variables M, S, and B in the formula by the given values and solve for R.

Solution
$$\begin{aligned} M &= S \cdot R + B \\ 3560 &= 42{,}500R + 500 \\ 3560 - 500 &= 42{,}500R + 500 - 500 \\ 3060 &= 42{,}500R \\ \frac{3060}{42{,}500} &= \frac{42{,}500R}{42{,}500} \\ 0.072 &= R \\ 7.2\% &= R \end{aligned}$$
Tina's commission rate was 7.2%.

Applying the Concepts

103.
$$\frac{2}{3}x - 4 = 10$$
$$\frac{2}{3}x - 4 + 4 = 10 + 4 \quad \text{Addition Property of Equations}$$
$$\frac{2}{3}x + 0 = 14 \quad \text{Addition Property of Zero}$$
$$\frac{2}{3}x = 14$$
$$\frac{3}{2}\left(\frac{2}{3}x\right) = \frac{3}{2}(14) \quad \text{Multiplication Property of Equations}$$
$$1x = 21 \quad \text{Multiplication Property of Reciprocals}$$
$$x = 21 \quad \text{Multiplication Property of One}$$

104. Answers will vary. For example, $2x + 5 = -1$ has the solution -3.

105. No, the sentence "Solve $3x + 4(x - 3)$" does not make sense because $3x + 4(x - 3)$ is an expression, and you cannot solve an expression. You can solve an equation.

Section 11.4

Objective A Exercises

1.
$$\begin{aligned} 6x + 3 &= 2x + 5 \\ 6x - 2x + 3 &= 2x - 2x + 5 \\ 4x + 3 &= 5 \\ 4x + 3 - 3 &= 5 - 3 \\ 4x &= 2 \\ \frac{4x}{4} &= \frac{2}{4} \\ x &= \frac{1}{2} \end{aligned}$$

2.
$$\begin{aligned} 7x + 1 &= x + 19 \\ 7x - x + 1 &= x - x + 19 \\ 6x + 1 &= 19 \\ 6x + 1 - 1 &= 19 - 1 \\ 6x &= 18 \\ \frac{6x}{6} &= \frac{18}{6} \\ x &= 3 \end{aligned}$$

3.
$$\begin{aligned} 3x + 3 &= 2x + 2 \\ 3x - 2x + 3 &= 2x - 2x + 2 \\ x + 3 &= 2 \\ x + 3 - 3 &= 2 - 3 \\ x &= -1 \end{aligned}$$

4.
$$\begin{aligned} 6x + 3 &= 3x + 6 \\ 6x - 3x + 3 &= 3x - 3x + 6 \\ 3x + 3 &= 6 \\ 3x + 3 - 3 &= 6 - 3 \\ 3x &= 3 \\ \frac{3x}{3} &= \frac{3}{3} \\ x &= 1 \end{aligned}$$

5.
$$\begin{aligned} 5x + 4 &= x - 12 \\ 5x - x + 4 &= x - x + 12 \\ 4x + 4 &= -12 \\ 4x + 4 - 4 &= -12 - 4 \\ 4x &= -16 \\ \frac{4x}{4} &= \frac{-16}{4} \\ x &= -4 \end{aligned}$$

6.
$$\begin{aligned} 3x - 12 &= x - 8 \\ 3x - x - 12 &= x - x - 8 \\ 2x - 12 &= -8 \\ 2x - 12 + 12 &= -8 + 12 \\ 2x &= 4 \\ \frac{2x}{2} &= \frac{4}{2} \\ x &= 2 \end{aligned}$$

7.
$$\begin{aligned} 7b - 2 &= 3b - 6 \\ 7b - 3b - 2 &= 3b - 3b - 6 \\ 4b - 2 &= -6 \\ 4b - 2 + 2 &= -6 + 2 \\ 4b &= -4 \\ \frac{4b}{4} &= \frac{-4}{4} \\ b &= -1 \end{aligned}$$

8.
$$\begin{aligned} 2d - 9 &= d - 8 \\ 2d - d - 9 &= d - d - 8 \\ d - 9 &= -8 \\ d - 9 + 9 &= -8 + 9 \\ d &= 1 \end{aligned}$$

9.
$$\begin{aligned} 9n - 4 &= 5n - 20 \\ 9n - 5n - 4 &= 5n - 5n - 20 \\ 4n - 4 &= -20 \\ 4n - 4 + 4 &= -20 + 4 \\ 4n &= -16 \\ \frac{4n}{4} &= \frac{-16}{4} \\ n &= -4 \end{aligned}$$

10.
$$\begin{aligned} 8x - 7 &= 5x + 8 \\ 8x - 5x - 7 &= 5x - 5x + 8 \\ 3x - 7 &= 8 \\ 3x - 7 + 7 &= 8 + 7 \\ 3x &= 15 \\ \frac{3x}{3} &= \frac{15}{3} \\ x &= 5 \end{aligned}$$

11.
$$\begin{aligned} 2x + 1 &= 16 - 3x \\ 2x + 3x + 1 &= 16 - 3x + 3x \\ 5x + 1 &= 16 \\ 5x + 1 - 1 &= 16 - 1 \\ 5x &= 15 \\ \frac{5x}{5} &= \frac{15}{5} \\ x &= 3 \end{aligned}$$

12.
$$\begin{aligned} 3x + 2 &= -23 - 2x \\ 3x + 2x + 2 &= -23 - 2x + 2x \\ 5x + 2 &= -23 \\ 5x + 2 - 2 &= -23 - 2 \\ 5x &= -25 \\ \frac{5x}{5} &= \frac{-25}{5} \\ x &= -5 \end{aligned}$$

13.
$$\begin{aligned}5x-2&=-10-3x\\5x+3x-2&=-10-3x+3x\\8x-2&=-10\\8x-2+2&=-10+2\\8x&=-8\\\frac{8x}{8}&=\frac{-8}{8}\\x&=-1\end{aligned}$$

14.
$$\begin{aligned}4x-3&=7-x\\4x+x-3&=7-x+x\\5x-3&=7\\5x-3+3&=7+3\\5x&=10\\\frac{5x}{5}&=\frac{10}{5}\\x&=2\end{aligned}$$

15.
$$\begin{aligned}2x+7&=4x+3\\2x-4x+7&=4x-4x+3\\-2x+7&=3\\-2x+7-7&=3-7\\-2x&=-4\\\frac{-2x}{-2}&=\frac{-4}{-2}\\x&=2\end{aligned}$$

16.
$$\begin{aligned}7m-6&=10m-15\\7m-10m-6&=10m-10m-15\\-3m-6&=-15\\-3m-6+6&=-15+6\\-3m&=-9\\\frac{-3m}{-3}&=\frac{-9}{-3}\\m&=3\end{aligned}$$

17.
$$\begin{aligned}c+4&=6c-11\\c-6c+4&=6c-6c-11\\-5c+4&=-11\\-5c+4-4&=-11-4\\-5c&=-15\\\frac{-5c}{-5}&=\frac{-15}{-5}\\c&=3\end{aligned}$$

18.
$$\begin{aligned}t-6&=4t-21\\t-4t-6&=4t-4t-21\\-3t-6&=-21\\-3t-6+6&=-21+6\\-3t&=-15\\\frac{-3t}{-3}&=\frac{-15}{-3}\\t&=5\end{aligned}$$

19.
$$\begin{aligned}3x-7&=x-7\\3x-x-7&=x-x-7\\2x-7&=-7\\2x-7+7&=-7+7\\2x&=0\\\frac{2x}{2}&=\frac{0}{2}\\x&=0\end{aligned}$$

20.
$$\begin{aligned}2x+6&=7x+6\\2x-7x+6&=7x-7x+6\\-5x+6&=6\\-5x+6-6&=6-6\\-5x&=0\\\frac{-5x}{-5}&=\frac{0}{-5}\\x&=0\end{aligned}$$

21.
$$\begin{aligned}3-4x&=5-3x\\3-4x+3x&=5-3x+3x\\3-x&=5\\3-3-x&=5-3\\-x&=2\\(-1)(-x)&=(-1)2\\x&=-2\end{aligned}$$

22.
$$\begin{aligned}6-2x&=9-x\\6-2x+x&=9-x+x\\6-x&=9\\6-6-x&=9-6\\-x&=3\\(-1)(-x)&=(-1)3\\x&=-3\end{aligned}$$

23.
$$\begin{aligned}7+3x&=9+5x\\7+3x-5x&=9+5x-5x\\7-2x&=9\\7-7-2x&=9-7\\-2x&=2\\\frac{-2x}{-2}&=\frac{2}{-2}\\x&=-1\end{aligned}$$

24.
$$\begin{aligned}12+5x&=9-3x\\12+5x+3x&=9-3x+3x\\12+8x&=9\\12-12+8x&=9-12\\8x&=-3\\\frac{8x}{8}&=\frac{-3}{8}\\x&=-\frac{3}{8}\end{aligned}$$

25.
$$\begin{aligned} 5 + 2y &= 7 + 5y \\ 5 + 2y - 5y &= 7 + 5y - 5y \\ 5 - 3y &= 7 \\ 5 - 5 - 3y &= 7 - 5 \\ -3y &= 2 \\ \frac{-3y}{-3} &= \frac{2}{-3} \\ y &= -\frac{2}{3} \end{aligned}$$

26.
$$\begin{aligned} 9 + z &= 2 + 3z \\ 9 + z - 3z &= 2 + 3z - 3z \\ 9 - 2z &= 2 \\ 9 - 9 - 2z &= 2 - 9 \\ -2z &= -7 \\ \frac{-2z}{-2} &= \frac{-7}{-2} \\ z &= \frac{7}{2} = 3\frac{1}{2} \end{aligned}$$

27.
$$\begin{aligned} 8 - 5w &= 4 - 6w \\ 8 - 5w + 6w &= 4 - 6w + 6w \\ 8 + w &= 4 \\ 8 - 8 + w &= 4 - 8 \\ w &= -4 \end{aligned}$$

28.
$$\begin{aligned} 9 - 4x &= 11 - 5x \\ 9 - 4x + 5x &= 11 - 5x + 5x \\ 9 + x &= 11 \\ 9 - 9 + x &= 11 - 9 \\ x &= 2 \end{aligned}$$

29.
$$\begin{aligned} 6x + 1 &= 3x + 2 \\ 6x - 3x + 1 &= 3x - 3x + 2 \\ 3x + 1 &= 2 \\ 3x + 1 - 1 &= 2 - 1 \\ 3x &= 1 \\ \frac{3x}{3} &= \frac{1}{3} \\ x &= \frac{1}{3} \end{aligned}$$

30.
$$\begin{aligned} 7x + 5 &= 4x + 7 \\ 7x - 4x + 5 &= 4x - 4x + 7 \\ 3x + 5 &= 7 \\ 3x + 5 - 5 &= 7 - 5 \\ 3x &= 2 \\ \frac{3x}{3} &= \frac{2}{3} \\ x &= \frac{2}{3} \end{aligned}$$

31.
$$\begin{aligned} 5x + 8 &= x + 5 \\ 5x - x + 8 &= x - x + 5 \\ 4x + 8 &= 5 \\ 4x + 8 - 8 &= 5 - 8 \\ 4x &= -3 \\ \frac{4x}{4} &= \frac{-3}{4} \\ x &= -\frac{3}{4} \end{aligned}$$

32.
$$\begin{aligned} 9x + 1 &= 3x - 4 \\ 9x - 3x + 1 &= 3x - 3x - 4 \\ 6x + 1 &= -4 \\ 6x + 1 - 1 &= -4 - 1 \\ 6x &= -5 \\ \frac{6x}{6} &= \frac{-5}{6} \\ x &= -\frac{5}{6} \end{aligned}$$

33.
$$\begin{aligned} 2x - 3 &= 6x - 4 \\ 2x - 6x - 3 &= 6x - 6x - 4 \\ -4x - 3 &= -4 \\ -4x - 3 + 3 &= -4 + 3 \\ -4x &= -1 \\ \frac{-4x}{-4} &= \frac{-1}{-4} \\ x &= \frac{1}{4} \end{aligned}$$

34.
$$\begin{aligned} 4 - 3x &= 4 - 5x \\ 4 - 3x + 5x &= 4 - 5x + 5x \\ 4 + 2x &= 4 \\ 4 - 4 + 2x &= 4 - 4 \\ 2x &= 0 \\ \frac{2x}{2} &= \frac{0}{2} \\ x &= 0 \end{aligned}$$

35.
$$\begin{aligned} 6 - 3x &= 6 - 5x \\ 6 - 3x + 5x &= 6 - 5x + 5x \\ 6 + 2x &= 6 \\ 6 - 6 + 2x &= 6 - 6 \\ 2x &= 0 \\ \frac{2x}{2} &= \frac{0}{2} \\ x &= 0 \end{aligned}$$

36.
$$\begin{aligned} 2x + 7 &= 4x - 3 \\ 2x - 4x + 7 &= 4x - 4x - 3 \\ -2x + 7 &= -3 \\ -2x + 7 - 7 &= -3 - 7 \\ -2x &= -10 \\ \frac{-2x}{-2} &= \frac{-10}{-2} \\ x &= 5 \end{aligned}$$

37.
$$\begin{aligned} 6x-2&=2x-9\\ 6x-2x-2&=2x-2x-9\\ 4x-2&=-9\\ 4x-2+2&=-9+2\\ 4x&=-7\\ \frac{4x}{4}&=\frac{-7}{4}\\ x&=-\frac{7}{4}\\ x&=-1\frac{3}{4} \end{aligned}$$

38.
$$\begin{aligned} 4x-7&=-3x+2\\ 4x+3x-7&=-3x+3x+2\\ 7x-7&=2\\ 7x-7+7&=2+7\\ 7x&=9\\ \frac{7x}{7}&=\frac{9}{7}\\ x&=\frac{9}{7}\\ x&=1\frac{2}{7} \end{aligned}$$

39.
$$\begin{aligned} 6x-3&=-5x+8\\ 6x+5x-3&=-5x+5x+8\\ 11x-3&=8\\ 11x-3+3&=8+3\\ 11x&=11\\ \frac{11x}{11}&=\frac{11}{11}\\ x&=1 \end{aligned}$$

40.
$$\begin{aligned} 7y-5&=3y+9\\ 7y-3y-5&=3y-3y+9\\ 4y-5&=9\\ 4y-5+5&=9+5\\ 4y&=14\\ \frac{4y}{4}&=\frac{14}{4}\\ y&=\frac{7}{2}\\ y&=3\frac{1}{2} \end{aligned}$$

41.
$$\begin{aligned} -6t-2&=-8t-4\\ -6t+8t-2&=-8t+8t-4\\ 2t-2&=-4\\ 2t-2+2&=-4+2\\ 2t&=-2\\ \frac{2t}{2}&=\frac{-2}{2}\\ t&=-1 \end{aligned}$$

42.
$$\begin{aligned} -7w+2&=3w-8\\ -7w-3w+2&=3w-3w-8\\ -10w+2&=-8\\ -10w+2-2&=-8-2\\ -10w&=-10\\ \frac{-10w}{-10}&=\frac{-10}{-10}\\ w&=1 \end{aligned}$$

43.
$$\begin{aligned} -3-4x&=7-2x\\ -3-4x+2x&=7-2x+2x\\ -3-2x&=7\\ -3+3-2x&=7+3\\ -2x&=10\\ \frac{-2x}{-2}&=\frac{10}{-2}\\ x&=-5 \end{aligned}$$

44.
$$\begin{aligned} -8+5x&=8+6x\\ -8+5x-6x&=8+6x-6x\\ -8-x&=8\\ -8+8-x&=8+8\\ -x&=16\\ (-1)(-x)&=(-1)(16)\\ x&=-16 \end{aligned}$$

45.
$$\begin{aligned} 3-7x&=-2+5x\\ 3-7x-5x&=-2+5x-5x\\ 3-12x&=-2\\ 3-3-12x&=-2-3\\ -12x&=-5\\ \frac{-12x}{-12}&=\frac{-5}{-12}\\ x&=\frac{5}{12} \end{aligned}$$

46.
$$\begin{aligned} 3x-2&=7-5x\\ 3x+5x-2&=7-5x+5x\\ 8x-2&=7\\ 8x-2+2&=7+2\\ 8x&=9\\ \frac{8x}{8}&=\frac{9}{8}\\ x&=1\frac{1}{8} \end{aligned}$$

47.
$$\begin{aligned} 5x+8&=4-2x\\ 5x+2x+8&=4-2x+2x\\ 7x+8&=4\\ 7x+8-8&=4-8\\ 7x&=-4\\ \frac{7x}{7}&=\frac{-4}{7}\\ x&=-\frac{4}{7} \end{aligned}$$

48. $$\begin{aligned} 4-3x &= 6x-8 \\ 4-3x-6x &= 6x-6x-8 \\ 4-9x &= -8 \\ 4-4-9x &= -8-4 \\ -9x &= -12 \\ \frac{-9x}{-9} &= \frac{-12}{-9} \\ x &= \frac{4}{3} \\ x &= 1\frac{1}{3} \end{aligned}$$

49. $$\begin{aligned} 12z-9 &= 3z+12 \\ 12z-3z-9 &= 3z-3z+12 \\ 9z-9 &= 12 \\ 9z-9+9 &= 12+9 \\ 9z &= 21 \\ \frac{9z}{9} &= \frac{21}{9} \\ z &= \frac{7}{3} \\ z &= 2\frac{1}{3} \end{aligned}$$

50. $$\begin{aligned} 4c+13 &= -6c+9 \\ 4c+6c+13 &= -6c+6c+9 \\ 10c+13 &= 9 \\ 10c+13-13 &= 9-13 \\ 10c &= -4 \\ \frac{10c}{10} &= \frac{-4}{10} \\ c &= -\frac{2}{5} \end{aligned}$$

51. $$\begin{aligned} \frac{5}{7}m-3 &= \frac{2}{7}m+6 \\ \frac{5}{7}m-\frac{2}{7}m-3 &= \frac{2}{7}m-\frac{2}{7}m+6 \\ \frac{3}{7}m-3 &= 6 \\ \frac{3}{7}m-3+3 &= 6+3 \\ \frac{3}{7}m &= 9 \\ \frac{7}{3}\cdot\frac{3}{7}m &= \frac{7}{3}\cdot 9 \\ m &= 21 \end{aligned}$$

52. $$\begin{aligned} \frac{4}{5}x-1 &= \frac{1}{5}x+5 \\ \frac{4}{5}x-\frac{1}{5}x-1 &= \frac{1}{5}x-\frac{1}{5}x+5 \\ \frac{3}{5}x-1 &= 5 \\ \frac{3}{5}x-1+1 &= 5+1 \\ \frac{3}{5}x &= 6 \\ \frac{5}{3}\cdot\frac{3}{5}x &= \frac{5}{3}\cdot 6 \\ x &= 10 \end{aligned}$$

53. $$\begin{aligned} \frac{3}{7}x+5 &= \frac{5}{7}x-1 \\ \frac{3}{7}x-\frac{5}{7}x+5 &= \frac{5}{7}x-\frac{5}{7}x-1 \\ \frac{-2}{7}x+5 &= -1 \\ \frac{-2}{7}x+5-5 &= -1-5 \\ \frac{-2}{7}x &= -6 \\ \left(\frac{-7}{2}\right)\left(\frac{-2}{7}x\right) &= \left(\frac{-7}{2}\right)(-6) \\ x &= 21 \end{aligned}$$

54. $$\begin{aligned} \frac{3}{4}x+2 &= \frac{1}{4}x-9 \\ \frac{3}{4}x-\frac{1}{4}x+2 &= \frac{1}{4}x-\frac{1}{4}x-9 \\ \frac{1}{2}x+2 &= -9 \\ \frac{1}{2}x+2-2 &= -9-2 \\ \frac{1}{2}x &= -11 \\ 2\cdot\frac{1}{2}x &= 2\cdot(-11) \\ x &= -22 \end{aligned}$$

Objective B Exercises

55. $$\begin{aligned} 6x+2(x-1) &= 14 \\ 6x+2x-2 &= 14 \\ 8x-2 &= 14 \\ 8x-2+2 &= 14+2 \\ 8x &= 16 \\ \frac{8x}{8} &= \frac{16}{8} \\ x &= 2 \end{aligned}$$

56.
$$\begin{aligned} 3x + 2(x+4) &= 13 \\ 3x + 2x + 8 &= 13 \\ 5x + 8 &= 13 \\ 5x + 8 - 8 &= 13 - 8 \\ 5x &= 5 \\ \frac{5x}{5} &= \frac{5}{5} \\ x &= 1 \end{aligned}$$

57.
$$\begin{aligned} -3 + 4(x+3) &= 5 \\ -3 + 4x + 12 &= 5 \\ 4x + 9 &= 5 \\ 4x + 9 - 9 &= 5 - 9 \\ 4x &= -4 \\ \frac{4x}{4} &= \frac{-4}{4} \\ x &= -1 \end{aligned}$$

58.
$$\begin{aligned} 8b - 3(b-5) &= 30 \\ 8b - 3b + 15 &= 30 \\ 5b + 15 &= 30 \\ 5b + 15 - 15 &= 30 - 15 \\ 5b &= 15 \\ \frac{5b}{5} &= \frac{15}{5} \\ b &= 3 \end{aligned}$$

59.
$$\begin{aligned} 6 - 2(d+4) &= 6 \\ 6 - 2d - 8 &= 6 \\ -2d - 2 &= 6 \\ -2d - 2 + 2 &= 6 + 2 \\ -2d &= 8 \\ \frac{-2d}{-2} &= \frac{8}{-2} \\ d &= -4 \end{aligned}$$

60.
$$\begin{aligned} 5 - 3(n+2) &= 8 \\ 5 - 3n - 6 &= 8 \\ -3n - 1 &= 8 \\ -3n - 1 + 1 &= 8 + 1 \\ -3n &= 9 \\ \frac{-3n}{-3} &= \frac{9}{-3} \\ n &= -3 \end{aligned}$$

61.
$$\begin{aligned} 5 + 7(x+3) &= 20 \\ 5 + 7x + 21 &= 20 \\ 7x + 26 &= 20 \\ 7x + 26 - 26 &= 20 - 26 \\ 7x &= -6 \\ \frac{7x}{7} &= \frac{-6}{7} \\ x &= -\frac{6}{7} \end{aligned}$$

62.
$$\begin{aligned} 6 - 3(x-4) &= 12 \\ 6 - 3x + 12 &= 12 \\ -3x + 18 &= 12 \\ -3x + 18 - 18 &= 12 - 18 \\ -3x &= -6 \\ \frac{-3x}{-3} &= \frac{-6}{-3} \\ x &= 2 \end{aligned}$$

63.
$$\begin{aligned} 2x + 3(x-5) &= 10 \\ 2x + 3x - 15 &= 10 \\ 5x - 15 &= 10 \\ 5x - 15 + 15 &= 10 + 15 \\ 5x &= 25 \\ \frac{5x}{5} &= \frac{25}{5} \\ x &= 5 \end{aligned}$$

64.
$$\begin{aligned} 3x - 4(x+3) &= 9 \\ 3x - 4x - 12 &= 9 \\ -x - 12 &= 9 \\ -x - 12 + 12 &= 9 + 12 \\ -x &= 21 \\ (-1)(-x) &= (-1)(21) \\ x &= -21 \end{aligned}$$

65.
$$\begin{aligned} 3(x-4) + 2x &= 3 \\ 3x - 12 + 2x &= 3 \\ 5x - 12 &= 3 \\ 5x - 12 + 12 &= 3 + 12 \\ 5x &= 15 \\ \frac{5x}{5} &= \frac{15}{5} \\ x &= 3 \end{aligned}$$

66.
$$\begin{aligned} 4 + 3(x-9) &= -12 \\ 4 + 3x - 27 &= -12 \\ 3x - 23 &= -12 \\ 3x - 23 + 23 &= -12 + 23 \\ 3x &= 11 \\ \frac{3x}{3} &= \frac{11}{3} \\ x &= 3\frac{2}{3} \end{aligned}$$

67.
$$\begin{aligned} 2x - 3(x-4) &= 12 \\ 2x - 3x + 12 &= 12 \\ -x + 12 &= 12 \\ -x + 12 - 12 &= 12 - 12 \\ -x &= 0 \\ (-1)(-x) &= (-1)0 \\ x &= 0 \end{aligned}$$

68.
$$\begin{aligned} 4x - 2(x - 5) &= 10 \\ 4x - 2x + 10 &= 10 \\ 2x + 10 &= 10 \\ 2x + 10 - 10 &= 10 - 10 \\ 2x &= 0 \\ \frac{2x}{2} &= \frac{0}{2} \\ x &= 0 \end{aligned}$$

69.
$$\begin{aligned} 2x + 3(x + 4) &= 7 \\ 2x + 3x + 12 &= 7 \\ 5x + 12 &= 7 \\ 5x + 12 - 12 &= 7 - 12 \\ 5x &= -5 \\ \frac{5x}{5} &= \frac{-5}{5} \\ x &= -1 \end{aligned}$$

70.
$$\begin{aligned} 3(x + 2) + 7 &= 12 \\ 3x + 6 + 7 &= 12 \\ 3x + 13 &= 12 \\ 3x + 13 - 13 &= 12 - 13 \\ 3x &= -1 \\ \frac{3x}{3} &= \frac{-1}{3} \\ x &= -\frac{1}{3} \end{aligned}$$

71.
$$\begin{aligned} 3(x - 2) + 5 &= 5 \\ 3x - 6 + 5 &= 5 \\ 3x - 1 &= 5 \\ 3x - 1 + 1 &= 5 + 1 \\ 3x &= 6 \\ \frac{3x}{3} &= \frac{6}{3} \\ x &= 2 \end{aligned}$$

72.
$$\begin{aligned} 4(x - 5) + 7 &= 7 \\ 4x - 20 + 7 &= 7 \\ 4x - 13 &= 7 \\ 4x - 13 + 13 &= 7 + 13 \\ 4x &= 20 \\ \frac{4x}{4} &= \frac{20}{4} \\ x &= 5 \end{aligned}$$

73.
$$\begin{aligned} 3y + 7(y - 2) &= 5 \\ 3y + 7y - 14 &= 5 \\ 10y - 14 &= 5 \\ 10y - 14 + 14 &= 5 + 14 \\ 10y &= 19 \\ \frac{10y}{10} &= \frac{19}{10} \\ y &= 1\frac{9}{10} \end{aligned}$$

74.
$$\begin{aligned} -3z - 3(z - 3) &= 3 \\ -3z - 3z + 9 &= 3 \\ -6z + 9 &= 3 \\ -6z + 9 - 9 &= 3 - 9 \\ -6z &= -6 \\ \frac{-6z}{-6} &= \frac{-6}{-6} \\ z &= 1 \end{aligned}$$

75.
$$\begin{aligned} 4b - 2(b + 9) &= 8 \\ 4b - 2b - 18 &= 8 \\ 2b - 18 &= 8 \\ 2b - 18 + 18 &= 8 + 18 \\ 2b &= 26 \\ \frac{2b}{2} &= \frac{26}{2} \\ b &= 13 \end{aligned}$$

76.
$$\begin{aligned} 3x - 6(x - 3) &= 9 \\ 3x - 6x + 18 &= 9 \\ -3x + 18 &= 9 \\ -3x + 18 - 18 &= 9 - 18 \\ -3x &= -9 \\ \frac{-3x}{-3} &= \frac{-9}{-3} \\ x &= 3 \end{aligned}$$

77.
$$\begin{aligned} 3x + 5(x - 2) &= 10 \\ 3x + 5x - 10 &= 10 \\ 8x - 10 &= 10 \\ 8x - 10 + 10 &= 10 + 10 \\ 8x &= 20 \\ \frac{8x}{8} &= \frac{20}{8} \\ x &= \frac{5}{2} = 2\frac{1}{2} \end{aligned}$$

78.
$$\begin{aligned} 3x - 5(x - 1) &= -5 \\ 3x - 5x + 5 &= -5 \\ -2x + 5 &= -5 \\ -2x + 5 - 5 &= -5 - 5 \\ -2x &= -10 \\ \frac{-2x}{-2} &= \frac{-10}{-2} \\ x &= 5 \end{aligned}$$

79.
$$\begin{aligned} 3x + 4(x + 2) &= 2(x + 9) \\ 3x + 4x + 8 &= 2x + 18 \\ 7x + 8 &= 2x + 18 \\ 7x - 2x + 8 &= 2x - 2x + 18 \\ 5x + 8 &= 18 \\ 5x + 8 - 8 &= 18 - 8 \\ 5x &= 10 \\ \frac{5x}{5} &= \frac{10}{5} \\ x &= 2 \end{aligned}$$

80. $5x + 3(x + 4) = 4(x + 2)$
$$5x + 3x + 12 = 4x + 8$$
$$8x + 12 = 4x + 8$$
$$8x - 4x + 12 = 4x - 4x + 8$$
$$4x + 12 = 8$$
$$4x + 12 - 12 = 8 - 12$$
$$4x = -4$$
$$\frac{4x}{4} = \frac{-4}{4}$$
$$x = -1$$

81. $2d - 3(d - 4) = 2(d + 6)$
$$2d - 3d + 12 = 2d + 12$$
$$-d + 12 = 2d + 12$$
$$-d - 2d + 12 = 2d - 2d + 12$$
$$-3d + 12 = 12$$
$$-3d + 12 - 12 = 12 - 12$$
$$-3d = 0$$
$$\frac{-3d}{-3} = \frac{0}{-3}$$
$$d = 0$$

82. $3t - 4(t - 1) = 3(t - 2)$
$$3t - 4t + 4 = 3t - 6$$
$$-t + 4 = 3t - 6$$
$$-t - 3t + 4 = 3t - 3t - 6$$
$$-4t + 4 = -6$$
$$-4t + 4 - 4 = -6 - 4$$
$$-4t = -10$$
$$\frac{-4t}{-4} = \frac{-10}{-4}$$
$$t = \frac{5}{2} = 2\frac{1}{2}$$

83. $7 - 2(x - 3) = 3(x - 1)$
$$7 - 2x + 6 = 3x - 3$$
$$-2x + 13 = 3x - 3$$
$$-2x - 3x + 13 = 3x - 3x - 3$$
$$-5x + 13 = -3$$
$$-5x + 13 - 13 = -3 - 13$$
$$-5x = -16$$
$$\frac{-5x}{-5} = \frac{-16}{-5}$$
$$x = 3\frac{1}{5}$$

84. $4 - 3(x + 2) = 2(x - 4)$
$$4 - 3x - 6 = 2x - 8$$
$$-3x - 2 = 2x - 8$$
$$-3x - 2x - 2 = 2x - 2x - 8$$
$$-5x - 2 = -8$$
$$-5x - 2 + 2 = -8 + 2$$
$$-5x = -6$$
$$\frac{-5x}{-5} = \frac{-6}{-5}$$
$$x = \frac{6}{5} = 1\frac{1}{5}$$

85. $6x - 2(x - 3) = 11(x - 2)$
$$6x - 2x + 6 = 11x - 22$$
$$4x + 6 = 11x - 22$$
$$4x - 11x + 6 = 11x - 11x - 22$$
$$-7x + 6 = -22$$
$$-7x + 6 - 6 = -22 - 6$$
$$-7x = -28$$
$$\frac{-7x}{-7} = \frac{-28}{-7}$$
$$x = 4$$

86. $9x - 5(x - 3) = 5(x + 4)$
$$9x - 5x + 15 = 5x + 20$$
$$4x + 15 = 5x + 20$$
$$4x - 5x + 15 = 5x - 5x + 20$$
$$-x + 15 = 20$$
$$-x + 15 - 15 = 20 - 15$$
$$-x = 5$$
$$(-1)(-x) = (-1)5$$
$$x = -5$$

87. $6c - 3(c + 1) = 5(c + 2)$
$$6c - 3c - 3 = 5c + 10$$
$$3c - 3 = 5c + 10$$
$$3c - 5c - 3 = 5c - 5c + 10$$
$$-2c - 3 = 10$$
$$-2c - 3 + 3 = 10 + 3$$
$$-2c = 13$$
$$\frac{-2c}{-2} = \frac{13}{-2}$$
$$c = -6\frac{1}{2}$$

88. $2w - 7(w - 2) = 3(w - 4)$
$$2w - 7w + 14 = 3w - 12$$
$$-5w + 14 = 3w - 12$$
$$-5w - 3w + 14 = 3w - 3w - 12$$
$$-8w + 14 = -12$$
$$-8w + 14 - 14 = -12 - 14$$
$$-8w = -26$$
$$\frac{-8w}{-8} = \frac{-26}{-8}$$
$$w = \frac{13}{4}$$
$$w = 3\frac{1}{4}$$

89. $7 - (x + 1) = 3(x + 3)$
$$7 - x - 1 = 3x + 9$$
$$-x + 6 = 3x + 9$$
$$-x - 3x + 6 = 3x - 3x + 9$$
$$-4x + 6 = 9$$
$$-4x + 6 - 6 = 9 - 6$$
$$-4x = 3$$
$$\frac{-4x}{-4} = \frac{3}{-4}$$
$$x = -\frac{3}{4}$$

90.
$$\begin{aligned}12 + 2(x - 9) &= 3(x - 12)\\ 12 + 2x - 18 &= 3x - 36\\ 2x - 6 &= 3x - 36\\ 2x - 3x - 6 &= 3x - 3x - 36\\ -x - 6 &= -36\\ -x - 6 + 6 &= -36 + 6\\ -x &= -30\\ (-1)(-x) &= (-1)(-30)\\ x &= 30\end{aligned}$$

91.
$$\begin{aligned}2x - 3(x + 4) &= 2(x - 5)\\ 2x - 3x - 12 &= 2x - 10\\ -x - 12 &= 2x - 10\\ -x - 2x - 12 &= 2x - 2x - 10\\ -3x - 12 &= -10\\ -3x - 12 + 12 &= -10 + 12\\ -3x &= 2\\ \frac{-3x}{-3} &= \frac{2}{-3}\\ x &= -\frac{2}{3}\end{aligned}$$

92.
$$\begin{aligned}3x + 2(x - 7) &= 7(x - 1)\\ 3x + 2x - 14 &= 7x - 7\\ 5x - 14 &= 7x - 7\\ 5x - 7x - 14 &= 7x - 7x - 7\\ -2x - 14 &= -7\\ -2x - 14 + 14 &= -7 + 14\\ -2x &= 7\\ \frac{-2x}{-2} &= \frac{7}{-2}\\ x &= -3\frac{1}{2}\end{aligned}$$

93.
$$\begin{aligned}x + 5(x - 4) &= 3(x - 8) - 5\\ x + 5x - 20 &= 3x - 24 - 5\\ 6x - 20 &= 3x - 29\\ 6x - 3x - 20 &= 3x - 3x - 29\\ 3x - 20 &= -29\\ 3x - 20 + 20 &= -29 + 20\\ 3x &= -9\\ \frac{3x}{3} &= \frac{-9}{3}\\ x &= -3\end{aligned}$$

94.
$$\begin{aligned}2x - 2(x - 1) &= 3(x - 2) + 7\\ 2x - 2x + 2 &= 3x - 6 + 7\\ 2 &= 3x + 1\\ 2 - 1 &= 3x + 1 - 1\\ 1 &= 3x\\ \frac{1}{3} &= \frac{3x}{3}\\ \frac{1}{3} &= x\end{aligned}$$

95.
$$\begin{aligned}9b - 3(b - 4) &= 13 + 2(b - 3)\\ 9b - 3b + 12 &= 13 + 2b - 6\\ 6b + 12 &= 2b + 7\\ 6b - 2b + 12 &= 2b - 2b + 7\\ 4b + 12 &= 7\\ 4b + 12 - 12 &= 7 - 12\\ 4b &= -5\\ \frac{4b}{4} &= \frac{-5}{4}\\ b &= -1\frac{1}{4}\end{aligned}$$

96.
$$\begin{aligned}3y - 4(y - 2) &= 15 - 3(y - 2)\\ 3y - 4y + 8 &= 15 - 3y + 6\\ -y + 8 &= -3y + 21\\ -y + 3y + 8 &= -3y + 3y + 21\\ 2y + 8 &= 21\\ 2y + 8 - 8 &= 21 - 8\\ 2y &= 13\\ \frac{2y}{2} &= \frac{13}{2}\\ y &= 6\frac{1}{2}\end{aligned}$$

97.
$$\begin{aligned}3(x - 4) + 3x &= 7 - 2(x - 1)\\ 3x - 12 + 3x &= 7 - 2x + 2\\ 6x - 12 &= -2x + 9\\ 6x + 2x - 12 &= -2x + 2x + 9\\ 8x - 12 &= 9\\ 8x - 12 + 12 &= 9 + 12\\ 8x &= 21\\ \frac{8x}{8} &= \frac{21}{8}\\ x &= 2\frac{5}{8}\end{aligned}$$

98.
$$\begin{aligned}2(x - 6) + 7x &= 5 - 3(x - 2)\\ 2x - 12 + 7x &= 5 - 3x + 6\\ 9x - 12 &= -3x + 11\\ 9x + 3x - 12 &= -3x + 3x + 11\\ 12x - 12 &= 11\\ 12x - 12 + 12 &= 11 + 12\\ 12x &= 23\\ \frac{12x}{12} &= \frac{23}{12}\\ x &= 1\frac{11}{12}\end{aligned}$$

99.
$$\begin{aligned}3.67x - 5.3(x - 1.932) &= 6.99\\ 3.67x - 5.3x + 10.2396 &= 6.99\\ -1.63x + 10.2396 &= 6.99\\ -1.63x + 10.2396 - 10.2396 &= 6.99 - 10.2396\\ -1.63x &= -3.2496\\ \frac{-1.63x}{-1.63} &= \frac{-3.2496}{-1.63}\\ x &\approx 1.9936196\end{aligned}$$

100.
$$\begin{aligned} 4.06x + 4.7(x + 3.22) &= 1.774 \\ 4.06x + 4.7x + 15.134 &= 1.774 \\ 8.76x + 15.134 &= 1.774 \\ 8.76x + 15.134 - 15.134 &= 1.774 - 15.134 \\ 8.76x &= -13.36 \\ \frac{8.76x}{8.76} &= \frac{-13.36}{8.76} \\ x &\approx -1.5251142 \end{aligned}$$

101.
$$\begin{aligned} 8.45(z - 10) &= 3(z - 3.854) \\ 8.45z - 84.5 &= 3z - 11.562 \\ 8.45z - 3z - 84.5 &= 3z - 3z - 11.562 \\ 5.45z - 84.5 &= -11.562 \\ 5.45z - 84.5 + 84.5 &= -11.562 + 84.5 \\ 5.45z &= 72.938 \\ \frac{5.45z}{5.45} &= \frac{72.938}{5.45} \\ z &\approx 13.3831193 \end{aligned}$$

102.
$$\begin{aligned} 4(d - 1.99) - 3.92 &= 3(d - 1.77) \\ 4d - 7.96 - 3.92 &= 3d - 5.31 \\ 4d - 11.88 &= 3d - 5.31 \\ 4d - 3d - 11.88 &= 3d - 3d - 5.31 \\ d - 11.88 &= -5.31 \\ d - 11.88 + 11.88 &= -5.31 + 11.88 \\ d &= 6.57 \end{aligned}$$

Applying the Concepts

103.
$$\begin{aligned} 2x - 2 &= 4x + 6 \\ 2x - 4x - 2 &= 4x - 4x + 6 \\ -2x - 2 &= 6 \\ -2x - 2 + 2 &= 6 + 2 \\ -2x &= 8 \\ x &= -4 \end{aligned}$$
Then $3x^2 = 3(-4)^2 = 48$.

104.
$$\begin{aligned} 3 + 2(4a - 3) &= 4 \\ 3 + 8a - 6 &= 4 \\ 8a - 3 &= 4 \\ 8a - 3 + 3 &= 4 + 3 \\ 8a &= 7 \\ a &= \frac{7}{8} \end{aligned} \qquad \begin{aligned} 4 - 3(2 - 3b) &= 11 \\ 4 - 6 + 9b &= 11 \\ -2 + 9b &= 11 \\ -2 + 2 + 9b &= 11 + 2 \\ 9b &= 13 \\ b &= \frac{13}{9} \end{aligned}$$
Thus b is larger.

105. Students should explain that the solution of the original equation is $x = 0$. Therefore, the fourth line, where each side of the equation is divided by x, involved division by zero, which is not defined.

106. Many beginning algebra students do not differentiate between an equation that has no solution and an equation whose solution is zero. Students should explain that zero is a (real) number and that the solution of the equation $2x + 3 = 3$ is the (real) number zero. However, there is no solution to the equation $x = x + 1$ because there is no (real) number that is equal to itself plus 1.

Section 11.5

Objective A Exercises

1. $y - 9$

2. $\frac{w}{7}$

3. $z + 3$

4. $-2x$

5. $\frac{2}{3}n + n$

6. $r^2 - r$

7. $\frac{m}{m - 3}$

8. $v + 2v$

9. $9(x + 4)$

10. $a + \frac{a}{7}$

11. $n - (-5)n$

12. $x - \frac{x}{2}$

13. $c\left(\frac{1}{4}c\right)$

14. $\frac{z - 3}{z}$

15. $m^2 + 2m^2$

16. $y(y + 4)$

17. $2(t + 6)$

18. $\frac{r}{8 - r}$

19. $\frac{x}{9 + x}$

20. $z + 6z$

21. $3(b + 6)$

22. $\frac{w}{w + 8}$

Objective B Exercises

23. The *square* of a number
The unknown number: x
x^2

24. Five *less than* some number
The unknown number: x
$x - 5$

25. A number *divided* by twenty
The unknown number: x
$\frac{x}{20}$

26. The *difference between* a number and twelve
The unknown number: x
$x - 12$

27. Four *times* some number
The unknown number: x
$4x$

28. The *quotient* of 5 and a number
The unknown number: x
$\frac{5}{x}$

29. Three-fourths *of* a number
The unknown number: x
$\frac{3}{4}x$

30. The *sum* of a number and seven
The unknown number: x
$x + 7$

31. Four *increased* by some number
The unknown number: x
$4 + x$

32. The *ratio* of a number to nine
The unknown number: x
$\frac{x}{9}$

33. The *difference between* five *times* a number and the number
The unknown number: x
Five times the number: $5x$
$5x - x$

34. Six *less than* the *total* of three and a number
The unknown number: x
The total of three and the number: $3 + x$
$(3 + x) - 6$

35. The *product* of a number and two *more than* the number
The unknown number: x
Two more than the number: $x + 2$
$x(x + 2)$

36. The *quotient* of six and the *sum* of nine and a number
The unknown number: x
The sum of nine and the number: $x + 9$
$\frac{6}{9 + x}$

37. Seven *times* the *total* of a number and eight
The unknown number: x
The total of the number and eight: $x + 8$
$7(x + 8)$

38. The *difference between* ten and the *quotient* of a number and two
The unknown number: x
The quotient of the number and two: $\frac{x}{2}$
$10 - \frac{x}{2}$

39. The *square* of a number *plus* the *product* of three and the number
The unknown number: x
The square of the number: x^2
The product of three and the number: $3x$
$x^2 + 3x$

40. A number *decreased* by the *product* of five and the number
The unknown number: x
The product of five and the number: $5x$
$x - 5x$

41. The *sum* of three *more than* a number and one-half *of* the number
The unknown number: x
Three more than the number: $x + 3$
One-half of the number: $\frac{1}{2}x$
$(x + 3) + \frac{1}{2}x$

42. Eight *more than* twice the sum of a number *and* seven
The unknown number: x
Twice the sum of the number and seven: $2(x + 7)$
$2(x + 7) + 8$

43. The *quotient* of three times a number and the number
The unknown number: x
Three times the number: $3x$
$\frac{3x}{x}$

44. The *square* of a number *divided* by the *sum* of the number and twelve
The unknown number: x
The square of the number: x^2
The sum of the number and twelve: $x + 12$
$\frac{x^2}{x + 12}$

Applying the Concepts

45a. $2x + 3$: Answers will vary. For example, the sum of twice a number and 3.

b. $2(x + 3)$: Answers will vary. For example, twice the sum of a number and 3.

46a. $\frac{2x}{7}$: Answers will vary. For example, the quotient of twice a number and 7.

b. $\frac{2 + x}{7}$: Answers will vary. For example, the quotient of the sum of 2 and a number, and 7.

47. Students will provide different explanations of how variables are used. Look for the idea that a variable is used to represent a number that is unknown or a number that can change, or vary.

48. $2x$

49. $\frac{1}{2}x$: number of carbon atoms

$\frac{1}{2}x$: number of oxygen atoms

Section 11.6

Objective A Exercises

1. The unknown number: x

$$x + 7 = 12$$
$$x + 7 - 7 = 12 - 7$$
$$x = 5$$

The number is 5.

2. The unknown number: x

$$x - 7 = 5$$
$$x - 7 + 7 = 5 + 7$$
$$x = 12$$

The number is 12.

3. The unknown number: x

$$3x = 18$$
$$\frac{3x}{3} = \frac{18}{3}$$
$$x = 6$$

The number is 6.

4. The unknown number: x

$$\frac{x}{3} = 1$$
$$3 \cdot \frac{x}{3} = 3 \cdot 1$$
$$x = 3$$

The number is 3.

5. The unknown number: x

$$x + 5 = 3$$
$$x + 5 - 5 = 3 - 5$$
$$x = -2$$

The number is -2.

6. The unknown number: x

$$\frac{x}{4} = 6$$
$$4 \cdot \frac{x}{4} = 4 \cdot 6$$
$$x = 24$$

The number is 24.

7. The unknown number: x

$$6x = 14$$
$$\frac{6x}{6} = \frac{14}{6}$$
$$x = \frac{7}{3} = 2\frac{1}{3}$$

The number is $2\frac{1}{3}$.

8. The unknown number: x

$$x - 7 = 3$$
$$x - 7 + 7 = 3 + 7$$
$$x = 10$$

The number is 10.

9. The unknown number: x

$$\frac{5}{6}x = 15$$
$$\frac{6}{5} \cdot \frac{5}{6}x = \frac{6}{5} \cdot 15$$
$$x = 18$$

The number is 18.

10. The unknown number: x

$$20 + x = 5$$
$$20 - 20 + x = 5 - 20$$
$$x = -15$$

The number is -15.

11. The unknown number: x

$$3x + 4 = 8$$
$$3x + 4 - 4 = 8 - 4$$
$$3x = 4$$
$$\frac{3x}{3} = \frac{4}{3}$$
$$x = \frac{4}{3} = 1\frac{1}{3}$$

The number is $1\frac{1}{3}$.

12. The unknown number: x

$$\frac{1}{3}x + 7 = 12$$
$$\frac{1}{3}x + 7 - 7 = 12 - 7$$
$$\frac{1}{3}x = 5$$
$$3 \cdot \frac{1}{3}x = 3 \cdot 5$$
$$x = 15$$

The number is 15.

13. The unknown number: x

$$\frac{1}{4}x - 7 = 9$$
$$\frac{1}{4}x - 7 + 7 = 9 + 7$$
$$\frac{1}{4}x = 16$$
$$4 \cdot \frac{1}{4}x = 4 \cdot 16$$
$$x = 64$$

The number is 64.

14. The unknown number: x

$$\frac{x}{4}+9=2$$
$$\frac{x}{4}+9-9=2-9$$
$$\frac{x}{4}=-7$$
$$4\cdot\frac{x}{4}=4(-7)$$
$$x=-28$$

The number is −28.

15. The unknown number: x

$$\frac{x}{9}=14$$
$$9\cdot\frac{x}{9}=9\cdot 14$$
$$x=126$$

The number is 126.

16. The unknown number: x

$$5+5x=30$$
$$5-5+5x=30-5$$
$$5x=25$$
$$\frac{5x}{5}=\frac{25}{5}$$
$$x=5$$

The number is 5.

17. The unknown number: x

$$\frac{x}{4}-6=-2$$
$$\frac{x}{4}-6+6=-2+6$$
$$\frac{x}{4}=4$$
$$4\cdot\frac{x}{4}=4\cdot 4$$
$$x=16$$

The number is 16.

18. The unknown number: x

$$(x+3)\cdot 2=8$$
$$2x+6=8$$
$$2x+6-6=8-6$$
$$2x=2$$
$$\frac{2x}{2}=\frac{2}{2}$$
$$x=1$$

The number is 1.

19. The unknown number: x

$$7-2x=13$$
$$7-7-2x=13-7$$
$$-2x=6$$
$$\frac{-2x}{-2}=\frac{6}{-2}$$
$$x=-3$$

The number is −3.

20. The unknown number: x

$$3x+5=8$$
$$3x+5-5=8-5$$
$$\frac{3x}{3}=\frac{3}{3}$$
$$x=1$$

The number is 1.

21. The unknown number: x

$$9-\frac{x}{2}=5$$
$$9-9-\frac{x}{2}=5-9$$
$$-\frac{x}{2}=-4$$
$$(-2)\left(-\frac{x}{2}\right)=(-2)(-4)$$
$$x=8$$

The number is 8.

22. The unknown number: x

$$10x+7=27$$
$$10x+7-7=27-7$$
$$10x=20$$
$$\frac{10x}{10}=\frac{20}{10}$$
$$x=2$$

The number is 2.

23. The unknown number: x

$$\frac{3}{5}x+8=2$$
$$\frac{3}{5}x+8-8=2-8$$
$$\frac{3}{5}x=-6$$
$$\frac{5}{3}\cdot\frac{3}{5}x=\frac{5}{3}\cdot(-6)$$
$$x=-10$$

The number is −10.

24. The unknown number: x

$$\frac{2}{3}x-5=3$$
$$\frac{2}{3}x-5+5=3+5$$
$$\frac{2}{3}x=8$$
$$\frac{3}{2}\cdot\frac{2}{3}x=\frac{3}{2}\cdot 8$$
$$x=12$$

The number is 12.

25. The unknown number: x

$$\frac{x}{4.186} - 7.92 = 12.529$$
$$\frac{x}{4.186} - 7.92 + 7.92 = 12.529 + 7.92$$
$$\frac{x}{4.186} = 20.449$$
$$4.186 \cdot \frac{x}{4.186} = 4.186(20.449)$$
$$x = 85.599514$$

The number is 85.599514.

26. The unknown number: x

$$5.68x + 132.7 = x - 29.265$$
$$5.68x - x + 132.7 = x - x - 29.265$$
$$4.68x + 132.7 = -29.265$$
$$4.68x + 132.7 - 132.7 = -29.265 - 132.7$$
$$4.68x = -161.965$$
$$\frac{4.68x}{4.68} = \frac{-161.965}{4.68}$$
$$x \approx -34.607906$$

The number is approximately -34.607906.

Objective B Exercises

27. Strategy To find the price of a pair of shoes at Target, write and solve an equation using P to represent the price at Target.

Solution

$$72.50 = P - 4.25$$
$$72.50 + 4.25 = P - 4.25 + 4.25$$
$$76.75 = P$$

The price at Target is \$76.75.

28. Strategy To find the weekly salary last year, write and solve an equation using s to represent last year's weekly salary.

Solution

$$832 = 58 + s$$
$$832 - 58 = 58 - 58 + s$$
$$774 = s$$

The manager's weekly salary last year was \$774.

29. Strategy To find the value of the SUV last year, write and solve an equation using V to represent the value of the SUV last year

Solution

$$\frac{4}{5}V = 16{,}000$$
$$\frac{5}{4} \cdot \frac{4}{5}V = \frac{5}{4} \cdot 16{,}000$$
$$V = 20{,}000$$

The value of the SUV last year was \$20,000.

30. Strategy To find the value of the cottage 6 years ago, write and solve an equation using V to represent the value 6 years ago.

Solution

$$175{,}000 = 2V$$
$$\frac{175{,}000}{2} = \frac{2V}{2}$$
$$87{,}500 = V$$

The value of the cottage 6 years ago was \$87,500.

31. Strategy To find the length of the Brooklyn Bridge, write and solve an equation using L to represent the length of the Brooklyn Bridge.

Solution

$$1991 = L + 1505$$
$$1991 - 1505 = L + 1505 - 1505$$
$$486 = L$$

The length of the Brooklyn Bridge is 486 m.

32. Strategy To find the average credit card balance today, write and solve an equation using D to represent the average credit card balance today.

Solution

$$3275 = D - 5665$$
$$3275 + 5665 = D - 5665 + 5665$$
$$8940 = D$$

The average credit card balance today is \$8940.

33. Strategy To find the family's monthly income, write and solve an equation using S to represent the family's income.

Solution

$$1360 = \frac{1}{4}S$$
$$4 \cdot 1360 = 4 \cdot \frac{1}{4}S$$
$$5440 = S$$

The family's monthly income is \$5440.

34. Strategy To find the cost of the calculator 5 years ago, write and solve an equation using C to represent the cost 5 years ago.

Solution

$$\frac{3}{4}C = 72$$
$$\frac{4}{3} \cdot \frac{3}{4}C = \frac{4}{3} \cdot 72$$
$$C = 96$$

The cost of the calculator 5 years ago was \$96.

35. Strategy To find the monthly output a year ago, write and solve an equation using M to represent the monthly output a year ago.

Solution

$$400 = 0.08M$$
$$\frac{400}{0.08} = \frac{0.08M}{0.08}$$
$$5000 = M$$

The monthly output a year ago was 5000 computers.

36. Strategy To find the average number of home runs per game 40 years ago, write and solve an equation using H to represent the average number of home runs per game 40 years ago.

Solution

$$2.21 = 1.35H$$
$$\frac{2.21}{1.35} = \frac{1.35H}{1.35}$$
$$1.637 \approx H$$

The average number of home runs per game 40 years ago was 1.64 home runs.

37. Strategy To find the recommended daily allowance of sodium:

- Write and solve an equation using x to represent the daily allowance of sodium.
- Convert the milligrams to grams.

Solution

$$8\% \cdot x = 200$$
$$0.08x = 200$$
$$\frac{0.08x}{0.08} = \frac{200}{0.08}$$
$$x = 2{,}500$$

2,500 mg = 2.5 g

The recommended daily allowance of sodium is 2.5 g.

38. Strategy To find the store's cost for the skis, write and solve an equation using C to represent the store's cost for the skis.

Solution

$$340 = C + 0.25C$$
$$340 = 1.25C$$
$$\frac{340}{1.25} = \frac{1.25C}{1.25}$$
$$272 = C$$

The store's cost for the skis is \$272.

39. Strategy To find the number of hours of labor required to install a water softener, write and solve an equation using T to represent the time it took to install the water softener.

Solution

$$400 = 310 + 30T$$
$$400 - 310 = 310 - 310 + 30T$$
$$90 = 30T$$
$$\frac{90}{30} = \frac{30T}{30}$$
$$3 = T$$

It took 3 h to install the water softener.

40. Strategy To find the total sales for the month, write and solve an equation using S to represent the total sales for the month.

Solution

$$2580 = 600 + 0.03S$$
$$2580 - 600 = 600 - 600 + 0.03S$$
$$1980 = 0.03S$$
$$\frac{1980}{0.03} = \frac{0.03S}{0.03}$$
$$66{,}000 = S$$

The total sales for the month were \$66,000.

41. Strategy To find the number of plants and animals known to be at risk, write and solve an equation using P to represent the number of plants and animals.

Solution

$$10.7\% \cdot P = 1184$$
$$0.107P = 1184$$
$$\frac{0.107P}{0.107} = \frac{1184}{0.107}$$
$$P \approx 11{,}065$$

About 11,065 plants and animals are known to be at risk of extinction in the world.

42. Strategy To find the number of business-related miles, write and solve an equation using M to represent the number of miles driven. 36 cents = \$.36

Solution

$$0.36M = 1728$$
$$\frac{0.36M}{0.36} = \frac{1728}{0.36}$$
$$M = 4800$$

There were 4800 business-related miles driven.

43. Strategy To find the percent spent in New York, write and solve the basic percent equation using P to represent the percent. The base is 295 and the amount is 9.8.

Solution Percent × base = amount

$$P \times 295 = 9.8$$
$$295P = 9.8$$
$$\frac{295P}{295} = \frac{9.8}{295}$$
$$P \approx 0.0332$$

The percent is 3.3%.

44. Strategy To find the number of yards of cement that can be purchased, write and solve an equation using C to represent the number of yards of cement.

Solution

$$363 = 75 + 24C$$
$$363 - 75 = 75 - 75 + 24C$$
$$288 = 24C$$
$$\frac{288}{24} = \frac{24C}{24}$$
$$12 = C$$

12 yd of cement can be purchased for $363.

45. Strategy To find the original rate of water flow, write and solve an equation using R to represent the original rate.

Solution

$$2 = \frac{3}{5}R - 1$$
$$2 + 1 = \frac{3}{5}R - 1 + 1$$
$$3 = \frac{3}{5}R$$
$$\frac{5}{3} \cdot 3 = \frac{5}{3} \cdot \frac{3}{5}R$$

The original water flow rate was 5 gal/min.

46. Strategy To find the Fahrenheit temperature, write and solve an equation using F to represent the Fahrenheit temperature.

Solution

$$40 = \frac{5}{9}(F - 32)$$
$$40 = \frac{5}{9}F - \frac{160}{9}$$
$$40 + \frac{160}{9} = \frac{5}{9}F - \frac{160}{9} + \frac{160}{9}$$
$$\frac{520}{9} = \frac{5}{9}F$$
$$\frac{9}{5} \cdot \frac{520}{9} = \frac{9}{5} \cdot \frac{5}{9}F$$
$$104 = F$$

The temperature is 104°F.

47. Strategy To find the total sales for the month, write and solve an equation using T to represent the total sales.

Solution

$$600 + 0.0825T = 4109.55$$
$$600 - 600 + 0.0825T = 4109.55 - 600$$
$$0.0825T = 3509.55$$
$$\frac{0.0825T}{0.0825} = \frac{3509.55}{0.0825}$$
$$T = 42{,}540$$

The total sales for the month were $42,540.

48. Strategy To find the world carbon dioxide emissions in 1998, write and solve an equation using T to represent the number of billions of metric tons of world carbon dioxide emissions in 1998.

Solution

$$9.85 = 1.604T$$
$$\frac{9.85}{1.604} = \frac{1.604T}{1.604}$$
$$6.14 \approx T$$

The world carbon dioxide emissions in 1998 were 6.14 billion metric tons.

49. Strategy To find the world carbon dioxide emissions in 1990, write and solve an equation using T to represent the number of billions of metric tons of world carbon dioxide emissions in 1990.

Solution

$$8.87 = 1.521T$$
$$\frac{8.87}{1.521} = \frac{1.521T}{1.521}$$
$$5.83 \approx T$$

The world carbon dioxide emissions in 1990 were 5.83 billion metric tons.

Applying the Concepts

50.

Boyhood	Football	Married	Daughter born	Daughter died	Man died
$\frac{1}{6}x$	$\frac{1}{8}x$	5 yr	$\frac{1}{12}x$	$\frac{1}{2}x$	6 yr

$$\frac{1}{6}x+\frac{1}{8}x+5+\frac{1}{12}x+\frac{1}{2}x+6=x$$
$$\frac{7}{8}x+11=x$$
$$\frac{7}{8}x-x+11=x-x$$
$$-\frac{1}{8}x+11=0$$
$$-\frac{1}{8}x+11-11=0-11$$
$$-\frac{1}{8}x=-11$$
$$-8\left(-\frac{1}{8}x\right)=-8(-11)$$
$$x=88$$

The man was 88 years old when he died.

51. The problem states that a 4-quart mixture of fruit juice is made from apple juice and cranberry juice. There are 6 more quarts of apple juice than of cranberry juice. If we let $x =$ the number of quarts of cranberry juice, then $x + 6 =$ the number of quarts of apple juice. The total number of quarts is 4. Therefore, we can write the equation $x + (x + 6) = 4$.

$$x+(x+6)=4$$
$$2x=-2$$
$$x=-1$$

Since $x =$ the number of quarts of cranberry juice, there are -1 qt of cranberry juice in the mixture. We cannot add -1 qt to a mixture. The solution is not reasonable.

We see from the original problem that the answer will not be reasonable. If the total number of quarts in the mixture is 4, we cannot have more than 6 qt of apple juice in the mixture.

52. Students should provide you with information concerning their majors, as well as two formulas from the field of study and explanations of the variables used in each formula.

Chapter 11 Review Exercises

1. $-2(a-b)=-2[a+(-b)]$
$=-2(a)+(-2)(-b)$
$=-2a+2b$

2.

$3x-2=-8$	
$3(-2)-2$	-8
$-6-2$	-8
$-6+(-2)$	-8
$-8=-8$	

Yes, -2 is a solution.

3.
$$x-3=-7$$
$$x-3+3=-7+3$$
$$x=-4$$

4.
$$-2x+5=-9$$
$$-2x+5-5=-9-5$$
$$-2x=-14$$
$$\frac{-2x}{-2}=\frac{-14}{-2}$$
$$x=7$$

5. $a^2-3b=2^2-3(-3)$
$=4+9=13$

6.
$$-3x=27$$
$$\frac{-3x}{-3}=\frac{27}{-3}$$
$$x=-9$$

7.
$$\frac{2}{3}x+3=-9$$
$$\frac{2}{3}x+3-3=-9-3$$
$$\frac{2}{3}x=-12$$
$$\frac{3}{2}\cdot\frac{2}{3}x=\frac{3}{2}(-12)$$
$$x=-18$$

8. $3x-2(3x-2)=3x+(-2)[3x+(-2)]$
$=3x+(-2)(3x)+(-2)(-2)$
$=3x+(-6x)+4$
$=-3x+4$

9.
$$\begin{aligned} 6x - 9 &= -3x + 36 \\ 6x + 3x - 9 &= -3x + 3x + 36 \\ 9x - 9 &= 36 \\ 9x - 9 + 9 &= 36 + 9 \\ 9x &= 45 \\ \frac{9x}{9} &= \frac{45}{9} \\ x &= 5 \end{aligned}$$

10.
$$\begin{aligned} x + 3 &= -2 \\ x + 3 - 3 &= -2 - 3 \\ x &= -5 \end{aligned}$$

11.
$$\begin{array}{r|l} 3x - 5 = & -10 \\ \hline 3(5) - 5 & -10 \\ 15 - 5 & -10 \\ 15 + (-5) & -10 \\ 10 \neq & -10 \end{array}$$

No, 5 is not a solution.

12.
$$\begin{aligned} a^2 - (b \div c) &= (-2)^2 - [8 \div (-4)] \\ &= 4 - (-2) = 6 \end{aligned}$$

13.
$$\begin{aligned} 3(x - 2) + 2 &= 11 \\ 3x - 6 + 2 &= 11 \\ 3x - 4 &= 11 \\ 3x - 4 + 4 &= 11 + 4 \\ 3x &= 15 \\ \frac{3x}{3} &= \frac{15}{3} \\ x &= 5 \end{aligned}$$

14.
$$\begin{aligned} 35 - 3x &= 5 \\ 35 - 35 - 3x &= 5 - 35 \\ -3x &= -30 \\ \frac{-3x}{-3} &= \frac{-30}{-3} \\ x &= 10 \end{aligned}$$

15.
$$\begin{aligned} &6bc - 7bc + 2bc - 5bc \\ &= 6bc + (-7)bc + 2bc + (-5)bc \\ &= (-1)bc + 2bc + (-5)bc \\ &= 1bc + (-5)bc \\ &= -4bc \end{aligned}$$

16.
$$\begin{aligned} 7 - 3x &= 2 - 5x \\ 7 - 3x + 5x &= 2 - 5x + 5x \\ 7 + 2x &= 2 \\ 7 - 7 + 2x &= 2 - 7 \\ 2x &= -5 \\ \frac{2x}{2} &= \frac{-5}{2} \\ x &= \frac{-5}{2} = -2\frac{1}{2} \end{aligned}$$

17.
$$\begin{aligned} -\frac{3}{8}x &= -\frac{15}{32} \\ -\frac{8}{3}\left(-\frac{3}{8}x\right) &= \left(-\frac{8}{3}\right)\left(-\frac{15}{32}\right) \\ x &= \frac{5}{4} = 1\frac{1}{4} \end{aligned}$$

18.
$$\begin{aligned} &\frac{1}{2}x^2 - \frac{1}{3}x^2 + \frac{1}{5}x^2 + 2x^2 \\ &= \frac{1}{2}x^2 + \left(-\frac{1}{3}\right)x^2 + \frac{1}{5}x^2 + 2x^2 \\ &= \frac{3}{6}x^2 + \left(-\frac{2}{6}\right)x^2 + \frac{1}{5}x^2 + 2x^2 \\ &= \frac{1}{6}x^2 + \frac{1}{5}x^2 + 2x^2 \\ &= \frac{5}{30}x^2 + \frac{6}{30}x^2 + 2x^2 \\ &= \frac{11}{30}x^2 + 2x^2 \\ &= \frac{11}{30}x^2 + \frac{60}{30}x^2 \\ &= \frac{71}{30}x^2 \end{aligned}$$

19.
$$\begin{aligned} 5x - 3(1 - 2x) &= 4(2x - 1) \\ 5x - 3 + 6x &= 8x - 4 \\ 11x - 3 &= 8x - 4 \\ 11x - 8x - 3 &= 8x - 8x - 4 \\ 3x - 3 &= -4 \\ 3x - 3 + 3 &= -4 + 3 \\ 3x &= -1 \\ \frac{3x}{3} &= \frac{-1}{3} \\ x &= -\frac{1}{3} \end{aligned}$$

20.
$$\begin{aligned} \frac{5}{6}x - 4 &= 5 \\ \frac{5}{6}x - 4 + 4 &= 5 + 4 \\ \frac{5}{6}x &= 9 \\ \frac{6}{5} \cdot \frac{5}{6}x &= \frac{6}{5} \cdot 9 \\ x &= \frac{54}{5} = 10\frac{4}{5} \end{aligned}$$

21. Strategy To find the number of miles per gallon of gas, replace D and G in the formula by the given values and solve for M.

Solution
$$\begin{aligned} D &= M \cdot G \\ 621 &= M \cdot 27 \\ \frac{621}{27} &= \frac{27M}{27} \\ 23 &= M \end{aligned}$$

The mileage obtained was 23 mi/gal.

22. **Strategy** To find the Celsius temperature, replace the variable F in the formula by the given value and solve for C.

Solution
$$F = 1.8C + 32$$
$$100 = 1.8C + 32$$
$$100 - 32 = 1.8C + 32 - 32$$
$$68 = 1.8C$$
$$37.8 \approx C$$
The temperature is 37.8°C.

23. The *total* of n and the *quotient* of n and 5
The unknown number: n
The quotient of n and 5: $\frac{n}{5}$

$n + \frac{n}{5}$

24. The *sum* of five more than a number and one-third *of* the number
The unknown number: n
Five more than the number: $n + 5$
One-third of the number: $\frac{1}{3}n$
$(n + 5) + \frac{1}{3}n$

25. The unknown number: x
$$9 - 2x = 5$$
$$9 - 9 - 2x = 5 - 9$$
$$-2x = -4$$
$$\frac{-2x}{-2} = \frac{-4}{-2}$$
$$x = 2$$
The number is 2.

26. The unknown number: p
$$5p = 50$$
$$\frac{5p}{5} = \frac{50}{5}$$
$$p = 10$$
The number is 10.

27. **Strategy** To find the regular price, write and solve an equation using R to represent the regular price.

Solution
$$228 = 60\% \cdot R$$
$$228 = 0.60R$$
$$\frac{228}{0.60} = \frac{0.60R}{0.60}$$
$$380 = R$$
The regular price of the CD player is \$380.

28. **Strategy** Let x represent last year's crop. Then $0.12x$ is the increase in last year's crop. Last year's crop plus the increase is this year's crop (28,336 bushels).

Solution
$$0.12x + x = 26{,}336$$
$$1.12x = 28{,}336$$
$$x = 25{,}300$$
Last year's crop was 25,300 bushels.

Chapter 11 Test

1.
$$\frac{x}{5} - 12 = 7$$
$$\frac{x}{5} - 12 + 12 = 7 + 12$$
$$\frac{x}{5} = 19$$
$$5 \cdot \frac{x}{5} = 5 \cdot 19$$
$$x = 95$$

2.
$$x - 12 = 14$$
$$x - 12 + 12 = 14 + 12$$
$$x = 26$$

3.
$$3y - 2x - 7y - 9x = 3y + (-2x) + (-7y) + (-9x)$$
$$= 3y + (-7y) + (-2x) + (-9x)$$
$$= -4y + (-2x) + (-9x)$$
$$= -4y + (-11x)$$
$$= -4y - 11x = -11x - 4y$$

4.
$$8 - 3x = 2x - 8$$
$$8 - 3x - 2x = 2x - 2x - 8$$
$$8 - 5x = -8$$
$$8 - 8 - 5x = -8 - 8$$
$$-5x = -16$$
$$\frac{-5x}{-5} = \frac{-16}{-5}$$
$$x = \frac{16}{5} = 3\frac{1}{5}$$

5.
$$3x - 12 = -18$$
$$3x - 12 + 12 = -18 + 12$$
$$3x = -6$$
$$\frac{3x}{3} = \frac{-6}{3}$$
$$x = -2$$

6.
$$c^2 - (2a + b^2) = (-2)^2 - [2(3) + (-6)^2]$$
$$= 4 - (6 + 36)$$
$$= 4 - (42)$$
$$= 4 + (-42) = -38$$

7.
$x^2 + 3x - 7$	$= 3x - 2$
$3^2 + 3(3) - 7$	$3(3) - 2$
$9 + 9 - 7$	$9 - 2$
$18 - 7$	7
$11 \neq 7$	

No, 3 is not a solution.

8. $9 - 8ab - 6ab = 9 - 14ab = -14ab + 9$

9.
$$-5x = 14$$
$$\frac{-5x}{-5} = \frac{14}{-5}$$
$$x = -2\frac{4}{5}$$

10.
$$\begin{aligned} 3y + 5(y-3) + 8 &= 3y + 5[y + (-3)] + 8 \\ &= 3y + 5y + 5(-3) + 8 \\ &= 8y + (-15) + 8 \\ &= 8y + (-7) \\ &= 8y - 7 \end{aligned}$$

11.
$$\begin{aligned} 3x - 4(x-2) &= 8 \\ 3x - 4x + 8 &= 8 \\ -x + 8 &= 8 \\ -x + 8 - 8 &= 8 - 8 \\ -x &= 0 \\ (-1)(-x) &= (-1)0 \\ x &= 0 \end{aligned}$$

12.
$$\begin{aligned} 5 &= 3 - 4x \\ 5 - 3 &= 3 - 3 - 4x \\ 2 &= -4x \\ \frac{2}{-4} &= \frac{-4x}{-4} \\ -\frac{1}{2} &= x \end{aligned}$$

13.
$$\begin{aligned} \frac{x^2}{y} - \frac{y^2}{x} &= \frac{3^2}{-2} - \frac{(-2)^2}{3} \\ &= \frac{9}{-2} - \frac{4}{3} \\ &= \frac{-27}{6} - \frac{8}{6} \\ &= \frac{-35}{6} = -5\frac{5}{6} \end{aligned}$$

14.
$$\frac{5}{8}x = -10$$
$$\frac{8}{5} \cdot \frac{5}{8}x = \frac{8}{5}(-10)$$
$$x = -16$$

15.
$$\begin{aligned} y - 4y + 3 &= 12 \\ -3y + 3 &= 12 \\ -3y + 3 - 3 &= 12 - 3 \\ -3y &= 9 \\ \frac{-3y}{-3} &= \frac{9}{-3} \\ y &= -3 \end{aligned}$$

16.
$$\begin{aligned} 2x + 4(x-3) &= 5x - 1 \\ 2x + 4x - 12 &= 5x - 1 \\ 6x - 12 &= 5x - 1 \\ 6x - 5x - 12 &= 5x - 5x - 1 \\ x - 12 &= -1 \\ x - 12 + 12 &= -1 + 12 \\ x &= 11 \end{aligned}$$

17. Strategy To find the monthly payment, replace the variables L and N in the formula by the given values and solve for P.

Solution
$$\begin{aligned} L &= P \cdot N \\ 6600 &= P \cdot 48 \\ \frac{6600}{48} &= \frac{48P}{48} \\ 137.50 &= P \end{aligned}$$
The monthly payment is \$137.50.

18. Strategy To find the number of clocks made during a month, replace the variables T, U, and F in the formula by the given values and solve for N.

Solution
$$\begin{aligned} T &= U \cdot N + F \\ 65{,}000 &= 15N + 5000 \\ 65{,}000 - 5000 &= 15N + 5000 - 5000 \\ 60{,}000 &= 15N \\ \frac{60{,}000}{15} &= \frac{15N}{15} \\ 4000 &= N \end{aligned}$$
4000 clocks were made during the month.

19. Strategy To find the time, replace the variables V and V_0 in the formula by the given values and solve for t.

Solution
$$\begin{aligned} V &= V_0 + 32t \\ 392 &= 24 + 32t \\ 392 - 24 &= 24 - 24 + 32t \\ 368 &= 32t \\ \frac{368}{32} &= \frac{32t}{32} \\ 11.5 &= t \end{aligned}$$
The object will fall for 11.5 s.

20. The *sum* of x and one-third *of* x
The unknown number: x
One-third of x: $\frac{1}{3}x$
$x + \frac{1}{3}x$

21. Five *times* the *sum* of a number and three
The unknown number: x
The sum of a number and three: $x + 3$
$5(x + 3)$

22. The unknown number: x
$$\begin{aligned} 2x - 3 &= 7 \\ 2x - 3 + 3 &= 7 + 3 \\ 2x &= 10 \\ \frac{2x}{2} &= \frac{10}{2} \\ x &= 5 \end{aligned}$$
The number is 5.

23. The unknown number: w

$$5 + 3w = w - 2$$
$$5 + 3w - w = w - w - 2$$
$$5 + 2w = -2$$
$$5 - 5 + 2w = -2 - 5$$
$$2w = -7$$
$$\frac{2w}{2} = \frac{-7}{2}$$
$$w = -3\frac{1}{2}$$

The number is $-3\frac{1}{2}$.

24. Strategy To find Santos's total sales for the month, write and solve an equation using T to represent the total sales.

Solution

$$3600 = 1200 + 0.06T$$
$$3600 - 1200 = 1200 - 1200 + 0.06T$$
$$2400 = 0.06T$$
$$\frac{2400}{0.06} = \frac{0.06T}{0.06}$$
$$40{,}000 = T$$

Santos's total sales for the month were $40,000.

25. Strategy To find the number of hours worked, write and solve an equation using h to represent the number of hours worked.

Solution

$$152 + 42h = 278$$
$$152 - 152 + 42h = 278 - 152$$
$$42h = 126$$
$$h = 3$$

The mechanic worked for 3 h.

Cumulative Review Exercises

1. $6^2 - (18 - 6) \div 4 + 8 = 36 - (12) \div 4 + 8$
$= 36 - 3 + 8$
$= 33 + 8 = 41$

2.

$$3\frac{1}{6} = 3\frac{5}{30} = 2\frac{35}{30}$$
$$-1\frac{7}{15} = 1\frac{14}{30} = 1\frac{14}{30}$$
$$1\frac{21}{30} = 1\frac{7}{10}$$

3. $\left(\frac{3}{8} - \frac{1}{4}\right) \div \frac{3}{4} + \frac{4}{9} = \left(\frac{3}{8} - \frac{2}{8}\right) \div \frac{3}{4} + \frac{4}{9}$
$= \frac{1}{8} \div \frac{3}{4} + \frac{4}{9}$
$= \frac{1}{8} \times \frac{4}{3} + \frac{4}{9}$
$= \frac{1}{6} + \frac{4}{9}$
$= \frac{3}{18} + \frac{8}{18} = \frac{11}{18}$

4.

$$\begin{array}{r} 9.67 \\ \times\ 0.0049 \\ \hline 8703 \\ 3868 \\ \hline 0.047383 \end{array}$$

5. $\frac{\$84}{20\text{ h}} = 4.20/\text{h}$

6. $\frac{2}{3} = \frac{n}{40}$
$2 \times 40 = 3 \cdot n$
$80 = 3 \cdot n$
$80 \div 3 = n$
$26.67 \approx n$

7. $5\frac{1}{3}\% = \frac{16}{3} \times \frac{1}{100} = \frac{16}{300} = \frac{4}{75}$

8. Percent × base = amount
$n \times 30 = 42$
$n = 42 \div 30$
$n = 1.40 = 140\%$

9. Percent × base = amount
$125\% \times n = 8$
$1.25 \times n = 8$
$n = 8 \div 1.25 = 6.4$

10.

$$\begin{array}{l} 3\text{ ft }9\text{ in.} \\ \times\qquad\ \ 5 \\ \hline 15\text{ ft }45\text{ in.} = 18\text{ ft }9\text{ in.} \end{array}$$

11. $1\frac{3}{8}\text{ lb} = \frac{11}{8}\text{ lb} \times \frac{16\text{ oz}}{1\text{ lb}} = \frac{11 \cdot 16\text{ oz}}{8} = 22\text{ oz}$

12. 282 mg = 0.282 g

13. $-2 + 5 + (-8) + 4 = 3 + (-8) + 4$
$= -5 + 4 = -1$

14. $13 - (-6) = 13 + 6 = 19$

15. $(-2)^2 - (-8) \div (3 - 5)^2 = (-2)^2 - (-8) \div (-2)^2$
$= 4 - (-8) \div 4$
$= 4 - (-2) = 4 + 2 = 6$

16. $3ab - 2ac = 3(-2)(6) - 2(-2)(-3)$
$= -36 - 12 = -36 + (-12) = -48$

17.
$$\begin{aligned}3z - 2x + 5z - 8x &= 3z + (-2x) + 5z + (-8x)\\ &= 3z + 5z + (-2x) + (-8x)\\ &= 8z + (-10x)\\ &= 8z - 10x = -10x + 8z\end{aligned}$$

18.
$$\begin{aligned}6y - 3(y-5) + 8 &= 6y + (-3)[y + (-5)] + 8\\ &= 6y + (-3)y + (-3)(-5) + 8\\ &= 6y + (-3y) + 15 + 8\\ &= 3y + 23\end{aligned}$$

19.
$$\begin{aligned}2x - 5 &= -7\\ 2x - 5 + 5 &= -7 + 5\\ 2x &= -2\\ 2x &= -2\\ \frac{2x}{2} &= \frac{-2}{2}\\ x &= -1\end{aligned}$$

20.
$$\begin{aligned}7x - 3(x-5) &= -10\\ 7x - 3x + 15 &= -10\\ 4x + 15 &= -10\\ 4x + 15 - 15 &= -10 - 15\\ 4x &= -25\\ \frac{4x}{4} &= \frac{-25}{4}\\ x &= -6\frac{1}{4}\end{aligned}$$

21.
$$\begin{aligned}-\frac{2}{3}x &= 5\\ \left(-\frac{3}{2}\right)\left(-\frac{2}{3}\right)x &= -\frac{3}{2}\cdot 5\\ x &= -\frac{15}{2} \quad = -7\frac{1}{2}\end{aligned}$$

22.
$$\begin{aligned}\frac{x}{3} - 5 &= -12\\ \frac{x}{3} - 5 + 5 &= -12 + 5\\ \frac{x}{3} &= -7\\ 3\cdot\frac{x}{3} &= 3(-7)\\ x &= -21\end{aligned}$$

23. Strategy To find the percent of the students who received an A grade, solve the basic percent equation for percent.

Solution Percent · base = amount
$$\begin{aligned}n \cdot 34 &= 6\\ n &= 6 \div 34\\ n &\approx 0.176 = 17.6\%\end{aligned}$$
The percent is 17.6%.

24. Strategy To find the price:
- Find the amount of the markup by solving the basic percent equation for amount. The base is \$28.50 and the percent is 40%.
- Add the amount of the markup to the cost.

Solution
$$\begin{aligned}0.40 \times 28.50 &= n\\ 11.40 &= n\end{aligned} \qquad \begin{array}{r}\$28.50\\ +11.40\\ \hline \$39.90\end{array}$$
The price of the piece of pottery is \$39.90.

25a. Strategy To find the discount subtract the sale price (\$369) from the regular price (\$450).

Solution $450 - 369 = 81$
The discount is \$81.

b. Strategy To find the discount rate, write and solve the basic percent equation for percent. The base is the regular price and the amount is the discount.

Solution Percent × base = amount
$$\begin{aligned}n \times 450 &= 81\\ n &= 81 \div 450\\ n &= 0.18\end{aligned}$$
The discount rate is 18%.

26. Strategy To find the simple interest due, multiply the principal and rate and time (in years).

Solution
$$\begin{aligned}\text{Interest} &= 80{,}000 \times 11\% \times \frac{4}{12}\\ &= 80{,}000 \times 0.11 \times \frac{4}{12}\\ &\approx 2933.33\end{aligned}$$
The simple interest due on the loan is \$2933.33.

27. The *sum* of three *times* a number and four
The unknown number: n
Three times the number: $3n$
$3n + 4$

28. Strategy To calculate the probability:
- Count the number of possible outcomes.
- Count the number of favorable outcomes.
- Use the probability formula.

Solution There are 16 possible outcomes.
There are 2 favorable outcomes: (3, 4), (4, 3).

$$\text{Probability} = \frac{2}{16} = \frac{1}{8}$$

The probability is $\frac{1}{8}$ that the sum of the upward faces on the two dice is 7.

29. Strategy To find the total sales, replace the variables M, R, and B in the formula with the given values and solve for S.

Solution

$$M = S \cdot R + B$$
$$3400 = S \cdot 0.08 + 800$$
$$3400 - 800 = S \cdot 0.08 + 800 - 800$$
$$2600 = S \cdot 0.08$$
$$\frac{2600}{0.08} = \frac{S \cdot 0.08}{0.08}$$
$$32{,}500 = S$$

The total sales were $32,500.

30. The unknown number: x

$$8x - 3 = 3 + 5x$$
$$8x - 5x - 3 = 3 + 5x - 5x$$
$$3x - 3 = 3$$
$$3x - 3 + 3 = 3 + 3$$
$$3x = 6$$
$$\frac{3x}{3} = \frac{6}{3}$$
$$x = 2$$

The number is 2.

Chapter 12: Geometry

Prep Test

1. $$\begin{aligned} x + 47 &= 90 \\ x + 47 - 47 &= 90 - 47 \\ x &= 43 \end{aligned}$$
The solution is 43.

2. $$\begin{aligned} 32 + 97 + x &= 180 \\ 129 + x &= 180 \\ 129 - 129 + x &= 180 - 129 \\ x &= 51 \end{aligned}$$
The solution is 51.

3. $2(18) + 2(10) = 36 + 20 = 56$

4. abc
$= (2)(3.14)(9)$
$= (6.28)(9)$
$= 56.52$

5. xyz^3
$= \left(\frac{4}{3}\right)(3.14)(3)^3$
$= 113.04$

6. $$\begin{aligned} \frac{5}{12} &= \frac{6}{x} \\ 5x &= 12 \times 6 \\ \frac{5x}{5} &= \frac{72}{5} \\ x &= 14.4 \end{aligned}$$

7. $$\begin{aligned} QS &= QR + RS \\ 28 &= 7 + RS \\ 28 - 7 &= 7 - 7 + RS \\ 21 &= RS \end{aligned}$$

8. $$\begin{aligned} QS &= QR + RS \\ 45 &= 15 + RS \\ 45 - 15 &= 15 - 15 + RS \\ 30 &= RS \end{aligned}$$

9. $$\begin{aligned} AD &= AB + BC + CD \\ 35 &= 12 + BC + 9 \\ 35 &= 21 + BC \\ 35 - 21 &= 21 - 21 + BC \\ 14 &= BC \end{aligned}$$

10. $$\begin{aligned} AD &= AB + BC + CD \\ 54 &= 21 + 14 + CD \\ 54 &= 35 + CD \\ 54 - 35 &= 35 - 35 + CD \\ 19 &= CD \end{aligned}$$

Go Figure

The first figure is a diamond (D) inside a square (S) inside a triangle (T) inside a circle (C), or DSTC.
The second figure is STCD.
The third figure is TCDS.
The next figure would be CDST: A circle inside a diamond inside a square inside a triangle.

Section 12.1

Objective A Exercises

1. 0°; 90°

2. 90°; 180°

3. 180°

4. Perpendicular

5. $EG = EF + FG$
$EG = 20 + 10 = 30$

6. $EG = EF + FG$
$EG = 18 + 6 = 24$

11. Let x represent the complement of 31°. The sum of complementary angles is 90°.
$$\begin{aligned} x + 31^\circ &= 90^\circ \\ x + 31^\circ - 31^\circ &= 90^\circ - 31^\circ \\ x &= 59^\circ \end{aligned}$$
59° is the complement of 31°.

12. Let x represent the complement of 62°. The sum of complementary angles is 90°.
$$\begin{aligned} x + 62^\circ &= 90^\circ \\ x + 62^\circ - 62^\circ &= 90^\circ - 62^\circ \\ x &= 28^\circ \end{aligned}$$
28° is the complement of 62°.

13. Let x represent the supplement of 72°. The sum of supplementary angles is 180°.
$$\begin{aligned} x + 72^\circ &= 180^\circ \\ x + 72^\circ - 72^\circ &= 180^\circ - 72^\circ \\ x &= 108^\circ \end{aligned}$$
108° is the supplement of 72°.

14. Let x represent the supplement of 162°. The sum of supplementary angles is 180°.
$$\begin{aligned} x + 162^\circ &= 180^\circ \\ x + 162^\circ - 162^\circ &= 180^\circ - 162^\circ \\ x &= 18^\circ \end{aligned}$$
18° is the supplement of 162°.

15. Let x represent the complement of 13°. The sum of complementary angles is 90°.
$$\begin{aligned} x + 13^\circ &= 90^\circ \\ x + 13^\circ - 13^\circ &= 90^\circ - 13^\circ \\ x &= 77^\circ \end{aligned}$$
77° is the complement of 13°.

16. Let x represent the complement of 88°. The sum of complementary angles is 90°.
$$x + 88° = 90°$$
$$x + 88° - 88° = 90° - 88°$$
$$x = 2°$$
2° is the complement of 88°.

17. Let x represent the supplement of 127°. The sum of supplementary angles is 180°.
$$x + 127° = 180°$$
$$x + 127° - 127° = 180° - 127°$$
$$x = 53°$$
53° is the supplement of 127°.

18. Let x represent the supplement of 7°. The sum of supplementary angles is 180°.
$$x + 7° = 180°$$
$$x + 7° - 7° = 180° - 7°$$
$$x = 173°$$
173° is the supplement of 7°.

19. $\angle AOB = 32° + 45° = 77°$

20. $\angle AOB = 64° + 72° = 136°$

21.
$$42° + \angle a = 160°$$
$$42° - 42° + \angle a = 160° - 42°$$
$$\angle a = 118°$$

22.
$$\angle a + 32° = 65°$$
$$\angle a - 32° - 32° = 65° - 32°$$
$$\angle a = 33°$$

23.
$$\angle a + 47° = 180°$$
$$\angle a + 47° - 47° = 180° - 47°$$
$$\angle a = 133°$$

24.
$$\angle a + 13° = 90°$$
$$\angle a + 13° - 13° = 90° - 13°$$
$$\angle a = 77°$$

25.
$$\angle LON = \angle LOM + \angle MON$$
$$139° = 53° + \angle MON$$
$$139° - 53° = 53° - 53° + \angle MON$$
$$86° = \angle MON$$

26.
$$\angle LON = \angle LOM + \angle MON$$
$$85° = \angle LOM + 38°$$
$$85° - 38° = \angle LOM$$
$$47° = \angle LOM$$

Objective B Exercises

27. 180°

28. Hypotenuse

29. Rectangle or square

30. Square

31. Cube

32. Sphere

33. Parallelogram, rectangle, or square

34. Circle

35. Cylinder

36. Rectangular solid or cube

37. The sum of the three angles of a triangle is 180°.
$$\angle A + \angle B + \angle C = 180°$$
$$\angle A + 13° + 65° = 180°$$
$$\angle A + 78° = 180°$$
$$\angle A + 78° - 78° = 180° - 78°$$
$$\angle A = 102°$$
The measure of the other angle is 102°.

38. The sum of the three angles of a triangle is 180°.
$$\angle A + \angle B + \angle C = 180°$$
$$\angle A + 105° + 32° = 180°$$
$$\angle A + 137° = 180°$$
$$\angle A + 137° - 137° = 180° - 137°$$
$$\angle A = 43°$$
The measure of the other angle is 43°.

39. In a right triangle, one angle measures 90° and the two acute angles are complementary.
$$\angle A + \angle B = 90°$$
$$\angle A + 45° = 90°$$
$$\angle A + 45° - 45° = 90° - 45°$$
$$\angle A = 45°$$
The other angles measure 90° and 45°.

40. In a right triangle, one angle measures 90° and the two acute angles are complementary.
$$\angle A + \angle B = 90°$$
$$\angle A + 62° = 90°$$
$$\angle A + 62° - 62° = 90° - 62°$$
$$\angle A = 28°$$
The other angles measure 90° and 28°.

41. The sum of the three angles of a triangle is 180°.
$$\angle A + \angle B + \angle C = 180°$$
$$\angle A + 62° + 104° = 180°$$
$$\angle A + 166° = 180°$$
$$\angle A + 166° - 166° = 180° - 166°$$
$$\angle A = 14°$$
The measure of the other angle is 14°.

42. The sum of the three angles of a triangle is 180°.
$$\angle A + \angle B + \angle C = 180°$$
$$\angle A + 30° + 45° = 180°$$
$$\angle A + 75° = 180°$$
$$\angle A + 75° - 75° = 180° - 75°$$
$$\angle A = 105°$$
The measure of the other angle is 105°.

43. In a right triangle, one angle measures 90° and the two acute angles are complementary.

$$\angle A + \angle B = 90^\circ$$
$$\angle A + 25^\circ = 90^\circ$$
$$\angle A + 25^\circ - 25^\circ = 90^\circ - 25^\circ$$
$$\angle A = 65^\circ$$

The other angles measure 90° and 65°.

44. The sum of the three angles of a triangle is 180°.

$$\angle A + \angle B + \angle C = 180^\circ$$
$$\angle A + 42^\circ + 105^\circ = 180^\circ$$
$$\angle A + 147^\circ = 180^\circ$$
$$\angle A + 147^\circ - 147^\circ = 180^\circ - 147^\circ$$
$$\angle A = 33^\circ$$

The measure of the other angle is 33°.

45. $r = \frac{1}{2}d$

$r = \frac{1}{2}(16\text{ in.}) = 8\text{ in.}$

The radius is 8 in.

46. $r = \frac{1}{2}d$

$r = \frac{1}{2}(9\text{ ft}) = 4\frac{1}{2}\text{ ft}$

The radius is $4\frac{1}{2}$ ft.

47. $d = 2r$

$d = 2\left(2\frac{1}{3}\text{ ft}\right)$

$d = 2\left(\frac{7}{3}\text{ ft}\right)$

$d = \frac{14}{3}\text{ ft} = 4\frac{2}{3}\text{ ft}$

The diameter is $4\frac{2}{3}$ ft.

48. $d = 2r$

$d = 2(24\text{ cm}) = 48\text{ cm}$

The diameter is 48 cm.

49. $d = 2r$

$d = 2(3.5\text{ cm}) = 7\text{ cm}$

The diameter is 7 cm.

50. $d = 2r$

$d = 2\left(1\frac{1}{2}\text{ ft}\right) = 3\text{ ft}$

The diameter is 3 ft.

51. $r = \frac{1}{2}d$

$r = \frac{1}{2}(4\text{ ft }8\text{ in.})$

$r = 2\text{ ft }4\text{ in.}$

The radius is 2 ft 4 in.

52. $r = \frac{1}{2}d$

$r = \frac{1}{2}(1.2\text{ m}) = 0.6\text{ m}$

The radius is 0.6 m.

Objective C Exercises

53. $\angle a + 74^\circ = 180^\circ$ supplementary angles

$$\angle a + 74^\circ - 74^\circ = 180^\circ - 74^\circ$$
$$\angle a = 106^\circ$$

$\angle b = 74^\circ$ vertical angles

54. $\angle a + 49^\circ = 180^\circ$ supplementary angles

$$\angle a + 49^\circ - 49^\circ = 180^\circ - 49^\circ$$
$$\angle a = 131^\circ$$

$\angle b = 49^\circ$ vertical angles

55. $\angle a = 112^\circ$ vertical angles

$\angle b + 112^\circ = 180^\circ$ supplementary angles

$$\angle b + 112^\circ - 112^\circ = 180^\circ - 112^\circ$$
$$\angle b = 68^\circ$$

56. $\angle a = 131^\circ$ vertical angles

$\angle b + 131^\circ = 180^\circ$ supplementary angles

$$\angle b + 131^\circ - 131^\circ = 180^\circ - 131^\circ$$
$$\angle b = 49^\circ$$

57. $\angle a = 38^\circ$ vertical angles

$\angle b + 38^\circ = 180^\circ$ supplementary angles

$$\angle b + 38^\circ - 38^\circ = 180^\circ - 38^\circ$$
$$\angle b = 142^\circ$$

58. $\angle b + 136^\circ = 180^\circ$ supplementary angles

$$\angle b + 136^\circ - 136^\circ = 180^\circ - 136^\circ$$
$$\angle b = 44^\circ$$

$\angle a = \angle b$ corresponding angles

$\angle a = 44^\circ$

$\angle b = 44^\circ$

59. $\angle a + 122^\circ = 180^\circ$ supplementary angles

$$\angle a + 122^\circ - 122^\circ = 180^\circ - 122^\circ$$
$$\angle a = 58^\circ$$

$\angle a = \angle b$ alternate interior angles

$\angle b = 58^\circ$

60. $\angle a = 55^\circ$ alternate interior angles

$\angle a + \angle b = 180^\circ$ supplementary angles

$$55^\circ + \angle b = 180^\circ$$
$$55^\circ - 55^\circ + \angle b = 180^\circ - 55^\circ$$
$$\angle b = 125^\circ$$

61. $\angle b + 28° = 180°$ supplementary angles
$\angle b + 28° - 28° = 180° - 28°$
$\angle b = 152°$
$\angle a = \angle b$ corresponding angles
$\angle a = 152°$

$\angle b = 152°$

62. $\angle b = 75°$ alternate exterior angles
$\angle a + \angle b = 180°$ supplementary angles
$\angle a + 75° = 180°$
$\angle a + 75° - 75° = 180° - 75°$
$\angle a = 105°$

$\angle b = 75°$ alternate exterior angles

63. $\angle a = 130°$ alternate interior angles

$\angle b + 130° = 180°$ supplementary angles
$\angle b + 130° - 130° = 180° - 130°$
$\angle b = 50°$

64. $\angle b = 118°$ corresponding angles
$\angle a + \angle b = 180°$ supplementary angles
$\angle a + 118° = 180°$
$\angle a + 118° - 118° = 180° - 118°$
$\angle a = 62°$

$\angle b = 118°$ corresponding angles

Applying the Concepts

65a. 1°

b. 90°

66a. Always true.

b. Always true.

c. Sometimes true.

67. $\angle AOC$ and $\angle BOC$ are supplementary angles. Therefore, $\angle AOC + \angle BOC = 180°$. Because $\angle AOC = \angle BOC$, by substitution $\angle AOC + \angle AOC = 180°$. Therefore, $2\angle AOC = 180°$ and $\angle AOC = 90°$. Therefore, AB is perpendicular to CD.

Section 12.2

Objective A Exercises

1. $P = a + b + c$
$= 12 \text{ in.} + 20 \text{ in.} + 24 \text{ in.}$
$= 56 \text{ in.}$
The perimeter of the triangle is 56 in.

2. $P = a + b + c$
$= 14 \text{ cm} + 13 \text{ cm} + 12 \text{ cm}$
$= 39 \text{ cm}$
The perimeter of the triangle is 39 cm.

3. $P = 4s$
$= 4(5 \text{ ft})$
$= 20 \text{ ft}$
The perimeter of the square is 20 ft.

4. $P = 4s$
$= 4(2 \text{ m})$
$= 8 \text{ m}$
The perimeter of the square is 8 m.

5. $P = 2L + 2W$
$= 2(32 \text{ cm}) + 2(14 \text{ cm})$
$= 64 \text{ cm} + 28 \text{ cm}$
$= 92 \text{ cm}$
The perimeter of the rectangle is 92 cm.

6. $P = 2L + 2W$
$= 2(18 \text{ ft}) + 2(5 \text{ ft})$
$= 36 \text{ ft} + 10 \text{ ft}$
$= 46 \text{ ft}$
The perimeter of the rectangle is 46 ft.

7. $C = \pi d$
$\approx 3.14(15 \text{ cm})$
$= 47.1 \text{ cm}$
The circumference of the circle is approximately 47.1 cm.

8. $C = 2\pi r$
$\approx 2(3.14)(4 \text{ in.})$
$= 25.12 \text{ in.}$
The circumference of the circle is approximately 25.12 in.

9. $P = 2 \text{ ft } 4 \text{ in.} + 3 \text{ ft} + 4 \text{ ft } 6 \text{ in.}$
$= 9 \text{ ft } 10 \text{ in.}$
The perimeter of the triangle is 9 ft 10 in.

10. $P = 2L + 2W$
$= 2(2 \text{ m}) + 2(0.8 \text{ m})$
$= 4 \text{ m} + 1.6 \text{ m}$
$= 5.6 \text{ m}$
The perimeter of the rectangle is 5.6 m.

11. $C = 2\pi r$
$\approx 2(3.14)(8 \text{ cm})$
$= 50.24 \text{ cm}$
The circumference of the circle is approximately 50.24 cm.

12. $C = \pi d$
$\approx \left(\frac{22}{7}\right)(14 \text{ in.})$
$= 44 \text{ in.}$
The circumference of the circle is approximately 44 in.

13. $P = 4s$
$= 4(60 \text{ m})$
$= 240 \text{ m}$
The perimeter of the square is 240 m.

14. $P = a + b + c$
$= 1\frac{2}{3} \text{ ft} + 1\frac{2}{3} \text{ ft} + 1\frac{2}{3} \text{ ft}$
$= 5 \text{ ft}$
The perimeter of the triangle is 5 ft.

15. Perimeter = sum of sides
$= 22 \text{ cm} + 47 \text{ cm} + 29 \text{ cm} + 42 \text{ cm} + 17 \text{ cm}$
$= 157 \text{ cm}$
The perimeter is 157 cm.

16. $P = 2L + 2W$
$= 2\left(\frac{3}{4} \text{ mi}\right) + 2\left(\frac{1}{2} \text{ mi}\right)$
$= \frac{3}{2} \text{ mi} + 1 \text{ mi}$
$= 2\frac{1}{2} \text{ mi}$
The perimeter of the rectangular farm is $2\frac{1}{2}$ mi.

Objective B Exercises

17. Perimeter = sum of sides
$= 19 \text{ cm} + 20 \text{ cm} + 8 \text{ cm} + 5 \text{ cm} + 27 \text{ cm} + 42 \text{ cm}$
$= 121 \text{ cm}$

18. Perimeter = sum of sides
$= 1\frac{1}{2} \text{ ft} + 6\frac{3}{4} \text{ ft} + 3 \text{ ft} + 2\frac{2}{3} \text{ ft} + 3\frac{1}{2} \text{ ft} + 2\frac{3}{4} \text{ ft}$
$= 20\frac{1}{6} \text{ ft}$

19. Perimeter of Composite Figure = 3 sides of a rectangle + $\frac{1}{2}$ the circumference of a circle
$= 2L + W + \frac{1}{2}\pi d$
$\approx 2(15 \text{ m}) + 8 \text{ m} + \frac{1}{2}(3.14)(8 \text{ m})$
$= 30 \text{ m} + 8 \text{ m} + 12.56 \text{ m}$
$= 50.56 \text{ m}$

20. Perimeter $= 4 \cdot \frac{1}{2}$ circumference of circle
$= 4 \cdot \frac{1}{2}(3.14 \cdot 4 \text{ cm})$
$= 25.12 \text{ cm}$

21. Perimeter = length of two sides $+ \frac{1}{2}$ circumference of circle
$= 2 \cdot 1 \text{ ft} + \frac{1}{2}(3.14 \cdot 1 \text{ ft})$
$= 2 \text{ ft} + 1.57 \text{ ft}$
$= 3.57 \text{ ft}$

22. Perimeter = length of two sides $+ \frac{3}{4}$ circumference of circle
$\approx 2 \cdot 6 \text{ cm} + \frac{3}{4}(2 \cdot 3.14 \cdot 6 \text{ cm})$
$= 12 \text{ cm} + 28.26 \text{ cm}$
$= 40.26 \text{ cm}$

23. Perimeter = sum of six sides of figure
$= 22.75 \text{ m} + 25.73 \text{ m} + 15.94 \text{ m} + 18.3 \text{ m} + 21.61 \text{ m} + 34.97 \text{ m}$
$= 139.3 \text{ m}$

24. Perimeter = length of side $+ 2$ times $\frac{1}{2}$ circumference of circle
$\approx (2.55 \text{ ft} + 2.55 \text{ ft}) + 2 \cdot \frac{1}{2}(3.14 \cdot 2.55 \text{ ft})$
$= 5.10 \text{ ft} + 8.007 \text{ ft}$
$= 13.107 \text{ ft}$

Objective C Exercises

25. **Strategy** To find the amount of fencing, use the formula for the perimeter of a rectangle.

Solution $P = 2L + 2W = 2 \cdot 18 + 2 \cdot 12$
$= 36 + 24 = 60$
The amount of fencing needed is 60 ft.

26. **Strategy** To find out how many feet must be nailed down, find the perimeter of a rectangle.

Solution $P = 2L + 2W = 2 \cdot 12 + 2 \cdot 10$
$= 24 + 20 = 44$
The amount of carpet that must be nailed is 44 ft.

27. **Strategy** To find the amount of binding, find the perimeter of a rectangle.

Solution $P = 2L + 2W = 2 \cdot 8.5 + 2 \cdot 3.5$
$= 17 + 7 = 24$
The amount of binding needed is 24 ft.

28. **Strategy** To find how much molding is needed, use the formula for the circumference of a circle.

Solution $C = \pi d$
$\approx 3.14 \cdot 3.8 \text{ ft}$
$= 11.932 \text{ ft}$
The amount of molding needed for the table is approximately 11.932 ft.

29. Strategy To find the cost of the fence:
- Find the length of fence that is not along the road.
- Multiply the length of fence not along the road by $5.85.
- Multiply the length along the road by $6.20.
- Add the two products to find the total cost.

Solution Length = 800 + 1250 + 800 = 2850
2850 × $5.85 = $16,672.50
1250 × $6.20 = $7,750
$16,672.50 + $7,750 = $24,422.50
The total cost of the fence is $24,422.50.

30. Strategy To find the amount of bias binding:
- Use the formula for the perimeter of a rectangle to find the amount of binding needed.
- Convert the amount to feet.
- Divide the amount by 15 to find the number of packages needed.

Solution $P = 2L + 2W = 2 \cdot 72 + 2 \cdot 45$
$= 144 + 90 = 234$
234 in. = 19.5 ft
$19.5 \div 15 = 1.3$
Since 1.3 packages are needed, 2 packages must be ordered.

31. Strategy To find the distance the bike travels:
- Convert diameter (24 in.) to feet.
- Use the formula for circumference to find the distance traveled in 1 revolution.
- Multiply the distance traveled in 1 revolution by the number of revolutions (5).

Solution $24 \text{ in.} = 24 \not{\text{in.}} \times \frac{1 \text{ ft}}{12 \not{\text{in.}}} = \frac{24}{12} \text{ ft} = 2 \text{ ft}$
$C = \pi d$
$\approx 3.14 \cdot 2 = 6.28 \text{ ft}$
$6.28 \text{ ft} \cdot 5 = 31.4 \text{ ft}$
The bicycle travels 31.4 ft.

32. Strategy To find the distance the tricycle travels:
- Convert the diameter (12 in.) to feet.
- Use the formula for circumference to find the distance traveled in 1 revolution.
- Multiply the distance traveled in 1 revolution by the number of revolutions (8).

Solution $12 \not{\text{in.}} \times \frac{1 \text{ ft}}{12 \not{\text{in.}}} = 1 \text{ ft}$
$C = \pi d$
$\approx 3.14 \cdot 1 = 3.14 \text{ ft}$
$3.14 \text{ ft} \times 8 = 25.12 \text{ ft}$
The bicycle travels 25.12 ft.

33a. Strategy To estimate whether the perimeter is more or less than 70 m, assume that the figure is a rectangle with length 25 m and width 10 m.

Solution $P = 2L + 2W = 2 \cdot 25 + 2 \cdot 10$
$= 50 + 20 = 70$
The perimeter of the rink is larger than the perimeter of the rectangle. The perimeter of the rink is more than 70 m.

b. Strategy To find the perimeter of the roller rink, find the perimeter of the composite figure.

Solution Perimeter
= sum of length of two sides
+ 2 times $\frac{1}{2}$ circumference of a circle
$\approx 2 \cdot 25 + 2 \cdot \frac{1}{2}(3.14 \cdot 10)$
$= 50 + 31.4 = 81.4$
The perimeter of the rink is 81.4 m.

34. Strategy To find the cost of the rain gutter:
- Subtract to find the unknown dimensions.
- Add to find the perimeter.
- Multiply the perimeter by the per-meter cost of the gutter.

Solution Unknown dimension = 14 m − 6 m
= 8 m
Unknown dimension = 8 m − 5 m
= 3 m
Perimeter = 6 m + 8 m + 14 m + 5 m
+ 8 m + 3 m = 44 m
44 × $11.30 = $497.20
It will cost $497.20 to install the rain gutter.

35. **Strategy** To find the length of weather stripping, find the perimeter of the composite figure.

Solution Perimeter
= sum of three sides of rectangle
$+\frac{1}{2}$ circumference of circle
$\approx (3\text{ ft}) + (2 \cdot 6\text{ ft }6\text{ in.}) + \frac{1}{2}(3.14 \cdot 3\text{ ft})$
$= 3\text{ ft} + 13\text{ ft} + 4.71\text{ ft} = 20.71\text{ ft}$
Approximately 20.71 ft of weather stripping are installed.

36. **Strategy** To find the distance Earth travels, use the formula for the circumference of a circle.

Solution $C = 2\pi r$
$\approx 2 \cdot 3.14 \cdot 93{,}000{,}000\text{ mi}$
$= 584{,}040{,}000\text{ mi}$
Earth travels approximately 584,040,000 mi in 1 revolution around the sun.

37. **Strategy** To find the circumference of Earth, use the formula for the circumference of a circle.

Solution $C = 2\pi r$
$\approx 2 \cdot 3.14 \cdot 6356\text{ km}$
$= 39{,}915.68\text{ km}$
The circumference of Earth is approximately 39,915.68 km.

Applying the Concepts

38a. Two. If the diameter is 1 ft, then $C = \pi$. If the diameter is 2 ft, then $C = 2\pi$.

b. Two. If the radius is 1 ft, then $C = 2\pi$. If the radius is 2 ft, then $C = 4\pi$.

39. Length = 8
Width = 3
$P = 2L + 2W = 2(8) + 2(3) = 16 + 6 = 22$ units

40.

41. The perimeter of one large triangle is 3 cm. (1 on each side) as in Figure A.
The perimeter of three medium triangles is $3\left(\frac{3}{2}\right)$ $\left(\frac{1}{2}\text{ on each side}\right)$ as in Figure B.
The perimeter of nine small triangles is $9\left(\frac{3}{4}\right)$ $\left(\frac{1}{4}\text{ on each side}\right)$ as in Figure C.

The perimeter of all shaded triangles
$= 3 + 3\left(\frac{3}{2}\right) + 9\left(\frac{3}{4}\right)$
$= 3 + \frac{9}{2} + \frac{27}{4}$
$= 13\frac{5}{4} = 14\frac{1}{4}$ cm

42. A square has 4 equal sides, so each side is $\frac{1}{4}$ the length of the wire. Each side $= \frac{1}{4}x$ or $\frac{x}{4}$

43. The ranger could measure the circumference of the trunk of the tree and then solve the equation $C = \pi d$ for d.

Section 12.3

Objective A Exercises

1. $A = LW = 24\text{ ft} \cdot 6\text{ ft} = 144\text{ ft}^2$

2. $A = LW = 18\text{ in.} \cdot 8\text{ in.} = 144\text{ in}^2$

3. $A = s^2 = (9\text{ in.})^2 = 81\text{ in}^2$

4. $A = s^2 = (4\text{ in.})^2 = 16\text{ in}^2$

5. $A = \pi r^2$
$\approx 3.14(4\text{ ft})^2 = 50.24\text{ ft}^2$

6. $A = \pi r^2$
$\approx 3.14(3\text{ cm})^2 = 28.26\text{ cm}^2$

7. $A = \frac{1}{2}bh$
$= \frac{1}{2} \cdot (10\text{ in.})(4\text{ in.}) = 20\text{ in}^2$

8. $A = \frac{1}{2}bh$
$= \frac{1}{2} \cdot 7\text{ m} \cdot 6\text{ m} = 21\text{ m}^2$

9. $A = \frac{1}{2}bh$
$= \frac{1}{2} \cdot 3\text{ cm} \cdot 1.42\text{ cm} = 2.13\text{ cm}^2$

10. $A = \frac{1}{2}bh$
$= \frac{1}{2} \cdot 3\text{ ft} \cdot \frac{2}{3}\text{ft} = 1\text{ ft}^2$

11. $A = s^2 = 4\text{ ft} \cdot 4\text{ ft} = 16\text{ ft}^2$

12. $A = s^2 = 10 \text{ cm} \cdot 10 \text{ cm} = 100 \text{ cm}^2$

13. $A = LW = 43 \text{ in.} \cdot 19 \text{ in.} = 817 \text{ in}^2$

14. $A = LW$
$= 82 \text{ cm} \cdot 20 \text{ cm} = 1640 \text{ cm}^2$

15. $A = \pi r^2 \approx \frac{22}{7} \cdot 7 \text{ in.} \cdot 7 \text{ in.} = 154 \text{ in}^2$

16. $r = \frac{1}{2} d = \frac{1}{2} \cdot 40 \text{ cm} = 20 \text{ cm}$
$A = \pi r^2 \approx 3.14(20 \text{ cm})^2$
$= 1256 \text{ cm}^2$

Objective B Exercises

17. Area = area of rectangle – area of triangle
$= (LW) - \left(\frac{1}{2} bh\right)$
$= (8 \text{ cm} \cdot 4 \text{ cm}) - \left(\frac{1}{2} \cdot 4 \text{ cm} \cdot 3 \text{ cm}\right)$
$= 32 \text{ cm}^2 - 6 \text{ cm}^2$
$= 26 \text{ cm}^2$

18. Area = $\frac{1}{2}$ area of circle + area of square
$= \frac{1}{2} \pi r^2 + s^2$
$\approx \frac{1}{2}(3.14)(3 \text{ in.})^2 + (6 \text{ in.})^2$
$= 14.13 \text{ in}^2 + 36 \text{ in}^2$
$= 50.13 \text{ in}^2$

19. Area = area of rectangle – area of triangle
$= (LW) - \left(\frac{1}{2} bh\right)$
$= (80 \text{ cm} \cdot 30 \text{ cm}) - \left(\frac{1}{2} \cdot 30 \text{ cm} \cdot 12 \text{ cm}\right)$
$= 2400 \text{ cm}^2 - 180 \text{ cm}^2$
$= 2220 \text{ cm}^2$

20. Area = area of rectangle – $\frac{1}{2}$ area of circle
$= (LW) - \frac{1}{2} \pi r^2$
$\approx (2 \text{ m} \cdot 0.8 \text{ m}) - \frac{1}{2}(3.14)(0.4 \text{ m})^2$
$= 1.6 \text{ m}^2 - 0.2512 \text{ m}^2$
$= 1.3488 \text{ m}^2$

21. Area = area of circle – $\frac{1}{4}$ area of circle
$= \pi r^2 - \frac{1}{4} \cdot \pi r^2$
$\approx 3.14(8 \text{ in.})^2 - \frac{1}{4} \cdot 3.14(8 \text{ in.})^2$
$= 200.96 \text{ in}^2 - 50.24 \text{ in}^2$
$= 150.72 \text{ in}^2$

22. Area = area of rectangle + area of triangle
$= (LW) + \left(\frac{1}{2} bh\right)$
$= (6 \text{ in.} \cdot 4 \text{ in.}) + \left(\frac{1}{2} \cdot 4 \text{ in.} \cdot 3 \text{ in.}\right)$
$= 24 \text{ in}^2 + 6 \text{ in}^2$
$= 30 \text{ in}^2$

23. Area = area of rectangle – $\frac{1}{2}$ area of circle
$= LW - \frac{1}{2} \cdot \pi r^2$
$\approx 4.38 \text{ ft} \cdot 3.74 \text{ ft} - \frac{1}{2} \cdot 3.14(2.19 \text{ ft})^2$
$= 16.3812 \text{ ft}^2 - 7.529877 \text{ ft}^2$
$= 8.851323 \text{ ft}^2$

24. Area = area of triangle + $\frac{1}{2}$ area of circle
$= \left(\frac{1}{2} bh\right) + \frac{1}{2} \cdot \pi r^2$
$\approx \left(\frac{1}{2} \cdot 22.4 \text{ cm} \cdot 22.4 \text{ cm}\right)$
$+ \frac{1}{2} \cdot 3.14(11.2 \text{ cm})^2$
$= 250.88 \text{ cm}^2 + 196.9408 \text{ cm}^2$
$= 447.8208 \text{ cm}^2$

Objective C Exercises

25. **Strategy** To find the area of the playing field, find the area of a rectangle with length 100 yd and width 75 yd.

Solution $A = LW$
$= 100 \text{ yd} \cdot 75 \text{ yd}$
$= 7500 \text{ yd}^2$
The area of the playing field is 7500 yd^2.

26. **Strategy** To find the area of the lens:
- Find the radius.
- Use the formula for the area of a circle.

Solution $r = \frac{1}{2} d = \frac{1}{2} \cdot 200 \text{ in.}$
$= 100 \text{ in.}$
$A = \pi r^2 = \pi(100 \text{ in.})^2$
$= 10{,}000\pi \text{ in}^2$
The area of the lens is $10{,}000\pi \text{ in}^2$.

27. **Strategy** To find the area of the field, find the area of a circle with a radius of 50 ft.

Solution $A = \pi r^2 \approx 3.14 \cdot 50 \text{ ft} \cdot 50 \text{ ft}$
$= 7850 \text{ ft}^2$
The area watered by the irrigation system is approximately 7850 ft^2.

28. Strategy To find the amount of fabric:
- Find the length and width of the fabric by adding 0.1 m to each side of the wall hanging.
- Find the area of a rectangle with the new length and new width.

Solution $5\text{ m} + 0.1\text{ m} + 0.1\text{ m} = 5.2\text{ m}$
$3.5\text{ m} + 0.1\text{ m} + 0.1\text{ m} = 3.7\text{ m}$
$A = LW$
$= 5.2\text{ m} \cdot 3.7\text{ m}$
$= 19.24\text{ m}^2$
The area of the fabric is 19.24 m^2.

29. Strategy To find the amount of stain:
- Find the area of a rectangle that measures 10 ft by 8 ft.
- Divide the area by the area that one quart of stain will cover(50 ft^2).

Solution $A = LW$
$= 10\text{ ft} \cdot 8\text{ ft}$
$= 80\text{ ft}^2$
$80\text{ ft}^2 \div 50\text{ ft}^2 = 1.6$
It will take 1.6 quarts of stain.
You should buy 2 qt.

30. Strategy To find the cost of the carpet:
- Find the area of the room and hallway. The total area is the sum of the areas of the two rectangles.
- Multiply the total area by \$18.50.

Solution $\text{Area} = 6.8 \cdot 4.5 + (10.8 - 6.8) \cdot 1$
$= 30.6 + 4 \cdot 1$
$= 30.6 + 4$
$= 34.6$
$\text{Cost} = (34.6)(\$18.50) = \$640.10$
The cost of the carpet is \$640.10.

31. Strategy To find the area of the driveway, subtract the area of the small rectangle from the area of the large rectangle.

Solution Area = area of large rectangle − area of small rectangle
$= (\text{length} \cdot \text{width}) - (\text{length} \cdot \text{width})$
$= (75\text{ ft} \cdot 30\text{ ft}) - (50\text{ ft} \cdot 20\text{ ft})$
$= 2250\text{ ft}^2 - 1000\text{ ft}^2$
$= 1250\text{ ft}^2$
The area of the driveway is 1250 ft^2.

32. Strategy To find the number of tiles to be purchased.
- Use the formula for the area of a rectangle to find the area of the kitchen floor.
- Divide the area of the kitchen floor by the area of one tile $\left(1\frac{1}{2}\text{ ft}\right)^2$.

Solution $A = LW$
$= 12\text{ ft} \cdot 9\text{ ft}$
$= 108\text{ ft}^2$
$108\text{ ft}^2 \div \left(1\frac{1}{2}\text{ ft}\right)^2 = 108 \div \frac{9}{4}$
$= 108 \cdot \frac{4}{9} = 48$
You should purchase 48 tiles for your kitchen floor.

33. Strategy To find the cost of the wallpaper:
- Use the formula for the area of a rectangle to find the areas of the two walls.
- Add the areas of the two walls.
- Divide the total area by the area in one roll (40 ft^2) to find the total number of rolls.
- Multiply the number of rolls by \$28.50.

Solution $\text{Area}_1 = 9\text{ ft} \cdot 8\text{ ft} = 72\text{ ft}^2$
$\text{Area}_2 = 11\text{ ft} \cdot 8\text{ ft} = 88\text{ ft}^2$
$\text{Total area} = 72\text{ ft}^2 + 88\text{ ft}^2 = 160\text{ ft}^2$
$160\text{ ft}^2 \div 40\text{ ft}^2 = 4$
$4 \cdot \$28.50 = \$114$
The cost to wallpaper the two walls is \$114.

34. Strategy To find the area of the boundary, subtract the area of the rectangular swimming pool from the area of the swimming pool and boundary.

Solution Area = area of swimming pool and boundary − area of swimming pool
$= (\text{length} \cdot \text{width}) - (\text{length} \cdot \text{width})$
$= (9\text{ m} \cdot 12\text{ m}) - (8\text{ m} \cdot 5\text{ m})$
$= 108\text{ m}^2 - 40\text{ m}^2$
$= 68\text{ m}^2$
The area of the boundary around the pool is 68 m^2.

35. Strategy To find the amount budgeted:
- Use the formula for the area of a square to find the area of the park.
- Divide the area by 1200 ft^2 to find the number of bags of seed.
- Multiply the number of bags of seed by \$5.75.

Solution $A = s^2$
$= (60\text{ ft})^2 = 3{,}600\text{ ft}^2$
$3{,}600\text{ ft}^2 \div 1{,}200\text{ ft}^2 = 3$
$3 \cdot \$5.75 = \$17.25$
\$17.25 should be budgeted for grass seed.

36a. Strategy To determine whether the area is more or less than 8000 ft^2:
- Assume that the area is a rectangle with dimensions 175 ft by 80 ft.
- Find the area and compare with 8000 ft^2.

Solution
$A = LW$
$= 175 \text{ ft} \cdot 80 \text{ ft}$
$= 14{,}000$
Since the area of the rink is greater than 14,000 ft^2 it is more than 8000 ft^2.

b. Strategy To find how much hardwood floor is needed, find the area of the composite figure.

Solution Area = area of rectangle + 2 times $\frac{1}{2}$ area of circle
$= (LW) + 2\left(\frac{1}{2}\pi r^2\right)$
$\approx (175 \text{ ft} \cdot 80 \text{ ft}) + \frac{1}{2} \cdot 3.14(40 \text{ ft})^2$
$= 14{,}000 \text{ ft}^2 + 5024 \text{ ft}^2$
$= 19{,}024 \text{ ft}^2$
To cover the rink, approximately 19,024 ft^2 of hardwood floor is needed.

37. Strategy To find the total area of the park:
- Find the area of the first rectangle.
- Find the area of the second rectangle.
- Find the area of the semicircle.
- Add all the areas together.

Solution
Area of first rectangle $= 12.7 \times 2.5 = 31.75$
Area of second rectangle $= 17.5 \times 4.3 = 75.25$
Area of semicircle $= \frac{1}{2} \times 3.14 \times (3.4)^2 = 18.1492$
Total area $= 31.75 + 75.25 + 18.1492 = 125.1492$
The total area of the park is 125.1492 mi^2.

38. Strategy To find the cost to plaster the room:
- Find the area of the two walls 25 ft 6 in. long and 8 ft high.
- Find the area of the two walls 22 ft long and 8 ft high.
- Add to find the area of the four walls.
- Subtract 120 ft^2 from the area of the four walls.
- Multiply the area by the cost per square foot ($2.50).

Solution
$2 \cdot 25.5 \text{ ft} \cdot 8 \text{ ft} = 408 \text{ ft}^2$ area of two walls
$2 \cdot 22 \text{ ft} \cdot 8 \text{ ft} = 352 \text{ ft}^2$ area of two walls
$408 \text{ ft}^2 + 352 \text{ ft}^2 = 760 \text{ ft}^2$ area of four walls
$760 \text{ ft}^2 - 120 \text{ ft}^2 = 640 \text{ ft}^2$ area of walls minus doors and windows
$640 \text{ ft}^2 \times \$2.50 = \$1600$
The cost to plaster the room is $1600.

39a. Strategy To find the increase in area:
- Find the area of the original circle.
- Find the area of the increased circle.
- Subtract the area of the original circle from the area of the larger circle.

Solution
Area of original circle $\approx (64)(3.14) = 200.96 \text{ in}^2$
Area of increased circle $\approx (100)(3.14) = 314 \text{ in}^2$
$314 - 200.96 = 113.04 \text{ in}^2$
The amount of the increase is about 113.04 in^2.

b. Strategy To find the increase in area:
- Find the area of the original circle.
- Find the area of the increased circle.
- Subtract the area of the original circle from the area of the larger circle.

Solution Area of original circle $\approx (25)(3.14) = 78.5$ cm^2
Area of increased circle $\approx (100)(3.14) = 314$ cm^2
$314 - 78.5 = 235.5$ cm^2
The amount of the increase is about 235.5 cm^2.

Applying the Concepts

40. Strategy To find what fractional part of the area of the larger of the two squares is the shaded area:
- Find the area of the larger square.
- Find the area of the smaller square.
- Find the area of the shaded area by multiplying $\frac{1}{4}$ times the area of the smaller square.
- Write as a fraction in simplest form the ratio of the area of the shaded area to the area of the larger square.

Solution Area of larger square $= s^2 = 12^2 = 144$
Area of smaller square $= s^2 = 3^2 = 9$
Area of shaded area $= \frac{1}{4}(9) = \frac{9}{4} = 2\frac{1}{4}$

$$\frac{2\frac{1}{4}}{144} = 2\frac{1}{4} \div 144 = \frac{9}{4} \div 144 = \frac{9}{4} \cdot \frac{1}{144} = \frac{1}{64}$$

The shaded area is $\frac{1}{64}$ of the area of the larger square.

41a. Area of original rectangle $= LW$
Area of doubled rectangle $= (2L)(2W)$
$= 4LW$
$= 4 \times$ Area of original rectangle
If the length and width are doubled, the area is increased 4 times.

b. Area of original circle $= \pi r^2$
Area with radius doubled $= \pi(2r)^2$
$= \pi\ 4r^2$
$= 4(\pi r^2)$
$= 4 \times$ Area of original circle
If the radius is doubled, the area is quadrupled.

c. If the diameter is doubled, the radius is doubled. From (b) if the radius is doubled, the area is quadrupled.

42. The area in the circles to the left of the line is equal to the area in the circles to the right of the line. Note that in the circle at the left in the top row, the line goes through the center of the circle; thus it is a diameter of the circle, and half the area lies on one side of the line and half lies on the other side of the line. A complete circle lies on each side of the line; the circle at the right in the top row is on one side, and the circle at the left in the bottom row lies on the other side. For the two circles at the right on the bottom row, half their combined area lies on the left side of the line, and half lies on the right side of the line.

43a. Sometimes true

b. Sometimes true

c. Always true

44. Area of Triangle = Area of rectangle around triangle − Areas of 3 triangles around original triangle and within rectangle

$$= LW - \frac{1}{2}bh - \frac{1}{2}bh - \frac{1}{2}bh$$
$$= (3\text{ in.})(2\text{ in.}) - \frac{1}{2}(2\text{ in.})(1\text{ in.}) - \frac{1}{2}(1\text{ in.})(3\text{ in.}) - \frac{1}{2}(2\text{ in.})(1\text{ in.})$$
$$= 6\text{ in}^2 - 1\text{ in}^2 - \frac{3}{2}\text{ in}^2 - 1\text{ in}^2$$
$$= \frac{12}{2}\text{ in}^2 - \frac{2}{2}\text{ in}^2 - \frac{3}{2}\text{ in}^2 - \frac{2}{2}\text{ in}^2$$
$$= \frac{12-2-3-2}{2}\text{ in}^2$$
$$= \frac{5}{2}\text{ in}^2$$
$$= 2\frac{1}{2}\text{ in}^2$$

The area of the triangle is $2\frac{1}{2}\text{ in}^2$.

Section 12.4

Objective A Exercises

1. $V = LWH$
$= 12\text{ cm} \cdot 4\text{ cm} \cdot 3\text{ cm} = 144\text{ cm}^3$

2. $V = LWH$
$= 6\text{ ft} \cdot 8\text{ ft} \cdot 5\text{ ft} = 240\text{ ft}^3$

3. $V = s^3 = (8\text{ in.})^3 = 512\text{ in}^3$

4. $V = s^3 = (12\text{ m})^3 = 1728\text{ m}^3$

5. $V = \frac{4}{3}\pi r^3 \approx \frac{4}{3}(3.14)(8\text{ in.})^3$
$\approx 2143.57\text{ in}^3$

6. $r = \frac{1}{2}d = \frac{1}{2}(7\text{ in.}) = 3.5\text{ in.}$
$V = \frac{4}{3}\pi r^3 \approx \frac{4}{3}(3.14)(3.5\text{ in.})^3$
$\approx 179.50\text{ in}^3$

7. $V = \pi r^2 h$
$\approx 3.14(2\text{ cm})^2 \cdot 12\text{ cm} = 150.72\text{ cm}^3$

8. $r = \frac{1}{2}d = \frac{1}{2} \cdot 5\text{ ft} = 2.5\text{ ft}$
$V = \pi r^2 h$
$\approx 3.14(2.5\text{ ft})^2 \cdot 8\text{ ft} = 157\text{ ft}^3$

9. $V = LWH$
$= 2\text{ m} \cdot 0.8\text{ m} \cdot 4\text{ m} = 6.4\text{ m}^3$

10. $V = \pi r^2 h$
$\approx \frac{22}{7}(7\text{ cm})^2(14\text{ cm})$
$= 2156\text{ cm}^3$

11. $V = \frac{4}{3}\pi r^3$
$\approx \frac{4}{3} \cdot 3.14(11\text{ mm})^3$
$\approx 5572.45\text{ mm}^3$

12. $V = s^3$
$= 2.14\text{ m} \cdot 2.14\text{ m} \cdot 2.14\text{ m}$
$\approx 9.8\text{ m}^3$

13. $r = \frac{1}{2}d = \frac{1}{2} \cdot 12\text{ ft} = 6\text{ ft}$
$V = \pi r^2 h$
$\approx 3.14(6\text{ ft})^2(30\text{ ft})$
$= 3391.2\text{ ft}^3$

14. $r = \frac{1}{2}d = \frac{1}{2} \cdot 6\text{ ft} = 3\text{ ft}$
$V = \frac{4}{3}\pi r^3$
$\approx \frac{4}{3} \cdot 3.14 \cdot 3\text{ ft} \cdot 3\text{ ft} \cdot 3\text{ ft} = 113.04\text{ ft}^3$

15. $V = s^3$
$= 3\frac{1}{2}\text{ ft} \cdot 3\frac{1}{2}\text{ ft} \cdot 3\frac{1}{2}\text{ ft} = 42\frac{7}{8}\text{ ft}^3$

16. $V = LWH$
$= 1.15\text{ m} \cdot 0.60\text{ m} \cdot 0.25\text{ m}$
$= 0.1725\text{ m}^3$

Objective B Exercises

17. Volume $= \frac{1}{2}$volume of cylinder + volume of rectangular solid

$= \left[\frac{1}{2} \cdot \pi(\text{radius})^2 \cdot \text{height}\right] + (\text{length} \cdot \text{width} \cdot \text{height})$

$\approx \left(\frac{1}{2} \cdot 3.14 \cdot 3 \text{ in.} \cdot 3 \text{ in.} \cdot 2 \text{ in.}\right) + (6 \text{ in.} \cdot 9 \text{ in.} \cdot 1 \text{ in.}) = 28.26 \text{ in}^3 + 54 \text{ in}^3 = 82.26 \text{ in}^3$

18. Volume = volume of cylinder + $\frac{1}{2}$volume of sphere $= [\pi(\text{radius})^2 \cdot \text{height}] + \frac{1}{2}\left[\frac{4}{3} \cdot \pi(\text{radius})^3\right]$

$\approx (3.14 \cdot 3 \text{ ft} \cdot 3 \text{ ft} \cdot 12 \text{ ft}) + \frac{1}{2}\left(\frac{4}{3} \cdot 3.14 \cdot 3 \text{ ft} \cdot 3 \text{ ft} \cdot 3 \text{ ft}\right)$

$= 339.12 \text{ ft}^3 + 56.52 \text{ ft}^3 = 395.64 \text{ ft}^3$

19. Volume = volume of rectangular solid – volume of cylinder = (length · width · height)

$- [\pi(\text{radius})^2 \cdot \text{height}]$

$\approx (1.20 \text{ m} \cdot 2 \text{ m} \cdot 0.80 \text{ m}) - (3.14 \cdot 0.20 \text{ m} \cdot 0.20 \text{ m} \cdot 2 \text{ m})$

$= 1.92 \text{ m}^3 - 0.2512 \text{ m}^3 = 1.6688 \text{ m}^3$

20. Volume = volume of rectangular solid + volume of rectangular solid

= (length · width · height) + (length · width · height)

$= (2 \text{ m} \cdot 1.5 \text{ m} \cdot 1.5 \text{ m}) + (2 \text{ m} \cdot 0.5 \text{ m} \cdot 0.5 \text{ m}) = 4.50 \text{ m}^3 + 0.50 \text{ m}^3 = 5 \text{ m}^3$

21. Volume = volume of cylinder + volume of cylinder

$= [\pi(\text{radius})^2 \cdot \text{height}] + [\pi(\text{radius})^2 \cdot \text{height}]$

$\approx (3.14 \cdot 3 \text{ in.} \cdot 3 \text{ in.} \cdot 2 \text{ in.}) + (3.14 \cdot 1 \text{ in.} \cdot 1 \text{ in.} \cdot 4 \text{ in.})$

$= 56.52 \text{ in}^3 + 12.56 \text{ in}^3 = 69.08 \text{ in}^3$

22. Volume = volume of large cylinder – volume of small cylinder

$= [\pi(\text{radius})^2 \cdot \text{height}] - [\pi(\text{radius})^2 \cdot \text{height}]$

$\approx (3.14 \cdot 9 \text{ cm} \cdot 9 \text{ cm} \cdot 24 \text{ cm}) - (3.14 \cdot 4.5 \text{ cm} \cdot 4.5 \text{ cm} \cdot 24 \text{ cm})$

$= 6104.16 \text{ cm}^3 - 1526.04 \text{ cm}^3 = 4578.12 \text{ cm}^3$

Objective C Exercises

23. Strategy To find the volume of the tank, use the formula for the volume of a rectangular solid.

Solution $V = LWH$

$= 9 \text{ m} \cdot 3 \text{ m} \cdot 1.5 \text{ m}$

$= 40.5 \text{ m}^3$

The volume of the water in the tank is 40.5 m^3.

24. Strategy To find the volume of the booster, use the formula for the volume of a cylinder.

Solution $V = \pi r^2 h$

$\approx 3.14(5 \text{ ft})^2 \cdot 52 \text{ ft}$

$= 4082 \text{ ft}^3$

The volume of the booster is approximately 4082 ft^3.

25. Strategy To find the volume of the balloon, use the formula for the volume of a sphere.

Solution $V = \frac{4}{3}\pi r^3$

$\approx \frac{4}{3} \cdot 3.14(16 \text{ ft})^3$

$\approx 17{,}148.59 \text{ ft}^3$

The volume is approximately $17{,}148.59 \text{ ft}^3$.

26. Strategy To find the volume of the storage tank, use the formula for the volume of a sphere.

Solution $V = \frac{4}{3}\pi r^3$

$\approx \frac{4}{3} \cdot 3.14(4.5 \text{ m})^3$

$= 381.51 \text{ m}^3$

The volume of the storage tank is approximately 381.51 m^3.

27. Strategy To find the amount of oil:
- Use the formula for the volume of a cylinder to find the volume of the tank.
- Multiply the volume by $\frac{2}{3}$ to find the amount of oil.

Solution $V = \pi r^2 h$
$\approx 3.14(3\text{ m})^2(4\text{ m})$
$= 113.04\text{ m}^3$

Amount of oil $= \frac{2}{3} \cdot 113.04\text{ m}^3$
$= 75.36\text{ m}^3$

The amount of oil is approximately 75.36 m^3.

28. Strategy To find the volume not used for storage:
- Use the formula for the volume of a cylinder to find the volume of the silo.
- Multiply the volume of the silo by $\frac{1}{4}$ to find the volume not used for storage.

Solution $V = \pi r^2 h$
$\approx 3.14(8\text{ ft})^2(30\text{ ft})$
$= 6028.80\text{ ft}^3$

Amount not used $= \frac{1}{4} \cdot 6028.80\text{ ft}^3$
$\approx 1507.2\text{ ft}^3$

Approximately 1507.2 ft^3 of the silo is not used for storage.

29. Strategy To find the volume of the auditorium, find the volume of the rectangular solid and add half the volume of the cylinder.

Solution $V = LWH + \frac{1}{2}[\pi r^2 h]$
$\approx 125\text{ ft} \cdot 94\text{ ft} \cdot 32\text{ ft} + \frac{1}{2}[3.14(47\text{ ft})^2 \cdot 125\text{ ft}]$
$= 376{,}000\text{ ft}^3 + 433{,}516.25\text{ ft}^3$
$= 809{,}516.25\text{ ft}^3$

The volume of the auditorium is approximately $809{,}516.25\text{ ft}^3$.

30. Strategy To find the weight of the water, multiply the volume in cubic feet by the weight per cubic foot.

Solution $V = LWH = 50\text{ ft} \times 13\text{ ft} \times 10\text{ ft}$
$= 6500\text{ ft}^3$
$6500 \times 62.4 = 405{,}600\text{ lb}$

The weight of the water is 405,600 lb.

31. Strategy To find the volume of the bushing, subtract the volume of the half-cylinder from the volume of the rectangular solid.

Solution $V = LWH - \frac{1}{2}[\pi r^2 h]$
$\approx (12\text{ in.} \cdot 84\text{ in.} \cdot 3\text{ in.}) - \frac{1}{2}(3.14)(2\text{ in.})^2(12\text{ in.})$
$= 288\text{ in}^3 - 75.36\text{ in}^3$
$= 212.64\text{ in}^3$

The volume of the bushing is approximately 212.64 in^3.

32. Strategy To find the number of gallons in the aquarium:
- Use the formula for the volume of a rectangular solid.
- Convert the volume to gallons.

Solution $V = LWH$
$= 18\text{ in} \cdot 12\text{ in} \cdot 16\text{ in}$
$= 3456\text{ in}^3$

$3456\text{ in}^3 = 3456\,\cancel{\text{in}^3} \times \frac{1\text{ gal}}{231\,\cancel{\text{in}^3}}$
$\approx 15.0\text{ gal}$

It will take 15.0 gal of water to fill the aquarium.

33. Strategy To find the number of gallons in the fish tank:
- Use the formula for the volume of a rectangular solid.
- Convert the volume to gallons.

Solution $V = LWH$
$= 12\text{ in.} \cdot 8\text{ in.} \cdot 9\text{ in.}$
$= 864\text{ in}^3$

$864\text{ in}^3 = 864\,\cancel{\text{in}^3} \times \frac{1\text{ gal}}{231\,\cancel{\text{in}^3}} \approx 3.7\text{ gal}$

The tank will hold 3.7 gal.

34a. Strategy To determine whether the volume is more or less than 240 ft^3, assume (conservatively) that the volume is a rectangular solid with length 30 ft, width 4 ft, and height 4 ft, and compare with 240 ft^3.

Solution
$$V = LWH$$
$$= 30 \text{ ft} \cdot 4 \text{ ft} \cdot 4 \text{ ft} = 480 \text{ ft}^3$$

Since 480 ft^3 > 240 ft^3, the volume of the truck is more than 240 ft^3.

b. Strategy To find the amount of oil the truck is carrying:
- The volume of the tank is equal to the volume of a cylinder plus the sum of two half-spheres. The radius of the sphere is one half the diameter of the cylinder.
- Multiply the volume by $\frac{1}{2}$.

Solution
$$\text{Volume} = \pi r^2 h + 2\left(\frac{1}{2}\cdot\frac{4}{3}\pi r^3\right)$$
$$\approx 3.14(4 \text{ ft})^2(30 \text{ ft}) + \frac{4}{3}(3.14)(4 \text{ ft})^3$$
$$\approx 1507.20 \text{ ft}^3 + 267.947 \text{ ft}^3$$
$$= 1775.147 \text{ ft}^3$$
$$\frac{1}{2}(1775.147) \approx 887.57$$

The volume of oil is approximately 887.57 ft^3.

35. Strategy To find the cost of the floor:
- Find the volume. The volume is equal to the volume of a rectangular solid plus one half the volume of the cylinder. The radius is one half the length of the rectangular solid.
- Multiply the volume by $5.85.

Solution
$$V = LWH + \frac{1}{2}\pi r^2 h$$
$$\approx 50 \text{ ft} \cdot 25 \text{ ft} \cdot \frac{1}{2} \text{ ft} + \frac{1}{2}(3.14)(25 \text{ ft})^2\left(\frac{1}{2} \text{ ft}\right)$$
$$= 625 \text{ ft}^3 + 490.625 \text{ ft}^3$$
$$= 1115.625 \text{ ft}^3$$

Cost = 1115.625 × \$5.85 ≈ 6526.41
The cost is approximately \$6526.41.

Applying the Concepts

36.
$$\text{Volume of a sphere} = \frac{4}{3}\pi r^3$$
$$\text{Volume of a hemisphere} = \frac{1}{2}\cdot\frac{4}{3}\pi r^3 = \frac{2}{3}\pi r^3$$

37a. Volume = length · width · height.
If the length and width are doubled,
Volume = 2 · length · 2 · width · height
= 4 · length · width · height
The volume will be 4 times larger.

b. Volume = length · width · height.
If the length, width and height are doubled,
Volume = 2 · length · 2 · width · 2 · height
= 8 · length · width · height
The volume will be 8 times larger.

c. Volume = $(\text{side})^3$. If the side is doubled,
Volume = $(2.\text{side})^3 = 8.(\text{side})^3$
The volume will be 8 times larger.

38. For example, a cut perpendicular to the top and bottom faces and parallel to two of the sides.

39. For example, beginning at an edge that is perpendicular to the bottom face, cut at an angle through to the bottom face.

40. For example, beginning at the top face, at a distance d from the vertex, cut at an angle to the bottom face, ending at a distance greater than d from the vertex directly below the first chosen vertex.

41. For example, beginning on the top face, at a distance d from a vertex, cut across the cube to a point just below the opposite vertex.

42. The length of the rectangular solid is equal to half the circumference of the base of the cylinder.
$$L = \frac{1}{2}C$$
The width of the rectangular solid is equal to the radius of the base of the cylinder.
$$W = r$$
The height of the rectangular solid is equal to the height of the cylinder.
$$H = h$$
For the base of the rectangular solid:
$$L = \frac{1}{2}C;\ W = r;$$
$$A = LW = \frac{1}{2}C(r) = \frac{1}{2}(\pi d)r = \frac{1}{2}\pi(2r)r = \pi r^2$$
The volume of the rectangular solid and of the cylinder is $V = LWH = (LW)h = \pi r^2 h$.

Section 12.5

Objective A Exercises

1. 2.646
2. 5.831
3. 6.481
4. 8
5. 12.845
6. 12
7. 13.748
8. 11.402

Objective B Exercises

9. $$\begin{aligned}\text{Hypotenuse} &= \sqrt{(\text{leg})^2 + (\text{leg})^2} \\ &= \sqrt{(3 \text{ in.})^2 + (4 \text{ in.})^2} \\ &= \sqrt{9 \text{ in}^2 + 16 \text{ in}^2} \\ &= \sqrt{25 \text{ in}^2} \\ &= 5 \text{ in.}\end{aligned}$$

10. $$\begin{aligned}\text{Hypotenuse} &= \sqrt{(\text{leg})^2 + (\text{leg})^2} \\ &= \sqrt{(5 \text{ in.})^2 + (12 \text{ in.})^2} \\ &= \sqrt{25 \text{ in}^2 + 144 \text{ in}^2} \\ &= \sqrt{169 \text{ in}^2} \\ &= 13 \text{ in.}\end{aligned}$$

11. $$\begin{aligned}\text{Hypotenuse} &= \sqrt{(\text{leg})^2 + (\text{leg})^2} \\ &= \sqrt{(5 \text{ cm})^2 + (7 \text{ cm})^2} \\ &= \sqrt{25 \text{ cm}^2 + 49 \text{ cm}^2} \\ &= \sqrt{74 \text{ cm}^2} \\ &\approx 8.602 \text{ cm}\end{aligned}$$

12. $$\begin{aligned}\text{Hypotenuse} &= \sqrt{(\text{leg})^2 + (\text{leg})^2} \\ &= \sqrt{(7 \text{ cm})^2 + (9 \text{ cm})^2} \\ &= \sqrt{49 \text{ cm}^2 + 81 \text{ cm}^2} \\ &= \sqrt{130 \text{ cm}^2} \\ &\approx 11.402 \text{ cm}\end{aligned}$$

13. $$\begin{aligned}\text{Leg} &= \sqrt{(\text{hypotenuse})^2 - (\text{leg})^2} \\ &= \sqrt{(15 \text{ ft})^2 - (10 \text{ ft})^2} \\ &= \sqrt{225 \text{ ft}^2 - 100 \text{ ft}^2} \\ &= \sqrt{125 \text{ ft}^2} \\ &\approx 11.180 \text{ ft}\end{aligned}$$

14. $$\begin{aligned}\text{Leg} &= \sqrt{(\text{hypotenuse})^2 - (\text{leg})^2} \\ &= \sqrt{(20 \text{ ft})^2 - (18 \text{ ft})^2} \\ &= \sqrt{400 \text{ ft}^2 - 324 \text{ ft}^2} \\ &= \sqrt{76 \text{ ft}^2} \\ &\approx 8.718 \text{ ft}\end{aligned}$$

15. $$\begin{aligned}\text{Leg} &= \sqrt{(\text{hypotenuse})^2 - (\text{leg})^2} \\ &= \sqrt{(6 \text{ cm})^2 - (4 \text{ cm})^2} \\ &= \sqrt{36 \text{ cm}^2 - 16 \text{ cm}^2} \\ &= \sqrt{20 \text{ cm}^2} \\ &\approx 4.472 \text{ cm}\end{aligned}$$

16. $$\begin{aligned}\text{Leg} &= \sqrt{(\text{hypotenuse})^2 - (\text{leg})^2} \\ &= \sqrt{(12 \text{ m})^2 - (9 \text{ m})^2} \\ &= \sqrt{144 \text{ m}^2 - 81 \text{ m}^2} \\ &= \sqrt{63 \text{ m}^2} \\ &\approx 7.937 \text{ m}\end{aligned}$$

17. $$\begin{aligned}\text{Hypotenuse} &= \sqrt{(\text{leg})^2 + (\text{leg})^2} \\ &= \sqrt{(9 \text{ yd})^2 + (9 \text{ yd})^2} \\ &= \sqrt{81 \text{ yd}^2 + 81 \text{ yd}^2} \\ &= \sqrt{162 \text{ yd}^2} \\ &\approx 12.728 \text{ yd}\end{aligned}$$

18. $$\begin{aligned}\text{Leg} &= \sqrt{(\text{hypotenuse})^2 - (\text{leg})^2} \\ &= \sqrt{(20 \text{ cm})^2 - (10 \text{ cm})^2} \\ &= \sqrt{400 \text{ cm}^2 - 100 \text{ cm}^2} \\ &= \sqrt{300 \text{ cm}^2} \\ &\approx 17.321 \text{ cm}\end{aligned}$$

19. $$\begin{aligned}\text{Leg} &= \sqrt{(\text{hypotenuse})^2 - (\text{leg})^2} \\ &= \sqrt{(12 \text{ ft})^2 - (6 \text{ ft})^2} \\ &= \sqrt{144 \text{ ft}^2 - 36 \text{ ft}^2} \\ &= \sqrt{108 \text{ ft}^2} \\ &\approx 10.392 \text{ ft}\end{aligned}$$

20. $$\begin{aligned}\text{Leg} &= \sqrt{(\text{hypotenuse})^2 - (\text{leg})^2} \\ &= \sqrt{(16 \text{ cm})^2 - (8 \text{ cm})^2} \\ &= \sqrt{256 \text{ cm}^2 - 64 \text{ cm}^2} \\ &= \sqrt{192 \text{ cm}^2} \\ &\approx 13.856 \text{ cm}\end{aligned}$$

21. $$\begin{aligned}\text{Hypotenuse} &= \sqrt{(\text{leg})^2 + (\text{leg})^2} \\ &= \sqrt{(15 \text{ cm})^2 + (15 \text{ cm})^2} \\ &= \sqrt{225 \text{ cm}^2 + 225 \text{ cm}^2} \\ &= \sqrt{450 \text{ cm}^2} \\ &\approx 21.213 \text{ cm}\end{aligned}$$

22. Hypotenuse $= \sqrt{(\text{leg})^2 + (\text{leg})^2}$
$= \sqrt{(6 \text{ in.})^2 + (6 \text{ in.})^2}$
$= \sqrt{36 \text{ in}^2 + 36 \text{ in}^2}$
$= \sqrt{72 \text{ in}^2}$
≈ 8.485 in.

23. Hypotenuse $= \sqrt{(\text{leg})^2 + (\text{leg})^2}$
$= \sqrt{(8 \text{ m})^2 + (4 \text{ m})^2}$
$= \sqrt{64 \text{ m}^2 + 16 \text{ m}^2}$
$= \sqrt{80 \text{ m}^2}$
≈ 8.944 m

24. Leg $= \sqrt{(\text{hypotenuse})^2 - (\text{leg})^2}$
$= \sqrt{(8.6 \text{ cm})^2 - (4.3 \text{ cm})^2}$
$= \sqrt{73.96 \text{ cm}^2 - 18.49 \text{ cm}^2}$
$= \sqrt{55.47 \text{ cm}^2}$
≈ 7.448 cm

25. Leg $= \sqrt{(\text{hypotenuse})^2 - (\text{leg})^2}$
$= \sqrt{(11.3 \text{ yd})^2 - (8.1 \text{ yd})^2}$
$= \sqrt{127.69 \text{ yd}^2 - 65.61 \text{ yd}^2}$
$= \sqrt{62.08 \text{ yd}^2}$
≈ 7.879 yd

26. Leg $= \sqrt{(\text{hypotenuse})^2 - (\text{leg})^2}$
$= \sqrt{(13.9 \text{ ft})^2 - (8.2 \text{ ft})^2}$
$= \sqrt{193.21 \text{ ft}^2 - 67.24 \text{ ft}^2}$
$= \sqrt{125.97 \text{ ft}^2}$
≈ 11.224 ft

Objective C Exercises

27. Strategy To find the length of the ramp, use the Pythagorean Theorem. The ramp is the hypotenuse of a right triangle.

Solution Hypotenuse $= \sqrt{(\text{leg})^2 + (\text{leg})^2}$
$= \sqrt{(9 \text{ ft})^2 + (3.5 \text{ ft})^2}$
$= \sqrt{81 \text{ ft}^2 + 12.25 \text{ ft}^2}$
$= \sqrt{93.25 \text{ ft}^2}$
≈ 9.66 ft

The ramp is 9.66 ft long.

28. Strategy To find the distance between the holes, use the Pythagorean Theorem. The distance is the hypotenuse of a right triangle. The legs are 6 and 2 in.

Solution Hypotenuse $= \sqrt{(\text{leg})^2 + (\text{leg})^2}$
$= \sqrt{(6 \text{ in.})^2 + (2 \text{ in.})^2}$
$= \sqrt{36 \text{ in}^2 + 4 \text{ in}^2}$
$= \sqrt{40 \text{ in}^2}$
≈ 6.32 in.

The distance between the holes is 6.32 in.

29. Strategy
- Traveling 18 mi east and then 12 mi north forms a right angle. The distance from the starting point is the hypotenuse of the triangle with legs 18 mi and 12 mi.
- Find the hypotenuse of the right triangle.

Solution Hypotenuse $= \sqrt{(\text{leg})^2 + (\text{leg})^2}$
$= \sqrt{(18 \text{ mi})^2 + (12 \text{ mi})^2}$
$= \sqrt{324 \text{ mi}^2 + 144 \text{ mi}^2}$
$= \sqrt{468 \text{ mi}^2}$
≈ 21.6 mi

The distance is 21.6 mi.

30. Strategy
- Traveling 12 mi west and then 16 mi south forms a right angle. The distance from the starting point is the hypotenuse of the triangle with legs 12 mi and 16 mi.
- Find the hypotenuse of the right triangle.

Solution Hypotenuse $= \sqrt{(\text{leg})^2 + (\text{leg})^2}$
$= \sqrt{(12 \text{ mi})^2 + (16 \text{ mi})^2}$
$= \sqrt{144 \text{ mi}^2 + 256 \text{ mi}^2}$
$= \sqrt{400 \text{ mi}^2}$
$= 20$ mi

You are 20 mi from your starting point.

31. Strategy
- The angles of a rectangle are right angles. The length (11 mi) and width (5 mi) are the legs of a right triangle. The diagonal is the hypotenuse.
- Find the length of the hypotenuse.

Solution Hypotenuse $= \sqrt{(\text{leg})^2 + (\text{leg})^2}$
$= \sqrt{(11 \text{ mi})^2 + (5 \text{ mi})^2}$
$= \sqrt{121 \text{ mi}^2 + 25 \text{ mi}^2}$
$= \sqrt{146 \text{ mi}^2}$
≈ 12.1 mi

The length of the diagonal is 12.1 mi.

32. Strategy • The angles of a rectangle are right angles. The length (8 m) and width (3.5 m) are the legs of a right triangle. The diagonal is the hypotenuse.
• Find the length of the hypotenuse.

Solution

$$\begin{aligned}\text{Hypotenuse} &= \sqrt{(\text{leg})^2 + (\text{leg})^2}\\ &= \sqrt{(8\text{ m})^2 + (3.5\text{ m})^2}\\ &= \sqrt{64\text{ m}^2 + 12.25\text{ m}^2}\\ &= \sqrt{76.25\text{ m}^2}\\ &\approx 8.7\text{ m}\end{aligned}$$

The length of the diagonal is 8.7 m.

33. Strategy • To find how high on the building the ladder reaches, use the Phythagorean Theorem. The hypotenuse is the length of the ladder (8 m). One leg is the distance from the base of the building to the base of the ladder (3 m). The distance from the ground to the top of the ladder is the unknown leg.

Solution

$$\begin{aligned}\text{Leg} &= \sqrt{(\text{hypotenuse})^2 - (\text{leg})^2}\\ &= \sqrt{(8\text{ m})^2 - (3\text{ m})^2}\\ &= \sqrt{64\text{ m}^2 - 9\text{ m}^2}\\ &= \sqrt{55\text{ m}^2}\\ &\approx 7.4\text{ m}\end{aligned}$$

The ladder is 7.4 m high on the building.

34. Strategy • Use the Pythagorean Theorem to find the length of the unknown side.
• Add the lengths of the sides to find the perimeter of the right triangle.

Solution

$$\begin{aligned}\text{Hypotenuse} &= \sqrt{(\text{leg})^2 + (\text{leg})^2}\\ &= \sqrt{(5\text{ cm})^2 + (9\text{ cm})^2}\\ &= \sqrt{25\text{ cm}^2 + 81\text{ cm}^2}\\ &= \sqrt{106\text{ cm}^2}\\ &\approx 10.30\text{ cm}\end{aligned}$$

$5\text{ cm} + 9\text{ cm} + 10.3\text{ cm} = 24.3\text{ cm}$
The perimeter is 24.3 cm.

35. Strategy • Use the Pythagorean Theorem to find the length of the unknown side.
• Add the lengths of the sides to find the perimeter of the right triangle.

Solution

$$\begin{aligned}\text{Hypotenuse} &= \sqrt{(\text{leg})^2 + (\text{leg})^2}\\ &= \sqrt{(6\text{ in.})^2 + (10\text{ in.})^2}\\ &= \sqrt{36\text{ in}^2 + 100\text{ in}^2}\\ &= \sqrt{136\text{ in}^2}\\ &\approx 11.7\text{ in.}\end{aligned}$$

$6\text{ in.} + 10\text{ in.} + 11.7\text{ in.} = 27.7\text{ in.}$
The perimeter is 27.7 in.

36. Strategy To find the distance between the holes, use the Pythagorean Theorem. The distance is the length of the hypotenuse of a right triangle. The legs are 4 cm and 9 cm.

Solution

$$\begin{aligned}\text{Hypotenuse} &= \sqrt{(\text{leg})^2 + (\text{leg})^2}\\ &= \sqrt{(4\text{ cm})^2 + (9\text{ cm})^2}\\ &= \sqrt{16\text{ cm}^2 + 81\text{ cm}^2}\\ &= \sqrt{97\text{ cm}^2}\\ &\approx 9.8\text{ cm}\end{aligned}$$

The distance is 9.8 cm.

37. Strategy To find the distance from the corner to the memorial, use the Pythagorean Theorem. The length of one leg is 600 ft. The length of the hypotenuse is 650 ft. The distance from the corner to the memorial is the length of the unknown side.

Solution

$$\begin{aligned}\text{Leg} &= \sqrt{(\text{hypotenuse})^2 - (\text{leg})^2}\\ &= \sqrt{(650\text{ ft})^2 - (600\text{ ft})^2}\\ &= \sqrt{422{,}500\text{ ft}^2 - 360{,}000\text{ ft}^2}\\ &= \sqrt{62{,}500\text{ ft}^2}\\ &= 250\text{ ft}\end{aligned}$$

The distance is 250 ft.

38. Strategy To find the cost of fencing the plot:
- Use the composite figures and the Pythagorean Theorem to find the length of the unknown side.
- Add the lengths of the sides to find the perimeter.
- Multiply the perimeter by the cost per meter ($11.40).

Solution The plot is a composite figure made up of a rectangle and a right triangle.

$$\begin{aligned}\text{Hypotenuse} &= \sqrt{(\text{leg})^2 + (\text{leg})^2}\\ &= \sqrt{(4\text{ m})^2 + (3\text{ m})^2}\\ &= \sqrt{16\text{ m}^2 + 9\text{ m}^2}\\ &= \sqrt{25\text{ m}^2}\\ &= 5\text{ m length of unknown side}\end{aligned}$$

$5\text{ m} + 7\text{ m} + 4\text{ m} + 10\text{ m}$
$= 26\text{ m}$ perimeter

$26 \times \$11.40 = \$296.40$
It will cost $296.40 to fence the plot.

39. Strategy To find the distance between the centers of adjacent holes, use the Pythagorean Theorem. The distance between holes is the hypotenuse of a right triangle. Each of the legs is 3 in. long.

Solution

$$\begin{aligned}\text{Hypotenuse} &= \sqrt{(\text{leg})^2 + (\text{leg})^2}\\ &= \sqrt{(3\text{ in.})^2 + (3\text{ in.})^2}\\ &= \sqrt{9\text{ in}^2 + 9\text{ in}^2}\\ &= \sqrt{18\text{ in}^2}\\ &\approx 4.243\text{ in.}\end{aligned}$$

The distance is 4.243 in.

40. Strategy To find the offset distance of the pipe:
- Find the length of the bent portion of the pipe by subtracting the straight portions of the pipe from the total length (62 in.).
- Use the Pythagorean Theorem to find the offset distance. The length of the bent portion is the hypotenuse. One leg is 9 in. and the other leg is the offset distance.

Solution

$$62\text{ in.} - \left(20\frac{3}{4}\text{ in.} + 31\frac{1}{2}\text{ in.}\right)$$
$$62\text{ in.} - \left(20\frac{3}{4}\text{ in.} + 31\frac{2}{4}\text{ in.}\right)$$
$$62\text{ in.} - \left(51\frac{5}{4}\text{ in.}\right)$$
$$62\text{ in.} - \left(52\frac{1}{4}\text{ in.}\right)$$
$$61\frac{4}{4}\text{ in.} - \left(52\frac{1}{4}\text{ in.}\right) = 9\frac{3}{4}\text{ in.}$$
$$\text{Leg} = \sqrt{\left(9\frac{3}{4}\text{ in.}\right)^2 - (9\text{ in.})^2}$$

The offset distance is $3\frac{3}{4}$ in.

Applying the Concepts

41a. Always true

b. Always true

42. Strategy
- To determine if a 25-foot ladder is long enough to reach 24 ft up the side of the home when the bottom of the ladder is 6 ft from the base of the side of the house, use the Pythagorean Theorem to find the hypotenuse of a right triangle with legs 24 ft and 6 ft.
- Compare the length of the hypotenuse with 25. If the length of the hypotenuse is less than 25 ft, the ladder will reach the gutter. If the length of the hypotenuse is more than 25 ft, the ladder will not reach the gutter.

Solution

$$\begin{aligned}\text{Hypotenuse} &= \sqrt{(\text{leg})^2 + (\text{leg})^2}\\ &= \sqrt{(24\text{ ft})^2 + (6\text{ ft})^2}\\ &= \sqrt{576\text{ ft}^2 + 36\text{ ft}^2}\\ &= \sqrt{612\text{ ft}^2}\\ &\approx 24.74\text{ ft}\end{aligned}$$

$24.74 < 25$
Yes, the hypotenuse is less than 25 ft. The ladder will reach the gutters.

43. No, the Pythagorean Theorem can be used only to find unknown lengths of sides of right triangles. No right angle is indicated in the triangle in the diagram.

44a. A Pythagorean triple is a triple A, B, C such that $A^2 + B^2 = C^2$.

b. Examples:
$3^2 + 4^2 = 5^2$
$5^2 + 12^2 = 13^2$
$7^2 + 24^2 = 25^2$

45. Strategy To find the total length of the pipe needed to connect the buildings:
- Use the Pythagorean Theorem to find the length of the middle section. The middle section is the hypotenuse of a right triangle with legs 4 m and 3 m.
- Find the sum of the three sections of pipe.

Solution

$$\begin{aligned}\text{Hypotenuse} &= \sqrt{(\text{leg})^2 + (\text{leg})^2}\\ &= \sqrt{(4\text{ m})^2 + (3\text{ m})^2}\\ &= \sqrt{16\text{ m}^2 + 9\text{ m}^2}\\ &= \sqrt{25\text{ m}^2}\\ &\approx 5\text{ m}\end{aligned}$$

Total length $= 2\text{ m} + 5\text{ m} + 1\text{ m} = 8\text{ m}$.
The total length of the pipe needed is 8 m.

Section 12.6

Objective A Exercises

1. $\dfrac{5\cancel{\text{m}}}{10\cancel{\text{m}}} = \dfrac{1}{2}$

2. $\dfrac{12\cancel{\text{ft}}}{36\cancel{\text{ft}}} = \dfrac{1}{3}$

3. $\dfrac{9\cancel{\text{in.}}}{12\cancel{\text{in.}}} = \dfrac{3}{4}$

4. $\dfrac{3\cancel{\text{m}}}{9\cancel{\text{m}}} = \dfrac{1}{3}$

5. $\angle CAB = \angle DEF$
$AC = ED$ and
$AB = EF$
Therefore SAS applies and the triangles are congruent.

6. $\angle CAB = \angle DEF$
$AB = EF$ and
$AC = ED$
Therefore SAS applies and the triangles are congruent.

7. $AC = EF$
$AB = DE$ and
$BC = FD$
Therefore SSS applies and the triangles are congruent.

8. $AC = DE$
$BC = FE$ and
$AB = DF$
Therefore SSS applies and the triangles are congruent.

9.
$$\begin{aligned}\frac{AC}{DF} &= \frac{AB}{DE}\\ \frac{5\cancel{\text{cm}}}{9\cancel{\text{cm}}} &= \frac{4\text{ cm}}{DE}\\ 5 \times DE &= 4\text{ cm} \times 9\\ 5 \times DE &= 36\text{ cm}\\ DE &= 36\text{ cm} \div 5\\ DE &= 7.2\text{ cm}\end{aligned}$$

10.
$$\begin{aligned}\frac{CB}{FE} &= \frac{AB}{DE}\\ \frac{7\cancel{\text{in.}}}{16\cancel{\text{in.}}} &= \frac{6\text{ in.}}{DE}\\ 7 \times DE &= 6\text{ in.} \times 16\\ 7 \times DE &= 96\text{ in.}\\ DE &= 96\text{ in.} \div 7\\ DE &\approx 13.7\text{ in.}\end{aligned}$$

11.
$$\begin{aligned}\frac{AC}{DF} &= \frac{\text{height of triangle } ABC}{\text{height of triangle } DEF}\\ \frac{3\cancel{\text{m}}}{5\cancel{\text{m}}} &= \frac{2\text{ m}}{\text{height}}\\ 3 \times \text{height} &= 5 \times 2\text{ m}\\ 3 \times \text{height} &= 10\text{ m}\\ \text{Height} &= 10\text{ m} \div 3\\ \text{Height} &\approx 3.3\text{ m}\end{aligned}$$

12.
$$\begin{aligned}\frac{CB}{EF} &= \frac{\text{height of triangle } ABC}{\text{height of triangle } DEF}\\ \frac{7\cancel{\text{ft}}}{20\cancel{\text{ft}}} &= \frac{\text{height}}{14\text{ ft}}\\ 20 \times \text{height} &= 7 \times 14\text{ ft}\\ 20 \times \text{height} &= 98\text{ ft}\\ \text{Height} &= 98\text{ ft} \div 20\\ \text{Height} &= 4.9\text{ ft}\end{aligned}$$

Objective B Exercises

13. Strategy To find the height of the building, solve a proportion.

Solution
$$\begin{aligned}\frac{\text{height}}{8\text{ m}} &= \frac{8\cancel{\text{m}}}{4\cancel{\text{m}}}\\ \text{Height} \times 4 &= 8\text{ m} \times 8\\ \text{Height} \times 4 &= 64\text{ m}\\ \text{Height} &= 64\text{ m} \div 4\\ \text{Height} &= 16\text{ m}\end{aligned}$$
The height of the building is 16 m.

14. Strategy To find the height of the building, solve a proportion.

Solution
$$\begin{aligned}\frac{5.2\cancel{\text{ft}}}{1.3\cancel{\text{ft}}} &= \frac{\text{height}}{5.2\text{ ft}}\\ 1.3 \times \text{height} &= 5.2 \times 5.2\text{ ft}\\ 1.3 \times \text{height} &= 27.04\text{ ft}\\ \text{height} &= 27.04\text{ ft} \div 1.3\\ \text{height} &= 20.8\text{ ft}\end{aligned}$$
The height of the building is 20.8 ft.

15. Strategy To find the perimeter:
- Solve a proportion to find the length of side BC.
- Add the three sides of triangle ABC.

Solution
$$\frac{AC}{DF} = \frac{BC}{EF}$$
$$\frac{4\text{ m}}{8\text{ m}} = \frac{BC}{6\text{ m}}$$
$$8 \times BC = 4 \times 6\text{ m}$$
$$8 \times BC = 24\text{ m}$$
$$BC = 24\text{ m} \div 8$$
$$BC = 3\text{ m}$$

$3\text{ m} + 4\text{ m} + 5\text{ m} = 12\text{ m}$

The perimeter is 12 m.

16. Strategy To find the perimeter:
- Solve a proportion to find the length of side DF.
- Add the lengths of the three sides of the triangle.

Solution
$$\frac{AB}{DE} = \frac{AC}{DF}$$
$$\frac{6\text{ cm}}{12\text{ cm}} = \frac{5\text{ cm}}{DF}$$
$$6 \times DF = 12 \times 5\text{ cm}$$
$$6 \times DF = 60\text{ cm}$$
$$DF = 60\text{ cm} \div 6$$
$$DF = 10\text{ cm}$$

$10\text{ cm} + 12\text{ cm} + 16\text{ cm} = 38\text{ cm}$

The perimeter is 38 cm.

17. Strategy To find the area:
- Solve a proportion to find the height of triangle ABC.
- Use the formula $A = \frac{1}{2}bh$.

Solution
$$\frac{AB}{DE} = \frac{\text{height of triangle } ABC}{\text{height of triangle } DEF}$$
$$\frac{15\text{ cm}}{40\text{ cm}} = \frac{\text{height}}{20\text{ cm}}$$
$$40 \times \text{height} = 15 \times 20\text{ cm}$$
$$40 \times \text{height} = 300\text{ cm}$$
$$\text{Height} = 300\text{ cm} \div 40$$
$$\text{Height} = 7.5\text{ cm}$$

$$A = \frac{1}{2}bh$$
$$= \frac{1}{2} \cdot 15\text{ cm} \cdot 7.5\text{ cm}$$
$$= 56.25\text{ cm}^2.$$

The area is 56.25 cm^2.

18. Strategy To find the area:
- Solve a proportion to find the length of side DE (the base of triangle DEF).
- Use the formula $A = \frac{1}{2}bh$

Solution
$$\frac{AB}{DE} = \frac{\text{height of triangle } ABC}{\text{height of triangle } DEF}$$
$$\frac{8\text{ m}}{DE} = \frac{4\text{ m}}{7\text{ m}}$$
$$DE \times 4 = 8\text{ m} \times 7$$
$$DE \times 4 = 56\text{ m}$$
$$DE = 56\text{ m} \div 4$$
$$DE = 14\text{ m}$$

$$A = \frac{1}{2}bh$$
$$= \frac{1}{2} \cdot 14\text{ m} \cdot 7\text{ m}$$
$$= 49\text{ m}^2$$

The area is 49 m^2.

Applying the Concepts

19a. Always true

b. Sometimes true

c. Always true

20. Yes. Given two squares, the ratios of corresponding sides are equal because the same number will be in the numerators (the length of a side of one square) and the same number will be in the denominators (the length of a side of the second square.).
No. The lengths of the sides of a rectangle vary. Therefore, given two rectangles, the ratios of corresponding sides may vary.

21. $\triangle ABC$ and $\triangle DEC$ are similar triangles.

$$\frac{8}{5} = \frac{6}{DE} \qquad \frac{8}{5} = \frac{10}{EC}$$
$$8DE = 30 \qquad 8EC = 50$$
$$DE = \frac{30}{8} = \frac{15}{4} \qquad EC = \frac{50}{8} = \frac{25}{4}$$

The perimeter of the trapezoid

$$ABED = AB + AD + DE + BE$$
$$= 6 + (8 - 5) + \frac{15}{4} + \left(10 - \frac{25}{4}\right)$$
$$= 6 + 3 + 3.75 + 3.75$$
$$= 16.5$$

22. To find the height of the tree, you could use similar triangles and a proportion. This method assumes that the sun is shining and is not directly overhead. Use the yardstick to measure the shadow of the tree. Then use the yardstick to measure the length of your own shadow. Write and solve a proportion. One possible proportion is as follows:
"Your height" over the "length of your shadow" equal to "height of the tree" over "length of the shadow cast by the tree."

Chapter 12 Review Exercises

1. $r = \frac{1}{2}d = \frac{1}{2}(1.5\text{ m}) = 0.75\text{ m}$

2. $C = 2\pi r$
$\approx 2(3.14)(5\text{ cm}) = 31.4\text{ cm}$

3. $P = 2L + 2W$
$= 2(8\text{ ft}) + 2(5\text{ ft})$
$= 16\text{ ft} + 10\text{ ft} = 26\text{ ft}$

4. $AD = AB + BC + CD$
$24 = 15 + BC + 6$
$24 = 21 + BC$
$24 - 21 = 21 - 21 + BC$
$3 = BC$

5. Volume = length · width · height
$= 10\text{ ft} \cdot 5\text{ ft} \cdot 4\text{ ft} = 200\text{ ft}^3$

6. Hypotenuse $= \sqrt{(\text{leg})^2 + (\text{leg})^2}$
$= \sqrt{(10\text{ cm})^2 + (24\text{ cm})^2}$
$= \sqrt{100\text{ cm}^2 + 576\text{ cm}^2}$
$= \sqrt{676\text{ cm}^2}$
$= 26\text{ cm}$

7. Let x represent the supplement of 105°. The sum of supplementary angles is 180°.
$x + 105° = 180°$
$x + 105° - 105° = 180° - 105°$
$x = 75°$
75° is the supplement of 105°.

8. $\sqrt{15} \approx 3.873$

9. $\frac{BC}{EF} = \frac{\text{height of triangle } ABC}{\text{height of triangle } DEF}$
$\frac{12\text{ cm}}{24\text{ cm}} = \frac{8\text{ cm}}{h}$
$12 \times h = 24 \times 8\text{ cm}$
$12 \times h = 192\text{ cm}$
$h = 192\text{ cm} \div 12 = 16\text{ cm}$

10. $A = \pi r^2$
$\approx 3.14 \cdot (4.5\text{ cm})^2$
$= 63.585\text{ cm}^2$

11a. Because line t is a transversal cutting parallel lines, $\angle b = 45°$.

b. $\angle a = 180° - 45° = 135°$

12. $A = LW$
$= 11\text{ m} \times 5\text{ m} = 55\text{ m}^2$

13. Volume = volume of larger rectangular solid − volume of smaller rectangular solid
= length · width · height − length · width · height
$= 8\text{ in.} \cdot 7\text{ in.} \cdot 6\text{ in.} - 8\text{ in.} \cdot 4\text{ in.} \cdot 3\text{ in.}$
$= 336\text{ in}^3 - 96\text{ in}^3 = 240\text{ in}^3$

14. Area = area of rectangle + $\frac{1}{2}$(area of circle)
= length · width + $\frac{1}{2}\pi(\text{radius})^2$
$\approx 8\text{ in.} \cdot 4\text{ in.} + \frac{1}{2}(3.14)(4\text{ in.})^2$
$= 32\text{ in}^2 + 25.12\text{ in}^2$
$= 57.12\text{ in}^2$

15. $V = \frac{4}{3}\pi r^3$
$\approx \frac{4}{3}(3.14)(4\text{ ft})^3$
$\approx 267.9\text{ ft}^3$

16. **Strategy** To find the area:
- Solve a proportion to find the length of side DF (the base of the triangle DEF).
- Use the formula $A = \frac{1}{2}bh$.

Solution
$\frac{AC}{DF} = \frac{\text{height of triangle } ABC}{\text{height of triangle } DEF}$
$\frac{8\text{ m}}{DF} = \frac{5\text{ m}}{9\text{ m}}$
$8\text{ m} \times 9 = 5 \times DF$
$72\text{ m} = 5 \times DF$
$72\text{ m} \div 5 = DF$
$14.4\text{ m} = DF$
$A = \frac{1}{2}bh$
$= \frac{1}{2}(14.4\text{ m})(9\text{ m}) = 64.8\text{ m}^2$
The area is 64.8 m^2.

17. Perimeter = length of two sides + $\frac{1}{2}$ circumference of circle
$\approx 2(16\text{ in.}) + \frac{1}{2}(2 \cdot 3.14 \cdot 5\text{ in.})$
$= 32\text{ in.} + 15.7\text{ in.} = 47.7\text{ in.}$

18a. Because line t is a transversal cutting parallel lines, $\angle b = 80°$

b. $\angle a = 180° - 80° = 100°$

19. Strategy To find how high on the building the ladder will reach, use the Pythagorean Theorem. The hypotenuse is 17 ft and one leg is 8 ft. The other leg is the height up the building.

Solution

$$\begin{aligned} \text{leg} &= \sqrt{(\text{hypotenuse})^2 - (\text{leg})^2} \\ &= \sqrt{(17\text{ ft})^2 - (8\text{ ft})^2} \\ &= \sqrt{289\text{ ft}^2 - 64\text{ ft}^2} \\ &= \sqrt{225\text{ ft}^2} \\ &= 15\text{ ft} \end{aligned}$$

The ladder will reach 15 ft up the building.

20. $90° - 32° = 58°$
The other angles of the triangle are 90° and 58°.

21. Strategy To find how many feet the bicycle travels, find how many feet the wheel travels if it makes 10 revolutions:
- Find how far the wheel travels when it makes 1 revolution by using the circumference formula.
- Convert the circumference to feet.
- Multiply the distance traveled in 1 revolution by 10.

Solution

$$\begin{aligned} C &= \pi d \\ &= \pi \cdot 28\text{ in.} \\ &\approx 3.14 \cdot (28\text{ in.}) \\ &= 87.92\text{ in.} \end{aligned}$$

$$\begin{aligned} 87.92\text{ in.} &= 87.92\cancel{\text{in.}} \times \frac{1\text{ ft}}{12\cancel{\text{in.}}} \\ &= \frac{87.92}{12}\text{ft} \approx 7.33\text{ ft} \end{aligned}$$

$10 \times 7.33\text{ ft} = 73.3\text{ ft}$
The bicycle travels approximately 73.3 ft in 10 revolutions.

22. Strategy To find the area of the room in square yards:
- Use the area of the rectangle formula.
- Convert square feet to square yards.

Solution

$$\begin{aligned} A &= LW \\ &= 18\text{ ft} \cdot 14\text{ ft} = 252\text{ ft}^2 \end{aligned}$$

$$\begin{aligned} 252\text{ ft}^2 &= 252\cancel{\text{ft}^2} \times \frac{1\text{ yd}^2}{9\cancel{\text{ft}^2}} \\ &= \frac{252}{9}\text{ yd}^2 = 28\text{ yd}^2 \end{aligned}$$

The area of the room is 28 yd^2.

23. Strategy To find the volume of the silo, use the formula for the volume of a cylinder.

Solution

$$\begin{aligned} V &= \pi r^2 h \\ &\approx 3.14(4.5\text{ ft})^2(18\text{ ft}) \\ &= 1144.53\text{ ft}^3 \end{aligned}$$

The volume of the silo is approximately 1144.53 ft^3.

24.

$$\begin{aligned} A &= \frac{1}{2}bh \\ &= \frac{1}{2}(8\text{ m})(2.75\text{ m}) \\ &= 11\text{ m}^2 \end{aligned}$$

25. Strategy
- Traveling 20 mi west and then 21 mi south forms a right angle. The distance from the starting point is the hypotenuse of the triangle with legs 20 mi and 21 mi.
- Find the hypotenuse of the right triangle.

Solution

$$\begin{aligned} \text{hypotenuse} &= \sqrt{(\text{leg})^2 + (\text{leg})^2} \\ &= \sqrt{(20\text{ mi})^2 + (21\text{ mi})^2} \\ &= \sqrt{400\text{ mi}^2 + 441\text{ mi}^2} \\ &= \sqrt{841\text{ mi}^2} \\ &= 29 \end{aligned}$$

The distance from the starting point is 29 mi.

Chapter 12 Test

1.

$$\begin{aligned} V &= \pi r^2 h \\ &\approx 3.14 \cdot (3\text{ m})^2 \cdot 6\text{ m} \\ &= 169.56\text{ m}^3 \end{aligned}$$

2.

$$\begin{aligned} P &= 2L + 2W \\ &= 2(2\text{ m}) + 2(1.4\text{ m}) \\ &= 4\text{ m} + 2.8\text{ m} \\ &= 6.8\text{ m} \end{aligned}$$

3. Strategy To find the volume of the composite figure, subtract the volume of the smaller cylinder from the volume of the larger cylinder.

Solution

$$\begin{aligned} \text{Volume} &= \text{volume of larger cylinder} \\ &\quad - \text{volume of smaller cylinder} \\ &= \pi(\text{radius})^2 \cdot \text{height} \\ &\quad - \pi \cdot (\text{radius})^2 \cdot \text{height} \\ &\approx 3.14(6\text{ cm})^2 \cdot 14\text{ cm} \\ &\quad - 3.14 \cdot (2\text{ cm})^2 \cdot 14\text{ cm} \\ &= 1582.56\text{ cm}^3 - 175.84\text{ cm}^3 \\ &= 1406.72\text{ cm}^3 \end{aligned}$$

The volume of the composite figure is approximately 1406.72 cm^3.

4. **Strategy** To find the missing length, use the Pythagorean Theorem. $AB = FE$ is the hypotenuse. The legs are 6 and 8 m.

Solution
$$\begin{aligned}\text{Hypotenuse} &= \sqrt{(8\text{ m})^2 + (6\text{ m})^2}\\ &= \sqrt{64\text{ m}^2 + 36\text{ m}^2}\\ &= \sqrt{100\text{ m}^2}\\ &= 10\text{ m}\end{aligned}$$
The length of FE is 10 m.

5. $90° - 32° = 58°$
58° is the complement of 32°.

6. $$\begin{aligned}A &= \pi r^2\\ &\approx \frac{22}{7}(1\text{ m})^2\\ &= \frac{22\text{ m}^2}{7} = 3\frac{1}{7}\text{ m}^2\end{aligned}$$

7. Angles x and z are supplementary; therefore, $\angle z = 180° - 30° = 150°$. $\angle y$ and $\angle z$ are corresponding angles; therefore, $\angle y = \angle z = 150°$.

8. $$\begin{aligned}\text{Perimeter} &= \text{two lengths} + \text{circumference of circle}\\ &= 2(4\text{ ft}) + \pi \cdot \text{diameter}\\ &= 8\text{ ft} + \pi\left(2\frac{1}{2}\text{ ft}\right)\\ &\approx 8\text{ ft} + 3.14(2.5\text{ ft})\\ &= 15.85\text{ ft}\end{aligned}$$

9. $\sqrt{189} \approx 13.748$

10. $$\begin{aligned}\text{Leg} &= \sqrt{(\text{hypotenuse})^2 - (\text{leg})^2}\\ &= \sqrt{(12\text{ ft})^2 - (7\text{ ft})^2} = \sqrt{144\text{ ft}^2 - 49\text{ ft}^2}\\ &= \sqrt{95\text{ ft}^2}\\ &\approx 9.747\text{ ft}\end{aligned}$$

11. $$\begin{aligned}\text{Area} &= \text{area of rectangle} - \text{area of triangle}\\ &= \text{length} \cdot \text{width} - \frac{1}{2} \cdot \text{base} \cdot \text{height}\\ &= 3\text{ ft} \cdot 4\frac{1}{2}\text{ ft} - \frac{1}{2}\left(4\frac{1}{2}\text{ ft}\right)\left(1\frac{1}{2}\text{ ft}\right)\\ &= 13.5\text{ ft}^2 - 3.375\text{ ft}^2 = 10.125\text{ ft}^2\end{aligned}$$

12. Angles x and b are supplementary angles.
$$\begin{aligned}\angle x + \angle b &= 180°\\ 45° + \angle b &= 180°\\ 45° - 45° + \angle b &= 180° - 45°\\ \angle b &= 135°\end{aligned}$$
$\angle a = \angle x$ because $\angle a$ and $\angle x$ are alternate exterior angles. $\angle a = 45°$

13. $$\begin{aligned}\frac{AB}{DE} &= \frac{BC}{EF}\\ \frac{\frac{3}{4}\text{ ft}}{2\frac{1}{2}\text{ ft}} &= \frac{BC}{4\text{ ft}}\\ \frac{3}{4} \times 4\text{ ft} &= 2\frac{1}{2} \times BC\\ 3\text{ ft} &= 2\frac{1}{2} \times BC\\ 3\text{ ft} \div 2\frac{1}{2} &= BC\\ 3\text{ ft} \times \frac{2}{5} &= BC\\ BC &= \frac{6}{5}\text{ ft} = 1\frac{1}{5}\text{ ft}\end{aligned}$$

14. $90° - 40° = 50°$
The other two angles of the triangle are 90° and 50°.

15. **Strategy** To find the width of the canal, solve a proportion.

Solution
$$\begin{aligned}\frac{5\text{ ft}}{\text{Width of canal}} &= \frac{12\text{ ft}}{60\text{ ft}}\\ 5\text{ ft} \times 60 &= 12 \times \text{width of canal}\\ 300\text{ ft} &= 12 \times \text{width of canal}\\ 300\text{ ft} \div 12 &= \text{width of canal}\\ 25\text{ ft} &= \text{width of canal}\end{aligned}$$
The width of the canal is 25 ft.

16. **Strategy** To find how much more pizza is contained in the larger pizza, subtract the area of the smaller pizza from the area of the larger pizza.

Solution
$$\begin{aligned}A &= \pi r^2\\ &\approx 3.14 \cdot (10\text{ in.})^2 = 314\text{ in}^2\\ A &= \pi r^2\\ &\approx 3.14 \cdot (8\text{ in.})^2 = 200.96\text{ in}^2\end{aligned}$$
$314\text{ in}^2 - 200.96\text{ in}^2 = 113.04\text{ in}^2$
The amount of extra pizza is 113.04 in^2

17. **Strategy** To find the cost of the carpet:
- Subtract the area of the smaller rectangle from the area of the larger rectangle.
- Convert the area to square yards.
- Multiply the area in square yards by the cost per square yard.

Solution
$$\begin{aligned}\text{Area} &= \text{area of larger rectangle}\\ &\quad - \text{area of smaller rectangle}\\ &= \text{length} \cdot \text{width} - \text{length} \cdot \text{width}\\ &= 20\text{ ft} \cdot 22\text{ ft} - 6\text{ ft} \cdot 11\text{ ft}\\ &= 440\text{ ft}^2 - 66\text{ ft}^2 = 374\text{ ft}^2\end{aligned}$$
$$374\text{ ft}^2 = 374\text{ ft}^2 \times \frac{1\text{ yd}^2}{9\text{ ft}^2} \approx 41.5556\text{ yd}^2$$
$$41.5556\text{ yd}^2 \times \$26.80 \approx \$1113.69$$
It will cost $1113.69 to carpet the area.

18. Strategy To find the cross-sectional area of the redwood tree:
- Convert the diameter (11 ft 6 in.) to feet.
- Use the formula $r = \frac{1}{2}d$ to find radius.
- Use the formula for area of a circle.

Solution $6 \text{ in.} = 6 \text{ in.} \times \frac{1 \text{ ft}}{12 \text{ in.}} = 0.5 \text{ ft}$

$11 \text{ ft } 6 \text{ in.} = 11.5 \text{ ft}$

$$r = \frac{1}{2}d = \frac{1}{2}(11.5 \text{ ft}) = 5.75 \text{ ft}$$

$$A = \pi r^2 \approx (3.14)(5.75 \text{ ft})^2 \approx 103.82 \text{ ft}^2$$

The cross-sectional area is approximately 103.82 ft^2.

19. Strategy To find the length of the rafter:
- Use the Pythagorean Theorem to find the part of the rafter that covers the roof.
- Find the total length of the rafter by adding the 2 ft overhang to the part that covers the roof.

Solution

$$\text{Hypotenuse} = \sqrt{(5 \text{ ft})^2 + (12 \text{ ft})^2} = \sqrt{25 \text{ ft}^2 + 144 \text{ ft}^2} = \sqrt{169 \text{ ft}^2} = 13 \text{ ft}$$

$13 \text{ ft} + 2 \text{ ft} = 15 \text{ ft}$

The length of the rafter is 15 ft.

20. Strategy To find the volume of the interior of the box, subtract the thickness of the sides and bottom of the box from the exterior dimensions of the box. Then use the formula for volume of a rectangular solid.

Solution

$$\text{Length} = 1 \text{ ft } 2 \text{ in.} - 2\left(\frac{1}{2} \text{ in.}\right) = 1 \text{ ft } 1 \text{ in.} = 13 \text{ in.}$$

$$\text{Width} = 9 \text{ in.} - 2\left(\frac{1}{2} \text{ in.}\right) = 8 \text{ in.}$$

$$\text{Height} = 8 \text{ in.} - \frac{1}{2} \text{ in.} = 7.5 \text{ in.}$$

$$V = LWH = 13 \text{ in.} \cdot 8 \text{ in.} \cdot 7.5 \text{ in.} = 780 \text{ in}^3$$

The volume of the interior of the toolbox is 780 in^3.

Cumulative Review Exercises

1.

$$96 = 2 \cdot 2 \cdot 2 \cdot 2 \cdot 2 \mid 3$$
$$144 = 2 \cdot 2 \cdot 2 \cdot 2 \mid 3 \cdot 3$$
$$\text{GCF} = 2 \cdot 2 \cdot 2 \cdot 2 \cdot 3 = 48$$

2.

$$3\frac{5}{12} = 3\frac{20}{48}$$
$$2\frac{9}{16} = 2\frac{27}{48}$$
$$+1\frac{7}{8} = 1\frac{42}{48}$$
$$6\frac{89}{48} = 7\frac{41}{48}$$

3. $4\frac{1}{3} \div 6\frac{2}{9} = \frac{13}{3} \div \frac{56}{9} = \frac{13}{3} \times \frac{9}{56} = \frac{13 \cdot \cancel{3} \cdot 3}{\cancel{3} \cdot 7 \cdot 2 \cdot 2 \cdot 2} = \frac{39}{56}$

4.

$$\left(\frac{2}{3}\right)^2 \div \left(\frac{1}{3} + \frac{1}{2}\right) - \frac{2}{5} = \left(\frac{2}{3} \cdot \frac{2}{3}\right) \div \left(\frac{2}{6} + \frac{3}{6}\right) - \frac{2}{5}$$
$$= \frac{4}{9} \div \frac{5}{6} - \frac{2}{5} = \frac{4}{9} \times \frac{6}{5} - \frac{2}{5} = \frac{2 \cdot 2 \cdot 2 \cdot \cancel{3}}{\cancel{3} \cdot 3 \cdot 5} - \frac{2}{5}$$
$$= \frac{8}{15} - \frac{2}{5} = \frac{8}{15} - \frac{6}{15} = \frac{2}{15}$$

5. $-\frac{2}{3} - \left(-\frac{5}{8}\right) = -\frac{16}{24} + \frac{15}{24} = -\frac{1}{24}$

6. $\frac{\$348.80}{40 \text{ h}} = \$8.72/\text{h}$

7.

$$\frac{3}{8} = \frac{n}{100}$$
$$3 \times 100 = n \times 8$$
$$300 = n \times 8$$
$$300 \div 8 = n$$
$$37.5 = n$$

8. $37\frac{1}{2}\% = \frac{75}{2}\% = \frac{75}{2} \times \frac{1}{100} = \frac{75}{200} = \frac{3}{8}$

9. $2^2 - [(-2)^2 - (-4)] = 4 - [4 + 4] = 4 - 8 = -4$

10. $36.4\% \times n = 30.94$
$0.364 \times n = 30.94$
$n = 30.94 \div 0.364$
$n = 85$

11. $\frac{x}{3} + 3 = 1$
$\frac{x}{3} = -2$
$x = -6$

12. $2(x-3) + 2 = 5x - 8$
$2x - 6 + 2 = 5x - 8$
$2x - 4 = 5x - 8$
$4 = 3x$
$\frac{4}{3} = x$

13. 32.5 km = 32,500 m

14. 32 m = 32.00 m
−42 cm = 0.42 m
31.58 m

15. $\frac{2}{3}x = -10$
$x = \frac{3}{2}(-10)$
$x = -15$

16. $2x - 4(x-3) = 8$
$2x - 4x + 12 = 8$
$-2x + 12 = 8$
$-2x = -4$
$x = 2$

17. Strategy To find the monthly payment:
- Find the amount paid in payments by the subtracting the down payment ($1000) from the price ($26,488).
- Divide the amount paid in payments by the number of payments (36).

Solution $26,488 − $1000 = $25,488
$25{,}488 \div 36 = 708$

The monthly payment is $708.

18. Strategy To find the sales tax, solve a proportion.

Solution $\frac{\$175}{\$6.75} = \frac{\$1220}{n}$
$175 \times n = 6.75 \times 1220$
$175 \times n = 8235$
$n = 8235 \div 175 \approx 47.06$
The sales tax on the stereo system is $47.06.

19. Strategy To find the operator's original wage, solve the basic percent equation for the base. The percent is 110% and the amount is $16.06.

Solution $110\% \times n = 16.06$
$1.10 \times n = 16.06$
$n = 16.06 \div 1.10 = 14.60$
The original wage was $14.60.

20. Strategy To find the sale price:
- Find the amount of the markdown by solving the basic percent equation for amount. The base is $120 and the percent is 55%.
- Subtract the amount of the markdown from the original price ($120).

Solution $55\% \times 120 = n$
$0.55 \times 120 = 66$

$120
−66
$54

The sale price of the dress is $54.

21. Strategy To find the value of the investment, multiply the amount invested by the compound interest factor.

Solution $25,000 × 4.05466 = 101,366.50
The value of the investment after 20 years would be $101,366.50.

22. Strategy To find the weight of the package:
- Find the weight of the package in ounces by multiplying the weight of one tile (6 oz) by the number of tiles in the package (144).
- Convert the weight in ounces to pounds.

Solution 6 oz × 144 = 864 oz
$864 \text{ oz} = 864 \cancel{\text{oz}} \times \frac{1 \text{ lb}}{16 \cancel{\text{oz}}} = 54 \text{ lb}$
The weight of the package is 54 lb.

23. Strategy To find the distance between the rivets:
- Divide the length of the plates (5.4 m) by the number of spaces (24).
- Convert the meters to centimeters.

Solution $5.400 \div 24 = 0.225$

0.225 m = 22.5 cm
The distance between the rivets is 22.5 cm.

24. Let x = the number.
$2 + 4x = -6$
$4x = -8$
$x = -2$
The number is −2.

25a. Because vertical angles have the same measure, $\angle a = 74°$.

b. $\angle a$ and $\angle b$ are supplementary; therefore, $\angle b = 180° - \angle a = 180° - 74° = 106°$.

26. $$\begin{aligned}\text{Perimeter} &= 2 \cdot \text{length} + \text{width} + \frac{1}{2}(\text{circumference}) \\ &\approx 2 \cdot (7 \text{ cm}) + 6 \text{ cm} + \frac{1}{2}(3.14 \cdot 6 \text{ cm}) \\ &= 14 \text{ cm} + 6 \text{ cm} + 9.42 \text{ cm} \\ &= 29.42 \text{ cm}\end{aligned}$$

27. $$\begin{aligned}\text{Area} &= \text{area of rectangle} + \text{area of triangle} \\ &= \text{length} \cdot \text{width} + \frac{1}{2} \cdot \text{base} \cdot \text{height} \\ &= 5 \text{ in.} \cdot 4 \text{ in.} + \frac{1}{2} \cdot 12 \text{ in.} \cdot 5 \text{ in.} \\ &= 20 \text{ in}^2 + 30 \text{ in}^2 = 50 \text{ in}^2\end{aligned}$$

28. $$\begin{aligned}\text{Volume} &= \text{volume of rectangular solid} \\ &\quad - \frac{1}{2}\text{volume of cylinder} \\ &= \text{length} \cdot \text{width} \cdot \text{height} \\ &\quad - \frac{1}{2}[\pi(\text{radius})^2 \cdot \text{height}] \\ &\approx 8 \text{ in.} \cdot 4 \text{ in.} \cdot 3 \text{ in.} \\ &\quad - \frac{1}{2}[3.14(0.5 \text{ in.})^2 \cdot 8 \text{ in.}] \\ &= 96 \text{ in}^3 - 3.14 \text{ in}^3 = 92.86 \text{ in}^3\end{aligned}$$

29. $$\begin{aligned}\text{Hypotenuse} &= \sqrt{(\text{leg})^2 + (\text{leg})^2} \\ &= \sqrt{(8 \text{ ft})^2 + (7 \text{ ft})^2} \\ &= \sqrt{64 \text{ ft}^2 + 49 \text{ ft}^2} \\ &= \sqrt{113 \text{ ft}^2} \approx 10.63 \text{ ft}\end{aligned}$$

30. Strategy To find the perimeter of DEF:

- Solve a proportion to find the length of side DF.
- Solve a proportion to find the length of side FE.
- Use the formula for perimeter to find the perimeter of triangle DEF.

Solution

$$\begin{aligned}\frac{CB}{DE} &= \frac{CA}{DF} \\ \frac{4 \text{ cm}}{12 \text{ cm}} &= \frac{3 \text{ cm}}{DF} \\ 4 \times DF &= 3 \text{ cm} \times 12 \\ 4 \times DF &= 36 \text{ cm} \\ DF &= 36 \text{ cm} \div 4 = 9 \text{ cm}\end{aligned}$$

$$\begin{aligned}\frac{CB}{DE} &= \frac{AB}{FE} \\ \frac{4 \text{ cm}}{12 \text{ cm}} &= \frac{5 \text{ cm}}{FE} \\ 4 \times FE &= 5 \text{ cm} \times 12 \\ 4 \times FE &= 60 \text{ cm} \\ FE &= 60 \text{ cm} \div 4 = 15 \text{ cm}\end{aligned}$$

$$\begin{aligned}P &= a + b + c \\ &= 12 \text{ cm} + 15 \text{ cm} + 9 \text{ cm} \\ &= 36 \text{ cm}\end{aligned}$$

The perimeter is 36 cm.

Final Exam

1.
$$\begin{array}{r} 100{,}914 \\ -97{,}655 \\ \hline 3\,259 \end{array}$$

2.
$$\begin{array}{r} 53 \\ 657\overline{)34{,}821} \\ -3285 \\ \hline 1971 \\ -1971 \\ \hline 0 \end{array}$$

3.
$$\begin{array}{r} 90{,}001 \\ -29{,}796 \\ \hline 60{,}205 \end{array}$$

4.
$$\begin{aligned} 3^2 \cdot (5-3)^2 \div 3 + 4 &= 3^2 \cdot (2)^2 \div 3 + 4 \\ &= 9 \cdot 4 \div 3 + 4 \\ &= 36 \div 3 + 4 \\ &= 12 + 4 \\ &= 16 \end{aligned}$$

5.

	2	3
9 =		(3 · 3)
12 =	2 · 2	3
16 =	(2 · 2 · 2 · 2)	

LCM = 2 · 2 · 2 · 2 · 3 · 3 = 144

6. $\frac{3}{8} + \frac{5}{6} + \frac{1}{5} = \frac{45}{120} + \frac{100}{120} + \frac{24}{120} = \frac{169}{120} = 1\frac{49}{120}$

7.
$$\begin{array}{r} 7\frac{5}{12} = 7\frac{20}{48} = 6\frac{68}{48} \\ -3\frac{13}{16} = 3\frac{39}{48} = 3\frac{39}{48} \\ \hline 3\frac{29}{48} \end{array}$$

8. $3\frac{5}{8} \times 1\frac{5}{7} = \frac{29}{8} \times \frac{12}{7} = \frac{29 \cdot \overset{3}{\cancel{12}}}{\underset{2}{\cancel{8}} \cdot 7} = \frac{87}{14} = 6\frac{3}{14}$

9. $1\frac{2}{3} \div 3\frac{3}{4} = \frac{5}{3} \div \frac{15}{4} = \frac{5}{3} \times \frac{4}{15} = \frac{5 \times 4}{3 \times 15} = \frac{20}{45} = \frac{4}{9}$

10. $\left(\frac{2}{3}\right)^3 \left(\frac{3}{4}\right)^2 = \left(\frac{2}{3} \cdot \frac{2}{3} \cdot \frac{2}{3}\right)\left(\frac{3}{4} \cdot \frac{3}{4}\right) = \left(\frac{8}{27}\right)\left(\frac{9}{16}\right)$

$= \frac{72}{432} = \frac{1}{6}$

11.
$$\begin{aligned} \left(\frac{2}{3}\right)^2 \div \left(\frac{3}{4} + \frac{1}{3}\right) - \frac{1}{3} &= \left(\frac{2}{3}\right)^2 \div \left(\frac{9}{12} + \frac{4}{12}\right) - \frac{1}{3} \\ &= \frac{4}{9} \div \frac{13}{12} - \frac{1}{3} \\ &= \frac{4}{\underset{3}{\cancel{9}}} \times \frac{\overset{4}{\cancel{12}}}{13} - \frac{1}{3} \\ &= \frac{16}{39} - \frac{1}{3} \\ &= \frac{16}{39} - \frac{13}{39} = \frac{3}{39} = \frac{1}{13} \end{aligned}$$

12.
$$\begin{array}{r} 4.972 \\ 28.6 \\ 1.88 \\ +128.725 \\ \hline 164.177 \end{array}$$

13.
$$\begin{array}{r} 2.97 \\ \times\ 0.0094 \\ \hline 1188 \\ 2673 \\ \hline 0.027918 \end{array}$$

14.
$$\begin{array}{r} 0.687 \\ 0.062.\overline{)0.042.600} \\ -372 \\ \hline 540 \\ -496 \\ \hline 440 \\ -434 \\ \hline 6 \end{array} \quad \approx 0.69$$

15. $0.45 = \frac{45}{100} = \frac{9}{20}$

16. $\frac{323.4 \text{ mi}}{13.2 \text{ gal}} = 24.5 \text{ mi/gal}$

17.
$$\begin{aligned} \frac{12}{35} &= \frac{n}{160} \\ 12 \times 160 &= n \times 35 \\ 1920 &= n \times 35 \\ 1920 \div 35 &= n \\ 54.9 &\approx n \end{aligned}$$

18. $22\frac{1}{2}\% = \frac{45}{2} \times \frac{1}{100} = \frac{45}{200} = \frac{9}{40}$

19. $1.35 = 1.35 \times 100\% = 135\%$

20. $\frac{5}{4} = \frac{5}{4} \times 100\% = \frac{500}{4}\% = 125\%$

21. Percent × base = amount
$$\begin{aligned} 120\% \times 30 &= n \\ 1.2 \times 30 &= n \\ 36 &= n \end{aligned}$$

22. Percent × base = amount
$n \times 9 = 12$
$n = 12 \div 9 = 1\frac{1}{3} = 133\frac{1}{3}\%$

23. Percent × base = amount
$60\% \times n = 42$
$0.60 \times n = 42$
$n = 42 \div 0.60 = 70$

24. $1\frac{2}{3}\text{ ft} = \frac{5}{3}\text{ ft} = \frac{5}{3}\cancel{\text{ft}} \times \frac{12\text{ in.}}{1\cancel{\text{ft}}} = 20\text{ in.}$

25.
3 ft 2 in. = 2 ft 14 in.
−1 ft 10 in. = 1 ft 10 in.
1 ft 4 in.

26. $40\text{ oz} = 40\cancel{\text{oz}} \times \frac{1\text{ lb}}{16\cancel{\text{oz}}} = \frac{40}{16}\text{ lb} = 2.5\text{ lb}$

27.
3 lb 12 oz
+2 lb 10 oz
5 lb 22 oz = 6 lb 6 oz

28. $18\text{ pt} = 18\cancel{\text{pt}} \times \frac{1\cancel{\text{qt}}}{2\cancel{\text{pt}}} \times \frac{1\text{ gal}}{4\cancel{\text{qt}}} = \frac{18\text{ gal}}{8} = 2.25\text{ gal}$

29.
1 gal 3 qt
3)5 gal 1 qt
−3 gal
2 gal = 8 qt
9 qt
−9 qt
0

30. 2.48 m = 248 cm

31. 4 m 62 cm = 4 m + 0.62 m = 4.62 m

32. 1 kg 614 g = 1 kg + 0.614 kg = 1.614 kg

33. 2 L 67 ml = 2000 ml + 67 ml = 2067 ml

34. $55\text{ mi} \approx 55\text{ mi} \times \frac{1.61\text{ km}}{1\text{ mi}} \approx 88.55\text{ km}$

35. **Strategy** To find the cost:
- Find the number of watt-hours by multiplying the number of watts (2,400) by the number of hours (6).
- Convert watt-hours to kilowatt-hours.
- Multiply the kilowatt-hours by $.08.

Solution 2,400 W × 6 h = 14,400 Wh
14,400 Wh = 14.4 kWh
14.43 × $.08 = $1.152
The cost is $1.15.

36. The number is less than 10. Move the decimal point 8 places to the right. The exponent on 10 is −8.

$0.0000000679 = 6.79 \times 10^{-8}$

37. $P = 2L + 2W$
$= 2(1.2\text{ m}) + 2(0.75\text{ m})$
$= 2.4\text{ m} + 1.5\text{ m} = 3.9\text{ m}$

38. $A = LW$
$= 9\text{ in.} \times 5\text{ in.} = 45\text{ in}^2$

39. $V = LWH$
$= 20\text{ cm} \times 12\text{ cm} \times 5\text{ cm}$
$= 1200\text{ cm}^3$

40. $-2 + 8 + (-10) = 6 + (-10) = -4$

41. $-30 - (-15) = -30 + 15 = -15$

42. $2\frac{1}{2} \times -\frac{1}{5} = \frac{5}{2} \times \frac{-1}{5} = -\frac{1}{2}$

43. $-1\frac{3}{8} \div 5\frac{1}{2} = \frac{-11}{8} \div \frac{11}{2} = \frac{-11}{8} \times \frac{2}{11} = \frac{-1}{4} = -\frac{1}{4}$

44. $(-4)^2 \div (1-3)^2 - (-2) = (-4)^2 \div (-2)^2 - (-2)$
$= 16 \div 4 - (-2)$
$= 4 - (-2)$
$= 4 + 2$
$= 6$

45. $2x - 3(x-4) + 5 = 2x + (-3)[x + (-4)] + 5$
$= 2x + (-3)x + (-3)(-4) + 5$
$= 2x + (-3)x + 12 + 5$
$= -x + 12 + 5$
$= -x + 17$

46.
$\frac{2}{3}x = -12$
$\frac{3}{2} \cdot \frac{2}{3}x = \frac{3}{2} \cdot (-12)$
$x = -18$

47.
$3x - 5 = 10$
$3x - 5 + 5 = 10 + 5$
$3x = 15$
$\frac{3x}{3} = \frac{15}{3}$
$x = 5$

48.
$8 - 3x = x + 4$
$8 - 3x - x = x - x + 4$
$8 - 4x = 4$
$8 - 8 - 4x = 4 - 8$
$-4x = -4$
$\frac{-4x}{-4} = \frac{-4}{-4}$
$x = 1$

49. Strategy To find your new balance, subtract the check amounts ($321.88 and $34.23) and add the amount of the deposit ($443.56).

Solution

$$\begin{array}{r} \$872.48 \\ -321.88 \\ \hline 550.60 \\ -34.23 \\ \hline 516.37 \\ +443.56 \\ \hline \$959.93 \end{array}$$

Your new balance is $959.93.

50. Strategy To find how many people will vote, solve a proportion.

Solution

$$\begin{aligned} \frac{5}{8} &= \frac{n}{102{,}000} \\ 5 \times 102{,}000 &= 8 \times n \\ 510{,}000 &= 8 \times n \\ 510{,}000 \div 8 &= n \\ 63{,}750 &= n \end{aligned}$$

63,750 people will vote.

51. Strategy To find the last year's dividend, solve the basic percent equation for the base, letting n represent the base. The percent is 80% and the amount is $1.60.

Solution

$$\begin{aligned} \text{Percent} \times \text{base} &= \text{amount} \\ 80\% \times n &= \$1.60 \\ 0.80 \times n &= \$1.60 \\ n &= \$1.60 \div 0.80 \\ n &= \$2.00 \end{aligned}$$

The dividend last year was $2.00.

52. Strategy To find the mean income for the 4 months, add the incomes and divide the sum by the number of incomes (4).

Solution

$$\begin{array}{r} \$4320 \\ 3572 \\ 2864 \\ +\ 4420 \\ \hline \$15{,}176 \end{array} \qquad 15{,}176 \div 4 = 3794$$

The mean income is $3794.

53. Strategy To find the simple interest due, multiply the principal ($120,000) by the interest rate by the time (in years).

Solution

$$\begin{aligned} \text{Interest} &= 120{,}000 \times 8\% \times \frac{9}{12} \\ &= 120{,}000 \times 0.08 \times \frac{9}{12} \\ &= 7200 \end{aligned}$$

The simple interest due is $7200.

54. Strategy To calculate the probability:

- Count the number of possible outcomes.
- Count the number of favorable outcomes.
- Use the probability formula.

Solution There are 36 possible outcomes. There are 12 favorable outcomes: (1, 2), (2, 1), (1, 5), (5, 1), (2, 4), (4, 2), (3, 3), (3, 6), (6, 3), (4, 5), (5, 4), (6, 6).

$$\text{Probability} = \frac{12}{36} = \frac{1}{3}$$

The probability is $\frac{1}{3}$ that the sum of the dots on upward faces of the two dice is divisible by 3.

55. Strategy To find the percent:

- Read the graph and find the death count of China.
- Read the circle graph and find the death count of the other three countries.
- Find the sum of the death counts by adding the four death counts.
- Solve the basic percent equation for percent. The base is the sum of the four death counts and the amount is the death count of China.

Solution

China:	1300 thousand
Japan:	1100 thousand
USSR:	13,600 thousand
Germany:	+ 3300 thousand
	19,300 thousand

$$\begin{aligned} \text{Percent} \times \text{base} &= \text{amount} \\ n \times 19{,}300 &= 1300 \\ n &= 1300 \div 19{,}300 \\ n &\approx 0.067 \end{aligned}$$

China has 6.7% of the death count of the four countries.

56. Strategy To find the discount rate:
- Subtract the sale price ($226.08) from the regular price ($314) to find the amount of the discount.
- Use the basic percent equation for percent. The base is the regular price and the amount is the amount of the discount.

Solution

$$\begin{array}{r} \$314.00 \\ -226.08 \\ \hline \$87.92 \end{array}$$

$$\begin{aligned} \text{Percent} \times \text{base} &= \text{amount} \\ n \times 314 &= 87.92 \\ n &= 87.92 \div 314 \\ n &= 0.28 = 28\% \end{aligned}$$

The discount rate for the compact disc player is 28%.

57. Strategy To find the weight of the box in pounds:
- Multiply the number of tiles in the box (144) by the weight of each tile (9 oz) to find the total weight of the box in ounces.
- Convert the weight in ounces to the weight in pounds.

Solution $144 \times 9 \text{ oz} = 1296 \text{ oz}$

$$\begin{aligned} 1296 \text{ oz} &= 1296 \cancel{\text{oz}} \times \frac{1 \text{ lb}}{16 \cancel{\text{oz}}} \\ &= \frac{1296}{16} \text{ lb} \\ &= 81 \text{ lb} \end{aligned}$$

The weight of the box is 81 lb.

58. Strategy To find the perimeter of the composite figure, add the sum of the two sides to $\frac{1}{2}$ the circumference of the circle.

Solution

$$\begin{aligned} \text{Perimeter} &= 2s + \frac{1}{2}\pi d \\ &\approx 2(8 \text{ in.}) + \frac{1}{2}(3.14)(8 \text{ in.}) \\ &= 16 \text{ in.} + 12.56 \text{ in.} \\ &= 28.56 \text{ in.} \end{aligned}$$

The perimeter is approximately 28.56 in.

59. Strategy To find the area of the composite figure, subtract the area of the two half circles from the area of the rectangle.

Solution

$$\begin{aligned} \text{Area} &= \text{area of rectangle} \\ &\quad -2\left(\frac{1}{2} \text{ area of circle}\right) \\ \text{Area} &= \text{length} \times \text{width} \\ &\quad -2\left[\frac{1}{2}\pi(\text{radius})^2\right] \\ &\approx 10 \text{ cm} \times 2 \text{ cm} \\ &\quad -2\left[\frac{1}{2}(3.14)(1 \text{ cm})^2\right] \\ &= 20 \text{ cm}^2 - 2(1.57 \text{ cm}^2) \\ &= 20 \text{ cm}^2 - 3.14 \text{ cm}^2 \\ &= 16.86 \text{ cm}^2 \end{aligned}$$

The area of the composite figure is approximately 16.86 cm^2.

60. The unknown number: n

$$\begin{aligned} \frac{n}{2} - 5 &= 3 \\ \frac{n}{2} - 5 + 5 &= 3 + 5 \\ \frac{n}{2} &= 8 \\ 2 \cdot \frac{n}{2} &= 2 \cdot 8 \\ n &= 16 \end{aligned}$$

The number is 16.